WAL-MART ATLAS

Published by
Roundabout Publications
PO Box 19235
Lenexa, KS 66285

Phone
800-455-2207

Our Web Sites
www.RoadNotes.com
www.RVdumps.com
www.ScenicDrivesUSA.com
www.TravelBooksUSA.com
www.WalmartAtlas.com

Library of Congress Control Number: 2008928061
ISBN-10: 1-885464-21-5
ISBN-13: 978-1-885464-21-7

Contents

Introduction

Wal-Mart Atlas is a comprehensive directory of more than 4,000 Wal-Mart stores, Supercenters (Super Wal-Marts), and Sam's Club stores across the United States. Understanding how to use this book will aid you in locating stores and the availability of services provided.

Identifying Store Types

There are three basic symbols used throughout this book for indicating each type of store. The symbols shown below are used on all *State Maps*, *Metro Area Charts*, and *Store Detail Charts*.

- ○ A circle is used to indicate Wal-Mart stores
- ◇ A diamond is used to indicate Wal-Mart Supercenters
- □ A square is used to indicate Sam's Club stores

Stores with Gas or Diesel Fuel

Using the same basic symbols described above, each may be filled with a shade of red to indicate the availability of gasoline or diesel fuel. An empty symbol (○ ◇ □) identifies stores where no fuel service is available. Any symbol with a light-red fill (● ◆ ■) indicates that gasoline is available. Any symbol with a dark-red fill (● ◆ ■) identifies locations with both gasoline and diesel fuel.

State Maps

The *State Maps* provide a quick and easy way to locate stores and identify the availability of gas or diesel fuel (see sample Colorado map at right). When there are multiple store locations in the same city, the total number of stores is indicated in parentheses following the city name. If one or more of the same type of store offers fuel, the store symbol will indicate that fuel is available. Refer to the *Store Details Chart* to find the specific store(s) with fuel service.

Some metropolitan areas with numerous store locations in multiple cities are identified on *State Maps* in **Bold Red** type, followed by the total number of stores in that area. The cities within a metropolitan area are listed in the *Metro Area Chart* (see sample of Denver Area at right) and an overview of the stores within each city is provided.

Sample State Map (central Colorado)

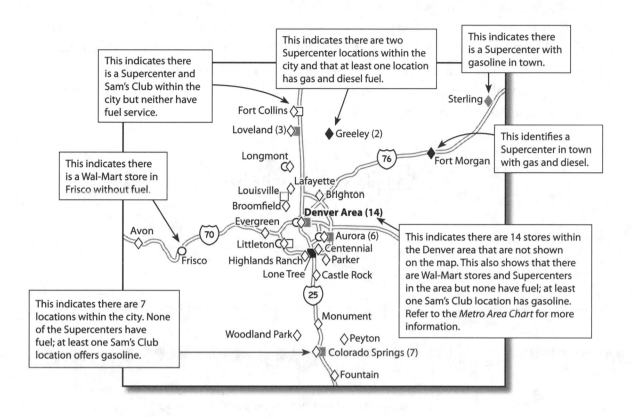

Sample Metro Area Chart (Denver Area)

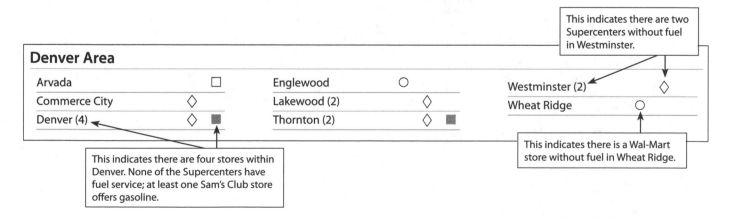

Store Detail Charts

Following the *State Map* and any *Metro Area Charts* are the details for each store. Store locations are listed alphabetically by city name. The same store symbols (○ ◇ □) as shown on the map are used in this chart, followed by four columns of "icons." A number in the column beneath the Interstate symbol (⬭) indicates a store's distance from an Interstate exit if within ten miles. The clock (🕐) indicates that a store is open 24 hours. If a store has a pharmacy within it, the ℞ symbol is used. Availability of auto service is indicated by the 🚐 symbol. Next in the chart is each store's address, zip code, phone number, and GPS coordinates followed by driving directions to the store.

Sample Store Detail Chart

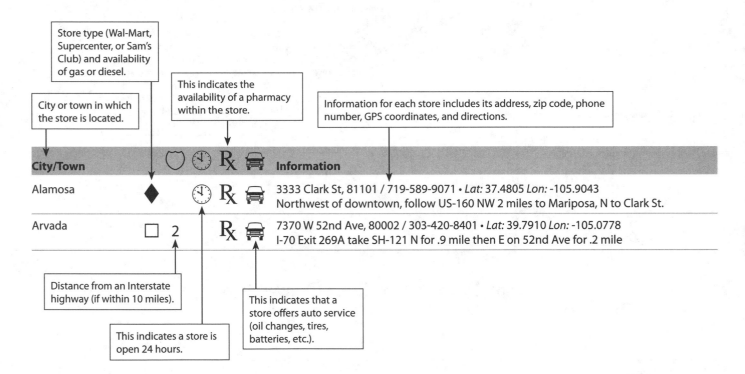

City/Town			℞	🚐	Information
Alamosa	◆	🕐	℞	🚐	3333 Clark St, 81101 / 719-589-9071 • *Lat:* 37.4805 *Lon:* -105.9043 Northwest of downtown, follow US-160 NW 2 miles to Mariposa, N to Clark St.
Arvada	□ 2		℞	🚐	7370 W 52nd Ave, 80002 / 303-420-8401 • *Lat:* 39.7910 *Lon:* -105.0778 I-70 Exit 269A take SH-121 N for .9 mile then E on 52nd Ave for .2 mile

Store type (Wal-Mart, Supercenter, or Sam's Club) and availability of gas or diesel.

This indicates the availability of a pharmacy within the store.

City or town in which the store is located.

Information for each store includes its address, zip code, phone number, GPS coordinates, and directions.

Distance from an Interstate highway (if within 10 miles).

This indicates a store is open 24 hours.

This indicates that a store offers auto service (oil changes, tires, batteries, etc.).

Alabama

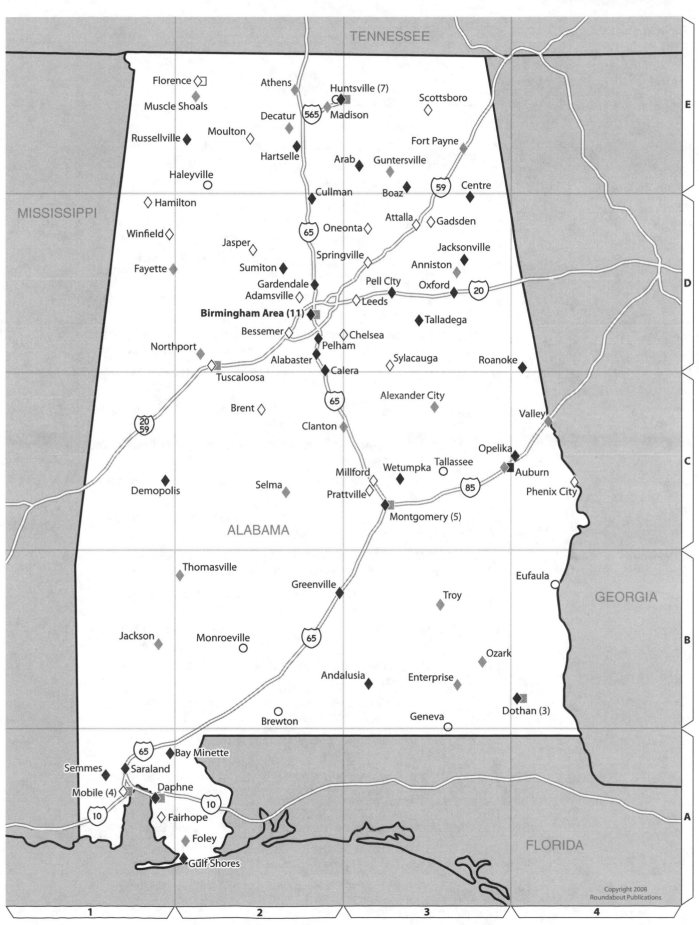

TENNESSEE

Florence ◇□
Muscle Shoals
Athens
Huntsville (7)
Scottsboro
Decatur
565
Madison
Russellville ◆
Moulton
Hartselle
Arab
Guntersville
Fort Payne
Haleyville ○
Hamilton ◇
Cullman
Boaz
59
Centre
MISSISSIPPI
Winfield ◇
Jasper ◇
Oneonta ◇
Attalla ◇ Gadsden
65
Springville
Jacksonville
Fayette ▨
Sumiton ◆
Anniston
Gardendale
Pell City
Oxford
20
Adamsville ◇
Leeds
Birmingham Area (11)
Bessemer ◇
Chelsea ◇
Talladega
Northport ▨
Pelham
Alabaster
Sylacauga ◇
Roanoke
Calera
Tuscaloosa
Alexander City
Valley
Brent ◇
65
Clanton ◇
Opelika
Millford ◇
Wetumpka Tallassee ○
Demopolis ◆
Selma
85
Auburn
20 59
Prattville ◇
Phenix City ◇
ALABAMA
Montgomery (5)

Thomasville
Eufaula ○
Greenville
Troy
GEORGIA
Jackson ◆
Monroeville ○
Ozark
65
Andalusia
Enterprise
Brewton ○
Geneva ○
Dothan (3)

65
Bay Minette
Semmes ◆ Saraland
Mobile (4) ◇
Daphne
10
Fairhope ◇
Foley
FLORIDA
Gulf Shores

1 2 3 4

Birmingham Area

Birmingham (4)	♦ ■	Homewood	◇ ■	Irondale	□
Fairfield	♦	Hoover (3)	◇ ■		

City/Town	⬭	🕐	℞	🚐	Information
Adamsville	◇	6	🕐	℞	🚐	2473 Hackworth Rd, 35214 / 205-798-9721 • *Lat:* 33.5808 *Lon:* -86.9232 I-20/59 Exit 123 go N on US-78 about 6 miles
Alabaster	♦	1	🕐	℞	🚐	630 Colonial Promenade Pkwy, 35007 / 205-620-0360 • *Lat:* 33.2358 *Lon:* -86.8040 I-65 Exit 238 go E .3 mile on US-31 then N .6 mile on Colonial Promenade Pkwy
Alexander City	♦		🕐	℞	🚐	2643 Hwy 280, 35010 / 256-234-0316 • *Lat:* 32.9351 *Lon:* -85.9726 West end of town near jct of US-280 and SH-22
Andalusia	♦			℞	🚐	1991 Dr M L K Jr Expy, 36420 / 334-222-6561 • *Lat:* 31.3186 *Lon:* -86.4440 East end of town near jct of US-84 and SH-100
Anniston	♦	8	🕐	℞	🚐	5560 McClellan Blvd, 36206 / 256-820-3326 • *Lat:* 33.7196 *Lon:* -85.8180 I-20 Exit 185 go N 6.2 miles on US-431 then N 1.8 miles on SH-21
Arab	♦		🕐	℞	🚐	1450 N Brindlee Mountain Pkwy, 35016 / 256-586-8168 • *Lat:* 34.3420 *Lon:* -86.5034 1.4 miles north of town on US-231
Athens	♦	2	🕐	℞	🚐	1011 US Hwy 72 E, 35611 / 256-230-2981 • *Lat:* 34.7869 *Lon:* -86.9594 I-65 Exit 351 go W 1.2 miles on US-72
Attalla	◇	1	🕐	℞	🚐	973 Gilbert Ferry Rd SE, 35954 / 256-538-3811 • *Lat:* 33.9970 *Lon:* -86.0938 I-59 Exit 181, west of exit
Auburn	■	1		℞	🚐	2335 Bent Creek Rd, 36830 / 334-821-0121 • *Lat:* 32.6025 *Lon:* -85.4268 I-85 Exit 57, east of exit
	♦	1	🕐	℞	🚐	1717 S College St, 36832 / 334-821-2493 • *Lat:* 32.5706 *Lon:* -85.4999 I-85 Exit 51 go W .9 mile on SH-147
Bay Minette	♦	7	🕐	℞	🚐	701 McMeans Ave, 36507 / 251-937-5558 • *Lat:* 30.8846 *Lon:* -87.7881 I-65 Exit 34 go SE 3.8 miles on AL-59 then S 2 miles on Bypass
Bessemer	◇	1	🕐	℞	🚐	750 Academy Dr, 35022 / 205-424-5890 • *Lat:* 33.3618 *Lon:* -86.9990 I-20/I-59 Exit 108, southeast of exit
Birmingham	■	1		℞	🚐	5940 Trussville Crossing Blvd, 35235 / 205-655-0505 • *Lat:* 33.6443 *Lon:* -86.6247 I-59 Exit 141 go W on Chalkville Rd .6 mile then N at Trussville Crossing
	◇	1	🕐	℞		1600 Montclair Rd, 35210 / 205-956-0416 • *Lat:* 33.5260 *Lon:* -86.7206 I-20 Exit 132, south of exit
	♦	1	🕐	℞	🚐	9248 Parkway E, 35206 / 205-833-7676 • *Lat:* 33.5886 *Lon:* -86.6990 I-59 Exit 134, north of exit
	◇	1	🕐	℞	🚐	5919 Trussville Crossing Pkwy, 35235 / 205-661-1957 • *Lat:* 33.6401 *Lon:* -86.6269 I-59 Exit 141, west of exit
Boaz	♦		🕐	℞	🚐	1972 US Hwy 431, 35957 / 256-593-0195 • *Lat:* 34.2146 *Lon:* -86.1567 Northeast side of town on US-431 at Butler Ave
Brent	◇			℞		10675 Hwy 5, 35034 / 205-926-4878 • *Lat:* 32.9142 *Lon:* -87.1924 2.3 miles southwest of town center near jct of SH-5 and SH-25
Brewton	○			℞		2041 Douglas Ave, 36426 / 251-867-4680 • *Lat:* 31.1412 *Lon:* -87.0690 2.6 miles north of town center on US-31 (Douglas Ave)
Calera	♦	1	🕐	℞	🚐	5100 Hwy 31, 35040 / 205-668-0831 • *Lat:* 33.1488 *Lon:* -86.7496 I-65 Exit 231, east of exit

○ Wal-Mart ◇ Supercenter □ Sam's Club ■ Gas ■ Gas & Diesel

City/Town	⬭	🕐	℞	🚗	Information
Centre	◆		🕐	℞ 🚗	1950 W Main St, 35960 / 256-927-9900 • *Lat:* 34.1611 *Lon:* -85.7140 Northwest of downtown about 2 miles on US-411/SH-25
Chelsea	◇		🕐	℞ 🚗	16077 Hwy 280, 35043 / 205-678-2222 • *Lat:* 33.3501 *Lon:* -86.6178 Northeast of town center about 1.5 miles on US-280/SH-38
Clanton	◆ 2		🕐	℞ 🚗	1415 7th St S, 35045 / 205-755-7574 • *Lat:* 32.8189 *Lon:* -86.6090 I-65 Exit 205 go W 2 miles on US-31
Cullman	◆ 3		🕐	℞ 🚗	626 Olive St SW, 35055 / 256-739-1664 • *Lat:* 34.1514 *Lon:* -86.8417 I-65 Exit 304 go E on SH-69 about 3 miles
Daphne	■ 1			℞ 🚗	29683 Frederick Blvd, 36526 / 251-626-6909 • *Lat:* 30.6599 *Lon:* -87.8570 I-10 Exit 38, south of exit
	◆ 6		🕐	℞ 🚗	27520 US Hwy 98, 36526 / 251-626-0923 • *Lat:* 30.5752 *Lon:* -87.8970 I-10 Exit 35 go S on US-98 for 5.6 miles
Decatur	◆ 6		🕐	℞ 🚗	2800 Spring Ave SW, 35603 / 256-350-4624 • *Lat:* 34.5575 *Lon:* -87.0002 I-65 Exit 334 go W 5.8 miles on SH-67, left at Spring Ave SW
Demopolis	◆		🕐	℞ 🚗	969 US Hwy 80 W, 36732 / 334-289-2385 • *Lat:* 32.4943 *Lon:* -87.8499 1.2 miles southwest of town via US-80
Dothan	■			🚗	3440 Ross Clark Cir, 36303 / 334-671-5005 • *Lat:* 31.2432 *Lon:* -85.4297 Northwest of town near US-231/SH-210 jct
	◆		🕐	℞ 🚗	3300 S Oates St, 36301 / 334-702-1310 • *Lat:* 31.1792 *Lon:* -85.4020 3.2 miles south of town center via US-231 BR (S Oates St)
	◆		🕐	℞ 🚗	4310 Montgomery Hwy, 36303 / 334-793-3099 • *Lat:* 31.2650 *Lon:* -85.4396 4.2 miles northwest of town center via US-231 BR (N Oates St) and US-231 (Montgomery Hwy)
Enterprise	◆		🕐	℞ 🚗	600 Boll Weevil Cir, 36330 / 334-347-5353 • *Lat:* 31.3157 *Lon:* -85.8301 From town center, go E 1.7 miles on SH-27/88/134, then N .6 miles on US-84
Eufaula	○			℞	1252 S Eufaula Ave, 36027 / 334-687-2218 • *Lat:* 31.8768 *Lon:* -85.1518 From jct of US-431 and SH-30 (south of town), go N 1.6 miles on US-431
Fairfield	◆ 2		🕐	℞ 🚗	7201 Aaron Aronov Dr, 35064 / 205-923-4423 • *Lat:* 33.4662 *Lon:* -86.9149 I-20/I-59 Exit 118, SW on Valley Rd .7 mile, left on Aaron Aronov Dr about 1 mile
Fairhope	◇		🕐	℞ 🚗	10040 Fairhope Ave Ext, 36532 / 251-990-9006 • *Lat:* 30.5236 *Lon:* -87.8520 From town center, go E on Fairhope Ave (CR-48) 3 miles
Fayette	◆		🕐	℞	3186 Hwy 171 N, 35555 / 205-932-5277 • *Lat:* 33.7313 *Lon:* -87.8116 3.5 miles north of town center via US-43
Florence	□			🚗	364 Cox Creek Pkwy, 35630 / 256-767-9960 • *Lat:* 34.8398 *Lon:* -87.6358 US-72 (east of town) go N on SH-133 .8 mile
	◇		🕐	℞ 🚗	3100 Hough Rd, 35630 / 256-767-7581 • *Lat:* 34.8360 *Lon:* -87.6262 From town center, follow US-43/US-72 E 3.7 miles, turn left (north) on SH-133 and go .5 mile to Hough Rd and turn right
Foley	◆		🕐	℞ 🚗	2200 S McKenzie St, 36535 / 251-943-3400 • *Lat:* 30.3829 *Lon:* -87.6835 1.6 miles south of town center via SH-59
Fort Payne	◆ 1		🕐	℞ 🚗	2001 Glenn Blvd SW, 35968 / 256-845-3163 • *Lat:* 34.4387 *Lon:* -85.7614 I-59 Exit 218, west of exit
Gadsden	◇ 6		🕐	℞ 🚗	340 E Meighan Blvd, 35903 / 256-547-2637 • *Lat:* 34.0100 *Lon:* -85.9887 I-59 Exit 183 go W 5.3 miles on US-278/US-431
Gardendale	◆ 1		🕐	℞ 🚗	890 Odum Rd, 35071 / 205-631-8110 • *Lat:* 33.6479 *Lon:* -86.8249 I-65 Exit 271 go E .3 mile on Fieldstown Rd then S .3 mile on Odum Rd
Geneva	○			℞	1608 W Magnolia Ave, 36340 / 334-684-3681 • *Lat:* 31.0460 *Lon:* -85.8926 Northwest of town near jct of Maple Ave (SH-52) and Magnolia Ave (SH-196)

○ Wal-Mart ◇ Supercenter □ Sam's Club ▨ Gas ■ Gas & Diesel

City/Town	🛡	🕐	Rx	🚗	Information
Greenville	◆ 1	🕐	Rx	🚗	501 Willow Ln, 36037 / 334-382-2655 • *Lat:* 31.8482 *Lon:* -86.6465 I-65 Exit 130 go N .2 mile on SH-185, W .1 mile on Cahaba Rd, then S .2 mile
Gulf Shores	◆	🕐	Rx	🚗	170 E Fort Morgan Rd, 36542 / 251-968-5871 • *Lat:* 30.2645 *Lon:* -87.6886 1.2 miles southwest of town near jct of Gulf Shores Pkwy (SH-59) and Fort Morgan Rd (SH-180)
Guntersville	◆	🕐	Rx	🚗	11697 US Hwy 431, 35976 / 256-878-0685 • *Lat:* 34.3019 *Lon:* -86.2787 From town center, follow US-431 S 4.8 miles
Haleyville	○		Rx		42417 Hwy 195, 35565 / 205-486-9498 • *Lat:* 34.2389 *Lon:* -87.5975 1.7 miles northeast of town center via SH-195
Hamilton	◇	🕐	Rx	🚗	1706 Military St S, 35570 / 205-921-3090 • *Lat:* 34.1181 *Lon:* -87.9895 From town center, S on US-43 for 1.5 miles
Hartselle	◆ 4	🕐	Rx	🚗	1201 Hwy 31 NW, 35640 / 256-773-1675 • *Lat:* 34.4555 *Lon:* -86.9473 I-65 Exit 328 go W 2.4 miles on Main St then N on US-31 about 1 mile
Homewood	■ 1		Rx	🚗	201 Lakeshore Pkwy, 35209 / 205-941-3326 • *Lat:* 33.4493 *Lon:* -86.8205 I-65 Exit 255 go W at Lakeshore Pkwy .2 mile
	◇ 1	🕐	Rx		209 Lakeshore Pkwy, 35209 / 205-945-8692 • *Lat:* 33.4477 *Lon:* -86.8231 I-65 Exit 255, west of exit
Hoover	■ 2		Rx	🚗	3053 John Hawkins Pkwy, 35244 / 205-982-0596 • *Lat:* 33.3744 *Lon:* -86.8093 I-459 Exit 13B take US-31S .8 mile & SW on SH-150 .4 mile
	◇ 2	🕐	Rx	🚗	2780 John Hawkins Pkwy, 35244 / 205-733-0303 • *Lat:* 33.3634 *Lon:* -86.8262 I-459 Exit 10 go E on SH-150 1.7 miles
	◇ 4	🕐	Rx	🚗	5335 Hwy 280, 35242 / 205-980-5156 • *Lat:* 33.4194 *Lon:* -86.6751 I-459 Exit 19 go E on US-280 3.6 miles
Huntsville	■ 5		Rx	🚗	5651 Holmes Ave NW, 35816 / 256-837-7323 • *Lat:* 34.7360 *Lon:* -86.6567 I-565 Exit 14 take SH-255N 3.2 miles, E on US-72 for .6 mile & S on Holmes Ave .4 mile
	■ 7		Rx	🚗	2235 National Blvd SW, 35803 / 256-881-8186 • *Lat:* 34.6248 *Lon:* -86.5848 I-565 Exit 19A take US-431S for 6.2 miles & W at National Blvd .2 mile
	○ 2		Rx		2900 S Memorial Pkwy, 35801 / 256-536-2870 • *Lat:* 34.7053 *Lon:* -86.5905 I-565 Exit 19A go S 1.8 miles on US-231 to Drake Ave SW
	◆	🕐	Rx	🚗	330 Sutton Rd, 35763 / 256-534-4140 • *Lat:* 34.6598 *Lon:* -86.4835 8 miles southeast of town via US-431
	◆ 2	🕐	Rx	🚗	2200 Sparkman Dr NW, 35810 / 256-852-2236 • *Lat:* 34.7633 *Lon:* -86.5942 From I-565/US-72 jct go W on US-72 (Sparkman Dr) 1.7 miles
	◇ 3	🕐	Rx	🚗	6140A University Dr, 35806 / 256-837-7272 • *Lat:* 34.7434 *Lon:* -86.6744 I-565 Exit 14 go N 2.2 miles on Research Park Blvd (SH-255) then W on University Dr. Westbound travelers use I-565 Exit 14B.
	◆ 8	🕐	Rx	🚗	11610 Memorial Pkwy SW, 35803 / 256-881-0581 • *Lat:* 34.6166 *Lon:* -86.5675 I-565 Exit 19A go S 8 miles on US-231 (S Memorial Pkwy)
Irondale	□ 1			🚗	3900 Grants Mill Rd, 35210 / 205-956-3987 • *Lat:* 33.5324 *Lon:* -86.6924 I-20 Exit 133, south of highway
Jackson	◆	🕐	Rx		4206 N College Ave, 36545 / 251-247-7101 • *Lat:* 31.5457 *Lon:* -87.8802 3 miles northeast of town center along US-43 at Industrial Bypass
Jacksonville	◆	🕐	Rx	🚗	1625 Pelham Rd S, 36265 / 256-435-8100 • *Lat:* 33.7883 *Lon:* -85.7614 I-20 Exit 185 go N 6 miles on US-431 then N 8 miles SH-21
Jasper	◇	🕐	Rx	🚗	1801 Hwy 78 E, 35501 / 205-384-1100 • *Lat:* 33.8447 *Lon:* -87.2539 2 miles east of town center on US-78 (or 30 miles west of I-65 Exit 299 via SH-69)
Leeds	◇ 1	🕐	Rx	🚗	8551 Whitfield Ave, 35094 / 205-699-0701 • *Lat:* 33.5633 *Lon:* -86.5220 I-20 Exit 144A, south of exit

○ Wal-Mart ◇ Supercenter □ Sam's Club ▨ Gas ■ Gas & Diesel

City/Town	⬡	🕐	℞	🚌	Information
Madison	◆ 1	🕐	℞	🚌	8650 Madison Blvd, 35758 / 256-461-7403 • *Lat:* 34.6815 *Lon:* -86.7402 I-565 Exit 8 go N to Madison Blvd and turn right
Millbrook	◇ 1	🕐	℞	🚌	145 Kelley Blvd, 36054 / 334-285-0311 • *Lat:* 32.4943 *Lon:* -86.4032 I-65 Exit 181, east of exit
Mobile	◼ 1		℞	🚌	601 E I-65 Service Rd S, 36606 / 251-479-1346 • *Lat:* 30.6779 *Lon:* -88.1262 I-65 Exit 3A go E on the Service Rd for .5 mile
	◇ 10	🕐	℞		2500 Dawes Rd, 36695 / 251-633-6023 • *Lat:* 30.6400 *Lon:* -88.2467 I-10 exit 10 take McDonald Rd (CR-39) N 3.6 miles, Three Notch Rd W 2 miles & Dawes Rd N 3.8 miles
	◇ 1	🕐	℞	🚌	5245 Rangeline Service Rd S, 36619 / 251-666-7972 • *Lat:* 30.5960 *Lon:* -88.1600 I-10 Exit 17, west of exit
	◇ 1	🕐	℞	🚌	101 E I-65 Service Rd S, 36606 / 251-471-1105 • *Lat:* 30.6843 *Lon:* -88.1266 I-65 Exit 4 go E .2 mile on Dauphin St, S .1 mile on Springdale Bld, W .3 mile on I-65 Service Rd
	◇ 7	🕐	℞	🚌	685 Schillinger Rd S, 36695 / 251-633-2211 • *Lat:* 30.6782 *Lon:* -88.2254 I-65 Exit 3 go W 6 miles on Airport Blvd then S .3 mile on Schillinger Rd
Monroeville	○		℞		465 Pike St, 36460 / 251-575-3333 • *Lat:* 31.5120 *Lon:* -87.3184 From town center, go S 1 mile on SH-41 to Pike St and turn left
Montgomery	◼ 1		℞	🚌	1080 Eastern Blvd, 36117 / 334-272-0277 • *Lat:* 32.3662 *Lon:* -86.2124 I-85 Exit 6 go NE on Eastern Blvd
	◆ 1	🕐	℞	🚌	851 Ann St, 36107 / 334-223-7177 • *Lat:* 32.3707 *Lon:* -86.2708 I-85 Exit 3, north of exit on Ann St
	◇ 1	🕐	℞	🚌	10710 Chantilly Pkwy, 36117 / 334-272-7377 • *Lat:* 32.3579 *Lon:* -86.1337 I-85 Exit 11, south of exit
	◆ 3	🕐	℞	🚌	6495 Atlanta Hwy, 36117 / 334-272-0263 • *Lat:* 32.3826 *Lon:* -86.1844 I-85 Exit 9 go N on SH-271 1.5 miles and then W .6 mile on US-80 (Atlanta Hwy)
	◇ 3	🕐	℞	🚌	3801 Eastern Blvd, 36116 / 334-284-4181 • *Lat:* 32.3289 *Lon:* -86.2335 I-85 Exit 6 go S on US-80 about 2.5 miles
Moulton	◇	🕐	℞	🚌	15445 AL Hwy 24, 35650 / 256-974-1128 • *Lat:* 34.4940 *Lon:* -87.2769 1.7 miles northeast of town center at jct of SH-24 and SH-157
Muscle Shoals	◆	🕐	℞	🚌	517 Avalon Ave, 35661 / 256-381-0987 • *Lat:* 34.7450 *Lon:* -87.6739 From jct of US-72 and US-43, go N on US-43 2.3 miles, left at Avalon Ave, .4 mile to store
Northport	◆ 9	🕐	℞	🚌	5710 McFarland Blvd, 35476 / 205-333-7820 • *Lat:* 33.2356 *Lon:* -87.6125 1.2 miles west of town center (or 9 Miles northwest of I-20/59 Exit 73 via US-82)
Oneonta	◇	🕐	℞	🚌	2453 2nd Ave E, 35121 / 205-625-6474 • *Lat:* 33.9727 *Lon:* -86.4482 2.2 miles northeast of town center via SH-75
Opelika	◆ 2	🕐	℞	🚌	2900 Pepperell Pkwy, 36801 / 334-745-9333 • *Lat:* 32.6357 *Lon:* -85.4207 I-85 Exit 58 go N about 1.6 miles to US-29 and then west about .5 mile
Oxford	◆ 1	🕐	℞	🚌	92 Plaza Ln, 36203 / 256-835-4701 • *Lat:* 33.6004 *Lon:* -85.8346 I-20 Exit 185 go S on SH-21 .3 mile, left on Plaza Ln
Ozark	◆	🕐	℞	🚌	1537 S US Hwy 231, 36360 / 334-774-0272 • *Lat:* 31.4438 *Lon:* -85.6514 1.8 miles southwest of town center near jct of US-231 and SH-249
Pelham	◆ 2	🕐	℞	🚌	2181 Pelham Pkwy, 35124 / 205-987-0108 • *Lat:* 33.3392 *Lon:* -86.7927 I-65 Exit 246 go W on SH-119 .7 mile and then N .5 mile on US-31
Pell City	◆ 1	🕐	℞	🚌	165 Vaughan Ln, 35125 / 205-338-5300 • *Lat:* 33.6082 *Lon:* -86.2770 I-20 Exit 158, north of exit
Phenix City	◇	🕐	℞	🚌	3700 Hwy 431 N, 36867 / 334-291-1700 • *Lat:* 32.4892 *Lon:* -85.0189 4 miles northwest of town center on US-431 at S Railroad St

○ Wal-Mart ◇ Supercenter ☐ Sam's Club ◼ Gas ◼ Gas & Diesel

City/Town	⬭	🕐	℞	🚐	Information
Prattville	◇ 2	🕐	℞	🚐	1903 Cobbs Ford Rd, 36066 / 334-361-2135 • *Lat:* 32.4607 *Lon:* -86.4177 I-65 Exit 179 go W 1.7 miles on Cobbs Ford Rd
Roanoke	◆	🕐	℞	🚐	4180 Hwy 431, 36274 / 334-863-2147 • *Lat:* 33.1629 *Lon:* -85.3661 1 mile north of town on US-431
Russellville	◆	🕐	℞	🚐	13675 Hwy 43, 35653 / 256-332-7382 • *Lat:* 34.4945 *Lon:* -87.7261 1.7 miles south of town center via Madison St and US-43
Saraland	◆ 1	🕐	℞	🚐	1095 Industrial Pkwy, 36571 / 251-675-8000 • *Lat:* 30.8020 *Lon:* -88.1016 I-65 Exit 13, east of exit
Scottsboro	◇	🕐	℞	🚐	24833 John T Reid Pkwy, 35768 / 256-574-1126 • *Lat:* 34.6691 *Lon:* -86.0092 On US-72 about .5 mile north of US-72/SH-35 jct
Selma	◈	🕐	℞	🚐	1501 AL Hwy 14 E, 36703 / 334-874-7793 • *Lat:* 32.4315 *Lon:* -87.0122 2 miles northeast of town center at US-80 and SH-14 jct
Semmes	◆ 8	🕐	℞	🚐	7855 Moffett Rd, 36575 / 251-645-8224 • *Lat:* 30.7633 *Lon:* -88.2268 I-65 Exit 5B go W 8 miles on US-98
Springville	◇ 2	🕐	℞	🚐	160 Springville Station Blvd, 35146 / 205-467-6656 • *Lat:* 33.7811 *Lon:* -86.4489 I-59 Exit 156 go N .4 mile on SH-23 then W 1 mile on US-11
Sumiton	◆	🕐	℞	🚐	690 Hwy 78, 35148 / 205-648-4100 • *Lat:* 33.7434 *Lon:* -87.0423 1 mile southeast of town center on US-78 at Bryan Rd
Sylacauga	◇	🕐	℞	🚐	41301 US Hwy 280, 35150 / 256-245-0356 • *Lat:* 33.1730 *Lon:* -86.2851 2.6 miles west of town center along US-280 near airport
Talladega	◆	🕐	℞	🚐	214 Haynes St, 35160 / 256-761-1681 • *Lat:* 33.4383 *Lon:* -86.0823 I-20 Exit 168 go S 12.7 miles on SH-7
Tallassee	◯ 9		℞		1300 Gilmer Ave, 36078 / 334-283-6841 • *Lat:* 32.5506 *Lon:* -85.9170 I-85 Exit 26 go N 9 miles on SH-229
Thomasville	◈	🕐	℞	🚐	34301 Hwy 43, 36784 / 334-636-0219 • *Lat:* 31.9402 *Lon:* -87.7373 1.8 miles north of town on US-43 at SH-5
Troy	◆	🕐	℞	🚐	1420 Hwy 231 S, 36081 / 334-566-8012 • *Lat:* 31.7788 *Lon:* -85.9405 3.6 miles southeast of town center via SH-87 and US-231
Tuscaloosa	◼ 1			🚐	1401 Skyland Blvd E, 35405 / 205-750-8559 • *Lat:* 33.1682 *Lon:* -87.5187 I-20/59 Exit 73 take US-82S .2 mile then E on Skyland .5 mile
	◇ 1	🕐	℞	🚐	1501 Skyland Blvd E, 35405 / 205-750-0823 • *Lat:* 33.1682 *Lon:* -87.5180 I-20/I-59 Exit 73 go S .2 mile on US-82 (McFarland Blvd) then E .3 mile on US-11 (Skyland Blvd)
Valley	◈ 1	🕐	℞	🚐	3501 20th Ave, 36854 / 334-768-2118 • *Lat:* 32.8377 *Lon:* -85.1776 I-85 Exit 79 go S .8 mile on US-29
Wetumpka	◆	🕐	℞	🚐	4538 US Hwy 231, 36092 / 334-567-3066 • *Lat:* 32.5073 *Lon:* -86.2144 I-85 Exit 6 go N 11.5 miles on US-231
Winfield	◇		℞		2575 US Hwy 43 W, 35594 / 205-487-4359 • *Lat:* 33.9358 *Lon:* -87.8366 From town center, follow US-43 NW about 1.5 miles

◯ Wal-Mart   ◇ Supercenter   ◻ Sam's Club   ◼ Gas   ◼ Gas & Diesel

Alraska

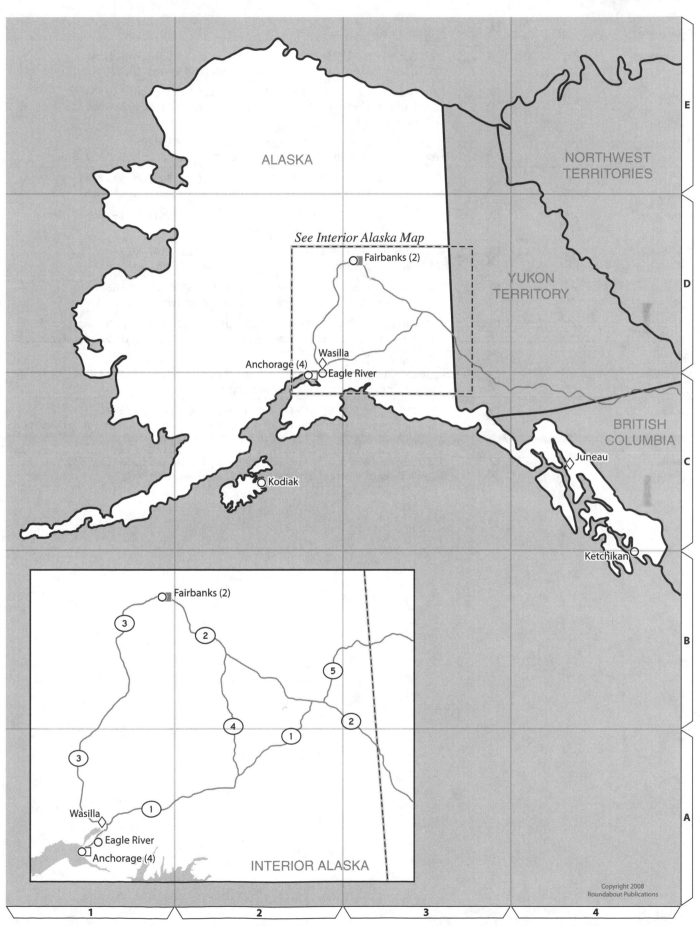

ALASKA

NORTHWEST
TERRITORIES

See Interior Alaska Map

○ Fairbanks (2)

YUKON
TERRITORY

Wasilla

Anchorage (4) ◇
○ Eagle River

BRITISH
COLUMBIA

◇ Juneau

○ Kodiak

Ketchikan ○

INTERIOR ALASKA

○ Fairbanks (2)

③

②

⑤

④ ① ②

③

①

Wasilla ◇

○ Eagle River
□○ Anchorage (4)

E

D

C

B

A

1   2   3   4

City/Town	🛡	🕐	℞	🚐	Information
Anchorage	□			🚐	3651 Penland Pkwy, 99508 / 907-276-2996 • Lat: 61.2159 Lon: -149.8124 Jct SH-3/SH-1 take SH-1 S 32.5 miles, E on Bragaw St .4 mile & S on Penland Pkwy
	□		℞	🚐	8801 Old Seward Hwy, 99515 / 907-522-2333 • Lat: 61.1410 Lon: -149.8638 Jct SH-3/SH-1 take SH-1 S 39.6 miles, Diamond Blvd W .1 mile, Briarwood St S .5 mile & Old Seward Hwy E
	○		℞		3101 A St, 99503 / 907-563-5900 • Lat: 61.1924 Lon: -149.8828 From SH-1 at Tudor Rd go W .6 mile, N on "C" St .2 mile, continue on "A" St .6 mile
	○		℞		8900 Old Seward Hwy, 99515 / 907-344-5300 • Lat: 61.1399 Lon: -149.8644 From SH-1 at Dimond Blvd go W .2 mile then S on Old Seward Hwy .3 mile
Eagle River	○		℞		18600 Eagle River Rd, 99577 / 907-694-9780 • Lat: 61.3106 Lon: -149.5357 From SH-1 at Eagle River Loop Rd go NE 2.6 miles
Fairbanks	■		℞	🚐	48 College Rd, 99701 / 907-451-4800 • Lat: 64.8520 Lon: -147.7079 SH-3 (west of town) take SH-2 NE for 2.2 miles, N on College Rd for .4 mile
	○		℞	🚐	537 Johansen Expy, 99701 / 907-451-9900 • Lat: 64.8586 Lon: -147.6862 Jct SH-2 & SH-3 go N on SH-2 for 3.2 miles then W on Johansen Expy .3 mile
Juneau	◇		℞		6525 Glacier Hwy, 99801 / 907-789-5000 • Lat: 58.3587 Lon: -134.5126 Jct Mendenhall Loop & SH-7 continue E on SH-7 for 2.7 miles, N on Switzer Access Rd then E on Glacier Hwy .1 mile
Ketchikan	○		℞		4230 Don King Rd, 99901 / 907-247-2156 • Lat: 55.3760 Lon: -131.7214 4 miles northwest of town via SH-7 and Signot Rd
Kodiak	○		℞		2911 Mill Bay Rd, 99615 / 907-481-1670 • Lat: 57.8104 Lon: -152.3633 From Abercrombie Historical Site (north of town) go S on Rezanof Dr .9 mile then SW on Mill Bay Rd .4 mile
Wasilla	◇	🕐	℞		1350 S Seward Meridian Pkwy, 99654 / 907-376-9780 • Lat: 61.5684 Lon: -149.3597 3.2 miles east of town center via SH-3 and Seward Meridian Pkwy

○ Wal-Mart ◇ Supercenter □ Sam's Club ■ Gas ■ Gas & Diesel

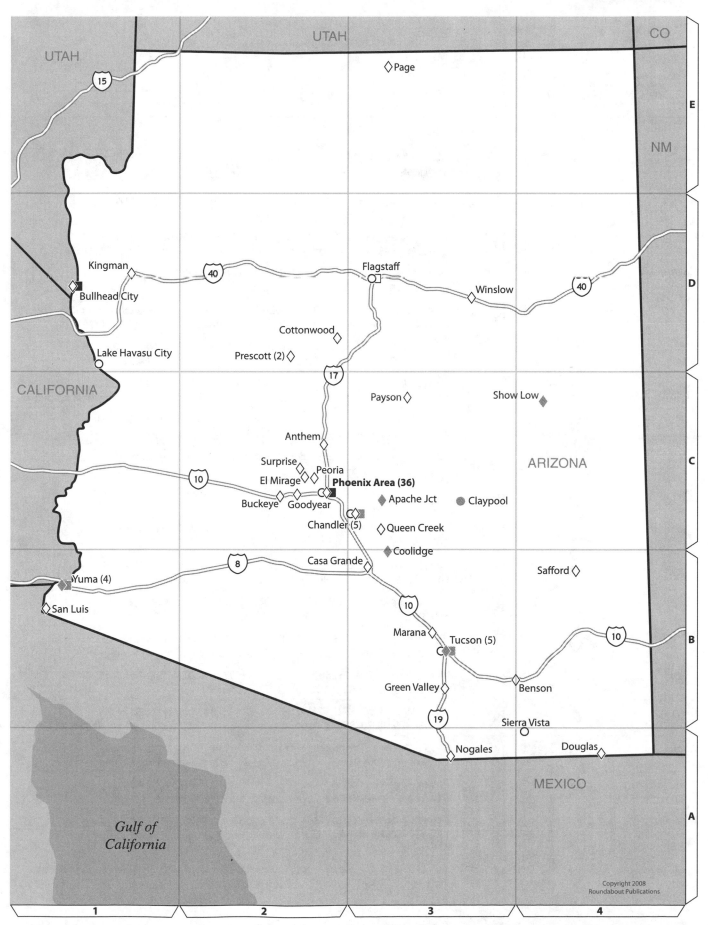

Arizona

○ Wal-Mart ◇ Supercenter □ Sam's Club ▨ Gas ■ Gas & Diesel

UTAH

CO

UTAH

E

NM

15

Kingman
Bullhead City
40
Flagstaff
Winslow
40

D

Lake Havasu City
Cottonwood
Prescott (2)
17
Payson
Show Low

CALIFORNIA

ARIZONA

C

Anthem
Surprise
El Mirage
Peoria
Phoenix Area (36)
Buckeye Goodyear
Apache Jct
Claypool
Chandler (5)
Queen Creek
Coolidge
Safford

10

Casa Grande
8
Yuma (4)
San Luis

10

Marana
Tucson (5)
B
Green Valley
Benson
19
Sierra Vista
Nogales
Douglas

MEXICO

A

Gulf of
California

Copyright 2008
Roundabout Publications

1   2   3   4

Phoenix Area

Avondale (2)	◇ ▨	Mesa (7)	◇	Scottsdale (3)	○ ◇ ▨
Gilbert (4)	◇ ■	Phoenix (14)	○ ◇ ■	Tempe	◇
Glendale (5)	○ ◇ ▨				

City/Town	🛡	🕐	℞	🚗	Information
Anthem	◇ 2	🕐	℞	🚗	4435 W Anthem Way, 85086 / 623-551-6314 • *Lat:* 33.8664 *Lon:* -112.1374 I-17 Exit 229 go E on Anthem Way 1.4 miles
Apache Junction	◆	🕐	℞	🚗	2555 W Apache Trl, 85220 / 480-380-3800 • *Lat:* 33.4150 *Lon:* -111.5738 US-60 Exit 193 go N on Signal Butte Rd 1.9 miles then E on Apache Trl 1.4 miles
Avondale	▨ 1		℞	🚗	1459 N Dysart Rd, 85323 / 623-882-3859 • *Lat:* 33.4493 *Lon:* -112.3409 I-10 Exit 129 go S on Dysart Rd for .6 mile
	◇ 1	🕐	℞	🚗	13055 W Rancho Santa Fe Blvd, 85323 / 623-935-4010 • *Lat:* 33.4608 *Lon:* -112.3386 I-10 Exit 129 go N on Dysart Rd .2 mile & east at W Rancho Santa Fe .1 mile
Benson	◇ 2	🕐	℞		201 S Prickly Pear Ave, 85602 / 520-586-0742 • *Lat:* 31.9687 *Lon:* -110.3155 I-10 Exit 303 continue I-10 BR/SH-80 E for .9 mile & S on Prickly Pear .2 mile
Buckeye	◇ 3	🕐	℞	🚗	1060 S Watson Rd, 85326 / 623-474-6728 • *Lat:* 33.4371 *Lon:* -112.5565 I-10 Exit 117 go S on Watson Rd 2.2 miles
Bullhead City	■		℞	🚗	600 Hwy 95 Ste 200, 86429 / 928-754-3900 • *Lat:* 35.1658 *Lon:* -114.5651 1.25 miles north of town center on SH-25
	◇	🕐	℞	🚗	2840 Hwy 95, 86442 / 928-758-7222 • *Lat:* 35.0827 *Lon:* -114.5969 I-40 Exit 1 go N on SH-95 for 16.4 miles
Casa Grande	◇ 2	🕐	℞	🚗	1741 E Florence Blvd, 85222 / 520-421-1200 • *Lat:* 32.8795 *Lon:* -111.7126 I-10 Exit 287 go W on SH-287/Florence Blvd 1.4 miles
Chandler	▨		℞	🚗	1375 S Arizona Ave, 85248 / 480-726-9383 • *Lat:* 33.2857 *Lon:* -111.8413 SH-202 Loop Exit 47 take SH-87 S for .4 mile
	▨ 1		℞	🚗	700 N 54th St, 85226 / 480-893-1555 • *Lat:* 33.3143 *Lon:* -111.9680 I-10 Exit 159 go E at Ray Rd for .3 mile & S at 54th for .4 mile
	○		℞		800 W Warner Rd, 85225 / 480-786-0062 • *Lat:* 33.3352 *Lon:* -111.8557 SH-101 Loop Exit 58 go E on Warner Rd 2.3 miles
	◇	🕐	℞	🚗	2750 E Germann Rd, 85249 / 480-812-2930 • *Lat:* 33.2784 *Lon:* -111.8031 SH-202 Loop Exit 44 go S on Gilbert .3 mile then W on Germann .3 mile
	◇ 9	🕐	℞	🚗	1175 S Arizona Ave, 85248 / 480-726-0841 • *Lat:* 33.2894 *Lon:* -111.8415 I-10 Exit 161 go E on SH-202 Loop 8 miles then SH-87 N .2 mile
Claypool	●		℞		100 S Ragus Rd, 85532 / 928-425-7171 • *Lat:* 33.4135 *Lon:* -110.8358 Jct US-60 & US-70 (SE of Claypool) take US-60 NW 5.5 miles then S on Ragus Rd
Coolidge	◆	🕐	℞		1695 N Arizona Blvd, 85228 / 520-723-0945 • *Lat:* 33.0002 *Lon:* -111.5238 I-10 Exit 185 take SH-387 E 7.3 miles, SH-87 SE 7 miles & S on N Arizona Blvd .2 mile
Cottonwood	◇	🕐	℞	🚗	2003 E Rodeo Dr, 86326 / 928-634-0444 • *Lat:* 34.7134 *Lon:* -112.0027 I-17 Exit 287 take SH-260/279 NW 11.9 miles then S at Rodeo Dr .2 mile
Douglas	◇	🕐	℞	🚗	199 W 5th St, 85607 / 520-364-1281 • *Lat:* 31.3399 *Lon:* -109.5250 From SH-80 (NE of town) go S on Washington Ave 2.1 miles, E on 8th .2 mile & S on Jefferson .2 mile
El Mirage	◇	🕐	℞		12900 W Thunderbird Rd, 85335 / 623-583-1321 • *Lat:* 33.6090 *Lon:* -112.3375 SH-101 Loop Exit 11 take US-60 NW 3.3 miles, S at "A" St .1 mile & W on Thunderbird 1.3 miles

○ Wal-Mart ◇ Supercenter ☐ Sam's Club ▨ Gas ■ Gas & Diesel

City/Town	⬡	🕐	℞	🚗	Information
Flagstaff	□	1	℞	🚗	1851 E Butler Ave, 86001 / 928-774-9444 • *Lat:* 35.1915 *Lon:* -111.6292 I-40 Exit 198 go W on Butler Ave for .5 mile
	○	1	℞		2750 S Woodlands Village Blvd, 86001 / 928-773-1117 • *Lat:* 35.1755 *Lon:* -111.6666 I-17 Exit 341 go W on McConnell Dr .2 mile, S on Beulah .2 mile & W on Woodlands Village .2 mile
Gilbert	■		℞	🚗	2621 S Market St, 85296 / 480-722-1447 • *Lat:* 33.3028 *Lon:* -111.7436 SH-202 Loop Exit 40 go W .3 mile on Williams Field Rd then S .3 mile on Market St
	▨		℞	🚗	1225 N Gilbert Rd, 85234 / 480-926-9006 • *Lat:* 33.3727 *Lon:* -111.7898 US-60 Exit 162 go S on Gilbert Rd for 1 mile
	◇	🕐	℞	🚗	2501 S Market St, 85296 / 480-224-6900 • *Lat:* 33.3047 *Lon:* -111.7437 SH-202 Loop Exit 40 go W .3 mile on Williams Field Rd then S .2 mile on Market St
	◇	🕐	℞	🚗	5290 S Power Rd, 85295 / 480-988-0012 • *Lat:* 33.2929 *Lon:* -111.6865 SH-202 Loop Exit 42 go S on Val Vista Dr 1.7 miles, E on Queen Creek Rd 4 miles & S on Power Rd .9 mile
Glendale	▨		℞	🚗	18501 N 83rd Ave, 85308 / 623-825-9257 • *Lat:* 33.6501 *Lon:* -112.2368 SH-101 Loop Exit 15 go W on Union Hills Dr .3 mile then S on 83rd .5 mile
	○		℞		5845 W Bell Rd, 85308 / 602-978-8205 • *Lat:* 33.6385 *Lon:* -112.1852 SH-101 Loop Exit 14 go E on Bell Rd for 3 miles
	◇	🕐	℞	🚗	18551 N 83rd Ave, 85308 / 623-825-1129 • *Lat:* 33.6504 *Lon:* -112.2369 SH-101 Loop Exit 15 go W on Union Hills Dr .4 mile & S on 83rd .5 mile
	◇	🕐	℞	🚗	5010 N 95th Ave, 85305 / 623-872-0058 • *Lat:* 33.5089 *Lon:* -112.2640 SH-101 Loop Exit 5 go E on Camelback Rd .4 mile & N at 95th
	◇	🕐	℞	🚗	5605 W Northern Ave, 85301 / 623-934-6920 • *Lat:* 33.5530 *Lon:* -112.1796 SH-101 Loop Exit 8 go E on Northern Ave 4.9 miles
Goodyear	◇	1 🕐	℞	🚗	1100 N Estrella Pkwy, 85338 / 623-925-9575 • *Lat:* 33.4571 *Lon:* -112.3924 I-10 Exit 126 go S on Estrella Pkwy .2 mile
Green Valley	◇	1 🕐	℞	🚗	18680 S Nogales Hwy, 85614 / 520-625-3808 • *Lat:* 31.9102 *Lon:* -110.9805 I-10 Exit 69 go NE on I-19 BR/Nogales Hwy 1 mile
Kingman	◇	1 🕐	℞	🚗	3396 N Stockton Hill Rd, 86409 / 928-692-0555 • *Lat:* 35.2216 *Lon:* -114.0357 I-40 Exit 51 go N on Stockton Hill Rd .3 mile
Lake Havasu City	○		℞		1795 Kiowa Ave, 86403 / 928-453-5655 • *Lat:* 34.5031 *Lon:* -114.3497 I-40 Exit 9 take SH-95 S 17.3 miles then W on Kiowa
Marana	◇	1 🕐	℞	🚗	8280 N Cortaro, 85743 / 520-744-3652 • *Lat:* 32.3568 *Lon:* -111.0921 I-10 Exit 246 go SW on Cortaro Rd for .2 mile
Mesa	◇	🕐	℞		6131 E Southern Ave, 85206 / 480-830-3919 • *Lat:* 33.3937 *Lon:* -111.6992 US-60 Exit 186 go N on Higley Rd .5 mile & E on Southern Ave 1.2 miles
	◇	🕐	℞	🚗	857 N Dobson Rd, 85201 / 480-962-0038 • *Lat:* 33.4332 *Lon:* -111.8710 SH-202 Loop Exit 10 go south on N Dobson Rd .3 mile
	◇	🕐	℞	🚗	1606 S Signal Butte Rd, 85206 / 480-358-1122 • *Lat:* 33.3856 *Lon:* -111.5983 US-60 Exit 193 take Signal Butte Rd N for 4 miles
	◇	🕐	℞	🚗	1710 S Greenfield Rd, 85206 / 480-892-3814 • *Lat:* 33.3828 *Lon:* -111.7388 US-60 Exit 185 go S on Greenfield Rd .3 mile
	◇	🕐	℞	🚗	1955 S Stapley Dr, 85204 / 480-892-9009 • *Lat:* 33.3796 *Lon:* -111.8070 US-60 Exit 193 go S on Stapley Dr .6 mile
	◇	🕐	℞	🚗	240 W Baseline Rd, 85210 / 480-668-9501 • *Lat:* 33.3788 *Lon:* -111.8370 US-60 Exit 179 go S on Country Club Dr .5 mile then E on Baseline Rd .2 mile
	◇	🕐	℞	🚗	4505 E McKellips Rd, 85215 / 480-641-6728 • *Lat:* 33.4517 *Lon:* -111.7337 SH-202 Loop Exit 21 go south on N Higley Rd 2.1 miles & W on McKellips .9 mile

○ Wal-Mart   ◇ Supercenter   □ Sam's Club   ▨ Gas   ■ Gas & Diesel

City/Town	⬡	🕐	℞	🚌	Information
Nogales	◇ 2	🕐	℞	🚌	100 W White Park Dr, 85621 / 520-281-4974 • *Lat:* 31.3630 *Lon:* -110.9310 I-19 Exit 4 go E on SH-189 for .4 mile & S on Southern Ave 1.2 miles
Page	◇	🕐	℞	🚌	1017 W Haul Rd, 86040 / 928-645-2622 • *Lat:* 39.9050 *Lon:* -111.4841 2 miles southeast of town along US-89 at Haul Rd
Payson	◇	🕐	℞		300 N Beeline Hwy, 85541 / 928-474-0029 • *Lat:* 34.2441 *Lon:* -111.3230 Jct SH-188 & SH-87 take SH-87 N 16.3 miles
Peoria	◇ 7	🕐	℞	🚌	7975 W Peoria Ave, 85345 / 623-878-9907 • *Lat:* 33.5819 *Lon:* -112.2360 SH-101 Loop Exit 10 go E 1.4 miles on Peoria Ave
Phoenix	▨ 1		℞	🚌	8340 W McDowell Rd, 85037 / 623-936-8528 • *Lat:* 33.4654 *Lon:* -112.2389 I-10 Exit 135 go N on 83rd Ave .2 mile then W on McDowell
	■ 2		℞	🚌	1525 W Bell Rd, 85023 / 602-439-9852 • *Lat:* 33.6400 *Lon:* -112.0921 I-17 Exit 212 go E on Bell Rd for 1.4 miles
	▨ 3		℞	🚌	2005 E Indian School Rd, 85016 / 602-954-3894 • *Lat:* 33.4947 *Lon:* -112.0386 I-10 Exit 147B go N 2.8 miles on US-51 to Exit 3 then E .2 mile on Indian School Rd
	○		℞		4617 E Bell Rd, 85032 / 602-482-7575 • *Lat:* 33.6404 *Lon:* -111.9814 SH-101 Loop Exit 29 take SH-51 S 2.2 miles then E on Bell Rd .3 mile
	◇ 9		℞		4747 E Cactus Rd, 85032 / 602-404-3712 • *Lat:* 33.5972 *Lon:* -111.9783 I-17 Exit 210 go E 8.3 miles on Thunderbird Rd (which becomes Cactus Rd)
	◇	🕐	℞		3721 E Thomas Rd, 85018 / 602-685-0555 • *Lat:* 33.4804 *Lon:* -112.0015 SH-202 Loop Exit 2 take 40th St N 1.5 miles & W on Thomas Rd .3 mile
	◇ 1	🕐	℞	🚌	1825 W Bell Rd, 85023 / 602-942-4138 • *Lat:* 33.6400 *Lon:* -112.0988 I-17 Exit 212 go E on Bell Rd for .9 mile
	◇ 1	🕐	℞	🚌	2020 N 75th Ave, 85035 / 623-849-1030 • *Lat:* 33.4705 *Lon:* -112.2210 I-10 Exit 136 go S on 75th Ave for .8 mile
	◇ 1	🕐	℞	🚌	2501 W Happy Valley Rd, 85085 / 623-780-5702 • *Lat:* 33.7128 *Lon:* -112.1093 I-17 Exit 218 go W on Happy Valley Rd .7 mile
	◇ 2	🕐	℞	🚌	1607 W Bethany Home Rd, 85015 / 602-246-1700 • *Lat:* 33.5239 *Lon:* -112.0936 I-17 Exit 204 go E on Bethany Home Rd 1.1 miles
	◇ 2	🕐	℞	🚌	6145 N 35th Ave, 85017 / 602-973-0774 • *Lat:* 33.5269 *Lon:* -112.1341 I-17 Exit 204 take Bethany Home Rd W 1.3 miles & N on 35th for .2 mile
	◇ 3	🕐	℞	🚌	5250 W Indian School Rd, 85031 / 623-845-8713 • *Lat:* 33.4951 *Lon:* -112.1722 I-10 Exit 139 take 51st Ave N 2.2 miles then W on Indian School Rd .2 mile
	◇ 3	🕐	℞	🚌	7575 W Lower Buckeye Rd, 85043 / 623-907-0007 • *Lat:* 33.4228 *Lon:* -112.2229 I-10 Exit 136 go S on 75th Ave 2.8 miles then W on Buckeye Rd
	◇ 5	🕐	℞	🚌	6150 S 35th Ave, 85041 / 602-243-8506 • *Lat:* 33.3850 *Lon:* -112.1076 I-17 Exit 197 take 19th Ave S 1.6 miles, Broadway W 2 miles & 35th Ave S 1.1 miles
Prescott	◇	🕐	℞	🚌	1280 Gail Gardner Way, 86305 / 928-541-0071 • *Lat:* 34.5629 *Lon:* -112.4882 Jct SH-69 & SH-89 (E of town) take SH-89 W 1 mile, N on Montezuma .7 mile, W on Whipple/Iron Springs 1.3 miles & NE on Gail Gardner Way
	◇	🕐	℞	🚌	3050 N Hwy 69, 86301 / 928-445-1113 • *Lat:* 34.5801 *Lon:* -112.4425 Jct SH-169 & SH-69 (E of town) go W on SH-69 for 12.5 miles
Queen Creek	◇	🕐	℞	🚌	1725 W Hunt Hwy, 85243 / 480-677-2149 • *Lat:* 33.1773 *Lon:* -111.5815 SH-202 Loop Exit 33 go E on Elliot Rd .4 mile, S on Ellsworth 10 miles & W on Hunt Hwy 6.4 miles
Safford	◇	🕐	℞	🚌	755 S 20th Ave, 85546 / 928-428-7990 • *Lat:* 32.8335 *Lon:* -109.7328 Jct US-191 & US-70 (E of town) take US-191/70 W 11.3 miles & 20th Ave S .8 mile
San Luis	◇	🕐	℞		1613 N Main St, 85349 / 928-722-7278 • *Lat:* 32.5077 *Lon:* -114.7864 1 mile north of town along US-95

○ Wal-Mart ◇ Supercenter ☐ Sam's Club ▨ Gas ■ Gas & Diesel

City/Town		🛡	🕘	Rx	🚚	Information
Scottsdale	■			Rx	🚚	15255 N Northsight Blvd, 85260 / 480-609-0550 • *Lat:* 33.6240 *Lon:* -111.8952 SH-101 Loop Exit 39 go W at Raintree .4 mile then N at Northsight .4 mile
	○			Rx	🚚	4915 N Pima Rd, 85251 / 480-941-0333 • *Lat:* 33.5081 *Lon:* -111.8914 SH-101 Loop Exit 46 go W on Chaparrel Rd .2 mile & S on Pima Rd
	◇		🕘	Rx	🚚	15355 N Northsight Blvd, 85260 / 480-348-5505 • *Lat:* 33.6250 *Lon:* -111.8947 SH-101 Loop Exit 39 go W on Raintree Dr .4 mile & N on Northsight Blvd .5 mile
Show Low	◆		🕘	Rx	🚚	5401 S White Mountain Rd, 85901 / 928-537-3141 • *Lat:* 34.1991 *Lon:* -110.0178 Jct US-60 & SH-77 (E of town) take US-60 W .5 mile & White Mountain Rd S 4.1 miles
Sierra Vista	○			Rx	🚚	657 AZ Hwy 90, 85635 / 520-458-8790 • *Lat:* 31.5602 *Lon:* -110.2571 I-10 Exit 302 take SH-90 S 31.5 miles
Surprise	◇		🕘	Rx	🚚	13770 W Bell Rd, 85374 / 623-544-2200 • *Lat:* 33.6388 *Lon:* -112.3560 SH-101 Loop Exit 11 go W on Grand Ave 6.2 miles & W on Bell Rd .3 mile
Tempe	◇	2	🕘	Rx		1380 W Elliot Rd, 85284 / 480-345-8686 • *Lat:* 33.3493 *Lon:* -111.9625 I-10 Exit 157 go E on Elliot Rd for 1.1mile
Tucson	■	5		Rx	🚚	4701 N Stone Ave, 85704 / 520-292-9789 • *Lat:* 32.2923 *Lon:* -110.9707 I-10 Exit 256 W on Grant Rd .8 mile, N on Oracle Rd 3.3 miles, W on River Rd .4 mile, N on Stone Ave
	○	5		Rx		455 E Wetmore Rd, 85705 / 520-292-2992 • *Lat:* 32.2867 *Lon:* -110.9645 I-10 Exit 256 go E on Grant Rd .8 mile, N on Oracle Rd 2.5 miles & E on Wetmore Rd .8 mile
	○	4		Rx	🚚	7150 E Speedway Blvd, 85710 / 520-751-1882 • *Lat:* 32.2354 *Lon:* -110.8399 I-10 Exit 254 go E on Prince Rd 2.3 miles, N on Stone Ave 1.1 miles & E on Wetmore Rd .3 mile
	◇	1	🕘	Rx	🚚	1650 W Valencia Rd, 85746 / 520-573-3777 • *Lat:* 32.1340 *Lon:* -111.0001 I-19 Exit 95 go east on W Valencia Rd .7 mile
	◆	4	🕘	Rx	🚚	7635 N La Cholla Blvd, 85741 / 520-297-0840 • *Lat:* 32.3459 *Lon:* -111.0130 I-10 Exit 248 go E on Ina Rd 3.2 miles & S on La Chella Blvd .4 mile
Winslow	◇	1		Rx	🚚	700 Mikes Pike St, 86047 / 928-289-4641 • *Lat:* 35.0410 *Lon:* -110.7013 I-40 Exit 253 go NE on Mikes Pike .2 mile
Yuma	■	1		Rx	🚚	1462 S Pacific Ave, 85365 / 928-783-3684 • *Lat:* 32.7013 *Lon:* -114.5990 I-8 Exit 2 go N on 16th St for .5 mile then W on Pacific Ave for .2 mile
	◆	3	🕘	Rx	🚚	2900 S Pacific Ave, 85365 / 928-344-0992 • *Lat:* 32.6753 *Lon:* -114.5989 I-8 Exit 2 go E on 16th St .5 mile then S on Pacific Ave 1.6 miles
	◇	3	🕘	Rx	🚚	8151 E 32nd St, 85365 / 928-344-5974 • *Lat:* 32.6692 *Lon:* -114.5477 I-8 Exit 3 go S on SH-280 for 1.4 miles then W on 32nd St .9 mile
	◇	4	🕘	Rx	🚚	2501 S Avenue B, 85364 / 928-317-2776 • *Lat:* 32.6817 *Lon:* -114.6502 I-8 Exit 2 go W on 16th St 2.5 miles then S on US-95 1.2 miles

Arkansas

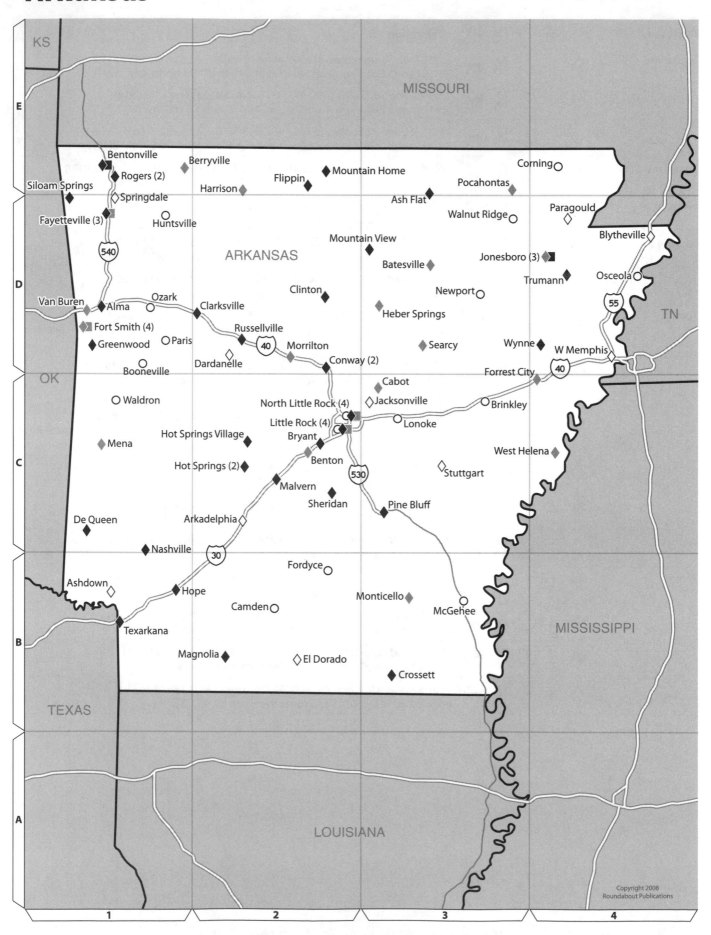

KS

MISSOURI

E

Bentonville
Berryville
Corning ○
Rogers (2)
Flippin
Mountain Home ◆
Pocahontas
Siloam Springs
Harrison
Ash Flat ◆
Walnut Ridge ○
Paragould ◇
Springdale ◇
Blytheville ◇
Fayetteville (3)
Mountain View
Jonesboro (3)
Huntsville ○
ARKANSAS
Batesville ◆
Osceola ○
D
Trumann ◆
Clinton ◆
Newport ○
540
TN
Van Buren
Ozark
Heber Springs
55
Alma
Clarksville ◆
Fort Smith (4)
Russellville
Searcy
Wynne ◆
Greenwood ◆
Paris ○
40 Morrilton
W Memphis
Dardanelle ◇
Conway (2)
Forrest City
40
OK
Booneville ○
Cabot
Waldron ○
Jacksonville ◇
Brinkley ○
North Little Rock (4)
Hot Springs Village ◆
Little Rock (4)
Lonoke ○
Mena ◆
Bryant
West Helena ◆
Benton
C
Hot Springs (2) ◆
530
Stuttgart ◇
Malvern ◆
Sheridan ◆
Pine Bluff ◆
De Queen ◆
Arkadelphia ◇
Nashville ◆
30
Fordyce ○
Ashdown ◇
Hope ◆
Monticello ◆
Camden ○
McGehee ○
MISSISSIPPI
B
Texarkana
Magnolia ◆
◇ El Dorado
Crossett ◆

TEXAS

A

LOUISIANA

1   2   3   4

City/Town	⬡	🕐	℞	🚍	Information
Alma	◆ 1	🕐	℞	🚍	367 W Cherry St, 72921 / 479-632-4585 • Lat: 35.4806 Lon: -94.2258 I-40 Exit 13 take US-71 S .5 mile then E on US-64
Arkadelphia	◇ 2	🕐	℞	🚍	109 WP Malone Dr, 71923 / 870-246-2459 • Lat: 34.1208 Lon: -93.0944 I-30 Exit 73 take SH-8 W .3 mile then Malone Dr N 1.4 miles
Ash Flat	◆	🕐	℞	🚍	219 Hwy 412, 72513 / 870-994-7520 • Lat: 36.2208 Lon: -91.6285 Jct SH-56 & US-167 (south of town) take US-167 N 1.7 miles then US-412/62 NW .6 mile
Ashdown	◇	🕐	℞		297 Hwy 32 Bypass, 71822 / 870-898-5126 • Lat: 33.6581 Lon: -94.1100 I-30 Exit 223B go N on US-59/71 for 14.6 miles then E on SH-32 Bypass
Batesville	◆	🕐	℞	🚍	3150 Harrison St, 72501 / 870-793-9004 • Lat: 35.7647 Lon: -91.6140 Jct SH-14 & US-167 (south of town) take US-167 N 2.6 miles then E on SH-69 for 1.7 miles
Benton	◆ 1	🕐	℞	🚍	17309 I-30, 72015 / 501-860-6135 • Lat: 34.5748 Lon: -92.5874 I-30 Exit 118 take the W Service Rd .5 mile
Bentonville	■ 1		℞	🚍	3500 SE Club Blvd, 72712 / 479-621-5537 • Lat: 36.3650 Lon: -94.2247 I-540 Exit 86 go E on US-62 for .3 mile then S on SE Club Blvd
	◆ 4	🕐	℞	🚍	406 S Walton Blvd, 72712 / 479-273-0060 • Lat: 36.3688 Lon: -94.2219 I-540 Exit 85 go NW on Walton Blvd 4 miles
Berryville	◆	🕐	℞	🚍	1000 W Trimble Ave, 72616 / 870-423-4636 • Lat: 36.3767 Lon: -93.5837 Jct SH-143 & US-62 (west of town) go E on US-62 for 2.2 miles
Blytheville	◇ 1	🕐	℞	🚍	3700 E AR Hwy 18, 72315 / 870-763-0440 • Lat: 35.9289 Lon: -89.8709 I-55 Exit 67 go E on SH-18 for .2 mile
Booneville	○		℞		1555 E Main St, 72927 / 479-675-3688 • Lat: 35.1421 Lon: -93.9021 Jct SH-109 & SH-10 (east of town) take SH-10 W 5.5 miles
Brinkley	○ 1				1419 Pinecrest Shopping Ctr, 72021 / 870-734-1811 • Lat: 34.9059 Lon: -91.2031 I-40 Exit 216 take US-49 S then W at Pinecrest Plaza
Bryant	◆ 1	🕐	℞	🚍	400 Bryant Ave, 72022 / 501-847-2857 • Lat: 34.6225 Lon: -92.4964 I-30 Exit 123 go W on Commerce .1 mile, N on Main St .1 mile & W on Bryant
Cabot	◆	🕐	℞	🚍	304 S Rockwood Dr, 72023 / 501-941-5200 • Lat: 34.9779 Lon: -92.0374 US-167/67 Exit 19 take SH-89 W .4 mile then S on Rockwood .2 mile
Camden	○		℞	🚍	1270 AR Hwy 4 Bypass SW, 71701 / 870-836-4538 • Lat: 33.5774 Lon: -92.8358 Jct SH-24 & US-278 (west of town) go SW on US-278 for 5 miles
Clarksville	◆ 1	🕐	℞	🚍	1230 E Market St, 72830 / 479-754-2046 • Lat: 35.4502 Lon: -93.4646 I-40 Exit 58 take SH-103 S .2 mile then E on Market St
Clinton	◆	🕐	℞	🚍	1966 Hwy 65 S, 72031 / 501-745-2498 • Lat: 35.5663 Lon: -92.4521 Jct SH-9 & US-65 (south of town) take US-65 N 2.8 miles
Conway	◆ 1	🕐	℞	🚍	1155 Hwy 65 N, 72032 / 501-329-0023 • Lat: 35.1544 Lon: -92.4003 I-40 Exit 125 take US-65 BR south .2 mile
	◆ 5	🕐	℞	🚍	3900 Dave Ward Dr, 72034 / 501-328-9570 • Lat: 35.0713 Lon: -92.4967 I-40 Exit 129 take SH-286 W 4.3 miles
Corning	○		℞		1900 W Main St, 72422 / 870-857-6914 • Lat: 36.4115 Lon: -90.5946 Jct US-62 & US-67 (in town) go W on US-67/Main St .5 mile
Crossett	◆	🕐	℞	🚍	910 Unity Rd, 71635 / 870-364-2165 • Lat: 33.1368 Lon: -91.9378 Jct US-425 & US-82 (east of town) take US-82 W 6.8 miles
Dardanelle	◇ 9	🕐	℞		1172 N State Hwy 7, 72834 / 479-229-2502 • Lat: 35.1871 Lon: -93.2042 I-40 Exit 81 take SH-7 S 8.3 miles
De Queen	◆	🕐	℞		926 E Collin Raye Dr, 71832 / 870-642-2794 • Lat: 34.0455 Lon: -94.3174 Jct US-371 & US-59/71 (southeast of town) take US-59/71 W 12.7 miles

○ Wal-Mart   ◇ Supercenter   □ Sam's Club   ▨ Gas   ■ Gas & Diesel

City/Town	⬡	🕐	℞	🚌	Information
El Dorado	◇		🕐	℞ 🚌	2730 N West Ave, 71730 / 870-862-2128 • *Lat:* 33.2395 *Lon:* -92.6658 Jct SH-7 & US-167 BR (northeast of town) follow US-167 BR for 1.5 miles
Fayetteville	■	1		℞ 🚌	3081 N Hwy 112, 72704 / 479-587-1840 • *Lat:* 36.1089 *Lon:* -94.1802 I-540 Exit 66, north of highway
	◆	1	🕐	℞ 🚌	2875 W 6th St, 72704 / 479-582-0428 • *Lat:* 36.0520 *Lon:* -94.2012 I-540 Exit 62 go W on US-62 for .5 mile
	◆	2	🕐	℞ 🚌	3919 N Mall Ave, 72703 / 479-443-7679 • *Lat:* 36.1242 *Lon:* -94.1500 I-540 Exit 67 go NE on US-71 BR 1.7 miles then W on Mall Dr
Flippin	◆		🕐	℞ 🚌	168 Wal-Mart Dr, 72634 / 870-453-2211 • *Lat:* 36.2752 *Lon:* -92.6009 West of town center, .5 mile south of US-62/SH-178 jct
Fordyce	○			℞	1123 N Hwy 79, 71742 / 870-352-5167 • *Lat:* 33.8248 *Lon:* -92.4276 Jct US-167 & US-79 (north of town) take US-79 N .4 mile
Forrest City	◆	1	🕐	℞ 🚌	205 Deadrick Rd, 72335 / 870-633-0021 • *Lat:* 35.0298 *Lon:* -90.7911 I-40 Exit 241 go S on Washington St .6 mile then W on Deadrick
Fort Smith	■	2		℞ 🚌	7700 Rogers Ave, 72903 / 479-484-5454 • *Lat:* 35.3513 *Lon:* -94.3481 I-540 Exit 8B take Rogers Ave SE for 1.4 miles
	◆	1	🕐	℞ 🚌	2425 Zero St, 72901 / 479-646-6382 • *Lat:* 35.3279 *Lon:* -94.4099 I-540 Exit 11 go W on SH-255 for .8 mile
	◇	1	🕐	℞ 🚌	2100 N 62nd St, 72904 / 479-785-5964 • *Lat:* 35.4034 *Lon:* -94.3654 I-540 Exit 5, east of exit
	◇	2	🕐	℞ 🚌	8301 Rogers Ave, 72903 / 479-484-5205 • *Lat:* 35.3488 *Lon:* -94.3413 I-540 Exit 8 take Rogers Ave SE for 1.9 miles
Greenwood	◆	10	🕐	℞	551 Liberty Dr, 72936 / 479-996-8500 • *Lat:* 35.2313 *Lon:* -94.3030 I-540 Exit 12 take US-71 SE 8.6 miles, E on SH-10 for .5 mile & S at Liberty Dr .2 mile
Harrison	◆		🕐	℞ 🚌	1417 Hwy 65 N, 72601 / 870-365-8400 • *Lat:* 36.2470 *Lon:* -93.1147 Jct SH-43 & US-62/65 (northwest of town) go NW on US-62/65 for .8 mile
Heber Springs	◆		🕐	℞	1500 Hwy 25B N, 72543 / 501-362-8188 • *Lat:* 35.5074 *Lon:* -92.0295 Jct SH-337 & SH-25 (south of town) follow SH-25 N 4.1 miles
Hope	◆	1	🕐	℞ 🚌	2400 N Hervey St, 71801 / 870-777-5500 • *Lat:* 33.6804 *Lon:* -93.6073 I-30 Exit 30 go S on US-278 for .3 mile
Hot Springs	◆		🕐	℞ 🚌	1601 Albert Pike Blvd, 71913 / 501-624-2498 • *Lat:* 34.4930 *Lon:* -93.0899 US-270 Exit 1 go E on US-270 BR for 1.2 miles
	◆		🕐	℞ 🚌	4019 Central Ave, 71913 / 501-623-7605 • *Lat:* 34.4555 *Lon:* -93.0635 US-270 Exit 5 go S on Central Ave .7 mile
Hot Springs Village	◆		🕐	℞	3604 N Hwy 7, 71909 / 501-318-0185 • *Lat:* 34.6301 *Lon:* -93.0576 Jct US-270 & SH-227 (northwest of town) go N on SH-227 for 5.6 miles, NE on Glazypeau Rd 7.9 miles & N on SH-7
Huntsville	○			℞	121 Lee St, 72740 / 479-738-2001 • *Lat:* 36.0854 *Lon:* -93.7361 Jct US-412 & US-412 BR (west of town) follow US-412 BR SE for 2.7 miles then S on Lee St
Jacksonville	◇		🕐	℞ 🚌	2000 John Harden Dr, 72076 / 501-985-8731 • *Lat:* 34.8847 *Lon:* -92.1095 At US-67/167 Exit 11 on John Harden Dr, 1.8 miles north of town center
Jonesboro	■			🚌	2405 S Caraway Rd, 72401 / 870-972-1644 • *Lat:* 35.8167 *Lon:* -90.6782 3 miles southeast of town center via Matthews Ave and Caraway Rd
	◆		🕐	℞ 🚌	1815 E Highland Dr, 72401 / 870-931-5001 • *Lat:* 35.8211 *Lon:* -90.6850 From US-63 Exit 42 go N on Caraway Rd .9 mile & W on Highland .4 mile
	◇		🕐	℞ 🚌	1911 W Parker Rd, 72404 / 870-972-6350 • *Lat:* 35.8234 *Lon:* -90.7409 From US-63 Exit 45 go W on Parker Rd 1.8 miles

○ Wal-Mart ◇ Supercenter ☐ Sam's Club ▧ Gas ■ Gas & Diesel

City/Town	⬡	🕐	℞	�	Information
Little Rock	▪ 1		℞	�	900 S Bowman Rd, 72211 / 501-227-7119 • *Lat:* 34.7470 *Lon:* -92.4074 I-430 Exit 6 go W on Financial Centre Pkwy for .8 mile then S on Bowman
	○ 1		℞		700 S Bowman Blvd, 72211 / 501-223-0604 • *Lat:* 34.7484 *Lon:* -92.4073 I-430 Exit 6 go W .5 mile on Financial Centre Pkwy then S .3 mile on Chenal Pkwy
	◇ 1	🕐	℞	🚗	8801 Baseline Rd, 72209 / 501-565-0274 • *Lat:* 34.6700 *Lon:* -92.3765 I-30 Exit 130 go E on Baseline Rd .2 mile
	◆ 6	🕐	℞	🚗	19301 Cantrell Rd, 72223 / 501-868-4659 • *Lat:* 34.8108 *Lon:* -92.4848 I-430 Exit 9 go W on Cantrell Rd 5.9 miles
Lonoke	○ 1		℞		1400 N Center St, 72086 / 501-676-3191 • *Lat:* 34.7953 *Lon:* -91.8950 I-40 Exit 175 go S on SH-31 for .6 mile
Magnolia	◆	🕐	℞	🚗	60 Hwy 79 N, 71753 / 870-234-7800 • *Lat:* 33.2553 *Lon:* -93.2086 Jct US-82 & US-79 (southeast of town) go N on US-79 for 1.5 miles
Malvern	◆ 1	🕐	℞	🚗	1910 Martin Luther King Blvd, 72104 / 501 337 9485 • *Lat:* 34.3849 *Lon:* -92.8282 I-30 Exit 98 take US-270 BR east .7 mile
McGehee	○		℞		1001 Hwy 65 S, 71654 / 870-222-4184 • *Lat:* 33.6242 *Lon:* -91.3781 Jct SH-278 & US-65 (south of town) take US-65 S .5 mile
Mena	◆	🕐	℞	🚗	600 Hwy 71 N, 71953 / 479-394-0025 • *Lat:* 34.5944 *Lon:* -94.2046 Jct US-270 & US-71 take US-71 S 5.1 miles
Monticello	◆	🕐	℞	🚗	427 Hwy 425 N, 71655 / 870-367-0409 • *Lat:* 33.6331 *Lon:* -91.8021 Jct SH-35 & US-425 (north of town) take US-425 S 1.1 miles
Morrilton	◆ 1	🕐	℞	🚗	1621 N Business 9, 72110 / 501-354-0290 • *Lat:* 35.1701 *Lon:* -92.7222 I-40 Exit 108 take SH-9 N .2 mile
Mountain Home	◆	🕐	℞	🚗	65 Wal-Mart Dr, 72653 / 870-492-9299 • *Lat:* 36.3701 *Lon:* -92.4476 From Hopper Bypass (northeast of town) go SW on US-62 for 2.3 miles
Mountain View	◆	🕐	℞	🚗	409 Sylamore Ave, 72560 / 870-269-4395 • *Lat:* 35.8673 *Lon:* -92.1054 Jct SH-14 & SH-5 (north of town) take SH-14/5/9 S 5.1 miles
Nashville	◆	🕐	℞	🚗	1710 S 4th St, 71852 / 870-845-1881 • *Lat:* 33.9277 *Lon:* -93.8515 Jct US-278 & SH-27 BR go W on E Russell St for .7 mile
Newport	○		℞	🚗	2500 Malcolm Ave, 72112 / 870-523-2500 • *Lat:* 35.5941 *Lon:* -91.2339 US-67 Exit 83 go W on SH-384 for .8 mile & S on SH-267 for .3 mile
North Little Rock	▪ 2		℞	🚗	5600 Landers Rd, 72117 / 501-945-2167 • *Lat:* 34.8047 *Lon:* -92.2112 I-40 Exit 155 take US-167 N for 1.9 miles then W on Landers Rd for .2 mile
	○ 1		℞		3801 Camp Robinson Rd, 72118 / 501-753-3003 • *Lat:* 34.7907 *Lon:* -92.2759 I-40 Exit 152 go W on 33rd St .1 mile & N on SH-176 for .4 mile
	◆ 1	🕐	℞	🚗	4450 E McCain Blvd, 72117 / 501-945-2700 • *Lat:* 34.7890 *Lon:* -92.2156 I-40 Exit 156 go N on Springfield Dr .8 mile & E on McCain Blvd .2 mile
	◇ 3	🕐	℞	🚗	12001 Maumelle Blvd, 72113 / 501-851-6102 • *Lat:* 34.8281 *Lon:* -92.3922 I-430 exit 12 take Maumelle Blvd (SH-100) W 2.6 miles
Osceola	○ 4		℞		1051 W Keiser Ave, 72370 / 870-563-3251 • *Lat:* 35.6976 *Lon:* -89.9801 I-55 Exit 48 go W on SH-140 for 3.6 miles
Ozark	○ 3		℞		1516 N 18th St, 72949 / 479-667-2143 • *Lat:* 35.5033 *Lon:* -93.8452 I-40 Exit 37 take SH-219 W .4 mile, SH-96 SW 1.8 miles & SH-23 W
Paragould	◇	🕐	℞	🚗	2802 W Kings Hwy, 72450 / 870-236-9707 • *Lat:* 36.0601 *Lon:* -90.5237 Jct SH-168 & US-412 (west of town) take US-412 E 7.2 miles
Paris	○		℞		1501 E Walnut St, 72855 / 479-963-2152 • *Lat:* 35.2920 *Lon:* -93.7147 Jct SH-109 & Airport Rd (east of town) go W on SH-109 for 1.6 miles

○ Wal-Mart ◇ Supercenter ▢ Sam's Club ▪ Gas ▪ Gas & Diesel

City/Town	🛡	🕐	Rx	🚐	Information
Pine Bluff	◆ 1	🕐	Rx	🚐	5501 S Olive St, 71603 / 870-534-7054 • *Lat:* 34.1693 *Lon:* -92.0064 I-530 Exit 43 go S on Olive St .1 mile
Pocahontas	◆	🕐	Rx	🚐	1415 Hwy 67 S, 72455 / 870-892-7703 • *Lat:* 36.2507 *Lon:* -90.9625 Jct US-63 & US-67 (south of town) go N on US-67 for 16 miles
Rogers	◆ 1	🕐	Rx	🚐	4208 Pleasant Crossing Blvd, 72758 / 479-621-9769 • *Lat:* 36.3180 *Lon:* -94.1579 I-540 Exit 81 go W on Pleasant Grove .4 mile
	◆ 2	🕐	Rx	🚐	2110 W Walnut St, 72756 / 479-636-3222 • *Lat:* 36.3340 *Lon:* -94.1478 I-540 Exit 85 go W on Walnut St 1.9 miles
Russellville	◆ 1	🕐	Rx	🚐	2409 E Main St, 72802 / 479-967-9777 • *Lat:* 35.2783 *Lon:* -93.1066 I-40 Exit 84 go S on SH-331 for .4 mile & W on Main St .6 mile
Searcy	◆	🕐	Rx	🚐	3509 E Race Ave, 72143 / 501-268-2207 • *Lat:* 35.2503 *Lon:* -91.6942 US-67/167 Exit 46 go W on Race Ave .3 mile
Sheridan	◆	🕐	Rx		1308 S Rock St, 72150 / 870-942-7171 • *Lat:* 34.3017 *Lon:* -92.3990 I-530 Exit 10 go S on US-167 for 20.8 miles
Siloam Springs	◆	🕐	Rx	🚐	2901 Hwy 412 E, 72761 / 479-524-5101 • *Lat:* 36.1811 *Lon:* -94.5130 I-540/US 71 Exit 72 go W on US-412 for 14.8 miles
Springdale	◇ 3	🕐	Rx	🚐	2004 S Pleasant St, 72764 / 479-751-4817 • *Lat:* 36.1672 *Lon:* -94.1438 I-540/US-71 go E on US-412 for 2.3 miles then S on Pleasant St .5 mile
Stuttgart	◇	🕐	Rx		406 E 22nd St, 72160 / 870-673-3349 • *Lat:* 34.4792 *Lon:* -91.5491 1.5 miles south of town center via US-79 BR (Main St) and SH-130 (22nd St)
Texarkana	◆	🕐	Rx	🚐	133 Arkansas Blvd, 71854 / 870-772-1501 • *Lat:* 33.4606 *Lon:* -94.0424 Jct US-82 & SH-245 Loop go N on 245 Loop for 1.9 miles then W on Arkansas Blvd 2.1 miles
Trumann	◆	🕐	Rx		512 Industrial Park Dr, 72472 / 870-483-6491 • *Lat:* 35.6919 *Lon:* -90.5392 From US-63 Exit 29 take SH-69 E .4 mile, Pecan Grove Rd N .7 mile, SH-212 E & Industrial Dr N .2 mile
Van Buren	◆ 1	🕐	Rx	🚐	2214 Fayetteville Rd, 72956 / 479-474-2314 • *Lat:* 35.4701 *Lon:* -94.3561 I-40 Exit 5 take SH-59 N .3 mile
Waldron	○		Rx	🚐	1359 W 2nd St, 72958 / 479-637-2169 • *Lat:* 34.9003 *Lon:* -94.1069 Jct SH-23 & US-71 (north of town) go S on US-71/71 BYP 8.2 miles & E on 2nd St
Walnut Ridge	○		Rx	🚐	1600 W Main St, 72476 / 870-886-6605 • *Lat:* 36.0750 *Lon:* -90.9710 Jct SH-25 & US-412 (west of town) take US-412 E 7.7 miles
West Helena	◆	🕐	Rx	🚐	602 Sheila Dr, 72390 / 870-572-2442 • *Lat:* 34.5557 *Lon:* -90.6530 1 mile northwest of town at jct of Quarles Ln and Sheila Dr
West Memphis	◇ 1	🕐	Rx	🚐	798 W Service Rd, 72301 / 870-732-0175 • *Lat:* 35.1665 *Lon:* -90.2028 I-40 Exit 276 take the Service Rd W .1 mile
Wynne	◆	🕐	Rx	🚐	800 Hwy 64 E, 72396 / 870-238-8129 • *Lat:* 35.2471 *Lon:* -90.7564 Jct SH-1 & US-64 (north of town) go W on US-64 for 9.9 miles

○ Wal-Mart   ◇ Supercenter   □ Sam's Club   ■ Gas   ■ Gas & Diesel

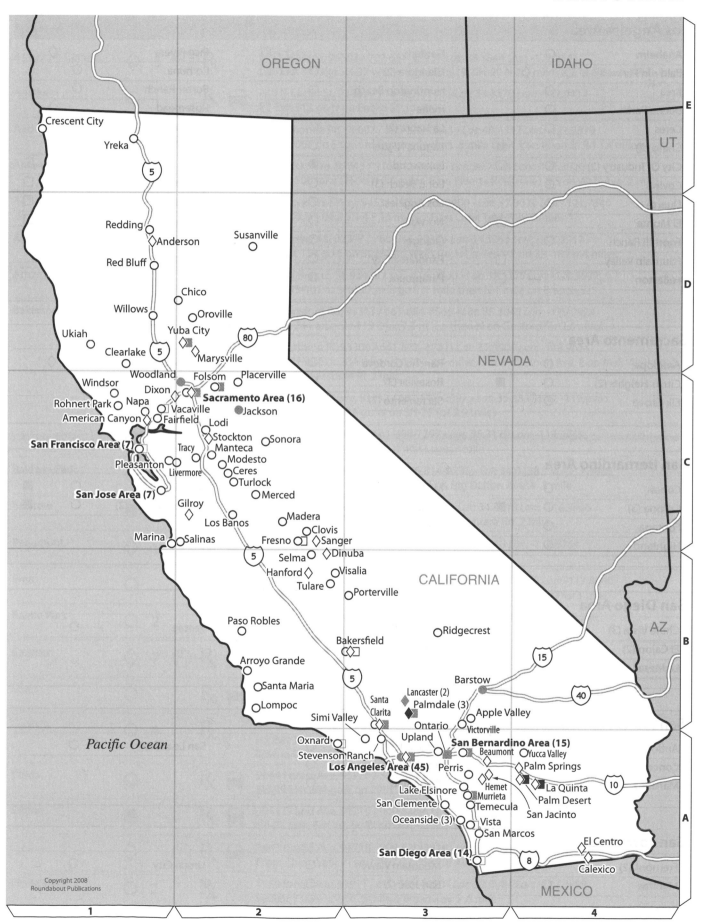

California

○ Wal-Mart ◇ Supercenter □ Sam's Club ▨ Gas ■ Gas & Diesel

OREGON

IDAHO

UT

NEVADA

CALIFORNIA

AZ

Pacific Ocean

MEXICO

Crescent City
Yreka
Redding
Anderson
Red Bluff
Susanville
Chico
Willows
Oroville
Ukiah
Yuba City
Clearlake
Marysville
Windsor
Woodland
Folsom
Placerville
Dixon
Sacramento Area (16)
Rohnert Park
Napa
Vacaville
Jackson
American Canyon
Fairfield
Lodi
San Francisco Area (7)
Stockton
Sonora
Tracy
Manteca
Pleasanton
Modesto
Livermore
Ceres
Turlock
San Jose Area (7)
Merced
Gilroy
Madera
Los Banos
Clovis
Marina
Salinas
Fresno
Sanger
Selma
Dinuba
Hanford
Visalia
Tulare
Porterville
Paso Robles
Ridgecrest
Bakersfield
Arroyo Grande
Barstow
Santa Maria
Lancaster (2)
Santa
Palmdale (3)
Clarita
Apple Valley
Lompoc
Simi Valley
Ontario
Victorville
Oxnard
Upland
San Bernardino Area (15)
Stevenson Ranch
Beaumont
Yucca Valley
Los Angeles Area (45)
Perris
Palm Springs
Lake Elsinore
Hemet
La Quinta
San Clemente
Murrieta
Palm Desert
Oceanside (3)
Temecula
San Jacinto
Vista
El Centro
San Marcos
San Diego Area (14)
Calexico

5
80
5
5
15
40
5
15
10
8

Copyright 2008
Roundabout Publications

E
D
C
B
A

1   2   3   4

City/Town	⬭	🕐	℞	🚗	Information
	○ 7		℞		1360 Eastlake Pkwy, 91915 / 619-421-3140 • *Lat:* 32.6333 *Lon:* -116.9675 I-805 Exit 6 go W on Telegraph Canyon & Otay Lake Roads 5.2 miles then S on Eastlake Pkwy 1.1 miles
	○ 1		℞	🚗	75 N Broadway, 91910 / 619-691-7945 • *Lat:* 32.6499 *Lon:* -117.0933 I-5 Exit 8B go E .4 mile on "E" St then N .5 mile on Broadway
Citrus Heights	■ 2		℞	🚗	7147 Greenback Ln, 95621 / 916-721-6499 • *Lat:* 38.6784 *Lon:* -121.2980 I-80 Exit 98 go E on Greenback for 2.1 miles
	○ 3	🕐	℞		7010 Auburn Blvd, 95621 / 916-729-8077 • *Lat:* 38.6929 *Lon:* -121.2949 I-80 Exit 98 go E on CR-14 for .9 mile then N on Auburn Blvd 1.7 miles
City Of Industry	☐			🚗	17835 Gale Ave, 91748 / 626-912-2010 • *Lat:* 33.9955 *Lon:* -117.9160 SH-60/Pomona Fwy Exit 19 go N on Azusa Ave for .3 mile & E on Gale for .9 mile
	○ 7		℞	🚗	17150 Gale Ave, 91745 / 626-854-1166 • *Lat:* 34.0002 *Lon:* -117.9322 I-605 Exit 19 take SH-60 E 6.6 miles, N on Aszusa .3 mile then W on Gale Ave
Clearlake	○		℞	🚗	15960 Dam Rd, 95422 / 707-994-6881 • *Lat:* 38.9262 *Lon:* -122.6125 Jct SH-20 & SH-53 (E of town) take SH-53 S 6 miles then E on Dam Rd
Clovis	○		℞	🚗	323 W Shaw Ave, 93612 / 559-297-4176 • *Lat:* 36.8086 *Lon:* -119.7164 SH-99 Exit 133 take SH-180 E 3.9 miles, SH-168 NE 4.2 miles & E on Shaw Ave 1 mile
Colton	○ 1		℞	🚗	1120 S Mount Vernon Ave, 92324 / 909-783-0497 • *Lat:* 34.0502 *Lon:* -117.3089 I-215 Exit 39 go N on Mt Vernon Ave .3 mile
Concord	☐ 1			🚗	1225 Concord Ave, 94520 / 925-687-8914 • *Lat:* 37.9810 *Lon:* -122.0542 I-680 Exit 52, E on Concord Ave .7 mile
Corona	■ 1		℞	🚗	1375 E Ontario Ave, 92881 / 951-582-0319 • *Lat:* 33.8455 *Lon:* -117.5374 I-15 Exit 93 go W on Ontario for .2 mile
	○ 1		℞	🚗	1290 E Ontario Ave, 92881 / 951-278-0924 • *Lat:* 33.8465 *Lon:* -117.5397 I-15 Exit 93 go NW on Ontario Ave .7 mile
	○ 3		℞	🚗	479 N McKinley St, 92879 / 951-270-0707 • *Lat:* 33.8895 *Lon:* -117.5202 I-5 Exit 96 take SH-91 W 1.8 miles & McKinley St N .3 mile
Covina	○ 3		℞	🚗	1275 N Azusa Ave, 91722 / 626-339-4161 • *Lat:* 34.1027 *Lon:* -117.9078 I-10 Exit 36 go N on Azusa Ave 2.3 miles
Crescent City	○		℞		900 E Washington Blvd, 95531 / 707-464-1198 • *Lat:* 41.7728 *Lon:* -124.1934 US-101 Exit 791 go W on Washington Blvd .2 mile
Dinuba	◇	🕐	℞	🚗	770 W El Monte Way, 93618 / 559-591-0380 • *Lat:* 36.5459 *Lon:* -119.4026 From SH-99 Exit 115 go E on Mountain View Ave 5.2 miles then continue on El Monte Way 5.5 miles
Dixon	◇ 1	🕐	℞	🚗	235 E Dorset Dr, 95620 / 707-693-6505 • *Lat:* 38.4709 *Lon:* -121.8189 I-80 Exit 66 take SH-113 S .4 mile
Duarte	○ 1		℞		1600 Mountain Ave, 91010 / 626-359-7708 • *Lat:* 34.1275 *Lon:* -117.9885 I-210 Exit 35 go S on Mountain Ave .1 mile
El Cajon	○ 1		℞		605 Fletcher Pkwy, 92020 / 619-440-2009 • *Lat:* 32.8075 *Lon:* -116.9700 I-8 Exit 17 go N on Johnson Ave .4 mile then E on Fletcher
	○ 1		℞	🚗	13487 Camino Canada, 92021 / 619-561-0828 • *Lat:* 32.8284 *Lon:* -116.9044 I-8 Exit 22 go N on Camino Canada .2 mile
El Centro	◇ 1	🕐	℞	🚗	2150 N Waterman Ave, 92243 / 760-337-1600 • *Lat:* 32.8071 *Lon:* -115.5740 I-8 Exit 114 go N on Bradshaw Rd .3 mile & W on Waterman .1 mile
El Monte	☐ 2			🚗	4901 Santa Anita Ave, 91731 / 626-575-0973 • *Lat:* 34.0947 *Lon:* -118.0277 I-605 Exit 24 go W on Lower Azusa Rd for 2.1 miles & N on Santa Anita for .2 mile
Elk Grove	○		℞		8465 Elk Grove Blvd, 95758 / 916-684-7100 • *Lat:* 38.4093 *Lon:* -121.3916 SH-99 Exit 286 go W on Elk Grove Blvd .4 mile

○ Wal-Mart　◇ Supercenter　☐ Sam's Club　■ Gas　■ Gas & Diesel

City/Town	⬡	🕐	℞	🚐	Information
Fairfield	○	1	℞	🚐	300 Chadbourne Rd, 94534 / 707-428-4792 • *Lat:* 38.2376 *Lon:* -122.0838 I-80 Exit 43 go S on Abernathy then Chalbourne Rd .7 mile
Folsom	■		℞	🚐	2495 Iron Point Rd #11, 95630 / 916-817-8965 • *Lat:* 38.6461 *Lon:* -121.1189 US-50 Exit 25 go N on Prairie City Rd for .7 mile, then E on Iron Point Rd for 1.4 miles
	○		℞	🚐	1018 Riley St, 95630 / 916-983-1090 • *Lat:* 38.6709 *Lon:* -121.1669 I-80 Exit 98 go E on Greenback Ln 8.9 miles, continue on Riley St 1.2 miles
Fontana	○	4	℞	🚐	17251 Foothill Blvd, 92335 / 909-355-6922 • *Lat:* 34.1065 *Lon:* -117.4282 I-10 Exit 64 take Sierra Ave N 2.7 miles then E on Foothill Blvd .4 mile
Foothill Ranch	○	6	℞	🚐	26502 Towne Centre Dr, 92610 / 949-588-7923 • *Lat:* 33.6804 *Lon:* -117.6681 I-5 Exit 92 go E 5 miles on Bake Pkwy then N .4 mile on Towne Centre Dr
Fountain Valley	□	1		🚐	17099 Brookhurst St, 92708 / 714-965-0410 • *Lat:* 33.7144 *Lon:* -117.9548 I-405 Exit 14 go N on Brookhurst for .7 mile
Fremont	○	1	℞		40580 Albrae St, 94538 / 510-440-8060 • *Lat:* 37.5192 *Lon:* -121.9869 I-880 Exit 16 go W on Stevenson Blvd then S on Albrae St .2 mile
	○	1	℞	🚐	44009 Osgood Rd, 94539 / 510-651-3301 • *Lat:* 37.5121 *Lon:* -121.9414 I-680 Exit 14 go W on Auto Mall Pkwy .3 mile then S on Osgood Rd .1 mile
Fresno	□		℞	🚐	7663 N Blackstone Ave, 93720 / 559-446-0106 • *Lat:* 36.8480 *Lon:* -119.7910 9 miles north of downtown via SH-41 (Yosemite Fwy). At Herndon Ave Exit, go W .4 mile, then N .7 mile on Blackstone Ave
	○		℞	🚐	7065 N Ingram Ave, 93650 / 559-431-0107 • *Lat:* 36.8386 *Lon:* -119.8021 SH-99 Exit 142 go E on Herndon Ave 6.5 miles then N on Ingram Ave .1 mile
	○		℞	🚐	3680 W Shaw Ave, 93711 / 559-277-8191 • *Lat:* 36.8084 *Lon:* -119.8591 SH-99 Exit 140 W on Shaw Ave 1.5 miles
	○		℞	🚐	5125 E Kings Canyon Rd, 93727 / 559-252-9457 • *Lat:* 36.7361 *Lon:* -119.7218 SH-99 Exit 133 take SH-180 E 5.2 miles, S on Peach Ave 1.1 miles & W on Kings Canyon Rd .2 mile
Fullerton	□	8		🚐	629 S Placentia Ave, 92831 / 714-738-1251 • *Lat:* 33.8656 *Lon:* -117.8816 I-5 Exit 114B take SH-91 E for 5.7 miles, S on State College Blvd for .2 mile, then N on Placentia for 1.2 miles
Gardena	□	2		🚐	1399 W Artesia Blvd, 90248 / 310-532-0779 • *Lat:* 33.8731 *Lon:* -118.2988 I-405 Exit 37B go N on Vermont Ave for 1 mile then W on Artesia for .5 mile
Gilroy	◇	🕐	℞	🚐	7150 Camino Arroyo, 95020 / 408-848-8161 • *Lat:* 37.0072 *Lon:* -121.5529 US-101 Exit 356 take SH-152 E .4 mile then N at Camino Arroyo
Glendora	□	1	℞	🚐	1301 S Lone Hill Ave, 91740 / 909-394-4556 • *Lat:* 34.1162 *Lon:* -117.8292 I-210 Exit 44 go S on Lone Hill for .3 mile
	○	1	℞	🚐	1950 Auto Centre Dr, 91740 / 909-592-4866 • *Lat:* 34.1174 *Lon:* -117.8269 I-210 Exit 44 go S on Lone Hill Ave .2 mile & E on Auto Centre Dr .1 mile
Hanford	◇	🕐	℞	🚐	250 S 12th Ave, 93230 / 559-583-6292 • *Lat:* 36.3132 *Lon:* -119.6730 SH-99 Exit 101 go W on SH-198 for 15.1 miles then N on 12th Ave .2 mile
Hemet	◇	🕐	℞	🚐	1231 S Sanderson Ave, 92545 / 951-766-1164 • *Lat:* 33.7246 *Lon:* -117.0068 I-215 Exit 15 take SH-74 E 11.1 miles then S on Sanderson Ave 1.5 miles
Highland	○	6	℞	🚐	4210 Highland Ave, 92346 / 909-425-8846 • *Lat:* 34.1359 *Lon:* -117.1972 I-80 Exit 79 take SH-30 N 4.6 miles, NE on SH-330 for .7 mile & W on Highland Ave .3 mile
Huntington Beach	○	3	℞		8230 Talbert Ave, 92646 / 714-841-5390 • *Lat:* 33.7011 *Lon:* -117.9862 I-405 Exit 15 go W on Warner Ave 1.5 miles, S on Beach Blvd 1 mile & E on Talbert Ave .2 mile
Irvine	□	3		🚐	16555 Von Karman Ave, 92606 / 949-553-9466 • *Lat:* 33.6979 *Lon:* -117.8341 I-405 Exit 9A take SH-55 N 1.6 miles to Exit 8 then go E 1 mile on Dyer Rd/Barranca Pkwy

○ Wal-Mart　◇ Supercenter　□ Sam's Club　■ Gas　■ Gas & Diesel

City/Town	🛡	🕐	℞	🚐	Information
Jackson	●		℞	🚐	10355 Wicklow Way, 95642 / 209-223-5384 • *Lat:* 38.3629 *Lon:* -120.7982 Jct SH-124 & SH-88 (W of town) take SH-88 NE 8 miles then S on Wicklow Way .2 mile
La Habra	■ 5		℞	🚐	1390 S Beach Blvd, 90631 / 562-697-9281 • *Lat:* 33.9150 *Lon:* -117.9697 I-5 Exit 117 go E on Artesia Blvd for .8 mile then NE on Beach Blvd for 3.4 miles
	○ 5		℞		1340 S Beach Blvd, 90631 / 562-694-2707 • *Lat:* 33.9155 *Lon:* -117.9691 I-5 Exit 117 go E on Artesia Blvd .8 mile & NE on Beach Blvd 3.4 miles
La Mesa	○ 2				5500 Grossmont Center Dr, 91942 / 619-337-3655 • *Lat:* 32.7798 *Lon:* -117.0097 I-8 Exit 12 go NE on Fletcher Pkwy 1.3 miles & S on Grossmont Center Dr .2 mile
La Quinta	■ 6		℞	🚐	79315 Hwy 111, 92253 / 760-771-3749 • *Lat:* 33.7076 *Lon:* -116.2817 I-10 Exit 137 go S on Washington St 4.3 miles then E on SH-111 for 1 mile
	◇ 6	🕐	℞	🚐	79295 Hwy 111, 92253 / 760-564-3313 • *Lat:* 33.7058 *Lon:* -116.2819 From I-10 Exit 137 go S on Washington St 4.3 miles then E on SH-111 for 1 mile
Laguna Niguel	○ 4		℞	🚐	27470 Alicia Pkwy, 92677 / 949-360-0758 • *Lat:* 33.5652 *Lon:* -117.7142 I-5 Exit 88 go W 1.9 miles on Oso Pkwy, continue .9 miles on Pacific Park Dr, then S .4 mile on Alicia Pkwy
Lake Elsinore	○ 1		℞	🚐	31700 Grape St, 92532 / 951-245-5990 • *Lat:* 33.6590 *Lon:* -117.2943 I-15 Exit 73 go E on Diamond Dr/Railroad Canyon Rd for .2 mile then S on Grape St .4 mile
Lakewood	● 2		℞	🚐	2770 Carson St, 90712 / 562-429-6239 • *Lat:* 33.8323 *Lon:* -118.1590 I-405 Exit 29 go N on Cherry Ave 1.4 miles & E on Carson St .5 mile
Lancaster	◆	🕐	℞	🚐	1731 E Avenue J, 93535 / 661-945-7848 • *Lat:* 34.6897 *Lon:* -118.0986 SH-114 Exit 44 go E 3.3 miles on Avenue I, S 1 mile on 10th St, E .8 mile on Avenue J
	◇	🕐	℞	🚐	44665 Valley Central Way, 93536 / 661-940-8744 • *Lat:* 34.6959 *Lon:* -118.1718 SH-14 Exit 44 go W .3 mile on Avenue I then S on Valley Central Way for .6 mile
Livermore	○ 2		℞	🚐	2700 Las Positas Rd, 94551 / 925-455-0215 • *Lat:* 37.6987 *Lon:* -121.7689 I-580 Exit 47 go S on 1st St .4 mile & W at Las Positas Rd 1.5 miles
Lodi	○ 6		℞		2350 W Kettleman Ln, 95242 / 209-368-6696 • *Lat:* 38.1154 *Lon:* -121.3038 I-5 Exit 485 go E on SH-12 for 5.1 miles
Lompoc	○		℞	🚐	701 W Central Ave, 93436 / 805-735-9088 • *Lat:* 34.6610 *Lon:* -120.4666 Jct SH-246 & SH-1 (N of town) go S on SH-1 for 1.2 miles then W on Central Ave .5 mile
Long Beach	■ 1		℞	🚐	7480 Carson Blvd, 90808 / 562-425-0662 • *Lat:* 33.8312 *Lon:* -118.0887 I-605 Exit 3 go W on Carson St for .2 mile
	○ 2		℞		151 E 5th St, 90802 / 562-435-8389 • *Lat:* 33.7731 *Lon:* -118.1913 From I-710 Exit 1 go E .8 mile on Anaheim St, S .6 mile on Pacific Ave, E .1 mile on 6th St
	○ 1		℞	🚐	7750 E Carson St, 90808 / 562-425-5113 • *Lat:* 33.8313 *Lon:* -118.0824 I-605 Exit 3 go E on Carson St for .1 mile
Los Angeles	○ 2		℞		4101 Crenshaw Blvd, 90008 / 323-299-8014 • *Lat:* 34.0101 *Lon:* -118.3353 I-10 Exit 9 go S on Crenshaw Blvd 1.8 miles
Los Banos	○ 6		℞	🚐	1575 W Pacheco Blvd, 93635 / 209-826-9655 • *Lat:* 37.0566 *Lon:* -120.8748 I-5 Exit 403 go E on SH-152 for 5.1 miles
Madera	○		℞		1977 W Cleveland Ave, 93637 / 559-675-9212 • *Lat:* 36.9747 *Lon:* -120.0810 SH-99 Exit 155 go W on Cleveland Ave for .2 mile
Manteca	○		℞		1205 S Main St, 95337 / 209-824-2000 • *Lat:* 37.7864 *Lon:* -121.2163 From SH-99 (SE of town) take SH-120 W for 1.8 miles then N on Main St .2 mile
Marina	○		℞	🚐	150 Beach Rd, 93933 / 831-883-9138 • *Lat:* 36.6945 *Lon:* -121.7996 SH-1 Exit 410 go E on Reservation Rd for .3 mile, continue on Beach Rd for .1 mile
Martinez	○ 3		℞		1021 Arnold Dr, 94553 / 925-313-5716 • *Lat:* 37.9959 *Lon:* -122.1095 I-680 Exit 53 take SH-4 W for 2 miles, N on Morello Ave for .1 mile & W on Arnold Dr for .5 mile

○ Wal-Mart   ◇ Supercenter   □ Sam's Club   ▨ Gas   ■ Gas & Diesel

City/Town	🛡	🕐	℞	🚗	Information
Marysville	◇	🕐	℞	🚗	1131 N Beale Rd, 95901 / 530-634-9751 • *Lat:* 39.1256 *Lon:* -121.5744 SH-99/70 Exit 18 go W on Lindenhurst Ave 1.2 miles then N on Beale Rd for .2 mile
Merced	○		℞	🚗	3055 Loughborough Dr, 95348 / 209-384-1275 • *Lat:* 37.3177 *Lon:* -120.4998 SH-99 Exit 188 take SH-59 N for .8 mile, E on Olive Ave for .3 mile & S on Loughborough
Milpitas	○ 3		℞	🚗	301 Ranch Dr, 95035 / 408-934-0304 • *Lat:* 37.4317 *Lon:* -121.9196 I-880 Exit 10 go S on Dixon Landing Rd/McCarthy Blvd for 1.9 miles then E on Ranch Dr for .2 mile
Modesto	○		℞		2225 Plaza Pkwy, 95350 / 209-524-4733 • *Lat:* 37.6718 *Lon:* -121.0358 SH-99 Exit 229 go NE on Briggsmore Ave for .3 mile, NW on Prescott for .1 mile & W on Plaza Pkwy for .2 mile
Moreno Valley	○		℞	🚗	12721 Moreno Beach Dr, 92555 / 951-242-1185 • *Lat:* 33.9362 *Lon:* -117.1788 From SH-60 Exit 65 go S on Moreno Beach Dr for .1 mile
Mountain View	○ 7		℞		600 Showers Dr, 94040 / 650-917-0796 • *Lat:* 37.4006 *Lon:* -122.1089 I-280 Exit 19 take SH-85 N 3.6 miles, NW on SH-82 for 3 miles & N on Showers Dr for .1 mile
Murrieta	▨ 4		℞	🚗	40500 Murrieta Hot Springs Rd, 92563 / 951-696-4500 • *Lat:* 33.5564 *Lon:* -117.1784 I-15 Exit 64 go E on Murieta for 3.3 miles
	○ 1		℞	🚗	41200 Murrieta Hot Springs Rd, 92562 / 951-696-7135 • *Lat:* 33.5533 *Lon:* -117.1952 I-15 Exit 64 go W on Murrieta Springs Rd for .2 mile
Napa	○		℞		681 Lincoln Ave, 94558 / 707-224-8797 • *Lat:* 38.3101 *Lon:* -122.2844 Jct SH-12 & SH-29 (SW of town) go N on SH-29/121 for 3.2 miles then E on Lincoln Ave 1.2 miles
National City	○ 1		℞		1200 Highland Ave, 91950 / 619-336-0395 • *Lat:* 32.6743 *Lon:* -117.0974 I-8 Exit 10 go W on Plaza Blvd for .8 mile & S on Highland Ave for .1 mile
Norwalk	○ 1		℞		11729 Imperial Hwy, 90650 / 562-929-6766 • *Lat:* 33.9172 *Lon:* -118.0832 I-5 Exit 122 go W on Imperial Hwy for .2 mile
Oakland	○ 1		℞	🚗	8400 Edgewater Dr, 94621 / 510-430-9606 • *Lat:* 37.7379 *Lon:* -122.1992 I-880 Exit 36 go S on Hegenberger .2 mile then W on Edgewater Dr .1 mile
Oceanside	○ 4		℞		3405 Marron Rd, 92056 / 760-730-1371 • *Lat:* 33.1777 *Lon:* -117.2985 I-5 Exit 51 take SH-78 E for 3.1 miles, S on College Blvd for .3 mile & W on Marron Rd for .3 mile
	○ 2		℞	🚗	2100 Vista Way, 92054 / 760-966-0026 • *Lat:* 33.1811 *Lon:* -117.3453 I-5 Exit 51 take SH-78 E for .5 mile, N on jefferson St for .2 mile & W on Vista Way for .4 mile
	○ 7		℞	🚗	705 College Blvd, 92057 / 760-631-0434 • *Lat:* 33.2415 *Lon:* -117.2899 I-5 Exit 54 take SH-76 E 6.6 miles then SE on College Blvd for .1 mile
Ontario	▨ 1		℞	🚗	951 N Milliken Ave, 91764 / 909-476-9259 • *Lat:* 34.0733 *Lon:* -117.5581 I-10 Exit 57 go N on Milliken for .4 mile
Orange	○		℞		2300 N Tustin St, 92865 / 714-998-4473 • *Lat:* 33.8278 *Lon:* -117.8363 From SH-91 take SH-55 S for .7 mile then Exit 17 go S on Tustin for .6 mile
Oroville	○		℞		355 Oro Dam Blvd E, 95965 / 530-534-1082 • *Lat:* 39.4979 *Lon:* -121.5766 From SH-70 (S of town) take Exit 46 & go E on Oroville Dam Blvd for .1 mile
Oxnard	□		℞	🚗	2401 N Rose Ave, 93036 / 805-983-2442 • *Lat:* 34.2221 *Lon:* -119.1596 US-101 Exit 61 go S on Rose Ave for .2 mile
	○		℞	🚗	2001 N Rose Ave, 93036 / 805-981-4884 • *Lat:* 34.2200 *Lon:* -119.1585 US-101 Exit 61 go S on Rose Ave for .4 mile
Palm Desert	■ 1		℞	🚗	34220 Monterey Ave, 92211 / 760-770-7146 • *Lat:* 33.7302 *Lon:* -116.3912 I-10 Monterey Ave Exit go S on Monterey for .4 mile

○ Wal-Mart ◇ Supercenter □ Sam's Club ▨ Gas ■ Gas & Diesel

City/Town	🛡	⏱	℞	🚐	Information
	◇ 1	⏱	℞		34500 Monterey Ave, 92211 / 760-328-4375 • *Lat:* 33.7217 *Lon:* -116.3839 I-10 Exit 131 go S on Monterey Ave for .6 mile
Palm Springs	◇ 4	⏱	℞	🚐	5601 E Ramon Rd, 92264 / 760-322-3906 • *Lat:* 33.8157 *Lon:* -116.4874 I-10 Exit 126 go S on Date Palm Dr 2.2 miles & W on Ramon Rd 1.7 miles
Palmdale	■		℞	🚐	39940 10th St W, 93551 / 661-575-9200 • *Lat:* 34.6081 *Lon:* -118.1475 SH-14 Exit 37 go W on Rancho Vista Blvd for .3 mile & N on 10th St for .4 mile
	◆	⏱	℞	🚐	37140 47th St E, 93552 / 661-533-0248 • *Lat:* 34.5568 *Lon:* -118.0451 From SH-14 (S of town) take Exit 30 Pearlblossom NE 3.6 miles then 47th St N 1 mile
	◇	⏱	℞	🚐	40130 10th St W, 93551 / 661-267-6496 • *Lat:* 34.6116 *Lon:* -118.1475 From SH-14 (SW of town) take Exit 37 W on Rancho Vista Blvd for .3 mile then N on 10th St for .7 mile
Panorama City	○ 2		℞		8333 Van Nuys Blvd, 91402 / 818-830-0350 • *Lat:* 34.2220 *Lon:* -118.4490 I-405 Exit 68 go E on Roscoe Blvd 1.4 miles & N at Van Nuys Blvd
Paramount	○ 1		℞	🚐	14501 Lakewood Blvd, 90723 / 562-531-8240 • *Lat:* 33.9023 *Lon:* -118.1431 I-105 Exit 16 go S on Lakewood Blvd for .8 mile
Paso Robles	○		℞	🚐	180 Niblick Rd, 93446 / 805-238-1212 • *Lat:* 35.6149 *Lon:* -120.6812 From US-101 take Spring St Exit, go S on Spring St for .2 mile & W on Niblick Rd for .5 mile
Perris	○ 4		℞	🚐	2560 N Perris Blvd, 92571 / 951-940-0440 • *Lat:* 33.8186 *Lon:* -117.2264 I-215 Exit 22 go E on Ramona Expy 1.4 miles & S on Perris Blvd 1.8 miles
Pico Rivera	◇ 2		℞	🚐	8500 Washington Blvd, 90660 / 562-801-2413 • *Lat:* 33.9866 *Lon:* -118.1039 I-605 Exit 13 go E on Washington Blvd 1.6 miles
Pittsburg	○		℞	🚐	2203 Loveridge Rd, 94565 / 925-427-2022 • *Lat:* 38.0097 *Lon:* -121.8700 I-680 Exit 53 take SH-4 E for 12.1 miles to Exit 24 then S on Loveridge Rd for .5 mile
Placerville	○		℞	🚐	4300 Missouri Flat Rd, 95667 / 530-621-2917 • *Lat:* 38.7062 *Lon:* -120.8306 From US-50 Exit 44A take Missouri Flat Rd SE .5 mile
Pleasanton	○ 2		℞	🚐	4501 Rosewood Dr, 94588 / 925-734-8744 • *Lat:* 37.7001 *Lon:* -121.8845 I-580 Exit 47 go S on Santa Rita Rd .6 mile then W on Rosewood Dr .7 mile
Pomona	○ 5		℞	🚐	80 Rio Rancho Rd, 91766 / 909-620-4602 • *Lat:* 34.0276 *Lon:* -117.7616 I-210 Exit 45 take SH-71 S 4 miles to Exit 13 then SW on Rio Rancho Rd .4 mile
Porter Ranch	○ 7		℞		19821 Rinaldi St, 91326 / 818-832-0643 • *Lat:* 34.2752 *Lon:* -118.5666 Jct I-405 & SH-118 go W on SH-118 for 5.4 miles, N on Tampa Ave .1 mile & W on Rinaldi St .6 mile
Porterville	○		℞	🚐	1250 W Henderson Ave, 93257 / 559-783-8195 • *Lat:* 36.0805 *Lon:* -119.0459 SH-99 Exit 76 go W on SH-190 for 15.3 miles, N on SH-65 for 1.9 miles & W on Henderson .4 mile
Poway	○ 5		℞	🚐	13425 Community Rd, 92064 / 858-486-1882 • *Lat:* 32.9591 *Lon:* -117.0404 I-15 Exit 22 go SE on Camino Del Norte/Twin Peaks Rd 3 miles then S on Community Rd 1.3 miles
Rancho Cordova	○		℞		10655 Folsom Blvd, 95670 / 916-361-0296 • *Lat:* 38.5953 *Lon:* -121.2909 SH-99 Exit 298 take US-50 E 11.1 miles, at Exit 17 go N on Zinfandel Dr for .5 mile & W on Folsom Blvd .1 mile
Rancho Cucamonga	○ 1		℞	🚐	12549 Foothill Blvd, 91739 / 909-899-1441 • *Lat:* 34.1061 *Lon:* -117.5293 I-15 Exit 112 go E on SH-66 for .4 mile & N on Foothill Blvd
Red Bluff	○ 1		℞	🚐	1025 S Main St, 96080 / 530-529-5540 • *Lat:* 40.1607 *Lon:* -122.2267 I-5 Exit 647 go NW on S Main St .4 mile
Redding	○ 1		℞	🚐	1515 Dana Dr, 96003 / 530-221-2800 • *Lat:* 40.5856 *Lon:* -122.3441 I-5 Exit 678 go N on Hilltop Dr .2 mile & E on Dana Dr .8 mile

○ Wal-Mart ◇ Supercenter ☐ Sam's Club ■ Gas ■ Gas & Diesel

City/Town	⬡	🕐	℞	🚗	Information
Redlands	○ 1		℞	🚗	2050 W Redlands Blvd, 92373 / 909-798-9114 • *Lat:* 34.0632 *Lon:* -117.2240 I-10 Exit 75 go S at California St .2 mile & E on Redlands Blvd .2 mile
Rialto	○ 1		℞	🚗	1610 S Riverside Ave, 92376 / 909-820-9912 • *Lat:* 34.0728 *Lon:* -117.3706 I-10 Exit 68 take Riverside Ave N .3 mile
Richmond	○ 1		℞		1400 Hilltop Mall Rd, 94806 / 510-669-1342 • *Lat:* 37.9783 *Lon:* -122.3241 I-80 Exit 19B go W .4 mile on Hilltop Dr
Ridgecrest	○		℞		911 S China Lake Blvd, 93555 / 760-371-4974 • *Lat:* 35.6076 *Lon:* -117.6708 From US-395 (SW of town) go NE on China Lake Blvd 4.5 miles
Riverside	■ 1		℞	🚗	6363 Valley Springs Pkwy, 92507 / 951-653-4840 • *Lat:* 33.9746 *Lon:* -117.3349 I-215 Exit 29 go E on Eucalyptus Ave for .3 mile then N on Valley Springs for .3 mile
	○		℞	🚗	2663 Canyon Springs Pkwy, 92507 / 951-653-4849 • *Lat:* 33.9415 *Lon:* -117.2843 From SH-60 Exit 60 take Frederick St S .3 mile, Towngate Blvd/Eucalyptus Ave W 1.5 miles, Valley Springs/Canyon Springs N .9 mile
	○ 9		℞	🚗	5200 Van Buren Blvd, 92503 / 951-689-4595 • *Lat:* 33.9368 *Lon:* -117.4543 I-15 Exit 96 take SH-91 E 6.6 miles, Van Buren Blvd NW 1.8 miles then W on Audrey St
Rohnert Park	○		℞		4625 Redwood Dr, 94928 / 707-586-3717 • *Lat:* 38.3687 *Lon:* -122.7150 Jct SH-116 & US-101 take US-101 N 1.9 miles, exit toward Golf Course Dr to Redwood Dr NW .3 mile
Rosemead	◇ 2		℞		1827 Walnut Grove Blvd, 91770 / 626-307-1531 • *Lat:* 34.0505 *Lon:* -118.0821 I-10 Exit 26A go S 1.5 miles on Walnut Grove Ave
Roseville	■ 3		℞	🚗	904 Pleasant Grove Blvd, 95678 / 916-781-8160 • *Lat:* 38.7839 *Lon:* -121.2865 I-80 exit at SH-65, go NW for 2.1 miles then S on Pleasant Grove for .3 mile
	○ 2		℞	🚗	1400 Lead Hill Blvd, 95661 / 916-783-8281 • *Lat:* 38.7486 *Lon:* -121.2582 I-80 Exit 103 take Harding Blvd N .7 mile & Lead Hill Blvd E .6 mile
	◇ 3	🕐	℞	🚗	900 Pleasant Grove Blvd, 95678 / 916-786-6768 • *Lat:* 38.7840 *Lon:* -121.2864 I-80 Exit 106 take SH-65 NW 2.4 miles then S on Pleasant Grove Blvd .3 mile
Sacramento	□			🚗	3360 El Camino Ave, 95821 / 916-487-8242 • *Lat:* 38.6104 *Lon:* -121.3861 From Capitol City Fwy go E on El Camino Ave for 2.1 miles
	□			🚗	7660 Stockton Blvd, 95823 / 916-688-3801 • *Lat:* 38.4795 *Lon:* -121.4215 SH-99 exit at Florin Rd & go E for 1 mile then S on Stockton for 1.2 miles
	■ 2		℞	🚗	3671 N Freeway Blvd, 95834 / 916-419-2165 • *Lat:* 38.6393 *Lon:* -121.4968 I-80 Exit 88 go N on Truxel Rd for .4 mile, E at Gateway Park Blvd for .2 mile & S at Freeway Blvd for .6 mile
	○		℞		4420 Florin Rd, 95823 / 916-422-5401 • *Lat:* 38.4960 *Lon:* -121.4543 From SH-99 take the Florin Rd Exit W for .5 mile
	○ 1		℞		3661 Truxel Rd, 95834 / 916-928-9668 • *Lat:* 38.6377 *Lon:* -121.5047 I-80 Exit 88 N on Truxel Rd for .5 mile
	○ 3		℞		3460 El Camino Ave, 95821 / 916-977-0201 • *Lat:* 38.6104 *Lon:* -121.3838 I-80 Exit 90 go S on Watt Ave 2.4 miles & W on El Camino .1 mile
	◇ 1	🕐	℞	🚗	5821 Antelope Rd, 95842 / 916-729-6162 • *Lat:* 38.7046 *Lon:* -121.3280 I-10 Exit 100 go SW on Antelope Rd 1 mile
Salinas	○		℞	🚗	1375 N Davis Rd, 93907 / 831-751-0231 • *Lat:* 36.7094 *Lon:* -121.6648 Jct SH-68 & US-101 take US-101 N 2.4 miles, Boronda Rd W .3 mile, continue on Davis Rd 1.5 miles
San Bernardino	■ 1		℞	🚗	1055 Harriman Pl, 92408 / 909-796-1505 • *Lat:* 34.0666 *Lon:* -117.2623 I-10 Exit 74 go N on Tippecanoe Ave for .2 mile then W at Harriman
	○ 1		℞		4001 Hallmark Pkwy, 92407 / 909-880-4038 • *Lat:* 34.1635 *Lon:* -117.3356 From I-210 take the University Pkwy Exit W .1 mile then N on Hallmark Pkwy

○ Wal-Mart ◇ Supercenter □ Sam's Club ▨ Gas ■ Gas & Diesel

City/Town	⬡	🕐	℞	🚐	Information
San Clemente	○ 2		℞	🚐	951 Avenida Pico, 92673 / 949-498-6669 • *Lat:* 33.4538 *Lon:* -117.6058 I-5 Exit 76 go NE on Avenida 1.8 miles
San Diego	□ 4		℞	🚐	6336 College Grove Way, 92115 / 619-858-0084 • *Lat:* 32.7380 *Lon:* -117.0577 I-8 Exit 10 go S on College Ave for 2.8 miles then W at College Grove Dr for .5 mile
	○ 1		℞		4840 Shawline St, 92111 / 858-268-2885 • *Lat:* 32.8298 *Lon:* -117.1640 I-805 Exit 22 take Clairmont Mesa Blvd E .2 mile & Shawline St S .2 mile
	○ 3		℞		3412 College Ave, 92115 / 619-858-0071 • *Lat:* 32.7431 *Lon:* -117.0521 I-8 Exit 10 go S on College Ave 3 miles
	○ 1		℞	🚐	3382 Murphy Canyon Rd, 92123 / 858-571-6094 • *Lat:* 32.8055 *Lon:* -117.1143 I-15 Exit 8 take Aero Dr W .3 mile & Murphy Canyon Rd S .3 mile
	○ 1		℞	🚐	710 Dennery Rd, 92154 / 619-428-4000 • *Lat:* 32.5790 *Lon:* -117.0349 I-805 Exit 2 take Palm Ave E .3 mile then Dennery Rd S .4 mile
San Jacinto	◇	🕐	℞	🚐	1861 S San Jacinto Ave, 92583 / 951-487-1492 • *Lat:* 33.7679 *Lon:* -116.9587 I-215 Exit 15 take SH-74 E 13.9 miles then San Jacinto Ave N 1.4 miles
San Jose	○		℞		5502 Monterey Hwy, 95138 / 408-363-9050 • *Lat:* 37.2548 *Lon:* -121.8004 From US-101 take the SH-82 Exit to Monterey Rd S for .4 mile
	○ 1		℞		777 Story Rd, 95122 / 408-885-1142 • *Lat:* 37.3294 *Lon:* -121.8589 From I-280 take the McLaughlin Ave Exit, S on McLaughlin .3 mile & W on Storey Rd .4 mile
San Leandro	○ 1		℞		1919 Davis St, 94577 / 510-569-0200 • *Lat:* 37.7180 *Lon:* -122.1808 I-880 take the Davis St Exit & go W for .3 mile
San Marcos	○ 2		℞		732 Center Dr, 92069 / 760-233-8009 • *Lat:* 33.1366 *Lon:* -117.1235 I-15 Exit 32 take US-78 W 1.2 miles, Nordahl Rd N .1 mile then W on Montiel/Center Dr .4 mile
Sanger	◇		℞		2761 Jensen Ave, 93657 / 559-875-4268 • *Lat:* 36.7056 *Lon:* -119.5744 SH-99 Exit 130 go 11 miles E on Jensen Ave
Santa Ana	○ 6		℞	🚐	3600 W McFadden Ave, 92704 / 714-775-1804 • *Lat:* 33.7382 *Lon:* -117.9172 I-5 Exit 106 take SH-22 W 3 miles, Harbor Blvd S 2.1 miles then E at McFadden Ave .2 mile
Santa Clarita	■ 6		℞	🚐	26468 Carl Boyer Dr, 91350 / 661-222-7408 • *Lat:* 34.4128 *Lon:* -118.5037 I-5 Exit 170 E on SH-126 for 2.6 miles, N on Boquet Canyon Rd .6 mile, E on Soledad Canyon 1.8 miles, E on Golden Triangle .4 mile & S on Carl Boyer Dr
	○ 3		℞		27931 Kelly Johnson Pkwy, 91355 / 661-294-5211 • *Lat:* 34.4142 *Lon:* -118.5699 I-5 Exit 170 go W then N on The Old Rd for .6 mile, NE on Rye Canyon Rd 1 mile, N on Aurora St .5 mile & E on Kelly J Pkwy .2 mile
	◇	🕐	℞	🚐	26471 Carl Boyer Dr, 91350 / 661-259-0863 • *Lat:* 34.4128 *Lon:* -118.5034 SH-14 Exit 5 go N on Golden Valley Rd 2.6 miles, W on Center Pointe Pkwy & N on Boyer Dr .2 mile
Santa Fe Springs	○ 4		℞	🚐	13310 Telegraph Rd, 90670 / 562-946-6343 • *Lat:* 33.9416 *Lon:* -118.0489 I-5 Exit 120 take Bloomfield Ave N 2.6 miles & Telegraph Rd E .9 mile
Santa Maria	○		℞	🚐	2220 S Bradley Rd, 93455 / 805-349-7885 • *Lat:* 34.9202 *Lon:* -120.4217 Jct SH-166 & US-101 (N of town) take US-101 S 5 miles, W on Betteravia Rd .2 mile & S on Bradley Rd .3 mile
Santee	○ 10		℞	🚐	170 Town Center Pkwy, 92071 / 619-449-7900 • *Lat:* 32.8425 *Lon:* -116.9876 I-15 Exit 11 take SH-52 E 7.7 miles, N on Mission Gorge Rd 1.4 miles, W on Cuyamaca St .3 mile & S at Town Center Pkwy .2 mile
Selma	○		℞	🚐	3400 Floral Ave, 93662 / 559-891-7190 • *Lat:* 36.5762 *Lon:* -119.6315 Jct SH-201 & SH-99 (S of town) take SH-99 N 5.2 miles & E on Floral Ave .3 mile
Simi Valley	○		℞	🚐	255 Cochran St, 93065 / 805-581-1666 • *Lat:* 34.2812 *Lon:* -118.7926 From SH-118 Exit 23 (Ronald Reagan Fwy/Simi Valley Fwy) go S .2 mile on 1st St then W .7 mile on Cochran St

○ Wal-Mart ◇ Supercenter □ Sam's Club ▨ Gas ■ Gas & Diesel

City/Town	⬡	🕐	℞	🚌	Information
Sonora	◯			℞ 🚌	1101 Sanguinetti Rd, 95370 / 209-533-2617 • *Lat:* 37.9737 *Lon:* -120.3678 1.4 miles southeast of town center near jct of SH-108 and Mono Way
South Gate	☐ 1			🚌	5871 Firestone Blvd, 90280 / 562-806-4725 • *Lat:* 33.9490 *Lon:* -118.1622 I-710 Exit 13 go E on Firestone Blvd for .6 mile
Stanton	☐ 1			🚌	12540 Beach Blvd, 90680 / 714-898-9891 • *Lat:* 33.7804 *Lon:* -117.9926 I-405 take SH-22 E for 3 miles then N on SH-39 for .7 mile
Stevenson Ranch	◯ 1			℞ 🚌	25450 The Old Rd, 91381 / 661-253-1911 • *Lat:* 34.3825 *Lon:* -118.5709 I-5 Exit 167 take Pico Canyon Rd W .3 mile
Stockton	◇ 5	🕐	℞	🚌	3223 E Hammer Ln, 95212 / 209-473-2796 • *Lat:* 38.0213 *Lon:* -121.2750 I-5 Exit 478 go E on Hammer Lane 4.7 miles
Susanville	◯		℞		2900 Main St, 96130 / 530-251-2000 • *Lat:* 40.4109 *Lon:* -120.6364 Jct SH-44 & SH-36 (W of town) take SH-36 E for 6.8 miles
Sylmar	☐ 1			🚌	12920 Foothill Blvd, 91342 / 818-365-7710 • *Lat:* 34.2953 *Lon:* -118.4173 I-210 Exit 5 go W on Maclay St for .1 mile, S .3 mile on Foothill Blvd
Temecula	◯ 1		℞	🚌	32225 Hwy 79, 92592 / 951-506-7613 • *Lat:* 33.4897 *Lon:* -117.2017 I-15 at Exit 58
Torrance	☐ 4		℞	🚌	2601 Skypark Dr, 90505 / 310-534-0134 • *Lat:* 33.8028 *Lon:* -118.3313 I-110 Exit 4 go W on SH-1 for 3 miles, N on Crenshaw Blvd for .8 mile & W on Skypark for .2 mile
	◯ 1		℞	🚌	19503 Normandie Ave, 90501 / 310-782-6022 • *Lat:* 33.8541 *Lon:* -118.2994 I-405 Exit 38 go S on Normandie for .5 mile
Tracy	◯ 1		℞	🚌	3010 W Grant Line Rd, 95304 / 209-836-5786 • *Lat:* 37.7538 *Lon:* -121.4710 I-205 Exit 6 go W on Grant Line Rd for .5 mile
Tulare	◯		℞	🚌	1110 E Prosperity Ave, 93274 / 559-684-1300 • *Lat:* 36.2259 *Lon:* -119.3306 SH-99 Exit 88 go E on Prosperity Ave for .2 mile
Turlock	◯		℞	🚌	2111 Fulkerth Rd, 95380 / 209-634-8543 • *Lat:* 37.5074 *Lon:* -120.8721 SH-99 Exit 214 go E on Fulkerth Rd for .3 mile
Ukiah	◯		℞	🚌	1155 Airport Park Blvd, 95482 / 707-468-0258 • *Lat:* 39.1341 *Lon:* -123.1986 Jct US-101 & SH-222 (S of town) go W on SH-222 for .3 mile then S on Airport Park Blvd .1 mile
Union City	◯ 1		℞	🚌	30600 Dyer St, 94587 / 510-475-5915 • *Lat:* 37.6033 *Lon:* -122.0693 I-880 Exit 23 go W on Alvarado Rd .4 mile & N on Dyer St .5 mile
Upland	◯ 2		℞	🚌	1540 W Foothill Blvd, 91786 / 909-920-4021 • *Lat:* 34.1068 *Lon:* -117.6786 I-210 Exit 52 go E on Base Line Rd for .8 mile, S on Benson Ave 1 mile & E on Foothill Blvd
Vacaville	☐ 2		℞	🚌	1500 Helen Power Dr, 95687 / 707-449-0290 • *Lat:* 38.3627 *Lon:* -121.9577 I-80 Exit 55 go NE on Monte Vista Ave for .4 mile, E on Nut Tree Rd for .5 mile & S on Burton Dr for .3 mile
	◯ 1		℞	🚌	1501 Helen Power Dr, 95687 / 707-451-0166 • *Lat:* 38.3624 *Lon:* -121.9579 I-80 Exit 56 follow signs to Orange Dr .1 mile, Nut Tree Dr S .3 mile, Burton Dr W .3 mile to Power Dr
Victorville	◯ 1		℞	🚌	15272 Bear Valley Rd, 92395 / 760-951-5005 • *Lat:* 34.4707 *Lon:* -117.3307 I-15 Exit 147 go E on Bear Valley Rd for .8 mile
Visalia	◯		℞	🚌	1819 E Noble Ave, 93292 / 559-636-2302 • *Lat:* 36.3260 *Lon:* -119.2725 SH-99 Exit 96 take SH-198 E 7.6 miles to Exit 107B then E on Noble Ave .2 mile
Vista	☐ 10		℞	🚌	1900 University Dr, 92083 / 760-732-1101 • *Lat:* 33.1706 *Lon:* -117.2180 I-5 Exit 51B take SH-78 E for 8.8 miles, E on Sycamore Ave for .2 mile & N on University for .3 mile
	◯ 9		℞	🚌	1800 University Dr, 92083 / 760-945-7995 • *Lat:* 33.1706 *Lon:* -117.2154 I-5 Exit 51 take US-78 E 8.8 miles, E on Sycamore Ave .2 mile & N on University Dr

◯ Wal-Mart ◇ Supercenter ☐ Sam's Club ▓ Gas ■ Gas & Diesel

Connecticut

○ Wal-Mart ◇ Supercenter □ Sam's Club ▨ Gas ■ Gas & Diesel

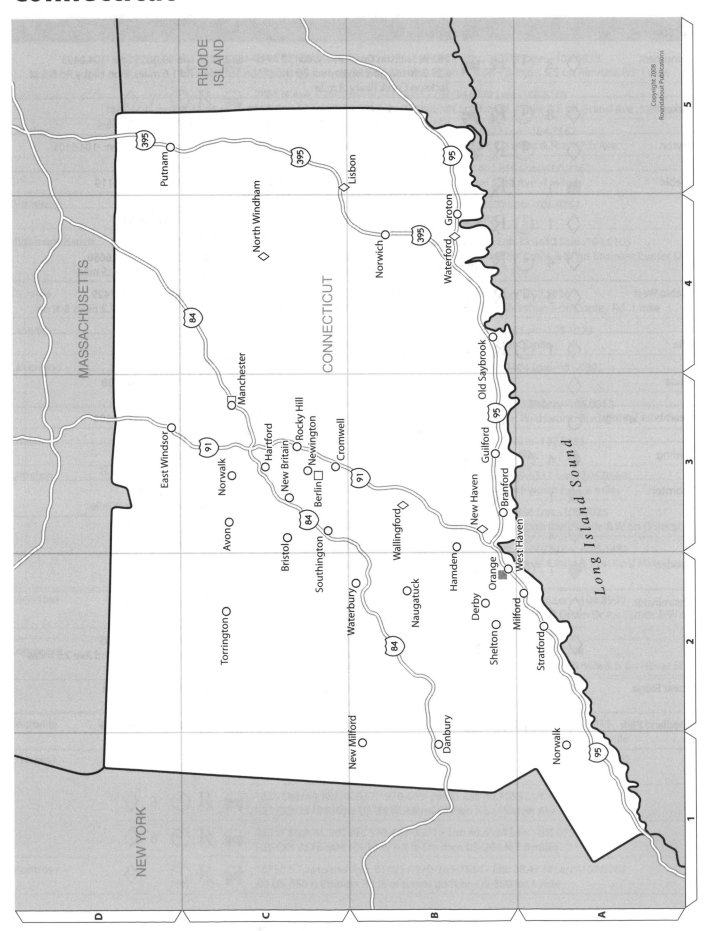

City/Town	⬭	🕐	℞	🚗	Information
Avon	◯		℞		255 W Main St, 06001 / 860-409-0404 • Lat: 41.8124 Lon: -72.8537 Jct US-44 & US-202 (E of town) take US-44 W for 1.2 miles
Berlin	☐ 4				245 Wilbur Cross Hwy, 06037 / 860-829-0841 • Lat: 41.6433 Lon: -72.7320 I-91 Exit 22 take SH-9 W 2.4 miles then SH-15 N 1.4 miles
Branford	◯ 2		℞		120 Commercial Pkwy, 06405 / 203-488-4106 • Lat: 41.2796 Lon: -72.8312 I-95 Exit 54 go S .2 mile on Cedar St, W .8 mile on US-1 (Main St), N .3 mile on Commercial Pkwy
Bristol	◯ 6		℞		1400 Farmington Ave, 06010 / 860-585-1700 • Lat: 41.6989 Lon: -72.8961 I-84 Exit 33 take SH-72 W 2.1 miles, SH-177 N 2 miles & US-6 S 1 mile
Cromwell	◯ 1		℞		161 Berlin Rd, 06416 / 860-635-0458 • Lat: 41.6069 Lon: -72.7121 I-91 Exit 21 go W on Berlin Rd for .3 mile
Danbury	◯ 1		℞		67 Newtown Rd, 06810 / 203-791-1929 • Lat: 41.4059 Lon: -73.4187 I-84 Exit 8 go S on Newtown Rd .7 mile
Derby	◯		℞		656 New Haven Ave, 06418 / 203-736-2660 • Lat: 41.3122 Lon: -73.0579 Jct SH-8 & SH-34 (W of town) follow SH-34 E for 2.2 miles
East Windsor	◯ 1		℞		69 Prospect Hill Rd, 06088 / 860-292-1235 • Lat: 41.9219 Lon: -72.6074 I-91 Exit 44 take US-5 N for .7 mile
Groton	◯ 1		℞		150 Gold Star Hwy, 06340 / 860-448-2022 • Lat: 41.3677 Lon: -72.0656 I-95 Exit 86 go NE on Gold Star Hwy .7 mile
Guilford	◯ 1				900 Boston Post Rd, 06437 / 203-458-1252 • Lat: 41.2884 Lon: -72.6790 I-95 Exit 59 go S on Goose Ln .2 mile then US-1 SE .8 mile
Hamden	◯ 6		℞		2300 Dixwell Ave, 06514 / 203-230-0285 • Lat: 41.3731 Lon: -72.9170 I-91 Exit 10 take US-40 N 3.1 miles then follow SH-10 S 2.5 miles
Hartford	◯ 1		℞	🚗	495 Flatbush Ave, 06106 / 860-953-0040 • Lat: 41.7424 Lon: -72.7124 I-84 Exit 45 take Flatbush Ave S .8 mile
Lisbon	◇ 1	🕐	℞	🚗	180 River Rd, 06351 / 860-376-3254 • Lat: 41.5846 Lon: -71.9944 I-395 Exit 84 go S on River Rd .3 mile
Manchester	☐ 1		℞	🚗	69 Pavilion Dr, 06042 / 860-644-5593 • Lat: 41.8037 Lon: -72.5501 I-84 Exit 62 go N on Buckland for .1 mile & E on Pavillion
	◯ 2		℞		420 Buckland Hills Dr, 06042 / 860-644-5100 • Lat: 41.8078 Lon: -72.5383 I-84 Exit 62 go W on Buckland St .4 mile then NW on Buckland Hills Dr 1 mile
Milford	◯ 1		℞	🚗	1365 Boston Post Rd, 06460 / 203-301-0559 • Lat: 41.2400 Lon: -73.0340 I-95 Exit 39B take Boston Post Rd (US-1) N for .3 mile
Naugatuck	◯ 7		℞		1100 New Haven Rd, 06770 / 203-729-9100 • Lat: 41.4692 Lon: -73.0277 I-84 Exit 19 take SH-8 S for 4.7 miles to Exit 26/SH-63 SE for 1.8 miles
New Britain	◯ 2		℞		655 Farmington Ave, 06053 / 860-223-2555 • Lat: 41.6957 Lon: -72.7909 I-84 Exit 37 take Feinmann Rd SE .5 mile then Farmington Ave S .6 mile
New Haven	◯ 1	🕐	℞		315 Foxon Blvd, 06513 / 203-467-7509 • Lat: 41.3206 Lon: -72.8736 I-91 Exit 8 go E on SH-80 for .6 mile
New Milford	◯		℞		164 Danbury Rd, 06776 / 860-350-4823 • Lat: 41.5514 Lon: -73.4175 I-84 Exit 7 take US-7 NW for 10.1 miles
Newington	◯ 5		℞	🚗	3164 Berlin Tpke, 06111 / 860-667-7657 • Lat: 41.6625 Lon: -72.7214 I-91 Exit 22N merge onto US-9 N 2.2 miles to Exit 21, Berlin Tpk/US-5 N 2.6 miles
North Windham	◇	🕐	℞	🚗	474 Boston Post Rd, 06256 / 860-456-4399 • Lat: 41.7446 Lon: -72.1701 Jct US-6 & SH-66 (SW of town) follow SH-66/Boston Post Rd for 1.3 miles
Norwalk	◯ 2		℞		680 Connecticut Ave, 06854 / 203-854-5236 • Lat: 41.8071 Lon: -72.7350 I-95 Exit 14 take US-1 S 1.1 miles

◯ Wal-Mart   ◇ Supercenter   ☐ Sam's Club   ▬ Gas   ▬ Gas & Diesel

City/Town	⬡	🕐	℞	🚐	Information
	○	5		℞	650 Main Ave, 06851 / 203-846-4514 • *Lat:* 41.1586 *Lon:* -73.4201 I-95 Exit 15 follow US-7 W 4.3 miles
Norwich	○	1	℞	🚐	220 Salem Tpke, 06360 / 860-889-7745 • *Lat:* 41.5074 *Lon:* -72.1227 I-395 Exit 80 (northbound travelers use Exit 80W) go W on Salem Tpk .4 mile
Old Saybrook	○	2	℞		665 Boston Post Rd, 06475 / 860-388-0584 • *Lat:* 41.2960 *Lon:* -72.3789 I-95-exit 68 take US-1 S for 1.6 miles
Orange	■	2		🚐	2 Boston Post Rd, 06477 / 203-795-8100 • *Lat:* 41.2808 *Lon:* -72.9834 I-95 Exit 42 go W on SH-162 for 1 mile then US-1 N .5 mile
Putnam	○	1	℞		625 School St, 06260 / 860-928-3999 • *Lat:* 41.9244 *Lon:* -71.8889 I-395 Exit 97 go W on US-44 for .3 mile
Rocky Hill	○	1	℞		80 Town Line Rd, 06067 / 860-563-4355 • *Lat:* 41.6820 *Lon:* -72.6581 I-91 Exit 24 take SH-99 W for .2 mile then S on Town Line Rd .2 mile
Shelton	○		℞		465 Bridgeport Ave, 06484 / 203-929-1110 • *Lat:* 41.2959 *Lon:* -73.1087 From SH-8 Exit 12 go W on Old Stratford Rd .3 mile then N on Bridgeport Ave 1.1 miles
Southington	○	1	℞		235 Queen St, 06489 / 860-621-9540 • *Lat:* 41.6219 *Lon:* -72.8730 I-84 Exit 32 go S on Queen St .8 mile
Stratford	○	2	℞		150 Barnum Ave Cutoff, 06614 / 203-502-7631 • *Lat:* 41.2005 *Lon:* -73.1169 I-95 Exit 34 follow US-1 S for 1.3 miles
Torrington	○		℞		970 Torringford St, 06790 / 860-496-8653 • *Lat:* 41.8190 *Lon:* -73.0814 From SH-8 Exit 44 go NE on US-202 for 1.9 miles then S on Torringford St .1 mile
Wallingford	◇	5	🕐 ℞		844 N Colony Rd, 06492 / 203-269-6622 • *Lat:* 41.4783 *Lon:* -72.8119 I-690 Exit 10 take SH-15 S for 3.7 miles to Exit 66/US-5 S for 1 mile
Waterbury	○	3	℞	🚐	910 Wolcott St, 06705 / 203-759-1000 • *Lat:* 41.5659 *Lon:* -73.0080 I-64 Exit 25 take E Main St .8 miles, N on Southmayd .6 mile & N on SH-69 for 1 mile
Waterford	◇	1	🕐 ℞	🚐	155 Waterford Pkwy N, 06385 / 860-447-3646 • *Lat:* 41.3715 *Lon:* -72.1250 I-95 Exit 81 go W on Cross Rd .1 mile to Waterford Pkwy N for .3 mile
West Haven	○	1	℞	🚐	515 Saw Mill Rd, 06516 / 203-931-2081 • *Lat:* 41.2700 *Lon:* -72.9753 I-95 Exit 42 go S on Sawmill Rd .1 mile

○ Wal-Mart   ◇ Supercenter   □ Sam's Club   ■ Gas   ■ Gas & Diesel

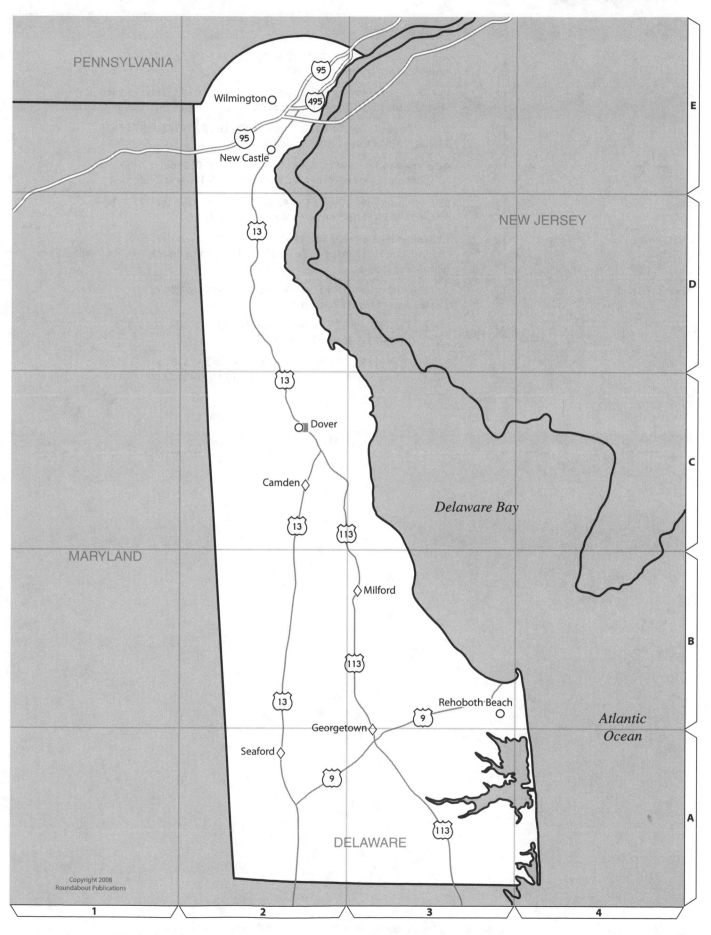

Delaware

○ Wal-Mart ◇ Supercenter □ Sam's Club ▨ Gas ■ Gas & Diesel

PENNSYLVANIA

Wilmington ○

New Castle

Dover

Camden

Milford

Rehoboth Beach

Georgetown

Seaford

MARYLAND

NEW JERSEY

Delaware Bay

Atlantic Ocean

DELAWARE

Copyright 2008
Roundabout Publications

City/Town	🛡	🕐	℞	🚐	Information
Camden	◇	🕐	℞	🚐	263 Wal-Mart Dr, 19934 / 302-698-9170 • *Lat:* 39.1016 *Lon:* -75.5441 1 mile south of town along US-13
Dover	■		℞	🚐	1572 N Dupont Hwy, 19901 / 302-678-4220 • *Lat:* 39.1932 *Lon:* -75.5466 SH-1 Exit 104 go SW on Scarborough Rd 1.5 miles then S on Dupont Hwy .7 mile
	○		℞		1574 N Dupont Hwy, 19901 / 302-674-2159 • *Lat:* 39.1938 *Lon:* -75.5475 3 miles north of town center along US-13
Georgetown	◇	🕐	℞		4 College Park Ln, 19947 / 302-854-9454 • *Lat:* 38.7013 *Lon:* -75.4062 1.7 miles northwest of town center near jct of US-113 and Bedford St
Milford	◇	🕐	℞	🚐	939 N Dupont Hwy, 19963 / 302-422-2854 • *Lat:* 38.9296 *Lon:* -75.4319 Jct SH-14 & US-13 go S on Dupont Hwy for .5 mile
New Castle	○ 4		℞	🚐	117 Wilton Blvd, 19720 / 302-324-0900 • *Lat:* 39.6524 *Lon:* -75.6231 I-95 Exit 3 go SE 2.2 miles on SH-273 (Christiana Rd), S on Appleby Rd .7 mile & E on Wilton Blvd .8 mile
Rehoboth Beach	○		℞		18922 Rehoboth Mall Blvd, 19971 / 302-644-8014 • *Lat:* 38.7296 *Lon:* -75.1313 3 miles west of town along SH-1
Seaford	◇	🕐	℞	🚐	751 N Dual Hwy, 19973 / 302-628-1668 • *Lat:* 38.6620 *Lon:* -75.5935 Jct US-9 & US-13 (S of town) take US-13 N 6.6 miles
Wilmington	○ 3		℞		1251 Centerville Rd, 19808 / 302-683-9312 • *Lat:* 39.7320 *Lon:* -75.6196 I-95 Exit 5 take SH-141 N 1.5 miles to Exit 5, merge onto Centerville Rd N for .6 mile

○ Wal-Mart   ◇ Supercenter   ☐ Sam's Club   ▧ Gas   ■ Gas & Diesel

Florida

○ Wal-Mart ◇ Supercenter □ Sam's Club ■ Gas ■ Gas & Diesel

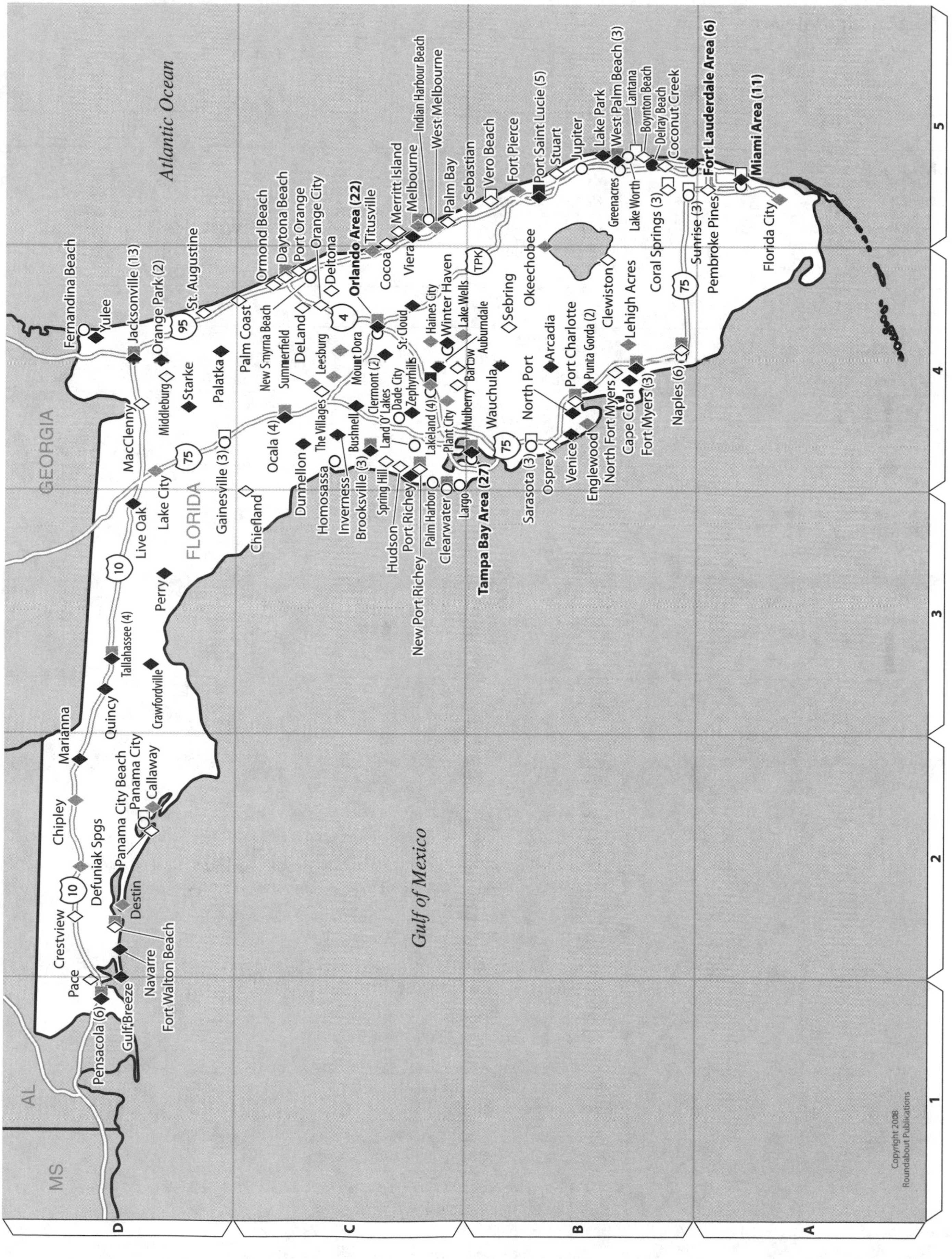

Fort Lauderdale Area

Cooper City	○	Margate	◇	Pompano Beach (2)	○	◆
Lauderdale Lakes	◇	North Lauderdale	○			

Miami Area

Doral	■	Hialeah Gardens	◆	Miramar (2)	○	□
Hallandale Beach	○	Miami (2)	○	North Miami Beach	◇	
Hialeah	◆	Miami Gardens (2)	◇			

Orlando Area

Altamonte Springs	○	Fern Park	□	Orlando (9)	○ ◆ ■	
Apopka	◇	Kissimmee (5)	◆ ■	Sanford (3)	◆ ■	
Casselberry	◇	Ocoee	◇			

Tampa Bay Area

Bradenton (4)	◇ ■	Palmetto	◆	Tampa (9)	○ ◆ ■	
Brandon (4)	○ ◆ ■	Pinellas Park (2)	◆ ■	Wesley Chapel	■	
Gibsonton	◆	Saint Petersburg (2)	○ ◇	Wimauma	◇	
Oldsmar	◇	Seffner	○			

City/Town		Information
Altamonte Springs	○ 4 ℞	200 S State Rd 434, 32714 / 407-774-9966 • *Lat:* 28.6606 *Lon:* -81.4193 I-4 Exit 90 go W on SH-414 for 2.1 miles then SH-434 N 1 mile
Apopka	◇ 7 🕐 ℞ 🚌	1700 S Orange Blossom Trl, 32703 / 407-889-8668 • *Lat:* 28.6525 *Lon:* -81.4684 I-4 Exit 90 go W on SH-414 for 4.9 miles & N on Orange Blosm Trl 1.8 miles
Arcadia	◆ 🕐 ℞ 🚌	2725 SE Hwy 70, 34266 / 863-993-1677 • *Lat:* 27.2088 *Lon:* -81.8338 Jct US-17 & SH-70 go E on SH-70 for .4 mile
Auburndale	◆ 🕐 ℞ 🚌	2120 US Hwy 92 W, 33823 / 863-967-1164 • *Lat:* 28.0574 *Lon:* -81.8160 I-4 Exit 41 take SH-570 (toll) S for 7.1 miles to Exit 17/US-92 E for 3.5 miles
Bartow	◇ 🕐 ℞ 🚌	1050 E Van Fleet Dr, 33830 / 863-533-5400 • *Lat:* 27.9042 *Lon:* -81.8322 Northwest of town at jct US-17 & US-98
Boynton Beach	◇ 3 🕐 ℞ 🚌	3200 Old Boynton Rd, 33436 / 561-742-0718 • *Lat:* 26.5317 *Lon:* -80.0946 I-95 Exit 59 go W on Gateway Blvd 1.3 miles, S on Congress Ave 1 mile & W on Old Boynton Rd .2 mile
Bradenton	■ 4 ℞ 🚌	5300 30th St E, 34203 / 941-739-2130 • *Lat:* 27.4472 *Lon:* -82.5263 I-75 Exit 217 (northbound use Exit 217B) go W 4 miles
	◇ 5 🕐 ℞ 🚌	2911 53rd Ave E, 34203 / 941-753-6751 • *Lat:* 27.4476 *Lon:* -82.5266 I-75 Exit 217 merge onto SH-70 W 4.5 miles

○ Wal-Mart ◇ Supercenter □ Sam's Club ■ Gas ■ Gas & Diesel

City/Town	⬡	⏰	℞	🚐	Information
	◇	1	⏰ ℞ 🚐		6225 E State Rd 64, 34208 / 941-708-2800 • *Lat:* 27.4933 *Lon:* -82.4825 I-75 Exit 220 go W on SH-64 for 1 mile
	◇		⏰ ℞ 🚐		5315 Cortez Rd W, 34210 / 941-798-9341 • *Lat:* 27.4624 *Lon:* -82.6149 I-75 Exit 217 take SH-70 W for 8 miles, 26th St N 1 mile & Cortez Rd W 1.7 miles
Brandon	■	1	℞ 🚐		2021 W Brandon Blvd, 33511 / 813-685-8223 • *Lat:* 27.9375 *Lon:* -82.3169 I-75 Exit 257 take SH-60 E 1 mile
	○	6	℞		949 E Bloomingdale Ave, 33511 / 813-681-8136 • *Lat:* 27.8935 *Lon:* -82.2700 I-75 Exit 254 take US-301 S .9 mile then E on Bloomingdale Ave 4.2 miles
	◆	6	⏰ ℞ 🚐		1208 E Brandon Blvd, 33511 / 813-651-9040 • *Lat:* 27.9380 *Lon:* -82.2662 I-75 Exit 257 go E on SH-60 for 5.8 miles
	◇	5	⏰ ℞ 🚐		11110 Causeway Blvd, 33511 / 813-661-4426 • *Lat:* 27.9233 *Lon:* -82.3265 I-75 Exit 254 take US-301 NW 2.5 miles then E on Causeway Blvd 1.7 miles
Brooksville	■		℞ 🚐		13360 Cortez Blvd, 34613 / 352-592-4737 • *Lat:* 28.5335 *Lon:* -82.5025 I-75 Exit 301 take US-50 W 17.4 miles
	◆		⏰ ℞ 🚐		7305 Broad St, 34601 / 352-796-5996 • *Lat:* 28.5363 *Lon:* -82.4064 Jct US-98 & SH-50 (SE of town) go W on SH-50 for 2.3 miles then S on US-41 for .3 mile
	◇		⏰ ℞ 🚐		13300 Cortez Blvd, 34613 / 352-597-3807 • *Lat:* 28.5335 *Lon:* -82.5036 From SH-589 (toll) Exit 46 take SH-50 W for 2 miles
Bushnell	◆	1	⏰ ℞ 🚐		2163 W C 48, 33513 / 352-793-1300 • *Lat:* 28.6685 *Lon:* -82.1399 I-75 Exit 314 go E on CR-48 for .3 mile
Callaway	◆		⏰ ℞ 🚐		725 N Tyndall Pkwy, 32404 / 850-785-6011 • *Lat:* 30.1597 *Lon:* -85.5914 Jct SH-22 & US-98 go N on US-98 for 1 mile
Cape Coral	◆	10	⏰ ℞ 🚐		1619 Del Prado Blvd S, 33990 / 239-772-9220 • *Lat:* 26.6220 *Lon:* -81.9406 I-75 Exit 136 take SH-884 W 7.6 miles, continue W on Veterans Pkwy 1.4 miles then N on Del Prado for 1 mile
Casselberry	◇	6	⏰ ℞ 🚐		1241 State Rd 436, 32707 / 407-679-0377 • *Lat:* 28.6360 *Lon:* -81.3211 I-4 Exit 92 go SE on SH-436 for 5.2 miles
Chiefland	◇		⏰ ℞ 🚐		2201 N Young Blvd, 32626 / 352-493-0758 • *Lat:* 29.5003 *Lon:* -82.8700 Jct US-129 & US-27 go NW on US-27/19/98 for 1.1 miles
Chipley	◆	1	⏰ ℞ 🚐		1621 Main St, 32428 / 850-638-2243 • *Lat:* 30.7512 *Lon:* -85.5506 I-10 Exit 120 merge onto SH-77 N .5 mile
Clearwater	■		℞ 🚐		2575 Gulf To Bay Blvd, 33765 / 727-791-8081 • *Lat:* 27.9604 *Lon:* -82.7317 I-275 Exit 39 take SH-60 W 13.4 miles
	○	7	℞		23106 US Hwy 19 N, 33765 / 727-724-7777 • *Lat:* 27.9833 *Lon:* -82.7300 I-275 Exit 30 take SH-686/Umberton Rd W 4.9 miles then US-19 N 1.4 miles
Clermont	◆		⏰ ℞ 🚐		1450 Johns Lake Rd, 34711 / 352-243-6151 • *Lat:* 28.5275 *Lon:* -81.7291 Jct US-50 & US-27 take US-27 S 1.6 miles & E on Johns Lake Rd 1.6 miles
	◇		⏰ ℞ 🚐		550 US Hwy 27, 34714 / 352-536-2746 • *Lat:* 28.3548 *Lon:* -81.6766 Jct CR-561 & US-27 (NE of Lake Minneola) take US-27 S .4 mile
Clewiston	◇		⏰ ℞ 🚐		1005 W Sugarland Hwy, 33440 / 863-983-4844 • *Lat:* 26.7545 *Lon:* -80.9474 Jct SH-80 & US-27 (S of Lake Oceechobee) go E on US-27 for 8.2 miles
Cocoa	◇	6	⏰ ℞ 🚐		2700 Clearlake Rd, 32922 / 321-639-1610 • *Lat:* 28.3946 *Lon:* -80.7549 I-95 Exit 201 take SH-520 E 2.4 miles & SH-501 N 2.7 miles
Coconut Creek	◇	5	⏰ ℞		5571 W Hillsboro Blvd, 33073 / 954-426-6101 • *Lat:* 26.3176 *Lon:* -80.2009 I-95 Exit 42B go W 5 miles on Hillsboro Blvd
Cooper City	○	4	℞		4700 S Flamingo Rd, 33330 / 954-680-7810 • *Lat:* 26.0608 *Lon:* -80.3131 I-595 Exit 1 follow SH-823 S 3.9 miles

○ Wal-Mart   ◇ Supercenter   □ Sam's Club   ■ Gas   ■ Gas & Diesel

City/Town	🛡	🕐	℞	🚐	Information
Coral Springs	☐ 8		℞	🚐	950 N University Dr, 33071 / 954-345-3443 • *Lat:* 26.2425 *Lon:* -80.2541 I-95 Exit 36B go W on Atlantic Blvd 7.7 miles then N on University .2 mile
	◇ 6	🕐	℞		3801 Turtle Creek Dr, 33067 / 954-341-4505 • *Lat:* 26.2778 *Lon:* -80.2057 I-95 Exit 39 take SH-834 W 5 miles then N at Turle Creek Dr .3 mile
	◇ 10	🕐	℞		6001 Coral Ridge Dr, 33076 / 954-757-0331 • *Lat:* 26.3044 *Lon:* -80.2785 I-95 Exit 41 go W on 10th St 2 miles, continue on SH-869 (toll) for 7.5 miles to Exit 10/ Coral Ridge Dr N .4 mile
Crawfordville	◆	🕐	℞	🚐	35 Mike Stewart, 32327 / 850-926-1560 • *Lat:* 30.2109 *Lon:* -84.3620 Jct CR-2204 & SH-363 take SH-363 S 3.7 miles, Commerce Blvd SE 1.2 miles & Wade Dr/Mike Stewart E for .7 mile
Crestview	◇ 1	🕐	℞	🚐	3351 S Ferdon Blvd, 32536 / 850-682-8001 • *Lat:* 30.7277 *Lon:* -86.5678 I-10 Exit 56 merge onto Ferdon Blvd N .1 mile
Dade City	○ 10		℞		12650 Hwy 301, 33525 / 352-567-1551 • *Lat:* 28.3415 *Lon:* -82.1872 I-75 Exit 285 take SH-52 E 5.6 miles, Clinton Ave SE 3.1 miles & US-301 N .9 mile
Daytona Beach	■ 3		℞	🚐	1175 Beville Rd, 32119 / 386-760-3330 • *Lat:* 29.1734 *Lon:* -81.0326 I-95 Exit 260A take SH-400 E 3 miles
	◇ 4	🕐	℞	🚐	1101 Beville Rd, 32119 / 386-760-7880 • *Lat:* 29.1740 *Lon:* -81.0312 I-95 Exit 206 take SH-200 E 3.1 miles
DeFuniak Springs	◆ 2	🕐	℞	🚐	1226 Freeport Hwy S, 32435 / 850-892-3138 • *Lat:* 30.7038 *Lon:* -86.1228 I-10 Exit 85 merge onto US-331 S 1.2 miles
DeLand	◇	🕐	℞	🚐	1699 N Woodland Blvd, 32720 / 386-734-4420 • *Lat:* 29.0609 *Lon:* -81.3042 Jct SH-472 & US-17 (S of town) take US-17 N 6.2 miles
Delray Beach	● 3		℞		16205 Military Trl, 33484 / 561-495-8127 • *Lat:* 26.4372 *Lon:* -80.1224 I-95 Exit 51 go W on Linton Blvd 2 miles & S on Military Trl .1 mile
Deltona	◇ 9	🕐	℞	🚐	101 Howland Blvd, 32738 / 407-328-8052 • *Lat:* 28.8723 *Lon:* -81.1638 I-4 Exit 114 go SE on Howland Blvd 9 miles
Destin	◆	🕐	℞	🚐	15017 Emerald Coast Pkwy, 32541 / 850-650-0341 • *Lat:* 30.3876 *Lon:* -86.4547 Jct US-331 & US-98 (E of town) take US-98 W 16.5 miles
Doral	■ 9		℞	🚐	8425 NW 13th Ter, 33126 / 305-463-9384 • *Lat:* 25.7852 *Lon:* -80.3328 I-95 Exit 3A take SH-838 W 8 miles, N on 12th St .2 mile & W on 84th .2 mile
Dunnellon	◆	🕐	℞	🚐	11012 N Williams St, 34432 / 352-489-4210 • *Lat:* 29.0497 *Lon:* -82.4613 Jct SH-40 & US-41 (N of town) take US-41 S 3.3 miles
Englewood	◆	🕐	℞	🚐	2931 S McCall Rd, 34224 / 941-475-9220 • *Lat:* 26.9343 *Lon:* -82.3100 I-75 Exit 191 merge onto River Rd SW 12.2 miles, Pine St S 1.6 miles & McCall Rd E .6 mile
Fern Park	☐ 4		℞	🚐	355 Semoran Blvd, 32730 / 407-260-8109 • *Lat:* 28.6498 *Lon:* -81.3318 I-4 Exit 92 take SH-436 E 3.4 miles
Fernandina Beach	○		℞		1385 Amelia Plaza, 32034 / 904-261-5306 • *Lat:* 30.6649 *Lon:* -81.4319 Jct Fletcher & Atlantic Avenues (NE of town) go W on Atlantic 1.1 miles & N on 15th St .7 mile
Florida City	◆	🕐	℞	🚐	33501 S Dixie Hwy, 33034 / 305-242-4447 • *Lat:* 25.4580 *Lon:* -80.4749 Florida's Tpk (toll) Exit 1 take US-1 N .2 mile
Fort Myers	■ 6		℞	🚐	5170 S Cleveland Ave, 33907 / 239-939-2442 • *Lat:* 26.5857 *Lon:* -81.8722 I-75 Exit 136 go W on Colonial Blvd 4.6 miles then S on Cleveland Ave .8 mile
	◆ 1	🕐	℞	🚐	4770 Colonial Blvd, 33966 / 239-274-2920 • *Lat:* 26.6125 *Lon:* -81.8105 I-75 Exit 136 go W on Colonial Blvd .7 mile
	◇ 6	🕐	℞	🚐	14821 Ben C Pratt / 6 Mile Cypress Pkwy, 33912 / 239-437-1880 • *Lat:* 26.5278 *Lon:* -81.8651 I-75 Exit 131 go W on Daniels Pkwy 2.6 miles & S on Pratt Pkwy 2.9 miles
Fort Pierce	◆ 2	🕐	℞	🚐	5100 Okeechobee Rd, 34947 / 772-468-0880 • *Lat:* 27.4201 *Lon:* -80.3766 I-95 Exit 129 merge onto SH-70 E 1.3 miles

○ Wal-Mart ◇ Supercenter ☐ Sam's Club ■ Gas ■ Gas & Diesel

City/Town	⬔	🕐	℞	🚘	Information
Fort Walton Beach	▪			🚘	740 Beal Pkwy NW, 32547 / 850-862-5330 • *Lat:* 30.4560 *Lon:* -86.6384 US-98 (south of town) go N on Beal Pkwy 3.6 miles
	◇	🕐	℞	🚘	748 Beal Pkwy NW, 32547 / 850-862-0700 • *Lat:* 30.4405 *Lon:* -86.6390 Jct SH-188 & SH-189 go S on SH-189 for .6 mile
Gainesville	▢ 6			🚘	2801 NW 13th St, 32609 / 352-375-8853 • *Lat:* 29.6786 *Lon:* -82.3388 I-75 Exit 384 take SH-24 E 3.2 miles then US-441 N 2.5 miles
	◯ 1		℞		3570 SW Archer Rd, 32608 / 352-371-3171 • *Lat:* 29.6228 *Lon:* -82.3772 I-75 Exit 384 take SH-24 E .8 mile
	◯ 6		℞		2649 NW 13th St, 32609 / 352-378-0619 • *Lat:* 29.6773 *Lon:* -82.3388 I-75 Exit 387 take SH-26 E 5.1 miles then US-441 N 1.7 miles
Gibsonton	◆ 1	🕐	℞	🚘	9205 Gibsonton Dr, 33534 / 813-672-0739 • *Lat:* 27.8496 *Lon:* -82.3548 I-75 Exit 250 merge onto Gibsonton Dr W .5 mile
Greenacres	◯ 5		℞		6294 Forest Hill Blvd, 33415 / 561-966-3101 • *Lat:* 26.6512 *Lon:* -80.1424 I-95 Exit 66 take SH-882/Forest Hill Blvd W 4.7 miles
Gulf Breeze	◆	🕐	℞	🚘	3767 Gulf Breeze Pkwy, 32563 / 850-934-0362 • *Lat:* 30.3897 *Lon:* -87.0664 I-10 Exit 22 take SH-821 (toll) S 11 miles then US-98 E .1 mile
Haines City	◆ 8	🕐	℞	🚘	36205 Hwy 27, 33844 / 863-422-7537 • *Lat:* 28.0938 *Lon:* -81.6132 I-4 Exit 55 take US-27 S 7.4 miles
Hallandale Beach	◯ 3		℞		2551 E Hallandale Beach Blvd, 33009 / 954-455-4700 • *Lat:* 25.9865 *Lon:* -80.1213 I-95 Exit 18 take SH-858 E 2.8 miles
Hialeah	◆ 6	🕐	℞	🚘	5851 NW 177th St, 33015 / 305-558-6069 • *Lat:* 25.9351 *Lon:* -80.2947 I-95 Exit 12 take SH-826 W 5.1 miles then SH-823 S .7 mile & W on 177th St
Hialeah Gardens	◆	🕐	℞	🚘	9300 NW 77th Ave, 33016 / 305-819-0672 • *Lat:* 25.8567 *Lon:* -80.3232 I-95 Exit 3 take SH-836 W 7.4 miles then SH-826 N 5 miles
Homosassa	◯		℞		3826 S Suncoast Blvd, 34448 / 352-628-4161 • *Lat:* 28.8066 *Lon:* -82.5766 Jct US-98 & US-19 go N on US-19/98 for 1.2 miles
Hudson	◇	🕐	℞	🚘	12610 US Hwy 19, 34667 / 727-861-0040 • *Lat:* 28.3411 *Lon:* -82.6992 Jct Suncoast Pkwy (toll) & SH-52 (E of town) take SH-52 W 9.3 miles & US-19 N .6 mile
Indian Harbour Beach	◯ 8		℞		1001 E Eau Gallie Blvd, 32937 / 321-777-5504 • *Lat:* 28.1385 *Lon:* -80.5828 I-95 Exit 183 take SH-318 E 7.4 miles
Inverness	◆	🕐	℞	🚘	2461 E Gulf To Lake Hwy, 34453 / 352-637-2300 • *Lat:* 28.8551 *Lon:* -82.3928 I-75 Exit 329 follow SH-44 W 17 miles
Jacksonville	▪ 8		℞	🚘	10690 Beach Blvd, 32246 / 904-928-0017 • *Lat:* 30.2866 *Lon:* -81.5392 I-95 Exit 340 take SH-115 N 6.2 miles then E at Beach Blvd 1.2 miles
	▪ 1		℞	🚘	300 Busch Dr, 32218 / 904-696-8842 • *Lat:* 30.4299 *Lon:* -81.6501 I-95 Exit 360 go E on Busch Dr .3 mile
	▪ 1		℞	🚘	6373 Youngerman Cir, 32244 / 904-573-9702 • *Lat:* 30.1966 *Lon:* -81.7441 I-295 Exit 12 go S on Blanding Blvd .2 mile then W on Youngerman Cir .3 mile
	◆ 1	🕐	℞		6830 Normandy Blvd, 32205 / 904-786-0390 • *Lat:* 30.3024 *Lon:* -81.7603 I-295 Exit 19 merge onto Normandy Blvd E 1 mile
	◆ 1	🕐	℞		4250 Phillips Hwy, 32207 / 904-737-7007 • *Lat:* 30.2798 *Lon:* -81.6283 I-95 Exit 347 go W on Emerson Rd .3 mile then US-1 N .2 mile
	◆	🕐	℞	🚘	8808 Beach Blvd, 32216 / 904-642-4999 • *Lat:* 30.2867 *Lon:* -81.5638 Jct SH-115 & US-90 take US-90 W 1.2 miles
	◆	🕐	℞	🚘	11900 Atlantic Blvd, 32225 / 904-641-8088 • *Lat:* 30.3207 *Lon:* -81.4953 SH-9A at Atlantic Blvd Exit, go E 2.1 miles
	◇ 1	🕐	℞	🚘	6767 103rd St, 32210 / 904-772-0011 • *Lat:* 30.2485 *Lon:* -81.7555 I-295 Exit 16 go E on 103rd St .5 mile

◯ Wal-Mart ◇ Supercenter ▢ Sam's Club ▪ Gas ▪ Gas & Diesel

City/Town	⬡	🕐	℞	🚗	Information
	◇ 1	🕐	℞	🚗	12100 Lem Turner Rd, 32218 / 904-764-2855 • *Lat:* 30.4526 *Lon:* -81.7054 I-295 Exit 32 merge onto SH-115 S .4 mile
	◇ 1	🕐	℞	🚗	13227 City Square Dr, 32218 / 904-751-5552 • *Lat:* 30.4910 *Lon:* -81.6258 I-95 Exit 363 take Duval Rd/CR-110 E .1 mile
	◇ 1	🕐	℞		10991 San Jose Blvd, 32223 / 904-260-4402 • *Lat:* 30.1756 *Lon:* -81.6276 I-295 Exit 5 merge onto San Jose Blvd S .4 mile
	◇	🕐	℞	🚗	9890 Hutchinson Park Dr, 32225 / 904-721-4941 • *Lat:* 30.3308 *Lon:* -81.5508 I-95 Exit 362A go S on SH-9A for 11.5 miles then W on Monument Rd
	◇ 10	🕐	℞		13490 Beach Blvd, 32224 / 904-223-0772 • *Lat:* 30.2867 *Lon:* -81.4556 I-95 Exit 344 take SH-202 E 7 miles then Hodges Blvd N 2.6 miles
Jupiter	○ 2		℞		2144 W Indiantown Rd, 33458 / 561-746-6422 • *Lat:* 26.9343 *Lon:* -80.1286 I-95 Exit 87 take SH-706 E for 1.7 miles
Kissimmee	■ 6		℞	🚗	4763 W Irlo Bronson Hwy, 34746 / 407-397-9910 • *Lat:* 28.3262 *Lon:* -81.4705 I-4 Exit 64A take US-192 E 5.1 miles
	◆ 10	🕐	℞	🚗	1471 E Osceola Pkwy, 34744 / 407-870-2277 • *Lat:* 28.3407 *Lon:* -81.3855 I-4 Exit 65 go E on Osceola Pkwy (toll) 9.4 miles
	◆ 4	🕐	℞	🚗	3250 Vineland Rd, 34746 / 407-397-1125 • *Lat:* 28.3454 *Lon:* -81.4866 I-4 Exit 67 follow SH-536 E 2.4 miles then S on SH-535 1.1 miles
	◆	🕐	℞	🚗	904 Cypress Pkwy, 34759 / 407-870-1903 • *Lat:* 28.1469 *Lon:* -81.4479 11 miles south of town via US-17, Pleasant Hill Rd, and Cypress Pkwy
	◇ 9	🕐	℞	🚗	4444 W Vine St, 34746 / 407-397-7000 • *Lat:* 28.3038 *Lon:* -81.4599 I-4 Exit 64 follow US-192 E for 9 miles
Lake City	◆ 6	🕐	℞	🚗	2767 W US Hwy 90, 32055 / 386-755-2427 • *Lat:* 30.1800 *Lon:* -82.6769 I-75 Exit 427 take US-90 E 5.7 miles
Lake Park	◆ 2		℞	🚗	101 N Congress Ave, 33403 / 561-842-8113 • *Lat:* 26.7654 *Lon:* -80.0880 I-95 Exit 77 go E on Northern Blvd .9 mile then S on Congress Ave 1 mile
Lake Wales	◆	🕐	℞	🚗	2000 State Rd 60 E, 33898 / 863-676-9425 • *Lat:* 27.8940 *Lon:* -81.5557 Jct US-27 & SH-60 (W of town) go W on SH-60 for 1.6 miles
Lake Worth	○ 3		℞		4545 Hypoluxo Rd, 33463 / 561-642-6005 • *Lat:* 26.5723 *Lon:* -80.1145 I-95 Exit 60 go W on Hypoluxo Rd for 2.7 miles
Lakeland	■ 9		℞	🚗	3530 Lakeland Highlands Rd, 33803 / 863-644-4730 • *Lat:* 28.0019 *Lon:* -81.9241 I-4 Exit 27 go SE on Polk Pkwy (SH-570) 8 miles, then N on Lakeland Highlands Rd .4 mile
	■ 2		℞	🚗	4600 US Hwy 98 N, 33809 / 863-853-2654 • *Lat:* 28.1013 *Lon:* -81.9740 I-4 Exit 32 take US-98 NW 1.5 miles
	○ 7		℞	🚗	3501 S Florida Ave, 33803 / 863-644-5676 • *Lat:* 28.0006 *Lon:* -81.9573 I-4 Exit 27 take SH-570 (toll) E for 6.6 miles to Exit 7/Florida Ave N for .4 mile
	◆ 5	🕐	℞	🚗	5800 Hwy 98 N, 33809 / 863-815-4498 • *Lat:* 28.1179 *Lon:* -81.9740 I-4 Exit 32 take US-98 S 2.8 miles, continue SE on Bartow Rd 2.1 miles
Land O'Lakes	○ 5		℞		21703 Village Lakes Shp Ctr Dr, 34639 / 813-949-4238 • *Lat:* 28.2183 *Lon:* -82.4318 I-75 Exit 275 take SH-56 W 1 mile, continue on SH-54 W 3.8 miles then N at Village Lakes Shp Ctr Dr .2 mile
Lantana	□ 1		℞	🚗	7233 Seacrest Blvd, 33462 / 561-586-9260 • *Lat:* 26.5653 *Lon:* -80.0665 I-95 Exit 60 go E on Hypoluxo Rd .2 mile & S on Seacrest .5 mile
Largo	○		℞		1111 Missouri Ave N, 33770 / 727-587-7822 • *Lat:* 27.9268 *Lon:* -82.7878 I-275 Exit 31 follow SH-686 W 9.9 miles then N on Missouri Ave .8 mile
Lauderdale Lakes	◇ 4		℞	🚗	3001 N State Rd 7, 33313 / 954-733-7473 • *Lat:* 26.1503 *Lon:* -80.2251 I-95 Exit 32 take SH-870 W for 3.2 miles then S on 40th Ave 1.2 miles

○ Wal-Mart ◇ Supercenter □ Sam's Club ▨ Gas ■ Gas & Diesel

City/Town	⬯	🕐	℞	🚗	Information
Leesburg	◆		🕐	℞		2501 Citrus Blvd, 34748 / 352-326-3900 • *Lat:* 28.8432 *Lon:* -81.8970 Jct SH-44 & US-27 (S of town) go N on US-27 for 3 miles
Lehigh Acres	◆ 10	🕐	℞	🚗	2523 Lee Blvd, 33971 / 239-368-5700 • *Lat:* 26.6146 *Lon:* -81.6641 I-75 Exit 136 follow SH-884/CR-884 E for 9.2 miles
Live Oak	◆ 1	🕐	℞	🚗	6868 US Hwy 129, 32060 / 386-330-2488 • *Lat:* 30.3240 *Lon:* -82.9668 I-10 Exit 283 go S on US-129 for .7 mile
MacClenny	◇ 1		℞	🚗	9218 S State Rd 228, 32063 / 904-259-4760 • *Lat:* 30.2652 *Lon:* -82.1087 I-10 Exit 336 go NW on SH-228 1 mile
Margate	◇ 5	🕐	℞		5555 W Atlantic Blvd, 33063 / 954-975-8682 • *Lat:* 26.2356 *Lon:* -80.2015 I-95 Exit 36 go W on Atlantic Blvd 4.4 miles
Marianna	◆ 2	🕐	℞	🚗	2255 Hwy 71, 32448 / 850-526-5744 • *Lat:* 30.7291 *Lon:* -85.1857 I-10 Exit 142 merge onto SH-71 N for 1.6 miles
Melbourne	■ 1		℞	🚗	4255 W New Haven Ave, 32904 / 321-768-8190 • *Lat:* 28.0787 *Lon:* -80.6960 I-95 Exit 180 go E on US-192 .7 mile
	◆ 3	🕐	℞		1000 N Wickham Rd, 32935 / 321-242-1601 • *Lat:* 28.1424 *Lon:* -80.6510 I-95 Exit 183 go E on SH-518 for 2.3 miles & S on Wickham .4 mile
Merritt Island	◇ 8	🕐	℞	🚗	1500 E Merritt Island Cswy, 32952 / 321-452-6058 • *Lat:* 28.3575 *Lon:* -80.6694 I-95 Exit 201 take SH-520 E for 7.6 miles
Miami	○ 9		℞		8651 NW 13th Ter, 33126 / 305-470-4510 • *Lat:* 25.7852 *Lon:* -80.3358 I-95 Exit 3A take SH-836 W 8 miles, exit at NW 12th W .1 mile, Galloway Rd N .1 mile & 13th Ter E .2 mile
	○		℞		15885 SW 88th St, 33196 / 305-383-3611 • *Lat:* 25.6845 *Lon:* -80.4501 Florida's Tpk (toll) Exit 20 go W on 88th St 4 miles
Miami Gardens	◇ 3	🕐	℞	🚗	17650 NW 2nd Ave, 33169 / 305-651-4661 • *Lat:* 25.9415 *Lon:* -80.2130 I-95 Exit 20 go W on Hollywood Blvd 2.7 miles & N on 70th Ave .1 mile
	◇ 4		℞	🚗	19501 NW 27th Ave, 33056 / 305-622-6664 • *Lat:* 25.9519 *Lon:* -80.2456 I-95 Exit 12 take SH-826 W 2.1 miles then SH-817 N 1.3 miles
Middleburg	◇ 10	🕐	℞	🚗	1580 Branan Field Rd, 32068 / 904-214-9411 • *Lat:* 30.0835 *Lon:* -81.8684 I-295 Exit 12 take Blanding Blvd/SH-21 S 9.2 miles then Branon Field Rd W .3 mile
Miramar	□ 6		℞	🚗	1900 S University Dr, 33025 / 954-433-8867 • *Lat:* 25.9931 *Lon:* -80.2479 I-95 Exit 19 take SH-824W 5.1 miles then S on University Dr .1 mile
	○ 6		℞		1800 S University Dr, 33025 / 954-433-9300 • *Lat:* 25.9926 *Lon:* -80.2487 I-95 Exit 19 take SH-824 (Pembroke Rd) W 5.1 miles then S on University Dr
Mount Dora	◆	🕐	℞		17030 US Hwy 441, 32757 / 352-735-3000 • *Lat:* 28.8208 *Lon:* -81.6749 Jct SH-46 & US-441 (E of town) take US-441 N 4.4 miles
Mulberry	◇	🕐	℞	🚗	6745 N Church Ave, 33860 / 863-701-2232 • *Lat:* 27.9031 *Lon:* -81.9737 From SH-570 (toll) Exit 7 take SH-37 S for 6.8 miles
Naples	■ 2		℞	🚗	2550 Immokalee Rd, 34110 / 239-592-6670 • *Lat:* 26.2723 *Lon:* -81.7690 I-75 Exit 111 take Immokalee Rd W 1.6 miles
	○ 7		℞		11225 Tamiami Trl N, 34110 / 239-591-4311 • *Lat:* 26.2736 *Lon:* -81.8019 I-75 Exit 116 merge onto Bonita Beach Rd SE 1.7 miles, Old US-41 S 2.8 miles & Tamiami Trl S 1.7 miles
	○ 6		℞	🚗	3451 Tamiami Trl E, 34112 / 239-793-5517 • *Lat:* 26.1244 *Lon:* -81.7633 I-75 Exit 107 take CR-896 W 4.3 miles then S on 9th St 1.6 miles
	◇ 1	🕐	℞	🚗	5420 Juliet Blvd, 34109 / 239-254-8310 • *Lat:* 26.2707 *Lon:* -81.7476 I-75 Exit 111 go W on Immolake Rd
	◇ 1	🕐	℞	🚗	9885 Collier Blvd, 34114 / 239-455-1131 • *Lat:* 26.1504 *Lon:* -81.6869 I-75 Exit 101 take Collier Blvd S .6 mile

○ Wal-Mart   ◇ Supercenter   □ Sam's Club   ■ Gas   ■ Gas & Diesel

City/Town	⬡	🕐	℞	🚐	Information
	◇ 8	🕐	℞	🚐	6650 Collier Blvd, 34114 / 239-417-1252 • *Lat:* 26.0565 *Lon:* -81.6997 I-75 Exit 101 go S on Collier Blvd 7.2 miles
Navarre	◆	🕐	℞	🚐	9360 Navarre Pkwy, 32566 / 850-939-3998 • *Lat:* 30.4099 *Lon:* -86.8309 Jct SH-87 & US-98 (W of town) take US-98 E for 2.6 miles
New Port Richey	▪		℞	🚐	4330 US Hwy 19, 34652 / 727-846-7300 • *Lat:* 28.2229 *Lon:* -82.7328 I-75 Exit 275 go W on SH-54 23.4 miles then N .3 mile on US-19
	◇	🕐	℞	🚐	8745 State Rd 54, 34655 / 727-376-3811 • *Lat:* 28.2060 *Lon:* -82.6696 I-75 Exit 275 take SH-54 W 17.8 miles
New Smyrna Beach	○ 3		℞		1998 State Rd 44, 32168 / 386-427-5767 • *Lat:* 29.0221 *Lon:* -80.9757 I-95 Exit 249 take SH-44 E for 2.6 miles
North Fort Myers	◇ 7	🕐	℞	🚐	545 Pine Island Rd, 33903 / 239-997-9991 • *Lat:* 26.6819 *Lon:* -81.8993 I-75 Exit 143 follow SH-78 W for 6.4 miles
North Lauderdale	○ 6		℞		7300 W McNab Rd, 33068 / 954-726-3388 • *Lat:* 26.2082 *Lon:* -80.2231 I-95 Exit 33 go W on Cypress Creek Rd 3.4 miles, continue W on McNab 1.9 miles
North Miami Beach	◇ 5		℞		1425 NE 163rd St, 33162 / 305-949-5881 • *Lat:* 25.9258 *Lon:* -80.1715 I-95 Exit 16 go E on 203rd 1.1 miles, S on US-1 for 2.7 miles & E on 163rd .6 mile
North Port	◆	🕐	℞	🚐	17000 Tamiami Trl, 34287 / 941-423-5266 • *Lat:* 27.0363 *Lon:* -82.2152 I-75 Exit 191 go SE on River Rd 5.5 miles then E on Tamiami Trl 5.4 miles
Ocala	▪ 1		℞	🚐	3921 SW College Rd, 34474 / 352-873-0500 • *Lat:* 29.1469 *Lon:* -82.1887 I-75 Exit 350 go SW on SH-200 .4 mile
	◆	🕐	℞		4980 E Silver Springs Blvd, 34470 / 352-236-1188 • *Lat:* 29.1942 *Lon:* -82.0912 Jct US-441/301 & SH-40 go E on SH-40 for 3.1 miles
	◆ 5	🕐	℞	🚐	9570 SW Hwy 200, 34481 / 352-291-7512 • *Lat:* 29.0586 *Lon:* -82.2780 I-75 Exit 350 follow SH-200 SW for 4.9 miles
	◇ 3	🕐	℞	🚐	2600 SW 19th Avenue Rd, 34474 / 352-237-7155 • *Lat:* 29.1599 *Lon:* -82.1673 I-75 Exit 350 take SH-200 NE 1.5 miles, S on 27th Ave .5 mile & E on 19th .1 mile
Ocoee	◇	🕐	℞	🚐	10500 W Colonial Dr, 34761 / 407-877-6900 • *Lat:* 28.5516 *Lon:* -81.5343 From SH-429 (toll) Exit 23 go W on Colonial Dr 1.5 miles
Okeechobee	◆	🕐	℞	🚐	2101 S Parrott Ave, 34974 / 863-763-7070 • *Lat:* 27.2232 *Lon:* -80.8287 1.3 miles south of town center on US-98/US-441
Oldsmar	◇	🕐	℞	🚐	3801 Tampa Rd, 34677 / 813-854-3261 • *Lat:* 28.0426 *Lon:* -82.6741 Jct SH-589 & SH-580 go W on Hillsborough Rd 7.1 miles, continue W on Tampa Rd 1.7 miles
Orange City	◇ 2	🕐	℞	🚐	2400 Veterans Memorial Pkwy, 32763 / 386-775-1500 • *Lat:* 28.9250 *Lon:* -81.2817 I-4 Exit 111 go W on Saxon Blvd .7 mile then N on Veterans Memorial Pkwy 1.1 miles
Orange Park	◆ 7	🕐	℞		1505 County Rd 220, 32003 / 904-278-1836 • *Lat:* 30.1021 *Lon:* -81.7072 I-295 Exit 10 take US-17 S 6.3 miles then W on CR-220 for .3 mile
	◇ 5	🕐	℞	🚐	899 Blanding Blvd, 32065 / 904-272-0036 • *Lat:* 30.1400 *Lon:* -81.7702 I-295 exit 12 go S on Blanding Blvd 4.7 miles
Orlando	▪		℞	🚐	7701 E Colonial Dr, 32807 / 407-384-7570 • *Lat:* 28.5685 *Lon:* -81.2833 SH-417 (toll rd) Exit 34 go W on SH-50 for 1 mile
	▪		℞	🚐	7810 W Colonial Dr, 32818 / 407-532-5212 • *Lat:* 28.5519 *Lon:* -81.4932 SH-408 (toll rd) Exit 4 go N on Hiawassee Rd .4 mile then SH-50 W 1 mile
	▪ 7		℞	🚐	9498 S Orange Blossom Trl, 32837 / 407-859-9056 • *Lat:* 28.4216 *Lon:* -81.4049 I-4 Exit 80 take US-441 S 6.1 miles
	○ 7		℞		3838 S Semoran Blvd, 32822 / 407-277-4314 • *Lat:* 28.5053 *Lon:* -81.3106 I-4 Exit 82 take SH-408 (toll) E 4.3 miles then S on Semoran Blvd 2.3 miles

○ Wal-Mart   ◇ Supercenter   □ Sam's Club   ▪ Gas   ■ Gas & Diesel

City/Town	⬡	🕐	℞	�	Information
	◆ 4	🕐	℞	🚗	2500 S Kirkman Rd, 32811 / 407-290-6977 • *Lat:* 28.5169 *Lon:* -81.4594 I-4 Exit 74 merge onto Lirkman Rd N 3.7 miles
	◇ 1	🕐	℞	🚗	8990 Turkey Lake Rd, 32819 / 407-351-2229 • *Lat:* 28.4424 *Lon:* -81.4749 I-4 Exit 74 follow Sand Lake Rd W .3 mile then S on Turkey Lake Rd .6 mile
	◇	🕐	℞	🚗	11250 E Colonial Dr, 32817 / 407-281-8941 • *Lat:* 28.5679 *Lon:* -81.2182 From SH-417 (toll) Exit 34 go E on Colonial Dr 2.8 miles
	◇ 6	🕐	℞	🚗	8101 S John Young Pkwy, 32819 / 407-354-5665 • *Lat:* 28.4501 *Lon:* -81.4273 I-4 Exit 72 take SH-528 (toll) E 2.9 miles to Exit 3/Young Pkwy N 2.3 miles
	◇	🕐	℞	🚗	5991 New Goldenrod Rd, 32822 / 407-382-8880 • *Lat:* 28.4733 *Lon:* -81.2899 From SH-528/Beachline Expy Exit 12 follow SH-551 N 1.7 miles
Ormond Beach	◇ 1	🕐	℞	🚗	1521 W Granada Blvd, 32174 / 386-672-2104 • *Lat:* 29.2578 *Lon:* -81.1136 I-95 Exit 268 go E on Grenada Blvd .1 mile
Osprey	◇ 6	🕐	℞	🚗	13140 S Tamiami Trail, 34229 / 941-918-1247 • *Lat:* 27.1909 *Lon:* -82.4878 I-75 Exit 205 follow SH-72 W 5.1 miles then S on Tamiami Trl .3 mile
Pace	◇ 7	🕐	℞	🚗	4965 Hwy 90, 32571 / 850-995-0542 • *Lat:* 30.6031 *Lon:* -87.1171 I-10 Exit 17 follow US-90 W for 6.6 miles
Palatka	◆	🕐	℞	🚗	1024 S State Rd 19, 32177 / 386-328-6733 • *Lat:* 29.6706 *Lon:* -81.6693 Jct SH-20 & SH-19 (W of town) go S on SH-19 for .2 mile
Palm Bay	◇ 1	🕐	℞	🚗	1040 Malabar Rd SE, 32907 / 321-723-2171 • *Lat:* 27.9986 *Lon:* -80.6406 I-95 Exit 173 go W on Malabar Rd .5 mile
Palm Coast	◇ 1	🕐	℞	🚗	174 Cypress Point Pkwy, 32164 / 386-446-8486 • *Lat:* 29.5510 *Lon:* -81.2265 I-95 Exit 289 go W on Palm Coast Pkwy .3 mile then S on Cypress Point Pkwy .3 mile
Palm Harbor	◯		℞		35404 US Hwy 19 N, 34684 / 727-784-8797 • *Lat:* 28.0938 *Lon:* -82.7397 Jct SH-584/Curlew Rd & US-19 go N on US-19 for .3 mile
Palmetto	◆ 4	🕐	℞	🚗	508 10th St E, 34221 / 941-723-2199 • *Lat:* 27.5155 *Lon:* -82.5552 I-75 Exit 224 go W on US-301 for 3.6 miles
Panama City	☐			🚗	1707 W 23rd St, 32405 / 850-769-2222 • *Lat:* 30.1897 *Lon:* -85.6874 Jct US-98 & SH-22 (east of town) take US-98 W 6.9 miles then N on Lisenby Ave 1 mile & W on 23rd
	◯		℞		513 W 23rd St, 32405 / 850-785-0307 • *Lat:* 30.1896 *Lon:* -85.6673 Jct SH-22 & US-98 (E of town) follow US-98 W 4.6 miles, N on Cove Blvd 1 mile & W on 23rd 1.1 miles
Panama City Beach	◇	🕐	℞	🚗	10270 Front Beach Rd, 32407 / 850-234-1989 • *Lat:* 30.1780 *Lon:* -85.8040 10 miles west of Panama City via US-98 and Front Beach Rd
Pembroke Pines	◇ 4	🕐	℞		151 SW 184th Ave, 33029 / 954-442-5822 • *Lat:* 26.0061 *Lon:* -80.3923 I-95 Exit 14 take SH-860 W for 2.9 miles then N on 17th Ave .7 mile & W on 19th St
Pensacola	▦ 3		℞	🚗	1250 Airport Blvd, 32504 / 850-484-7508 • *Lat:* 30.4805 *Lon:* -87.2157 I-10 Exit 13 take SH-291 S 1.7 miles then E on Airport Rd .5 mile
	◆ 3	🕐	℞	🚗	2650 Creighton Rd, 32504 / 850-479-2101 • *Lat:* 30.4953 *Lon:* -87.1922 I-10 Exit 13 go S on SH-291 for .6 mile & E on Creighton Rd 1.8 miles
	◆	🕐	℞	🚗	2951 S Blue Angel Pkwy, 32506 / 850-458-5550 • *Lat:* 30.3613 *Lon:* -87.3594 I-110 Exit 5 take SH-296/CR-296 W 5.8 miles & S on Blue Angel Pkwy 7.6 miles
	◆ 2	🕐	℞	🚗	8970 Pensacola Blvd, 32534 / 850-484-3771 • *Lat:* 30.5272 *Lon:* -87.2747 I-10 Exit 10 go N on Pensacola Blvd 1.8 miles
	◇ 4	🕐	℞		4600 Mobile Hwy, 32506 / 850-455-4320 • *Lat:* 30.4365 *Lon:* -87.2782 I-110 Exit 4 go W on Fairfield Dr 3.5 miles then N on Mobile Hwy .2 mile
	◇ 6		℞		501 N Navy Blvd, 32507 / 850-453-6311 • *Lat:* 30.3951 *Lon:* -87.2782 I-110 Exit 4 follow SH-295 S for 6 miles

◯ Wal-Mart ◇ Supercenter ☐ Sam's Club ▦ Gas ■ Gas & Diesel

City/Town	⬭	🕐	℞	🚐	Information
Perry	◆	🕐	℞	🚐	1900 S Jefferson St, 32348 / 850-223-4179 • *Lat:* 30.1029 *Lon:* -83.5825 1 mile south of town center on US-221
Pinellas Park	■ 5		℞	🚐	7001 Park Blvd, 33781 / 727-547-8955 • *Lat:* 27.8393 *Lon:* -82.7353 I-275 Exit 28 go W on SH-694 for 4.3 miles
	◆ 1	🕐	℞	🚐	8001 US Hwy 19 N, 33781 / 727-576-1770 • *Lat:* 27.8453 *Lon:* -82.6877 I-275 Exit 28 take SH-694 W .9 mile & US-19 N .1 mile
Plant City	◆ 5	🕐	℞		2602 James L Redman Pkwy, 33566 / 813-752-1188 • *Lat:* 27.9865 *Lon:* -82.1214 I-4 Exit 22 go SW on Park Rd 3.7 miles & S on Redman Pkwy 1 mile
Pompano Beach	○ 1		℞		300 W Copans Rd, 33064 / 954-784-0220 • *Lat:* 26.2597 *Lon:* -80.1275 I-95 Exit 38 go E on Copans Rd .3 mile
	◆ 2	🕐	℞	🚐	2300 W Atlantic Blvd, 33069 / 954-971-7170 • *Lat:* 26.2311 *Lon:* -80.1541 I-95 Exit 36 go W on Atlantic Blvd 1.4 miles
Port Charlotte	■ 7		℞	🚐	17700 Murdock Cir, 33948 / 941-255-5556 • *Lat:* 27.0089 *Lon:* -82.1532 I-75 Exit 179 go S on Toledo Blade Blvd 6.3 miles then E on El Jobean Rd .6 mile & S on Murdock Cir
	◇ 8	🕐	℞	🚐	19100 Murdock Cir, 33948 / 941-625-2399 • *Lat:* 27.0126 *Lon:* -82.1407 I-75 Exit 179 go S on Toledo Blade Blvd 5.7 miles & SE on Tamiami Trl 1.5 miles
Port Orange	◇ 1	🕐	℞	🚐	1590 Dunlawton Ave, 32127 / 386-756-2711 • *Lat:* 29.1169 *Lon:* -81.0227 I-95 Exit 256 go E on SH-321 for .9 mile
Port Richey	◆	🕐	℞	🚐	8701 US Hwy 19, 34668 / 727-846-9504 • *Lat:* 28.2833 *Lon:* -82.7159 Jct SH-52 & US-19 (N of town) go S on US-19 for 3.6 miles
Port Saint Lucie	■ 2		℞	🚐	1750 SW Gatlin Blvd, 34953 / 772-878-4881 • *Lat:* 27.2645 *Lon:* -80.4025 I-95 Exit 118 go E 1.2 miles on Gatlin Blvd
	■ 10			🚐	10900 S US Hwy 1, 34952 / 772-335-3225 • *Lat:* 27.2654 *Lon:* -80.2847 I-95 Exit 129 take SH-70 E 4.1 miles then US-1S 5.5 miles
	◆ 1	🕐	℞	🚐	1675 NW Saint Lucie West Blvd, 34986 / 772-873-2221 • *Lat:* 27.3114 *Lon:* -80.4075 I-95 Exit 121 go W on Saint Lucie Blvd .3 mile
	◇ 10	🕐	℞	🚐	10855 S US Hwy 1, 34952 / 772-335-5359 • *Lat:* 27.2909 *Lon:* -80.2975 I-95 Exit 118 go E on Gatin Blvd 3.2 miles & Port Saint Lucie Blvd 5.8 miles then US-1 S .4 mile
	◇ 1	🕐	℞	🚐	1850 SW Gatlin Blvd, 34953 / 772-336-8212 • *Lat:* 27.2645 *Lon:* -80.4050 I-95 Exit 118 go E on Gatlin Blvd 1 mile
Punta Gorda	◆ 1	🕐	℞	🚐	375 Kings Hwy, 33983 / 941-625-1201 • *Lat:* 27.0244 *Lon:* -82.0450 I-75 Exit 170 go NE on Kings Hwy .2 mile
	◇ 1	🕐	℞	🚐	5001 Taylor Rd, 33950 / 941-637-3800 • *Lat:* 26.8938 *Lon:* -82.0102 I-75 exit 161 take Jones Loop Rd W .5 mile then Taylor Rd S .1 mile
Quincy	◆ 2	🕐	℞		1940 Pat Thomas Pkwy, 32351 / 850-875-1661 • *Lat:* 30.5561 *Lon:* -84.5929 I-10 Exit 181 go N 1.2 miles on SH-267
Saint Augustine	◇ 6	🕐	℞	🚐	2355 US Hwy 1 S, 32086 / 904-797-3309 • *Lat:* 29.8089 *Lon:* -81.3183 I-95 Exit 311 take SH-207 N 4.1 miles, SH-312 E 1 mile & US-1 S .8 mile
Saint Cloud	◆	🕐	℞	🚐	4400 13th St, 34769 / 407-957-1300 • *Lat:* 28.2538 *Lon:* -81.3167 From Florida's Tpk (toll) Exit 242 take US-192 E 1.3 miles
Saint Petersburg	○ 8		℞		3993 Tyrone Blvd N, 33709 / 727-347-1188 • *Lat:* 27.8088 *Lon:* -82.7528 I-275 Exit 28 take SH-694 W 3.9 miles, 66th St S 2.3 miles, 38th Ave W 1.3 miles & Tyrone Blvd N .3 mile
	◇ 1	🕐	℞	🚐	3501 34th St S, 33711 / 727-906-4647 • *Lat:* 27.7369 *Lon:* -82.6796 I-275 Exit 19 take 22nd Ave W .2 mile & 34th St S .8 mile
Sanford	■ 1		℞	🚐	1101 Rinehart Rd, 32771 / 407-302-8355 • *Lat:* 28.7913 *Lon:* -81.3449 I-4 Exit 101A go E on CR-46A .2 mile then N on Rinehart Rd .4 mile

○ Wal-Mart ◇ Supercenter □ Sam's Club ■ Gas ■ Gas & Diesel

City/Town	🛡	🕐	℞	🚗	Information
	◆ 1	🕐	℞	🚗	1601 Rinehart Rd, 32771 / 407-321-1540 • *Lat:* 28.8033 *Lon:* -81.3309 I-4 Exit 101 go S on Rinehart Rd .8 mile
	◇ 1	🕐	℞		3653 S Orlando Dr, 32773 / 407-321-1371 • *Lat:* 28.7608 *Lon:* -81.2850 I-4 Exit 101 take SH-417 (toll) to Exit 50/US-17 SW 1 mile
Sarasota	□ 1		℞	🚗	300 N Cattlemen Rd, 34232 / 941-341-9274 • *Lat:* 27.3395 *Lon:* -82.4523 I-75 Exit 210, west of exit
	○ 2		℞		4381 Cattlemen Rd, 34233 / 941-379-3550 • *Lat:* 27.2913 *Lon:* -82.4519 I-75 Exit 207 go W on Bee Ridge Rd .4 mile & S on Cattlemen Rd .7 mile
	○ 4		℞		8320 Lockwood Ridge Rd, 34243 / 941-351-6969 • *Lat:* 27.3920 *Lon:* -82.5058 I-75 Exit 213 go W on University Pkwy 3.6 miles & N at Lockwood Ridge Rd .2 mile
Sebastian	◆ 10	🕐	℞	🚗	2001 US Hwy 1, 32958 / 772-589-8528 • *Lat:* 27.7890 *Lon:* -80.4778 I-95 Exit 156 follow CR-512 E 3.7 miles, Roseland Rd N 4.7 miles & US-1 S .8 mile
Scbring	◇	🕐	℞		3525 US Hwy 27 N, 33870 / 863-471-1200 • *Lat:* 27.5130 *Lon:* -81.4947 Jct US-98 & US-27 (N of town) go S on US-27/98 for 16.6 miles
Seffner	○ 2		℞		11720 Martin Luther King Blvd, 33584 / 813-681-6654 • *Lat:* 27.9818 *Lon:* -82.3015 I-75 Exit 160 go E on Martin Luther King Blvd 1.9 miles
Spring Hill	◇	🕐	℞	🚗	1485 Commercial Way, 34606 / 352-686-0744 • *Lat:* 28.4573 *Lon:* -82.6287 From SH-589 (toll) Exit 46 go W 5.8 miles on SH-50 then S 5.5 miles on US-19
Starke	◆	🕐	℞	🚗	14500 US Hwy 301 S, 32091 / 904-964-3286 • *Lat:* 29.9202 *Lon:* -82.1290 Jct SH-100 & US-301 (S of town) go S on US-301 for 2 miles
Stuart	◇ 6	🕐	℞	🚗	4001 SE Federal Hwy, 34997 / 772-288-4749 • *Lat:* 27.1528 *Lon:* -80.2186 I-95 Exit 101 take SH-76 NE 1 mile, Cove Rd W 3.2 miles & US-1 N 1.7 miles
Summerfield	◆	🕐	℞	🚗	17861 S US Hwy 441, 34491 / 352-307-4400 • *Lat:* 28.9623 *Lon:* -81.9671 Jct SH-42 & US-441 (S of town) take US-441 S 1.9 miles
Sunrise	□ 2		℞	🚗	13550 W Sunrise Blvd, 33323 / 954-846-7001 • *Lat:* 26.1456 *Lon:* -80.3280 I-75 Exit 19 follow Sawgrass Expy N 1 mile then go east on Sunrise Blvd 1.3 miles
	○ 3		℞		12555 W Sunrise Blvd, 33323 / 954-845-0581 • *Lat:* 26.1459 *Lon:* -80.3176 I-75 Exit 19 take SH-869 (toll) N .5 mile to Exit 1/Sunrise Blvd E for 2.2 miles
	○ 7		℞		3306 N University Dr, 33351 / 954-749-3111 • *Lat:* 26.1687 *Lon:* -80.2554 I-95 Exit 31 go W 6 miles on Oakland Park Blvd then N .1 mile on Unversity Dr
Tallahassee	■ 5		℞	🚗	3122 Dick Wilson Blvd, 32301 / 850-671-5959 • *Lat:* 30.4311 *Lon:* -84.2254 I-10 Exit 203 go S 5 miles on US-319
	◆ 8	🕐	℞		3535 Apalachee Pkwy, 32311 / 850-656-2732 • *Lat:* 30.4280 *Lon:* -84.2146 I-10 Exit 209 take US-90 W 4.8 miles, US-319 S 2.3 miles & US-27 E .7 mile
	◆ 4	🕐	℞	🚗	5500 Thomasville Rd, 32312 / 850-668-2511 • *Lat:* 30.5421 *Lon:* -84.2286 I-10 Exit 203 take SH-61 N 3.4 miles
	◇ 3	🕐	℞	🚗	4400 W Tennessee St, 32304 / 850-574-3588 • *Lat:* 30.4596 *Lon:* -84.3566 I-10 Exit 196 take SH-263 S 1.5 miles then US-90 E .7 mile
Tampa	■ 4		℞	🚗	15835 N Dale Mabry Hwy, 33618 / 813-960-2110 • *Lat:* 28.0963 *Lon:* -82.5020 I-275 Exit 53 go W on Bearss Ave 3.1 miles then N on Dale Mabry .8 mile
	□ 5		℞	🚗	5135 S Dale Mabry Hwy, 33611 / 813-805-6602 • *Lat:* 27.8911 *Lon:* -82.5085 I-275 Exit 41A go S 4.4 miles on Dale Mabry Hwy
	○ 2		℞		1505 N Dale Mabry Hwy, 33607 / 813-872-6992 • *Lat:* 27.9565 *Lon:* -82.5054 I-275 Exit 41 go W on Dale Mabry Hwy 1.7 miles
	○ 6		℞		2701 E Fletcher Ave, 33612 / 813-558-0994 • *Lat:* 28.0691 *Lon:* -82.4293 I-75 Exit 270 go SW on Downs Blvd 5.3 miles then W at University Plaza St .4 mile

○ Wal-Mart   ◇ Supercenter   □ Sam's Club   ■ Gas   ■ Gas & Diesel

City/Town	○	🕐	℞	🚌	Information
	○	7	℞		7011 W Waters Ave, 33634 / 813-881-0402 • *Lat:* 28.0260 *Lon:* -82.5584 I-275 Exit 50 go W 1.8 miles on Busch Blvd, S .6 mile on Armenia Ave, W 4.5 miles on Waters Ave
	○	3	℞		14941 N Dale Mabry Hwy, 33618 / 813-968-3544 • *Lat:* 28.0858 *Lon:* -82.5042 I-275 Exit 53 take Bearss Ave W 3 miles
	◆	7	🕐 ℞	🚌	6192 Gunn Hwy, 33625 / 813-968-6477 • *Lat:* 28.0640 *Lon:* -82.5516 I-275 Exit 50 go W 3.2 miles on Busch Blvd then continue W 3.4 miles on Gunn Hwy
	◇	8	🕐 ℞		8220 N Dale Mabry Hwy, 33614 / 813-887-5175 • *Lat:* 28.0229 *Lon:* -82.5052 I-275 Exit 53 take Bearss Ave W 3.2 miles & Dale Mabry Hwy S 4.3 miles
	◇	5	🕐 ℞		19910 Bruce B Downs Blvd, 33647 / 813-994-6543 • *Lat:* 28.1535 *Lon:* -82.3537 I-75 Exit 275 take SH-56 E 2.1 miles & Downs Blvd S 2.2 miles
The Villages	◇		🕐 ℞	🚌	4085 Wedgewood Ln, 32162 / 352-259-0128 • *Lat:* 28.9282 *Lon:* -82.0121 Jct SH-42 & US-301 (NW of town) take US-301 S 3.3 miles, CR-105 S .7 mile & E on Wedgewood Ln
Titusville	◆	1	🕐 ℞	🚌	3175 Cheney Hwy, 32780 / 321-267-5825 • *Lat:* 28.5565 *Lon:* -80.8440 I-95 Exit 215 take SH-50 E .6 mile
Venice	◆	5	🕐 ℞	🚌	4150 Tamiami Trl S, 34293 / 941-497-2523 • *Lat:* 27.0495 *Lon:* -82.3956 I-75 Exit 193 go S on Jacaranda Blvd 4.5 miles & E on Tamiami Trl .1 mile
Vero Beach	☐	5		🚌	5565 20th St, 32966 / 772-978-9385 • *Lat:* 27.6386 *Lon:* -80.4437 I-95 Exit 147 go E on SH-60 for 4.7 miles
	◇	5	🕐 ℞	🚌	5555 20th St, 32966 / 772-778-6677 • *Lat:* 27.6386 *Lon:* -80.4436 I-95 Exit 147 take 20th St/SH-60 E 4.7 miles
Viera	◆	1	🕐 ℞	🚌	8500 N Wickham Rd, 32940 / 321-242-0225 • *Lat:* 28.2304 *Lon:* -80.7233 I-95 Exit 191 go W on Wickham Rd .3 mile
Wauchula	◆		🕐 ℞		1480 US Hwy 17 N, 33873 / 863-773-6419 • *Lat:* 27.5881 *Lon:* -81.8213 Jct SH-62 & US-17 (N of town) take US-17 S 3 miles
Wesley Chapel	■	3	℞	🚌	27727 State Road 56, 33543 / 813-929-7010 • *Lat:* 28.1867 *Lon:* -82.3734 I-75 Exit 275 take SH-56 E for 2.2 miles
West Melbourne	◆	1	🕐 ℞	🚌	845 Palm Bay Rd NE, 32904 / 321-984-2715 • *Lat:* 28.0354 *Lon:* -80.6480 I-95 Exit 176 take Palm Bay Rd E .8 mile
West Palm Beach	■	1	℞	🚌	4295 45th St, 33407 / 561-687-0098 • *Lat:* 26.7599 *Lon:* -80.1067 I-95 Exit 74 go W on 45th St for .9 mile
	◆	4	🕐 ℞		4375 Belvedere Rd, 33406 / 561-242-8889 • *Lat:* 26.6921 *Lon:* -80.1101 I-95 Exit 70 merge onto Okeechobee Blvd W .9 mile, S on Congress Ave 1 mile & W on Belvedere Rd 1.5 miles
	◆	9	🕐 ℞	🚌	9990 Belvedere Rd, 33411 / 561-795-0017 • *Lat:* 26.6914 *Lon:* -80.2008 I-95 Exit 68 take US-98 W 8.1 miles, SH-7 N .8 mile then E on Belvedere Rd
Wimauma	◇	3	🕐 ℞	🚌	4928 State Rd 674, 33598 / 813-633-1467 • *Lat:* 27.7125 *Lon:* -82.3328 I-75 Exit 240 follow SH-674 E 3 miles
Winter Haven	○		℞		355 Cypress Gardens Blvd, 33880 / 863-299-5527 • *Lat:* 28.0042 *Lon:* -81.7229 2 miles southeast of town center via US-17 and Cypress Gardens Blvd (SH-540)
	◆		🕐 ℞	🚌	7450 Cypress Gardens Blvd, 33884 / 863-318-0752 • *Lat:* 27.9783 *Lon:* -81.6493 Jct SH-60 & US-27 (SE of town) take US-27 N 5.9 miles then W on Cypress Gardens Blvd 1.3 miles
Yulee	◆	8	🕐 ℞	🚌	464016 State Rd 200, 32097 / 904-261-9410 • *Lat:* 30.6227 *Lon:* -81.5356 I-95 Exit 373 take SH-200 E 7.1 miles
Zephyrhills	◆		🕐 ℞	🚌	7631 Gall Blvd, 33541 / 813-782-1957 • *Lat:* 28.2680 *Lon:* -82.1884 Jct SH-52 & US-301 (N of town) go S on US-301 for 4.2 miles

○ Wal-Mart   ◇ Supercenter   ☐ Sam's Club   ■ Gas   ■ Gas & Diesel

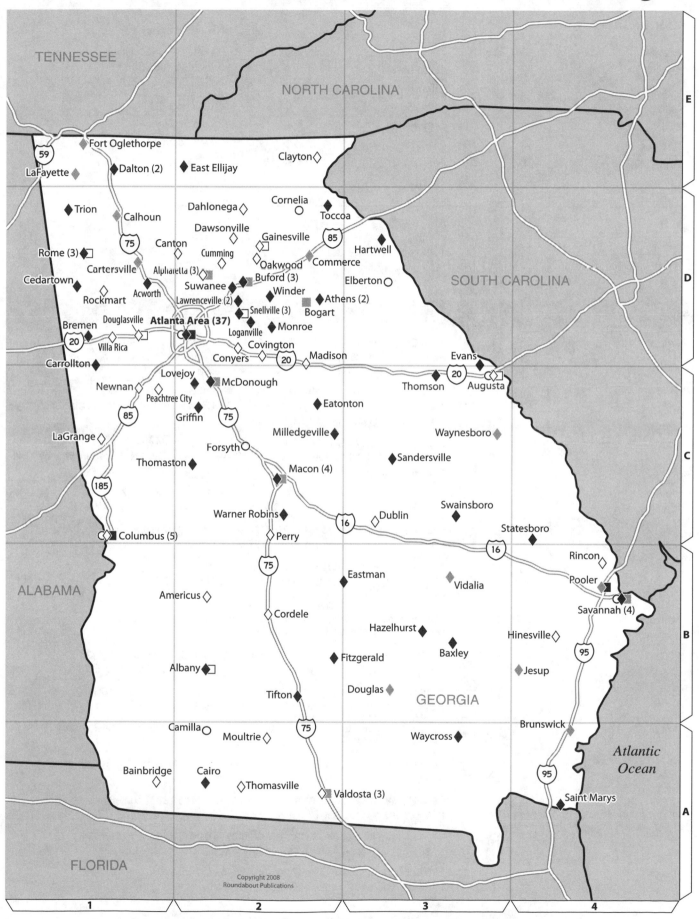

Georgia

○ Wal-Mart ◇ Supercenter □ Sam's Club ▧ Gas ■ Gas & Diesel

TENNESSEE

NORTH CAROLINA

SOUTH CAROLINA

ALABAMA

GEORGIA

FLORIDA

Atlantic Ocean

Fort Oglethorpe
LaFayette
Dalton (2)
East Ellijay
Clayton
Trion
Calhoun
Dahlonega
Cornelia
Toccoa
Dawsonville
Gainesville
Hartwell
Canton
Commerce
Rome (3)
Cumming
Oakwood
Cartersville
Alpharetta (3)
Buford (3)
Elberton
Cedartown
Suwanee
Winder
Athens (2)
Acworth
Rockmart
Lawrenceville (2)
Snellville (3)
Bogart
Bremen
Douglasville
Atlanta Area (37)
Loganville
Monroe
Villa Rica
Covington
Conyers
Madison
Evans
Carrollton
Lovejoy
Thomson
Augusta
Newnan
McDonough
Peachtree City
Eatonton
LaGrange
Griffin
Milledgeville
Waynesboro
Forsyth
Thomaston
Sandersville
Macon (4)
Swainsboro
Warner Robins
Dublin
Statesboro
Columbus (5)
Perry
Rincon
Pooler
Eastman
Vidalia
Americus
Savannah (4)
Cordele
Hazelhurst
Hinesville
Albany
Baxley
Jesup
Tifton
Douglas
Camilla
Brunswick
Moultrie
Waycross
Bainbridge
Cairo
Thomasville
Valdosta (3)
Saint Marys

Copyright 2008
Roundabout Publications

Atlanta Area

Atlanta (4)	◇	■	Hiram (2)	◇	▨	Roswell	◇		
Austell	◇		Kennesaw	◆		Stockbridge (2)	◆		
Chamblee	◇		Lilburn	◆		Stone Mountain	◆		
College Park	◇		Lithia Springs	◇		Tucker (2)	○	▨	
Dallas	◆		Lithonia (2)	◆	▨	Union City	◇		
Decatur	◇		Marietta (6)	○ ◆	▨	Woodstock (2)	◇		
Duluth (2)	◆	☐	Morrow (2)	◆	▨				
Fayetteville	◇		Riverdale	◇					

City/Town	🛡	🕐	℞	🚐	Information
Acworth	◆ 3	🕐	℞		3826 Cobb Pkwy NW, 30101 / 770-966-1226 • *Lat:* 34.0463 *Lon:* -84.6956 I-75 Exit 278 go S .5 mile on Glade Rd, turn right and continue S 2.2 miles on Lake Acworth Dr, then turn left and go .3 mile on Kemp Rd
Albany	☐			🚐	1201 N Westover Blvd, 31707 / 229-888-3400 • *Lat:* 31.6170 *Lon:* -84.2111 Jct US-19/US-82 (north of town) take US-82 W 1.3 miles to Exit 7, S on Nottingham Way .3 mile & W on Westover .5 mile
	◆	🕐	℞	🚐	2825 Ledo Rd, 31707 / 229-889-9655 • *Lat:* 31.6227 *Lon:* -84.2141 Jct US-19 & US-82 (N of town) take US-82 W 1.3 miles to Exit 7/Nottingham Way N .2 mile then W on Ledo Rd .6 mile
Alpharetta	▨ 10		℞	🚐	10600 Davis Dr, 30004 / 770-992-4568 • *Lat:* 34.0411 *Lon:* -84.3147 I-285 Exit 27 go N 9 miles on US-19, W on Mansell Rd .4 mile & N on Davis Dr
	◇	🕐	℞	🚐	5200 Windward Pkwy, 30004 / 770-772-9033 • *Lat:* 34.0923 *Lon:* -84.2766 SH-400 (toll) Exit 11 follow Windward Pkwy W 1 mile
	◇	🕐	℞	🚐	5455 Atlanta Hwy, 30004 / 770-475-4101 • *Lat:* 34.1504 *Lon:* -84.2517 From US-19/SH-400 Exit 12B follow McFarland Hwy NW 2.5 miles then Atlanta Hwy N 1.1 mile
Americus	◇	🕐	℞	🚐	1711 E Lamar St, 31709 / 229-928-0653 • *Lat:* 32.0711 *Lon:* -84.2125 Jct US-19 & US-280 (W of town) follow US-280 E for 1.9 miles
Athens	◆	🕐	℞	🚐	1911 Epps Bridge Pkwy, 30606 / 706-549-1423 • *Lat:* 33.9186 *Lon:* -83.4428 From US-441/Athens Perimeter Exit 1 go N on Epps Bridge Pkwy .7 mile
	◇	🕐	℞	🚐	4375 Lexington Rd, 30605 / 706-355-3966 • *Lat:* 33.9331 *Lon:* -83.3116 From US-441/Athens Perimeter Exit 8 go E on US-78 for 2.8 miles
Atlanta	■ 1		℞	🚐	2901-A Clairmont Rd NE, 30329 / 404-325-4000 • *Lat:* 33.8422 *Lon:* -84.3128 I-85 Exit 91 go NW on Clairtmont for .1 mile
	◇ 1	🕐	℞	🚐	2427 Gresham Rd SE, 30316 / 404-244-3034 • *Lat:* 33.7176 *Lon:* -84.3106 I-20 Exit 63 go N on Gresham Rd .3 mile
	◇ 1	🕐	℞		1801 Howell Mill Rd NW, 30318 / 404-352-5252 • *Lat:* 33.8037 *Lon:* -84.4138 I-75 Exit 252 go S on Howell Mill Rd .2 mile
	◇ 1		℞		4725 Ashford Dunwoody Rd, 30338 / 770-395-0199 • *Lat:* 33.9342 *Lon:* -84.3375 I-285 Exit 29 go N on Ashford Dunwoody 1 mile
Augusta	☐ 1			🚐	596 Bobby Jones Expy, 30907 / 706-863-7846 • *Lat:* 33.5004 *Lon:* -82.0866 I-20 Exit 196B go N .4 mile on Bobby Jones Expy

○ Wal-Mart ◇ Supercenter ☐ Sam's Club ▨ Gas ■ Gas & Diesel

City/Town	⬡	🕐	℞	🚗	Information
	◯ 1		℞	🚗	260 Bobby Jones Expy, 30907 / 706-860-0170 • *Lat:* 33.5056 *Lon:* -82.0906 I-20 Exit 196B follow I-520 W for 1 mile
	◇ 1	🕐	℞		3209 Deans Bridge Rd, 30906 / 706-792-9323 • *Lat:* 33.4218 *Lon:* -82.0637 I-520 Exit 5 go SW on Deans Bridge Rd/US-1 S .1 mile
Austell	◇ 7	🕐	℞	🚗	1133 E West Connector, 30106 / 770-863-9300 • *Lat:* 33.8561 *Lon:* -84.5859 I-20 Exit 44 go NW 1.3 miles on Thornton Rd, turn right and go N 1.8 miles on Maxham Rd, then continue N on SH-5 (Austell Rd) 2.9 miles, turn right and go E 1.1 miles on East-West Connector
Bainbridge	◇	🕐	℞	🚗	500 E Alice St, 39819 / 229-246-2404 • *Lat:* 30.8916 *Lon:* -84.5685 Jct US-84 & US-27 (S of town) go N on US-27 BR .1 mile then W on Alice St .1 mile
Baxley	◆	🕐	℞	🚗	980 W Parker St, 31513 / 912-367-3117 • *Lat:* 31.7823 *Lon:* -82.3597 Jct US-1 & US-341 (in town) go W on US-341 for .7 mile
Bogart	▨		℞	🚗	4365 Atlanta Hwy, 30622 / 706-548-3666 • *Lat:* 33.9402 *Lon:* -83.4863 Athens Perimeter Hwy Exit 18 take US-78BR W 1.5 miles
Bremen	◆ 2	🕐	℞	🚗	404 US Hwy 27 Byp, 30110 / 770-537-5531 • *Lat:* 33.7180 *Lon:* -85.1438 I-20 Exit 11 follow US-27 N 2 miles, US-78 E 1.2 miles & N on US-27 BR .2 mile
Brunswick	◈ 3	🕐	℞	🚗	150 Altama Connector, 31525 / 912-261-1616 • *Lat:* 31.2150 *Lon:* -81.4831 I-95 Exit 38 take SH-25 Spur SE for 2.3 miles then N on Altama Connector .3 mile
Buford	▨ 2		℞	🚗	3383 Buford Dr, 30519 / 770-831-7122 • *Lat:* 34.0735 *Lon:* -83.9838 I-85 Exit 115 go N on Buford Dr (SH 20) for 1.1 miles
	◆ 3	🕐	℞	🚗	3250 Sardis Church Rd, 30519 / 678-546-6464 • *Lat:* 34.0783 *Lon:* -83.9179 I-85 Exit 120 go N on Hamilton Mill Rd .4 mile then NE on Sardis Church Rd 1.7 miles
	◇ 1	🕐	℞	🚗	3795 Buford Dr, 30519 / 770-271-8210 • *Lat:* 34.0851 *Lon:* -83.9899 I-985 Exit 4 take Buford Dr SE .5 mile
Cairo	◆	🕐	℞		361 8th Ave NE, 39828 / 229-377-1394 • *Lat:* 30.8857 *Lon:* -84.2044 Jct SH111/93 & US-84 go E on US-84 for .2 mile
Calhoun	◈ 2	🕐	℞	🚗	450 W Belmont Dr, 30701 / 706-625-4274 • *Lat:* 34.4808 *Lon:* -84.9451 I-75 Exit 312 go W on SH-53 for 1.7 miles
Camilla	◯		℞		131 US 19 N, 31730 / 229-336-0920 • *Lat:* 31.2341 *Lon:* -84.1995 .5 mile northeast of town center, .2 mile north of US-19/SH37 jct
Canton	◇ 1	🕐	℞	🚗	1550 Riverstone Pwky, 30114 / 770-479-9891 • *Lat:* 34.2527 *Lon:* -84.4695 I-575 Exit 20 go SW on Riverstone Pkwy .1 mile
Carrollton	◆	🕐	℞	🚗	1735 S Hwy 27, 30117 / 770-834-3513 • *Lat:* 33.5433 *Lon:* -85.0741 Jct SH-166 & SH-1 (S of town) go S on SH-1 for 1.1 miles
Cartersville	◈ 2	🕐	℞	🚗	101 Market Place Blvd, 30121 / 770-382-0182 • *Lat:* 34.2020 *Lon:* -84.7903 I-75 Exit 290 take SH-20 W 1.8 miles
Cedartown	◆	🕐	℞	🚗	1585 Rome Hwy, 30125 / 770-748-1636 • *Lat:* 34.0399 *Lon:* -85.2402 Jct US-278 & US-27 (E of town) go NW on US-27 for 2.3 miles then S on US-27 BR .2 mile
Chamblee	◇ 3		℞		1871 Chamblee Tucker Rd, 30341 / 770-455-0422 • *Lat:* 33.8887 *Lon:* -84.3099 I-85 Exit 94 go W on Chamblee-Tucker Rd for 2.3 miles
Clayton	◇ 2	🕐	℞	🚗	1455 Hwy 441 S, 30525 / 706-782-3039 • *Lat:* 34.8674 *Lon:* -83.4021 Jct US-76 & US-441 (in town) go N on US-441 for 1.5 miles
College Park	◇ 3	🕐	℞	🚗	6149 Old National Hwy, 30349 / 770-994-9440 • *Lat:* 33.5876 *Lon:* -84.4693 I-285 Exit 62 take Old Nat'l Hwy/SH-279 S 2.4 miles
Columbus	◼ 1			🚗	5448 Whittlesey Blvd, Ste A, 31909 / 706-649-6799 • *Lat:* 32.5433 *Lon:* -84.9477 I-185 Exit 10 E to US-27, S .2 mile, E on Adams Farm Dr .4 mile & NE on Whittlesey .5 mile
	◯ 1		℞		4701 Buena Vista Rd, 31907 / 706-568-3222 • *Lat:* 32.4672 *Lon:* -84.9143 I-185 Exit 4 go S on Buena Vista Rd 1 mile

◯ Wal-Mart   ◇ Supercenter   ▢ Sam's Club   ▨ Gas   ◼ Gas & Diesel

City/Town	⬡	🕐	℞	🚗	Information
	◇ 3	🕐	℞	🚗	5448 Whittlesey Blvd, 31909 / 706-322-8801 • *Lat:* 32.5383 *Lon:* -84.9276 I-185 Exit 10 take US-80 E 1 mile, US-27 S .5 mile, Adams Farm Rd S .4 mile & Whittlesey Blvd E .5 mile
	◇ 1	🕐	℞		2801 Airport Thruway, 31909 / 706-653-4227 • *Lat:* 32.5202 *Lon:* -84.9487 I-185 Exit 8 go E at Airport Thruwy .5 mile
	◇ 6	🕐	℞	🚗	6475 Gateway Rd, 31909 / 706-563-5979 • *Lat:* 32.5361 *Lon:* -84.8765 I-185 Exit 10 follow US-80 E 5.8 miles then S on Gateway Rd
Commerce	◆ 1	🕐	℞	🚗	30983 Hwy 441 S, 30529 / 706-335-7563 • *Lat:* 34.2488 *Lon:* -83.4599 I-85 Exit 149 go S on US-441 for .4 mile
Conyers	◇ 1	🕐	℞	🚗	1436 Dogwood Dr SE, 30013 / 770-860-8544 • *Lat:* 33.6515 *Lon:* -84.0002 I-20 Exit 82 follow signs for SH-138 E .3 mile then E on Dogwood Dr .4 mile
Cordele	◇ 1	🕐	℞	🚗	1215 E 16th Ave, 31015 / 229-273-9270 • *Lat:* 31.9624 *Lon:* -83.7636 I-75 Exit 101 take SH-30 W .8 mile
Cornelia	○		℞		308 Habersham Hills Cir, 30531 / 706-776-3060 • *Lat:* 34.5460 *Lon:* -83.5432 From US-23 Level Grove Exit (W of town) take Old Level Rd W .5 mile, Old Athens Rd N .4 mile & Hill Mill Rd W .2 mile
Covington	◇ 1	🕐	℞	🚗	10300 Industrial Blvd NE, 30014 / 770-787-8030 • *Lat:* 33.6118 *Lon:* -83.8280 I-20 Exit 93, south of exit
Cumming	◇	🕐	℞	🚗	1500 Market Place Blvd, 30041 / 770-889-3436 • *Lat:* 34.1864 *Lon:* -84.1324 SH-400 (toll) Exit 14 merge onto Buford Hwy .6 mile then E on Market Pl Blvd .5 mile
Dahlonega	◇	🕐	℞		270 Wal-Mart Way, 30533 / 706-867-6912 • *Lat:* 34.5379 *Lon:* -83.9728 1 mile northeast of town center via SH-52
Dallas	◆	🕐	℞	🚗	3615 Marietta Hwy, 30157 / 770-445-2141 • *Lat:* 33.9325 *Lon:* -84.7327 7 miles east of town via SH-120 (or 14 miles west of I-75 Exit 263 via SH-120)
Dalton	◆ 1	🕐	℞	🚗	815 Shugart Rd, 30720 / 706-281-2855 • *Lat:* 34.7856 *Lon:* -84.9967 I-75 Exit 336 E .2 mile on US-41 then S .7 mile on Shugart Rd
	◇ 10	🕐	℞	🚗	2545 E Walnut Ave, 30721 / 706-279-1905 • *Lat:* 34.7671 *Lon:* -84.9274 I-75 Exit 328 follow S Dalton Bypass 7.9 miles then NW on Airport Rd .8 mile & E on Walnut Ave .4 mile
Dawsonville	◇	🕐	℞	🚗	156 Power Center Dr, 30534 / 706-265-8787 • *Lat:* 34.3567 *Lon:* -84.0452 7.2 miles southeast of town center via SH-53 and SH-400, across from North Georgia Premium Outlets
Decatur	◇	🕐	℞		3580 Memorial Dr, 30032 / 404-284-0500 • *Lat:* 33.7552 *Lon:* -84.2671 I-285 Exit 41 go SW 2.2 miles on SH-154 (Cynthia McKinney Pkwy)
Douglas	◆	🕐	℞	🚗	1450 Bowens Mill Rd SE, 31533 / 912-384-4600 • *Lat:* 31.4895 *Lon:* -82.8359 From Jct US-41 & Bowens Mill Rd/SH135 (S of town) go E on Bowens Mill Rd .9 mile
Douglasville	□ 1		℞	🚗	6995 Concourse Pkwy, 30134 / 770-489-6167 • *Lat:* 33.7303 *Lon:* -84.7585 I-20 Exit 34 take SH-5 N for .1 mile & E on Concourse Pkwy .2 mile
	◇ 1	🕐	℞	🚗	7001 Concourse Pkwy, 30134 / 770-489-7057 • *Lat:* 33.7303 *Lon:* -84.7575 I-20 Exit 34 go N on SH-5 for .1 mile then E on Concourse Pkwy .2 mile
Dublin	◇ 8	🕐	℞	🚗	2423 US Hwy 80 W, 31021 / 478-272-7017 • *Lat:* 32.5495 *Lon:* -82.9722 I-16 Exit 42 take SH-338 NE 2 miles then US-80 E 5.8 miles
Duluth	□ 1		℞	🚗	3450 Steve Reynolds Blvd, 30096 / 770-497-1165 • *Lat:* 33.9504 *Lon:* -84.1389 I-85 Exit 103 go NW on Reynolds Blvd .2 mile
	◆ 2	🕐	℞	🚗	2635 Pleasant Hill Rd, 30096 / 770-418-0162 • *Lat:* 33.9707 *Lon:* -84.1478 I-85 Exit 103 take Steve Reynolds Blvd NW 1.4 miles & Pleasant Hill Rd NW .5 mile

○ Wal-Mart　◇ Supercenter　□ Sam's Club　◼ Gas　◼ Gas & Diesel

City/Town	🛡	🕐	Rx	🚐	Information
East Ellijay	◆		🕐	Rx	🚐	88 Highland Crossing, 30540 / 706-276-1170 • *Lat:* 34.8012 *Lon:* -84.4337 From Jct SH-382 & SH-515 (S of town) take SH-515/Zell Miller Pkwy N for 2.9 miles then E on Highland Crossing
Eastman	◆		🕐	Rx	🚐	1099 Indian Dr, 31023 / 478-374-7782 • *Lat:* 32.1793 *Lon:* -83.1798 1.4 miles south of town at US-341/SH-87 jct
Eatonton	◆		🕐	Rx	🚐	201 Wal-Mart Dr, 31024 / 706-485-5052 • *Lat:* 33.2966 *Lon:* -83.3872 2 miles south of town at US-129/Gray Hwy jct
Elberton	○			Rx		955 Elbert St, 30635 / 706-283-8660 • *Lat:* 34.0931 *Lon:* -82.8467 Jct SH-72 & SH-17 (SE of town) go N on SH-72/17 for .2 mile
Evans	◆	6	🕐	Rx	🚐	4469 Washington Rd, 30809 / 706-854-9892 • *Lat:* 33.5439 *Lon:* -82.1407 I-20 Exit 194 take SH-383 N 4.2 miles then Washington Rd NW 1 mile
Fayetteville	◇		🕐	Rx	🚐	125 Pavilion Pkwy, 30214 / 770-460-0947 • *Lat:* 33.4794 *Lon:* -84.4418 From Jct SH-92 & SH-85 (in town) go N on SH-85/Glynn St 1.9 miles then W on Pavillion Pkwy .4 mile
Fitzgerald	◆		🕐	Rx	🚐	120 Benjamin H Hill Dr W, 31750 / 229-423-4353 • *Lat:* 31.6925 *Lon:* -83.2564 Jct SH-125 & SH-107 (SW of town) take SH-107 E 3.4 miles
Forsyth	○	1		Rx		120 N Lee St, 31029 / 478-994-0163 • *Lat:* 33.0388 *Lon:* -83.9386 I-75 Exit 187 follow SH-83 SW .3 mile
Fort Oglethorpe	◆	5	🕐	Rx	🚐	3040 Battlefield Pkwy, 30742 / 706-861-4698 • *Lat:* 34.9405 *Lon:* -85.2184 I 75 Exit 350 take Battlefield Pkwy W 4.2 miles
Gainesville	☐	1			🚐	3137 Frontage Rd, 30504 / 770-287-7716 • *Lat:* 34.2296 *Lon:* -83.8641 I-985 Exit 16 go NW on SH-53 for .2 mile then N on Frontage Rd .2 mile
	◇	4	🕐	Rx	🚐	400 Shallowford Rd NW, 30504 / 770-503-9300 • *Lat:* 34.2916 *Lon:* -83.8463 I-985 Exit 20 take SH-60 N 2.1 miles then SH-369 SW .8 mile & Shallowford Rd NW .3 mile
Griffin	◆		🕐	Rx	🚐	1569 N Expressway, 30223 / 770-229-5040 • *Lat:* 33.2755 *Lon:* -84.2915 I-75 Exit 205 take SH-16 W 12.9 miles and SH-92 N .9 mile
Hartwell	◆		🕐	Rx	🚐	1572 Anderson Hwy, 30643 / 706-376-5400 • *Lat:* 34.3473 *Lon:* -82.8962 I-85 Exit 177 follow SH-77 SE for 12.7 miles then US-29 N .1 mile
Hazlehurst	◆		🕐	Rx		136 E Jarman St, 31539 / 912-375-3627 • *Lat:* 31.8648 *Lon:* -82.5868 Jct US-23 & SH-27 (S of town) go NE on SH-27 for .1 mile
Hinesville	◇		🕐	Rx	🚐	751 W Oglethorpe Hwy, 31313 / 912-369-3600 • *Lat:* 31.8283 *Lon:* -81.5981 I-95 Exit 76 take US-84/SH-38 W for 16 miles
Hiram	◼			Rx	🚐	4798 Jimmy Lee Smith Pkwy, 30141 / 678-567-5990 • *Lat:* 33.8890 *Lon:* -84.7487 Jct SH-92/US-278 in Hiram, go SE on US-278 for .4 mile
	◇		🕐	Rx		4166 Jimmy Lee Smith Pkwy, 30141 / 770-439-1028 • *Lat:* 33.8921 *Lon:* -84.7572 I-20 Exit 36 go N on Campbellton St 1.5 miles, N on SH-92 for 10 miles & W on US-278 .2 mile
Jesup	◆		🕐	Rx	🚐	1100 N 1st St, 31545 / 912-530-6335 • *Lat:* 31.6167 *Lon:* -81.8744 1 mile northeast of town center on US-84 (N 1st St)
Kennesaw	◆	6	🕐	Rx	🚐	3105 N Cobb Pkwy, 30152 / 770-974-9291 • *Lat:* 34.0299 *Lon:* -84.6570 I-75 Exit 269 go W on Barrett Pkwy 1.3 miles then NW 4.7 miles on Cobb Pkwy
La Fayette	◆		🕐	Rx	🚐	2625 N Hwy 27, 30728 / 706-639-4900 • *Lat:* 34.7463 *Lon:* -85.2700 Jct SH-136 & US-27 (N of town) go N on US-27 for .2 mile
Lagrange	◇	6	🕐	Rx	🚐	803 New Franklin Rd, 30240 / 706-812-0225 • *Lat:* 33.0668 *Lon:* -85.0286 I-85 Exit 18 take SH-109 W 3.4 miles then US-27/SH-1 N 1.9 miles
Lawrenceville	◆	6	🕐	Rx	🚐	1400 Lawrenceville Hwy, 30044 / 770-682-1992 • *Lat:* 33.9380 *Lon:* -84.0254 I-85 Exit 107 take SH-120 E 1 mile, Sugarloaf Pkwy S 3.6 miles & Lawrenceville Hwy E .5 mile

○ Wal-Mart   ◇ Supercenter   ☐ Sam's Club   ◼ Gas   ◼ Gas & Diesel

City/Town	⛨	🕐	℞	🚌	Information
	◇ 7	🕐	℞	🚌	630 Collins Hill Rd, 30045 / 770-995-0102 • *Lat:* 33.9725 *Lon:* -83.9932 I-85 Exit 107 take SH-120 E 1 mile, Sugarloaf Pkwy SE 1.4 miles, SH-316 E 4 miles & Collins Hill Rd S .3 mile
Lilburn	◆ 5	🕐	℞	🚌	4004 Lawrenceville Hwy NW, 30047 / 770-921-9224 • *Lat:* 33.9044 *Lon:* -84.1131 I-85 Exit 102 take Beaver Ruin Rd SE 3.7 miles then US-29 E .5 mile
Lithia Springs	◇ 1	🕐	℞	🚌	1100 Thornton Rd, 30122 / 770-819-1123 • *Lat:* 33.7784 *Lon:* -84.6061 I-20 Exit 44 merge onto Thornton Rd/SH-6 W .1 mile
Lithonia	■ 1		℞	🚌	2994 Turner Hill Rd, 30038 / 770-482-2077 • *Lat:* 33.6956 *Lon:* -84.0885 I-20 Exit 75 go S on Turner Hill Rd .3 mile
	◆ 1	🕐	℞	🚌	5401 Fairington Rd, 30038 / 770-593-3540 • *Lat:* 33.7024 *Lon:* -84.1685 I-20 Exit 71, south of exit
Loganville	◆	🕐	℞	🚌	4221 Atlanta Hwy, 30052 / 770-554-7481 • *Lat:* 33.8421 *Lon:* -83.9082 Jct SH-20 & US-78 (W of town) go NW on US-78 for .5 mile
Lovejoy	◆ 8	🕐	℞	🚌	11465 Tara Blvd, 30250 / 770-471-4451 • *Lat:* 33.4361 *Lon:* -84.3144 I-75 Exit 221 go W on Jonesboro Rd 5.3 miles, continue on McDonough Rd 1.9 miles then S on Tara Blvd .5
Macon	■ 2		℞	🚌	4701 Log Cabin Dr, 31204 / 478-788-6121 • *Lat:* 32.8158 *Lon:* -83.7084 I-475 Exit 3 go E on SH-22 for 1.2 miles then S at Log Cabin Dr
	◆ 1	🕐	℞	🚌	6020 Harrison Rd, 31206 / 478-781-0086 • *Lat:* 32.8105 *Lon:* -83.7221 I-475 Exit 3 take US-80 E .3 mile
	◆ 1	🕐	℞	🚌	5955 Zebulon Rd, 31210 / 478-471-9150 • *Lat:* 32.8346 *Lon:* -83.6365 I-475 Exit 9 go E on Zebulon Rd .7 mile
	◇ 2	🕐	℞	🚌	1401 Gray Hwy, 31211 / 478-745-3999 • *Lat:* 32.8639 *Lon:* -83.6125 I-16 Exit 1B go N on 2nd St .5 mile, continue on Gray Hwy .9 mile
Madison	◇ 1	🕐	℞	🚌	1681 Eatonton Rd, 30650 / 706-342-9988 • *Lat:* 33.5654 *Lon:* -83.4784 I-20 Exit 114 follow US-441/Eatonton Rd N .7 mile
Marietta	■ 2		℞	🚌	150 S Cobb Pkwy, 30062 / 770-423-7018 • *Lat:* 33.9486 *Lon:* -84.5193 I-75 Exit 263 go W on Marietta Pkwy .5 mile then N on Cobb Pkwy .6 mile
	○ 3		℞		1785 Cobb Pkwy S, 30060 / 770-955-0626 • *Lat:* 33.9094 *Lon:* -84.4932 I-285 Exit 19 take Cobb Pkwy/US-41 N 2.1 miles
	◆ 1	🕐	℞	🚌	2795 Chastain Meadows Pkwy, 30066 / 770-427-4933 • *Lat:* 34.0215 *Lon:* -84.5526 I-575 Exit 1 go E on Barrett Pkwy .2 mile then N on Chastain Meadows Pkwy .6 mile
	◇ 2	🕐	℞	🚌	210 Cobb Pkwy S, 30060 / 770-429-9029 • *Lat:* 33.9468 *Lon:* -84.5187 I-75 Exit 263 merge onto Marietta Pkwy NW .6 mile then N on Cobb Pkwy .6 mile
	◇ 7	🕐	℞		3100 Johnson Ferry Rd, 30062 / 770-640-7225 • *Lat:* 34.0231 *Lon:* -84.4257 I-75 Exit 263 take SH-120 N 1.1 miles, Sewell Mill Rd NE 3.8 miles & Johnson Ferry Rd N 2.1 miles
	◇ 8	🕐	℞		6520 Ernest W Barrett Pkwy SW, 30064 / 770-222-6666 • *Lat:* 33.8672 *Lon:* -84.6342 I-20 Exit 44 take SH-6 NW 1.3 miles, Maxham Rd N 1.8 miles, Austell Rd N 2.9 miles, East-West Connector W 2 miles
McDonough	■ 1		℞	🚌	1765 Jonesboro Rd, 30253 / 770-914-0488 • *Lat:* 33.4636 *Lon:* -84.2144 I-75 Exit 221 go W on Jonesboro Rd for .2 mile
	◆ 1	🕐	℞	🚌	135 Willow Ln, 30253 / 678-432-2023 • *Lat:* 33.4329 *Lon:* -84.1809 I-75 Exit 218 go E on SH-20 for .4 mile & N on Willow Ln for .2 mile
Milledgeville	◆	🕐	℞	🚌	2592 N Columbia St, 31061 / 478-453-0667 • *Lat:* 33.1101 *Lon:* -83.2559 From SH-22 (NW of town) continue E to Jct US-441, then N on US-441 for 1.1 miles
Monroe	◆	🕐	℞	🚌	2050 W Spring St, 30655 / 770-267-4527 • *Lat:* 33.7964 *Lon:* -83.7436 I-20 Exit 98 follow SH-11 N 13.9 miles then SH-10 W 1.9 miles

○ Wal-Mart ◇ Supercenter □ Sam's Club ■ Gas ■ Gas & Diesel

City/Town	🛡	🕐	Rx	🚗	Information
Morrow	■	3		Rx	🚗	7325 Jonesboro Rd, 30260 / 770-960-8228 • *Lat:* 33.5558 *Lon:* -84.3468 I-75 Exit 231 go S on Mount Zion Blvd 1.1 miles then W on Battle Creek Rd .8 mile & N on Jonesboro .2 mile
	◆	1	🕐	Rx		6065 Jonesboro Rd, 30260 / 770-968-0774 • *Lat:* 33.5892 *Lon:* -84.3380 I-75 Exit 233 take SH-54 N .8 mile
Moultrie	◇		🕐	Rx	🚗	641 Veterans Pkwy S, 31788 / 229-985-3697 • *Lat:* 31.1709 *Lon:* -83.7613 Jct SH-37 & US-319 (E of town) go S on US-319 for 1.3 miles
Newnan	◇	1	🕐	Rx	🚗	1025 Bullsboro Dr, 30265 / 770-502-0677 • *Lat:* 33.3953 *Lon:* -84.7447 I-85 Exit 47, east of exit
Oakwood	◇	1	🕐	Rx	🚗	3875 Mundy Mill Rd, 30566 / 770-535-6543 • *Lat:* 34.2337 *Lon:* -83.8720 I-985 Exit 16 take Mundy Mill Rd/SH-53 W .5 mile
Peachtree City	◇		🕐	Rx	🚗	2717 Hwy 54, 30269 / 770-632-6373 • *Lat:* 33.3970 *Lon:* -84.6001 I-85 Exit 61 follow SH-74 S 11 miles then E at SH-54
Perry	◇	1	🕐	Rx	🚗	1009 Saint Patricks Dr, 31069 / 478-987-1444 • *Lat:* 32.4714 *Lon:* -83.7427 I-75 Exit 136 go SE on Sam Nunn Blvd .1 mile & N on St. Patricks Dr
Pooler	■	1		Rx	🚗	15 Mill Creek Cir, 31322 / 912-748-3767 • *Lat:* 32.1383 *Lon:* -81.2438 I-95 Exit 104 go W on Pooler Pkwy .3 mile then S at Mill Creek Cir .2 mile
	◆	1	🕐	Rx	🚗	160 Pooler Pkwy, 31322 / 912-748-2677 • *Lat:* 32.1410 *Lon:* -81.2445 I-95 Exit 104 follow Pooler Pkwy W .4 mile
Rincon	◇	8	🕐	Rx	🚗	434 S Columbia Ave, 31326 / 912-826-4030 • *Lat:* 32.2808 *Lon:* -81.2320 I-95 Exit 109 follow SH-21 N for 7.2 miles
Riverdale	◇	5	🕐	Rx	🚗	7050 Hwy 85, 30274 / 770-994-1670 • *Lat:* 33.5630 *Lon:* -84.4132 I-75 Exit 237A follow SH-85 S 4.5 miles
Rockmart	◇		🕐	Rx	🚗	1801 Nathan Dean Byp, 30153 / 678-757-8766 • *Lat:* 34.0099 *Lon:* -85.0329 1 mile northeast of town center on US-278 (Nathan Dean Pkwy)
Rome	☐				🚗	2550 Redmond Cir NW, 30165 / 706-236-9765 • *Lat:* 34.2725 *Lon:* -85.2296 4.4 miles northwest of town center via SH-20
	◆		🕐	Rx	🚗	825 Cartersville Hwy SE, 30161 / 706-292-0838 • *Lat:* 34.2170 *Lon:* -85.1228 Jct SH-101 & US-411 (S of town) go E on US-411 for 2.9 miles
	◇		🕐	Rx	🚗	2510 Redmond Cir NW, 30165 / 706-236-9595 • *Lat:* 34.2736 *Lon:* -85.2289 Jct SH-20 & SH-1 Loop (W of town) go N on SH-1 for .2 mile
Roswell	◇		🕐	Rx	🚗	970 Mansell Rd, 30076 / 770-993-0533 • *Lat:* 34.0430 *Lon:* -84.3343 SH-400 (toll) Exit 8 go W on Mansell Rd 1.5 miles
Saint Marys	◆	6	🕐	Rx	🚗	6586 GA Hwy 40 E, 31558 / 912-510-9216 • *Lat:* 30.7522 *Lon:* -81.5764 I-95 Exit 1 follow St Marys Rd E 3.3 miles, exit at Cumberland Island & take SH-40 S for 1.8 miles
Sandersville	◆		🕐	Rx	🚗	1308 S Harris St, 31082 / 478-552-1988 • *Lat:* 32.9561 *Lon:* -82.8094 Jct SH-68 & SH-15 (S of town) go N on SH-15 for 1 mile
Savannah	■			Rx	🚗	1975 E Montgomery Cross Rd, 31406 / 912-352-3330 • *Lat:* 31.9898 *Lon:* -81.0809 7 miles south of downtown via Harry Truman Pkwy at Montgomery Cross Rd
	○			Rx		4725 Hwy 80 E, 31410 / 912-898-1391 • *Lat:* 32.0426 *Lon:* -81.0053 6 miles east of town at jct of Island Expy and US-80
	◆	3	🕐	Rx	🚗	6000 Ogeechee Rd, 31419 / 912-921-0882 • *Lat:* 31.9974 *Lon:* -81.2598 I-95 Exit 94 take SH-204 E 1.8 miles then US-17 S .9 mile
	◇	8	🕐	Rx	🚗	1955 E Montgomery Cross Rd, 31406 / 912-354-0335 • *Lat:* 31.9898 *Lon:* -81.0808 I-16 Exit 164A follow SH-21 S 5.9 miles then Truman Pkwy S 1.9 miles & E on Montgomery Cross Rd .2 mile

○ Wal-Mart   ◇ Supercenter   ☐ Sam's Club   ■ Gas   ■ Gas & Diesel

City/Town	🛡	⏱	℞	🚌	Information
Snellville	☐ 10		℞	🚌	1520 Scenic Hwy N, 30078 / 770-979-0492 • *Lat:* 33.8886 *Lon:* -84.0089 I-85 Exit 107 go E on Duluth Hwy 1 mile, SE on Sugarloaf Pkwy 6.3 miles then S on Scenic Hwy 2.1 miles
	◆ 10	⏱	℞	🚌	3435 Centerville Hwy, 30039 / 770-972-7572 • *Lat:* 33.8048 *Lon:* -84.0456 I-20 Exit 75 follow SH-124 N for 9.2 miles then go W .2 mile on Annistown Rd
	◇	⏱	℞	🚌	1550 Scenic Hwy N, 30078 / 770-979-2447 • *Lat:* 33.8875 *Lon:* -84.0093 I-20 Exit 75 follow SH-124 N for 15.6 miles
Statesboro	◆	⏱	℞		730 Northside Dr E, 30458 / 912-489-1910 • *Lat:* 32.4357 *Lon:* -81.7587 I-16 Exit 127 take SH-67 N 10.8 miles, N on Veterans Memorial Pkwy 2.1 miles, W on US-80 for .2 mile
Stockbridge	◆ 1		℞	🚌	1400 Hudson Bridge Rd, 30281 / 770-474-0123 • *Lat:* 33.5056 *Lon:* -84.2325 I-75 Exit 224 go W on Hudson Bridge Rd .3 mile
	◆ 1	⏱	℞		5600 N Henry Blvd, 30281 / 770-389-1709 • *Lat:* 33.5534 *Lon:* -84.2588 I-675 Exit 1 take SH-138 SE .6 mile
Stone Mountain	◆ 9	⏱	℞	🚌	1825 Rockbridge Rd, 30087 / 770-469-8660 • *Lat:* 33.8257 *Lon:* -84.1237 I-285 Exit 39B merge onto US-78 E for 8.1 miles to Exit 9, W on Park Pl Blvd .1 mile & N on Rockbridge Rd .2 mile
Suwanee	◆ 1	⏱	℞	🚌	3245 Lawrenceville Suwanee Rd, 30024 / 678-482-5441 • *Lat:* 34.0368 *Lon:* -84.0529 I-85 Exit 111 take SH-317 N for .6 mile
Swainsboro	◆	⏱	℞	🚌	414 S Main St, 30401 / 478-237-3318 • *Lat:* 32.5892 *Lon:* -82.3274 I-16 Exit 90 take US-1 N 10.3 miles, then US-1 BR 3.5 miles
Thomaston	◆	⏱	℞	🚌	855 N Church St, 30286 / 706-648-2105 • *Lat:* 32.9100 *Lon:* -84.3305 1.6 miles north of town center via Center St and Church St
Thomasville	◇	⏱	℞	🚌	15328 US Hwy 19 S, 31757 / 229-228-0144 • *Lat:* 30.8583 *Lon:* -83.9469 Jct US-84 & US-19 (E of town) go N on US-19 for 1.7 miles
Thomson	◆ 4	⏱	℞		2205 Harrison Rd SE, 30824 / 706-595-5530 • *Lat:* 33.4739 *Lon:* -82.4832 I-20 Exit 172 follow US-78 S for 3.3 miles
Tifton	◆ 1	⏱	℞	🚌	1830 US Hwy 82 W, 31793 / 229-386-0263 • *Lat:* 31.4460 *Lon:* -83.5419 I-75 Exit 62 take US-82 W .8 mile
Toccoa	◆	⏱	℞	🚌	3886 Hwy 17, 30577 / 706-886-9775 • *Lat:* 34.5638 *Lon:* -83.3154 I-85 Exit 173 go N on SH-17 for 11.9 miles then W on Veterans Memorial Way/SH-17 for 1.5 miles
Trion	◆	⏱	℞	🚌	13427 Hwy 27, 30753 / 706-734-2931 • *Lat:* 34.5205 *Lon:* -85.3142 3.7 miles north of Summerville along US-27
Tucker	▪ 6		℞	🚌	1940 Mountain Industrial Blvd, 30084 / 770-908-8408 • *Lat:* 33.8400 *Lon:* -84.2011 I-85 Exit 99 take SH-140S 3.4 miles, continue S on Mountain Industrial Blvd 2.4 miles
	○ 4		℞	🚌	4375 Lawrenceville Hwy, 30084 / 770-939-2671 • *Lat:* 33.8571 *Lon:* -84.2064 I-285 Exit 38 merge onto Lawrenceville Hwy/US-29 N for 3.4 miles
Union City	◇ 1	⏱	℞	🚌	4375 Jonesboro Rd, 30291 / 770-964-6921 • *Lat:* 33.5671 *Lon:* -84.5321 I-85 Exit 64 go E on Jonesboro Rd/SH-138 for .2 mile
Valdosta	▪ 1		℞	🚌	450 Norman Dr, 31601 / 229-244-3939 • *Lat:* 30.8288 *Lon:* -83.3191 I-75 Exit 16 take US-221 E .3 mile then N on Norman Dr .6 mile
	◇ 1	⏱	℞	🚌	340 Norman Dr, 31601 / 229-249-8400 • *Lat:* 30.8264 *Lon:* -83.3176 I-75 Exit 16 go E on US-221 for .2 mile then N on Norman Dr .5 mile
	◇ 5	⏱	℞	🚌	3274 Inner Perimeter Rd, 31602 / 229-253-0312 • *Lat:* 30.8822 *Lon:* -83.2915 I-75 Exit 22 merge onto US-41 S for 3.8 miles then E on Inner Perimeter Rd .5 mile

○ Wal-Mart   ◇ Supercenter   ☐ Sam's Club   ▪ Gas   ■ Gas & Diesel

City/Town	⬡	🕐	℞	🚗	Information
Vidalia	◆		🕐 ℞	🚗	3109 E 1st St, 30474 / 912-537-0889 • *Lat:* 32.2072 *Lon:* -82.3787 I-16 Exit 84 take SH-297 S 13.8 miles, SH-292/North St E 1.7 miles, Stockyard Rd S .2 mile & 1st St E .5 mile
Villa Rica	◇	1	🕐 ℞	🚗	600 Carrollton Villa Rica Hwy, 30180 / 770-459-6601 • *Lat:* 33.7155 *Lon:* -84.9375 I-20 Exit 24 take SH-61 S for .5 mile
Warner Robins	◆	9	🕐 ℞	🚗	502 Booth Rd, 31088 / 478-918-0338 • *Lat:* 32.5923 *Lon:* -83.6092 I-75 Exit 144 go E on Russell Pkwy 7.8 miles then S on Booth Rd .5 mile
	◆	5	🕐 ℞	🚗	2720 Watson Blvd, 31093 / 478-953-7070 • *Lat:* 32.6183 *Lon:* -83.6721 I-75 Exit 146 follow SH-247 (Watson Blvd) E 4.1 miles
Waycross	◆		🕐 ℞	🚗	2425 Memorial Dr, 31503 / 912-283-9000 • *Lat:* 31.1965 *Lon:* -82.3222 Jct State St/US-1 BR & Waring St (NW of town) go E on Waring St 1.5 miles then N on Steve St .2 mile
Waynesboro	◆		🕐 ℞		1500 N Liberty St, 30830 / 706-437-8380 • *Lat:* 33.1058 *Lon:* -82.0258 Jct SH-56/80 & US-25 BYP (E of town) take US-25 BYP W for 1.7 miles then N on Liberty St .1 mile
Winder	◆	3	🕐 ℞	🚗	440 Atlanta Hwy NW, 30680 / 770-867-8642 • *Lat:* 33.9921 *Lon:* -83.7576 I-75 Exit 126 follow SH-211 S for 9 miles then W on US-29/Atlanta Hwy for 1.4 miles
Woodstock	◇	4	🕐 ℞	🚗	12182 Hwy 92, 30188 / 770-516-4719 • *Lat:* 34.0872 *Lon:* -84.4813 I-575 Exit 7 take SH-92 E for 3.2 miles
	◇	4	🕐 ℞	🚗	6435 Bells Ferry Rd, 30189 / 770-926-2606 • *Lat:* 34.1134 *Lon:* -84.5825 I-575 Exit 8 go W on Towne Lake Pkwy 1.4 miles, continue on Eagle Dr 1.7 miles then N on Bells Ferry Rd .3 mile

○ Wal-Mart ◇ Supercenter ☐ Sam's Club ▨ Gas ■ Gas & Diesel

Hawaii

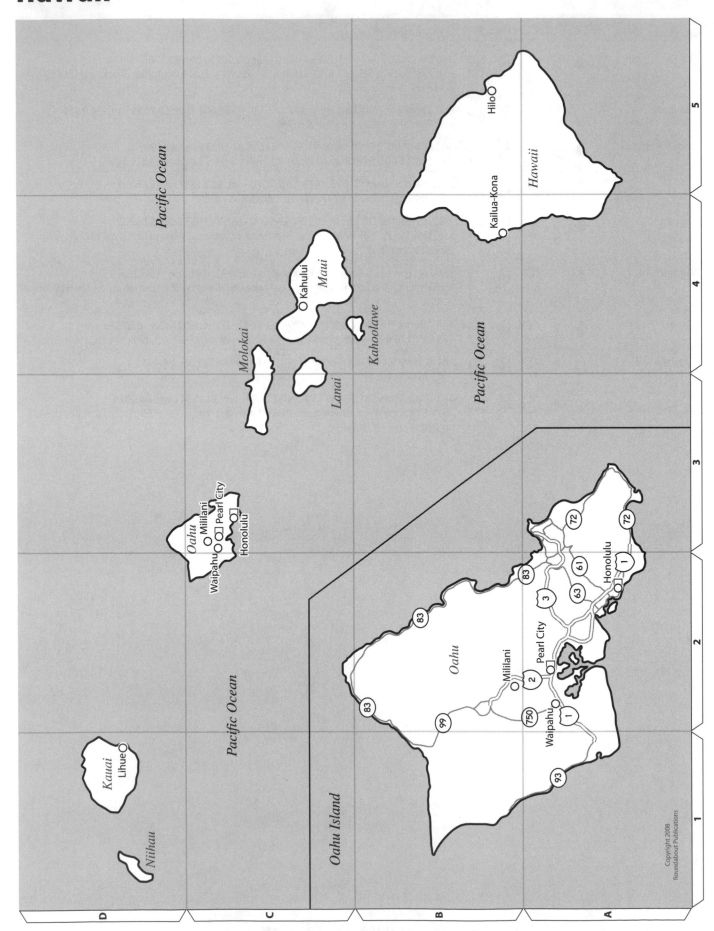

Pacific Ocean

Hilo ○

Hawaii

Kailua-Kona ○

Kahului ○

Maui

Molokai

Kahoolawe

Lanai

Pacific Ocean

Oahu

Mililani ○
Pearl City ☐
Waipahu ○ ○ ☐ Honolulu

72

72

Honolulu

83

61

1

63

3

83

Oahu

Mililani ○

Pearl City ☐

2

99

750

93

Waipahu ○ 1

Pacific Ocean

Oahu Island

Kauai
Lihue ○

Niihau

D   C   B   A

5   4   3   2   1

City/Town	🛡	🕐	℞	🚗	Information
Hilo	○		℞		325 Makaala St, 96720 / 808-961-9115 • *Lat:* 19.6994 *Lon:* -155.0639 Jct SH-130 & SH-11 take SH-11 N 5.1 miles then E at Makaala St
Honolulu	□		℞	🚗	750 Keeaumoku St, 96814 / 808-945-9841 • *Lat:* 21.2954 *Lon:* -157.8417 I-H1 Exit 22 take Kinou St S for 1 mile then W on Keeaumoku St
	○		℞		700 Keeaumoku St, 96814 / 808-955-8441 • *Lat:* 21.2948 *Lon:* -157.8420 I-H1 Exit 22 merge onto Kinau St 1 mile then S on Keeaumoku St .5 mile
Kahului	○		℞	🚗	101 Pakaula St, 96732 / 808-871-7820 • *Lat:* 20.8766 *Lon:* -156.4551 Jct SH-340 & SH-36 take SH-36 E 1.5 miles, SH-38/Dairy Rd S .6 mile & Pakaula St E .3 mile
Kailua Kona	○		℞		75-1015 Henry St, 96740 / 808-334-0466 • *Lat:* 19.6470 *Lon:* -155.9891 Jct Hualalai Rd & SH-11 take SH-11 N 1.3 miles then Henry St NE .1 mile
Lihue	○		℞		3-3300 Kuhio Hwy, 96766 / 808-246-1599 • *Lat:* 21.9822 *Lon:* -159.3672 .5 mile north of town center on SH-56 (Kuhio Hwy)
Mililani	○				95-550 Lanikuhana Ave, 96789 / 808-623-6711 • *Lat:* 21.4515 *Lon:* -158.0050 I-H2 Exit 5B go SW .8 mile on Mehula Pkwy, turn left at Lanikuhana Ave .4 mile
Pearl City	□		℞	🚗	1000 Kamehameha Hwy Ste 100, 96782 / 808-456-7788 • *Lat:* 21.3951 *Lon:* -157.9727 I-H201 (east of town) take SH-99 for 3.1 miles
	○		℞		1131 Kuala St, 96782 / 808-454-8785 • *Lat:* 21.3985 *Lon:* -157.9751 From I-H201 W exit onto SH-99 for 3.6 miles then N on Kuala St .2 mile
Waipahu	○		℞		94-595 Kupuohi St, 96797 / 808-688-0066 • *Lat:* 21.3910 *Lon:* -158.0337 I-H1 Exit 5B merge onto SH-750 N/Kunia Rd .7 mile, E at Kupuna Loop & N on Kupuohi St .2 mile

Idaho

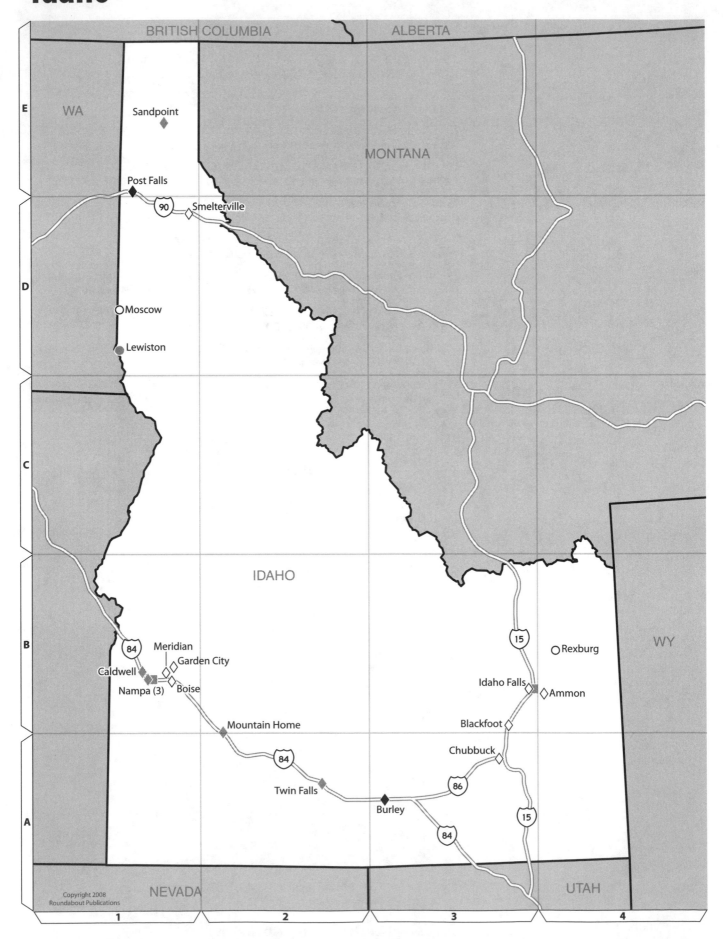

Legend: ○ Wal-Mart ◇ Supercenter □ Sam's Club ▨ Gas ■ Gas & Diesel

BRITISH COLUMBIA — ALBERTA

WA

MONTANA

E

Sandpoint ◆

Post Falls ◆
90
◇ Smelterville

D

○ Moscow

● Lewiston

IDAHO

C

WY

B

84
Meridian ◇
◇ Garden City
Caldwell ◆ ◇
Nampa (3) ◇ Boise

15
○ Rexburg

Idaho Falls ▨ ◇ Ammon

Blackfoot ◇

Mountain Home ▨

Chubbuck ◇

84

86

Twin Falls ▨

Burley ◆

A

84

15

NEVADA

UTAH

1   2   3   4

City/Town	⬡	🕐	℞	🚗	Information
Ammon	◇	6	🕐	℞ 🚗	1201 S 25th E, 83406 / 208-522-0204 • Lat: 43.4825 Lon: -111.9844 I-15 Exit 116 go E on 33rd St 1.1 miles, N on Yellowstone Hwy 1.2 miles, E on 17th St 3 miles
Blackfoot	◇	1	🕐	℞	565 Jensen Grove Dr, 83221 / 208-785-6937 • Lat: 43.1986 Lon: -112.3577 I-15 Exit 93 follow I-15 BR E .4 mile & N on Pkwy Dr to Jensen Grove Dr .3 mile
Boise	◇	1	🕐	℞ 🚗	8300 W Overland Rd, 83709 / 208-321-9077 • Lat: 43.5904 Lon: -116.2854 I-84 Exit 50A merge onto Cole Rd .4 mile then W Overland Rd for .6 mile
Burley	◆	2	🕐	℞ 🚗	385 N Overland Ave, 83318 / 208-677-4709 • Lat: 42.5600 Lon: -113.7931 I-84 Exit 208 merge onto SH-27 S/I-84 BR E for 1.5 miles
Caldwell	◆	4	🕐	℞ 🚗	5108 Cleveland Blvd, 83607 / 208-455-0066 • Lat: 43.6332 Lon: -116.6443 I-84 Exit 33A, SH-55 S .5 mile, Nampa-Cldwell Blvd W 1.5 miles, continue on Cleveland Blvd 1.4 miles
Chubbuck	◇	1	🕐	℞ 🚗	4240 Yellowstone Ave, 83202 / 208-237-5090 • Lat: 42.9097 Lon: -112.4661 I-86 Exit 61 go S on US-91 for .1 mile
Garden City	◇	6	🕐	℞	7319 W State St, 83714 / 208-853-0541 • Lat: 43.6687 Lon: -116.2799 I-84 Exit 50, Cole Rd N 3.4 miles, Mt View Dr W .2 mile, Glenwood St N 1.7 miles, State St W .3 mile
Idaho Falls	▣	4		℞ 🚗	700 E 17th St, 83404 / 208-529-2300 • Lat: 43.4824 Lon: -112.0197 I-15 Exit 116 go E on 33rd St/Sunnyside Rd 1.5 miles, N on Yellowstone Hwy 1.2 miles & E on 17th St 1.3 miles
	◇	1	🕐	℞ 🚗	500 S Utah Ave, 83402 / 208-528-8735 • Lat: 43.4912 Lon: -112.0510 I-15 Exit 118 take W Broadway/I-15 BR E .3 mile, then Utah Ave S .3 mile
Jerome	◆	1	🕐	℞ 🚗	2680 S Lincoln Ave, 83338 / 208-324-4333 • Lat: 42.6969 Lon: -114.5183 I-84 Exit 168 take SH-79 N for .4 mile
Lewiston	●			℞	2981 Thain Grade, 83501 / 208-746-8364 • Lat: 46.3928 Lon: -116.9906 From US-12/US-95 (NE of town), US-12 SW .6 mile, Memorial Bridge S .4 mile, 21st St S 1 mile & Thain Grade .8 mile
Meridian	◇	3	🕐	℞ 🚗	4051 E Fairview Ave, 83642 / 208-373-7908 • Lat: 43.6194 Lon: -116.3446 I-84 Exit 46 go N on SH-55 for 1.9 miles then E on Fairview Ave .5 mile
Moscow	○			℞	2470 W Pullman Rd, 83843 / 208-883-8828 • Lat: 46.7326 Lon: -117.0350 Jct US-95 & SH-8 (in town) go W on SH-8/West 3rd St for 1.6 miles
Mountain Home	◆	1	🕐	℞ 🚗	2745 American Legion Blvd, 83647 / 208-587-0601 • Lat: 43.1358 Lon: -115.6658 I-84 Exit 95 (toward Mountain Home) go S on SH-51 for .2 mile
Nampa	▣	1		℞ 🚗	5725 E Franklin Rd, 83687 / 208-442-8136 • Lat: 43.6049 Lon: -116.5094 I-84 Exit 38 go N .4 mile then E on Franklin Rd for .2 mile
	◆	4	🕐	℞ 🚗	2100 12th Ave Rd, 83686 / 208-467-5047 • Lat: 43.5493 Lon: -116.5726 I-84 Exit 36 go S on Franklin Blvd .9 mile, SW on 11th Ave .8 mile, S on SH-45 for 2.2 miles
	◇	1	🕐	℞ 🚗	5875 E Franklin Rd, 83687 / 208-461-6481 • Lat: 43.5955 Lon: -116.5373 I-84 Exit 38 go N on I-84 BR .5 mile then E on Franklin Rd .1 mile
Ponderay	◆		🕐	℞ 🚗	476999 Hwy 95, 83852 / 208-265-8332 • Lat: 48.3055 Lon: -116.5327 From Jct US-2 & US-95 (in Sandpoint) go N on US-95 for 2.3 miles
Post Falls	◆	1	🕐	℞ 🚗	3050 E Mullan Ave, 83854 / 208-457-9866 • Lat: 47.7158 Lon: -116.9070 I-90 Exit 7 go N on SH-41 for .3 mile then W on Mullan Ave .6 mile
Rexburg	○			℞	530 N 2nd E, 83440 / 208-359-2809 • Lat: 43.8347 Lon: -111.7779 I-15 Exit 143 take SH-28/33 E for 21 miles then N on 2nd St for .6 mile
Smelterville	◇	1	🕐	℞	583 Commerce Dr, 83868 / 208-783-0426 • Lat: 47.5438 Lon: -116.1857 I-90 Exit 48 go S on Airport Rd then W on Commerce Dr

○ Wal-Mart ◇ Supercenter ☐ Sam's Club ▣ Gas ◼ Gas & Diesel

Illinois

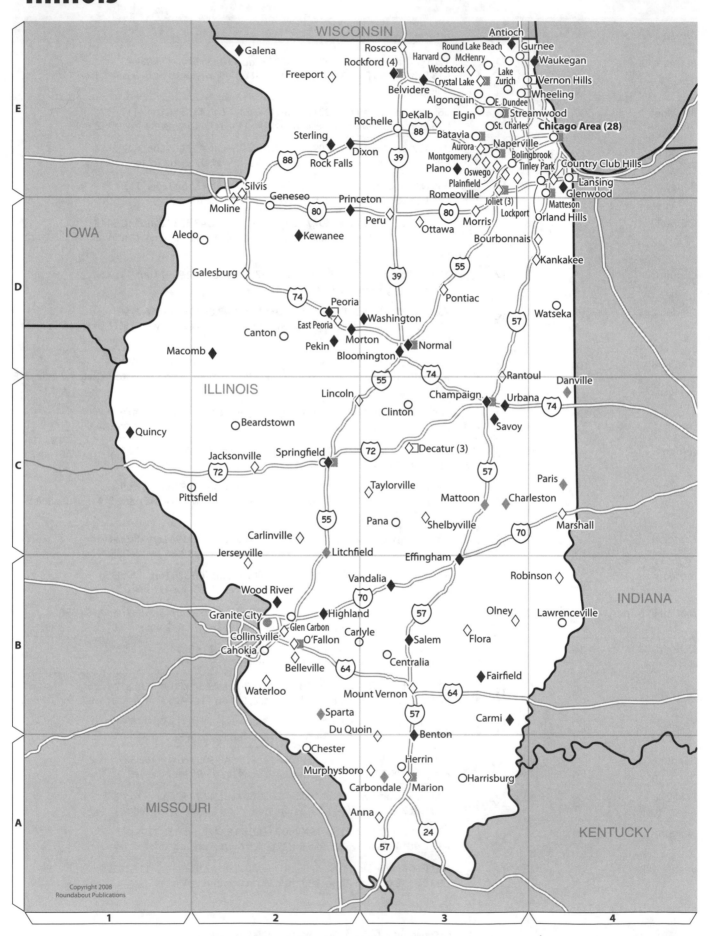

Wal-Mart ◇ Supercenter ☐ Sam's Club ▨ Gas ◼ Gas & Diesel

WISCONSIN

Galena
Roscoe
Antioch
Round Lake Beach
Gurnee
Rockford (4)
Harvard McHenry
Waukegan
Freeport
Woodstock
Lake Zurich
Vernon Hills
Belvidere
Crystal Lake
Wheeling
Rochelle
DeKalb
Algonquin
E. Dundee
Streamwood
Elgin
St. Charles
Chicago Area (28)
Sterling
Batavia
Naperville
Dixon
Aurora
Bolingbrook
Rock Falls
Montgomery
Tinley Park
Country Club Hills
Plano
Oswego
Lansing
Silvis
Plainfield
Glenwood
Moline
Geneseo
Princeton
Romeoville
Joliet (3)
Matteson
Lockport
Orland Hills
Aledo
Peru
Morris
Ottawa
Bourbonnais
Kewanee
Kankakee

IOWA

Galesburg
Pontiac
Watseka
Peoria
Washington
East Peoria
Canton
Morton
Normal
Macomb
Pekin
Bloomington
Rantoul
Danville

ILLINOIS

Lincoln
Champaign
Urbana
Clinton
Beardstown
Savoy
Quincy
Decatur (3)
Paris
Jacksonville
Springfield
Taylorville
Mattoon
Charleston
Pittsfield
Pana
Shelbyville
Marshall
Carlinville
Jerseyville
Litchfield
Effingham
Robinson
Wood River
Vandalia
INDIANA
Granite City
Highland
Olney
Lawrenceville
Glen Carbon
Carlyle
Collinsville
O'Fallon
Salem
Flora
Cahokia
Belleville
Centralia
Fairfield
Waterloo
Mount Vernon
Sparta
Carmi
Du Quoin
Benton
Chester
Herrin
Murphysboro
Harrisburg
Carbondale
Marion
Anna

MISSOURI

KENTUCKY

Copyright 2008
Roundabout Publications

1   2   3   4

Chicago Area

Addison (2)	○	□	Des Plaines	■		Mount Prospect	○	
Bedford Park	○		Elk Grove Village	○		Niles (2)	○	
Bloomingdale	○		Evanston	■		Northlake (2)	○	■
Bridgeview	○		Evergreen Park (2)	○	□	Palatine	○	
Chicago	○		Forest Park	○		Rolling Meadows (2)	○	□
Cicero		■	Glen Ellyn	○		Villa Park	○	
Crestwood	○		Hodgkins (2)	○	■	Woodridge		■
Darien	○							

City/Town	⬡	🕐	℞	🚌	Information
Addison	□ 2			🚌	1006 N Rohlwing Rd, 60101 / 630-932-7770 • *Lat:* 41.9474 *Lon:* -88.0320 I-355 Exit 31 go E on Army Trail Rd .4 mile then N on SH-53 1.1 miles
	○ 1		℞	🚌	1050 N Rohlwing Rd, 60101 / 630-889-1826 • *Lat:* 41.9492 *Lon:* -88.0320 I-290 Exit 7 go S on Lake St .2 mile then E on Rohlwing Rd .1 mile
Aledo	○ 8		℞		1500 SE 5th St, 61231 / 309-582-5617 • *Lat:* 41.1975 *Lon:* -90.7278 Jct US-67 & SH-17 (E of town) go W on SH-17 for 7.4 miles & S on 19 Ave .1 mile
Algonquin	○ 6		℞	🚌	1410 S Randall Rd, 60102 / 847-458-5620 • *Lat:* 42.1589 *Lon:* -88.3358 From I-90 (toll) Randall Rd Exit, go N on Randall Rd 5.3 miles
Anna	◇ 5	🕐	℞		300 Leigh Ave, 62906 / 618-833-8592 • *Lat:* 37.4627 *Lon:* -89.2228 I-57 Exit 30 take SH-146 W 4.6 miles then S on Leigh St .1 mile
Antioch	◆ 5	🕐	℞	🚌	475 E Hwy 173, 60002 / 847-838-2148 • *Lat:* 42.4671 *Lon:* -88.0642 I-94 (toll) Rosencrans Rd Exit (northbound access only) follow SH-173 W 5 miles
Aurora	○ 3		℞		2131 W Galena Blvd, 60506 / 630-264-1804 • *Lat:* 41.7649 *Lon:* -88.3683 I-88 (toll) Orchard Rd Exit go S on Orchard 2.2 miles & E on Galena Blvd .6 mile
	◇ 2	🕐	℞	🚌	2900 Kirk Rd, 60502 / 630-375-6207 • *Lat:* 41.8170 *Lon:* -88.2797 I-88 (toll) at Farnsworth Ave exit go N 1 mile, continue on Kirk Rd .3 mile
Batavia	■ 6		℞	🚌	501 N Randall Rd, 60510 / 630-761-9100 • *Lat:* 41.8618 *Lon:* -88.3406 I-88 (toll rd) go NE on Orchard Rd 2.6 miles then N on Randall Rd 2.9 miles
	○ 6		℞	🚌	801 N Randall Rd, 60510 / 630-879-3970 • *Lat:* 41.8640 *Lon:* -88.3407 I-88 (toll) Orchard Rd Exit go NE on Orchard 2.6 miles & N on Randall Rd 3.3 miles
Beardstown	○		℞	🚌	61 Plaza Dr, 62618 / 217-323-1340 • *Lat:* 40.0030 *Lon:* -90.4387 Jct SH-125 & US-67 (S of town) take US-67 S .1 mile & W at Plaza Dr .1 mile
Bedford Park	○ 4		℞		7050 S Cicero Ave, 60638 / 708-496-0230 • *Lat:* 41.7647 *Lon:* -87.7426 I-55 Exit 286 take Cicero Ave S 3.6 miles
Belleville	◇ 4	🕐	℞	🚌	2601 Green Mount Commons Dr, 62221 / 618-236-2200 • *Lat:* 38.5214 *Lon:* -89.9284 I-64 Exit 16 go S 3.7 miles on Green Mount Rd
Belvidere	◆ 9	🕐	℞	🚌	2101 Gateway Center Dr, 61008 / 815-547-5447 • *Lat:* 42.2399 *Lon:* -88.8186 I-39 Exit 122 take US-20 E 8.1 miles, S at Farmington Way & W at Gateway Center Dr .3 mile
Benton	◆ 1	🕐	℞	🚌	919 Giacone Dr, 62812 / 618-439-9453 • *Lat:* 37.9945 *Lon:* -88.9312 I-57 Exit 71 go E on SH-14/Main St .3 mile then S on Giacone Dr
Bloomingdale	○ 4		℞		314 W Army Trail Rd, 60108 / 630-893-5000 • *Lat:* 41.9390 *Lon:* -88.1057 I-290 Exit 7 merge onto I-355 S 2.2 miles then W on Army Trail Rd 1.1 miles
Bloomington	◆ 1	🕐	℞	🚌	2225 W Market St, 61704 / 309-828-5646 • *Lat:* 40.4871 *Lon:* -89.0416 I-55/74 Exit 160 go W on Market St .8 mile

○ Wal-Mart ◇ Supercenter □ Sam's Club ■ Gas ■ Gas & Diesel

City/Town	🛡	🕐	℞	🚐	Information
Bolingbrook	○ 1		℞		200 S Bolingbrook Dr, 60440 / 630-739-4800 • *Lat:* 41.6950 *Lon:* -88.0680 I-55 Exit 267 take Bolingbrook Dr/SH-53 N for .6 mile
Bourbonnais	◇ 2	🕐	℞	🚐	2080 N State Rt 50, 60914 / 815-937-5100 • *Lat:* 41.1881 *Lon:* -87.8508 I-57 exit 315 take SH-50 N 1.2 miles
Bridgeview	○ 1		℞		10260 S Harlem Ave, 60455 / 708-499-2088 • *Lat:* 41.7054 *Lon:* -87.7983 I-294 US-20 E Exit, take US-20 E .2 mile then SH-43 S .7 mile
Cahokia	○ 1		℞		1511 Camp Jackson Rd, 62206 / 618-332-1771 • *Lat:* 38.5551 *Lon:* -90.1671 I-255 Exit 13 go W on SH-157 for .3 mile
Canton	○		℞		2071 N Main St, 61520 / 309-647-7000 • *Lat:* 40.5926 *Lon:* -90.0353 Jct SH-116 & SH-78 (N of town) take Main St/SH-78 S 7.9 miles
Carbondale	◆	🕐	℞	🚐	1450 E Main St, 62901 / 618-457-2033 • *Lat:* 37.7373 *Lon:* -89.1838 I-57 Exit 54 merge onto SH-13 W 12.6 miles
Carlinville	◇	🕐	℞		18600 Shipman Rd, 62626 / 217-854-4402 • *Lat:* 39.2695 *Lon:* -89.8956 I-55 Exit 60 take SH-108 W 13.5 miles then Shipman Rd/Alton Rd S .8 mile
Carlyle	○		℞		2517 Franklin St, 62231 / 618-594-2465 • *Lat:* 38.6101 *Lon:* -89.3915 Jct SH-127 & US-50 (in town) go W on Franklin St 1 mile
Carmi	◆	🕐	℞		1344 IL Hwy 1, 62821 / 618-382-5856 • *Lat:* 38.0978 *Lon:* -88.1460 1.5 miles northeast of town on SH-1
Centralia	○		℞		1340 W McCord St, 62801 / 618-533-1700 • *Lat:* 38.5329 *Lon:* -89.1575 I-64 Exit 61 take US-51 N 10.5 miles then W on McCord St 1.5 miles
Champaign	■ 1		℞	🚐	915 W Marketview Dr, 61822 / 217-355-2223 • *Lat:* 40.1381 *Lon:* -88.2597 I-74 Exit 181 go N on Prospect Ave .1 mile & W at Marketview Dr
	◆ 1	🕐	℞	🚐	2610 N Prospect Ave, 61822 / 217-352-0700 • *Lat:* 40.1463 *Lon:* -88.2578 I-74 Exit 181 go N on Prospect Ave .7 mile
Charleston	◆ 9	🕐	℞	🚐	2250 Lincoln Ave, 61920 / 217-345-1222 • *Lat:* 39.4850 *Lon:* -88.1610 I-57 Exit 190A take SH-16 E 8.9 miles
Chester	○		℞		2206 State St, 62233 / 618-826-5041 • *Lat:* 37.9239 *Lon:* -89.8111 Jct SH-3 & SH-150 (NE of town) take SH-150 S 9.6 miles
Chicago	○ 4		℞		4650 W North Ave, 60639 / 773-252-7465 • *Lat:* 41.9098 *Lon:* -87.7424 I-90/94 Exit 48B take North Ave/SH-64 W 4 miles
Cicero	■ 2		℞	🚐	2601 S Cicero Ave, 60804 / 708-656-6256 • *Lat:* 41.8430 *Lon:* -87.7438 I-290 Exit 24 go S on SH-50 for 2 miles
Clinton	○		℞		10 Clinton Plz, 61727 / 217-935-9586 • *Lat:* 40.1494 *Lon:* -88.9744 .5 mile west of town off SH-10 at Illini Dr
Collinsville	◇ 1	🕐	℞	🚐	1040 Collinsville Crossing Blvd, 62234 / 618-344-4480 • *Lat:* 38.6751 *Lon:* -90.0156 I-55/I-70 Exit 11 go S .3 mile on SH-157, turn right at Collinsville Crossing Blvd .2 mile
Country Club Hills	◇ 1	🕐	℞	🚐	4005 167th St, 60478 / 708-647-1689 • *Lat:* 41.5861 *Lon:* -87.7142 I-57 Exit 346 go E on 167th St for .5 mile
Crestwood	○ 2		℞	🚐	4700 135th St, 60445 / 708-489-5547 • *Lat:* 41.6473 *Lon:* -87.7360 From I-294 (toll) exit onto Cicero Ave/SH-50 S 1.6 miles then E on 135th St .1 mile
Crystal Lake	■		℞	🚐	5670 Northwest Hwy, 60014 / 815-477-9876 • *Lat:* 42.2263 *Lon:* -88.3076 I-90 (toll rd) go N on Randall/Rakow Rd 9.9 miles, N on CR-V32 1 mile & E on US-14 .4 mile
	◇	🕐	℞	🚐	1205 S Hwy 31, 60014 / 815-455-4200 • *Lat:* 42.2116 *Lon:* -88.2865 4 miles southeast of town center on SH-31 at James R Rakow Rd (south of US-14)
Danville	◆ 8	🕐	℞	🚐	4101 N Vermilion St, 61834 / 217-443-9520 • *Lat:* 40.1963 *Lon:* -87.6294 I-74 Exit 215 follow SH-1 N 7.6 miles
Darien	○ 4		℞	🚐	2189 75th St, 60561 / 630-434-0490 • *Lat:* 41.7512 *Lon:* -87.9984 I-55 Exit 271 go N on Lemont Rd 2.4 miles then E on 75th St .7 mile

○ Wal-Mart ◇ Supercenter □ Sam's Club ■ Gas ■ Gas & Diesel

City/Town	⬡	🕐	℞	🚐	Information
Decatur	☐ 1			🚐	4334 N Prospect St, 62526 / 217-876-9202 • Lat: 39.9002 Lon: -88.9538 I-72 Exit 141 go S on US-51BR .8 mile & W on Ash Ave & Prospect Dr .2 mile
	◇ 10	🕐	℞	🚐	4625 E Maryland St, 62521 / 217-864-6927 • Lat: 39.8198 Lon: -88.8851 I-72 Exit 133 take US-36 E 9.6 miles, 44th St S .2 mile & Maryland St E .1 mile
	◇ 1	🕐	℞	🚐	4224 N Prospect St, 62526 / 217-875-0016 • Lat: 39.8993 Lon: -88.9537 I-72 Exit 141 take US-51 BR S .8 mile & E on Ash Ave
Dekalb	◇ 5	🕐	℞	🚐	2300 Sycamore Rd, 60115 / 815-758-6225 • Lat: 41.9511 Lon: -88.7266 I-88 (toll) Peace Rd Exit, take Peace Rd N 3.6 miles, Barber Green Rd W .7 mile & Sycamre Rd S .2 mile
Des Plaines	▨ 2		℞	🚐	101 W Oakton St, 60018 / 847-296-5050 • Lat: 42.0227 Lon: -87.9233 I-90 (toll rd) go N on Wolf Rd .9 mile then W on Oakton .7 mile
Dixon	◆ 1	🕐	℞	🚐	1640 S Galena Ave, 61021 / 815-288-7770 • Lat: 41.8260 Lon: -89.4754 I-88 (toll) Dixon Exit take SH-26 N .4 mile
Du Quoin	◇	🕐	℞		215 E Grantway St, 62832 / 618-542-8438 • Lat: 37.9984 Lon: -89.2358 I-57 Exit 71 take SH-14 W for 15.8 miles then N on US-51 for 1.8 miles
East Dundee	○ 2		℞		620 Dundee Ave, 60118 / 847-426-2800 • Lat: 42.0946 Lon: -88.2577 From I-90 take SH-25/Dundee Ave N 2 miles
East Peoria	◇ 1	🕐	℞	🚐	401 River Rd, 61611 / 309-694-0513 • Lat: 40.6824 Lon: -89.5874 I-74 Exit 94 take SH-40 N .1 mile then River Rd E .2 mile
Effingham	◆ 1	🕐	℞	🚐	1204 Avenue Of Mid America, 62401 / 217-347-5171 • Lat: 39.1385 Lon: -88.5616 I-70 Exit 160 take SH-32 N .1 mile then E at Ave of Mid-America .2 mile
Elgin	○ 2		℞		1001 N Randall Rd, 60123 / 847-468-9600 • Lat: 42.0528 Lon: -88.3397 I-90 Randall Rd Exit, go S on Randall Rd/CR-34 for 1.8 miles
Elk Grove Village	○ 2		℞		801 Meacham Rd, 60007 / 847-584-7080 • Lat: 42.0024 Lon: -88.0457 I-290 Exit 4 go W on SH-53/Biesterfield Rd 1 mile then S on Meacham Rd .3 mile
Evanston	▨ 4		℞	🚐	2450 Main St, 60202 / 847-491-9000 • Lat: 42.0336 Lon: -87.7079 I-94 Exit 37 go E on Dempster 2.5 miles, S on McCormick Blvd .5 mile & E on Main St .2 mile
Evergreen Park	☐ 3		℞	🚐	9400 S Western Ave, 60805 / 708-422-7417 • Lat: 41.7226 Lon: -87.6822 I-57 Exit 355 go W on 111th St 1 mile then N on Western Ave 1.8 miles
	○ 4		℞	🚐	2500 W 95th St, 60805 / 708-229-0611 • Lat: 41.7210 Lon: -87.6859 I-57 Exit 355, W on Monterey Ave/111th St 1.1 miles, N on Western Ave 2 miles & W on 95th St .2 mile
Fairfield	◆	🕐	℞	🚐	150 Commerce Dr, 62837 / 618-842-7633 • Lat: 38.3795 Lon: -88.3805 Jct US-12 & SH-22/W Main St go E on Main St 2.2 miles & N on Telser Rd .9 mile
Flora	◇	🕐	℞	🚐	1540 N Worthey St, 62839 / 618-662-4491 • Lat: 38.6782 Lon: -88.4984 Jct US-45 & US-50 (E of town) take US-45/50 W 2.8 miles, CR-1 S .1 mile, 12th St W .5 mile & Worthey St S .4 mile
Forest Park	○ 1		℞	🚐	1300 Des Plaines Ave, 60130 / 708-771-2270 • Lat: 41.8626 Lon: -87.8188 I-290 Exit 21A go S on Des Plaines Ave .7 mile
Freeport	◇	🕐	℞	🚐	2445 IL Route 26 S, 61032 / 815-232-8120 • Lat: 42.2621 Lon: -89.6312 3 miles south of town center via SH-26
Galena	◆	🕐	℞		10000 Bartel Blvd, 61036 / 815-777-0507 • Lat: 42.4326 Lon: -90.4456 Jct SH-84 & US-20 (S of town) take The Great River Road N 13.6 miles & E on Bartell Blvd
Galesburg	◇ 2	🕐	℞	🚐	659 Knox Square Dr, 61401 / 309-344-1180 • Lat: 40.9765 Lon: -90.3640 I-74 Exit 46A go W on US-34 for 1.1 miles then Seminary St S .6 mile
Geneseo	○ 1		℞		125 E Bestor Dr, 61254 / 309-944-2145 • Lat: 41.4329 Lon: -90.1575 I-80 Exit 19 go N on SH-82 for .3 mile

○ Wal-Mart ◇ Supercenter ☐ Sam's Club ▨ Gas ▧ Gas & Diesel

City/Town	⬭	🕐	℞	🚌	Information
Glen Carbon	○ 1		℞	🚌	400 Junction Dr, 62034 / 618-692-0550 • *Lat:* 38.7759 *Lon:* -89.9548 I-270 Exit 12 go N on SH-82 for .3 mile
Glen Ellyn	○ 2		℞		3 S 100 Rt 53, 60137 / 630-545-1060 • *Lat:* 41.8276 *Lon:* -88.0545 I-355 Butterfield Rd/SH-56 Exit go W 1.3 miles then S .2 mile on SH-53
Glenwood	● 3		℞	🚌	103 W Holbrook Rd, 60425 / 708-755-1660 • *Lat:* 41.5389 *Lon:* -87.6288 I-294/I-80 take Halsted St/SH-1 S 2.5 miles then Holbrook Rd E .3 mile
Granite City	● 4		℞	🚌	379 W Pontoon Rd, 62040 / 618-451-4201 • *Lat:* 38.7357 *Lon:* -90.1434 I-270 Exit 3A take SH-3 S 2.9 miles then Pontoon Rd W .2 mile
Gurnee	□ 1		℞	🚌	6570 Grand Ave, 60031 / 847-855-1130 • *Lat:* 42.3856 *Lon:* -87.9652 I-94 Exit 69 go W on SH-132/Grand Ave 1 mile
	○ 2		℞		6590 Grand Ave, 60031 / 847-855-1230 • *Lat:* 42.3856 *Lon:* -87.9657 I-94 Exit 69 take Grand Ave//SH-132 W 1.1 miles
Harrisburg	○		℞	🚌	16 Arrowhead Point Shopping Ctr, 62946 / 618-252-8361 • *Lat:* 37.7295 *Lon:* -88.5451 Jct US-45 & SH-13 (NE of town) go N on US-45 for .2 mile
Harvard	○		℞		1201 S Division St, 60033 / 815-943-7496 • *Lat:* 42.4017 *Lon:* -88.6135 Jct SH-23 & US-14 (S of town) go N on US-14/Division St for .2 mile
Herrin	○ 7		℞		1713 S Park Ave, 62948 / 618-942-7386 • *Lat:* 37.7891 *Lon:* -89.0279 I-57 Exit 59 go W on CR-2/Herron Rd 4.6 miles then S on SH-148 for 1.5 miles
Highland	◆ 4	🕐	℞	🚌	12495 IL Hwy 143, 62249 / 618-654-4596 • *Lat:* 38.7586 *Lon:* -89.6846 I-70 Exit 24 go E on SH-143 for 3.3 miles
Hodgkins	■ 2		℞	🚌	9500 Joliet Rd, 60525 / 708-387-7030 • *Lat:* 41.7806 *Lon:* -87.8640 I-55 Exit 279 take US-12 N 1.2 miles & E on Joliet Rd .6 mile
	○ 2		℞		9450 Joliet Rd, 60525 / 708-387-2090 • *Lat:* 41.7807 *Lon:* -87.8638 I-55 Exit 279 merge onto LaGrange Rd N 1.2 miles then NE on Joliet Rd .6 mile
Jacksonville	◇ 4	🕐	℞	🚌	1941 W Morton Ave, 62650 / 217-245-5146 • *Lat:* 39.7230 *Lon:* -90.2692 I-72 exit 60B go N 2.4 miles on US-67/I-72 BR then E 1.3 miles on I-72 BR
Jerseyville	◇	🕐	℞	🚌	1316 S State St, 62052 / 618-498-7744 • *Lat:* 39.1052 *Lon:* -90.3158 Jct CR-25 & US-67 (S of town) go N on US-67 for 5.2 miles
Joliet	■ 1			🚌	321 S Larkin Ave, 60436 / 815-744-2525 • *Lat:* 41.5169 *Lon:* -88.1247 I-80 Exit 130 take SH-7/Larkin Ave N .4 mile
	◇ 1	🕐	℞	🚌	2424 W Jefferson St, 60435 / 815-744-7575 • *Lat:* 41.5221 *Lon:* -88.1431 I-80 Exit 130B go N .8 mile on SH-7 then W 1 mile on US-52 (or from I-55 Exit 253 go E 2.4 miles on US-52)
	◇ 3	🕐	℞	🚌	1401 IL Rt 59, 60431 / 815-609-3381 • *Lat:* 41.5350 *Lon:* -88.1768 I-55 Exit 253 take W Jefferson St/US-52 W for .6 mile & N on SH-59 for 1.8 miles
Kankakee	◇ 1	🕐	℞	🚌	505 Riverstone Pkwy, 60901 / 815-802-1884 • *Lat:* 41.0781 *Lon:* -87.8612 I-57 exit 308 take US-52 N .3 mile then Riverstone Pkwy E .4 mile
Kewanee	◆	🕐	℞	🚌	730 Tenney St, 61443 / 309-853-2020 • *Lat:* 41.2220 *Lon:* -89.9263 I-80 Exit 33 go S on SH-78 for 13.3 miles
Lake Zurich	○		℞		820 S Rand Rd, 60047 / 847-438-2200 • *Lat:* 42.1839 *Lon:* -88.0877 Jct Lake Cook Rd & US-12 (SE of town) go NW on US-12 for 3.3 miles
Lansing	□ 1			🚌	17555 Torrence Ave, 60438 / 708-895-1759 • *Lat:* 41.5750 *Lon:* -87.5587 I-80 Exit 161 go S on Torrence Ave for .2 mile
	○ 1		℞		16771 Torrence Ave, 60438 / 708-474-6405 • *Lat:* 41.5910 *Lon:* -87.5586 I-294//I-80 Exit 161 go N on Torrence Ave/US-6 for .9 mile
Lawrenceville	○		℞		2610 W Haven Rd, 62439 / 618-943-7551 • *Lat:* 38.7278 *Lon:* -87.6992 .7 mile west of town center via SH-250

○ Wal-Mart   ◇ Supercenter   □ Sam's Club   ■ Gas   ■ Gas & Diesel

City/Town	⬭	⏰	℞	🚐	Information
Lincoln	◇ 2	⏰	℞	🚐	825 Malerich Dr, 62656 / 217-735-2314 • *Lat:* 40.1577 *Lon:* -89.3942 I-55 Exit 126 take SH-10 E 1.3 miles
Litchfield	◆ 2	⏰	℞	🚐	1205 W Ferdon St, 62056 / 217-324-6195 • *Lat:* 39.1827 *Lon:* -89.6614 I-55 Exit 52 take SH-16 E .9 mile, Coluimbia Blvd N .3 mile & Ferdon St E .3 mile
Lockport	◇ 6	⏰	℞	🚐	16241 S Farrell Rd, 60441 / 815-838-1027 • *Lat:* 41.5937 *Lon:* -88.0262 I-80 Exit 140 follow I-355 (toll) N 4.3 miles, W .9 mile on SH-7 (159th St), S .3 mile on Farrell Rd
Macomb	◆	⏰	℞	🚐	1730 E Jackson St, 61455 / 309-836-3311 • *Lat:* 40.4587 *Lon:* -90.6440 Jct SH-2 & US-136 (E of town) go W on US-136 for 4.4 miles
Marion	▪ 2			🚐	2709 Walton Way, 62959 / 618-993-5568 • *Lat:* 37.7444 *Lon:* -88.9760 I-57 Exit 54 take SH-13 W for 1.1 miles
	◇ 2	⏰	℞	🚐	2802 Outer Dr, 62959 / 618-997-5618 • *Lat:* 37.7463 *Lon:* -88.9739 I-57 Exit 54B take SH-13 W 1.3 miles
Marshall	◇ 1	⏰	℞		108 Kyden Dr, 62441 / 217-826-8061 • *Lat:* 39.4145 *Lon:* -87.6935 I-70 Exit 147, south of exit
Matteson	▪ 3		℞	🚐	21430 S Cicero Ave, 60443 / 708-747-7979 • *Lat:* 41.5003 *Lon:* -87.7326 I-57 Exit 339 go E on Sauk Trl .9 mile & S on Cicero Ave 1.5 miles
	○ 1		℞		21410 S Cicero Ave, 60443 / 708-503-0440 • *Lat:* 41.5007 *Lon:* -87.7325 I-57 Exit 340 go E .5 mile on US-30 (Lincoln Hwy) then S .4 mile on SH-50
Mattoon	◆ 2	⏰	℞	🚐	101 Dettro Dr, 61938 / 217-234-2266 • *Lat:* 39.4769 *Lon:* -88.3352 I-57 Exit 190B merge onto SH-16 W .9 mile then S on Dettro Dr .5 mile
McHenry	○		℞		2019 N Richmond Rd, 60050 / 815-363-0100 • *Lat:* 42.3560 *Lon:* -88.2675 Jct SH-120 & N Chapel Hill Rd (E of town) take SH-120 W 1.5 miles & N on Richmond Rd .7 mile
Moline	◇ 1	⏰	℞		3930 44th Avenue Dr, 61265 / 309-736-2270 • *Lat:* 41.4704 *Lon:* -90.4820 I-74 Exit 4B go E .5 mile on SH-5, turn right at 38th St then left 41st Ave Dr .1 mile
Montgomery	◇ 5	⏰	℞	🚐	2000 Orchard Rd, 60538 / 630-844-0292 • *Lat:* 41.7205 *Lon:* -88.3753 I-88 (toll) Orchard Rd Exit go S 4.7 miles
Morris	◇ 3	⏰	℞	🚐	333 E US Rt 6, 60450 / 815-942-6306 • *Lat:* 41.3764 *Lon:* -88.3894 I-80 Exit 112 follow US-6 S & W for 2.4 miles
Morton	◆ 1	⏰	℞	🚐	155 E Courtland St, 61550 / 309-263-7898 • *Lat:* 40.6286 *Lon:* -89.4630 I-74 Exit 102 go N on Morton Ave .3 mile then E on Courtland St
Mount Prospect	○ 4		℞		930 Mount Prospect Plz, 60056 / 847-590-0002 • *Lat:* 42.0688 *Lon:* -87.9243 From I-294 (toll) take the Dempster Rd Exit to Rand Rd NW 3.4 miles
Mount Vernon	◇ 1	⏰	℞	🚐	110 Davidson Rd, 62864 / 618-244-7119 • *Lat:* 38.3125 *Lon:* -88.9602 I-57 Exit 95 go W on Broadway/SH-15 for .3 mile
Murphysboro	◇	⏰	℞	🚐	6495 Country Club Rd, 62966 / 618-684-5041 • *Lat:* 37.7599 *Lon:* -89.2808 3 miles east of town center off SH-13 at Country Club Rd
Naperville	▪ 5		℞	🚐	808 S State Rt 59, 60540 / 630-527-0880 • *Lat:* 41.7569 *Lon:* -88.2057 I-55 Exit 263 go W on 127th St 3.3 miles & N on SH-59 for 1.4 miles
	○ 5		℞		776 S State Rt 59, 60540 / 630-416-1000 • *Lat:* 41.7628 *Lon:* -88.1472 I-55 Exit 261 go N on Errington Rd .4 mile, W on 135th St 2 miles & N on SH-59 for 2.4 miles
Niles	○ 3		℞	🚐	8500 W Golf Rd, 60714 / 847-966-7904 • *Lat:* 42.0548 *Lon:* -87.8372 I-294 (toll) take Dempster St/US-14 E .3 mile, Potter Rd N 1 mile & Golf Rd/SH-58 E 1.2 miles
	○ 1		℞	🚐	5630 W Touhy Ave, 60714 / 847-647-8641 • *Lat:* 42.0121 *Lon:* -87.7684 I-94 Exit 39A take W Touhy Ave .7 mile

○ Wal-Mart ◇ Supercenter ☐ Sam's Club ▪ Gas ■ Gas & Diesel

City/Town	🛡	🕐	℞	🚐	Information
Normal	■ 2		℞	🚐	2151 Shepard Rd, 61761 / 309-454-3138 • *Lat:* 40.5243 *Lon:* -88.9494 I-55 Exit 167 go S on Veterans Pkwy 1.2 miles & E on Shepard .1 mile
	◆ 3	🕐	℞	🚐	300 Greenbriar Dr, 61761 / 309-451-1100 • *Lat:* 40.5141 *Lon:* -88.9517 I-55 Exit 167 take Veterans Pkwy/I-55 BR S 2 miles then E at Pkwy Plaza Dr
Northlake	■ 1		℞	🚐	141 W North Ave, 60164 / 708-531-0807 • *Lat:* 41.9068 *Lon:* -87.9101 I-290 Exit 13 take US-20 E .3 mile then N on Railroad Ave .1 mile & E at North Ave
	○ 1		℞		137 W North Ave, 60164 / 708-409-0049 • *Lat:* 41.9068 *Lon:* -87.9099 I-290 Exit 13A take Lake St/US-20 E .3 mile, Railroad Ave N .1 mile & North Ave/SH-64 E .2 mile
O Fallon	■ 1		℞	🚐	1350 W Hwy 50, 62269 / 618-632-4373 • *Lat:* 38.5920 *Lon:* -89.9120 I-64 Exit 14 go S on US-50 for .2 mile
	◇ 1	🕐	℞	🚐	1530 W Hwy 50, 62269 / 618-632-9066 • *Lat:* 38.5920 *Lon:* -89.9120 I-64 Exit 14 go W on US-50 for .6 mile
Olney	◇	🕐	℞	🚐	1001 N West St, 62450 / 618-395-7317 • *Lat:* 38.7393 *Lon:* -88.0947 Jct US-50 & SH-130 (S of town) take SH-130/West St N 1.7 miles
Orland Hills	○ 5		℞		9265 159th St, 60487 / 708-349-4300 • *Lat:* 41.6009 *Lon:* -87.8002 I-80 Exit 145 take US-45 N 3.5 miles then US-6 E .9 mile
Oswego	◇	🕐	℞	🚐	2300 Rt 34, 60543 / 630-554-3014 • *Lat:* 41.7033 *Lon:* -88.3092 Jct US-30 & US-34 (NE of town) take US-34 SW 1.3 miles
Ottawa	◇ 1	🕐	℞	🚐	4041 Veterans Dr, 61350 / 815-434-0120 • *Lat:* 41.3123 *Lon:* -88.8703 I-80 Exit 90 take SH-23/Columbus St S .4 mile
Palatine	○ 7		℞	🚐	1555 N Rand Rd, 60074 / 847-202-9189 • *Lat:* 42.1386 *Lon:* -88.0207 I-90 & SH-53 (S of town) go N on SH-53 for 5.3 miles then W on Rand Rd for 1.1 miles
Pana	○		℞		10 W 2nd St, 62557 / 217-562-5081 • *Lat:* 39.3898 *Lon:* -89.0844 Jct US-51 & SH-16 (E of town) go W on SH-16 for 5.2 miles
Paris	◆	🕐	℞		15150 US Hwy 150, 61944 / 217-466-5428 • *Lat:* 39.6041 *Lon:* -87.6774 Jct US-150 & SH-1 (E of town) take US-150 W 4.8 miles
Pekin	◆ 8	🕐	℞	🚐	3320 Veterans Dr, 61554 / 309-353-1123 • *Lat:* 40.5419 *Lon:* -89.5946 I-55 Exit 28 take Broadway/CR-19 W 5.5 miles & S on Veterans Dr 2.1 miles
Peoria	□ 4		℞	🚐	4100 W Willow Knolls Dr, 61615 / 309-691-4545 • *Lat:* 40.7761 *Lon:* -89.6557 I-74 Exit 88 go N on Sterling Ave .7 mile, NW on US-150 for 2.3 miles, N on CR-D37 for .3 mile, N on Brauer Rd
	○ 2		℞	🚐	3315 N University St, 61604 / 309-682-0055 • *Lat:* 40.7268 *Lon:* -89.6130 I-74 Exit 91 go N on University St 1.3 miles
	◆ 6	🕐	℞	🚐	8915 N Allen Rd, 61615 / 309-693-0525 • *Lat:* 40.7949 *Lon:* -89.6312 I-74 Exit 87B take US-6 N 5.3 miles to Exit 5 then S on Allen Rd .3 mile
Peru	◇ 1	🕐	℞	🚐	5307 State Rt 251, 61354 / 815-224-2396 • *Lat:* 41.3732 *Lon:* -89.1256 I-80 Exit 75, north of exit
Pittsfield	○ 7		℞		151 Shetland Dr, 62363 / 217-285-9621 • *Lat:* 39.5963 *Lon:* -90.7860 I-72 Exit 35 take SH-107/US-54 S 5.3 miles, Washington St W 1.2 miles & Shetland Dr N
Plainfield	◇ 6	🕐	℞	🚐	12690 S Rt 59, 60585 / 815-267-3041 • *Lat:* 41.6516 *Lon:* -88.2058 I-55 Exit 263 take Weber Rd N .8 mile, Rodeo Dr W 2.6 miles, 119th St W 1.4 miles & SH-59 S 1 mile
Plano	◆	🕐	℞	🚐	6800 W US Hwy 34, 60545 / 630-552-1580 • *Lat:* 41.6604 *Lon:* -88.5419 Jct SH-15 & US-34 (W of town) go W on US-34 for 1.2 miles
Pontiac	◇ 1	🕐	℞	🚐	1706 W Reynolds St, 61764 / 815-844-3600 • *Lat:* 40.8734 *Lon:* -88.6599 I-55 Exit 197 go E on Reynolds St .7 mile

○ Wal-Mart ◇ Supercenter □ Sam's Club ■ Gas ■ Gas & Diesel

City/Town	⬡	🕐	℞	🚌	Information
Princeton	◆ 1	🕐	℞	🚌	2111 Claude Bailey Pkwy, 61356 / 815-875-4521 • Lat: 41.3952 Lon: -89.4678 I-80 Exit 56, south of exit
Quincy	◆ 1	🕐	℞	🚌	5211 Broadway St, 62305 / 217-223-9930 • Lat: 39.9354 Lon: -91.3335 I-172 Exit 14 go W on SH-104/Broadway St .6 mile
Rantoul	◇ 1	🕐	℞	🚌	845 Broadmeadow Dr, 61866 / 217-892-9151 • Lat: 40.3073 Lon: -88.1795 I-57 Exit 250, east of exit
Robinson	◇	🕐	℞	🚌	1304 E Main St, 62454 / 618-546-5676 • Lat: 39.0061 Lon: -87.7256 Jct SH-33 & SH-1 (E of town) go W on SH-33 for 2.2 miles
Rochelle	○ 3		℞		1240 N 7th St, 61068 / 815-562-3424 • Lat: 41.9373 Lon: -89.0683 I-39 Exit 99 take SH-38 W 2.4 miles & N on 7th St .2 mile
Rock Falls	○ 1		℞		1901 1st Ave, 61071 / 815-626-6800 • Lat: 41.7633 Lon: -89.6891 I-88 Exit 41 take SH-40/88 N 1 mile
Rockford	■ 2		℞	🚌	7151 Walton St, 61108 / 815-394-1212 • Lat: 42.2677 Lon: -88.9779 I-90 Exit 63 go W on US-20BR 1.5 miles & S on Buckley Dr .2 mile
	◆ 8	🕐			3902 W Riverside Blvd, 61101 / 815-962-4071 • Lat: 42.3153 Lon: -89.1139 From I-90/39 take Riverside Blvd W 7.8 miles
	◇ 1	🕐	℞	🚌	7219 Walton St, 61108 / 815-399-7143 • Lat: 42.2681 Lon: -88.9744 I-90/39 Exit 63 take US-20 BR W .7 mile & Buckley Dr S for .2 mile
	◇ 4	🕐	℞	🚌	3849 Northridge Dr, 61114 / 815-636-0101 • Lat: 42.3166 Lon: -89.0322 I-90/39 take Riverside Blvd W 3.6 miles, S on Forest Hills Rd .2 mile & N on Northridge .2 mile
Rolling Meadows	□ 2		℞	🚌	1470 Golf Rd, 60008 / 847-357-1558 • Lat: 42.0514 Lon: -88.0003 I-90 go N on Arlington Heights Rd .4 mile, NW on Algonquin Rd .8 mile, W on Golf Rd .2 mile
	○ 2		℞	🚌	1460 Golf Rd, 60008 / 847-734-0456 • Lat: 42.0513 Lon: -87.9982 I-90 (toll) exit at Arlington Heights Rd Ext go N .2 mile, NW on Algonquin Rd .8 mile & W on Golf Rd .2 mile
Romeoville	◇ 4	🕐	℞	🚌	420 N Weber Rd, 60446 / 815-439-1666 • Lat: 41.6098 Lon: -88.1233 I-55 Exit 263 take Weber Rd S 3.3 miles
Roscoe	◇ 1	🕐	℞	🚌	4781 E Rockton Rd, 61073 / 815-389-4055 • Lat: 42.4564 Lon: -89.0265 I-90/39 Exit 3 go W on Rockton Rd for 1.6 miles
Round Lake Beach	○ 7		℞		772 E Rollins Rd, 60073 / 847-546-0043 • Lat: 42.3795 Lon: -88.0644 I-94 (toll) Grand Ave Exit go W 2.5 miles, turn left and follow CR-A20/Rollins Rd W 3.8 miles
Saint Charles	○		℞		150 Smith Rd, 60174 / 630-513-9559 • Lat: 41.9236 Lon: -88.2621 Jct SH-59 & SH-64 (E of town) go W on SH-64/North Ave 2.8 miles then N on Smith Rd .1 mile
Salem	◆ 1	🕐	℞	🚌	1870 W Main St, 62881 / 618-548-4383 • Lat: 38.6237 Lon: -88.9786 I-57 Exit 116 take US-50 W .3 mile
Savoy	◆ 6	🕐	℞	🚌	505 S Dunlap Ave, 61874 / 217-355-5845 • Lat: 40.0488 Lon: -88.2526 I-74 Exit 182 go S on Neil St 3.5 miles, continue S on Dunlap Ave 2.4 miles
Shelbyville	◇	🕐	℞		RR 2 Box 149, 62565 / 217-774-1560 • Lat: 39.4055 Lon: -88.8292 1.6 miles west of town center along SH-16
Silvis	◇ 6	🕐	℞	🚌	1601 18th St, 61282 / 309-796-3526 • Lat: 41.4963 Lon: -90.4040 I-80 exit 7 take Cleveland Rd & SH-84 W 3.6 miles, continue W .9 mile on Colona Rd, then N .9 mile on John Deere Rd
Sparta	◆	🕐	℞	🚌	1410 N Market St, 62286 / 618-443-5800 • Lat: 38.1390 Lon: -89.7033 On SH-4 1 mile north of town

○ Wal-Mart   ◇ Supercenter   □ Sam's Club   ▨ Gas   ■ Gas & Diesel

City/Town		🛡	🕓	Rx	🚗	Information
Springfield	■	2		Rx	🚗	2300 W White Oaks Dr, 62704 / 217-787-4070 • *Lat:* 39.7730 *Lon:* -89.7096 I-72 Exit 93 take SH-4 N 1.7 miles, W on Iles .2 mile & N on White Oaks Dr
	○	1		Rx	🚗	3401 Freedom Dr, 62704 / 217-793-3310 • *Lat:* 39.7530 *Lon:* -89.7080 I-72 Exit 93 take SH-4 for .4 mile then W on Lindbergh Blvd
	◆	2	🕓	Rx	🚗	2760 N Dirksen Pkwy, 62702 / 217-522-3090 • *Lat:* 39.8410 *Lon:* -89.6043 I-55 Exit 100 take SH-54 W .9 mile then N on Dirksen Pkwy .6 mile
Sterling	◆		🕓	Rx	🚗	4115 E Lincolnway, 61081 / 815-626-7200 • *Lat:* 41.8124 *Lon:* -89.6530 Jct SH-40/88 & SH-2 (S of town) follow SH-2 NE 2.8 miles
Streamwood	■	7		Rx	🚗	900 S Barrington Rd, 60107 / 630-213-8622 • *Lat:* 42.0134 *Lon:* -88.1449 I-290 Exit 5 go W on Elgin/Ohare Expy 4.2 miles, NW on SH-19 for 1.7 miles & N on Barrington .6 mile
	○			Rx		850 S Barrington Rd, 60107 / 630-213-7000 • *Lat:* 42.0147 *Lon:* -88.1449 Jct SH-59 & SH-19 (W of town) go E on SH-19 for 3.2 miles & N on Burlington Rd .6 mile
Taylorville	◇		🕓	Rx	🚗	1530 W Springfield Rd, 62568 / 217-287-7219 • *Lat:* 39.5727 *Lon:* -89.3155 Jct SH-104 & SH-29 (N of town) go N on SH-29 for .5 mile
Tinley Park	□	4			🚗	16100 Harlem Ave, 60477 / 708-429-6069 • *Lat:* 41.5984 *Lon:* -87.7944 I-80 Exit 148 take SH-43 N for 3.7 miles
Urbana	◆	2	🕓	Rx	🚗	100 High Cross Rd, 61802 / 217-344-6148 • *Lat:* 40.1284 *Lon:* -88.1628 I-74 Exit 185 take SH-130 S .8 mile, E on US-150/University Ave 1.2 miles & S at High Cross Rd
Vandalia	◆	1	🕓	Rx	🚗	201 Mattes Ave, 62471 / 618-283-4777 • *Lat:* 38.9670 *Lon:* -89.1305 I-70 Exit 61, south of exit
Vernon Hills	□	3		Rx	🚗	335 N Milwaukee Ave, 60061 / 847-955-9260 • *Lat:* 42.2328 *Lon:* -87.9428 I-94 take SH-60 W 2.1 miles then S on SH-21 for .4 mile
	○	3		Rx		555 E Townline Rd, 60061 / 847-918-0555 • *Lat:* 42.2398 *Lon:* -87.9482 From I-94 go W on Townline Rd/SH-60 for 2.6 miles
Villa Park	○			Rx		900 S Rt 83, 60181 / 630-530-2550 • *Lat:* 41.8725 *Lon:* -87.9618 Jct SH-64 & SH-83/Kingery Hwy go S on SH-83 for 2.2 miles
Washington	◆		🕓	Rx	🚗	1980 Freedom Pkwy, 61571 / 309-745-3339 • *Lat:* 40.6896 *Lon:* -89.3632 Jct SH-8 & US-24 (W of town) go NW on US-24 BR/Mcclugage Rd .3 mile & E on Freedom Pkwy .2 mile
Waterloo	◇		🕓	Rx	🚗	961 N Market St, 62298 / 618-939-3416 • *Lat:* 38.3587 *Lon:* -90.1552 Jct SH-158 & SH-3 (N of town) go S on SH-3 for 5.7 miles then W on HH Rd & S on Market St
Watseka	○			Rx	🚗	1200 E Walnut St, 60970 / 815-432-2200 • *Lat:* 40.7756 *Lon:* -87.7058 I-57 Exit 283 follow US-24 E for 16.5 miles
Waukegan	◆	4	🕓	Rx	🚗	3900 Fountain Square Pl, 60085 / 847-473-2193 • *Lat:* 42.3432 *Lon:* -87.8986 I-94 (toll) at Buckley Rd (SH-137) go E .6 mile then N 2.3 miles on IL-43 (Waukegan Rd) and left .2 mile
Wheeling	□	5		Rx	🚗	1055 McHenry Rd, 60090 / 847-541-9040 • *Lat:* 42.1508 *Lon:* -87.9532 I-94 take Lake-Cook Rd for 4.3 miles, then S at SH-83 for .4 mile
	○			Rx		1455 E Lake Cook Rd, 60090 / 847-537-5090 • *Lat:* 42.1535 *Lon:* -87.9526 Jct Arlington Heights Rd & Lake Cook Rd (W of town) go E on Lake Cook Rd 1.7 miles
Wood River	◆	9	🕓	Rx	🚗	610 Wesley Dr, 62095 / 618-259-0290 • *Lat:* 38.8664 *Lon:* -90.0678 I-270 & SH-255 follow SH-255 N 8.1 miles to Exit 8 then follow SH-111 W .5 mile
Woodridge	■	1			🚗	7300 Woodward Ave, 60517 / 630-663-9600 • *Lat:* 41.7547 *Lon:* -88.0313 I-355 go E on 75th St for .3 mile & N on Woodward .3 mile
Woodstock	◇		🕓	Rx	🚗	1275 Lake Ave, 60098 / 815-206-0256 • *Lat:* 42.2955 *Lon:* -88.4232 Jct Ridgefield Rd & US-14 (S of town) take US-14 N 2.8 miles & continue on Lake Ave .1 mile

○ Wal-Mart ◇ Supercenter □ Sam's Club ■ Gas ■ Gas & Diesel

Indiana

Legend: ○ Wal-Mart ◇ Supercenter □ Sam's Club ▦ Gas ◼ Gas & Diesel

MICHIGAN

ILLINOIS

OHIO

KENTUCKY

Michigan City
Hammond
Schererville
Merrillville
Portage
Valparaiso
La Porte
Plymouth
Mishawaka
South Bend (2)
Elkhart (2)
Goshen
Angola
Kendallville
Auburn
Columbia City
Warsaw
Rochester
Fort Wayne (5)
Rensselaer
Huntington
Decatur
Monticello
Logansport
Wabash
Bluffton
West Lafayette
Lafayette (3)
Kokomo
Marion
Portland
Frankfort
Muncie (2)
Winchester
Lebanon
Noblesville
Anderson
Crawfordsville
Carmel
Brownsburg
Fishers
New Castle
Avon
Greenfield
Richmond
Plainfield
Indianapolis (11)
Clinton
Greencastle
Greenwood
Rushville
Connersville
Brazil
Franklin
Shelbyville
Terre Haute (3)
Martinsville
Greensburg
Spencer
Columbus (3)
Sullivan
Bloomington
Aurora
Linton
North Vernon
Seymour
Washington
Bedford
Madison
Vincennes
Scottsburg
Paoli
Jasper
Princeton
New Albany
Clarksville
Corydon
Evansville (3)
Boonville
Tell City

INDIANA

1   2   3   4

A B C D E

City/Town	⬡	🕐	℞	🚍	Information
Anderson	◇ 1	🕐	℞	🚍	2321 Charles St, 46013 / 765-642-5025 • *Lat:* 40.0663 *Lon:* -85.6531 I-69 Exit 26 take SH-9 N for 1 mile
Angola	◆ 5	🕐	℞	🚍	2016 N Wayne St, 46703 / 260-665-7313 • *Lat:* 41.6587 *Lon:* -84.9993 I-69 Exit 148 go E on US-20 for 2.5 miles then N on Wayne St for 1.7 miles
Auburn	◇ 1	🕐	℞	🚍	505 Touring Dr, 46706 / 260-925-8080 • *Lat:* 41.3626 *Lon:* -85.0788 I-69 Exit 129 take SH-8 E .1 mile then S on Touring Dr .3 mile
Aurora	◇ 10	🕐	℞	🚍	100 Sycamore Estates Dr, 47001 / 812-926-4322 • *Lat:* 39.0746 *Lon:* -84.8930 I-275 Exit 21 take US-50 W for 9.8 miles
Avon	◆ 5	🕐	℞	🚍	9500 E US Hwy 36, 46123 / 317-209-0857 • *Lat:* 39.7628 *Lon:* -86.4022 I-465/74 Exit 13B take US-36 W for 4.6 miles
Bedford	◇	🕐	℞	🚍	3200 John Williams Blvd, 47421 / 812-275-0335 • *Lat:* 38.8680 *Lon:* -86.5154 Jct US-50 & SH-37 go N on SH-37 for 3.2 miles & E at Williams Blvd .2 mile
Bloomington	▪		℞	🚍	3205 W State Hwy 45, 47403 / 812-331-0003 • *Lat:* 39.1467 *Lon:* -86.5745 Southwest of town at the jct of SH-45 and SH-37
	◆	🕐	℞	🚍	3313 W State Rt 45, 47403 / 812-337-0002 • *Lat:* 39.1447 *Lon:* -86.5780 Jct SH-46 & SH-45 (W of town) follow SH-45 S 3.6 miles
Bluffton	◆	🕐	℞	🚍	2100 N Main St, 46714 / 260-824-0296 • *Lat:* 40.7425 *Lon:* -85.1712 I-69 Exit 86 take US-224 E .2 mile, SH-116 E 10.2 miles & S on Main St 1.2 miles
Boonville	◇	🕐	℞	🚍	1115 American Way, 47601 / 812-897-5964 • *Lat:* 38.0488 *Lon:* -87.3057 I-164 Exit 10 go E on Lynch Rd 1.8 miles then SH-62 E for 8.2 miles & N on American Way
Brazil	○ 7		℞		2150 E National Ave, 47834 / 812-443-0667 • *Lat:* 39.5295 *Lon:* -87.1009 I-70 Exit 23 take SH-59 N 5.1 miles then US-40 NE 1.4 miles
Brownsburg	◇ 1	🕐	℞	🚍	400 W Northfield Dr, 46112 / 317-858-0206 • *Lat:* 39.8573 *Lon:* -86.3927 I-74 Exit 66 go S on SH-267 for .2 mile
Carmel	○ 7		℞	🚍	2001 E 151st St, 46033 / 317-844-0096 • *Lat:* 40.0074 *Lon:* -86.1235 I-465 Exit 33 take SH-431 N 5.7 miles, US-31 N .5 mile & E at 151st St .1 mile
Clarksville	▪ 1		℞	🚍	1301 Veterans Pkwy, 47129 / 812-218-0310 • *Lat:* 38.3242 *Lon:* -85.7694 I-65 Exit 5 go W on Veterans Pkwy for .3 mile
	◇ 1	🕐	℞	🚍	1351 Veterans Pkwy, 47129 / 812-284-9926 • *Lat:* 38.3292 *Lon:* -85.7586 I-65 Exit 5, west of exit
Clinton	○		℞		1795 E IN Hwy 163, 47842 / 765-832-3533 • *Lat:* 39.6574 *Lon:* -87.4312 I-70 Exit 7 go N on 3rd St/US-150 for 4.2 miles, SH-63 N 11.9 miles & SH-163 E .2 mile
Columbia City	◇	🕐	℞	🚍	402 W Plaza Dr, 46725 / 260-244-4060 • *Lat:* 41.1702 *Lon:* -85.4929 I-69 Exit 109B take US-30 W 17.2 miles then N on SH-109 & W on Plaza Dr
Columbus	▪ 1		℞	🚍	2715 Merchant Mile, 47201 / 812-373-9226 • *Lat:* 39.1978 *Lon:* -85.9482 I-65 Exit 68 east of exit
	◆ 2	🕐	℞	🚍	735 Whitfield Dr, 47201 / 812-372-0227 • *Lat:* 39.2085 *Lon:* -85.8807 I-65 Exit 76A take US-31 S 9 miles & 10th St W .3 mile
	◇ 2	🕐	℞	🚍	2025 Merchant Mile, 47201 / 812-376-8680 • *Lat:* 39.1979 *Lon:* -85.9455 I-65 Exit 68, take SH-46 W .5 mile, Goller & Terrace Lake Blvd S 1.1 miles, Carr Hill Rd E .2 mile
Connersville	○		℞		2100 N Park Rd, 47331 / 765-827-1255 • *Lat:* 39.6590 *Lon:* -85.1290 I-70 Exit 137 follow SH-1 S 14.4 miles
Corydon	◇ 2	🕐	℞	🚍	2363 Hwy 135 NW, 47112 / 812-738-4551 • *Lat:* 38.2262 *Lon:* -86.1396 I-64 Exit 105 take SH-135 S 1.3 miles
Crawfordsville	◆ 7	🕐	℞	🚍	1835 S US Hwy 231, 47933 / 765-362-5930 • *Lat:* 40.0125 *Lon:* -86.9040 I-74 Exit 39 take SH-32 E 4.9 miles & US-231 S 2.1 miles

○ Wal-Mart ◇ Supercenter □ Sam's Club ▪ Gas ■ Gas & Diesel

City/Town	⬟	🕐	℞	🚐	Information
Decatur	◆	🕐	℞	🚐	1700 S 13th St, 46733 / 260-724-9990 • *Lat:* 40.8089 *Lon:* -84.9372 2 miles south of town on US-27/US-33
Elkhart	◇ 1	🕐	℞	🚐	175 County Rd 6 W, 46514 / 574-266-7448 • *Lat:* 41.7127 *Lon:* -85.9748 I-80/90 (toll) Exit 92 go S on SH-19 for .7 mile & W on CR-6 for .2 mile
	◇ 8	🕐		🚐	30830 Old US 20, 46514 / 574-674-2656 • *Lat:* 41.6885 *Lon:* -86.0583 I-80/I-90 Exit 83 go S 3.8 miles on Capital Ave (SH-331) then E 4.2 miles on McKinley Hwy/Old US-20
Evansville	▪ 2		℞	🚐	6700 E Virginia St, 47715 / 812-473-2518 • *Lat:* 37.9816 *Lon:* -87.4738 I-164 Exit 7B go W on SH-66 for 1 mile, N on Burkhardt Rd .3 mile then E on Virginia St
	◆	🕐	℞	🚐	335 S Red Bank Rd, 47712 / 812-424-5475 • *Lat:* 37.9660 *Lon:* -87.6469 I-164 Exit 7B take Lloyd Expy W for 9.8 miles & N on Red Bank Rd .4 mile
	◇ 2	🕐	℞	🚐	401 N Burkhardt Rd, 47715 / 812-473-1815 • *Lat:* 37.9785 *Lon:* -87.4737 I-164 Exit 7B take SH-66 W 1 mile & Burkhardt Rd W .1 mile
Fishers	◆ 1	🕐	℞	🚐	8300 E 96th St, 46037 / 317-578-4336 • *Lat:* 39.9274 *Lon:* -86.0217 I-69 Exit 3 go E on 96th St .5 mile
Fort Wayne	▪ 1		℞	🚐	6736 Lima Rd, 46818 / 260-490-0626 • *Lat:* 41.1387 *Lon:* -85.1617 I-69 Exit 111B take SH-3 N for .9 mile
	◆ 9	🕐	℞	🚐	7502 Southtown Crossing, 46816 / 260-441-7071 • *Lat:* 41.0074 *Lon:* -85.0825 I-69 Exit 99 go E on Lower Huntington & Airport Expy 7.3 miles, E on Tillman 1.1 miles, S on Phoenix Pkwy .1 mile
	◆ 1	🕐	℞	🚐	10420 Maysville Rd, 46835 / 260-492-5845 • *Lat:* 41.1314 *Lon:* -85.0094 I-469 Exit 25 go W on Maysville Rd .3 mile
	◆ 2	🕐	℞	🚐	1710 Apple Glen Blvd, 46804 / 260-436-0113 • *Lat:* 41.0694 *Lon:* -85.1988 I-69 Exit 105 go E on Illinois Rd 1.2 miles & S on Apple Glen Blvd .2 mile
	◇ 1	🕐	℞		5311 Coldwater Rd, 46825 / 260-484-4198 • *Lat:* 41.1274 *Lon:* -85.1359 I-69 Exit 112A take Coldwater Rd E .6 mile
Frankfort	◆	🕐	℞	🚐	2460 E Wabash St, 46041 / 765-654-5528 • *Lat:* 40.2790 *Lon:* -86.4805 I-65 Exit 146 take SH-47 E 1.8 miles, SH-39 N 10.8 miles & US-421 E 1.7 miles
Franklin	◆ 6	🕐	℞	🚐	2125 N Morton St, 46131 / 317-736-5377 • *Lat:* 39.5003 *Lon:* -86.0674 I-65 Exit 95 take Whiteland Rd W 1.6 miles then US-31 S 3.7 miles
Goshen	☐			🚐	4024 Elkhart Rd Ste1, 46526 / 574-875-7099 • *Lat:* 41.6207 *Lon:* -85.8979 Jct US-20 & US-33 (NW of town) go SE on US-33 for 3 miles
	○		℞	🚐	4024 Elkhard Rd, 46526 / 574-875-6601 • *Lat:* 41.6207 *Lon:* -85.8979 Jct US-20 & US-33 (NW of town) go SE on US-33/Elkhart Rd for 3.2 miles
	◇	🕐	℞	🚐	2304 Lincolnway E, 46526 / 574-534-4094 • *Lat:* 41.5560 *Lon:* -85.7894 I-80/90 (toll) Exit 101 follow SH-15 S for 11.7 miles then US-33 SE 3.1 miles
Greencastle	◇ 10	🕐	℞	🚐	1750 Indianapolis Rd, 46135 / 765-653-2481 • *Lat:* 39.6461 *Lon:* -86.8201 I-70 Exit 41 take US-231 N 7.8 miles then follow SH-240 E 1.8 miles
Greenfield	◆ 1	🕐	℞	🚐	1965 N State St, 46140 / 317-462-8850 • *Lat:* 39.8134 *Lon:* -85.7696 I-70 Exit 104 go S on State St .4 mile
Greensburg	◇ 1	🕐	℞	🚐	790 Greensburg Commmons Shopping Ctr, 47240 / 812-663-3434 • *Lat:* 39.3317 *Lon:* -85.4681 I-74 Exit 134A take SH-3 S .1 mile & E at Freeland Rd .2 mile
Greenwood	☐ 1		℞	🚐	1101 Windhorst Way, 46143 / 317-889-2582 • *Lat:* 39.6179 *Lon:* -86.0825 I-65 Exit 99 go W on Main St .6 mile, N on Emerson Ave .3 mile
	◆ 1	🕐	℞	🚐	1133 N Emerson Rd, 46143 / 317-885-9059 • *Lat:* 39.6344 *Lon:* -86.0825 I-65 Exit 101 go W on County Line Rd .3 mile then S on Emerson Rd .1 mile
Hammond	○ 2		℞	🚐	1828 E 165th St, 46320 / 219-989-0258 • *Lat:* 41.5956 *Lon:* -87.4851 I-80/94 Exit 2 take SH-152 N 1.7 miles then W on 165th St .2 mile

○ Wal-Mart ◇ Supercenter ☐ Sam's Club ▪ Gas ■ Gas & Diesel

City/Town			℞	🚗	Information
Huntington	◇		℞	🚗	2800 Wal-Mart Dr, 46750 / 260-358-8311 • *Lat:* 40.8990 *Lon:* -85.5138 I-69 Exit 86 follow US-224 W 10.4 miles
Indianapolis	■	4	℞	🚗	10859 E Washington St, 46229 / 317-897-2582 • *Lat:* 39.7756 *Lon:* -85.9736 I-70 Exit 91 go S on Post Rd 1.7 miles then E on Washington St 1.9 miles
	■	2	℞	🚗	3015 W 86th St, 46268 / 317-871-7135 • *Lat:* 39.9117 *Lon:* -86.2119 I-465 Exit 27 go S on Michigan Rd .8 mile then E on 86th .6 mile
	■	2	℞	🚗	7235 E 96th St, 46250 / 317-585-1619 • *Lat:* 39.9269 *Lon:* -86.0417 I-69 Exit 3 go W on 96th St 1.2 miles
	□	1	℞	🚗	5805 Rockville Rd, 46224 / 317-248-3577 • *Lat:* 39.7649 *Lon:* -86.2604 I-465/I-74 Exit 13A go E on Rockville Rd .4 mile
	◆	1	🕐 ℞	🚗	4650 S Emerson Ave, 46203 / 317-783-0950 • *Lat:* 39.6996 *Lon:* -86.0828 I-74/I-465 Exit 52, south of exit
	◆	4	🕐 ℞	🚗	10735 Pendleton Pike, 46236 / 317-823-1054 • *Lat:* 39.8604 *Lon:* -85.9766 I-465 Exit 42 take US-36 E 3.9 miles
	◇	4	🕐 ℞	🚗	7245 US Hwy 31 S, 46227 / 317-888-7906 • *Lat:* 39.6603 *Lon:* -86.1441 I-465 Exit 2B follow US-31 S 3.7 miles
	◇	2	🕐 ℞	🚗	3221 W 86th St, 46268 / 317-875-0273 • *Lat:* 39.9116 *Lon:* -86.2172 I-465 Exit 27 go S on Michigan Rd .8 mile then E on 86th St .3 mile
	◇	3	🕐 ℞	🚗	10617 E Washington St, 46229 / 317-895-0065 • *Lat:* 39.7754 *Lon:* -85.9777 I-465 Exit 46 follow US-40 E 2.7 miles
	◇	7	🕐 ℞	🚗	7325 N Keystone Ave, 46240 / 317-202-9720 • *Lat:* 39.8886 *Lon:* -86.1217 I-70 Exit 85B go N on Keystone Ave 6.4 miles
	◇	1	🕐 ℞		4545 Lafayette Rd, 46254 / 317-328-0325 • *Lat:* 39.8377 *Lon:* -86.2482 I-65 Exit 121, south of exit
Jasper	◇		🕐 ℞	🚗	4040 N Newton St, 47546 / 812-634-1233 • *Lat:* 38.4279 *Lon:* -86.9377 1 mile north of town center on US-231
Kendallville	◆	9	🕐 ℞	🚗	2501 E North St, 46755 / 260-347-4300 • *Lat:* 41.4450 *Lon:* -85.2203 I-69 Exit 134 take US-6 W 8.9 miles
Kokomo	■			🚗	1917 E Markland Ave, 46901 / 765-868-7025 • *Lat:* 40.4766 *Lon:* -86.1059 2 miles southeast of town center, east of US-31
	◇		🕐 ℞	🚗	1920 E Markland Ave, 46901 / 765-456-3550 • *Lat:* 40.4768 *Lon:* -86.1059 Jct US-33 & US-35 (E of town) go E on US-35/Markland Ave .1 mile
La Porte	○	7	℞	🚗	333 Boyd Blvd, 46350 / 219-325-3130 • *Lat:* 41.6198 *Lon:* -86.6933 I-80/90 (toll) follow SH-39 S 4.4 miles, SH-2 E 1.6 miles & Boyd Blvd S .2 mile
Lafayette	■	1		🚗	3819 State Rd 26 E, 47905 / 765-449-4309 • *Lat:* 40.4175 *Lon:* -86.8379 I-65 Exit 172 take SH-26 W 1 mile
	◇	1	🕐 ℞	🚗	4205 Commerce Dr, 47905 / 765-446-0100 • *Lat:* 40.4157 *Lon:* -86.8288 I-65 Exit 172 take SH-26 W .4 mile, Well Spring Dr S .1 mile & Commerce Dr E
	◇	5	🕐 ℞	🚗	2347 E 350 S, 47909 / 765-477-9379 • *Lat:* 40.3671 *Lon:* -86.8602 I-65 Exit 168 go W on SH-25/39 for 1.5 miles, continue W on "E-350-S" 2.8 miles
Lebanon	○	6	℞		2440 N Lebanon St, 46052 / 765-482-6070 • *Lat:* 40.0718 *Lon:* -86.4742 I-65 Exit 146 take SH-47 E 2 miles then SH-39 S 3.8 miles
Linton	◆		🕐 ℞	🚗	2251 E IN Hwy 54, 47441 / 812-847-2127 • *Lat:* 39.0381 *Lon:* -87.0951 Jct SH-59 & SH-54 (in town) go E on SH-54 for 3.8 miles
Logansport	○		℞		3919 E Market St, 46947 / 574-732-0221 • *Lat:* 40.7571 *Lon:* -86.3127 2.5 miles east of town center on US-24 (Market St)
Madison	◆		🕐 ℞	🚗	567 Ivy Tech Dr, 47250 / 812-273-4993 • *Lat:* 38.7805 *Lon:* -85.3749 Jct SH-7 & SH-62 (NW of town) take SH-62 E 2.4 miles then S on Ivy Tech Dr .1 mile

○ Wal-Mart ◇ Supercenter □ Sam's Club ■ Gas ■ Gas & Diesel

City/Town	⬡	🕐	℞	🚗	Information
Marion	◇ 9	🕐	℞		3240 S Western Ave, 46953 / 765-662-0809 • *Lat:* 40.5308 *Lon:* -85.6739 I-69 Exit 64 take SH-18 W 5 miles, Penn St & Lincoln Blvd W 1.7 miles, 30th St W 1.6 miles & Western Ave S .2 mile
Martinsville	◆	🕐	℞	🚗	410 Grand Valley Blvd, 46151 / 765-342-3786 • *Lat:* 39.4167 *Lon:* -86.4070 From SH-39/SH-37 jct south of town, follow SH-37 N 2.3 miles
Merrillville	■ 2		℞	🚗	3134 E 79th Ave, 46410 / 219-942-3711 • *Lat:* 41.4735 *Lon:* -87.2979 I-65 Exit 253 take US-30 E 1.2 miles then N on Colorado St .2 mile
	◇ 2	🕐	℞		2936 E 79th Ave, 46410 / 219-947-1309 • *Lat:* 41.4735 *Lon:* -87.3000 I-65 Exit 253 take US-30 E 1.3 miles then N at Merrillville Crossing .2 mile
Michigan City	◇ 1	🕐	℞	🚗	5780 Franklin St, 46360 / 219-879-3620 • *Lat:* 41.6671 *Lon:* -86.8938 I-94 exit 34B take US-421 N .7 mile
Mishawaka	☐ 3		℞	🚗	120 Indian Ridge Blvd, 46545 / 574-243-8048 • *Lat:* 41.7129 *Lon:* -86.1795 I-80/90 Exit 83, N on Capitol Ave .3 mile, SW on SH-23 for 1.6 miles, S on Main St .8 mile & W on Indian Ridge Blvd
	◇ 4	🕐	℞		316 Indian Ridge Blvd, 46545 / 574-243-9188 • *Lat:* 41.7129 *Lon:* -86.1851 I-80/90 (toll) Exit 77, follow Douglas Rd E 3.3 miles, Grape Rd N .2 mile & Indian Ridge Blvd E .1 mile
Monticello	◇	🕐	℞	🚗	1088 W Broadway St, 47960 / 574-583-2063 • *Lat:* 40.7451 *Lon:* -86.7796 Jct SH-43 & US-24 (W of town) take US-24 E 5.1 miles
Muncie	◆	🕐	℞	🚗	1501 E 29th St, 47302 / 765-282-7467 • *Lat:* 40.1601 *Lon:* -85.3711 Jct SH-67 & SH-3 (S of town) go N on Old SH-3 for 1 mile then W on 29th St .2 mile
	◇ 7	🕐	℞	🚗	4801 W Clara Ln, 47304 / 765-284-7181 • *Lat:* 40.2181 *Lon:* -85.4417 I-69 Exit 41 take SH-332 E 6.4 miles, S at Morrison Rd .1 mile & W at Clara Ln .1 mile
New Albany	◆ 2	🕐	℞	🚗	2910 Grant Line Rd, 47150 / 812-944-0635 • *Lat:* 38.3194 *Lon:* -85.8201 I-64 Exit 3 take Grant Line Rd S 1.3 miles
New Castle	◆ 4	🕐	℞	🚗	3167 S State Rd 3, 47362 / 765-529-5990 • *Lat:* 39.8864 *Lon:* -85.3860 I-70 Exit 123 follow SH-3 N 3.2 miles
Noblesville	◇ 7	🕐	℞	🚗	16865 Clover Rd, 46060 / 317-773-5212 • *Lat:* 40.0365 *Lon:* -85.9971 I-69 Exit 5 go N on SH-37 for 5.7 miles, W at Town & Country Blvd & N on Clover Rd .3 mile
North Vernon	○		℞		2110 N IN Hwy 3, 47265 / 812-346-5100 • *Lat:* 39.0158 *Lon:* -85.6397 1 mile northwest of town near jct of SH-3 and SH-7
Paoli	◇	🕐	℞		735 N Gospel St, 47454 / 812-723-4444 • *Lat:* 38.5642 *Lon:* -86.4662 Jct US-150 & SH-37 (in town) go N on SH-37 for .7 mile
Plainfield	◆ 4	🕐	℞	🚗	2373 E Main St, 46168 / 317-839-2261 • *Lat:* 39.7139 *Lon:* -86.3676 I-70 Exit 66 take SH-267 N 3 miles then E on Main St .5 mile
Plymouth	◆	🕐	℞	🚗	2505 N Oak Rd, 46563 / 574-935-9000 • *Lat:* 41.3635 *Lon:* -86.3291 Jct US-30 & US-31 (E of town) go W on US-30 for 3.2 miles then N on Oak Rd .1 mile
Portage	◇ 3	🕐	℞	🚗	6087 US Hwy 6, 46368 / 219-759-5900 • *Lat:* 41.5494 *Lon:* -87.1794 I-80/90 Exit 23 go S on Willowcreek Rd 2.4 miles then E on US-6 for .2 mile
Portland	◆	🕐	℞	🚗	950 W Votaw St, 47371 / 260-726-3682 • *Lat:* 40.4394 *Lon:* -84.9904 Jct US-27 & SH-67/26 (in town) go W on SH-67/26 (Votaw St) for .6 mile
Princeton	○		℞	🚗	2700 W Broadway St, 47670 / 812-386-6620 • *Lat:* 38.3556 *Lon:* -87.5931 I-64 Exit 25B merge onto US-41 N 14 miles then E on SH-64/65 for .5 mile
Rensselaer	○ 8		℞		905 S College Ave, 47978 / 219-866-0266 • *Lat:* 40.9273 *Lon:* -87.1558 I-65 Exit 205 go N on US-231 for 8 miles
Richmond	◆ 2	🕐	℞	🚗	3601 E Main St, 47374 / 765-965-5387 • *Lat:* 39.8308 *Lon:* -84.8532 I-70 Exit 156A take US-40 W 1.8 miles

○ Wal-Mart ◇ Supercenter ☐ Sam's Club ■ Gas ■ Gas & Diesel

City/Town	⬭	🕑	℞	🚌	Information
Rochester	◯		℞		2100 Peace Tree Vlg, 46975 / 574-223-9481 • *Lat:* 41.0512 *Lon:* -86.2186 Jct US-31 & SH-25 (S of town) go N on SH-25 for .3 mile
Rushville	◯		℞		1850 N Main St, 46173 / 765-932-2133 • *Lat:* 39.6298 *Lon:* -85.4447 Jct US-52 & SH-3 (S of town) go N on SH-3/N Main St for 1.5 miles
Schererville	◯ 9		℞		1555 US Hwy 41, 46375 / 219-865-6309 • *Lat:* 41.4938 *Lon:* -87.4707 I-65 Exit 253 follow US-30 W for 7.9 miles then US-41 N for .2 mile
Scottsburg	◆ 1	🕑	℞	🚌	1618 W McClain Ave, 47170 / 812-752-7122 • *Lat:* 38.6851 *Lon:* -85.7959 I-65 Exit 29B take SH-56 W for .3 mile
Seymour	◇ 2	🕑	℞	🚌	1600 E Tipton St, 47274 / 812-522-8838 • *Lat:* 38.9581 *Lon:* -85.8656 I-65 Exit 50B take US-50 W 1.1 miles
Shelbyville	◆ 1	🕑	℞	🚌	2500 Progress Pkwy, 46176 / 317-392-4940 • *Lat:* 39.5272 *Lon:* -85.7416 I-74 Exit 116 take SH-44 W .2 mile & Lee Blvd N .3 mile
South Bend	◆ 5	🕑	℞	🚌	3701 Portage Rd, 46628 / 574-243-4915 • *Lat:* 41.7269 *Lon:* -86.2889 I-80/90 Exit 72 take US-31 N 1.6 miles, Breck Rd E 2.3 miles & Portage Rd S .8 mile
	◇	🕑	℞	🚌	700 W Ireland Rd, 46614 / 574-299-1284 • *Lat:* 41.6288 *Lon:* -86.2584 I-80/90 Exit 72 take US-31 S 9.5 miles, exit at US-31 BR N .6 mile & W on Ireland Rd .4 mile
Spencer	◯		℞		823 W IN Hwy 46, 47460 / 812-829-2251 • *Lat:* 39.2894 *Lon:* -86.7754 I-70 Exit 23 take SH-59 S for 5 miles then SH-46 E for 9.6 miles
Sullivan	◯		℞		757 W Wolfe St, 47882 / 812-268-3381 • *Lat:* 39.1028 *Lon:* -87.4229 Jct US-41 & SH-154 (W of town) go E on SH-154/Wolfe St for .1 mile
Tell City	◆	🕑	℞	🚌	730 USHwy 66 E, 47586 / 812-547-8434 • *Lat:* 37.9360 *Lon:* -86.7555 Jct SH-237 & SH-66 (S of town) go N on SH-66 for 1.7 miles
Terre Haute	▪ 7		℞	🚌	4350 S US Hwy 41, 47802 / 812-235-5660 • *Lat:* 39.3959 *Lon:* -87.3985 I-70 Exit 7 take US-41 N for 7 miles
	◆ 3	🕑	℞	🚌	5555 S US Hwy 41, 47802 / 812-299-4677 • *Lat:* 39.3959 *Lon:* -87.3985 I-70 Exit 7 take US-150 E/US-41 S for 2.2 miles
Terre Haute	◇ 3	🕑	℞	🚌	2399 S State Rd 46, 47803 / 812-872-2520 • *Lat:* 39.4437 *Lon:* -87.3326 I-70 Exit 11 go N on SH-46 for 2.1 miles
Valparaiso	◇	🕑	℞	🚌	2400 Morthland Dr, 46383 / 219-465-2799 • *Lat:* 41.4585 *Lon:* -87.0299 I-65 Exit 253 follow US-30 E 15 miles
Vincennes	◇	🕑	℞	🚌	650 Kimmel Rd, 47591 / 812-886-0312 • *Lat:* 38.6602 *Lon:* -87.5060 Jct US-50/150 & US-41 (E of town) take US-41 S 1.7 miles, Hart St E .3 mile & Kimmel Rd N .1 mile
Wabash	◇	🕑	℞	🚌	1601 N Cass St, 46992 / 260-563-5536 • *Lat:* 40.8174 *Lon:* -85.8402 2 miles northwest of town center near US-24/SH-15 jct
Warsaw	◆	🕑	℞	🚌	2501 Walton Blvd, 46582 / 574-269-7811 • *Lat:* 41.2722 *Lon:* -85.8541 Jct US-30 & SH-15 (N of town) take Detroit St/SH-15 N .3 mile, Jalynn St W & Walton Blvd N .1 mile
Washington	◇	🕑	℞	🚌	1801 S State Rd 57, 47501 / 812-254-6681 • *Lat:* 38.6308 *Lon:* -87.1808 2 miles south of town near the jct of US-50 and SH-57
West Lafayette	◇ 5	🕑	℞	🚌	2801 Northwestern Ave, 47906 / 765-463-0201 • *Lat:* 40.4502 *Lon:* -86.9252 I-65 Exit 175 go W on Schuyler Ave 1.3 miles, continue on US-52 W 3.1 miles, Yeager Rd S .2 mile & US-231 N
Winchester	◇	🕑	℞	🚌	950 E Greenville Pike, 47394 / 765-584-2199 • *Lat:* 40.1652 *Lon:* -84.9650 I-70 Exit 151B take US-27 N 21.2 miles then Greenville Pike E .1 mile

◯ Wal-Mart　◇ Supercenter　☐ Sam's Club　▪ Gas　▪ Gas & Diesel

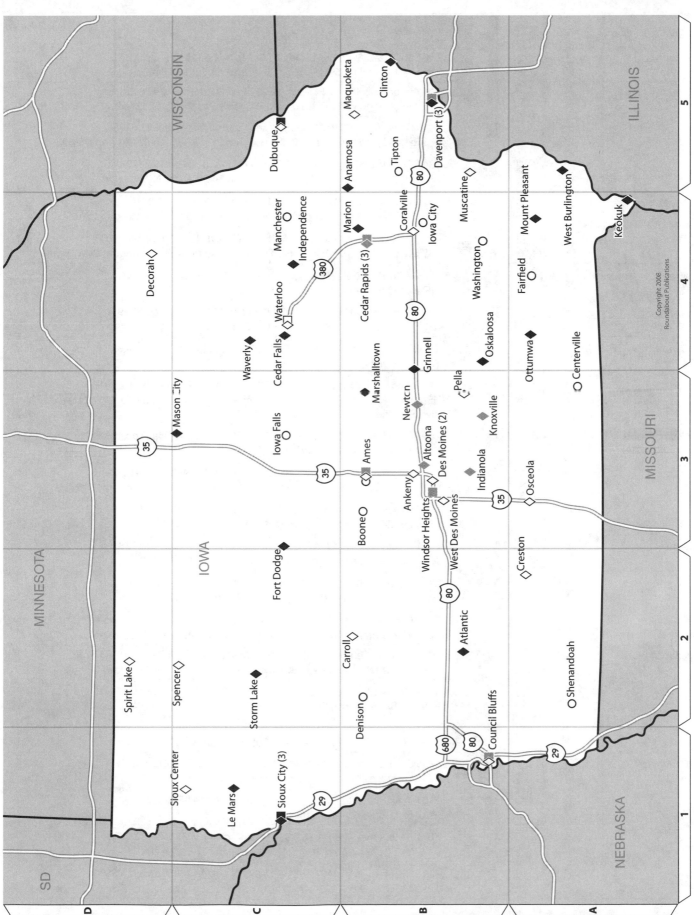

Wal-Mart ○ Supercenter ◇ Sam's Club □ Gas ▨ Gas & Diesel ■

City/Town	⬠	🕐	℞	🚌	Information
Altoona	◆ 2	🕐	℞	🚌	3501 8th St SW, 50009 / 515-967-1711 • *Lat:* 41.6443 *Lon:* -93.5050 I-80 Exit 142A take US-6 W for .5 mile then S on 56th St .8 mile
Ames	■ 2			🚌	305 Airport Rd, 50010 / 515-233-9750 • *Lat:* 42.0012 *Lon:* -93.6138 I-35 Exit 111B go W 1.5 miles on US-30 to Exit 148 then S on US-69, W at Airport Rd
	○ 4		℞		3015 Grand Ave, 50010 / 515-233-1345 • *Lat:* 42.0514 *Lon:* -93.6208 I-35 Exit 113 go W on 13th St 2.2 miles, N on Duff Ave 1.5 miles & W on US-69
	◇ 3	🕐	℞	🚌	534 S Duff Ave, 50010 / 515-956-3536 • *Lat:* 42.0174 *Lon:* -93.6103 I-35 Exit 111B take US-30 W 1.7 miles to Exit 148 then go N .8 mile on Duff Ave
Anamosa	◆	🕐	℞		101 115th St, 52205 / 319-462-4311 • *Lat:* 42.0997 *Lon:* -91.2570 Jct US-150 & SH-64 (E of town) go SE on SH-64 for .5 mile then W on 115th St .2 mile
Ankeny	◇ 1	🕐	℞	🚌	1002 SE National Dr, 50021 / 515-963-1111 • *Lat:* 41.7050 *Lon:* -93.5831 I-35 Exit 90 take SH-160 W .4 mile, Delaware Ave N .1 mile & National Dr W .1 mile
Atlantic	◆ 9	🕐	℞	🚌	1905 E 7th St, 50022 / 712-243-5214 • *Lat:* 41.4038 *Lon:* -94.9873 I-80 Exit 60 merge onto US-71 S 8.9 miles
Boone	○		℞		1815 S Story St, 50036 / 515-432-2416 • *Lat:* 42.0356 *Lon:* -93.8799 I-35 Exit 111B take US-30 W 16.7 miles then N on Story St
Carroll	◇	🕐	℞	🚌	2014 Kittyhawk Rd, 51401 / 712-792-2280 • *Lat:* 42.0785 *Lon:* -94.8917 1.6 miles northwest of town center along US-30
Cedar Falls	◆	🕐	℞	🚌	525 Brandilynn Blvd, 50613 / 319-277-6391 • *Lat:* 42.4853 *Lon:* -92.4418 US-20 Exit 225 take SH-27/58 N 1.3 miles, Viking Rd E .1 mile, Andrea Dr N & Brandilynn Blvd E .2 mile
Cedar Rapids	■ 1		℞	🚌	2605 Blairs Ferry Rd NE, 52402 / 319-393-7746 • *Lat:* 42.0346 *Lon:* -91.6806 I-380 Exit 24B go W on Blairs Ferry Rd .2 mile
	◆	🕐	℞	🚌	3601 29th Ave SW, 52404 / 319-390-9922 • *Lat:* 41.9492 *Lon:* -91.7180 From US-30 Exit 250 go N .7 mile on Edgewood Rd then W .1 mile on 29th Ave
	◇ 1	🕐	℞		2645 Blairs Ferry Rd NE, 52402 / 319-393-0444 • *Lat:* 42.0346 *Lon:* -91.6808 I-380 Exit 24 go W on Blairs Ferry Rd .2 mile
Centerville	○		℞		1101 N 18th St, 52544 / 641-437-7181 • *Lat:* 40.7425 *Lon:* -92.8678 Jct SH-2 & SH-5 (in town) take SH-5 N .7 mile
Clinton	◆	🕐	℞	🚌	2715 S 25th St, 52732 / 563-243-0001 • *Lat:* 41.8166 *Lon:* -90.2446 Jct US-30 & US-61 (W of town) tke US-30 E for 17.2 miles then N on 25th St
Coralville	◇ 1	🕐	℞	🚌	2801 Commerce Dr, 52241 / 319-545-6400 • *Lat:* 41.6957 *Lon:* -91.6132 I-80 Exit 240 merge onto US-6 W .4 mile then Commerce Dr W .3 mile
Council Bluffs	■ 1			🚌	3221 Manawa Centre Dr, 51501 / 712-366-0130 • *Lat:* 41.2486 *Lon:* -95.8753 I-80 Exit 3 take SH-192 S .4 mile, E on 32nd Ave .2 mile & S at Manawa Centre
	◇ 1	🕐	℞	🚌	3201 Manawa Centre Dr, 51501 / 712-366-3326 • *Lat:* 41.2280 *Lon:* -95.8473 I-29/I-80 Exit 3 go S on Expy St/SH-192 for .2 mile & E at 32nd Ave .2 mile
Creston	◇	🕐	℞	🚌	806 Laurel St, 50801 / 641-782-6954 • *Lat:* 41.0470 *Lon:* -94.3725 1 mile southwest of town center off US-34 at Laurel St
Davenport	■ 1		℞	🚌	3845 Elmore Ave, 52807 / 563-355-3939 • *Lat:* 41.5597 *Lon:* -90.5270 I-74 Exit 2 take US-6 W .1 mile then N at Elmore Ave .3 mile
	◆ 4	🕐	℞	🚌	3101 W Kimberly Rd, 52806 / 563-445-0272 • *Lat:* 41.5601 *Lon:* -90.6213 I-280 Exit 1 take US-6 E 3.6 miles
	◆ 1	🕐	℞	🚌	5811 Elmore Ave, 52807 / 563-359-0023 • *Lat:* 41.5773 *Lon:* -90.5284 I-74 Exit 1 go W on 53rd St .2 mile & N on Elmore Ave .2 mile
Decorah	◇	🕐	℞	🚌	1798 Old Stage Rd, 52101 / 563-382-8737 • *Lat:* 43.2890 *Lon:* -91.7550 Jct US-52 & SH-9 (SW of town) go E on SH-9 for 2.6 miles then NE on Old Stage Coach Rd

○ Wal-Mart   ◇ Supercenter   □ Sam's Club   ■ Gas   ■ Gas & Diesel

City/Town	🍎	🕐	℞	🚗	Information
Denison	○		℞		404 Arrowhead Dr, 51442 / 712-263-2000 • *Lat:* 42.0184 *Lon:* -95.3753 Jct US-59 & US-30 (SW of town) take US-30 W .3 mile & N on Arrowhead Dr 1.1 miles
Des Moines	◇ 5	🕐	℞	🚗	5101 SE 14th St, 50320 / 515-287-7700 • *Lat:* 41.5380 *Lon:* -93.5966 I-235 Exit 8B go S 4.1 miles on US-69 (14th St)
	◇ 1	🕐	℞	🚗	1001 73rd St, 50311 / 515-274-6224 • *Lat:* 41.5965 *Lon:* -93.7184 I-235 Exit 3 go N on 73rd St .1 mile
Dubuque	■		℞	🚗	4400 Asbury Rd, 52002 / 563-587-0576 • *Lat:* 42.5152 *Lon:* -90.7362 US-20 (SE of town) go N on SH-32 for 1.9 miles then E on Asbury Rd .2 mile
	◇	🕐	℞	🚗	4200 Dodge St, 52003 / 563-582-1003 • *Lat:* 42.4890 *Lon:* -90.7369 Jct SH-32 & US-20 (W of town) go E on US-20 for .1 mile
Fairfield	○		℞		1800 W Burlington Ave, 52556 / 641-472-6858 • *Lat:* 41.0063 *Lon:* -91.9866 Jct SH-1/Main St & US-34/Burlington Ave (in town) go W on US-34 for 1.2 miles
Fort Dodge	◆	🕐	℞	🚗	3036 1st Ave S, 50501 / 515-576-7400 • *Lat:* 42.5054 *Lon:* -94.1556 US-20 Exit 124 take CR-P59 N 3.5 miles, US-20 BR W 1.5 miles, 29th St N .3 mile & 1st St E .1 mile
Grinnell	◆ 2	🕐	℞		415 Industrial Ave, 50112 / 641-236-4999 • *Lat:* 41.7209 *Lon:* -92.7270 I-80 Exit 182 take SH-146 N 1.8 miles then E on Industrial Ave
Independence	◆	🕐	℞		302 Enterprise Dr, 50644 / 319-334-7128 • *Lat:* 42.4437 *Lon:* -91.8671 US-20 Exit 254 follow SH-150 N 2.1 miles, 8th St E .2 mile & Park Ave N .1 mile
Indianola	◆	🕐	℞	🚗	1500 N Jefferson Way, 50125 / 515-961-8955 • *Lat:* 41.3740 *Lon:* -93.5584 I-35 Exit 56 go E 11.9 miles on SH-92 then N 1.1 miles on US-69
Iowa City	○ 7		℞		1001 Hwy 1 W, 52246 / 319-337-3116 • *Lat:* 41.6460 *Lon:* -91.5533 I-80 Exit 239A take US-218 S 5.6 miles then SH-1 NE 1.1 miles
Iowa Falls	○		℞		840 S Oak St, 50126 / 641-648-5145 • *Lat:* 42.5037 *Lon:* -93.2622 I-35 Exit 142A merge onto US-20 E 15.6 miles to Exit 168 then US-65 N 3.9 miles
Keokuk	◆	🕐	℞	🚗	300 N Park Dr, 52632 / 319-524-6941 • *Lat:* 40.4172 *Lon:* -91.4080 Jct US-61 & US-218 (NW of town) follow US-218/Main St SE 1.9 miles then W at Park Ave
Knoxville	◆	🕐	℞		814 W Bell Ave, 50138 / 641-828-7584 • *Lat:* 41.3050 *Lon:* -93.1054 Jct SH-5 & SH-14 (S of town) go N on SH-14 for .2 mile & E on Bell Ave .2 mile
Le Mars	◆	🕐	℞	🚗	1111 Holton Dr, 51031 / 712-546-4900 • *Lat:* 42.7747 *Lon:* -96.1607 Jct SH-60 & US-75 (N of town) go S on US-75 1.5 miles
Manchester	○		℞		1220 W Main St, 52057 / 563-927-3377 • *Lat:* 42.4838 *Lon:* -91.4772 1 mile west of town on SH-13
Maquoketa	◇		℞		103 E Carlisle, 52060 / 563-652-6703 • *Lat:* 42.0484 *Lon:* -90.6655 1.4 miles south of town center at US-61 Exit 156
Marion	◆ 7	🕐	℞	🚗	5491 Hwy 151, 52302 / 319-447-2395 • *Lat:* 42.0428 *Lon:* -91.5838 I-380 Exit 24 go E on SH-100/Collins Rd for 6.5 miles & S on US-151 for .5 mile
Marshalltown	◆	🕐	℞	🚗	2802 S Center St, 50158 / 641-753-7846 • *Lat:* 42.0139 *Lon:* -92.9122 Jct US-30 & SH-14 (S of town) take SH-14 N for .6 mile
Mason City	◆ 5	🕐	℞	🚗	4151 4th St SW, 50401 / 641-423-6767 • *Lat:* 43.1481 *Lon:* -93.2600 I-35 Exit 194 take US-18 BR E 4.8 miles
Mount Pleasant	◆	🕐	℞	🚗	1045 N Grand Ave, 52641 / 319-385-4600 • *Lat:* 40.9785 *Lon:* -91.5392 From US-218 (N of town) take Exit 45 toward Jewel Ave .4 mile, merge on Grand Ave .9 mile
Muscatine	◇	🕐	℞	🚗	3003 N Hwy 61, 52761 / 563-263-8312 • *Lat:* 41.3579 *Lon:* -91.1517 Jct US-61 & SH-92 (S of town) continue to follow US-61 S 4.3 miles
Newton	◆ 2	🕐	℞	🚗	300 Iowa Speedway Dr, 50208 / 641-791-5322 • *Lat:* 41.6970 *Lon:* -93.0143 I-80 Exit 168, N onto E 44th St .1 mile, continue on SE Beltline Dr 1.2 miles

○ Wal-Mart ◇ Supercenter □ Sam's Club ▨ Gas ■ Gas & Diesel

City/Town	🛡	🕐	℞	🚐	Information
Osceola	◇ 1	🕐	℞		2400 College Dr, 50213 / 641-342-1650 • *Lat:* 41.0245 *Lon:* -93.8024 I-35 exit 33, west of exit
Oskaloosa	◆	🕐	℞	🚐	2203 Avenue A West, 52577 / 641-673-3839 • *Lat:* 41.2963 *Lon:* -92.6698 Jct US-63 & SH-92 (in town) go W on SH-92/Ave A for 1.3 miles
Ottumwa	◆	🕐	℞	🚐	1940 Venture Dr, 52501 / 641-682-1715 • *Lat:* 41.0159 *Lon:* -92.4569 3 miles west of town center on US-34
Pella	◇	🕐	℞		1650 Washington St, 50219 / 641-628-9881 • *Lat:* 41.4102 *Lon:* -92.9329 1 mile west of town center via Washington St
Shenandoah	○		℞		524 S Fremont St, 51601 / 712-246-4044 • *Lat:* 40.7619 *Lon:* -95.3853 Jct SH-27 & US-59 (S of town) go N on US-59 for 1.2 miles
Sioux Center	◇	🕐	℞		255 16th St SW, 51250 / 712-722-1990 • *Lat:* 43.0603 *Lon:* -96.1753 1 mile south of town on US-75
Sioux City	■ 1			🚐	4201 S York St, 51106 / 712-233-3133 • *Lat:* 42.4319 *Lon:* -96.3700 I-29 Exit 143 go E on Industrial Rd .2 mile then S on York Rd .3 mile
	◆ 1	🕐	℞	🚐	3400 Singing Hills Blvd, 51106 / 712-252-0210 • *Lat:* 42.4360 *Lon:* -96.3638 I-29 Exit 143 go E on Industrial Rd .3 mile & continue E on Singing Hills Blvd .3 mile
	◆ 4	🕐	℞	🚐	3101 Floyd Blvd, 51108 / 712-239-8901 • *Lat:* 42.5309 *Lon:* -96.3727 I-29 Exit 147A go NE on Floyd Blvd 3.3 miles
Spencer	◇	🕐	℞	🚐	500 11th St SW, 51301 / 712-262-5001 • *Lat:* 43.1267 *Lon:* -95.1516 Jct US-18 & US-71 (S of town) go S on US-71 for .4 mile
Spirit Lake	◇	🕐	℞	🚐	2200 17th St, 51360 / 712-336-1339 • *Lat:* 43.4237 *Lon:* -95.1240 Jct SH-9 & US-71 (N of town) go E on 17th St .2 mile
Storm Lake	◆	🕐	℞	🚐	1831 Lake Ave, 50588 / 712-732-7940 • *Lat:* 42.6637 *Lon:* -95.2006 1.2 miles north of town on SH-71
Tipton	○		℞		1126 Hwy 38, 52772 / 563-886-3153 • *Lat:* 41.7881 *Lon:* -91.1273 I-80 Exit 267 take SH-38 N 10.4 miles
Washington	○		℞		530 Hwy 1 S, 52353 / 319-653-7213 • *Lat:* 41.2949 *Lon:* -91.7081 1 mile west of town center on SH-1, south of Madison St
Waterloo	□ 9			🚐	210 E Tower Park Dr, 50701 / 319-236-9933 • *Lat:* 42.4561 *Lon:* -92.3536 I-380 take US-20 E for 7.8 miles to Exit 230 then N .2 mile on SH-21, San Marnan Rd W .3 mile & S on Shoppers Blvd
	◇ 1	🕐	℞		1334 Flammang Dr, 50702 / 319-232-3661 • *Lat:* 42.4600 *Lon:* -92.3307 I-380 Exit 72 go SW .8 mile on San Marnan Dr then left at Flammang Dr
Waverly	◆	🕐	℞	🚐	2700 4th St SW, 50677 / 319-352-5260 • *Lat:* 42.7023 *Lon:* -92.4755 From US-218 Exit 198 (S of town) merge onto Easton Ave/US-218 BR N .5 mile
West Burlington	◆	🕐	℞	🚐	324 W Agency Rd, 52655 / 319-753-6526 • *Lat:* 40.8132 *Lon:* -91.1588 Jct US-34 & US-61 (in town) go S on US-61 for .3 mile & W on Agency St for 1 mile
West Des Moines	◇ 2	🕐	℞	🚐	6365 Stagecoach Dr, 50266 / 515-453-2747 • *Lat:* 41.5439 *Lon:* -93.7923 I-35 Exit 70 go W on Mills Pkwy .8 mile then S on Stagecoach Dr .4 mile
Windsor Heights	▪ 1		℞	🚐	1101 73rd St, 50311 / 515-255-2252 • *Lat:* 41.5990 *Lon:* -93.7179 I-235 Exit 3 go N on 73rd St .2 mile

○ Wal-Mart ◇ Supercenter □ Sam's Club ▪ Gas ■ Gas & Diesel

Kansas

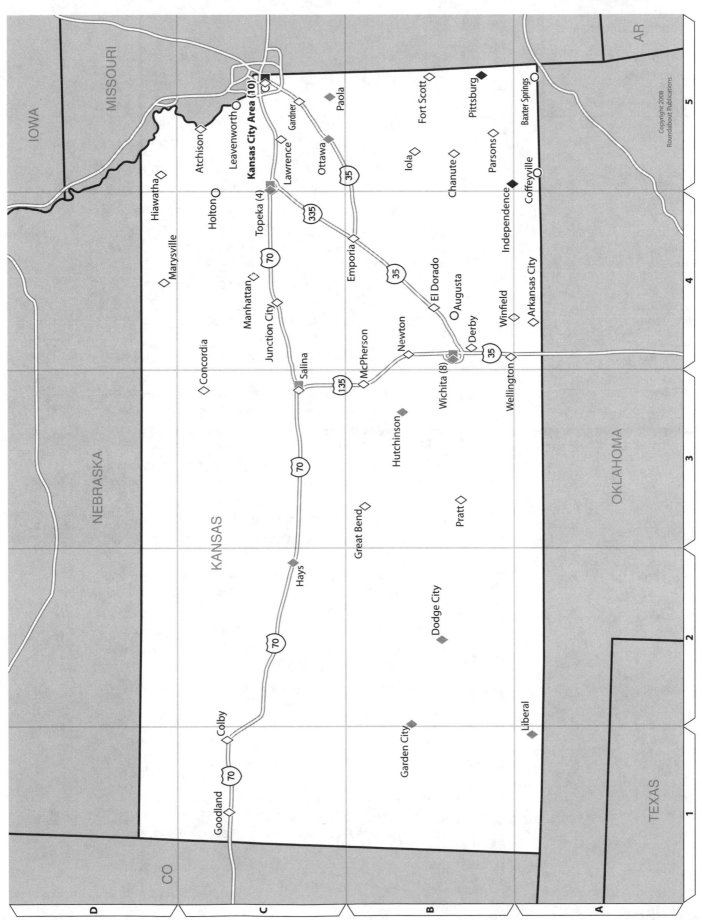

○ Wal-Mart ◇ Supercenter ☐ Sam's Club ▨ Gas ■ Gas & Diesel

Copyright 2008
Roundabout Publications

MISSOURI

IOWA

NEBRASKA

KANSAS

CO

OKLAHOMA

TEXAS

AR

Atchison
Leavenworth
Kansas City Area (10)
Gardner
Paola
Fort Scott
Pittsburg
Baxter Springs

Hiawatha
Holton
Topeka (4)
Lawrence
Ottawa
Iola
Chanute
Parsons
Coffeyville
Independence

Marysville

Manhattan
Junction City
Emporia
El Dorado
Augusta
Winfield
Arkansas City

Concordia
Salina
McPherson
Newton
Wichita (8)
Derby
Wellington

Hutchinson

Great Bend
Pratt

Hays

Dodge City

Colby

Garden City

Liberal

Goodland

335
70
35
135
35
70
70
70

Kansas City Area

Bonner Springs	◇	Olathe	◇	Shawnee	◇
Kansas City	○	Overland Park (4)	○ ◇ ■		
Lenexa	■	Roeland Park	○		

City/Town	🛡		🕐	℞	🚌	Information
Arkansas City	◇		🕐	℞	🚌	2701 N Summit St, 67005 / 620-442-2063 • *Lat:* 37.0927 *Lon:* -97.0404 I-35 Exit 4 take US-166 E 16 miles then Summit St N 2.5 miles
Atchison	◇		🕐	℞	🚌	1920 US Hwy 73, 66002 / 913-367-4062 • *Lat:* 39.5475 *Lon:* -95.1336 Jct US-59 & US-73 (S of town) go S on US-73 for 4.8 miles
Augusta	○			℞		1618 Ohio St, 67010 / 316-775-2254 • *Lat:* 37.6906 *Lon:* -96.9712 I-35 Exit 71 take SH-254 W 4.1 miles & S on Ohio St for 8 miles
Baxter Springs	○			℞		2970 Military Ave, 66713 / 620-856-2327 • *Lat:* 37.0066 *Lon:* -94.7387 Jct US-166 & US-69 (in town) take US-69 S 1.2 miles
Bonner Springs	◇	2	🕐	℞	🚌	12801 Kansas Ave, 66012 / 913-441-6751 • *Lat:* 39.0870 *Lon:* -94.8778 I-70 Exit 224 take SH-7 S .9 mile then E on Kansas Ave .2 mile
Chanute	◇		🕐	℞	🚌	2700 S Santa Fe Ave, 66720 / 620-431-3077 • *Lat:* 37.6540 *Lon:* -95.4524 From US-169 (S of town) take 35th St Exit E 1.4 miles then N on Santa Fe Ave .6 mile
Coffeyville	○			℞	🚌	1705 W 11th St, 67337 / 620-251-2290 • *Lat:* 37.0332 *Lon:* -95.6430 Jct US-75 & US-166 (W of town) go E on US-166 for 16 miles
Colby	◇	1	🕐	℞		115 W Willow St, 67701 / 785-462-8634 • *Lat:* 39.3655 *Lon:* -101.0465 I-70 Exit 54 go N on Country Club Dr .1 mile & W on CR-20 for .5 mile
Concordia	◇		🕐	℞		140 E College Dr, 66901 / 785-243-2602 • *Lat:* 39.5552 *Lon:* -97.6665 On west side of US-81 on the south edge of town
Derby	◇	4	🕐	℞	🚌	2020 N Southeast Blvd, 67037 / 316-788-9400 • *Lat:* 37.5577 *Lon:* -97.2748 I-35 Exit 45 take SH-15 S 3.6 miles
Dodge City	◆		🕐	℞	🚌	1905 N 14th Ave, 67801 / 620-225-3917 • *Lat:* 37.7674 *Lon:* -100.0330 Jct US-283 & US-400 (S of town) take US-400 W .8 mile & N on 14th Ave 1 mile
El Dorado	◇	1	🕐	℞	🚌	301 S Village Rd, 67042 / 316-322-8100 • *Lat:* 37.8200 *Lon:* -96.8898 I-35 Exit 71 take 6th Ave E .2 mile, 3rd Ave N .5 mile & Village Rd E
Emporia	◇	1	🕐	℞	🚌	2301 Industrial Rd, 66801 / 620-343-1500 • *Lat:* 38.4261 *Lon:* -96.2172 I-35 Exit 128 go N on Industrial Rd .4 mile
Fort Scott	◇		🕐	℞	🚌	2500 S Main St, 66701 / 620-223-2867 • *Lat:* 37.8084 *Lon:* -94.7053 2.5 miles south of town on US-69
Garden City	◆		🕐	℞	🚌	3101 E Kansas Ave, 67846 / 620-275-0775 • *Lat:* 37.9818 *Lon:* -100.8393 Jct SH-156 & US-83 (E of town) go W on SH-156/Kansas Ave for 1.9 miles
Gardner	◇	1	🕐	℞	🚌	1725 E Santa Fe St, 66030 / 913-884-8004 • *Lat:* 38.8108 *Lon:* -94.8915 I-35 Exit 210 merge onto US-56 W .2 mile then S at Cedar Niles Rd
Goodland	◇	1	🕐	℞		2160 Commerce Rd, 67735 / 785-899-2111 • *Lat:* 39.3409 *Lon:* -101.7481 I-70 Exit 17 go N on US-24 BR .3 mile then W on Commerce Rd
Great Bend	◆		🕐	℞	🚌	3503 10th St, 67530 / 620-792-3632 • *Lat:* 38.3617 *Lon:* -98.7862 Jct US-281 & US-56 (S of town) take US-56 W 1.2 miles
Hays	◆	1	🕐	℞	🚌	4301 N Vine St, 67601 / 785-625-0001 • *Lat:* 38.9019 *Lon:* -99.3180 I-70 Exit 159 take US-183 N .2 mile

○ Wal-Mart　◇ Supercenter　□ Sam's Club　■ Gas　■ Gas & Diesel

City/Town	⬡	🕐	℞	🚗	Information
Hiawatha	◇		🕐	℞	🚗	701 Hopi St, 66434 / 785-742-7445 • *Lat:* 39.8523 *Lon:* -95.5544 Jct US-73 & US-36 (S of town) take US-36 W .8 mile, 12th St N .5 mile & E on Iowa St
Holton	○			℞		209 Arizona Ave, 66436 / 785-364-4148 • *Lat:* 39.4650 *Lon:* -95.7479 Jct SH-16 & US-75 (W of town) go S on US-75/Arizona Ave .2 mile
Hutchinson	◆		🕐	℞	🚗	1905 E 17th Ave, 67501 / 620-669-9090 • *Lat:* 38.0722 *Lon:* -97.8877 Jct US-50 & SH-61 (SE of town), N on SH-61/Kennedy Pkwy 3.3 miles & E on 17th Ave .3 mile
Independence	◆		🕐	℞	🚗	121 Peter Pan Rd, 67301 / 620-331-5805 • *Lat:* 37.2265 *Lon:* -95.7427 Jct US-160 & US-75 (W of town), E on US-160/75 for 1.3 miles & N on Peter Pan Rd
Iola	◇		🕐	℞	🚗	2200 N State St, 66749 / 620-365-6981 • *Lat:* 37.9440 *Lon:* -95.4090 2 miles northwest of town center via US-54 and State St
Junction City	◇ 1		🕐	℞	🚗	521 E Chestnut St, 66441 / 785-238-8229 • *Lat:* 39.0216 *Lon:* -96.8210 I-70 Exit 298 go W on Chestnut St .2 mile
Kansas City	○ 2			℞	🚗	6565 State Ave, 66102 / 913-788-3331 • *Lat:* 39.1166 *Lon:* -94.7301 I-70 Exit 415B merge onto Turner Diagonal N .8 mile & E on State Ave .7 mile
Lawrence	◇ 5		🕐	℞	🚗	3300 Iowa St, 66046 / 785-832-8600 • *Lat:* 38.9244 *Lon:* -95.2594 I-70 Exit 202 take S McDonald Dr 1.2 miles, US-59 S 3.2 miles & 33rd St E .1 mile
Leavenworth	○			℞	🚗	3450 S 4th St, 66048 / 913-758-1915 • *Lat:* 39.2835 *Lon:* -94.9035 I-435 Exit 18 follow SH-5 N 10 miles & 4th St N .7 mile
Lenexa	■ 1			℞	🚗	12200 W 95th St, 66215 / 913-894-0084 • *Lat:* 38.9567 *Lon:* -94.7271 I-35 Exit 224 go E on 95th St .6 mile
Liberal	◆		🕐	℞	🚗	250 E Tucker Rd, 67901 / 620-624-0106 • *Lat:* 37.0686 *Lon:* -100.9194 Jct SH-51 & US-83 (N of town), US-83 S 6.8 miles, Kansas Ave W 1.3 miles, 15th St N 1 mile & Western Ave E .1 mile
Manhattan	◇ 10		🕐	℞	🚗	101 Bluemont Ave, 66502 / 785-776-4897 • *Lat:* 39.1866 *Lon:* -96.5591 I-70 Exit 313 follow SH-177 N 8.9 miles, US-24 E .5 mile & W at Bluemont Ave
Marysville	◇		🕐	℞		1174 Pony Express Hwy, 66508 / 785-562-2390 • *Lat:* 39.8419 *Lon:* -96.6054 Jct US-77 & US-36 (W of town) take US-36 E 3.3 miles
McPherson	◇ 1		🕐	℞	🚗	205 S Centennial Dr, 67460 / 620-241-0800 • *Lat:* 38.3691 *Lon:* -97.6301 I-135 Exit 60, west of exit
Newton	◇ 1		🕐	℞	🚗	1701 S Kansas Rd, 67114 / 316-284-0555 • *Lat:* 38.0236 *Lon:* -97.3369 I-135 Exit 30 take US-50 W .6 mile then SH-15 S .4 mile
Olathe	◇ 2		🕐	℞	🚗	13600 S Alden St, 66062 / 913-829-4404 • *Lat:* 38.8826 *Lon:* -94.7565 I-35 Exit 218 take Santa Fe St E 1.8 miles then S on Alden St
Ottawa	◆ 1		🕐	℞	🚗	2101 S Princeton St, 66067 / 785-242-9222 • *Lat:* 38.5820 *Lon:* -95.2676 I-35 Exit 183 take US-59 N .4 mile
Overland Park	■ 5			℞	🚗	8300 W 135th St, 66223 / 913-402-1405 • *Lat:* 38.8839 *Lon:* -94.6820 I-435 Exit 81 take US-69 S 4.2 miles then W on 135th .2 mile
	○ 1			℞	🚗	7701 Frontage Rd, 66204 / 913-648-5885 • *Lat:* 38.9895 *Lon:* -94.7003 I-35 Exit 227 go E on Frontage Rd .4 mile
	○ 2			℞	🚗	11701 Metcalf Ave, 66210 / 913-338-2202 • *Lat:* 38.9149 *Lon:* -94.6683 I-435 Exit 79 take Metcalf Ave S 1.3 miles
	◇ 8		🕐	℞	🚗	15700 Metcalf Ave, 66223 / 913-685-9959 • *Lat:* 38.8439 *Lon:* -94.6680 I-435 Exit 81 take US-69 S 6.3 miles, 151st St E .5 mile & Metcalf Ave S .7 mile
Paola	◆		🕐	℞		310 Hedge Ln, 66071 / 913-294-5400 • *Lat:* 38.5715 *Lon:* -94.8563 From US-69 (W of town) take 311th St W 8.3 miles, Baptiste Dr W .8 mile & Hedge Ln N .1 mile

○ Wal-Mart   ◇ Supercenter   □ Sam's Club   ▨ Gas   ■ Gas & Diesel

City/Town	⬠	🕐	Rx	🚐	Information
Parsons	◇		🕐	Rx 🚐	3201 N 16th St, 67357 / 620-421-0375 • *Lat:* 37.3541 *Lon:* -95.2589 Jct US-400 & US-59 (N of town) go S on US-59 for 1.4 miles
Pittsburg	◆		🕐	Rx 🚐	2710 N Broadway St, 66762 / 620-232-1593 • *Lat:* 37.4333 *Lon:* -94.7047 Jct SH-126 & US-69/160 (W of town), N on US-69/160 for 2.3 miles & S on Broadway .5 mile
Pratt	◇		🕐	Rx 🚐	2003 E 1st St, 67124 / 620-672-7548 • *Lat:* 37.6457 *Lon:* -98.7191 Jct SH-61 & US-400 (E of town) go W on US-400 for .2 mile
Roeland Park	○	1		Rx	5150 Roe Blvd, 66205 / 913-236-8898 • *Lat:* 39.0358 *Lon:* -94.6401 I-35 Exit 232B go E on 18th St Expy .4 mile, continue on Roe Blvd .3 mile
Salina	■	1		Rx 🚐	2919 Market Pl, 67401 / 785-825-2229 • *Lat:* 38.7853 *Lon:* -97.6112 I-135 Exit 89 go E on Schilling Rd .4 mile then N at Market Pl .1 mile
	◇	2	🕐	Rx 🚐	2900 S 9th St, 67401 / 785-825-6800 • *Lat:* 38.7860 *Lon:* -97.6132 I-135 Exit 90 go E on Magnolia Rd .4 mile & S on 9th St .8 mile
Shawnee	◇	2	🕐	Rx 🚐	16100 W 65th St, 66217 / 913-268-3468 • *Lat:* 39.0103 *Lon:* -94.7729 I-435 Exit 6A go E .8 mile on Shawnee Mission Pkwy, N .3 mile on Maurer Rd, W .2 mile on 65th St
Topeka	■	1		Rx 🚐	1401 SW Wanamaker Rd, 66604 / 785-273-5181 • *Lat:* 39.0411 *Lon:* -95.7620 I-470 Exit 1B, south of exit
	◆	1	🕐	Rx 🚐	1301 SW 37th St, 66611 / 785-267-7900 • *Lat:* 39.0005 *Lon:* -95.6943 I-470 Exit 5 take Burlington Rd N .1 mile & 37th St E .6 mile
	◇	2	🕐	Rx 🚐	1501 SW Wanamaker Rd, 66604 / 785-271-6444 • *Lat:* 39.0396 *Lon:* -95.7620 I-70 Exit 356 go S on Wannamaker Rd 1.1 miles (or south of I-470 Exit 1B)
	◇	5	🕐	Rx 🚐	2600 NW Rochester Rd, 66617 / 785-357-4827 • *Lat:* 39.0936 *Lon:* -95.6731 I-70 Exit 358A take US-75 N 1.5 miles, US-24 E 3.1 miles & Rochester Rd N .2 mile
Wellington	◇	2	🕐	Rx	2022 E 16th St, 67152 / 620-326-2261 • *Lat:* 37.2754 *Lon:* -97.3788 I-35 Exit 19 go W on US-160 for 2 miles
Wichita	■	1		Rx 🚐	6200 W Kellogg Dr, 67209 / 316-945-3010 • *Lat:* 37.6733 *Lon:* -97.4147 I-235 Exit 7B go W on Kellogg Dr .1 mile
	■	6		Rx 🚐	3415 N Rock Rd, 67226 / 316-634-6007 • *Lat:* 37.7452 *Lon:* -97.2448 I-35 Exit 53 take SH-96 W 5.7 miles then N on Rock Rd .2 mile
	◆	4	🕐	Rx 🚐	10600 W 21st St N, 67205 / 316-729-5446 • *Lat:* 37.7228 *Lon:* -97.4649 I-235 Exit 10 go NW on Zoo Blvd .8 mile & W on 21st St 3 miles
	◇	2	🕐	Rx 🚐	6110 W Kellogg Dr, 67209 / 316-945-2800 • *Lat:* 37.6733 *Lon:* -97.4135 I-235 Exit 7B take W Kellogg Dr 1.6 miles
	◇	2	🕐	Rx 🚐	501 E Pawnee St, 67211 / 316-267-2400 • *Lat:* 37.6496 *Lon:* -97.3327 I-135 Exit 3B go W on Pawnee St 1.2 miles
	◇	3	🕐	Rx 🚐	5475 N Meridian Ave, 67204 / 316-831-9425 • *Lat:* 37.7831 *Lon:* -97.3718 I-135 exit 13 take 53rd St W 2.5 miles then N on Meridian Ave .1 mile
	◇	3	🕐	Rx 🚐	11411 E Kellogg Dr, 67207 / 316-683-0735 • *Lat:* 37.6792 *Lon:* -97.2055 I-35 Exit 50 take US-400/Kellogg Dr E 2.1 miles
	◇	4	🕐	Rx 🚐	3030 N Rock Rd, 67226 / 316-636-4482 • *Lat:* 37.7390 *Lon:* -97.2445 I-135 Exit 10 follow SH-96 E 3.5 miles then S on Rock Rd .4 mile
Winfield	◇		🕐	Rx 🚐	2202 Pike Rd, 67156 / 620-221-6233 • *Lat:* 37.2281 *Lon:* -96.9958 Jct US-160 & US-77 (W of town) take US-77/Main St S .8 mile & E at Sunnyside Ave

○ Wal-Mart ◇ Supercenter ☐ Sam's Club ■ Gas ■ Gas & Diesel

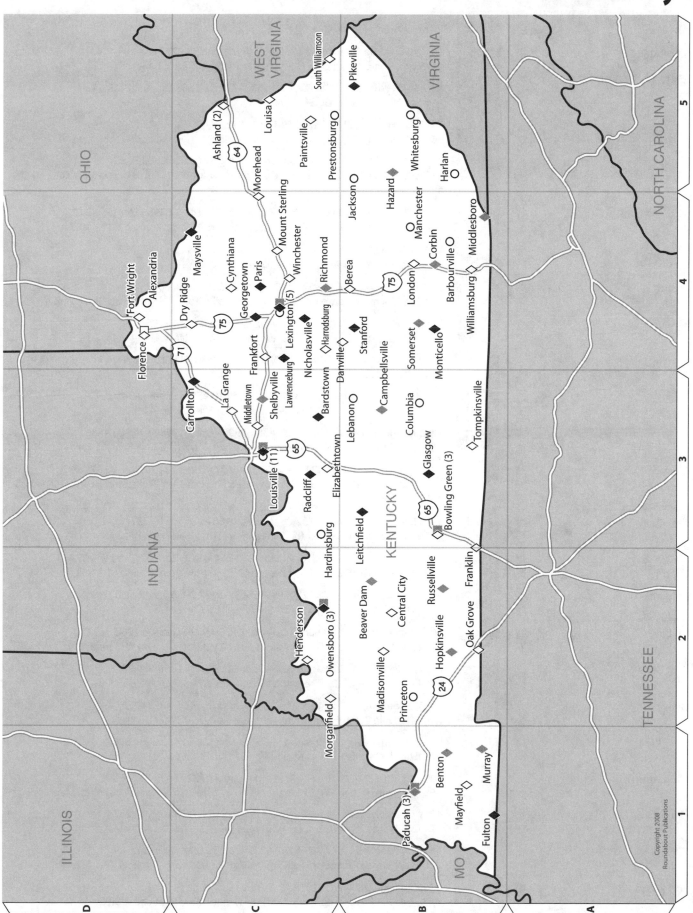

Kentucky

○ Wal-Mart ◇ Supercenter ☐ Sam's Club ▨ Gas ■ Gas & Diesel

City/Town	🛡	🕐	℞	🚐	Information
Alexandria	◯ 5		℞		6711 Alexandria Pike, 41001 / 859-635-8800 • *Lat:* 38.9877 *Lon:* -84.4049 I-275 Exit 77 merge onto SH-9 S 3.2 miles then US-27 S 1.3 miles
Ashland	◇ 5	🕐	℞	🚐	12504 US Hwy 60, 41102 / 606-929-9510 • *Lat:* 38.3883 *Lon:* -82.7153 I-64 Exit 181 follow US-60 E 4.2 miles
	◇	🕐	℞	🚐	351 River Hill Dr, 41101 / 606-329-0012 • *Lat:* 38.4700 *Lon:* -82.6442 I-64 Exit 181 take US-60 N 2.2 miles, follow SH-5 N 10.4 miles, then SH-1093 NE 1.7 miles
Barbourville	◯		℞		301 Parkway Plz, 40906 / 606-546-5454 • *Lat:* 36.8695 *Lon:* -83.9085 I-75 Exit 29 take US-24E S 18.7 miles, W on Treuhaft Blvd .2 mile & S on Hurricane Ln .3 mile
Bardstown	◆	🕐	℞	🚐	3795 E John Rowan Blvd, 40004 / 502-349-6007 • *Lat:* 37.7986 *Lon:* -85.4342 From ML Collins Blue Grass Pkwy Exit 25 take US-150/Springfield Rd N for .2 mile
Beaver Dam	◆	🕐	℞	🚐	1701 N Main St, 42320 / 270-274-9608 • *Lat:* 37.4165 *Lon:* -86.8782 From Westrn KY Pkwy Exit 75 take US-231 N 4.2 miles
Benton	◆ 10	🕐	℞	🚐	310 W 5th St, 42025 / 270-527-1605 • *Lat:* 36.8664 *Lon:* -88.3578 I-24 Exit 25A merge onto Carroll Pkwy S 9.1 miles to Exit 43, then SH-348 E .5 mile
Berea	◇ 1	🕐	℞	🚐	120 Jill Dr, 40403 / 859-986-2324 • *Lat:* 37.5671 *Lon:* -84.3105 I-75 Exit 76 take SH-21 E .3 mile then S at McKinney Dr
Bowling Green	▨ 1		℞	🚐	3200 Ken Bale Blvd, 42103 / 270-781-7775 • *Lat:* 36.9431 *Lon:* -86.4160 I-65 Exit 22, west of exit
	◇ 2	🕐	℞	🚐	150 Walton Ave, 42104 / 270-781-7903 • *Lat:* 36.9517 *Lon:* -86.4340 I-65 Exit 22 take US-231 N 1.6 miles then W on SH-880 for .4 mile
	◇ 10	🕐	℞	🚐	1201 Morgantown Rd, 42101 / 270-780-9996 • *Lat:* 36.9887 *Lon:* -86.4836 I-65 Exit 20 take Natcher Pkwy N 8 miles to Exit 7, then US-231 S for 1.1 miles
Campbellsville	◆	🕐	℞	🚐	725 Campbellsville Byp, 42718 / 270-789-0707 • *Lat:* 37.3461 *Lon:* -85.3716 From Cumberland Pkwy Exit 49 follow SH-55 N for 18.1 miles, continue on SH-210 for 1 mile
Carrollton	◆ 2	🕐	℞		200 Floyd Dr, 41008 / 502-732-0645 • *Lat:* 38.6675 *Lon:* -85.1231 I-71 Exit 44 go W on SH-227 for .9 mile then N on Floyd Dr .2 mile
Central City	◇	🕐	℞	🚐	1725 W Everely Brothers Blvd, 42330 / 270-754-4512 • *Lat:* 37.2749 *Lon:* -87.1419 From Western KY Pkwy Exit 58 take US-431 N .6 mile then US-62 W 1.8 miles
Columbia	◯		℞		809 Jamestown St, 42728 / 270-384-4745 • *Lat:* 37.0936 *Lon:* -85.3032 From Nunn Cumberland Pkwy Exit 49 take SH-55 N .4 mile
Corbin	◆ 1	🕐	℞	🚐	60 S Stewart Rd, 40701 / 606-523-1770 • *Lat:* 36.9720 *Lon:* -84.1062 I-75 Exit 29 take US-25E S for .5 mile then Sawyers/Stewart Rd W .3 mile
Cynthiana	◇	🕐	℞	🚐	805 US Hwy 27 S, 41031 / 859-234-3232 • *Lat:* 38.4054 *Lon:* -84.2878 I-75 Exit 126 take US-62 E 15.3 miles, continue on US-27 N for 2.8 miles
Danville	◇	🕐	℞	🚐	100 Walton Ave, 40422 / 859-236-9572 • *Lat:* 37.6141 *Lon:* -84.7732 From Danville Bypass (S of town) continue S on US-127 for .2 mile
Dry Ridge	◇ 1	🕐	℞	🚐	20 Ferguson Blvd, 41035 / 859-824-0575 • *Lat:* 38.6814 *Lon:* -84.5965 I-75 Exit 159 take SH-22 E .2 mile & S on Ferguson Blvd
Elizabethtown	◇ 5	🕐	℞		100 Wal-Mart Dr, 42701 / 270-763-1600 • *Lat:* 37.7329 *Lon:* -85.8855 I-65 Exit 94 take US-62 W .5 mile then NW on Ring Rd 3.9 miles & N on Wal Mart Ln
Florence	▢ 1		℞	🚐	4949 Houston Rd, 41042 / 859-283-5515 • *Lat:* 39.0150 *Lon:* -84.6374 I-71 Exit 182 go NW on Turfway Rd .4 mile then S on Houston Rd .2 mile
	◇ 1	🕐	℞	🚐	7625 Doering Dr, 41042 / 859-282-8333 • *Lat:* 39.0099 *Lon:* -84.6494 I-75 Exit 181 go W on SH-18 for .3 mile, N on Houston Rd .5 mile & W at Kiley Pl
Fort Wright	◇ 2	🕐	℞	🚐	3450 Valley Plaza Pkwy, 41017 / 859-341-7900 • *Lat:* 39.0341 *Lon:* -84.5348 I-275 Exit 79 merge onto Taylor Mill Rd 1.8 miles then W at Valley Sq Dr .1 mile

◯ Wal-Mart ◇ Supercenter ▢ Sam's Club ▨ Gas ▧ Gas & Diesel

City/Town	🛡	🕐	℞	🚗	Information
Frankfort	◇ 2	🕐	℞	🚗	301 Leonardwood Rd, 40601 / 502-875-5533 • *Lat:* 38.1609 *Lon:* -84.9006 I-64 Exit 53B follow US-127 N .7 mile then S on Leonardville Rd .7 mile
Franklin	◇ 3	🕐	℞	🚗	1550 Nashville Rd, 42134 / 270-586-9281 • *Lat:* 36.6893 *Lon:* -86.5689 I-65 Exit 2 take US-31 W 2.3 miles
Fulton	◆	🕐	℞		1405 Middle Rd, 42041 / 270-472-1426 • *Lat:* 36.5156 *Lon:* -88.9004 Purchase Pkwy Exit 1 go S .3 mile on Noland Ave then W .6 mile on SH-166 (Middle Rd)
Georgetown	◆ 1	🕐	℞	🚗	112 Osbourne Way, 40324 / 502-867-0547 • *Lat:* 38.2317 *Lon:* -84.5378 I-75 Exit 126 take US-62 NE .5 mile then W at Osbourne Way
Glasgow	◆	🕐	℞	🚗	2345 Happy Valley Rd, 42141 / 270-651-1136 • *Lat:* 37.0213 *Lon:* -85.9336 From Nunn Cumberland Pkwy Exit 11 follow US-31E N 2.5 miles & SH-90 NW 1.1 miles
Hardinsburg	◯				1002 Old Hwy 60, 40143 / 270-756-6012 • *Lat:* 37.7846 *Lon:* -86.4554 Jct SH-259 & US-60 (SE of town) go W on US-60 for 1.9 miles & N on 3rd St .5 mile
Harlan	◯		℞		201 Waldon Dr, 40831 / 606-573-2206 • *Lat:* 36.8211 *Lon:* -83.3188 Jct US-119 & US-421 (N of town) take US-421 S 2.9 miles, then W at Walton Rd
Harrodsburg	◇		℞	🚗	591 Joseph Dr, 40330 / 859-734-5721 • *Lat:* 37.7441 *Lon:* -84.8422 From ML Collins Blue Grass Pkwy Exit 59A take US-127 S 15.9 miles & W on Joseph Dr
Hazard	◆	🕐	℞	🚗	120 Daniel Boone Plz, 41701 / 606-439-1882 • *Lat:* 37.2517 *Lon:* -83.2983 From Jct SH-15 & SH-80/Hal Rogers Pkwy, go E on Hal Rogers Pkwy
Henderson	◇	🕐	℞	🚗	1195 Barrett Blvd, 42420 / 270-826-6036 • *Lat:* 37.8620 *Lon:* -87.5705 From Audubon Pkwy Exit 1A take Pennyrile Pkwy N 3.4 miles, then US-41 N .7 mile & E on Barrett Blvd
Hopkinsville	◆ 10	🕐	℞	🚗	300 Clinic Dr, 42240 / 270-886-1900 • *Lat:* 36.8308 *Lon:* -87.4711 I-24 Exit 86 take US-41 ALT N 8.9 miles then E at Clinic Dr .3 mile
Jackson	◯		℞		1589 Hwy 15 S, 41339 / 606-666-4907 • *Lat:* 37.5348 *Lon:* -83.3450 Jct SH-205 & SH-15 (N of town) go S on SH-15 for 6.1 miles
La Grange	◇ 1	🕐	℞	🚗	1015 New Moody Ln, 40031 / 502-222-4260 • *Lat:* 38.3978 *Lon:* -85.3717 I-71 Exit 22 take SH-53 E .1 mile then S at New Moody Ln .2 mile
Lawrenceburg	◆ 1	🕐	℞	🚗	1000 Bypass N, 40342 / 502-839-5178 • *Lat:* 38.0353 *Lon:* -84.9121 I-64 Exit 53A merge onto US-127 S for 1 mile then E at Laurenceburg Rd
Lebanon	◯		℞		180 Lebanon Trade Ctr, 40033 / 270-692-1880 • *Lat:* 37.5603 *Lon:* -85.2697 Jct US-150 & SH-55 (N of town) follow SH-55 S for 9.8 miles
Leitchfield	◆	🕐	℞	🚗	1801 Elizabethtown Rd, 42754 / 270-259-5622 • *Lat:* 37.4879 *Lon:* -86.2653 From Ford Western KY Pkwy Exit 112 take SH-224 W .7 mile & US-62 S 2.5 miles
Lexington	▪ 3		℞	🚗	1063 E New Circle Rd, 40505 / 859-253-2885 • *Lat:* 38.0589 *Lon:* -84.4580 I-75 Exit 110 take US-60 E 1.4 miles, S on Fortune Dr .4 mile, W at Trade Center Dr .3 mile & N on New Circle Rd
	◯ 3		℞	🚗	3180 Richmond Rd, 40509 / 859-268-2001 • *Lat:* 38.0012 *Lon:* -84.4463 I-75 Exit 108 follow Man O'War Blvd W 2.5 miles then N at Richmond Rd .2 mile
	◆ 1	🕐	℞	🚗	2350 Grey Lag Way, 40509 / 859-263-0999 • *Lat:* 38.0369 *Lon:* -84.4254 I-75 Exit 110 take US-60 W .4 mile, Sir Barton Way S .4 mile
	◇ 3	🕐	℞		500 W New Circle Rd, 40511 / 859-381-9370 • *Lat:* 38.0725 *Lon:* -84.4829 I-64 Exit 113 take US-68 W 1 mile & S on New Circle Rd 1.2 miles
	◇	🕐	℞	🚗	4051 Nicholasville Rd, 40503 / 859-971-0572 • *Lat:* 37.9779 *Lon:* -84.5296 I-64 Exit 115 merge onto Newtown Pike 1.5 miles, W on New Circle Rd 9.2 miles & US-27 S 1.2 miles
London	◇ 1	🕐	℞	🚗	1851 Hwy 192 W, 40741 / 606-878-6119 • *Lat:* 37.1110 *Lon:* -84.0925 I-75 Exit 38 take SH-192 E .6 mile

◯ Wal-Mart   ◇ Supercenter   ☐ Sam's Club   ▪ Gas   ■ Gas & Diesel

City/Town	🛡	🕐	℞	🚗	Information
Louisa	◇		🕐	℞		275 Walton Dr, 41230 / 606-673-4427 • *Lat:* 38.1029 *Lon:* -82.6244 2 miles southwest of town near US-23/SH-32 jct
Louisville	■ 2			℞	🚗	1401 Alliant Ave, 40299 / 502-267-0432 • *Lat:* 38.1891 *Lon:* -85.5545 I-64 Exit 17 go S on Blankenbaker Pkwy .6 mile, E on Bluegrass .1 mile & N on Alliant .4 mile
	■ 3			℞	🚗	6622 Preston Hwy, 40219 / 502-964-0379 • *Lat:* 38.1563 *Lon:* -85.6968 I-65 Exit 127 go E on SH-1065 for .9 mile then N on Preston Hwy 1.3 miles
	○ 1			℞		1915 S Hurstbourne Pkwy, 40220 / 502-499-1050 • *Lat:* 38.2181 *Lon:* -85.5852 I-64 Exit 15 take SH-1747/Hurstbourne Pkwy S 1 mile
	○ 2			℞		4840 Outer Loop, 40219 / 502-968-7884 • *Lat:* 38.1376 *Lon:* -85.6713 I-65 Exit 127 take Outer Loop/SH-1065 E 1.7 miles
	○ 7			℞		10445 Dixie Hwy, 40272 / 502-935-3233 • *Lat:* 38.1038 *Lon:* -85.8689 I-264 Exit 8A go S on Dixie Hwy 6.3 miles
	◆ 1		🕐	℞	🚗	7101 Cedar Springs Blvd, 40291 / 502-231-4880 • *Lat:* 38.1471 *Lon:* -85.5860 I-265 Exit 17 take US-150 N .6 mile
	◆ 2		🕐	℞	🚗	2020 Bashford Manor Ln, 40218 / 502-451-6766 • *Lat:* 38.1999 *Lon:* -85.6699 I-264 Exit 16 follow US-150/31 E .7 mile then S at Bashford Manor Ln .4 mile
	◇ 1		🕐	℞		3706 Diann Marie Rd, 40241 / 502-326-9166 • *Lat:* 38.2999 *Lon:* -85.5431 I-265 Exit 32 take SH-1447 E .3 mile & N at Chamberlain Ln .1 mile
	◇ 2		🕐	℞	🚗	11901 Standiford Plaza Dr, 40229 / 502-968-6800 • *Lat:* 38.0879 *Lon:* -85.6665 I-265 Exit 12 take SH-61 S 1.5 miles then E on Antle Dr
	◇ 3		🕐	℞	🚗	7100 Raggard Rd, 40216 / 502-447-4677 • *Lat:* 38.1765 *Lon:* -85.8670 I-264 Exit 5B follow SH-1934 (Cane Run Rd) S 3 miles
	◇ 5		🕐	℞	🚗	175 Outer Loop, 40214 / 502-361-0225 • *Lat:* 38.1267 *Lon:* -85.7795 I-65 Exit 125B merge onto Snyder Fwy W 4.3 miles to Exit 6, New Cut Rd N .3 mile & Outer Loop W .2 mile
Madisonville	◇		🕐	℞	🚗	1756 E Center St, 42431 / 270-821-6388 • *Lat:* 37.3267 *Lon:* -87.4793 Western KY Pkwy Exit 38B take US-41 N 8.2 miles to Exit 42, W on SH-70/85 for .3 mile
Manchester	○					240 Manchester Square Shpg Ctr, 40962 / 606-598-6123 • *Lat:* 37.1380 *Lon:* -83.7687 Hal Rogers Pkwy Exit 20, north of exit
Mayfield	◇		🕐	℞	🚗	1225 Paris Rd, 42066 / 270-247-0358 • *Lat:* 36.7262 *Lon:* -88.6295 From JM Carroll Pkwy Exit 22 take SH-80 E for 1.8 miles then S on SH-121 for 1.3 miles
Maysville	◆		🕐	℞	🚗	240 Wal-Mart Way, 41056 / 606-759-5040 • *Lat:* 38.6593 *Lon:* -83.7847 Jct US 62/68 & SH-546 (W of town) go NW on SH-546/Gov Brown Hwy for .6 mile
Middlesboro	◆		🕐	℞		US Hwy 25E at Hwy 441, 40965 / 606-248-9087 • *Lat:* 36.6215 *Lon:* -83.7042 1.5 miles northeast of town center at US25E/SH-441 jct
Middletown	◇ 1		🕐	℞	🚗	12981 Shelbyville Rd, 40243 / 502-244-2551 • *Lat:* 38.2431 *Lon:* -85.5153 I-265 Exit 27 take US-60 W .7 mile
Monticello	◆		🕐	℞	🚗	1461 E Hwy 90 Byp, 42633 / 606-348-3331 • *Lat:* 36.9757 *Lon:* -84.6700 Jct SH-92 & SH-90 (W of town) go S on SH-90/Bypass 3.3 miles
Morehead	◇ 1		🕐	℞	🚗	2233 Flemingsburg Rd, 40351 / 606-784-3262 • *Lat:* 38.1996 *Lon:* -83.4786 I-64 Exit 137 take SH-32 N .6 mile
Morganfield	◇		🕐	℞		901 US Hwy 60 E, 42437 / 270-389-1828 • *Lat:* 37.6894 *Lon:* -87.9032 From Pennyride Pkwy Exit 76 follow US-60 W for 22.7 miles
Mount Sterling	◇ 1		🕐	℞	🚗	499 Indian Mound Dr, 40353 / 859-497-9401 • *Lat:* 38.0731 *Lon:* -83.9522 I-64 Exit 110 take US-460 S .3 mile then SH-686 W .7 mile
Murray	◆		🕐	℞	🚗	809 N 12th St, 42071 / 270-753-2195 • *Lat:* 36.6260 *Lon:* -88.3147 From JM Carroll Pkwy Exit 41 follow US-641 S 17.5 miles

○ Wal-Mart ◇ Supercenter □ Sam's Club ■ Gas ■ Gas & Diesel

City/Town	⬥	⏱	℞	🚗	Information
Nicholasville	◆		⏱	℞	🚗	1024 N Main St, 40356 / 859-885-3299 • Lat: 37.8993 Lon: -84.5648 Jct US-27 & New Circle Rd (in Lexington) follow US-27 S for 7.3 miles
Oak Grove	◇ 3		⏱	℞	🚗	14800 Fort Campbell Blvd, 42262 / 270-640-4744 • Lat: 36.6669 Lon: -87.4435 I-24 Exit 86 merge onto US-41 ALT S 2.5 miles
Owensboro	▪			℞	🚗	5420 Frederica St, 42301 / 270-683-1930 • Lat: 37.7118 Lon: -87.1270 4.5 miles south of town center via US-431 (south of Owensboro Beltline)
	◆		⏱	℞	🚗	3151 Leitchfield Rd, 42303 / 270-683-5553 • Lat: 37.7386 Lon: -87.0223 Audubon Pkwy Exit 24A go E on US-60 BYP for 7.4 miles to Exit 9, S on Leitchfld Rd .5 mile
	◇		⏱	℞	🚗	5031 Frederica St, 42301 / 270-685-2060 • Lat: 37.7215 Lon: -87.1240 Audubon Pkwy Exit 24A go E on US-60 BYP for 3.1 miles to Exit 4 & S on Frederica Rd .4 mile
Paducah	▪ 1			℞	🚗	3550 James Sanders Blvd, 42001 / 270-444-6500 • Lat: 37.0842 Lon: -88.6905 I-24 Exit 4 take US-60 W for .1 mile then N on James Sanders Blvd .7 mile
	◆ 1		⏱	℞	🚗	5130 Hinkleville Rd, 42001 / 270-444-0066 • Lat: 37.0762 Lon: -88.6878 I-24 Exit 4 follow US-60 W for .5 mile
	◇ 6		⏱	℞	🚗	3220 Irvin Cobb Dr, 42003 / 270-444-6941 • Lat: 37.0522 Lon: -88.5681 I-24 Exit 16 take US-68 N .3 mile then follow US-62/I-24 BR for 5.7 miles
Paintsville	◇		⏱	℞	🚗	470 N Mayo Trail, 41240 / 606-789-8920 • Lat: 37.8171 Lon: -82.8159 Jct US-460 & SH-40/321 (NW of town) go S on SH-40/321 for 1 mile
Paris	◆		⏱	℞	🚗	305 Letton Dr, 40361 / 859-987-2817 • Lat: 38.2008 Lon: -84.2757 I-64 Exit 113 follow US-27 N 13.5 miles
Pikeville	◆		⏱	℞	🚗	254 Cassidy Blvd, 41501 / 606-432-6177 • Lat: 37.5048 Lon: -82.5361 Jct US-23/460 & US-119 (NE of town) go W on Cassidy Blvd .2 mile
Prestonsburg	○			℞		477 Village Dr, 41653 / 606-886-6681 • Lat: 37.6599 Lon: -82.7835 1 mile southwest of town at US-23/SH-114 jct
Princeton	○			℞		500 US Hwy 62 W, 42445 / 270-365-7692 • Lat: 37.1172 Lon: -87.8661 Western KY Pkwy Exit 12 take SH-139/91 W .3 mile & W on US-62 for 1.1 miles
Radcliff	◆		⏱	℞	🚗	1165 Wal-Mart Way, 40160 / 270-352-2720 • Lat: 37.8542 Lon: -85.9441 I-65 Exit 102 take SH-313 W .4 mile, SH-434 W for 9.9 miles & Dixie Hwy N 4 miles
Richmond	◆ 3		⏱	℞	🚗	820 Eastern Byp, 40475 / 859-624-4330 • Lat: 37.7329 Lon: -84.2753 I-75 Exit 87 go E on SH-876/Bypass 2.8 miles
Russellville	◆		⏱	℞	🚗	120 Sam Walton Dr, 42276 / 270-726-2880 • Lat: 36.9205 Lon: -86.9265 Jct US-431 & US-68 BYP (NW of town) go S on US-68 BYP for 1 mile
Shelbyville	◆ 1		⏱	℞	🚗	500 Taylorsville Rd, 40065 / 502-633-0705 • Lat: 38.1892 Lon: -85.2759 I-64 Exit 32A take SH-55 S .3 mile
Somerset	◆		⏱	℞	🚗	177 Washington Dr, 42501 / 606-679-9204 • Lat: 37.0677 Lon: -84.6222 Jct SH-80 BYP & US-27 (W of town) go S on US-27 for 2 miles & W on Washington Dr .1 mile
South Williamson	◇		⏱	℞		28402 US Hwy 119, 41503 / 606-237-0477 • Lat: 37.6667 Lon: -82.2832 Jct SH-319 & US-119 (S of town) go N on US-119 for 1.7 miles
Stanford	◆		⏱	℞		1283 US Hwy 27 N, 40484 / 606-365-2153 • Lat: 37.5417 Lon: -84.6516 Jct US-150 BYP & US-27 go S on US-27 for 2.3 miles
Tompkinsville	◇			℞		1650 Edmonton Rd, 42167 / 270-487-0780 • Lat: 36.7273 Lon: -85.6875 Jct SH-678 & SH-163 (N of town) go S on SH-163 for 6.2 miles
Whitesburg	○					350 Whitesburg Plaza, 41858 / 606-633-0152 • Lat: 37.1176 Lon: -82.7938 Jct SH-15 & US-119 (W of town) go NE on US-119 for .7 mile & E at Whitesburg Plaza
Williamsburg	◇ 1		⏱	℞	🚗	589 W Hwy 92, 40769 / 606-549-4075 • Lat: 36.7212 Lon: -84.1467 I-75 Exit 11 go E on SH-92 for .2 mile
Winchester	◇ 2		⏱	℞	🚗	1859 Bypass Rd, 40391 / 859-744-5070 • Lat: 37.9893 Lon: -84.2099 I-64 Exit 94 follow SH-1958 S 1.7 miles

○ Wal-Mart ◇ Supercenter □ Sam's Club ▪ Gas ▪ Gas & Diesel

Louisiana

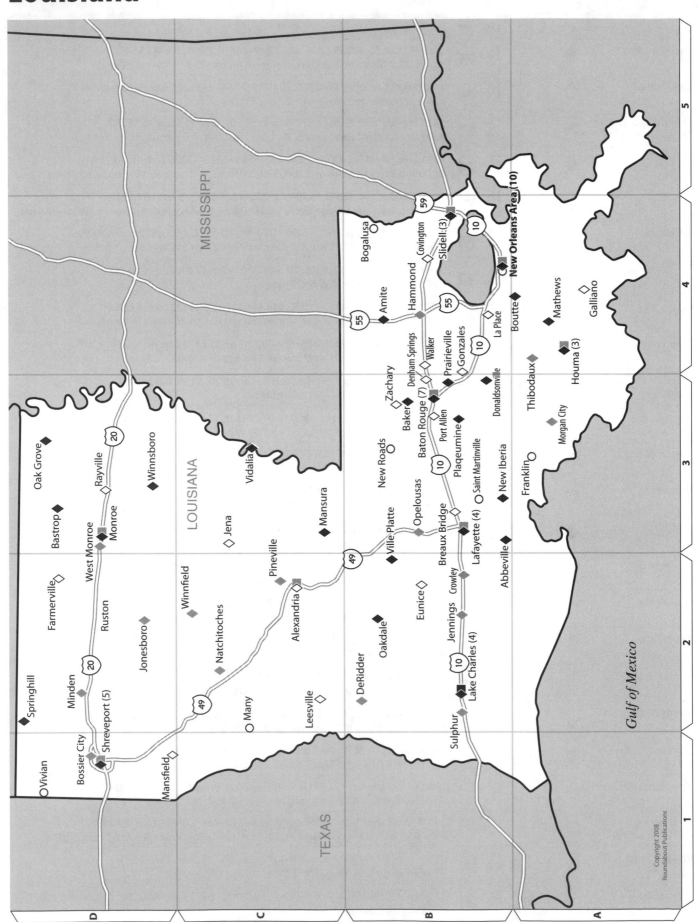

MISSISSIPPI

Bogalusa

Covington
Slidell (3)
59
10

New Orleans Area (10)

Hammond
Amite
55
55
10
La Place
Boutte
Mathews
Galliano

55

Zachary
Denham Springs
Walker
Prairieville
Gonzales
Donaldsonville
Thibodaux
Houma (3)

Baker
Baton Rouge (7)
Port Allen
Plaquemine
Saint Martinville
Morgan City

LOUISIANA

Oak Grove

Rayville
20
Winnsboro

Vidalia

New Roads
Opelousas
New Iberia
Franklin

Bastrop

Monroe
West Monroe

Jena

Mansura

Ville Platte
Breaux Bridge
Lafayette (4)
Abbeville

10

Farmerville

Ruston
Jonesboro

Winnfield
Pineville

Eunice
Crowley
Jennings

49

Alexandria
49

Oakdale

Springhill
Minden
20

Natchitoches

DeRidder

Sulphur
Lake Charles (4)
10

Vivian
Bossier City
Shreveport (5)

Many

Leesville

Mansfield

TEXAS

Gulf of Mexico

Copyright 2008
Roundabout Publications

D C B A

1 2 3 4 5

New Orleans Area

Harahan	◆		Kenner (2)	◇ ■		Metairie (2)	○	■
Harvey (2)	◇ ■		Marrero	◆		New Orleans (2)	◆	

City/Town	🛡	⏰	℞	🚗	Information
Abbeville	◆	⏰	℞	🚗	3005 Charity St, 70510 / 337-893-6485 • *Lat:* 29.9704 *Lon:* -92.0957 2.4 miles east of town center on SH-14
Alexandria	■ 4			🚗	3805 North Blvd, 71301 / 318-442-9730 • *Lat:* 31.2931 *Lon:* -92.4608 I-49 Exit 80 go NW on Jefferson Hwy 3.1 miles then N on Baldwin Ave/North Blvd .3 mile
	◇ 2	⏰	℞	🚗	2050 N Mall Dr, 71301 / 318-445-2300 • *Lat:* 31.2774 *Lon:* -92.4560 I-49 Exit 83, Broadway W .7 mile, Lee St N .2 mile, Memorial Dr W .6 mile & North Blvd S .2 mile
Amite	◆ 1	⏰	℞	🚗	1200 W Oak St, 70422 / 985-748-7707 • *Lat:* 30.7266 *Lon:* -90.5264 I-55 Exit 46 take SH-16 E .7 mile
Baker	◆ 7	⏰	℞	🚗	14507 Plank Rd, 70714 / 225-774-2050 • *Lat:* 30.5787 *Lon:* -91.1275 I-110 Exit 6 take Plank Rd/SH-67 NE 6.8 miles
Bastrop	◆		℞	🚗	6091 Hwy 165, 71220 / 318 281-9304 • *Lat:* 32.7733 *Lon:* -91.8690 3 miles east of town center on US-165
Baton Rouge	■ 1		℞	🚗	10444 N Mall Dr, 70809 / 225-295-1353 • *Lat:* 30.3794 *Lon:* -91.0649 I-10 Exit 163 go W on Siegen Lane .1 mile then S on Mall Dr .1 mile
	■ 5		℞	🚗	7685 Airline Hwy, 70814 / 225-929-9892 • *Lat:* 30.4721 *Lon:* -91.1094 I-12 Exit 2B go N on Airline Hwy 4.2 miles
	◆ 4	⏰	℞	🚗	9350 Cortana Pl, 70815 / 225-923-3400 • *Lat:* 30.4590 *Lon:* -91.0892 I-12 Exit 2B take US-61 N 2.9 miles, E at Florline Blvd .1 mile & S on Cortana Pl .6 mile
	◆ 10	⏰	℞	🚗	10200 Sullivan Rd, 70818 / 225-262-6599 • *Lat:* 30.5414 *Lon:* -91.0283 I-110 Exit 6 take Harding Blvd/SH-408 E 8.4 miles then Sullivan Rd S 1.1 miles
	◇ 1	⏰	℞	🚗	3132 College Dr, 70808 / 225-952-9022 • *Lat:* 30.4195 *Lon:* -91.1415 I-10 Exit 158 merge onto College Dr S .2 mile
	◇ 1	⏰	℞	🚗	10606 N Mall Dr, 70809 / 225-291-8104 • *Lat:* 30.3791 *Lon:* -91.0622 I-10 Exit 163 merge onto SH-3246 S/Siegen Ln .3 mile & S on N Mall Dr .3 mile
	◇ 3	⏰	℞	🚗	2171 O'Neal Ln, 70816 / 225-751-3505 • *Lat:* 30.4374 *Lon:* -91.0074 I-12 Exit 7 go S on O'Neal Lane 2.5 miles
Bogalusa	○			🚗	218 Cumberland St, 70427 / 985-732-5870 • *Lat:* 30.7890 *Lon:* -89.8642 Jct SH-10 & SH-21 (E of town) go W on SH-10/Louisiana Ave .9 mile & S on Cumberland St
Bossier City	◆ 2	⏰	℞	🚗	2536 Airline Dr, 71111 / 318-747-0173 • *Lat:* 32.5478 *Lon:* -93.7091 I-20 Exit 22 take Airline Dr N 1.7 miles (or .6 mile south of I-220 Exit 12)
Boutte	◆	⏰	℞	🚗	13001 Hwy 90, 70039 / 985-785-0855 • *Lat:* 29.9066 *Lon:* -90.3698 I-10 Exit 220 go SE on I-310 for 10.9 miles then US-90 E for 2 miles
Breaux Bridge	◇ 1	⏰	℞	🚗	1932 Rees St, 70517 / 337-332-1280 • *Lat:* 30.2904 *Lon:* -91.9121 I-10 Exit 109 take SH-328 S .5 mile
Covington	◇ 2	⏰	℞	🚗	880 N Hwy 190, 70433 / 985-867-8701 • *Lat:* 30.4436 *Lon:* -90.0822 I-12 Exit 63A merge onto US-190 E 1.6 miles
Crowley	◆ 1	⏰	℞	🚗	729 Odd Fellows Rd, 70526 / 337-783-6387 • *Lat:* 30.2309 *Lon:* -92.3648 I-10 Exit 82 follow SH-111 S .6 mile

○ Wal-Mart ◇ Supercenter ☐ Sam's Club ▨ Gas ■ Gas & Diesel

City/Town	⛊	🕐	℞	🚌	Information
Denham Springs	◇ 2	🕐	℞	🚌	904 S Range Ave, 70726 / 225-665-0270 • *Lat:* 30.4722 *Lon:* -90.9565 I-12 Exit 10 take SH-3002/Range Ave N 1.1 miles
Deridder	◆	🕐	℞	🚌	1125 N Pine St, 70634 / 337-462-0259 • *Lat:* 30.8653 *Lon:* -93.2856 Jct SH-3226 & US-171 (N of town) take US-171 S 2.5 miles
Donaldsonville	◆ 9		℞		37000 Hwy 3089, 70346 / 225-473-6687 • *Lat:* 30.0867 *Lon:* -90.9712 I-10 Exit 177 take SH-30 W 1.1 miles, SH-3251 SW 3.8 miles & SH-75 S 3.3 miles
Eunice	◇	🕐	℞	🚌	1538 Hwy 190, 70535 / 337-457-7392 • *Lat:* 30.4949 *Lon:* -92.4470 2 miles west of town center on US-190
Farmerville	◇		℞		833 Sterlington Hwy, 71241 / 318-368-2535 • *Lat:* 32.7705 *Lon:* -92.3947 I-20 Exit 86 take SH-33 N 21.5 miles then SH-2 E .7 mile
Franklin	◯		℞		200 Northwest Blvd, 70538 / 337-828-2418 • *Lat:* 29.8127 *Lon:* -91.5133 Jct US-90 & SH-3211 (N of town) go E on SH-3211/NW Blvd 1.7 miles
Galliano	◇	🕐	℞	🚌	16759 Hwy 3235, 70354 / 985-632-4040 • *Lat:* 29.4697 *Lon:* -90.3254 Jct US-90 & SH-1 follow SH-1 S 25.5 miles, 107th St W .5 mile & SH-3235 S .7 mile
Gonzales	◇ 9	🕐	℞	🚌	308 N Airline Hwy, 70737 / 225-647-8950 • *Lat:* 30.2337 *Lon:* -90.9091 I-10 Exit 187 merge onto US-61 N 8.7 miles
Hammond	◆ 1	🕐	℞	🚌	2799 W Thomas St, 70401 / 985-345-8876 • *Lat:* 30.5026 *Lon:* -90.4921 I-55 Exit 31 take US-190 E .9 mile
Harahan	◆ 8	🕐	℞	🚌	5110 Jefferson Hwy, 70123 / 504-733-4923 • *Lat:* 29.9497 *Lon:* -90.1813 I-10 Exit 226 merge onto Clearview Pkwy S 3.3 miles then SH-48/Jefferson Hwy W 4 miles
Harvey	◼ 8		℞	🚌	1527 Manhattan Blvd, 70058 / 504-361-3966 • *Lat:* 29.8925 *Lon:* -90.0588 I-10 Exit 234 take US-90BR W 6.3 miles to Exit 6 then S on Manhattan Blvd 1 mile
	◇ 1	🕐	℞	🚌	1501 Manhattan Blvd, 70058 / 504-366-5255 • *Lat:* 29.8931 *Lon:* -90.0591 I-10 Exit 6 merge onto Westbank Expy .1 mile then S on Manhattan Blvd .9 mile
Houma	◼		℞	🚌	2174 Martin Luther King Jr Blvd, 70360 / 985-851-3631 • *Lat:* 29.6332 *Lon:* -90.7617 Jct US-90 & SH-24 (north of town) go SE on SH-24 for 3.2 miles, S on SH-3040 for 3.5 miles
	◆	🕐	℞	🚌	933 Grand Caillou Rd, 70363 / 985-917-0151 • *Lat:* 29.5830 *Lon:* -90.6953 Jct US-90 & SH-182 take SH-182 S 3.2 miles, SH-3087 S 5 miles, Prospect Blvd S 1.1 miles & SH-57 W .5 mile
	◇	🕐	℞	🚌	1633 Martin Luther King Jr Blvd, 70360 / 985-851-6373 • *Lat:* 29.6106 *Lon:* -90.7522 Jct US-90 & SH-24 (NW of town) take SH-24 SE 6.3 miles, SH-664 S .5 mile & SH-3040 S .1 mile
Jena	◇	🕐	℞		3670 W Oak St, 71342 / 318-992-1351 • *Lat:* 31.6908 *Lon:* -92.1413 .8 mile northwest of town center on US-84
Jennings	◆ 1	🕐	℞	🚌	303 E Interstate Dr, 70546 / 337-824-4838 • *Lat:* 30.2454 *Lon:* -92.6553 I-10 Exit 64, on Frontage Rd W
Jonesboro	◆	🕐	℞		184 Old Winnfield Rd, 71251 / 318-259-4149 • *Lat:* 32.2287 *Lon:* -92.7082 I-20 Exit 85 follow US-167 S 24.8 miles
Kenner	◼ 1		℞	🚌	455 31st St, 70065 / 504-467-9677 • *Lat:* 30.0103 *Lon:* -90.2638 I-10 Exit 221 go N on Loyola Dr .2 mile & E on 31st .2 mile
	◇ 2	🕐	℞	🚌	300 W Esplanade Ave, 70065 / 504-464-1653 • *Lat:* 30.0231 *Lon:* -90.2693 I-10 Exit 221 take Loyola Dr N 1.1 miles then E on W Esplanade Ave
La Place	◇ 3	🕐	℞	🚌	1616 W Airline Hwy, 70068 / 985-652-8994 • *Lat:* 30.0728 *Lon:* -90.4967 I-10 Exit 206 take SH-3188 S 2.5 miles then E on Airline Hwy .3 mile
Lafayette	◼ 5		℞	🚌	3222 Ambassador Caffery Pkwy, 70506 / 337-216-0633 • *Lat:* 30.1847 *Lon:* -92.0752 I-10 Exit 100 go S on Ambassador Caffery Pkwy 4.9 miles

◯ Wal-Mart ◇ Supercenter ◻ Sam's Club ◼ Gas ◼ Gas & Diesel

City/Town	🛡	🕐	℞	🚗	Information
	◆ 5	🕐	℞	🚗	3142 Ambassador Caffery Pkwy, 70506 / 337-989-4082 • *Lat:* 30.1880 *Lon:* -92.0753 I-10 Exit 100 take Ambassador Caffery Pkwy/SH-3184 S 4.7 miles
	◆ 7	🕐	℞	🚗	2428 W Pinhook Rd, 70508 / 337-231-1852 • *Lat:* 30.1814 *Lon:* -92.0055 I-10 Exit 103A take US-167 S 2.6 miles, continue on Evangeline Trwy 1.9 miles, then W on Saloom Rd 1.2 miles, and S on Pinhook Rd .7 mile
	◆ 2	🕐	℞	🚗	1229 NE Evangeline Trwy, 70501 / 337-232-1677 • *Lat:* 30.2400 *Lon:* -92.0132 I-10 Exit 103A go S 1.3 miles on US-167
Lake Charles	■ 3		℞	🚗	2025 Sams Way, 70601 / 337-477-2668 • *Lat:* 30.2031 *Lon:* -93.2040 I-10 Exit 34 take I-210 Loop W 2.2 miles then N on Nelson Rd
	◆ 2	🕐	℞	🚗	2500 N Martin Luther King Hwy, 70601 / 337-436-3909 • *Lat:* 30.2696 *Lon:* -93.1816 I-10 Exit 33 take US-71 N 1.8 miles
	◆ 2	🕐	℞	🚗	3451 Nelson Rd, 70605 / 337-477-3785 • *Lat:* 30.1954 *Lon:* -93.2492 I-210 Exit 4 go SE on Nelson Rd 1.3 miles
	◆ 8	🕐	℞	🚗	3415 Hwy 14, 70607 / 337-477-7799 • *Lat:* 30.1142 *Lon:* -93.2014 I-10 Exit 36 take SH-397 S 6.1 miles then SH-14 W 1.7 miles
Leesville	◇	🕐	℞	🚗	2204 S 5th St, 71446 / 337-238-9041 • *Lat:* 31.1199 *Lon:* -93.2696 Jct SH-10 & US-171 (S of town) go N on US-171 for 6.5 miles
Mansfield	◇ 7	🕐	℞		7292 Hwy 509, 71052 / 318-872-5711 • *Lat:* 32.0490 *Lon:* -93.6856 I-49 Exit 177 take SH-509 S 7 miles
Mansura	◆	🕐	℞	🚗	7162 Hwy 1, 71350 / 318-253-4069 • *Lat:* 31.0958 *Lon:* -92.0595 Jct SH-452/Preston St & SH-1 (N of town) go S on SH-1 for 1.4 miles
Many	○		℞		155 San Antonio Ave, 71449 / 318-256-9207 • *Lat:* 31.5652 *Lon:* -93.4919 I-49 Exit 138 take SH-6 SW 24.1 miles
Marrero	◆ 10	🕐	℞	🚗	4810 Lapalco Blvd, 70072 / 504-341-0075 • *Lat:* 29.8763 *Lon:* -90.0936 From I-10 Exit 234 (near the Superdome) follow US-90BR/Westbank Expy 8 miles to Exit 4B, then go S 1.1 miles on Barataria Blvd and W .5 mile on Promenade Blvd
Mathews	◆		℞	🚗	4858 Hwy 1, 70375 / 985-532-6936 • *Lat:* 29.6922 *Lon:* -90.5505 Jct US-90 & SH-1 (S of town) go N on SH-1 for .5 mile
Metairie	■ 2		℞	🚗	3900 Airline Dr, 70001 / 504-831-2911 • *Lat:* 29.9752 *Lon:* -90.1702 I-10 Exit 226 go S on Clearview Pkwy 1.5 miles then E on Airline Hwy .5 mile
	○ 2		℞	🚗	8843 Veterans Memorial Blvd, 70003 / 504-465-0155 • *Lat:* 30.0058 *Lon:* -90.2253 I-10 Exit 223 take SH-49 S/Williams Blvd .2 mile then Veterans Memorial Blvd W 1 mile
Minden	◆ 4	🕐	℞	🚗	1379 Homer Rd, 71055 / 318-371-9290 • *Lat:* 32.6259 *Lon:* -93.2506 I-20 Exit 49 take SH-531 N 3.2 miles then W at Homer Rd
Monroe	■ 1			🚗	5400 Frontage Rd, 71202 / 318-345-5615 • *Lat:* 32.4928 *Lon:* -92.0526 I-20 Exit 120, south of exit
	◆ 3	🕐	℞	🚗	2701 Louisville Ave, 71201 / 318-324-0016 • *Lat:* 32.5247 *Lon:* -92.0914 I-20 Exit 118B take US-165 N 1.5 miles then US-165 BR/US-80 W 1 mile
Morgan City	◆	🕐	℞	🚗	973 Hwy 90 E, 70380 / 985-395-2094 • *Lat:* 29.6807 *Lon:* -91.2722 Jct SH-662 & US-90 Exit 182 (E of town) take US-90 W 5.8 miles
Natchitoches	◆ 7	🕐	℞	🚗	925 Keyser Ave, 71457 / 318-352-5607 • *Lat:* 31.7525 *Lon:* -93.0646 I-49 Exit 138 take SH-6 N 3.5 miles, follow SH-6 BR 1.5 miles & E on Keyser Ave 1.3 miles
New Iberia	◆	🕐	℞	🚗	1205 E Admiral Doyle Dr, 70560 / 337-367-9333 • *Lat:* 29.9840 *Lon:* -91.8173 Jct US-90 & SH-14 (W of town) take SH-14 E 1.8 miles then S on SH-674 for 1 mile
New Orleans	◆ 6	🕐	℞	🚗	4001 Behrman Pl, 70114 / 504-364-0414 • *Lat:* 29.9130 *Lon:* -90.0179 I-10 Exit 234 (near the Superdome) follow US-90 BR E .7 mile to Exit 9B, then go SE on SH-428 1.7 miles

○ Wal-Mart ◇ Supercenter □ Sam's Club ▨ Gas ■ Gas & Diesel

City/Town	🛡	⏰	Rx	🚗	Information
	◇ 3		Rx		1901 Tchoupitoulas St, 70130 / 504-522-4142 • *Lat:* 29.9256 *Lon:* -90.0683 I-10 Exit 234 (near the Superdome) follow US-90 BR E 1.2 miles to Exit 11C, merge onto Calliope St .1 mile, then S .8 mile on Tchoupitoulas/Religious Streets, E on Felicity & S on Tchoupitoulas
New Roads	◯		Rx	🚗	2050 False River Dr, 70760 / 225-638-8609 • *Lat:* 30.6848 *Lon:* -91.4576 Jct SH-3131 & SH-1 (S of town) go N on SH-1 for .3 mile
Oak Grove	◆		Rx		705 S Constitution Ave, 71263 / 318-428-9631 • *Lat:* 32.8548 *Lon:* -91.3924 Jct SH-589 & SH-17 (S of town) go N on SH-17 for 4.5 miles
Oakdale	◆	⏰	Rx	🚗	1900 Hwy 165 S, 71463 / 318-335-2502 • *Lat:* 30.7742 *Lon:* -92.6846 Jct Allen Parish Airport Rd & US-165 (S of town) go N on US-165 for 3.3 miles
Opelousas	◆ 1	⏰	Rx	🚗	1629 Cresswell Ln Ext, 70570 / 337-942-9853 • *Lat:* 30.5186 *Lon:* -92.0668 I-49 Exit 18 follow Creswell Ln E .4 mile
Pineville	◆ 5	⏰	Rx	🚗	3636 Monroe Hwy, 71360 / 318-640-6900 • *Lat:* 31.3663 *Lon:* -92.4101 I-49 Exit 84 take US-167 NE 4.1 miles then US-165 N .8 mile
Plaquemine	◆		Rx		59690 Belleview Dr, 70764 / 225-687-2550 • *Lat:* 30.2643 *Lon:* -91.2501 I-10 Exit 153 take SH-1 S 12.7 miles then SW on SH-75/Belleview Rd 1.8 miles
Port Allen	◇ 2		Rx	🚗	3255 LA Hwy 1 S, 70767 / 225-749-7455 • *Lat:* 30.4249 *Lon:* -91.2167 I-10 Exit 153 go S on SH-1 for 1.8 miles
Prairieville	◆ 5	⏰	Rx	🚗	17585 Airline Hwy, 70769 / 225-677-7375 • *Lat:* 30.3297 *Lon:* -90.9837 I-10 Exit 166 follow Highland Rd/SH-42 E 1.6 miles then S on Airline Hwy 2.5 miles
Rayville	◇ 1		Rx		1806 Julia St, 71269 / 318-728-6437 • *Lat:* 32.4641 *Lon:* -91.7603 I-20 Exit 138 take SH-137 N .6 mile then W at Glenda St
Ruston	◆ 1	⏰	Rx	🚗	1201 N Service Rd E, 71270 / 318-251-1168 • *Lat:* 32.5408 *Lon:* -92.6233 I-20 Exit 86 merge onto Woodward Ave & go W on Service Rd E .3 mile
Saint Martinville	◯		Rx		2310 N Main St, 70582 / 337-394-5525 • *Lat:* 30.1460 *Lon:* -91.8228 I-10 Exit 109 take SH-328 S 1.7 miles, Bridge St W .2 mile & follow SH-31 S 11.6 miles
Shreveport	▣ 3		Rx	🚗	7400 Youree Dr, 71105 / 318-798-2043 • *Lat:* 32.4366 *Lon:* -93.7150 I-49 Exit 202 go E 2.1 miles on SH-511 then S .5 mile on SH-1
	◆ 5	⏰	Rx	🚗	9550 Mansfield Rd, 71118 / 318-688-0538 • *Lat:* 32.3880 *Lon:* -93.8162 I-49 Exit 199 take Ind Loop/SH-526 W 3.2 miles then Mansfield Rd/US-171 S 1.2 miles
	◆ 1	⏰	Rx	🚗	6235 W Port Ave, 71129 / 318-688-7700 • *Lat:* 32.4488 *Lon:* -93.8669 I-20 Exit 10 go S on Pines Rd then W on Port Ave .1 mile
	◆ 4	⏰	Rx	🚗	1645 E Bert Kouns Loop, 71105 / 318-797-5970 • *Lat:* 32.4306 *Lon:* -93.7143 I-49 Exit 199 merge onto Ind Loop/SH-526 E for 3.4 miles
	◇ 3	⏰	Rx	🚗	1125 Shreveport Barksdale Hwy, 71105 / 318-861-9202 • *Lat:* 32.4852 *Lon:* -93.7079 I-49 Exit 205 go E 2.2 miles on Kings Hwy then continue E .7 mile on SH-3032 (Shreveport Barksdale Hwy)
Slidell	▣ 1		Rx	🚗	181 Northshore Blvd, 70460 / 985-641-1401 • *Lat:* 30.3083 *Lon:* -89.8260 I-12 Exit 80 go S on Northshore .1 mile
	◆ 1	⏰	Rx	🚗	39142 Natchez Dr, 70461 / 985-641-8572 • *Lat:* 30.2809 *Lon:* -89.7486 I-10 Exit 266 take Gause Blvd/US-190 E .2 mile, Tyler Dr S .2 mile & Natchez Dr W
	◇ 1	⏰	Rx	🚗	167 Northshore Blvd, 70460 / 985-690-0123 • *Lat:* 30.3073 *Lon:* -89.8260 I-12 Exit 80 go S on Northshore Blvd .2 mile
Springhill	◆		Rx		1920 S Arkansas St, 71075 / 318-539-5660 • *Lat:* 32.9854 *Lon:* -93.4599 Jct SH-2 & US-371 (S of town) go N on US-371 for 6.5 miles
Sulphur	◆ 2	⏰	Rx	🚗	525 N Cities Service Hwy, 70663 / 337-625-2849 • *Lat:* 30.2318 *Lon:* -93.3257 I-10 Exit 23 take SH-108 N for 1.3 miles

◯ Wal-Mart ◇ Supercenter ▢ Sam's Club ▨ Gas ▣ Gas & Diesel

City/Town	⬢	🕐	℞	🚐	Information
Thibodaux	◆	🕐	℞	🚐	410 N Canal Blvd, 70301 / 985-446-2257 • *Lat:* 29.8053 *Lon:* -90.8161 Jct SH-1 & SH-20 (N of town) go N on SH-20/Canal Blvd .4 mile
Vidalia	◆		℞		4283 Carter St, 71373 / 318-336-8996 • *Lat:* 31.5699 *Lon:* -91.4373 Jct SH-131 & US-84/65 (W of town) go W on US-84/65 for .8 mile
Ville Platte	◆	🕐	℞	🚐	891 E Lasalle St, 70586 / 337-363-5623 • *Lat:* 30.6844 *Lon:* -92.2620 I-49 Exit 23 take US-167 N 15.2 miles
Vivian	○		℞		929 S Pine St, 71082 / 318-375-4810 • *Lat:* 32.8601 *Lon:* -93.9861 Jct US-7 & SH-2 (E of town) follow SH-2 W 6.7 miles then Pine St/SH-2 S .2 mile
Walker	◇ 1	🕐	℞	🚐	28270 Walker Rd S, 70785 / 225-667-2335 • *Lat:* 30.4758 *Lon:* -90.8631 I-12 Exit 15 take Walker Rd/SH-447 S .6 mile
West Monroe	◆ 1	🕐	℞	🚐	1025 Glenwood Dr, 71291 / 318-322-0127 • *Lat:* 32.5014 *Lon:* -92.1496 I-20 Exit 114 take Thomas Rd/SH-617 N .1 mile then Glenwood Dr S .8 mile
Winnfield	◆	🕐	℞		5940 Hwy 167 N, 71483 / 318-628-2194 • *Lat:* 31.9389 *Lon:* -92.6542 Jct SH-156 & US-167 (N of town) go S on US-167 for .3 mile
Winnsboro	◆	🕐	℞	🚐	3360 Front St, 71295 / 318-435-3438 • *Lat:* 32.1797 *Lon:* -91.7265 Jct SH-130 & SH-15 (N of town) go N on SH-15 .9 mile
Zachary	◇ 9	🕐	℞	🚐	5801 Main St, 70791 / 225-654-0313 • *Lat:* 30.6487 *Lon:* -91.1432 I-110 Exit 8 take SH-19 N 7.9 miles then E on Main St .5 mile

○ Wal-Mart   ◇ Supercenter   □ Sam's Club   ▨ Gas   ■ Gas & Diesel

Maine

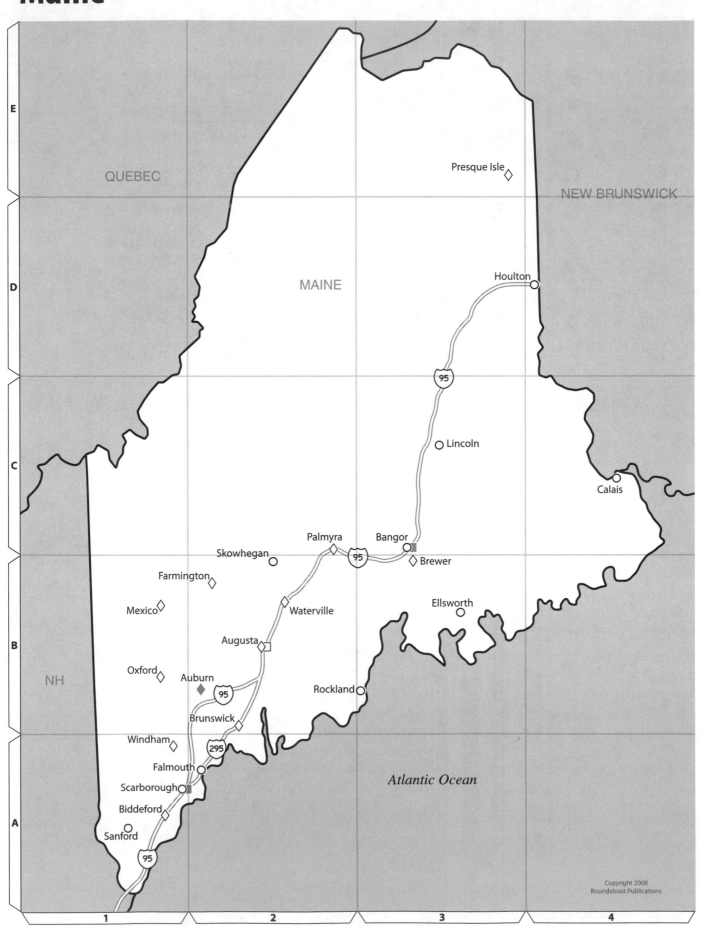

QUEBEC

NEW BRUNSWICK

MAINE

Presque Isle ◇

Houlton ○

95

Lincoln ○

Calais ○

Palmyra ◇   Bangor ○■
Skowhegan ○   95   Brewer ◇

Farmington ◇

Mexico ◇   Waterville ◇   Ellsworth ○

Augusta □

Oxford ◇   Auburn ◆
95   Rockland ○

Brunswick ◇

Windham ◇   295

Falmouth ○

Scarborough ○▨   *Atlantic Ocean*

Biddeford ◇

Sanford ○

95

NH

E

D

C

B

A

1   2   3   4

City/Town	⬠	🕐	℞	🚐	Information
Auburn	◆		🕐 ℞	🚐	100 Mount Auburn Ave, 04210 / 207-784-0738 • Lat: 44.1201 Lon: -70.2333 1.8 miles north of town center, west of SH-4 (Center St)
Augusta	□ 1			🚐	45 Marketplace Dr, 04330 / 207-623-2757 • Lat: 44.3425 Lon: -69.7879 I-95 Exit 112 (northbound travelers use Exit 112A) go SE on SH-27 .5 mile, N on Xavier Loop .2 mile to Marketplace Dr
	◇ 1	🕐 ℞			201 Civic Center Dr, 04330 / 207-623-8223 • Lat: 44.3435 Lon: -69.7931 I-95 Exit 112A take Civic Center Dr E .1 mile
Bangor	■ 1		℞	🚐	47 Haskell Rd, 04401 / 207-947-4606 • Lat: 44.8292 Lon: -68.7390 I-95 Exit 187 go S on Hogan Rd .1 mile & N on Haskell
	○ 1		℞		70 Springer Dr, 04401 / 207-947-5254 • Lat: 44.8363 Lon: -68.7397 I-95 Exit 187 go NW on Hogan Rd .3 mile then E on Springer Rd .1 mile
Biddeford	◇ 1	🕐 ℞		🚐	525 Alfred St, 04005 / 207-286-9551 • Lat: 43.4774 Lon: -70.4996 I-95 Exit 32 go W on Alfred St .5 mile
Brewer	◇ 1	🕐 ℞		🚐	24 Walton Dr, 04412 / 207-989-5068 • Lat: 44.7760 Lon: -68.7339 I-395 Exit 1A merge onto Wilson St/US-1A W .5 mile then S at Walton Dr
Brunswick	◇ 5	🕐 ℞		🚐	15 Tibbetts Dr, 04011 / 207-725-0773 • Lat: 43.9083 Lon: -69.9104 I-295 Exit 28 follow US-1 N 4.4 miles, SH-24 W .6 mile & Tibbets Dr S
Calais	○		℞	🚐	91 South St, 04619 / 207-454-8178 • Lat: 45.1838 Lon: -67.2681 On US-1/Main St (NW edge of town)
Ellsworth	○		℞		461 High St, 04605 / 207-667-6780 • Lat: 44.5132 Lon: -68.3944 2.7 miles southeast of town center along SH-3
Falmouth	○ 1		℞		206 US Hwy 1, 04105 / 207-781-3879 • Lat: 43.7204 Lon: -70.2326 I-295 Exit 10 take Bucknam Rd E .3 mile & US-1 S .5 mile
Farmington	◇	🕐 ℞		🚐	615 Wilton Rd, 04938 / 207-778-5344 • Lat: 44.6291 Lon: -70.1554 Jct SH-27/Famington Falls Rd & US-2 (S of town) take US-2 S for 2.5 miles
Houlton	○ 1		℞		17 Ludlow Rd, 04730 / 207-532-2181 • Lat: 46.1417 Lon: -67.8407 I-95 Exit 302 take US-1 N .2 mile then E on Ludlow Rd
Lincoln	○ 5		℞		250 W Broadway, 04457 / 207-794-8436 • Lat: 45.3557 Lon: -68.5279 I-95 Exit 227 go E 4 miles on Penobscot Valley Ave then N .2 mile on Broadway
Mexico	◇		℞		258 River Rd, 04257 / 207-364-2557 • Lat: 44.5398 Lon: -70.5176 Jct SH-142/Weld St & US-2/River Rd (SE of town) go NW on US-2 for 3.2 miles
Oxford	◇	🕐 ℞		🚐	1240 Main St, 04270 / 207-743-0882 • Lat: 44.1774 Lon: -70.5148 Jct SH-121/King St & SH-26/Main St (E of town) go N on Main St 3.1 miles
Palmyra	◇ 2	🕐 ℞			1573 Main St, 04965 / 207-368-2448 • Lat: 44.8389 Lon: -69.2976 I-95 Exit 157 follow US-2 NW 1.1 miles
Presque Isle	◇	🕐 ℞		🚐	781 Main St, 04769 / 207-764-8485 • Lat: 46.6978 Lon: -68.0115 Jct SH-227/Parsons Rd & US-1/Main St (N of town) go S on Main St .2 mile
Rockland	○		℞		265 Camden St, 04841 / 207-596-0885 • Lat: 44.1250 Lon: -69.0982 Jct SH-17/Maverick St & US-1/Camden St go N on Camden St .7 mile
Sanford	○		℞		1327 Main St, 04073 / 207-490-1988 • Lat: 43.4156 Lon: -70.7501 I-95 Exit 19 follow SH-109 W 10.5 miles
Scarborough	■ 1			🚐	440 Payne Rd, 04074 / 207-883-5553 • Lat: 43.6223 Lon: -70.3501 I-95 Exit 45 go E to Maine Mall Rd exit, then S on Maine Mall Rd/Payne Rd .6 mile
	○ 2		℞		451 Payne Rd, 04074 / 207-885-5567 • Lat: 43.6211 Lon: -70.3508 I-95 Exit 45 take Maine Mall Rd SE .9 mile, continue S on Payne Rd .5 mile
Skowhegan	○		℞	🚐	60 Fairgrounds Market Pl, 04976 / 207-474-2126 • Lat: 44.7752 Lon: -69.7242 Jct SH-148 & US-201 (N of town) take US-201 S 3.1 miles then Fairgrounds Market Pl E .2 mile

○ Wal-Mart ◇ Supercenter □ Sam's Club ■ Gas ■ Gas & Diesel

City/Town	⬭	🕐	℞	🚐	Information
Waterville	◇	1 🕐	℞	🚐	80 Waterville Commons Dr, 04901 / 207-877-8774 • *Lat:* 44.5703 *Lon:* -69.6443 I-95 Exit 130 go E on SH-104 for .2 mile & S on Waterville Commons .2 mile
Windham	◇	7 🕐	℞	🚐	30 Landing Rd, 04062 / 207-893-0603 • *Lat:* 43.8388 *Lon:* -70.4440 I-95 Exit 63 follow SH-115 W 6.6 miles, N on US-302 for .4 mile & W at Landing Rd

○ Wal-Mart   ◇ Supercenter   ☐ Sam's Club   ▮ Gas   ▮ Gas & Diesel

Maryland

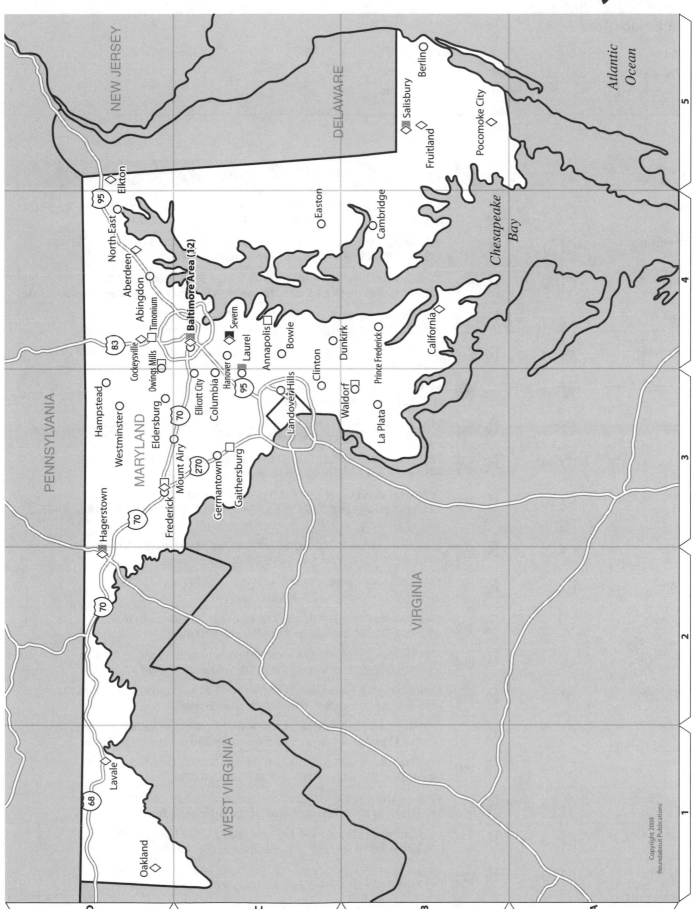

Baltimore Area

Arbutus	◇	Dundalk	○	Towson	○
Baltimore (5)	○ ■	Glen Burnie	○		
Catonsville (2)	○ ■	Nottingham	○		

City/Town	🛡	🕐	℞	🚐	Information
Aberdeen	◇ 4	🕐	℞		645 S Philadelphia Blvd, 21001 / 410-273-9200 • *Lat:* 39.4976 *Lon:* -76.1746 I-95 Exit 85 take SH-22 E .7 mile, SH-132 E 1.6 miles & US-40 W 1.7 miles
Abingdon	○ 1		℞		401 Constant Friendship Blvd, 21009 / 410-569-9403 • *Lat:* 39.4639 *Lon:* -76.3163 I-95 Exit 77B take SH-24 N .8 mile then S on Tollgate Rd .1 mile
Annapolis	□ 2		℞	🚐	2100 Generals Hwy, 21401 / 410-573-1112 • *Lat:* 38.9896 *Lon:* -76.5491 I-97 Exit 22 take US-50 E 1.3 miles, NW on West St .3 mile & N on Generals Hwy .2 mile
Arbutus	◇ 2	🕐	℞	🚐	3601 Washington Blvd, 21227 / 410-737-7700 • *Lat:* 39.2491 *Lon:* -76.6702 I-95 Exit 50 take Caton Ave S .6 mile then right at Washington Blvd .6 mile
Baltimore	■ 1		℞	🚐	2601 Port Covington Dr, 21230 / 410-837-1142 • *Lat:* 39.2609 *Lon:* -76.6088 I-95 Exit 54 (northbound only), go .2 mile E on SH-2, left at Cromwell St .3 mile
	■ 1		℞	🚐	6410 Petrie Way Rd, 21237 / 410-686-2683 • *Lat:* 39.3353 *Lon:* -76.4857 I-695 Exit 34 or I-695 Exit 35B, east of exit
	○ 1		℞	🚐	6420 Petrie Way Rd, 21237 / 410-687-4858 • *Lat:* 39.3355 *Lon:* -76.4860 I-695 Exit 35B merge onto Pulaski Hwy/US-40 E .2 mile
	○ 3		℞	🚐	2701 Port Covington Dr, 21230 / 410-625-1971 • *Lat:* 39.2592 *Lon:* -76.6086 I-95 Exit 59 take US-150 W 2.5 miles then S on Milton Ave
	○ 6		℞	🚐	112 Carroll Island Rd, 21220 / 410-335-5669 • *Lat:* 39.3377 *Lon:* -76.3997 Jct I-695 & SH-702 take SH-702 S 1.5 miles, SH-150 E 3.5 miles & Carroll Island Rd E .2 mile
Berlin	○		℞	🚐	11416 Ocean Gtwy, 21811 / 410-629-0502 • *Lat:* 38.3424 *Lon:* -75.1594 Jct US-113 & US-50 (W of town) take US-50 E for 3.4 miles
Bowie	○		℞		3300 Crain Hwy, 20716 / 301-805-8850 • *Lat:* 38.9359 *Lon:* -76.7182 US-50 Exit 13 merge onto US-301 S 2.4 miles
California	◇	🕐	℞	🚐	45485 Miramar Way, 20619 / 301-737-4420 • *Lat:* 38.2934 *Lon:* -76.5005 Jct SH-4 & SH-235 (in town) go S on SH-235 for 1.3 miles
Cambridge	○		℞	🚐	2775 Dorchester Sq, 21613 / 410-221-0292 • *Lat:* 38.5555 *Lon:* -76.0566 Jct SH-16 & US-50 (E of town) go W on US-50/Ocean Gateway 3.1 miles
Catonsville	■ 1		℞	🚐	5702 Baltimore National Pike, 21228 / 410-744-7174 • *Lat:* 39.2879 *Lon:* -76.7330 I-695 Exit 15A go E on Baltimore National Pike .5 mile
	○ 3		℞		6205 Baltimore National Pike, 21228 / 410-719-0600 • *Lat:* 39.2834 *Lon:* -76.7505 I-70 Exit 91 merge onto I-695 S 1.7 miles to Exit 15B then US-40 W .7 mile
Clinton	○ 4		℞	🚐	8745 Branch Ave, 20735 / 301-877-0502 • *Lat:* 38.7737 *Lon:* -76.8871 I-95/495 Exit 7A merge onto Branch Ave/SH-5 S 4 miles
Cockeysville	◇ 2	🕐	℞		1 Frankel Way, 21030 / 410-628-0980 • *Lat:* 39.4715 *Lon:* -76.6396 I-83 Exit 17 go E .7 mile on Padonia Rd then N 1 mile on York Rd
Columbia	○ 3		℞		6405 Dobbin Rd, 21045 / 410-740-2448 • *Lat:* 39.1968 *Lon:* -76.8205 I-95 Exit 41 follow SH-175 W 2.3 miles then S at Dobbin Rd .2 mile
Dundalk	○ 3		℞	🚐	2399 N Point Blvd, 21222 / 410-284-5412 • *Lat:* 39.2860 *Lon:* -76.4969 I-95 Exit 59 take SH-150 E .8 mile then S on N Point Blvd 1.3 miles

○ Wal-Mart ◇ Supercenter □ Sam's Club ■ Gas ■ Gas & Diesel

City/Town	⬡	🕐	℞	🚗	Information
Dunkirk	○		℞		10600 Towne Center Blvd, 20754 / 410-257-2610 • *Lat:* 38.7231 *Lon:* -76.6561 I-95/495 Exit 11A follow SH-4 SE 16.6 miles then left on Town Center Blvd .1 mile
Easton	○		℞		8155 Elliott Rd, 21601 / 410-819-0140 • *Lat:* 38.7733 *Lon:* -76.0572 Jct US-50 & SH-328 (E of town) go E on SH-328 for .2 mile & S on Elliott Rd .4 mile
Eldersburg	○ 8		℞	🚗	1320 Liberty Rd, 21784 / 410-549-5400 • *Lat:* 39.4040 *Lon:* -76.9496 I-70 Exit 80 merge onto Sykesville Rd N 7.6 miles then E on Liberty Rd
Elkton	◇ 6	🕐	℞	🚗	1000 E Pulaski Hwy, 21921 / 410-398-1070 • *Lat:* 39.6042 *Lon:* -75.7931 I-95 Exit 109 take SH-279 S 2.7 miles, SH-213 S 1.4 miles & US-40 E 1.9 miles
Ellicott City	○ 3		℞		3200 N Ridge Rd, 21043 / 410-418-5780 • *Lat:* 39.2821 *Lon:* -76.8190 I-70 Exit 87 merge onto US-29 S 1.5 miles to Exit 24 - US-40 E .6 mile & N on Ridge Rd .2 mile
Frederick	☐ 1		℞	🚗	5604 Buckeystown Pike, 21704 / 301-698-1692 • *Lat:* 39.3870 *Lon:* -77.4097 I-270 Exit 31 go N on SH-85 (Buckeystown Pike) .3 mile
	○ 6		℞	🚗	1811 Monocacy Blvd, 21701 / 301-644-2440 • *Lat:* 39.4388 *Lon:* -77.3802 I-70 Exit 53B take US-40 W 1.2 miles, US-15 N 2.4 miles, Liberty Rd E 1.1 miles & Monocacy Blvd S .8 mile
	◇ 1	🕐	℞	🚗	7400 Guilford Dr, 21704 / 301-631-0805 • *Lat:* 39.3946 *Lon:* -77.4131 I-70 Exit 54 go S on SH-355/Market St .8 mile then W on Guilford Dr .2 mile
Fruitland	◇	🕐	℞	🚗	409 N Fruitland, 21804 / 410-341-4803 • *Lat:* 38.3549 *Lon:* -75.5662 Jct SH-513/E Cedar Ln & SH-13 BR/Fruitland Blvd (in town) go S on SH-13 BR .2 mile
Gaithersburg	☐ 1		℞	🚗	610 N Frederick Ave, 20877 / 301-216-2550 • *Lat:* 39.1503 *Lon:* -77.2096 I-270 Exit 11 take SH-124 NE .5 mile then S on Frederick Ave .2 mile
Germantown	○ 1		℞	🚗	20910 Frederick Rd, 20876 / 301-515-6700 • *Lat:* 39.1986 *Lon:* -77.2452 I-270 Exit 16 merge onto Hurley Blvd E .3 mile then S on Observation Blvd .3 mile
Glen Burnie	○ 1		℞		6721 Chesapeake Center Dr, 21060 / 410-863-1280 • *Lat:* 39.1923 *Lon:* -76.6088 I-695 Exit 3B take I-895 Spur S .2 mile, SH-2 S .6 mile, SH-710 E .2 mile & S at Chesapeake Center Dr
Hagerstown	▣ 2		℞	🚗	1700 Wesel Blvd, 21740 / 301-714-0096 • *Lat:* 39.6306 *Lon:* -77.7626 I-81 Exit 5 go E on Halfway Blvd .4 mile & NE on Massey/Wesel Blvd 1.1 miles
	◇ 2	🕐	℞	🚗	17850 Garland Groh Blvd, 21740 / 301-714-1373 • *Lat:* 39.6568 *Lon:* -77.7473 I-81 Exit 6B take US-40 W .8 mile, Centre Blvd N & Garland Groh Blvd E .7 mile
Hampstead	○		℞	🚗	2320 Hanover Pike, 21074 / 410-374-5344 • *Lat:* 39.6387 *Lon:* -76.8678 2.5 miles north of town on SH-30
Hanover	○ 5		℞	🚗	7081 Arundel Mills Cir, 21076 / 410-579-8725 • *Lat:* 39.1543 *Lon:* -76.7306 I-95 Exit 43A take SH-100 E 3.9 miles to Exit 10A then SH-713 S .3 mile, Bass Pro Dr W & Arundel Mills Cir S .1 mile
La Plata	○		℞	🚗	40 Drury Dr, 20646 / 301-392-9112 • *Lat:* 38.5497 *Lon:* -76.9841 Jct SH-225/Hawthorne Rd & US-301 (N of town) go N on US-301 .6 mile
Landover Hills	○ 3		℞	🚗	6210 Annapolis Rd, 20784 / 301-773-7848 • *Lat:* 38.9419 *Lon:* -76.9071 I-95/495 Exit 20 go SW 2.7 miles on Annapolis Rd
Laurel	▣ 7		℞	🚗	3535 Russett Green, 20724 / 301-604-2060 • *Lat:* 39.0995 *Lon:* -76.8052 I-95 Exit 38 take SH-32 E 4.2 miles, SH-295 S 1.9 miles, SH-198 W .1 mile & N at Russett Green
	○ 6		℞	🚗	3549 Russett Grn, 20724 / 301-604-0180 • *Lat:* 39.1000 *Lon:* -76.8050 I-95 Exit 38 take SH-32 E 3.9 miles, SH-295 S 1.9 miles, Laurel Rd W .1 mile & Russett Grn E .1 mile
Lavale	◇ 2	🕐	℞	🚗	12500 Country Club Mall Rd, 21502 / 301-729-5081 • *Lat:* 39.6247 *Lon:* -78.8372 I-68 Exit 44 take SH-639 E .7 mile & Country Club Rd N 1 mile

○ Wal-Mart   ◇ Supercenter   ☐ Sam's Club   ▨ Gas   ■ Gas & Diesel

City/Town	⬡	🕐	℞	🚐	Information
Mount Airy	○ 1		℞	🚐	209 E Ridgeville Blvd, 21771 / 301-829-4433 • *Lat:* 39.3649 *Lon:* -77.1629 I-70 Exit 68 merge onto SH-27 N .4 mile then W on Ridgeville Blvd .2 mile
North East	○ 2		℞	🚐	75 N East Plz, 21901 / 410-287-2915 • *Lat:* 39.5803 *Lon:* -75.9663 I-95 Exit 100 follow SH-272 S for 1.9 miles
Nottingham	○ 3		℞		8118 Perry Hills Ct, 21236 / 410-882-9815 • *Lat:* 39.3790 *Lon:* -76.5063 I-95 Exit 67 take SH-43 W 2.8 miles then S on Perry Hills Ct
Oakland	◇	🕐	℞	🚐	13164 Garrett Hwy, 21550 / 301-334-8400 • *Lat:* 39.4259 *Lon:* -79.3914 On US-219 N of town
Owings Mills	☐ 3		℞	🚐	9750 Reisterstown Rd, 21117 / 410-654-6930 • *Lat:* 39.4063 *Lon:* -76.7651 I-695 Exit 20 go NW on SH-140 (Reisterstown Rd) 2.1 miles
	○ 2		℞		9750 Reisterstown Rd, 21117 / 443-394-0168 • *Lat:* 39.4072 *Lon:* -76.7670 I-695 Exit 20 go NW on SH-140 (Reisterstown Rd) 2.1 miles
Pocomoke City	◇	🕐	℞	🚐	2132 Old Snow Hill Rd, 21851 / 410-957-9600 • *Lat:* 38.0750 *Lon:* -75.5563 Jct US-13/Bypass & US-13 (E of town) go N on US-13 for .9 mile then E on Old Snow Hill Rd
Prince Frederick	○		℞		150 Solomons Island Rd N, 20678 / 410-535-3790 • *Lat:* 38.5395 *Lon:* -76.5895 Jct SH-231 & SH-2/SH-4 (E of town) go N on SH-2/SH-4 for .4 mile
Salisbury	▥		℞	🚐	2700 N Salisbury Blvd, 21801 / 410-860-8466 • *Lat:* 38.4152 *Lon:* -75.5668 Jct US-50 & US-13BR (northeast of town) go E on US-13BR (Salisbury Bypass) 1.7 miles
	◇	🕐	℞	🚐	2702 N Salisbury Blvd, 21801 / 410-860-5095 • *Lat:* 38.4152 *Lon:* -75.5668 Jct US-50 & US-13 BR (N of town) go N on US-13 BR 1.7 miles
Severn	■ 1		℞	🚐	424 George Claus Blvd, 21144 / 410-837-1142 • *Lat:* 39.1440 *Lon:* -76.6474 I-97 Exit 13, west side of highway
	◇ 1	🕐	℞	🚐	407 George Clauss Blvd, 21144 / 410-969-1050 • *Lat:* 39.1437 *Lon:* -76.6472 I-97 Exit 13 west side of the interstate at Quarterfield Rd
Timonium	☐ 1		℞	🚐	15 Texas Station Ct, 21093 / 410-628-6207 • *Lat:* 39.4579 *Lon:* -76.6401 I-83 Exit 17 go E on Pandonia Rd .4 mile, N on Beaver Dam Rd .2 mile & E on Texas Station
Towson	○ 2		℞		1238 Putty Hill Ave, 21286 / 410-494-4610 • *Lat:* 39.3933 *Lon:* -76.5809 I-695 Exit 29B merge on Loch Raven Blvd S .8 mile & W on Putty Hill Ave .9 mile
Waldorf	☐		℞	🚐	2365 Crain Hwy, 20601 / 301-645-7711 • *Lat:* 38.6459 *Lon:* -76.8904 I-95/495 Exit 7A take SH-5 S 12.3 miles then US-301 SW 1.1 miles
Waldorf	○		℞		11930 Acton Ln, 20601 / 301-705-7070 • *Lat:* 38.6385 *Lon:* -76.8967 I-95/495 Exit 7A take SH-5 S 12.3 miles, continue S on US-301 for 1.7 miles then E on Acton Ln
Westminster	○		℞		280 Woodward Rd, 21157 / 410-857-8307 • *Lat:* 39.5851 *Lon:* -76.9857 Jct SH-97 & SH-140 (N of town) take SH-140 S .9 mile, Englar Rd E .2 mile & Woodward Rd S .1 mile

○ Wal-Mart   ◇ Supercenter   ☐ Sam's Club   ▥ Gas   ■ Gas & Diesel

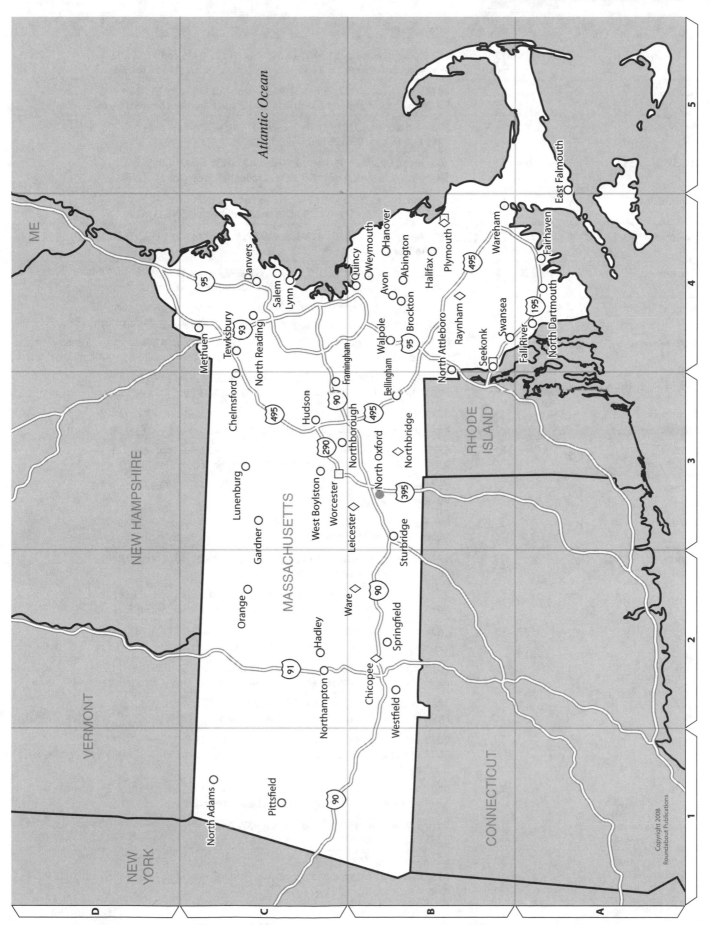

Massachusetts

○ Wal-Mart ◇ Supercenter □ Sam's Club ▬ Gas ▬ Gas & Diesel

Atlantic Ocean

ME

NEW HAMPSHIRE

VERMONT

NEW YORK

CONNECTICUT

RHODE ISLAND

MASSACHUSETTS

Methuen
Tewksbury
North Reading
Chelmsford
Danvers
Salem
Lynn
Quincy
Weymouth
Hanover
Abington
Avon
Brockton
Halifax
Plymouth
Wareham
Fairhaven
East Falmouth
Walpole
Framingham
Hudson
Bellingham
Northborough
North Oxford
Northbridge
North Attleboro
Raynham
Seekonk
Swansea
Fall River
North Dartmouth
Lunenburg
West Boylston
Worcester
Leicester
Gardner
Sturbridge
Orange
Ware
Springfield
Hadley
Chicopee
Northampton
Westfield
North Adams
Pittsfield

95
93
495
290
90
395
395
91
90
195
495

Copyright 2008
Roundabout Publications

City/Town	⬡	🕐	℞	🚗	Information
Abington	○		℞		777 Brockton Ave, 02351 / 781-857-2345 • *Lat:* 42.0935 *Lon:* -70.9692 SH-24 Exit 18A follow SH-27 SE 2.8 miles, continue on SH-123 for 2.6 miles
Avon	○		℞		30 Memorial Dr, 02322 / 508-427-9460 • *Lat:* 42.1215 *Lon:* -71.0328 SH-24 Exit 19A merge onto Harrison Blvd E 1.9 miles then S on SH-28 for .3 mile
Bellingham	○	1	℞		250 Hartford Ave, 02019 / 508-966-7633 • *Lat:* 42.1146 *Lon:* -71.4627 I-495 Exit 18 take SH-126 N .1 mile
Brockton	○		℞		700 Oak St, 02301 / 508-584-2333 • *Lat:* 42.1013 *Lon:* -71.0555 SH-24 Exit 18B merge onto SH-27 N .9 mile then E on Oak St .5 mile
Chelmsford	○	2	℞		66 Parkhurst Rd, 01824 / 978-459-1818 • *Lat:* 42.6230 *Lon:* -71.3601 I-495 Exit 33 follow SH-4 N 1.1 miles then Parkhurst Rd NE .6 mile
Chicopee	◇	1	🕐 ℞	🚗	591 Memorial Dr, 01020 / 413-593-3192 • *Lat:* 42.1738 *Lon:* -72.5762 I-90 (toll) Exit 5 take Memorial Dr N .3 mile
Danvers	○	1	℞		55 Brooksby Village Way, 01923 / 978-777-6977 • *Lat:* 42.5536 *Lon:* -70.9658 I-95 Exit 47A take SH-114 E .7 mile then S at Brooksby Village Dr .1 mile
East Falmouth	○		℞		137 Teaticket Hwy, 02536 / 508-540-8995 • *Lat:* 41.5639 *Lon:* -70.5961 Jct Sandwich Rd & Teaticket Highway/SH-28 (W of town) go NE on Teaticket Hwy .3 mile
Fairhaven	○	2			42 Fairhaven Commons Way, 02719 / 508-993-8100 • *Lat:* 41.6444 *Lon:* -70.8861 I-195 Exit 18 merge onto SH-240 S 1 mile, W at Bridge St .2 mile & S at Alden Rd .1 mile
Fall River	○	3	℞		374 William S Canning Blvd, 02721 / 508-730-2677 • *Lat:* 41.6735 *Lon:* -71.1611 I-195 Exit 8A take SH-24 S 1.7 miles then SH-81 N .4 mile
Framingham	○	2	℞		121 Worcester Rd, 01701 / 508-872-6575 • *Lat:* 42.2989 *Lon:* -71.3977 I-90 (toll) Exit 13 take SH-30 W .9 mile, S on Ring Rd .5 mile & W on Worchester Rd
Gardner	○		℞	🚗	677 Timpany Blvd, 01440 / 978-630-3244 • *Lat:* 42.5506 *Lon:* -71.9921 I-190 Exit 8A merge onto SH-2 W 15.4 miles then follow SH-68 S 1.3 miles
Hadley	○	5	℞		337 Russell St, 01035 / 413-586-4231 • *Lat:* 42.3552 *Lon:* -72.5557 I-91 Exit 20 follow SH-9 NE 4.8 miles
Halifax	○		℞		295 Plymouth St, 02338 / 781-294-9339 • *Lat:* 41.9956 *Lon:* -70.8449 From SH-24 Exit 15 follow SH-104 E 7.3 miles, continue E on SH-106 3.6 miles
Hanover	○		℞		1775 Washington St, 02339 / 781-826-0606 • *Lat:* 42.1461 *Lon:* -70.8447 From SH-3/SE Expy Exit 13 follow SH-53 S .4 mile
Hudson	○	2	℞		280 Washington St, 01749 / 978-568-3383 • *Lat:* 42.3730 *Lon:* -71.5622 I-495 Exit 25A take Hudston St E 1.6 miles then S at Washington St .3 mile
Leicester	◇		🕐 ℞	🚗	1620 Main St, 01524 / 508-892-9461 • *Lat:* 42.2474 *Lon:* -71.9374 1.6 miles west of town center along SH-9 (Main St)
Lunenburg	○		℞	🚗	301 Massachusetts Ave, 01462 / 978-582-6000 • *Lat:* 42.5925 *Lon:* -71.7586 From SH-2 Exit 32 take SH-13 N 4.1 miles then W at SH-2A/Massachusetts Ave .1 mile
Lynn	○	7	℞		780 Lynnway, 01905 / 781-592-4300 • *Lat:* 42.4492 *Lon:* -70.9634 From I-90 (toll) Exit 26 follow US-1A N 6.1 miles
Methuen	○	2	℞		70 Pleasant Valley St, 01844 / 978-686-2633 • *Lat:* 42.7420 *Lon:* -71.1659 I-93 Exit 48 follow SH-213 E 1.6 miles to Exit 3 then turn left and continue E .2 mile on Pleasant Valley St
North Adams	○		℞		830 Curran Hwy, 01247 / 413-664-4004 • *Lat:* 42.6784 *Lon:* -73.1067 Jct SH-2 & SH-8 (W of town) go S on SH-8 for 1.6 miles
North Attleboro	○	2	℞		1470 S Washington St, 02760 / 508-699-0277 • *Lat:* 41.9347 *Lon:* -71.3511 I-295 Exit 1A take US-1 S 1.5 miles
North Dartmouth	○	3	℞		506 State Rd, 02747 / 508-984-7771 • *Lat:* 41.6411 *Lon:* -71.0073 I-195 Exit 12 go S on Faunce Corner Rd .3 mile, Cross Rd SE 1.8 miles & E on State Rd .1 mile

○ Wal-Mart ◇ Supercenter □ Sam's Club ▓ Gas ▉ Gas & Diesel

City/Town	⬤⏱️℞🚗				Information
North Oxford	⬤	5		℞	742 Main St, 01537 / 508-987-1444 • *Lat:* 42.1690 *Lon:* -71.8827 I-395 Exit 4B go W on Sutton Ave .9 mile then N on Main St 4.1 miles
North Reading	◯	3		℞	72 Main St, 01864 / 978-664-3262 • *Lat:* 42.5718 *Lon:* -71.1100 I-93 Exit 39 go E on Concord St & Park St for 1.7 miles then N on Main St .5 mile
Northampton	◯	2		℞	180 N King St, 01060 / 413-587-0001 • *Lat:* 42.3431 *Lon:* -72.6422 I-91 Exit 21 go S on US-5/King St 1.4 miles
Northborough	◯	6		℞	200 Otis St, 01532 / 508-393-4385 • *Lat:* 42.2877 *Lon:* -71.6561 I-495 Exit 23B merge onto SH-9 W 4.9 miles then N on Otis St .4 mile
Northbridge	◇		⏱️	℞	100 Valley Pkwy, 01534 / 508-234-9034 • *Lat:* 42.1050 *Lon:* -71.6990 From SH-146 at Main St Exit, go E .4 mile on Main St
Orange	◯			℞	555 E Main St, 01364 / 978-544-5800 • *Lat:* 42.5869 *Lon:* -72.2845 Jct SH-122/S Main St & SH-2A/E Main St (in town) take E Main St E 1.3 miles
Pittsfield	◯			℞ 🚗	555 Hubbard Ave, 01201 / 413-442-1971 • *Lat:* 42.4681 *Lon:* -73.1961 Jct SH-8 & SH-9 (E of town) go E on SH-9 for .4 mile then S on Hubbard Ave .1 mile
Plymouth	☐			℞ 🚗	500 Colony Place Rd, 02360 / 508-747-2047 • *Lat:* 41.9532 *Lon:* -70.7195 Jct SH-3 & US-44 (NE of town) US-44 W .9 mile, exit at Cherry St, S on Commerce Way .6 mile, W on Colony Pl
	◇			℞ 🚗	300 Colony Place Rd, 02360 / 508-830-9555 • *Lat:* 41.9527 *Lon:* -70.7128 I-495 Exit 4 take SH-105 E 2.9 miles, US-44 E 9.6 miles & SH-80/Commerce Way S .2 mile
Quincy	◯			℞	301 Falls Blvd, 02169 / 617-745-4390 • *Lat:* 42.2382 *Lon:* -70.9851 Jct SH-53 & SH-3A (in town) go S on SH-53/Quincy Ave .9 mile & W on Falls Blvd .1 mile
Raynham	◇	5	⏱️	℞	36 Paramount Dr, 02767 / 508-822-4900 • *Lat:* 41.9050 *Lon:* -71.0353 I-495 Exit 6 take US-44 W 3.4 miles, S on Commerce Way .3 mile & W on Paramount Dr .4 mile
Salem	◯			℞	450 Highland Ave, 01970 / 978-825-1713 • *Lat:* 42.4935 *Lon:* -70.9343 Jct SH-129 & SH-107 (S of town) go N on SH-107/Highland Ave .8 mile
Seekonk	☐	1		🚗	1098 Fall River Ave, 02771 / 508-336-8262 • *Lat:* 41.7971 *Lon:* -71.3304 I-195 Exit 1 take SH-114A S for .6 mile then E on Fall River Ave
	◯	1		℞	1180 Fall River Ave, 02771 / 508-336-0290 • *Lat:* 41.7935 *Lon:* -71.3267 I-195 Exit 1 follow SH-114A S .6 mile
Springfield	◯	3		℞	1105 Boston Rd, 01119 / 413-782-6699 • *Lat:* 42.1389 *Lon:* -72.5071 I-90 (toll) Exit 7 follow SH-21 S 2.2 miles then W on US-20/Boston Rd .6 mile
Sturbridge	◯	2		℞	100 Charlton Rd, 01566 / 508-347-4993 • *Lat:* 42.1266 *Lon:* -72.0538 I-84 Exit 3A merge onto US-20 E 1.9 miles
Swansea	◯	1		℞	262 Swansea Mall Dr, 02777 / 508-677-3775 • *Lat:* 41.7577 *Lon:* -71.2181 I-195 Exit 3 take US-6 SE .1 mile then SH-118 N .3 mile
Tewksbury	◯	1		℞	333 Main St, 01876 / 978-851-6265 • *Lat:* 42.6214 *Lon:* -71.2624 I-495 Exit 38 take SH-38 E .5 mile
Walpole	◯	2		℞	550 Providence Hwy, 02081 / 508-668-4144 • *Lat:* 42.1345 *Lon:* -71.2224 I-95 Exit 9 follow US-1 N 1.4 miles
Ware	◇	6		℞	352 Palmer Rd, 01082 / 413-967-0040 • *Lat:* 42.2393 *Lon:* -72.2812 I-90 (toll) Exit 8 follow SH-32 N 6 miles
Wareham	◯	5		℞	3005 Cranberry Hwy, 02538 / 508-295-8890 • *Lat:* 41.7648 *Lon:* -70.6553 I-195 Exit 22A merge onto SH-25 E 2.8 miles then US-6 E 1.5 miles
West Boylston	◯	6		℞	137 W Boylston St, 01583 / 508-835-1101 • *Lat:* 42.3537 *Lon:* -71.7845 I-290 Exit 23 merge onto SH-140 N 4.9 miles then SH-12 S .7 mile
Westfield	◯	4		℞	141 Springfield Rd, 01085 / 413-572-0400 • *Lat:* 42.1086 *Lon:* -72.7066 I-90 (toll) Exit 3 take US-202 S 1 mile, Union St SE 2.3 miles, continue on US-20 E .4 mile

◯ Wal-Mart ◇ Supercenter ☐ Sam's Club ▧ Gas ▩ Gas & Diesel

City/Town			R_X		Information
Weymouth	○		R_X		740 Middle St, 02188 / 781-331-0063 • *Lat:* 42.1995 *Lon:* -70.9459 From Pilgrims Hwy (SH-3) at Main St Exit, go N .2 mile on Main St, E .5 mile on Winter St, S .1 mile on Middle St
Worcester	☐	1		🚍	301 Barber Ave, 01606 / 508-852-7717 • *Lat:* 42.2955 *Lon:* -71.7967 I-190 Exit 1 take SH-12 N .4 mile & S on Barber Ave .4 mile

Michigan

ONTARIO

Lake Superior

Houghton ◆

◇ Ironwood   Marquette ◇

Sault Sainte Marie ○

Iron Mountain ◆   Escanaba ◇

WISCONSIN

Cheboygan ◇
75

Petoskey ◇

Gaylord ◇   Alpena ◆

Lake Huron

Traverse City ○■

Houghton Lake ◆
West Branch ◇   Tawas City ◆
Cadillac ◆   75

MICHIGAN

Ludington ◆

Big Rapids ◇   Midland ◆   Bad Axe ◇

Mount Pleasant ◇   Bay City ▨   Caro ◆

Fremont ◆   Alma ○   Saginaw (3) ◆   Sandusky ◆

Muskegon (3) ◇   Comstock Park □   Greenville ◇   Clio ◆   Lapeer ◆   Fort Gratiot ◆
                                            Saint Johns ▨ Owosso ◇ Flint   Burton ◇
Grand Haven ◇ 96 Grand Rapids ○   69
Grandville ◇   Ionia ◇   Grand Blanc ◇   Port Huron ▨
Holland ◇   Kentwood ◇   69   Fenton ○   75   94
           Lansing ◇◇   White Lake ◇
Hastings ○   Charlotte ◇   Okemos ◇ 96 Howell ◇ Commerce Twp ◇
196   Fowlerville ◇
Plainwell ◇   New Hudson ◇
South Haven ◆ Kalamazoo (2) ◆   Battle Creek ◇   **Detroit Area (21)** ◆
                              94   Ypsilanti ○   Woodhaven ○
Benton Harbor ◇   94 Portage □ 69   Jackson ◇ Jonesville ◇   Monroe ◆
Three Rivers ◇ Sturgis ◇ Coldwater ◇ Adrian ◆   75
Niles ▨

ILLINOIS

INDIANA   OHIO

1   2   3   4

E
D
C
B
A

Detroit Area

Auburn Hills	■	Livonia	◇	Southgate	■
Belleville	○	Madison Heights	■	Sterling Heights (2)	○ ◇
Canton (2)	○ □	Rochester Hills	◇	Taylor	◇
Chesterfield	◇	Roseville (2)	○ ■	Troy	○
Dearborn	◇	Shelby Township	◆	Utica	■
Farmington Hills	□	Southfield	■	Waterford	□

City/Town	🛡	🕐	℞	🚌	Information
Adrian	◆		🕐	℞ 🚌	1601 E US Hwy 223, 49221 / 517-265-9771 • *Lat:* 41.8750 *Lon:* -84.0313 Jct SH-34 & US-223 (W of town) go N on US-223 for 1.5 miles
Alma	○			℞	7945 N Alger Rd, 48801 / 989-463-6770 • *Lat:* 43.4067 *Lon:* -84.6670 From US-127 at SH-46 (Monroe Rd) Exit, go W .3 mile on Monroe Rd then S .1 mile on Alger Rd
Alpena	◆		🕐	℞ 🚌	1180 MI Hwy 32 W, 49707 / 989-354-0830 • *Lat:* 45.0616 *Lon:* -83.4796 Jct US-32 & SH-65 (W of town) take SH-65 N 15 miles then SH-32 E 3.3 miles
Auburn Hills	■ 1			℞ 🚌	4350 Joslyn Rd, 48326 / 248-391-6910 • *Lat:* 42.7052 *Lon:* -83.2848 I-75 Exit 83 go N on Joslyn Rd .5 mile
Bad Axe	◇		🕐	℞ 🚌	901 N Van Dyke Rd, 48413 / 989-269-9506 • *Lat:* 43.8220 *Lon:* -83.0012 Jct SH-142/Pigeon Rd & SH-53 (N of town) go S on SH-53 for .1 mile
Battle Creek	■ 1			℞ 🚌	12737 6 Mile Rd, 49014 / 269-979-5327 • *Lat:* 42.2584 *Lon:* -85.1791 I-94 Exit 94A go S .5 mile on SH-66, E on B Drive
	◇ 2		🕐	℞ 🚌	6020 B Dr N, 49014 / 269-979-1628 • *Lat:* 42.2610 *Lon:* -85.1786 I-94 Exit 97 go E on B Dr N for 1.1 miles
Bay City	◇ 3		🕐	℞	3921 Wilder Rd, 48706 / 989-684-0430 • *Lat:* 43.6239 *Lon:* -83.8981 I-75 Exit 164 take Wilder Rd E 2.4 miles
Belleville	○ 1			℞ 🚌	10562 Belleville Rd, 48111 / 734-697-2078 • *Lat:* 42.2259 *Lon:* -83.4852 I-94 Exit 190 take Belleville Rd N .4 mile
Benton Harbor	◇ 1		🕐	℞ 🚌	1400 Mall Dr, 49022 / 269-927-6025 • *Lat:* 42.0790 *Lon:* -86.4229 I-94 Exit 29 go N on Pipestone Rd .2 mile & W on Mall Dr .3 mile
Big Rapids	◇		🕐	℞ 🚌	21400 Perry Ave, 49307 / 231-796-1443 • *Lat:* 43.6884 *Lon:* -85.5131 From US-131 Exit 139 take SH-20 E .5 mile
Burton	◇ 1		🕐	℞ 🚌	5323 E Court St N, 48509 / 810-744-9690 • *Lat:* 43.0204 *Lon:* -83.5993 I-69 Exit 141 go N .2 mile on Belsay Rd then W .3 mile on Court St
Cadillac	◆		🕐	℞ 🚌	8917 E 34 Rd, 49601 / 231-775-8778 • *Lat:* 44.2815 *Lon:* -85.4002 US-131 Exit 183 take 34 Rd W for .7 mile
Canton	□ 1			℞ 🚌	39800 Ford Rd, 48187 / 734-981-4460 • *Lat:* 42.3236 *Lon:* -83.4327 I-275 Exit 25 go E on Ford Rd .7 mile
	○ 1			℞	39500 Ford Rd, 48187 / 734-983-0538 • *Lat:* 42.3236 *Lon:* -83.4300 I-275 Exit 25 go E on Ford Rd .6 mile
Caro	◆		🕐	℞ 🚌	1121 E Caro Rd, 48723 / 989-673-7900 • *Lat:* 43.4994 *Lon:* -83.3830 Jct SH-24 & SH-81 (NE of town) go NE on SH-81 for .3 mile
Charlotte	◇ 2		🕐	℞ 🚌	1680 Packard Hwy, 48813 / 517-543-0300 • *Lat:* 42.5820 *Lon:* -84.8042 I-69 Exit 61 go N on Lansing Rd .9 mile then E on Packard Hwy .2 mile
Cheboygan	◇		🕐	℞ 🚌	1150 S Main St, 49721 / 231-627-2769 • *Lat:* 45.6267 *Lon:* -84.4779 I-75 Exit 313 follow SH-27 NE 14.6 miles

○ Wal-Mart ◇ Supercenter □ Sam's Club ■ Gas ■ Gas & Diesel

City/Town	🛡	🕐	℞	🚐	Information
Chesterfield	◇ 1	🕐	℞	🚐	45400 Marketplace Blvd, 48051 / 586-421-0451 • *Lat:* 42.6359 *Lon:* -82.8544 I-94 Exit 240 go W on Rosso Hwy .1 mile & N on Marketplace Blvd .4 mile
Clio	◆ 1	🕐	℞	🚐	11493 N Linden Rd, 48420 / 810-564-3149 • *Lat:* 43.1771 *Lon:* -83.7745 I-75 Exit 131 take SH-57 W .2 mile & S on Linden Rd
Coldwater	◇ 1	🕐	℞	🚐	800 E Chicago St, 49036 / 517-278-2240 • *Lat:* 41.9350 *Lon:* -84.9674 I-69 Exit 13 take US-12 E .4 mile
Commerce Township	◇ 6	🕐	℞	🚐	3301 N Pontiac Trail, 48390 / 248-668-0274 • *Lat:* 42.5574 *Lon:* -83.4422 I-96 Exit 164 follow SH-5 N 5.5 miles & NE on Pontiac Trail .3 mile
Comstock Park	▪ 2		℞	🚐	3901 Alpine Ave NW, 49321 / 616-785-0001 • *Lat:* 43.0340 *Lon:* -85.6898 I-96 Exit 30 go N on Alpine Ave 1.1 miles
	○ 2		℞	🚐	3999 Alpine Ave NW, 49321 / 616-784-2047 • *Lat:* 43.0359 *Lon:* -85.6899 I-96 Exit 30 take SH-37 N 1.2 miles
Dearborn	◇ 4		℞		5851 Mercury Dr, 48126 / 313-441-0194 • *Lat:* 42.3299 *Lon:* -83.2079 I-96 Exit 183 take SH-39 S 2.7 miles to Exit 7 then go E .7 mile on Ford Rd (SH-153)
Escanaba	◇	🕐	℞	🚐	601 N Lincoln Rd, 49829 / 906-786-7717 • *Lat:* 45.7523 *Lon:* -87.0807 1.7 miles northwest of town center, about .5 mile north of US-2/US-41/SH-35 jct
Farmington Hills	▢ 3		℞		32625 Northwestern Hwy, 48334 / 248-539-3066 • *Lat:* 42.5257 *Lon:* -83.3529 I-696 Exit 5 go N on Orchard Lake Rd 2.4 miles then SE on SH-10 for .5 mile
Fenton	○		℞		3700 Owen Rd, 48430 / 810-750-1132 • *Lat:* 42.7897 *Lon:* -83.7445 From US-23 Exit 78 take Owen Rd W .2 mile
Flint	▪ 1		℞	🚐	4373 Corunna Rd, 48532 / 810-230-6700 • *Lat:* 43.0020 *Lon:* -83.7670 I-75 Exit 118 go W on Corumma Rd 1 mile
	◇ 1	🕐	℞	🚐	4313 Corunna Rd, 48532 / 810-733-5055 • *Lat:* 43.0020 *Lon:* -83.7658 I-75 Exit 118 go W on Corunna Rd .9 mile
Fort Gratiot	◆ 4	🕐	℞	🚐	4845 24th Ave, 48059 / 810-385-1904 • *Lat:* 43.0490 *Lon:* -82.4574 I-69/94 Exit 274 take I-69/94 BR N then SH-25 N 3.6 miles
Fowlerville	◇ 1	🕐	℞	🚐	970 Gehringer Dr, 48836 / 517-223-8605 • *Lat:* 42.4903 *Lon:* -84.0726 I-96 Exit 129, north of exit
Fremont	◆	🕐	℞	🚐	7083 W 48th St, 49412 / 231-924-5000 • *Lat:* 43.4673 *Lon:* -85.9766 Jct SH-120/Maple Island Rd & SH-82/48th St (W of town) go E on 48th St 3.1 miles
Gaylord	◇ 1	🕐	℞	🚐	950 Edelweiss Pkwy, 49735 / 989-732-8090 • *Lat:* 45.0232 *Lon:* -84.6909 I-75 Exit 282 merge onto Dickerson Rd S .4 mile then W at Edelweiss Pkwy
Grand Blanc	▪ 2		℞	🚐	6160 S Saginaw Rd, 48439 / 810-603-9540 • *Lat:* 42.9415 *Lon:* -83.6470 I-475 Exit 2 go E at Hill Rd 1.4 miles then Saginaw Rd SE for .3 mile
	◇ 2	🕐	℞	🚐	6170 S Saginaw Rd, 48439 / 810-603-9739 • *Lat:* 42.9413 *Lon:* -83.6468 I-475 Exit 2 go E on Hill Rd 1.7 miles then S on Saginaw Rd .3 mile
Grand Haven	◆ 10	🕐	℞	🚐	14700 US Hwy 31, 49417 / 616-844-3074 • *Lat:* 43.0371 *Lon:* -86.2190 I-96 Exit 1 follow US-31 S 9.5 miles
Grand Rapids	○ 1		℞		5859 28th St SE, 49546 / 616-949-7670 • *Lat:* 42.9132 *Lon:* -85.5232 I-96 Exit 43 merge onto 28th St E .7 mile
Grandville	○ 1		℞	🚐	4542 Kenowa Ave SW, 49418 / 616-667-9724 • *Lat:* 42.8825 *Lon:* -85.7821 I-196 Exit 67 go W on 44th St .1 mile then S on Kenowa Ave .2 mile
	◇	🕐	℞	🚐	10772 W Carson City Rd, 48838 / 616-754-3062 • *Lat:* 43.1772 *Lon:* -85.2894 US-131 Exit 101 take SH-57 E 14.5 miles
Hastings	○		℞		1618 W MI Hwy 43, 49058 / 269-948-0470 • *Lat:* 42.6481 *Lon:* -85.3131 Jct SH-37 & SH-43 (W of town) go E on SH-37 for .6 mile
Holland	▢ 8			🚐	2190 N Park Dr, 49424 / 616-395-3190 • *Lat:* 42.8069 *Lon:* -86.0913 I-196 Exit 44 take US-31 N 6.8 miles, W on Lakewood Blvd .5 mile & N on Park Dr

○ Wal-Mart ◇ Supercenter ▢ Sam's Club ▪ Gas ■ Gas & Diesel

City/Town	🛡	🕐	℞	🚐	Information
	◇ 7	🕐	℞	🚐	2629 N Park Dr, 49424 / 616-393-2018 • *Lat:* 42.8111 *Lon:* -86.0903 I-196 Exit 55 take I-196 BR W 3.8 miles, 12th Ave N .1 mile, Lakewood Blvd W 1.7 miles & Park Dr N .5 mile
Houghton	◆	🕐	℞		995 Razorback Dr, 49931 / 906-482-0639 • *Lat:* 47.1129 *Lon:* -88.5865 Jct US-41 & SH-26 (N of town) go S on SH-26/Memorial Dr .9 mile & E on Sharon Ave .1 mile
Houghton Lake	◆	🕐	℞	🚐	2129 W Houghton Lake Dr, 48629 / 989-366-9766 • *Lat:* 44.3298 *Lon:* -84.7821 I-75 Exit 227 merge onto SH-55 W 15.3 miles then N on Heightsview Dr .1 mile
Howell	◇ 5	🕐	℞		3850 E Grand River Ave, 48843 / 517-548-9500 • *Lat:* 42.5879 *Lon:* -83.8775 I-96 Exit 137 follow CR-D19 N 1.3 miles & Grand River Ave SE 3 miles
Ionia	◇ 5	🕐	℞	🚐	3062 S State Rd, 48846 / 616-527-1392 • *Lat:* 42.9427 *Lon:* -85.0749 I-96 Exit 67 take SH-66 N 4.7 miles
Iron Mountain	◆	🕐	℞	🚐	1920 S Stephenson Ave, 49801 / 906-779-7180 • *Lat:* 45.8091 *Lon:* -88.0414 1.7 miles southeast of town via US-2/US-141
Ironwood	◇	🕐	℞	🚐	10305 Country Club Rd, 49938 / 906-932-0713 • *Lat:* 46.4688 *Lon:* -90.1248 2 miles east of town off US-2 at Country Club Rd, south of US-2
Jackson	■ 1		℞	🚐	3600 O'Neil Dr, 49202 / 517-788-6075 • *Lat:* 42.2667 *Lon:* -84.4554 I-94 Exit 137 go S on Airport Rd .1 mile then W on Oneil Dr .2 mile
	◇ 2	🕐	℞		1700 W Michigan Ave, 49202 / 517-817-0326 • *Lat:* 42.2476 *Lon:* -84.4346 I-94 Exit 137 take Airport Rd S .6 mile, Laurence Ave S .7 mile & Michigan Ave E .7 mile
Jonesville	◇	🕐	℞	🚐	701 Olds St, 49250 / 517-849-7000 • *Lat:* 41.9666 *Lon:* -84.6703 Jct US-12 & SH-99 (in town) go S on SH-99 for 1.1 miles
Kalamazoo	◆ 6	🕐	℞	🚐	6065 Gull Rd, 49048 / 269-373-1314 • *Lat:* 42.3287 *Lon:* -85.5113 I-94 Exit 80 take Sprinkle Rd N 4.4 miles then NE on Gull Rd .7 mile
	◇ 4	🕐	℞	🚐	501 N 9th St, 49009 / 269-544-0718 • *Lat:* 42.2843 *Lon:* -85.6781 I-94 Exit 74 take US-131 N 2.4 miles to Exit 38-Main St W 1 mile & 9th St S .2 mile
Kentwood	■ 2		℞	🚐	4326 28th St SE, 49512 / 616-942-2656 • *Lat:* 42.9125 *Lon:* -85.5597 I-96 Exit 43 go W on 28th for 1.6 miles
Lansing	■ 3		℞	🚐	340 E Edgewood Blvd, 48911 / 517-887-1052 • *Lat:* 42.6638 *Lon:* -84.5463 I-96 Exit 101 go E on Edgewood Blvd 2.6 miles
	■ 4		℞	🚐	2925 Towne Centre Blvd, 48912 / 517-482-9149 • *Lat:* 42.7630 *Lon:* -84.5179 I-69 Exit 89 take US-127 S 3.3 miles then W on Lake Lansing Rd .2 mile & N on Towne Centre .1 mile
	○		℞	🚐	3225 Towne Centre Blvd, 48912 / 517-487-9150 • *Lat:* 42.7645 *Lon:* -84.5179 US-127 Exit 79 go W on Lake Lansing Rd .3 mile & N on Centre Blvd
	◇ 1	🕐	℞	🚐	409 N Marketplace Blvd, 48917 / 517-622-1431 • *Lat:* 42.7382 *Lon:* -84.6728 I-69/96 Exit 93 merge E onto Saginaw Hwy .4 mile & S at Marketplace Blvd .2 mile
Lapeer	◆ 3	🕐	℞	🚐	555 E Genesee St, 48446 / 810-664-3062 • *Lat:* 43.0511 *Lon:* -83.3006 I-69 Exit 155 go N on SH-24 for 2 miles & E on Genesse St .3 mile
Livonia	◇ 2	🕐	℞	🚐	29555 Plymouth Rd, 48150 / 734-524-0577 • *Lat:* 42.3679 *Lon:* -83.3367 I-96 Exit 176 go S on Middlebelt Rd 1 mile then W at Plymouth Rd .1 mile
Ludington	◆	🕐	℞	🚐	4854 W US Hwy 10, 49431 / 231-843-1816 • *Lat:* 43.9555 *Lon:* -86.4001 Jct US-31 & US-10 (E of town) go W on US-10 for .8 mile
Madison Heights	■ 2		℞	🚐	31020 John R Rd, 48071 / 248-589-1208 • *Lat:* 42.5204 *Lon:* -83.1062 I-75 Exit 65 go E on 14 Mile Rd .5 mile then S on John R Rd 1 mile
Marquette	◇	🕐	℞	🚐	3225 US 41 W, 49855 / 906-226-7982 • *Lat:* 46.5320 *Lon:* -87.3998 Jct SH-35 & US-41 (SW of town) go N on US-41 for 4.5 miles
Midland	◆	🕐	℞	🚐	910 Joe Mann Blvd, 48642 / 989-835-6069 • *Lat:* 43.6602 *Lon:* -84.2372 I-75 Exit 162 follow US-10 W 16.9 miles, Eastman Ave N .3 mile & Mann Blvd E .5 mile

○ Wal-Mart   ◇ Supercenter   □ Sam's Club   ■ Gas   ■ Gas & Diesel

City/Town	⬤	🕐	℞	🚗	Information
Monroe	◯ 6		℞	🚗	2155 N Telegraph Rd, 48162 / 734-242-2280 • *Lat:* 41.9517 *Lon:* -83.3990 I-275 Exit 2 take US-24 S 5.3 miles
Mount Pleasant	☐		℞		4850 Encore Blvd, 48858 / 989-772-0974 • *Lat:* 43.5711 *Lon:* -84.7577 Jct US-127 & US-127 BR go W on US-127 BR 1.5 miles, E on Blue Grass Rd .5 mile & S on Encore Blvd .3 mile
	◇	🕐	℞	🚗	4730 Encore Blvd, 48858 / 989-772-6300 • *Lat:* 43.5730 *Lon:* -84.7576 2 miles south of town off US-127 BR at Blue Grass Rd to Encore Blvd
Muskegon	■ 3		℞	🚗	1707 E Sherman Blvd, 49444 / 231-733-2575 • *Lat:* 43.2050 *Lon:* -86.2020 I-96 Exit 1 take US-31 N 2.2 miles then E on Sherman Blvd .1 mile
	◇ 3	🕐	℞	🚗	1879 E Sherman Blvd, 49444 / 231-739-6202 • *Lat:* 43.2053 *Lon:* -86.2001 I-96 Exit 1 take US-31 N 2.2 miles then Sherman Blvd E .2 mile
	◇ 4	🕐	℞	🚗	3285 Henry St, 49441 / 231-739-4710 • *Lat:* 43.1926 *Lon:* -86.2636 I-96 Exit 1 continue W on Seaway Dr 3.3 miles, W on Norton .2 mile & N on Henry St .1 mile
New Hudson	◇ 1	🕐	℞	🚗	30729 Lyon Center Dr E, 48165 / 248-486-0445 • *Lat:* 42.5164 *Lon:* -83.6133 I-96 Exit 155 go S on Milford Rd .2 mile & E on Lynn Center Dr .2 mile
Niles	◆	🕐	℞	🚗	2107 S 11th St, 49120 / 269-683-2773 • *Lat:* 41.7891 *Lon:* -86.2503 US-31 Exit 3 take Pulaski Hwy E 3.6 miles & S on 11th St .7 mile
Novi	■ 1				27300 Wixom Rd, 48374 / 248-349-3057 • *Lat:* 42.4897 *Lon:* -83.5353 I-96 Exit 159 go S on Wixom Rd .5 mile
Okemos	◯ 5		℞	🚗	5110 Times Square Pl, 48864 / 517-381-5243 • *Lat:* 42.7278 *Lon:* -84.4091 I-69 Exit 94 take Saginaw St S 1.3 miles, Marsh Rd SE 3.1 miles & Times Sq Dr E .3 mile
Owosso	◆	🕐	℞	🚗	1621 E MI Hwy 21, 48867 / 989-723-2552 • *Lat:* 42.9980 *Lon:* -84.1391 US-127 Exit 96 follow SH-21 E 19.1 miles
Petoskey	◇	🕐	℞	🚗	1600 Anderson Rd, 49770 / 231-439-0200 • *Lat:* 45.3543 *Lon:* -84.9711 Jct US-31 & US-131 (W of town) take US-131 S .7 mile & W at Anderson Rd .4 mile
Plainwell	◇	🕐	℞	🚗	412 Oaks Xing, 49080 / 269-685-6191 • *Lat:* 42.4496 *Lon:* -85.6697 Located between Otsego and Plainwell. From US-131 Exit 49, go W .9 mile on SH-89
Port Huron	■ 1		℞	🚗	1237 32nd St, 48060 / 810-984-5355 • *Lat:* 42.9694 *Lon:* -82.4624 I-69 Exit 199 (nb only) or I-94 Exit 271 (eb only), southeast of exit
Portage	☐ 2		℞	🚗	7021 S Westnedge Ave, 49002 / 269-327-0534 • *Lat:* 42.2151 *Lon:* -85.5892 I-94 Exit 76 go S on Westnedge 1.1 miles
	◯ 4		℞		8350 Shaver Rd, 49024 / 269-323-2460 • *Lat:* 42.1937 *Lon:* -85.5975 I-94 Exit 76 go S on Westnedge Ave 2.3 miles, continue on Shaver Rd .8 mile
Rochester Hills	◇ 2	🕐	℞	🚗	2500 S Adams Rd, 48309 / 248-853-0433 • *Lat:* 42.6426 *Lon:* -83.1989 I-75 Exit 77A go E 1.8 miles on SH-59 (Veterans Memorial Fwy) to Adams Rd and go S .2 mile
Roseville	■ 1		℞	🚗	31720 Gratiot Ave, 48066 / 586-415-9987 • *Lat:* 42.5299 *Lon:* -82.9149 I-94 Exit 231 go N on Gratiot Ave .5 mile
	◯ 2		℞		28804 Gratiot Ave, 48066 / 586-777-0221 • *Lat:* 42.5090 *Lon:* -82.9285 I-696 Exit 27 go N on Gratiot Ave 1.1 miles
Saginaw	■ 2		℞	🚗	5656 Bay Rd, 48604 / 989-790-0954 • *Lat:* 43.4895 *Lon:* -83.9739 I-675 Exit 6 go W on Tittabawassee Rd 1.1 miles then N at Bay Rd .7 mile
	◇ 2	🕐	℞	🚗	5650 Bay Rd, 48604 / 989-790-3990 • *Lat:* 43.4894 *Lon:* -83.9739 I-675 Exit 6 go W on Tittabawassee Rd 1.1 miles then N on Bay Rd .7 mile
	◇ 5	🕐	℞	🚗	5825 Brockway Rd, 48638 / 989-497-8102 • *Lat:* 43.4352 *Lon:* -84.0309 I-675 Exit 3 take Davenport Ave W 4.6 miles, S on Wieneke Rd .1 mile & W on Brockway Rd
Saint Johns	◆	🕐	℞	🚗	1165 Superior Dr, 48879 / 989-224-8099 • *Lat:* 42.9773 *Lon:* -84.5405 From US-127 Exit 91, follow US-127 BR 5.2 miles then E on Superior Dr .1 mile

◯ Wal-Mart   ◇ Supercenter   ☐ Sam's Club   ■ Gas   ■ Gas & Diesel

City/Town	🛡	🕐	℞	🚐	Information
Sandusky	◆		🕐	℞	🚐	655 W Sanilac Rd, 48471 / 810-648-2728 • *Lat:* 43.4206 *Lon:* -82.8562 Jct SH-53 & SH-46 (W of town) go E on SH-46 for 11.6 miles
Sault Sainte Marie	○ 3			℞		4516 I-75 Business Spur, 49783 / 906-632-0572 • *Lat:* 46.4640 *Lon:* -84.3725 I-75 Exit 392 follow I-75 Spur/3 Mile Rd NE 2.3 miles then E at Marquette Ave .4 mile
Shelby Township	◆		🕐	℞	🚐	51450 Shelby Pkwy, 48315 / 586-997-6905 • *Lat:* 42.6729 *Lon:* -83.0136 Jct SH-59 & SH-53 (S of town) take SH-53 N 2.7 miles, 23 Mile Rd E .4 mile & Shelby Pkwy N .3 mile
South Haven	◆ 1		🕐	℞	🚐	201 73rd St, 49090 / 269-639-2260 • *Lat:* 42.4157 *Lon:* -86.2516 I-196 Exit 20 W on Phoenix St & N on 73rd St .1 mile
Southfield	▣ 5				🚐	22500 W 8 Mile Rd, 48033 / 248-354-1108 • *Lat:* 42.4434 *Lon:* -83.2636 I-96 Exit 179 go N 4 miles on US-24, E on 8 Mile Rd
Southgate	▣ 1			℞	🚐	15700 Northline Rd, 48195 / 734-285-0030 • *Lat:* 42.2137 *Lon:* -83.2154 I-75 Exit 37 go E on Northline Rd 1 mile
Sterling Heights	○			℞	🚐	44575 Mound Rd, 48314 / 586-323-2394 • *Lat:* 42.6216 *Lon:* -83.0523 I-75 Exit 77 merge onto SH-59 E 9.8 miles, Hall Rd E .2 mile & Mound Rd S .2 mile
	◇ 5		🕐	℞	🚐	33201 Van Dyke Ave, 48312 / 586-939-7208 • *Lat:* 42.5377 *Lon:* -83.0305 I-75 Exit 65 go E 4.5 miles on 14 Mile Rd
Sturgis	◆ 3		🕐	℞	🚐	1500 S Centerville Rd, 49091 / 269-651-8580 • *Lat:* 41.7862 *Lon:* -85.4281 I-80/90 (toll-IN) Exit 121 take SH-9 N .7 mile & continue on Centerville Rd 1.7 miles
Tawas City	◆		🕐	℞	🚐	621 E Lake St, 48763 / 989-984-0854 • *Lat:* 44.2751 *Lon:* -83.5061 Jct SH-55 & US-23 go N on US-23 for .2 mile
Taylor	◇ 1		🕐	℞	🚐	7555 Telegraph Rd, 48180 / 313-292-3474 • *Lat:* 42.2526 *Lon:* -83.2697 I-94 Exit 202 take US-24 S .9 mile
Three Rivers	◇		🕐	℞	🚐	101 S Tolbert Dr, 49093 / 269-273-7820 • *Lat:* 41.9425 *Lon:* -85.6517 1 mile west of town center near US-131/SH-60 jct
Traverse City	▣			℞	🚐	2401 US Hwy 31 S, 49684 / 231-946-8777 • *Lat:* 44.7213 *Lon:* -85.6462 Jct SH-37 & US-31 (S of town) take US-31 N 3.5 miles
	○			℞		2640 Crossing Cir, 49684 / 231-933-8800 • *Lat:* 44.7250 *Lon:* -85.6344 Jct US-31 & SH-37 (S of town) go N on US-31 for 3.6 miles then E on Airport Rd .6 mile
Troy	○ 4			℞		2001 W Maple Rd, 48084 / 248-435-4035 • *Lat:* 42.5475 *Lon:* -83.1766 I-75 Exit 69 take Big Beaver Rd W 1.2 miles, Livermore Rd S 1 mile & Maple Rd W 1.5 miles
Utica	▣ 9			℞	🚐	45600 Utica Park Blvd, 48315 / 586-726-9800 • *Lat:* 42.6295 *Lon:* -83.0089 I-94 Exit 240 take SH-59 W 7.9 miles then N at Utica Park Blvd .2 mile
Waterford	□ 7			℞	🚐	495 Summit Dr, 48328 / 248-738-5400 • *Lat:* 42.6461 *Lon:* -83.3336 I-75 Exit 77 take SH-59 W 5.3 miles then Telegraph Rd N .8 mile & Mall Dr W .3 mile
West Branch	◆ 1		🕐	℞	🚐	2750 Cook Rd, 48661 / 989-343-1309 • *Lat:* 44.2536 *Lon:* -84.2254 I-75 Exit 212 go N on Cook Rd .4 mile
White Lake	○			℞	🚐	9190 Highland Rd, 48386 / 248-698-9601 • *Lat:* 42.6571 *Lon:* -83.4677 Jct S Williams Lake Rd & Highland Rd/SH-59 (E of town) go W on SH-59 for 1.4 miles
Woodhaven	○ 2			℞	🚐	23800 Allen Rd, 48183 / 734-675-4360 • *Lat:* 42.1354 *Lon:* -83.2261 I-75 Exit 32 go E on "W" Rd .8 mile then S on Allen Rd .3 mile
Ypsilanti	▣ 2				🚐	5450 Carpenter Rd, 48197 / 734-434-1326 • *Lat:* 42.2093 *Lon:* -83.6797 I-94 Exit 180 take US-23 S 1.4 miles to Exit 34, US-12 NE .4 mile then N on Carpenter Rd
	○ 2			℞		2515 Ellsworth Rd, 48197 / 734-434-5620 • *Lat:* 42.2304 *Lon:* -83.6494 I-94 Exit 181, NE on Michigan Ave .6 mile, N on Hewitt Rd .2 mile & W on Ellsworth Rd .3 mile

○ Wal-Mart   ◇ Supercenter   □ Sam's Club   ▣ Gas   ■ Gas & Diesel

Minnesota

○ Wal-Mart ◇ Supercenter ☐ Sam's Club ▨ Gas ■ Gas & Diesel

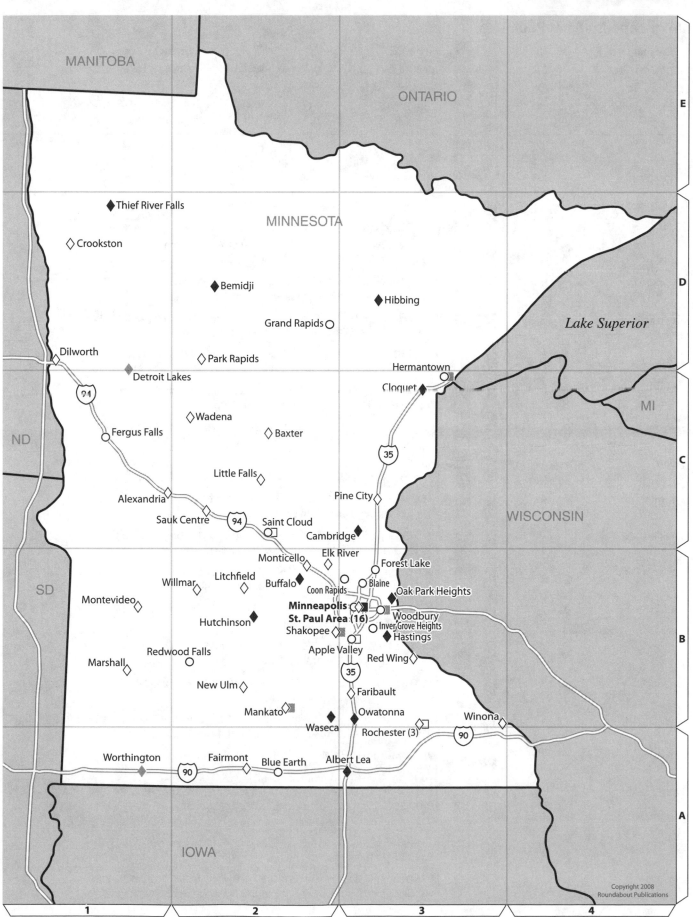

MANITOBA

ONTARIO

MINNESOTA

◆ Thief River Falls

◇ Crookston

◆ Bemidji

◆ Hibbing

Grand Rapids ○

Lake Superior

◇ Park Rapids

Dilworth

Hermantown ○
Cloquet ◆

◆ Detroit Lakes

ND

◇ Wadena

◇ Baxter

Fergus Falls ○

MI

Little Falls ◇

Alexandria ◇

Pine City ◇

WISCONSIN

Sauk Centre ◇ 94

Saint Cloud ☐

Cambridge ◆

Elk River

Monticello ◇

Forest Lake ○

SD

Litchfield ◇

Willmar ◇

Buffalo ◆

Blaine ○

Coon Rapids ○

Oak Park Heights ◆

Montevideo ◇

Minneapolis
St. Paul Area (16)

Woodbury
Inver Grove Heights

Hutchinson ◆

Shakopee ◇ ▨

Hastings ■

Redwood Falls ◇

Apple Valley ☐

Marshall ◇

Red Wing ◇

New Ulm ◇

Faribault ◇

Mankato ▨

Owatonna ◇

Winona ☐

Waseca ◆

Rochester (3) ☐

90

Worthington ▨

Fairmont ◇

Blue Earth ○

Albert Lea ◆

90

IOWA

Minneapolis / Saint Paul Area

Bloomington	○	Fridley (2)	○	□	Vadnais Heights	○
Brooklyn Park	○	Maple Grove (2)	◇	■	White Bear Lake	□
Eagan (2)	○ ■	Minneapolis (3)	○	■		
Eden Prairie	○	Saint Paul (2)	○			

City/Town	⬠	🕐	℞	🚌	Information
Albert Lea	◆ 1	🕐	℞	🚌	1550 Blake Ave, 56007 / 507-377-2998 • *Lat:* 43.6560 *Lon:* -93.3287 I-35 Exit 11 take CR-46 W .4 mile then S at Olsen Dr .2 mile
Alexandria	◇ 1	🕐	℞	🚌	4611 MN Hwy 29 S, 56308 / 320-762-8945 • *Lat:* 45.8478 *Lon:* -95.3878 I-94 Exit 103 take SH-29 N .4 mile
Apple Valley	□ 4		℞	🚌	14940 Florence Trl, 55124 / 952-432-1200 • *Lat:* 44.7331 *Lon:* -93.2022 I-35E Exit 88B go E 4 miles on SH-42, left at Foliage Ave, right at Florence Trail
	○ 6		℞	🚌	7835 150th St W, 55124 / 952-431-9700 • *Lat:* 44.7321 *Lon:* -93.2240 I-35E Exit 92 merge onto SH-77 S 4 miles then E on 150th St 2 miles
Baxter	◇	🕐	℞	🚌	7295 Glory Rd, 56425 / 218-829-2220 • *Lat:* 46.3444 *Lon:* -94.2529 Jct SH-210 & SH-371 (in town) take SH-371 S .5 mile & Glory Rd W .3 mile
Bemidji	◆	🕐	℞	🚌	2025 Paul Bunyan Dr NW, 56601 / 218-755-6120 • *Lat:* 47.4951 *Lon:* -94.9081 2.7 miles northwest of town via SH-197, just east of US-71
Blaine	○ 1		℞	🚌	4405 Pheasant Ridge Dr NE, 55449 / 763-784-0147 • *Lat:* 45.1646 *Lon:* -93.1577 I-35W Exit 33 take CR-17 N .1 mile & Pheasant Ridge Dr NE .4 mile
Bloomington	○ 1		℞		715 E 78th St, 55420 / 952-854-5600 • *Lat:* 44.8618 *Lon:* -93.2653 I-494 Exit 3 merge onto 78th St SE .1 mile
Blue Earth	○ 1		℞		1210 Giant Dr, 56013 / 507-526-4766 • *Lat:* 43.6515 *Lon:* -94.0950 I-90 Exit 119 take US-169 S .6 mile & W on Fairgrounds Rd
Brooklyn Park	○ 2		℞		8000 Lakeland Ave N, 55445 / 763-424-4842 • *Lat:* 45.0995 *Lon:* -93.3871 I-94 Exit 31 take CR-81 N .9 mile, 73rd Ave E .1 mile & Broadway S .1 mile
Buffalo	◆ 9	🕐	℞	🚌	1315 Hwy 25 N, 55313 / 763-682-2958 • *Lat:* 45.1881 *Lon:* -93.8763 I-94 Exit 193 take SH-25 S 8.6 miles
Cambridge	◆	🕐	℞	🚌	2101 2nd Ave SE, 55008 / 763-689-0606 • *Lat:* 45.5713 *Lon:* -93.2054 I-35 Exit 147 take SH-95 NW 11.8 miles & S at McKinley .1 mile
Cloquet	◆ 2	🕐	℞	🚌	1308 Hwy 33 S, 55720 / 218-878-0737 • *Lat:* 46.7016 *Lon:* -92.4567 I-35 Exit 237 merge onto SH-33 N 1.2 miles
Coon Rapids	○		℞		13020 Riverdale Dr NW, 55448 / 763-421-2622 • *Lat:* 45.2072 *Lon:* -93.3593 I-35W Exit 30 take US-10 W 10.5 miles, CR-9 N .1 mile & Northdale Blvd W
Crookston	◇	🕐	℞		1930 Sahlstrom Dr, 56716 / 218-281-2970 • *Lat:* 47.7935 *Lon:* -96.6104 1.7 miles north of town off US-2 at Acres Dr
Detroit Lakes	◆	🕐	℞	🚌	1583 Hwy 10 W, 56501 / 218-847-1126 • *Lat:* 46.8286 *Lon:* -95.8788 Jct US-59 & US-10 (NW of town) take US-10 W 1.2 miles, Airport Rd S .1 mile & Frontage Rd E
Dilworth	◇ 3	🕐	℞	🚌	415 34th St N, 56529 / 218-233-9822 • *Lat:* 46.8836 *Lon:* -96.7256 I-94 Exit 2 go N on 34th St 2.2 miles
Eagan	■ 1		℞	🚌	3035 Denmark Ave, 55121 / 651-405-0079 • *Lat:* 44.8467 *Lon:* -93.1498 I-35E Exit 98 go E on Lone Oak Rd .1 mile & S at Denmark Ave .1 mile

○ Wal-Mart   ◇ Supercenter   □ Sam's Club   ■ Gas   ■ Gas & Diesel

City/Town	⬤	🕐	℞	🚗	Information
	○ 1		℞		1360 Town Centre Dr, 55123 / 651-686-7428 • *Lat:* 44.8298 *Lon:* -93.1647 I-35E Exit 97 take Pine Knob Rd S .1 mile, Duckwood Dr E .1 mile & Town Centre Dr N .2 mile
Eden Prairie	○ 2		℞		12195 Singletree Ln, 55344 / 952-829-9040 • *Lat:* 44.8570 *Lon:* -93.4317 I-494 Exit 11A take US-212 W .9 mile, Prairie Center Dr W .4 mile & Singletree Ln N .2 mile
Elk River	◇ 9	🕐	℞	🚗	18185 Zane St NW, 55330 / 763-441-3461 • *Lat:* 45.2994 *Lon:* -93.5507 I-94 Exit 207 go N 6.9 miles on SH-101 and .8 mile N on US-169 to Main St then E .1 mile and S .3 mile on Zane St
Fairmont	◇ 1	🕐	℞	🚗	1250 Goemann Rd, 56031 / 507-235-2500 • *Lat:* 43.6816 *Lon:* -94.4478 I-90 Exit 102, north of exit
Faribault	◇ 1	🕐	℞	🚗	150 Western Ave NW, 55021 / 507-332-0232 • *Lat:* 44.2912 *Lon:* -93.3031 I-35 Exit 56 take SH-60 E .6 mile & S on Western Ave .2 mile
Fergus Falls	○ 1		℞		3300 MN Hwy 210 W, 56537 / 218-739-5552 • *Lat:* 46.2894 *Lon:* -96.1166 I-94 Exit 54 take SH-210 W .3 mile
Forest Lake	○ 1		℞	🚗	200 12th St SW, 55025 / 651-464-9740 • *Lat:* 45.2769 *Lon:* -92.9990 I-35 Exit 131 take CR-2 E .1 mile & 12th St S .2 mile
Fridley	□ 2		℞	🚗	8150 University Ave NE, 55432 / 763-784-4102 • *Lat:* 45.1158 *Lon:* -93.2634 I-694 Exit 37 go N on University Ave 1.7 miles
	○ 2		℞		8450 University Ave NE, 55432 / 763-780-9400 • *Lat:* 45.1235 *Lon:* -93.2655 I-694 Exit 37 take University Ave N 1.7 miles
Grand Rapids	○		℞		1400 S Pokegama Ave, 55744 / 218-326-9682 • *Lat:* 47.2166 *Lon:* -93.5286 Jct US-2 & US-169 (in town) go S on US-169 for 1.3 miles
Hastings	◆	🕐	℞	🚗	1752 N Frontage Rd, 55033 / 651-438-2400 • *Lat:* 44.7393 *Lon:* -92.8918 2 miles west of town off SH-55 at General Sieben Dr
Hermantown	▪ 6		℞	🚗	4743 Maple Grove Rd, 55811 / 218-722-1241 • *Lat:* 46.8077 *Lon:* -92.1789 I-35 Exit 255 take US-53 N 4.7 miles then W on Maple Grove Rd .7 mile
	○ 7		℞		4740 Mall Dr, 55811 / 218-727-1310 • *Lat:* 46.8128 *Lon:* -92.1766 I-35 Exit 255 take US-53 N 6.5 miles, Haines Rd S .1 mile & Mall Dr W .3 mile
Hibbing	◆	🕐	℞	🚗	12080 Hwy 169 W, 55746 / 218-262-2351 • *Lat:* 47.3989 *Lon:* -92.9767 Jct SH-73 & US-169 (SW of town) take US-169 E .2 mile
Hutchinson	◆	🕐	℞	🚗	1300 Hwy 15 S, 55350 / 320-587-1020 • *Lat:* 44.8948 *Lon:* -94.3928 Jct 5th Ave & Main St (in town) go S on Main St for 1.2 miles
Inver Grove Heights	○ 3		℞		9165 Cahill Ave, 55076 / 651-451-3975 • *Lat:* 44.8113 *Lon:* -93.0382 I-494 Exit 65 take 7th Ave S .6 mile, continue S on Cahill Ave 1.9 miles
Litchfield	◇		℞	🚗	2301 E Frontage Rd, 55355 / 320-693-1022 • *Lat:* 45.1183 *Lon:* -94.4920 1.8 miles east of town center along US-12
Little Falls	◇	🕐	℞	🚗	15091 18th St NE, 56345 / 320-632-9268 • *Lat:* 45.9754 *Lon:* -94.3346 1.8 miles east of town center along SH-27 at 18th St
Mankato	▪			🚗	1831 E Madison Ave, 56001 / 507-386-7600 • *Lat:* 44.1668 *Lon:* -93.9540 Jct of US-14/SH-22 east of town, S .5 mile on SH-22 then W on Madison Ave .2 mile
	◇	🕐	℞		1881 E Madison Ave, 56001 / 507-625-9318 • *Lat:* 44.1667 *Lon:* -93.9509 Jct US-14 & SH-22 (E of town) take SH-22 S .5 mile
Maple Grove	◼ 1		℞	🚗	16701 94th Ave N, 55311 / 763-416-5320 • *Lat:* 45.1248 *Lon:* -93.4923 I-94 Exit 213 go SW on 95th Ave .4 mile & Dunkirk Ln W .1 mile
	◇ 1	🕐	℞	🚗	9451 Dunkirk Ln N, 55311 / 763-420-3500 • *Lat:* 45.1258 *Lon:* -93.4916 I-94 Exit 213 take 95th Ave W .2 mile & Dunkirk Ln S
Marshall	◇	🕐	℞	🚗	1221 E Main St, 56258 / 507-532-9383 • *Lat:* 44.4339 *Lon:* -95.7709 Jct US-59 & SH-68 (NW of town) go N on SH-68 for 1 mile

○ Wal-Mart　◇ Supercenter　□ Sam's Club　▪ Gas　◼ Gas & Diesel

City/Town	⬡	🕐	℞	🚐	Information
Minneapolis	▣ 1		℞	🚐	200 American Blvd W, 55420 / 952-888-1050 • *Lat:* 44.8596 *Lon:* -93.2817 I-494 Exit 4A go S on Nicollet Ave .2 mile, W at American Blvd .2 mile
	☐ 5		℞	🚐	3745 Louisiana Ave S, 55426 / 952-924-9452 • *Lat:* 44.9354 *Lon:* -93.3680 I-394 Exit 3 take US-169 S for 2.7 miles, SH-7 E 1.5 miles & S at Louisiana Ave .2 mile
	○ 2		℞	🚐	3800 Silver Lake Rd NE, 55421 / 612-788-1303 • *Lat:* 45.0376 *Lon:* -93.2187 I-694 Exit 39 take CR-44 S 1.8 miles
Montevideo	◇	🕐	℞		3001 E Hwy 7, 56265 / 320-269-5390 • *Lat:* 44.9491 *Lon:* -95.6865 1.5 miles east of town center on SH-7
Monticello	◇ 1	🕐	℞	🚐	9320 Cedar St, 55362 / 763-295-9800 • *Lat:* 45.3033 *Lon:* -93.7941 I-94 Exit 193 take SH-25 N .3 mile & E at 7th St
New Ulm	◇	🕐	℞	🚐	1720 Westridge Rd, 56073 / 507-354-0900 • *Lat:* 44.3262 *Lon:* -94.4941 2.5 miles northwest of town center along US-14
Oak Park Heights	◇ 7	🕐	℞	🚐	5815 Norell Ave N, 55082 / 651-439-7476 • *Lat:* 45.0327 *Lon:* -92.8342 I-694 Exit 52 take SH-36 E 6.7 miles & S at Norrelle Ave .3 mile
Owatonna	◆ 1	🕐	℞	🚐	1130 W Frontage Rd, 55060 / 507-455-0049 • *Lat:* 44.0966 *Lon:* -93.2458 I-35 Exit 42 go W on US-14 to Frontage Rd N for .1 mile
Park Rapids	◇	🕐	℞	🚐	1303 Charles St, 56470 / 218-732-0339 • *Lat:* 46.9237 *Lon:* -95.0349 1.3 miles east of town center off SH-34 at SH-81 (Henrietta Ave)
Pine City	◇ 1	🕐	℞	🚐	950 11th St SW, 55063 / 320-629-5845 • *Lat:* 45.8224 *Lon:* -92.9775 I-35 Exit 169 take CR-7 W .3 mile & N at 11th St
Red Wing	◇	🕐	℞	🚐	295 Tyler Rd S, 55066 / 651-385-0003 • *Lat:* 44.5662 *Lon:* -92.5851 Jct SH-19 & US-61 (E of town) take US-61 S 2.8 miles & S at Tyler Rd
Redwood Falls	○		℞		1410 E Bridge St, 56283 / 507-644-6278 • *Lat:* 44.5413 *Lon:* -95.0915 Jct SH-101 & US-71 (E of town) go E on US-71/Bridge St for .2 mile
Rochester	☐			🚐	3410 55th St NW, 55901 / 507-281-8355 • *Lat:* 44.0794 *Lon:* -92.5130 I-90 Exit 218 take US-52 N 13.4 miles to Exit 59 then W at 55th St .3 mile
	◇ 7	🕐	℞	🚐	25 25th St SE, 55904 / 507-292-0909 • *Lat:* 43.9856 *Lon:* -92.4612 I-90 Exit 218 take US-52 N 5.5 miles then US-63 N .8 mile & 25th St E
	◇	🕐	℞	🚐	3400 55th St NW, 55901 / 507-280-7733 • *Lat:* 44.0794 *Lon:* -92.5129 Jct US-14 & CR-22 (W of town) go N on CR-22 for 3.3 miles
Saint Cloud	☐ 5			🚐	3601 2nd St S, 56301 / 320-253-8882 • *Lat:* 45.5498 *Lon:* -94.2020 I-94 Exit 167 take SH-15 N 4.1 miles then E at 2nd St .2 mile
	○ 5		℞		380 33rd Ave S, 56301 / 320-259-1527 • *Lat:* 45.5455 *Lon:* -94.1971 I-94 Exit 167 take SH-15 N 4.1 miles, 2nd St E .3 mile & 33rd Ave S .4 mile
Saint Paul	○ 1		℞		1450 University Ave W, 55104 / 651-644-0020 • *Lat:* 44.9555 *Lon:* -93.1614 I-94 Exit 239 merge onto St Anthony Ave W .3 mile, Pascal St N .2 mile & University Ave E
	○ 2		℞	🚐	1644 Robert St S, 55118 / 651-453-0343 • *Lat:* 44.8967 *Lon:* -93.0804 I-494 Exit 67 take SH-3 N 1.7 miles
Sauk Centre	◇ 1	🕐	℞	🚐	205 12th St S, 56378 / 320-352-7954 • *Lat:* 45.7233 *Lon:* -94.9472 I-94 Exit 127 take US-71 N .1 mile & 12th St E .2 mile
Shakopee	▣ 7		℞	🚐	8201 Old Carriage Ct, 55379 / 952-496-1979 • *Lat:* 44.7798 *Lon:* -93.4150 I-494 Exit 10 take US-169 S 5.7 miles then CR-18 S .9 mile & W on Old Carriage Rd .1 mile
	◇ 7	🕐	℞	🚐	8101 Old Carriage Ct, 55379 / 952-445-8013 • *Lat:* 44.7779 *Lon:* -93.4153 I-494 Exit 10 take US-169 S 5.7 miles, CR-18 S .9 mile & Old Carriage Rd W .1 mile
Thief River Falls	◆	🕐	℞	🚐	1755 Hwy 59 S, 56701 / 218-683-3643 • *Lat:* 48.1080 *Lon:* -96.1490 Jct CR-7 & US-59 (S of town) take US-59 N 2.6 miles
Vadnais Heights	○ 1		℞	🚐	850 County Rd E E, 55127 / 651-486-7001 • *Lat:* 45.0501 *Lon:* -93.0650 I-35E Exit 115 go W on CR-E .3 mile

○ Wal-Mart   ◇ Supercenter   ☐ Sam's Club   ▨ Gas   ▪ Gas & Diesel

City/Town	⬡	⏲	℞	🚐	Information
Wadena	◇	⏲	℞		100 Juniper Ave, 56482 / 218-631-1068 • Lat: 46.4579 Lon: -95.1532 Jct US-71 & US-10 (in town) take US-10 W 1 mile, 640th Ave N .6 mile & Juniper Ave E .2 mile
Waseca	◆	⏲	℞		2103 State St N, 56093 / 507-835-2250 • Lat: 44.0967 Lon: -93.5073 I-35 Exit 42 take US-14 W 13.4 miles & SH-13 N 1.3 miles
White Bear Lake	☐ 1		℞	🚐	1850 Buerkle Rd, 55110 / 651-779-6535 • Lat: 45.0398 Lon: -93.0218 I-694 Exit 50 go NW on White Bear Ave .2 mile & W at Buerkle Rd .2 mile
Willmar	◇	⏲	℞		700 19th Ave SE, 56201 / 320-231-3456 • Lat: 45.1034 Lon: -95.0354 2 miles southeast of town center, east of US-71 at 19th Ave
Winona	◇ 1	⏲	℞	🚐	955 Frontenac Dr, 55987 / 507-452-0102 • Lat: 44.0347 Lon: -91.6193 I-90 Exit 252 follow SH-43 N 7.2 miles & Frontenac Dr E .2 mile
Woodbury	◼ 1		℞	🚐	9925 Hudson Pl, 55125 / 651-702-7970 • Lat: 44.9451 Lon: -92.9053 I-94 Exit 251 go S on CR-19 for .2 mile then W on Hudson Rd .1 mile
	○ 1		℞	🚐	10240 Hudson Rd, 55129 / 651-735-5181 • Lat: 44.9451 Lon: -92.9001 I-94 Exit 251 take CR-19 S .3 mile & Hudson Rd E .4 mile
Worthington	◆ 1	⏲	℞	🚐	1055 Ryans Rd, 56187 / 507-376-6446 • Lat: 43.6349 Lon: -95.5934 I-90 Exit 43 take US-59 S .3 mile & Ryans Rd E

Mississippi

○ Wal-Mart   ◇ Supercenter   □ Sam's Club   ▮ Gas   ■ Gas & Diesel

TENNESSEE

Southhaven   Olive Branch   Corinth
Hernando   Holly Springs   Iuka
Senatobia   Ripley   Booneville
New Albany
Batesville   Oxford   Tupelo (3)
Clarksdale   Pontotoc   Fulton

ARKANSAS

55

Amory

Cleveland   Houston

West Point   Columbus
Indianola   Grenada
Greenwood   Winona   Starkville
Greenville

Louisville

MISSISSIPPI   Kosciusko

Philadelphia
Carthage

Madison
Ridgeland
Clinton   Flowood   Forest
20   Jackson   Pearl   Newton   20   Meridian (3)
Vicksburg   Richland

LOUISIANA   ALABAMA

59

Hazlehurst   Magee

55   Laurel   Waynesboro

Natchez   Brookhaven   Petal

McComb   Columbia   Hattiesburg (3)

Lucedale
59   Wiggins

Picayune   Diberville   Ocean Springs
Gulfport   10
Waveland   Biloxi   Pascagoula

Gulf of Mexico

Copyright 2008
Roundabout Publications

1   2   3   4

City/Town	🛡	🕐	Rx	🚗	Information
Amory	◆		🕐 Rx 🚗		1515 Hwy 278 E, 38821 / 662-256-1590 • Lat: 33.9833 Lon: -88.4671 Jct SH-25 & US-278 (S of town) go E on US-278 for 2 miles
Batesville	◆ 2		🕐 Rx 🚗		205 House Carlson Dr, 38606 / 662-563-3100 • Lat: 34.3090 Lon: -89.9165 I-55 Exit 243A take US-278 E .7 mile, Medical Center Dr S & House Carlson Dr W .4 mile
Biloxi	○ 6		Rx 🚗		2381 Pass Rd, 39531 / 228-385-1046 • Lat: 30.4018 Lon: -88.9749 I-110 Exit 1B take US-90 W 5.2 miles, Beauvoir Ave N .7 mile & Pass Rd W
Booneville	○		Rx		200 Wal-Mart Cir, 38829 / 662-728-6211 • Lat: 34.6773 Lon: -88.5617 Jct US-45 & SH-145 (N of town) take SH-145 S 3.7 miles & W at Wal-Mart Cir
Brookhaven	◆ 1		🕐 Rx 🚗		960 Brookway Blvd, 39601 / 601-835-0232 • Lat: 31.5792 Lon: -90.4652 I-55 Exit 40 take Brookway Blvd E .9 mile
Carthage	◆		🕐 Rx		905 Hwy 16 W, 39051 / 601-267-8374 • Lat: 32.7291 Lon: -89.5450 Jct SH-35 & SH-16 (in town) take SH-16 E .3 mile
Clarksdale	◆		🕐 Rx 🚗		1000 S State St, 38614 / 662-627-1133 • Lat: 34.1829 Lon: -90.5923 Jct US-278 & SH-322 (S of town) follow SH-322 W 4.2 miles
Cleveland	◆		🕐 Rx 🚗		710 N Davis Ave, 38732 / 662-843-6567 • Lat: 33.7561 Lon: -90.7156 .5 mile north of town along US-61/US-278
Clinton	◆ 3		🕐 Rx 🚗		950 Hwy 80 E, 39056 / 601-924-9096 • Lat: 32.3286 Lon: -90.3047 I-20 Exit 35 take US-80 E 2.2 miles
Columbia	◆		🕐 Rx 🚗		1001 Hwy 98 Byp, 39429 / 601-731-1193 • Lat: 31.2421 Lon: -89.8116 Jct SH-13 & US-98 (S of town) go E on US-98 for 1.1 miles
Columbus	◆		🕐 Rx 🚗		1913 Hwy 45 N, 39705 / 662-329-4810 • Lat: 33.5314 Lon: -88.4370 Jct US-82 & US-45 (SW of town) follow US-45 N 5.7 miles
Corinth	◆		🕐 Rx 🚗		2301 S Harper Rd, 38834 / 662-287-3148 • Lat: 34.9279 Lon: -88.4951 Jct US-72 & CR-404/Harper Rd (SE of town) go S on Harper Rd .2 mile
Diberville	◇ 1		🕐 Rx 🚗		3615 Sangani Blvd, 39540 / 228-396-4740 • Lat: 30.4586 Lon: -88.8947 I-10 Exit 46 take SH-15 N .6 mile then E on Sangani Blvd
Flowood	◇		🕐 Rx 🚗		5341 Lakeland Dr, 39232 / 601-992-8898 • Lat: 32.3527 Lon: -90.0240 I-55 Exit 98B go E 8.5 miles on Lakeland Dr (SH-25)
Forest	◆ 4		Rx 🚗		1309 Hwy 35 S, 39074 / 601-469-2122 • Lat: 32.3431 Lon: -89.4830 I-20 Exit 88 take SH-35 N 3.6 miles
Fulton	◆		🕐 Rx		100 Interchange Dr, 38843 / 662-862-2143 • Lat: 34.2611 Lon: -88.4017 From US-78 Exit 104 take SH-25 S
Greenville	◆		🕐 Rx 🚗		1831 Martin Luther King Blvd N, 38703 / 662-332-9026 • Lat: 33.3664 Lon: -91.0354 Jct US-82 & Old Hwy 61 (E of town) go S on Old Hwy 61 for 5.2 miles
Greenwood	◆		🕐 Rx 🚗		2202 Hwy 82 W, 38930 / 662-453-4656 • Lat: 33.5271 Lon: -90.2150 Jct US-278 & SH-1 (in town) follow SH-1 S 5 miles & Wilcox Rd E 1.4 miles
Grenada	◇ 1		🕐 Rx 🚗		1655 Sunset Dr, 38901 / 662-229-0114 • Lat: 33.7843 Lon: -89.8333 I-55 Exit 206 take SH-8 E 1 mile
Gulfport	□ 1		🚗		15065 Creosote Rd, 39503 / 228-864-3061 • Lat: 30.4275 Lon: -89.0894 I-10 Exit 34 take US-49 S .6 mile then E on Creosote Rd .2 mile
	◆ 2		🕐 Rx 🚗		9350-A Hwy 49, 39503 / 228-864-5197 • Lat: 30.4219 Lon: -89.0921 I-10 Exit 34 take US-49 S 1.1 miles
Hattiesburg	■ 3		🚗		6080 US Hwy 98, 39402 / 601-261-2171 • Lat: 31.2369 Lon: -89.2109 I-59 Exit 65 take US-98 W 2.5 miles
	◇ 2		🕐 Rx 🚗		6072 US Hwy 98, 39402 / 601-261-9393 • Lat: 31.3215 Lon: -89.3794 I-59 Exit 65 merge onto US-98 W 1.9 miles
	◇ 4		🕐 Rx 🚗		5901 Hwy 49, 39402 / 601-296-6855 • Lat: 31.3503 Lon: -89.3387 I-59 Exit 67 merge onto US-49 S 3.9 miles

○ Wal-Mart   ◇ Supercenter   □ Sam's Club   ▨ Gas   ■ Gas & Diesel

City/Town	⬡	🕐	℞	🚗	Information
Hazlehurst	◇ 1	🕐	℞	🚗	527 Lake St, 39083 / 601-894-1673 • Lat: 31.8667 Lon: -90.4022 I-55 Exit 61 take SH-28 E .4 mile then Lake St S .6 mile
Hernando	◆ 1	🕐	℞	🚗	2600 Mcingvale Rd, 38632 / 662-429-3456 • Lat: 34.8224 Lon: -89.9718 I-55 Exit 280 take SH-340 E .3 mile then Mcingvale Rd S .1 mile
Holly Springs	◇	🕐	℞		950 Mackie Dr, 38635 / 662-252-2211 • Lat: 34.7452 Lon: -89.4574 1.9 miles south of town center, south of US-78 Exit 30 at SH-4/SH-7
Houston	○		℞		660 E Madison St, 38851 / 662-456-5711 • Lat: 33.8960 Lon: -88.9898 Jct SH-15 & SH-8 go E on SH-8/Madison St .6 mile
Indianola	◆	🕐	℞	🚗	633 Hwy 82 W, 38751 / 662-887-3320 • Lat: 33.4577 Lon: -90.6615 Jct US-49W & US-82 (NE of town) take US-82 W .5 mile
Iuka	○		℞		1110 Battleground Dr, 38852 / 662-423-3054 • Lat: 34.8046 Lon: -88.2026 Jct US-72 & SH-25 (S of town) take SH-25 N 1.1 miles
Jackson	■ 1		℞	🚗	6360 Ridgewood Court Dr, 39211 / 601-977-0139 • Lat: 32.3961 Lon: -90.1436 I-55 Exit 102 merge onto Frontage Rd N .8 mile then E on Ridgewood Ct Dr
	◆ 1	🕐	℞	🚗	2711 Greenway Dr, 39204 / 601-922-3406 • Lat: 32.2906 Lon: -90.2643 I-20 Exit 40B go S on Robinson Rd .5 mile & Greenway Dr W .2 mile
Kosciusko	◇	🕐	℞		220 Veterans Memorial Dr, 39090 / 662-289-3422 • Lat: 33.0373 Lon: -89.5571 Jct SH-12 & SH-35 (in town) follow SH-35 SE for 1.4 miles
Laurel	◇ 2	🕐	℞	🚗	1621 Hwy 15 N, 39440 / 601-649-6191 • Lat: 31.7090 Lon: -89.1484 I-59 Exit 95 merge onto CR-15 N 1.7 miles
Louisville	◆	🕐	℞		159 Hwy 15 S, 39339 / 662-773-7823 • Lat: 33.1216 Lon: -89.0843 1.8 miles west of town center at SH-14/SH-15 jct
Lucedale	◆	🕐	℞	🚗	11228 Old 63 S, 39452 / 601-947-6991 • Lat: 30.9026 Lon: -88.5980 1.6 miles south of town center via SH-63
Madison	◇	🕐	℞	🚗	127 Grandview Dr, 39110 / 601-605-9662 • Lat: 32.5368 Lon: -90.1950 I-20 Exit 48 take SH-468 E 6.9 miles, SH-469 S 2.1 miles, Monterey Rd S 1.9 miles & Grandview Dr W
Magee	◆	🕐	℞	🚗	1625 Simpson Hwy 49, 39111 / 601-849-2628 • Lat: 31.8687 Lon: -89.7442 Jct SH-541 & US-49 (W of town) take US-49 N .4 mile
McComb	◇ 1	🕐	℞	🚗	1608 Veterans Blvd, 39648 / 601-684-1074 • Lat: 31.2605 Lon: -90.4719 I-55 Exit 18 go E on Smithdale Rd .5 mile
Meridian	■ 2			🚗	715 Bonita Dr, 39301 / 601-482-4833 • Lat: 32.3710 Lon: -88.6536 I-20/I-59 Exit 157A go S on US-45 .8 mile, W on SH-19 300 feet, right on Bonita Dr 1 mile
	◆ 1	🕐	℞	🚗	1733 2nd St S, 39301 / 601-485-2250 • Lat: 32.3651 Lon: -88.6949 I-20 Exit 153 take 22nd Ave NW .7 mile & 2nd St NE .3 mile
	◇ 3	🕐			2400 Hwy 19 N, 39307 / 601-482-0425 • Lat: 32.3840 Lon: -88.7508 I-20/59 Exit 150 follow SH-19 N 3 miles
Natchez	◆	🕐	℞	🚗	314 Sergeant Prentiss Dr, 39120 / 601-442-2895 • Lat: 31.5540 Lon: -91.3687 Jct US-84/98 & US-61 (W of town) follow US-61 SW 3.9 miles
New Albany	◆	🕐	℞	🚗	202 Park Plaza Dr, 38652 / 662-534-9374 • Lat: 34.4946 Lon: -89.0313 From US-78 Exit 61 take SH-30 W to Park Plaza Dr S .2 mile
Newton	◇ 2	🕐	℞		231 Eastside Dr, 39345 / 601-683-3393 • Lat: 32.3348 Lon: -89.1413 I-20 Exit 109 take SH-15 S 1.5 miles
Ocean Springs	◇ 6	🕐	℞	🚗	3911 Bienville Blvd, 39564 / 228-875-4036 • Lat: 30.4094 Lon: -88.7608 I-10 Exit 57 take SH-57 S 2.8 miles then US-90 W 2.5 miles
Olive Branch	◇ 10	🕐	℞	🚗	7950 Craft Goodman Frontage Rd, 38654 / 662-890-2500 • Lat: 34.9563 Lon: -89.9113 I-55 Exit 289 take SH-302 E 9 miles then Goodman Rd N .2 mile

○ Wal-Mart   ◇ Supercenter   □ Sam's Club   ▨ Gas   ■ Gas & Diesel

City/Town		🛡	🕐	℞	🚗	Information
Oxford	◇		🕐	℞	🚗	2530 Jackson Ave W, 38655 / 662-234-9131 • *Lat:* 34.3619 *Lon:* -89.5659 From US-278/SH-6 (W of town) take Jackson Ave W/SH-6 Bypass .4 mile
Pascagoula	◇	9	🕐	℞	🚗	4253 Denny Ave, 39581 / 228-762-9662 • *Lat:* 30.3840 *Lon:* -88.5183 I-10 Exit 75 take Franklin Creek Rd S .5 mile & US-90 W 7.6 miles
Pearl	◆	1	🕐	℞	🚗	5520 Hwy 80 E, 39208 / 601-939-0281 • *Lat:* 32.2839 *Lon:* -90.0469 I-20 Exit 54 take Greenfield Rd N .3 mile then US-80 W .6 mile
Petal	◇	8	🕐	℞		805 Hwy 42, 39465 / 601-584-6025 • *Lat:* 31.3495 *Lon:* -89.2343 I-59 Exit 67 merge onto US-49 S 1.3 miles then SH-42 E 6.1 miles
Philadelphia	◆		🕐	℞	🚗	1002 W Beacon St, 39350 / 601-656-4166 • *Lat:* 32.7697 *Lon:* -89.1287 Jct CR-15 & SH-16 (W of town) take SH-16 E .6 mile
Picayune	◆	1	🕐	℞	🚗	235 Frontage Rd, 39466 / 601-799-3455 • *Lat:* 30.5104 *Lon:* -89.6657 I-59 Exit 4 take SH-43 S .3 mile then S on Frontage Rd .6 mile
Pontotoc	◆		🕐	℞	🚗	100 McCord Rd, 38863 / 662-489-7451 • *Lat:* 34.2846 *Lon:* -89.0257 From US-78 Exit 64 take SH-15 S 13.2 miles
Richland	◆	5	🕐	℞	🚗	200 Market Place, 39218 / 601-939-0538 • *Lat:* 32.2149 *Lon:* -90.1543 I-20 Exit 47 take US-49 S 4.3 miles
Ridgeland	◇	2	🕐	℞		815 S Wheatley St, 39157 / 601-956-2717 • *Lat:* 32.4079 *Lon:* -90.1323 I-59 Exit 103 go E on County Line Rd .7 mile & N on Wheatley St .6 mile
Ripley	○			℞		822 City Ave S, 38663 / 662-837-0011 • *Lat:* 34.7228 *Lon:* -88.9497 Jct SH-4 & SH-15 (in town) take SH-15 S .6 mile
Senatobia	◆	2	🕐	℞	🚗	5219 Hwy 51 N, 38668 / 662-562-6202 • *Lat:* 34.6299 *Lon:* -89.9688 I-55 Exit 265 follow SH-4 W 1.5 miles then US-51 N .1 mile
Southaven	◇	1	🕐	℞	🚗	6811 Southcrest Pkwy, 38671 / 662-349-1838 • *Lat:* 34.9629 *Lon:* -89.9948 I-55 Exit 289 take SH-302 E .5 mile
	■	1		℞	🚗	465 Goodman Rd E, 38671 / 662-349-0723 • *Lat:* 34.9626 *Lon:* -89.9816 I-55 Exit 289 merge onto Goodman Rd E .4 mile
Starkville	◆		🕐	℞	🚗	1010 Hwy 12 W, 39759 / 662-324-0374 • *Lat:* 33.4451 *Lon:* -88.8462 Jct US-82 & SH-25 (NW of town) take SH-25 S 3.5 miles & SH-12 E .5 mile
Tupelo	■					🚗	3833 N Gloster St, 38804 / 662-840-6459 • *Lat:* 34.3128 *Lon:* -88.7071 Jct US-78 & US-45 (north of town) go N on US-45 for 1.2 miles, W on Barnes Crossing .5 mile, S on Gloster .2 mile
	◇		🕐	℞	🚗	2270 W Main St, 38801 / 662-844-4011 • *Lat:* 34.2561 *Lon:* -88.7404 US-78 Exit 85 take Natchez Trace Pkwy S 3.6 miles then SH-6 E 1.1 miles
	◇		🕐	℞	🚗	3929 N Gloster St, 38804 / 662-840-8401 • *Lat:* 34.3280 *Lon:* -88.7061 US-78 Exit 86 take US-45 N 1.5 miles, Barnes Crossing W .5 mile & Gloster St S .4 mile
Vicksburg	◇	2	🕐	℞	🚗	2150 Iowa Blvd, 39180 / 601-638-9164 • *Lat:* 32.3026 *Lon:* -90.8913 I-20 Exit 1C merge onto Halls Ferry Rd .3 mile, W on Frontage Rd .9 mile & Iowa Ave NW
Waveland	◆		🕐	℞	🚗	460 Hwy 90, 39576 / 228-467-4371 • *Lat:* 30.3046 *Lon:* -89.3835 I-10 Exit 2 take SH-607 S 5.8 miles & US-90 E 7.6 miles
Waynesboro	◆		🕐	℞	🚗	1350 Azalea Dr, 39367 / 601-735-9716 • *Lat:* 31.6711 *Lon:* -88.6531 Jct US-84 & SH-184 (W of town) go SE on SH-184/Azelea Dr 2.3 miles
West Point	◇		🕐	℞		1313 Hwy 45 S, 39773 / 662-494-1551 • *Lat:* 33.5863 *Lon:* -88.6590 1.5 miles south of town along US-45/SH-25
Wiggins	◆		🕐	℞	🚗	1053 Frontage Dr E, 39577 / 601-928-9119 • *Lat:* 30.8547 *Lon:* -89.1569 Jct SH-26 & US-49 (W of town) go NW on Frontage Rd .3 mile
Winona	○	3		℞		620 S Applegate St, 38967 / 662-283-3814 • *Lat:* 33.4705 *Lon:* -89.7356 I-55 Exit 185 take US-82 & US-182 E 1.7 miles & US-51 S 1.2 miles

○ Wal-Mart ◇ Supercenter □ Sam's Club ■ Gas ■ Gas & Diesel

Missouri

○ Wal-Mart ◇ Supercenter ☐ Sam's Club ▮ Gas ▮ Gas & Diesel

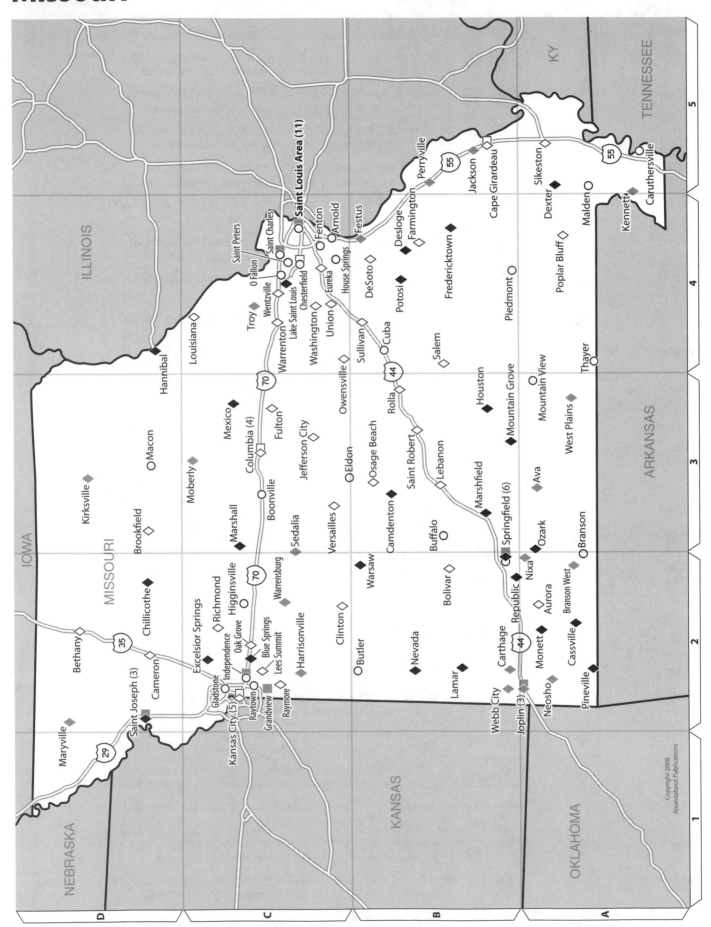

Copyright 2008
Roundabout Publications

Saint Louis Area

Ballwin	○		Kirkwood	○		Saint Ann	○
Des Peres	■		Maplewood (2)	○ ■		Saint Louis (5)	○ ■

City/Town	🛡	🕐	℞	🚗	Information
Arnold	○ 2		℞	🚗	2201 Michigan Ave, 63010 / 636-282-0297 • *Lat:* 38.4385 *Lon:* -90.3785 I-55 Exit 191 merge onto Big Bill Rd N .6 mile, US-67 S .5 mile & Michigan Ave W .4 mile
Aurora	◇	🕐	℞		3020 S Elliott Ave, 65605 / 417-678-5800 • *Lat:* 36.9475 *Lon:* -93.7188 I-44 Exit 46 follow SH-39 S 12.4 miles
Ava	◆	🕐	℞		1309 NW 12th Ave, 65608 / 417-683-4194 • *Lat:* 36.9624 *Lon:* -92.6773 Jct SH-5 & SH-14 (NW of town) go W on SH-14/12th Ave .2 mile
Ballwin	○ 3		℞	🚗	13901 Manchester Rd, 63011 / 636-256-0697 • *Lat:* 38.5967 *Lon:* -90.4855 I-270 Exit 9 take Manchester Rd W 2.2 miles
Bethany	◇ 1	🕐	℞		810 S 37th St, 64424 / 660-425-4410 • *Lat:* 40.2636 *Lon:* -94.0159 I-35 Exit 92 go W on US-136 .1 mile then S on 37th St .1 mile
Blue Springs	◆ 1	🕐	℞	🚗	600 NE Coronado, 64014 / 816-224-4800 • *Lat:* 39.0256 *Lon:* -94.2504 I-70 Exit 21 take Adams Pkwy S .2 mile & Coronado Dr E .1 mile
Bolivar	◇	🕐	℞	🚗	2451 S Springfield Ave, 65613 / 417-326-8424 • *Lat:* 37.5908 *Lon:* -93.4017 Jct SH-32 & SH-13/Springfield Ave (in town) go S on SH-13 for 1.7 miles
Boonville	○ 2		℞		1920 Main St, 65233 / 660-882-7422 • *Lat:* 38.9574 *Lon:* -92.7405 I-70 Exit 103 go N on SH-B 1.5 miles
Branson	○		℞	🚗	2050 W 76 Country Blvd, 65616 / 417-334-5005 • *Lat:* 36.6405 *Lon:* -93.2591 Jct US-65 & SH-76 (in town) go W on West 76 Country Blvd 2.2 miles
Branson West	◆	🕐	℞	🚗	18401 MO Hwy 13, 65737 / 417-272-8044 • *Lat:* 36.7008 *Lon:* -93.3698 Jct SH-265/413 & SH-13/76 (N of town) go S on SH-13 for .6 mile
Brookfield	◇	🕐	℞		937 Park Circle Dr, 64628 / 660-258-7416 • *Lat:* 39.7701 *Lon:* -93.0720 1.3 miles south of town center at US-36/SH-11 jct
Buffalo	○		℞		1250 W Dallas St, 65622 / 417-345-6166 • *Lat:* 37.6407 *Lon:* -93.1052 Jct US-65 & SH-32 (W of town) go W on SH-32/Dallas St .1 mile
Butler	○		℞	🚗	1005 W Fort Scott St, 64730 / 660-679-3151 • *Lat:* 38.2568 *Lon:* -94.3455 Jct US-71 & SH-52 (W of town) take SH-52 E .7 mile
Camdenton	◆	🕐	℞	🚗	94 Cecil St, 65020 / 573-346-3588 • *Lat:* 38.0229 *Lon:* -92.7256 Jct SH-5/7 & US-54 (in town) take US-54 NE 1.5 miles
Cameron	◇ 1	🕐	℞	🚗	2000 N Walnut St, 64429 / 816-632-9900 • *Lat:* 39.7532 *Lon:* -94.2341 I-35 Exit 54 follow I-35 BR .8 mile
Cape Girardeau	□ 1			🚗	232 Shirley Dr, 63701 / 573-334-8484 • *Lat:* 37.2983 *Lon:* -89.5837 I-55 Exit 96 go W on SH-K .1 mile, S on Siemers Dr .2 mile & W at Lambert Dr .2 mile
	◇ 1	🕐	℞	🚗	3439 William St, 63701 / 573-335-4600 • *Lat:* 37.3027 *Lon:* -89.5786 I-55 Exit 96 go W on SH-K .1 mile
Carthage	◆ 5	🕐	℞	🚗	2705 Grand Ave, 64836 / 417-358-3000 • *Lat:* 37.1420 *Lon:* -94.3107 I-44 Exit 18B take US-71 N 3.6 miles, SH-571 N .9 mile & Grand Ave N .2 mile
Caruthersville	○ 4		℞		1500 State Hwy 84 W, 63830 / 573-333-1262 • *Lat:* 36.2009 *Lon:* -89.6687 I-55 Exit 19 go E 4 miles on SH-84
Cassville	◆	🕐	℞	🚗	1401 Old Exeter Rd, 65625 / 417-847-3138 • *Lat:* 36.6758 *Lon:* -93.8832 Jct SH-76 & SH-37 (W of town) go N on SH-37 for .5 mile & E at Old Exeter Rd .1 mile

○ Wal-Mart ◇ Supercenter □ Sam's Club ■ Gas ■ Gas & Diesel

City/Town	♡	⏲	℞	🚐	Information
Chesterfield	□ 1		℞	🚐	196 THF Blvd, 63005 / 636-728-0359 • *Lat:* 38.6674 *Lon:* -90.5948 I-64 Exit 17 go S at Boone's Crossing .3 mile & E at THF Blvd .3 mile
	○ 1		℞	🚐	100 THF Blvd, 63005 / 636-536-4601 • *Lat:* 38.6675 *Lon:* -90.5903 I-64 Exit 17 take Boones Crossing S .2 mile, Airport Rd E .5 mile & Chesterfield Commons S .1 mile
Chillicothe	♦	⏲	℞	🚐	1000 Graves St, 64601 / 660-646-6000 • *Lat:* 39.7775 *Lon:* -93.5543 1 mile south of town off US-65 near intersection with US-36
Clinton	◇	⏲	℞	🚐	1712 E Ohio St, 64735 / 660-885-5536 • *Lat:* 38.3661 *Lon:* -93.7492 Jct SH-7 & SH-13 (E of town) go E on SH-7 for .2 mile
Columbia	□ 1		℞	🚐	101 Conley Rd, 65201 / 573-875-2979 • *Lat:* 38.9490 *Lon:* -92.2942 I-70 Exit 128A take US-63 S .2 mile, W on Interstate 70 Dr then S on Conley Rd
	◇ 1	⏲	℞	🚐	415 Conley Rd, 65201 / 573-499-4935 • *Lat:* 38.9527 *Lon:* -92.2938 I-70 Exit 128A go S on US-63 for .2 mile, W on Interstate Dr .1 mile & S on Conley Rd .5 mile
	◇ 2	⏲	℞	🚐	3001 W Broadway, 65203 / 573-445-9506 • *Lat:* 38.9549 *Lon:* -92.3810 I-70 Exit 124 take Stadium Blvd S .9 mile & SH-TT W .5 mile
	◇ 4	⏲	℞	🚐	1201 Grindstone Pkwy, 65201 / 573-449-0815 • *Lat:* 38.9130 *Lon:* -92.2982 I-70 Exit 128A go S on US-63 for 3 miles then W on SH-AC .8 mile
Cuba	○ 1		℞		100 Ozark Dr, 65453 / 573-885-2501 • *Lat:* 38.0730 *Lon:* -91.4046 I-44 Exit 208 go S on SH-19 & E on Ozark Dr .1 mile
De Soto	◇	⏲	℞	🚐	12862 Hwy 21, 63020 / 636-586-6878 • *Lat:* 38.1477 *Lon:* -90.5788 Jct SH-CC & SH-21 (S of town) take SH-21 N for 1.6 miles
Des Peres	▪ 2		℞	🚐	13455 Manchester Rd, 63131 / 314-822-7200 • *Lat:* 38.5995 *Lon:* -90.4690 I-270 Exit 9 go W on Manchester Rd 1.3 miles
Desloge	♦	⏲	℞	🚐	407 N State St, 63601 / 573-431-5094 • *Lat:* 37.8815 *Lon:* -90.5115 1.2 miles northeast of town center, just west of US-67 at Cedar Falls Rd Exit
Dexter	♦	⏲	℞	🚐	2025 W Business Hwy 60, 63841 / 573-624-5514 • *Lat:* 36.7996 *Lon:* -89.9613 Jct US-60 & SH-25 (NE of town) take US-60 W 1.7 miles, One Mile Rd S .5 mile & US-60 BR W .3 mile
Eldon	○		℞		1802 Hwy 54, 65026 / 573-392-3114 • *Lat:* 38.3202 *Lon:* -92.5878 Jct US-54 & US-54 BR (S of town) go N on US-54 BR 2.4 miles
Eureka	◇ 2	⏲	℞	🚐	131 Eureka Towne Center Dr, 63025 / 636-587-9836 • *Lat:* 38.5067 *Lon:* -90.6555 I-44 Exit 261 go N on Six Flags Rd .2 mile & E on 5th St 1.2 miles
Excelsior Springs	♦ 10	⏲	℞	🚐	2203 Patsy Ln, 64024 / 816-630-1003 • *Lat:* 39.3315 *Lon:* -94.2635 I-35 Exit 20 merge onto US-69 N 9.4 miles then S at McCleary Rd .1 mile
Farmington	◇	⏲	℞	🚐	701 Walton Dr, 63640 / 573-756-8448 • *Lat:* 37.7888 *Lon:* -90.4343 Jct US-67 & SH-32 (NW of town) take SH-32 SE .5 mile & Walton Dr S .2 mile
Fenton	○ 4		℞	🚐	653 Gravois Bluffs Blvd, 63026 / 636-349-3116 • *Lat:* 38.5080 *Lon:* -90.4411 I-270 Exit 3 follow SH-30 W 2.5 miles, SH-141 S .5 mile & Gravois Blvd E .1 mile
Festus	◆ 2	⏲	℞	🚐	650 S Truman Blvd, 63028 / 636-937-8441 • *Lat:* 38.2127 *Lon:* -90.3910 I-55 Exit 174A merge onto S Truman Blvd 1.4 miles
Fredericktown	♦	⏲	℞		1025 Walton Dr, 63645 / 573-783-5581 • *Lat:* 37.5600 *Lon:* -90.3219 1.7 miles west of town center near US-67/SH-72 jct
Fulton	◇ 6	⏲	℞		1701 N Bluff St, 65251 / 573-642-6877 • *Lat:* 38.8665 *Lon:* -91.9440 I-70 Exit 148 go S on US-54W 3.7 miles & US-54 BR/Bluff St S 1.5 miles
Gladstone	○ 4		℞	🚐	7207 North M1 Hwy, 64119 / 816-436-8900 • *Lat:* 39.2061 *Lon:* -94.5212 I-435 Exit 49A merge onto SH-152 W 1.9 miles then SH-1 S 1.6 miles

○ Wal-Mart   ◇ Supercenter   □ Sam's Club   ▪ Gas   ■ Gas & Diesel

City/Town	🛡	🕐	℞	🚗	Information
Grandview	■ 2			🚗	12420 S US Hwy 71, 64030 / 816-765-0600 • *Lat:* 38.8992 *Lon:* -94.5251 I-470 Exit 1 at US-71 go S 1.4 miles to Blue Ridge Blvd exit, go S .5 mile on Frontage Rd
Hannibal	◆ 1	🕐	℞	🚗	3650 Stardust Dr, 63401 / 573-221-5610 • *Lat:* 39.7230 *Lon:* -91.3993 From I-72/US-36 exit at US-61 and go N .5 mile then W at Stardust Dr .5 mile
Harrisonville	◆	🕐	℞	🚗	1700 N MO Hwy 291, 64701 / 816-884-5635 • *Lat:* 38.6659 *Lon:* -94.3670 Jct US-71 & SH-291 (NW of town) follow SH-291 N 1.9 miles
Higginsville	○ 6		℞	🚗	1180 W 19th St, 64037 / 660-584-7717 • *Lat:* 39.0769 *Lon:* -93.7369 I-70 Exit 49 take SH-13 N 5.4 miles then E on 19th St
House Springs	○ 10		℞		4550 Gravois Rd, 63051 / 636-375-3201 • *Lat:* 38.4095 *Lon:* -90.5723 I-44 Exit 264 follow SH-W 8.5 miles, continue on Gravois Rd .6 mile
Houston	◆	🕐	℞		1433 S Sam Houston Blvd, 65483 / 417-967-3302 • *Lat:* 37.3130 *Lon:* -91.9604 Jct SH-17 & US-63 (S of town) go S on US-63 for .3 mile
Independence	■ 1		℞	🚗	4100 S Bolger Rd, 64055 / 816-350-1687 • *Lat:* 39.0468 *Lon:* -94.3647 I-70 Exit 15B go W on 39th St .4 mile then N on Bolger .2 mile
	○ 1		℞	🚗	4000 S Bolger Rd, 64055 / 816-478-4090 • *Lat:* 39.0471 *Lon:* -94.3652 I-70 Exit 15B take SH-291 N .2 mile, 39th St W .4 mile & Bolger St N .2 mile
Jackson	◆ 2	🕐	℞		3051 E Jackson Blvd, 63755 / 573-243-3909 • *Lat:* 37.3640 *Lon:* -89.6333 I-55 Exit 99 follow I-55 BR/Jackson Blvd 1.9 miles
Jefferson City	◇	🕐	℞	🚗	724 W Stadium Blvd, 65109 / 573-635-8283 • *Lat:* 38.5719 *Lon:* -92.2474 Jct SH-179 & US-50 BR (W of town) go E on US-50 BR for .9 mile then S at Stadium Blvd
Joplin	■ 1		℞	🚗	3536 Hammons Blvd, 64804 / 417-623-6200 • *Lat:* 37.0488 *Lon:* -94.4748 I-44 Exit 8B, N to Hammons Blvd, turn right
	◆	🕐	℞	🚗	2623 W 7th St, 64801 / 417-206-4644 • *Lat:* 37.0847 *Lon:* -94.5458 I-44 Exit 15 follow I-44 BR/SH-66 W for 10.2 miles
	◇ 3	🕐	℞	🚗	1501 S Range Line Rd, 64804 / 417-781-0100 • *Lat:* 37.0740 *Lon:* -94.4775 I-44 Exit 8B go N on US-71 BR/Range Line Rd 2.4 miles
Kansas City	□ 1		℞	🚗	5110 N Oak Trfy, 64118 / 816-452-0005 • *Lat:* 39.1856 *Lon:* -94.5768 I-29 Exit 1C go N for .3 mile
	◇ 1	🕐	℞	🚗	11601 E US Hwy 40, 64133 / 816-313-1183 • *Lat:* 39.0466 *Lon:* -94.4421 I-70 Exit 11 take US-40 E .3 mile
	◇ 1	🕐	℞	🚗	8301 N Church Rd, 64158 / 816-792-4644 • *Lat:* 39.2427 *Lon:* -94.4616 I-35 Exit 16 go W on Barry Rd .3 mile & S on Church Rd .1 mile
	◇ 2	🕐	℞	🚗	8551 N Boardwalk Ave, 64154 / 816-741-1099 • *Lat:* 39.2491 *Lon:* -94.6566 I-29 Exit 8 go E on Barry Rd 1 mile then N on Boardwalk Ave .2 mile
	◇ 4	🕐	℞	🚗	1701 W 133rd St, 64145 / 816-942-3847 • *Lat:* 38.8864 *Lon:* -94.6059 I-435 Exit 75B go S on State Line Rd 3.5 miles & E at 133rd St .1 mile
Kennett	◆	🕐	℞	🚗	1500 1st St, 63857 / 573-888-2084 • *Lat:* 36.2368 *Lon:* -90.0400 I-55 Exit 17B take US-412 W 16.8 miles, continue on SH-84 .1 mile
Kirksville	◆	🕐	℞	🚗	2206 N Baltimore St, 63501 / 660-627-7100 • *Lat:* 40.2156 *Lon:* -92.5824 Jct US-63 & SH-6 (N of town) go S on US-63 for .1 mile
Kirkwood	○ 1		℞	🚗	1202 S Kirkwood Rd, 63122 / 314-835-9406 • *Lat:* 38.5629 *Lon:* -90.4067 I-44 Exit 277 follow US-61 N .3 mile
Lake Saint Louis	◆ 5	🕐	℞	🚗	6100 Ronald Reagan Dr, 63367 / 636-625-2101 • *Lat:* 38.7661 *Lon:* -90.7851 I-70 Exit 214 take Lake St Louis Blvd SW 3.2 miles then Reagan Dr S .9 mile
Lamar	◆	🕐	℞	🚗	29 SW 1st Ln, 64759 / 417-682-5516 • *Lat:* 37.4956 *Lon:* -94.3009 Jct US-71 & US-160 (W of town) take US-160 W .1 mile & 1st Ln N .1 mile

○ Wal-Mart ◇ Supercenter □ Sam's Club ■ Gas ■ Gas & Diesel

City/Town	⬡	🕐	℞	🚗	Information
Lebanon	◇ 1	🕐	℞	🚗	1800 S Jefferson Ave, 65536 / 417-588-2268 • *Lat:* 37.6631 *Lon:* -92.6493 I-44 Exit 129 take SH-5 S .5 mile
Lees Summit	◇ 3	🕐	℞	🚗	1000 NE Sam Walton Ln, 64086 / 816-246-4555 • *Lat:* 38.9293 *Lon:* -94.3647 I-470 Exit 10B merge onto SH-291 for 1.4 miles, Tudor Rd W .1 mile & Sam Walton Way S .3 mile
Louisiana	○		℞		3310 Georgia St, 63353 / 573-754-4573 • *Lat:* 39.4346 *Lon:* -91.0692 Jct SH-UU & US-54 (W of town) take US-54 N 1.8 miles then E on Kelly Ln .7 mile
Macon	○		℞	🚗	705 E Briggs Dr, 63552 / 660-385-5783 • *Lat:* 39.7522 *Lon:* -92.4640 Jct US-63 & US-36 (in town) go S on US-63 for .2 mile & E on Briggs Dr .2 mile
Malden	○		℞		1007 N Douglass St, 63863 / 573-276-5735 • *Lat:* 36.5701 *Lon:* -89.9708 Jct SH-153 & US-62 (E of town) take US-62 W 8.2 miles, SH-25 N 1 mile, Tom St W .7 mile & S on Douglass St
Maplewood	■ 1		℞	🚗	2100 Maplewood Commons Dr, 63143 / 314-644-7791 • *Lat:* 38.6211 *Lon:* -90.3330 I-64 Exit 32 go S on Hanley Rd .5 mile then E on Corcoran
	○ 1		℞	🚗	1900 Maplewood Commons Dr, 63143 / 314-781-2165 • *Lat:* 38.6226 *Lon:* -90.3329 I-64 Exit 32B go S on Hanley Rd .5 mile & E at Bruno Ave
Marshall	◆	🕐	℞	🚗	855 Cherokee Dr, 65340 / 660-886-6852 • *Lat:* 39.1131 *Lon:* -93.2136 I-70 Exit 78B take US-65 N 11.1 miles then W at Cherokee Dr
Marshfield	◆ 1	🕐	℞	🚗	14740 MO Hwy 38, 65706 / 417-468-3518 • *Lat:* 37.3314 *Lon:* -92.9100 I-44 Exit 100 follow SH-38 W .6 mile
Maryville	◆	🕐	℞	🚗	1605 S Main St, 64468 / 660-562-2994 • *Lat:* 40.3299 *Lon:* -94.8737 Jct SH-V & US-71 BR/S Main St (S of town) go S on US-71 BR .3 mile
Mexico	◆	🕐	℞	🚗	4820 S Clark St, 65265 / 573-581-4500 • *Lat:* 39.1517 *Lon:* -91.8879 I-70 Exit 148 go N on US-54 for 13.4 miles & US-54 BR N 2.4 miles
Moberly	◆	🕐	℞	🚗	1301 E Hwy 24, 65270 / 660-263-3113 • *Lat:* 39.4463 *Lon:* -92.4187 Jct US-63 & US-24 (NE of town) go E on US-24 for .2 mile
Monett	◆	🕐	℞	🚗	885 High St 60, 65708 / 417-235-6292 • *Lat:* 36.9270 *Lon:* -93.9395 I-44 Exit 44 follow SH-H 14.2 miles, Cleveland St W 1 mile, Eisenhower St S .1 mile & Scott St W .2 mile
Mountain Grove	◆	🕐	℞	🚗	2100 N Main Ave, 65711 / 417-926-5107 • *Lat:* 37.1463 *Lon:* -92.2626 Jct SH-95 & US-60 (N of town) go S on SH-95 for .3 mile
Mountain View	○		℞	🚗	101 W US Hwy 60, 65548 / 417-934-6000 • *Lat:* 37.0015 *Lon:* -91.7026 Jct SH-17 & US-60 (E of town) go W on US-60 for .8 mile
Neosho	◆	🕐	℞	🚗	3200 Lusk Dr, 64850 / 417-451-5544 • *Lat:* 36.8387 *Lon:* -94.3947 I-44 Exit 11 take US-71 S 16.1 miles, US-60 E 1.2 miles & Lusk Dr S
Nevada	◆	🕐	℞	🚗	2250 Lincoln Ave, 64772 / 417-667-3630 • *Lat:* 37.8336 *Lon:* -94.3278 From US-71 at Austin Blvd go W .4 mile then S on Barrett St .2 mile
Nixa	◆	🕐	℞	🚗	1102 N Massey Blvd, 65714 / 417-724-1097 • *Lat:* 37.0657 *Lon:* -93.3033 Jct SH-14 & US-160 (in town) go N on US-160/Massey Blvd 1.5 miles
O Fallon	○ 1		℞	🚗	1307 Hwy K, 63366 / 636-980-3700 • *Lat:* 38.7906 *Lon:* -90.6991 I-70 Exit 217 go S on SH-K .6 mile
Oak Grove	◇ 1	🕐	℞		201 S Salem St, 64075 / 816-690-4900 • *Lat:* 39.0154 *Lon:* -94.1238 I-70 Exit 28 go S on SH-H .3 mile, 4th St E .2 mile & Salem St N .2 mile
Osage Beach	◇	🕐	℞	🚗	4252 Hwy 54, 65065 / 573-348-6445 • *Lat:* 38.1477 *Lon:* -92.6206 Jct SH-134 & US-54 (N of town) go S on US-54 for .8 mile
Owensville	◇	🕐	℞		1888 Hwy 28, 65066 / 573-437-4156 • *Lat:* 38.3540 *Lon:* -91.4838 Jct SH-19 & SH-28 (S of town) go N on SH-28 for .9 mile

○ Wal-Mart ◇ Supercenter ☐ Sam's Club ▨ Gas ■ Gas & Diesel

City/Town	🛡	⏰	℞	🚗	Information
Ozark	◆		⏰	℞	🚗	2004 W Marler Ln, 65721 / 417-581-2761 • Lat: 37.0036 Lon: -93.2272 I-44 Exit 82A take US-65 S 17.2 miles, SH-F E .2 mile & Marler Ln S .1 mile
Perryville	◇ 8	⏰	℞		1750 S Perryville Blvd, 63775 / 573-547-2577 • Lat: 37.7041 Lon: -89.8945 I-55 Exit 129 take SH-51 S 7.8 miles
Piedmont	○		℞		15 Halls Plaza, 63957 / 573-223-7330 • Lat: 37.1433 Lon: -90.7009 Jct SH-34 & SH-49 (NE of town) go S on SH-49 for 2 miles & W at Hals Plaza Dr
Pineville	◆	⏰	℞	🚗	100 Commercial Ln, 64856 / 417-226-5800 • Lat: 36.5084 Lon: -94.2806 9 miles south of town along US-71
Poplar Bluff	◇	⏰	℞	🚗	333 S Westwood Blvd, 63901 / 573-686-6420 • Lat: 36.7555 Lon: -90.4083 Jct US-67 & SH-53 (SW of town) go N on US-67 BR .8 mile
Potosi	◆	⏰	℞		1 Memorial Dr, 63664 / 573-438-5441 • Lat: 37.9251 Lon: -90.7744 1.2 miles southeast of town center on SH-21, near the hospital
Raymore	◇	⏰	℞	🚗	2015 W Foxwood Dr, 64083 / 816-322-5455 • Lat: 38.8126 Lon: -94.4899 I-470 Exit 1 merge onto US-71 S 9.1 miles then E on SH-58 for 1.6 miles
Raytown	○ 2		℞	🚗	6709 Blue Ridge Blvd, 64133 / 816-358-7790 • Lat: 39.0022 Lon: -94.4821 I-435 Exit 67 take Gregory Blvd E 1 mile & N on Blue Ridge Blvd
Republic	◆	⏰	℞	🚗	1150 US Hwy 60 E, 65738 / 417-732-1473 • Lat: 37.1162 Lon: -93.4732 Jct SH-M & US-60 (N of town) go SW on US-60 for 1.5 miles
Richmond	◇	⏰	℞	🚗	908 Walton Way, 64085 / 816-776-5834 • Lat: 39.2645 Lon: -93.9619 1.5 miles southeast of town, south of SH-10/SH-13 jct
Rolla	◇ 2	⏰	℞	🚗	500 S Bishop Ave, 65401 / 573-341-9145 • Lat: 37.9393 Lon: -91.7775 I-44 Exit 185 go E on SH-E .3 mile, S on I-44 BR .6 mile & US-63 S .5 mile
Saint Ann	○ 2		℞		10835 Saint Charles Rock Rd, 63074 / 314-291-2300 • Lat: 38.7336 Lon: -90.3917 I-70 Exit 235 take Cypress Rd S .8 mile & St Charles Rock Rd E .4 mile
Saint Charles	■ 1		℞	🚗	2855 Veterans Memorial Pkwy, 63303 / 636-946-7002 • Lat: 38.7838 Lon: -90.5252 I-70 Exit 227 go S .1 mile to Veterans Memorial Pkwy then E .4 mile to store
	○ 2		℞	🚗	2897 Veterans Memorial Pkwy, 63303 / 636-947-8732 • Lat: 38.7844 Lon: -90.5262 I-70 Exit 228 take 1st Capitol Dr S .2 mile then Veterans Memorial Pkwy W .9 mile
Saint Joseph	■ 2		℞	🚗	5201 N Belt Hwy Bldg A, 64506 / 816-279-2192 • Lat: 39.8027 Lon: -94.8149 I-29 Exit 50 take US-169 S .7 mile, N at Green Acres Rd .4 mile & W on Blackwell Rd .2 mile
	◆ 2	⏰	℞	🚗	3022 S Belt Hwy, 64503 / 816-232-9819 • Lat: 39.7391 Lon: -94.8014 I-29 Exit 44 follow I-29 BR 1.7 miles
	◇ 2	⏰	℞	🚗	4201 N Belt Hwy, 64506 / 816-390-8400 • Lat: 39.8055 Lon: -94.8149 I-29 Exit 50 follow US-169 S 1.3 miles
Saint Louis	■ 1		℞	🚗	10248 Big Bend Rd, 63122 / 314-965-7076 • Lat: 38.5677 Lon: -90.3967 I-44 Exit 278 go W on Big Bend Blvd .2 mile
	■ 1		℞	🚗	10735 W Florissant Ave, 63136 / 314-521-3800 • Lat: 38.7650 Lon: -90.2807 I-270 Exit 29 go S on Florissant Ave .4 mile
	■ 2		℞	🚗	4512 Lemay Ferry Rd, 63129 / 314-892-9620 • Lat: 38.4988 Lon: -90.3361 I-55 Exit 195 go E on Butler Hill Rd .3 mile then N on Lemay Ferry Rd 1.3 miles
	○ 1		℞	🚗	3270 Telegraph Rd, 63125 / 314-845-8544 • Lat: 38.4978 Lon: -90.3002 I-255 Exit 2 go N on Telegraph Rd .3 mile
	○ 1		℞	🚗	10741 W Florissant Ave, 63136 / 314-521-3422 • Lat: 38.7651 Lon: -90.2807 I-270 Exit 29 go S on Florissant Ave .4 mile
Saint Peters	○ 2		℞	🚗	1661 Jungermann Rd, 63304 / 636-447-4450 • Lat: 38.7448 Lon: -90.5915 I-70 Exit 225 take Cave Springs Rd S .2 mile, Mexico Rd W .6 mile & Jungermann Rd S 1.1 miles

○ Wal-Mart   ◇ Supercenter   □ Sam's Club   ■ Gas   ■ Gas & Diesel

City/Town	⬡	🕐	℞	🚗	Information
Saint Robert	◇ 1	🕐	℞	🚗	185 Saint Robert Blvd, 65584 / 573-336-5103 • *Lat:* 37.8262 *Lon:* -92.1456 I-44 Exit 161B take SH-Y N .1 mile & Saint Robert Blvd W .6 mile
Salem	◇	🕐	℞		1101 W Hwy 32, 65560 / 573-729-6151 • *Lat:* 37.6360 *Lon:* -91.5463 Jct SH-19 & SH-32/72 (S of town) go W on SH-32/72 .6 mile
Sedalia	◆	🕐	℞	🚗	3201 W Broadway Blvd, 65301 / 660-826-7800 • *Lat:* 38.7092 *Lon:* -93.2675 I-70 Exit 78A take US-65 S 18.9 miles & US-50 W 1 mile
Sikeston	◇ 6	🕐	℞	🚗	1303 S Main St, 63801 / 573-472-3020 • *Lat:* 36.8546 *Lon:* -89.5826 I-55 Exit 67 take US-62 W 2.6 miles & US-61 NW 1.6 miles
Springfield	■ 6		℞	🚗	3660 E Sunshine St, 65809 / 417-882-5037 • *Lat:* 37.1800 *Lon:* -93.2197 I-44 Exit 82 take US-65 S 4.9 miles then E on Sunshine St .3 mile
	○ 3		℞	🚗	1923 E Kearney St, 65803 / 417-865-4545 • *Lat:* 37.2401 *Lon:* -93.2584 I-44 Exit 82A take US-65 S .8 mile & SH-744 W 1.8 miles
	◆ 5	🕐	℞	🚗	3520 W Sunshine St, 65807 / 417-862-7447 • *Lat:* 37.1828 *Lon:* -93.3499 I-44 Exit 72 take Chestnut Expy E 2.1 miles, US-160 S 2 miles & W on Sunshine St
	◇ 1	🕐	℞	🚗	2825 N Kansas Expy, 65803 / 417-865-8865 • *Lat:* 37.2479 *Lon:* -93.3111 I-44 Exit 77 follow SH-13 S .2 mile
	◇	🕐	℞	🚗	2021 E Independence St, 65804 / 417-886-8209 • *Lat:* 37.1415 *Lon:* -93.2575 I-44 Exit 82A take US-65 S 8.6 miles, follow US-65 BR 1.9 miles & W at Indpendence St .2 mile
	◇	🕐	℞		3315 S Campbell Ave, 65807 / 417-887-0855 • *Lat:* 37.1551 *Lon:* -93.2958 I-44 Exit 82A take US-65 S 6.4 miles, Battlefld St W 3.9 miles & Campbell Ave S .3 mile
Sullivan	◇ 1	🕐	℞	🚗	350 Park Ridge Rd, 63080 / 573-468-7030 • *Lat:* 38.2209 *Lon:* -91.1581 I-44 Exit 226 go E on SH-H .2 mile, Service Rd S .1 mile & E toward Park Ridge Rd
Thayer	○		℞		333 E Walnut St, 65791 / 417-264-7195 • *Lat:* 36.5233 *Lon:* -91.5408 Jct SH-19 & US-63 (N of town) take US-63 S 1.4 miles & W on Public Rd/Walnut St .3 mile
Troy	◆	🕐	℞	🚗	101 Hwy 47 E, 63379 / 636-528-8901 • *Lat:* 38.9855 *Lon:* -90.9843 I-70 Exit 193 follow SH-47 NE 18.9 miles
Union	◇ 4	🕐	℞		1445 E Central Ct, 63084 / 636-583-2355 • *Lat:* 38.4337 *Lon:* -90.9721 I-44 Exit 247 take US-50 W 3.2 miles, N on Prairie Dell & E at Central Ct
Versailles	◇	🕐	℞		1003 W Newton St, 65084 / 573-378-4668 • *Lat:* 38.4273 *Lon:* -92.8403 Jct SH-5 & SH-52 (W of town) take SH-52 W for .2 mile
Warrensburg	◆	🕐	℞	🚗	301 E Cooper St, 64093 / 660-747-1505 • *Lat:* 38.7793 *Lon:* -93.7371 Jct US-50 & SH-13 (N of town) go N on SH-13 for .2 mile
Warrenton	◇ 1	🕐	℞	🚗	500 Warren County Ctr, 63383 / 636-456-4600 • *Lat:* 38.8221 *Lon:* -91.1414 I-70 Exit 193, north of exit on Service Rd
Warsaw	◆	🕐	℞		103 W Polk St, 65355 / 660-438-7394 • *Lat:* 38.2438 *Lon:* -93.3833 Jct US-65 & SH-7 (N of town) take SH-7 SW 1.3 miles then S on Main St .2 mile
Washington	◇	🕐	℞	🚗	1701 Aroy Dr, 63090 / 636-239-1993 • *Lat:* 38.5427 *Lon:* -90.9956 Jct SH-47 & SH-100 (S of town) go E on SH-100 for .3 mile
Webb City	◆ 8	🕐	℞	🚗	1212 S Madison St, 64870 / 417-673-8288 • *Lat:* 37.1335 *Lon:* -94.4754 I-44 Exit 11 take SH-249 N 3.7 miles, W on Zora St 2.4 miles & N on US-71 BR 1.4 miles
Wentzville	◇ 1	🕐	℞	🚗	1971 Wentzville Pkwy, 63385 / 636-327-5155 • *Lat:* 38.8136 *Lon:* -90.8756 I-70 Exit 208 go N on Pearce Blvd/Wentzville Pkwy .2 mile
West Plains	◆	🕐	℞	🚗	1310 Preacher Rd, 65775 / 417-257-2800 • *Lat:* 36.7157 *Lon:* -91.8736 Jct US-63 & US-160 (S of town) take US-160 S .2 mile

○ Wal-Mart   ◇ Supercenter   ☐ Sam's Club   ■ Gas   ■ Gas & Diesel

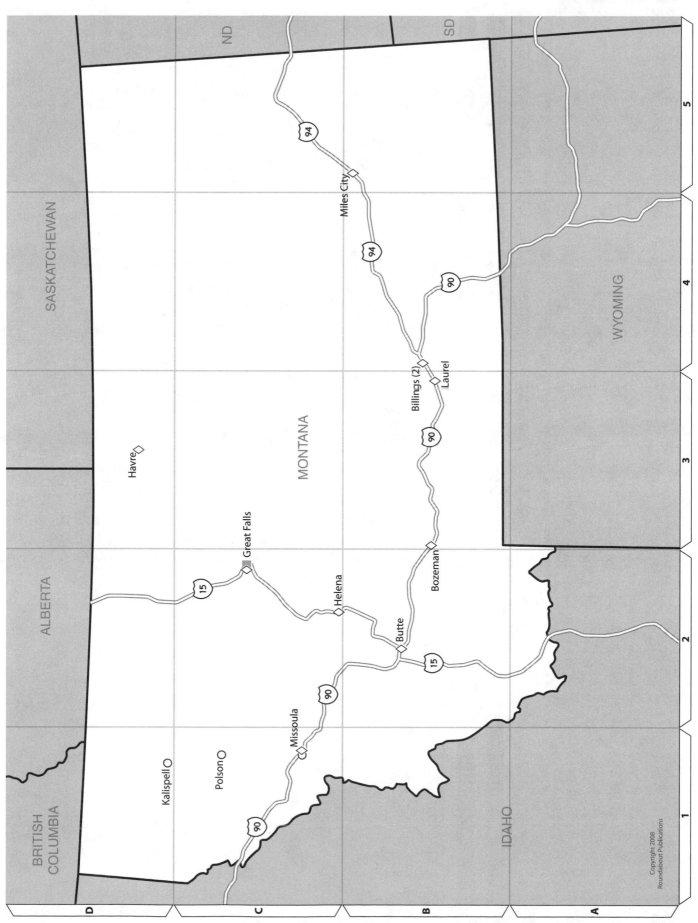

Montana

○ Wal-Mart ◇ Supercenter ☐ Sam's Club ▨ Gas ▮ Gas & Diesel

SASKATCHEWAN

ALBERTA

BRITISH COLUMBIA

ND

SD

WYOMING

IDAHO

MONTANA

Miles City

Billings (2)

Laurel

Havre

Great Falls

Helena

Butte

Bozeman

Missoula

Kalispell ○

Polson ○

94

94

90

90

90

15

15

90

90

City/Town	🛡	⏱	℞	🚐	Information
Billings	◇	2	⏱	℞ 🚐	2525 King Ave W, 59102 / 406-652-9692 • *Lat:* 45.7553 *Lon:* -108.5793 I-90 Exit 446 take I-90 BR W .4 mile then King Ave W 1.2 miles
	◇	3	⏱	℞ 🚐	1649 Main St, 59105 / 406-254-2842 • *Lat:* 45.8287 *Lon:* -108.4708 I-90 Exit 452 follow US-87 N for 2.8 miles
Bozeman	◇	1	⏱	℞ 🚐	1500 N 7th Ave, 59715 / 406-585-8788 • *Lat:* 45.6948 *Lon:* -111.0460 I-90 Exit 306 go S on 7th Ave .1 mile
Butte	◇	2	⏱	℞ 🚐	3901 Harrison Ave, 59701 / 406-494-1420 • *Lat:* 45.9642 *Lon:* -112.5083 I-15/90 Exit 127A go S on Harrison Ave 1.3 miles
Great Falls	■	3		℞ 🚐	401 Northwest Bypass, 59404 / 406-453-0018 • *Lat:* 47.5163 *Lon:* -111.3203 I-5 Exit 280 go E on Central Ave 1.2 miles, N on 3rd St .6 mile & W on Northwest Bypass .4 mile
	◇	3	⏱	℞ 🚐	701 Smelter Ave NE, 59404 / 406-761-5426 • *Lat:* 47.5248 *Lon:* -111.2970 I-15 Exit 280 take Central Ave E 1.2 miles, 3rd St N 1.3 miles & Smelter Ave NE .3 mile
Havre	◇		⏱	℞ 🚐	3510 US Hwy 2 W, 59501 / 406-262-9162 • *Lat:* 48.5564 *Lon:* -109.7312 Jct US-87 & US-2 (W of town) go E on US-2 for .7 mile
Helena	◇	1	⏱	℞ 🚐	2750 Prospect Ave, 59601 / 406-443-3220 • *Lat:* 46.5914 *Lon:* -111.9916 I-15 Exit 192 go E on US-12 for .4 mile
Kalispell	○			℞ 🚐	1150 E Idaho St, 59901 / 406-756-7250 • *Lat:* 48.2087 *Lon:* -114.2932 Jct US-93 & US-2 (in town) go NE on US-2/Idaho St 1.2 miles
Laurel	◇	1	⏱	℞	101 Bernhardt Rd, 59044 / 406-628-3000 • *Lat:* 45.6672 *Lon:* -108.7609 I-90 Exit 434 go N .4 mile on 1st Ave then E .5 mile on Railroad St
Miles City	◇	1	⏱	℞ 🚐	3205 Stower St, 59301 / 406-232-0022 • *Lat:* 46.4029 *Lon:* -105.8223 I-94 Exit 138 take SH-59 N .6 mile
Missoula	○	7		℞	4000 US Hwy 93 S, 59804 / 406-251-6060 • *Lat:* 46.8580 *Lon:* -114.1090 I-90 Exit 104 take Orange St SW 1.4 miles, Stephens Ave S .9 mile & US-12 S 4 miles
	◇	4	⏱	℞ 🚐	3555 Mullan Rd, 59808 / 406-829-8489 • *Lat:* 46.8854 *Lon:* -114.0449 I-90 Exit 104 take Orange St S .6 mile, Broadway W 1.3 miles & Mullen Rd W 1.2 miles
Polson	○			℞	170 Heritage Ln, 59860 / 406-883-9211 • *Lat:* 47.6878 *Lon:* -114.1214 Jct US-93 & SH-35/S Shore Rd (E of town) take South Shore Rd E .1 mile, Heritage Ln S .1 mile

○ Wal-Mart ◇ Supercenter ☐ Sam's Club ▨ Gas ■ Gas & Diesel

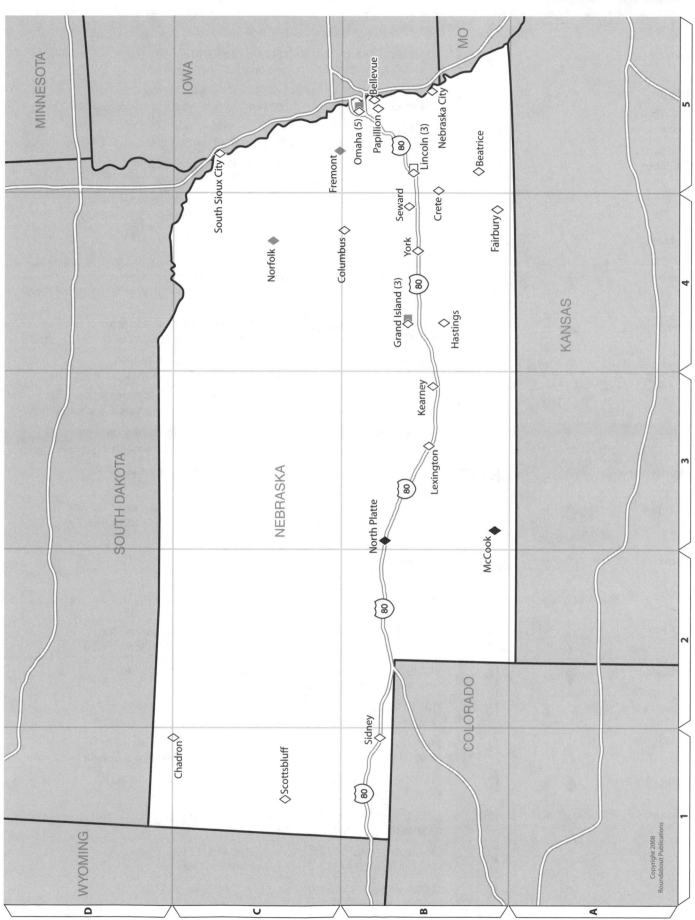

Nebraska

○ Wal-Mart   ◇ Supercenter   □ Sam's Club   ▮ Gas   ▮ Gas & Diesel

MINNESOTA

IOWA

MO

SOUTH DAKOTA

NEBRASKA

KANSAS

WYOMING

COLORADO

Bellevue
Omaha (5)
Papillion
Lincoln (3)
Nebraska City
Beatrice
South Sioux City
Fremont
Seward
Crete
Fairbury
Norfolk
Columbus
York
Grand Island (3)
Hastings
Kearney
Lexington
North Platte
McCook
Sidney
Chadron
Scottsbluff

Copyright 2008
Roundabout Publications

City/Town	⬡	🕐	℞	🚌	Information
Beatrice	◇		🕐	℞ 🚌	3620 N 6th St, 68310 / 402-228-1244 • *Lat:* 40.3007 *Lon:* -96.7466 Jct SH-34D & US-77 (N of town) go S on US-77 for 5.5 miles
Bellevue	◇ 6		🕐	℞ 🚌	10504 S 15th St, 68123 / 402-292-0156 • *Lat:* 41.1548 *Lon:* -95.9346 I-80 Exit 452 take US-75 S 4.9 miles then Cornhusker Rd E .2 mile & 15th St S .3 mile
Chadron	◇		🕐	℞	510 Linden St, 69337 / 308-432-6999 • *Lat:* 42.8292 *Lon:* -103.0231 Jct US-385 & US-20 (W of town) go W on US-20/4th St .3 mile
Columbus	◇		🕐	℞ 🚌	818 E 23rd St, 68601 / 402-564-1668 • *Lat:* 41.4387 *Lon:* -97.3186 Jct SH-15 & US-30 (E of town) go W on US-30 for 14.3 miles
Crete	◇		🕐	℞	1800 E 29th St, 68333 / 402-826-1002 • *Lat:* 40.6406 *Lon:* -96.9425 I-80 Exit 388 follow SH-103 S 12.2 miles then go W .6 mile on SH-33/SH-103
Fairbury	◇		🕐	℞	2831 Hwy 15, 68352 / 402-729-3394 • *Lat:* 40.1625 *Lon:* -97.1727 1.5 miles north of town along SH-15
Fremont	◆		🕐	℞ 🚌	3010 E 23rd St, 68025 / 402-727-0414 • *Lat:* 41.4515 *Lon:* -96.4784 Jct US-275 & US-30 BR (E of town) take US-30 BR W 1 mile, Luther Rd S .9 mile, Peterson Ave W .1 mile & 10th St W .3 mile
Grand Island	■ 8			🚌	1510 N Diers Ave, 68803 / 308-384-0622 • *Lat:* 40.9328 *Lon:* -98.3840 I-80 Exit 312 take US-281 N for 7.6 miles then W on 13th & S on Diers
	◇ 7		🕐	℞ 🚌	3501 S Locust St, 68801 / 308-381-4970 • *Lat:* 40.8853 *Lon:* -98.3395 I-80 Exit 312 follow US-281 N 4.7 miles then US-34 E 2 miles & Locust St S .1 mile
	◇ 9		🕐	℞ 🚌	2250 N Diers Ave, 68803 / 308-381-0333 • *Lat:* 40.9446 *Lon:* -98.3850 I-80 Exit 312 follow US-281 N 8.8 miles then Capitol Ave W & Diers Ave S .1 mile
Hastings	◇		🕐	℞ 🚌	3803 Osborne Dr W, 68901 / 402-462-6000 • *Lat:* 40.6219 *Lon:* -98.3845 I-80 Exit 312 take US-281 S 13.9 miles then 42nd St W & Osborne Dr S .2 mile
Kearney	◇ 5		🕐	℞ 🚌	5411 2nd Ave, 68847 / 308-234-8448 • *Lat:* 40.7267 *Lon:* -99.0836 I-80 Exit 272 follow SH-44 N 4.1 miles
Lexington	◇ 5		🕐	℞ 🚌	200 Frontier St, 68850 / 308-324-7427 • *Lat:* 40.7491 *Lon:* -99.7394 I-80 Exit 237 follow US-283 N 2.5 miles, 7th St E .5 mile, Taft St N .5 mile & 13th St E .7 mile
Lincoln	□ 2			℞ 🚌	4900 N 27th St, 68521 / 402-438-3540 • *Lat:* 40.8599 *Lon:* -96.6818 I-80 Exit 403 go S on 27th St 1.9 miles
	◇ 2		🕐	℞ 🚌	4700 N 27th St, 68521 / 402-438-4377 • *Lat:* 40.8580 *Lon:* -96.6818 I-80 Exit 403 take 27th St S 1.8 miles
	◇		🕐	℞ 🚌	8700 Andermatt Dr, 68526 / 402-484-6166 • *Lat:* 40.7344 *Lon:* -96.6006 I-80 Exit 397 take US-77 S 2.5 miles, SH-2 SE 8.2 miles & 87th St NE .1 mile
McCook	◆		🕐	℞ 🚌	1902 West B St, 69001 / 308-345-1800 • *Lat:* 40.1993 *Lon:* -100.6442 1 mile west of town on US-6/US-34
Nebraska City	◇ 6		🕐	℞ 🚌	2101 S 11th St, 68410 / 402-874-9080 • *Lat:* 40.6583 *Lon:* -95.8590 I-29 Exit 10 follow SH-2 W 5.1 miles then 11th St N .8 mile
Norfolk	◆		🕐	℞ 🚌	2400 W Pasewalk Ave, 68701 / 402-371-5452 • *Lat:* 42.0231 *Lon:* -97.4437 Jct US-21 & US-275 (S of town) take US-275 W .9 mile then S on Pasewalk Ave .2 mile
North Platte	◆ 1		🕐	℞	1401 S Dewey St, 69101 / 308-532-5529 • *Lat:* 41.1206 *Lon:* -100.7631 I-80 Exit 177 take US-83 N .5 mile
Omaha	■ 2			℞ 🚌	13130 L St, 68137 / 402-334-1526 • *Lat:* 41.2130 *Lon:* -96.1146 I-80 Exit 445 go W on L St 1.7 miles
	◇ 1		🕐	℞ 🚌	6304 N 99th St, 68134 / 402-492-9344 • *Lat:* 41.3153 *Lon:* -96.0668 I-680 Exit 6 take SH-133 E .2 mile then 99th St S .3 mile
	◇ 3		🕐	℞ 🚌	12850 L St, 68137 / 402-697-1054 • *Lat:* 41.2125 *Lon:* -96.1132 I-80 Exit 446 take SH-92/L St W 3 miles

○ Wal-Mart ◇ Supercenter □ Sam's Club ■ Gas ■ Gas & Diesel

City/Town	⬡	🕐	℞	🚌	Information
	◇ 6	🕐	℞	🚌	16960 W Maple Rd, 68116 / 402-289-9238 • *Lat:* 41.2923 *Lon:* -96.1804 I-680 Exit 4 take Maple Rd W 5.6 miles
	◇ 7	🕐	℞	🚌	18201 Wright St, 68130 / 402-330-4400 • *Lat:* 41.2331 *Lon:* -96.1989 I-80 Exit 445 follow US-275 W 6.8 miles then S on 183rd St & E on Wright St
Papillion	◇ 5	🕐	℞	🚌	8525 S 71st St Plaza, 68132 / 402-597-8977 • *Lat:* 41.1442 *Lon:* -96.0048 I-80 Exit 449 take 72nd St S 4.2 miles
Scottsbluff	◇	🕐	℞	🚌	3322 Avenue I, 69361 / 308-632-2666 • *Lat:* 41.8792 *Lon:* -103.6758 1.9 miles northwest of town center near US-26/SH-71 jct
Seward	◇ 4	🕐	℞		1326 280th, 68434 / 402-643-6631 • *Lat:* 40.8762 *Lon:* -97.1014 I-80 Exit 379 take SH-15 N 3.9 miles
Sidney	◇ 1	🕐	℞		3001 Silverberg Dr, 69162 / 308-254-9138 • *Lat:* 41.1169 *Lon:* -102.9471 I-80 Exit 59 follow I-80 BR W .3 mile then E at Old Post Rd
South Sioux City	◇ 2	🕐	℞	🚌	1601 Cornhusker Dr, 68776 / 402-494-8858 • *Lat:* 42.4693 *Lon:* -96.4274 I-129 Exit 1B merge onto US-77 N 1.4 miles & W on 25th St
York	◇ 1	🕐	℞	🚌	101 E David Dr, 68467 / 402-362-3366 • *Lat:* 40.8266 *Lon:* -97.5973 I-80 Exit 353 take US-81 N .5 mile

○ Wal-Mart   ◇ Supercenter   ☐ Sam's Club   ▨ Gas   ▨ Gas & Diesel

Nevada

○ Wal-Mart ◇ Supercenter ☐ Sam's Club ▨ Gas ■ Gas & Diesel

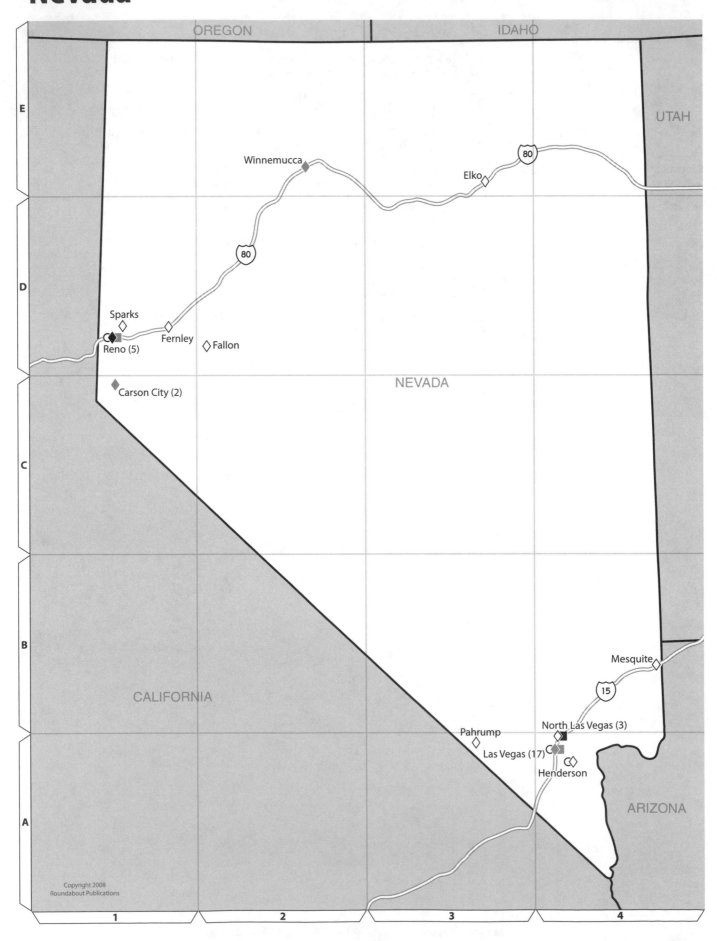

OREGON

IDAHO

UTAH

E

Winnemucca

80

Elko

80

NEVADA

D

Sparks

80

Fernley

Fallon

Reno (5)

Carson City (2)

C

CALIFORNIA

B

Mesquite

15

Pahrump

North Las Vegas (3)

Las Vegas (17)

Henderson

ARIZONA

A

1   2   3   4

City/Town	⬡	🕐	℞	🚌	Information
Carson City	◆	🕐	℞	🚌	3770 US Hwy 395 S, 89705 / 775-267-2158 • *Lat:* 39.0935 *Lon:* -119.7918 Jct US-50 & US-395 (in town) go S on US-395 for 5.3 miles
	◇	🕐	℞	🚌	3200 Market St, 89706 / 775-883-6415 • *Lat:* 39.1890 *Lon:* -119.7566 US-395 Exit 41 go W .1 mile on College Pkwy
Elko	◇ 1	🕐	℞	🚌	2944 Mountain City Hwy, 89801 / 775-778-6778 • *Lat:* 40.8393 *Lon:* -115.7930 I-80 Exit 301 take SH-225 N .4 mile
Fallon	◇	🕐	℞	🚌	2333 Reno Hwy, 89406 / 775-428-1700 • *Lat:* 39.4783 *Lon:* -118.8091 Jct US-95 & US-50 (in town) go W on US-50 for 1.7 miles
Fernley	◇ 1	🕐	℞		1550 Newlands Dr E, 89408 / 775-575-4832 • *Lat:* 39.6104 *Lon:* -119.2183 I-80 Exit 48, south of exit
Henderson	◯ 3		℞	🚌	300 E Lake Mead Pkwy, 89015 / 702-564-3665 • *Lat:* 36.0426 *Lon:* -114.9776 I-515 Exit 61 take SH-564 E for 2.4 miles
	◇ 1	🕐	℞	🚌	540 Marks St, 89014 / 702-547-0551 • *Lat:* 36.0614 *Lon:* -115.0362 I-515 Exit 64 take Sunset Rd W .3 mile then Marks St S .2 mile
Las Vegas	▨ 1		℞	🚌	1910 E Serene Ave, 89123 / 702-614-3372 • *Lat:* 36.0206 *Lon:* -115.1261 I-215 Exit 7 go S on Eastern Ave .3 mile & W on Serene Ave .4 mile
	▨ 3		℞	🚌	7100 Arroyo Crossing Pkwy, 89113 / 702-260-9003 • *Lat:* 36.0613 *Lon:* -115.2472 I-15 Exit 34 go W 2.6 miles on SH-215 (Bruce Woodbury Belt) to Exit 15 then S .4 mile
	▨ 4		℞	🚌	7175 Spring Mountain Rd, 89117 / 702-253-0072 • *Lat:* 36.1255 *Lon:* -115.2492 I-215 Exit 19 go E on Flamingo Rd 2.4 miles, N on Buffalo Dr .8 mile & E on Spring Mtn .7 mile
	▨		℞	🚌	8080 W Tropical Pkwy, 89149 / 702-515-7200 • *Lat:* 36.2703 *Lon:* -115.2752 US-95 Exit 91 go SE on Centennial Center Blvd .3 mile & W on Tropical Pkwy .6 mile
	□ 2		℞	🚌	5101 S Pecos Rd, 89120 / 702-456-5596 • *Lat:* 36.0967 *Lon:* -115.1012 I-515 Exit 68 go W on Tropicana 1 mile & S on Pecos Rd .2 mile
	◯ 3		℞		201 N Nellis Blvd, 89110 / 702-452-9998 • *Lat:* 36.1642 *Lon:* -115.0624 I-515 Exit 72 take Charleston Blvd E 1.7 miles & Nellis Blvd N .5 mile
	◯		℞		3041 N Rainbow Blvd, 89108 / 702-656-0199 • *Lat:* 36.2160 *Lon:* -115.2425 US-95 Exit 83 take Cheyenne Ave E .2 mile & Rainbow Blvd S .2 mile
	◆ 3	🕐	℞	🚌	4350 N Nellis Blvd, 89115 / 702-643-1500 • *Lat:* 36.2386 *Lon:* -115.0620 I-15 Exit 48 go E 2.2 miles on Craig Rd (NV-573) then S .1 mile on Nellis Blvd
	◇ 1	🕐	℞	🚌	2310 E Serene Ave, 89123 / 702-270-7831 • *Lat:* 36.0206 *Lon:* -115.1201 I-215 Exit 7 take Eastern Ave SE .2 mile & Serene Ave S
	◇ 1	🕐	℞	🚌	6464 N Decatur Blvd, 89131 / 702-515-7050 • *Lat:* 36.2778 *Lon:* -115.2064 I-215 Exit 13 take Decatur Blvd N .4 mile
	◇ 3	🕐	℞	🚌	4505 W Charleston Blvd, 89102 / 702-258-4540 • *Lat:* 36.1590 *Lon:* -115.2015 I-15 Exit 41 take Charleston Blvd W 2.3 miles
	◇ 3	🕐	℞	🚌	7200 Arroyo Crossing Pkwy, 89113 / 702-270-6003 • *Lat:* 36.0613 *Lon:* -115.2472 I-15 Exit 34 go W 2.6 miles on SH-215 (Bruce Woodbury Belt) to Exit 15 then S .4 mile
	◇ 3	🕐	℞	🚌	5198 Boulder Hwy, 89122 / 702-434-5595 • *Lat:* 36.1093 *Lon:* -115.0608 I-515 Exit 70 go S on Boulder Hwy 2.5 miles
	◇ 4	🕐	℞	🚌	6005 S Eastern Ave, 89119 / 702-451-8900 • *Lat:* 36.0807 *Lon:* -115.1189 I-515 Exit 68 go W on Tropicana 2 miles & S on Eastern Ave 1.3 miles
	◇ 5	🕐	℞		3615 S Rainbow Blvd, 89103 / 702-367-9999 • *Lat:* 36.1231 *Lon:* -115.2433 I-15 Exit 38A take Flamingo Rd W 3.3 miles & Rainbow Blvd N .8 mile
	◇ 5	🕐	℞	🚌	8060 W Tropical Pkwy, 89149 / 702-839-3620 • *Lat:* 36.2703 *Lon:* -115.2740 I-15 Exit 37 go W on Tropicana 4.8 miles

◯ Wal-Mart ◇ Supercenter □ Sam's Club ▨ Gas ■ Gas & Diesel

City/Town	🛡	⏰	℞	🚌	Information
	◇		⏰	℞	🚌	5200 S Fort Apache Rd, 89148 / 702-367-4001 • *Lat:* 36.0942 *Lon:* -115.2972 US-95 Exit 90 take Ann Rd W 2.5 miles then S on Ft Apache Rd .5 mile
Mesquite	◇ 1	⏰	℞	🚌	1120 W Pioneer Blvd, 89027 / 702-346-0208 • *Lat:* 36.8075 *Lon:* -114.1082 I-15 Exit 120, west of exit
North Las Vegas	■ 1		℞	🚌	2650 E Craig Rd, 89030 / 702-399-0347 • *Lat:* 36.2401 *Lon:* -115.1144 I-15 Exit 48 go W .7 mile on Craig Rd
	◇ 3	⏰	℞	🚌	3950 W Lake Mead Blvd, 89032 / 702-631-0421 • *Lat:* 36.1990 *Lon:* -115.1912 I-15 Exit 45 follow Lake Mead Blvd W 3 miles
	◇ 4	⏰	℞	🚌	1807 W Craig Rd, 89032 / 702-633-6521 • *Lat:* 36.2393 *Lon:* -115.1668 I-15 Exit 48 take Craig Rd W 3.7 miles
Pahrump	◇	⏰	℞	🚌	300 S Hwy 160, 89048 / 775-537-1400 • *Lat:* 36.2123 *Lon:* -115.9901 Jct SH-372 & SH-160 (in town) go N on SH-160 for .4 mile
Reno	■ 5		℞	🚌	4835 Kietzke Ln, 89509 / 775-829-7900 • *Lat:* 39.4804 *Lon:* -119.7936 I-80 Exit 15 take US-395 S 4.4 miles to Exit 63, N on Virginia St .2 mile & SW on Kietzke .2 mile
	○ 2		℞	🚌	2863 Northtowne Ln, 89512 / 775-359-8200 • *Lat:* 39.5559 *Lon:* -119.7822 I-80 Exit 15 merge onto US-395 N 1.1 miles then Exit 70-North McCarren Blvd E .2 mile
	◆ 9	⏰	℞	🚌	155 Damonte Ranch Pkwy, 89521 / 775-853-6400 • *Lat:* 39.4200 *Lon:* -119.7544 I-80 Exit 15 take US-395 S 8.8 miles to Exit 59-Damonte Pkwy W .2 mile
	◇ 1	⏰	℞	🚌	5260 W 7th St, 89523 / 775-624-2000 • *Lat:* 39.5369 *Lon:* -119.8667 I-80 Exit 10 go N .9 mile on McCarran Blvd then .1 mile on 7th St
	◇	⏰	℞	🚌	4855 Kietzke Lane, 89509 / 775-829-8088 • *Lat:* 39.4803 *Lon:* -119.7966 US-395 Exit 64 go W .2 mile on Moana Ln, S 1 mile on Kietzke Ln, W .1 mile on Redfield Pkwy
Sparks	◇ 3	⏰	℞		5065 Pyramid Way, 89436 / 775-425-9300 • *Lat:* 39.5752 *Lon:* -119.7462 I-80 Exit 18 go N on Pyramid Way 2.9 miles
Winnemucca	◆ 1	⏰	℞	🚌	3010 Potato Rd, 89445 / 775-625-3777 • *Lat:* 40.9542 *Lon:* -117.7445 I-80 Exit 176 take I-80 BR/W Winnemucca Blvd .4 mile & follow Potato Rd E .5 mile

○ Wal-Mart   ◇ Supercenter   □ Sam's Club   ■ Gas   ■ Gas & Diesel

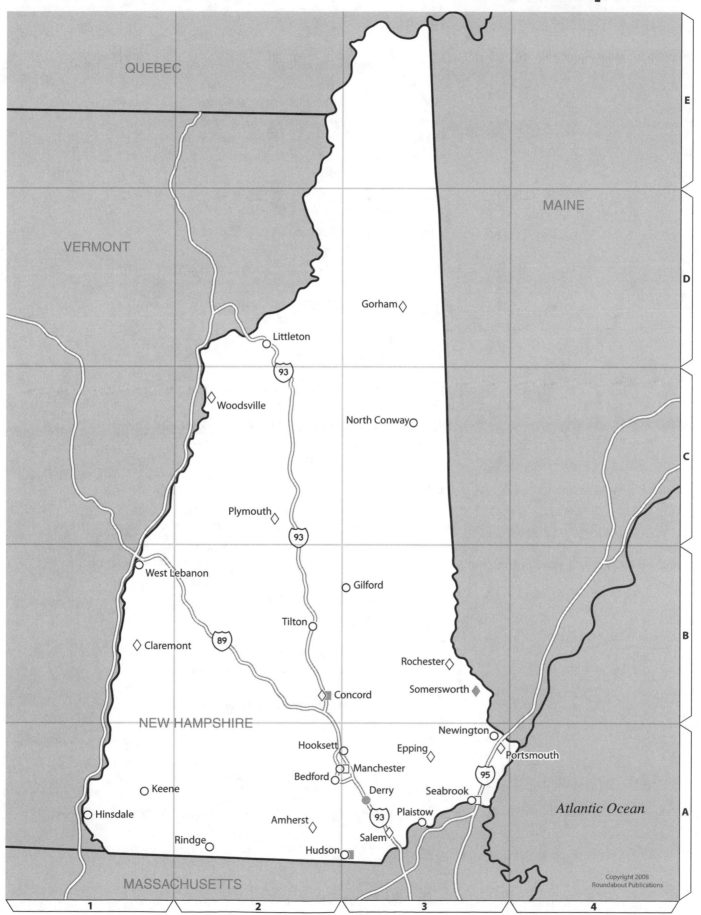

New Hampshire

○ Wal-Mart ◇ Supercenter ☐ Sam's Club ▨ Gas ■ Gas & Diesel

QUEBEC

MAINE

VERMONT

E

D

Gorham ◇

Littleton ○

93

Woodsville ◇

North Conway ○

C

Plymouth ◇

93

West Lebanon ○

Gilford ○

Tilton ○

89

◇ Claremont

B

Rochester ◇

Somersworth ◆

Concord ◇▨

NEW HAMPSHIRE

Newington ○

Hooksett ○

Epping ◇

Manchester ☐

95

Portsmouth ◇

Bedford ○

Derry

Seabrook ○☐

○ Keene

Plaistow ○

Atlantic Ocean

A

○ Hinsdale

93

Amherst ◇

Salem ◇

Rindge ○

Hudson ▨

MASSACHUSETTS

Copyright 2008
Roundabout Publications

| 1 | 2 | 3 | 4 |

City/Town	⬡	🕐	℞	🚐	Information
Amherst	◇ 5	🕐	℞		85 NH Hwy 101A, 03031 / 603-672-3421 • *Lat:* 42.8114 *Lon:* -71.5810 I-293 Exit 8 go W on Southwood Dr .1 mile then follow SH-101A W 4.5 miles
Bedford	○ 1		℞		17 Colby Ct, 03110 / 603-626-6733 • *Lat:* 42.9638 *Lon:* -71.4815 I-293 Exit 4 follow US-3 S .6 mile then W on Colby Ct
Claremont	◇ 6	🕐	℞	🚐	14 Bowen St, 03743 / 603-542-2703 • *Lat:* 43.3758 *Lon:* -72.3280 I-91 Exit 8 (in VT) go E on SH-12 3.7 miles, North St S 1.2 miles & SH-11 E .4 mile
Concord	■ 1			🚐	304 Sheep Davis Rd, 03301 / 603-226-1255 • *Lat:* 43.2283 *Lon:* -71.4764 I-393 Exit 3 take SH-106 S .5 mile
	◇ 2	🕐	℞		344 Loudon Rd, 03301 / 603-226-9312 • *Lat:* 43.2292 *Lon:* -71.4815 I-393 Exit 2 take Eastside Dr E .4 mile & Louden Rd N 1.5 miles
Derry	● 3		℞		30 Manchester Rd, 03038 / 603-434-3589 • *Lat:* 42.8983 *Lon:* -71.3347 I-93 Exit 5 follow SH-28 S 2.6 miles
Epping	◇	🕐	℞	🚐	35 Fresh River Rd, 03042 / 603-679-5919 • *Lat:* 43.0285 *Lon:* -71.0701 SH-101 Exit 7 take SH-125 N .4 mile then E at Fresh River Rd .2 mile
Gilford	○		℞		1458 Lake Shore Rd, 03249 / 603-528-8011 • *Lat:* 43.5639 *Lon:* -71.4399 I-93 Exit 20 follow US-3 NE 12.8 miles
Gorham	◇	🕐	℞		561 Main St, 03581 / 603-752-4621 • *Lat:* 44.4247 *Lon:* -71.1935 3.3 miles north of town center via US-2/SH-16
Hinsdale	○ 3		℞		18 Georges Fld, 03451 / 603-256-6723 • *Lat:* 42.8516 *Lon:* -72.5474 I-91 Exit 2 (in VT) take SH-9 E 1.1 miles, US-5 S .2 mile, SH-119 E .6 mile & Georges Fld N .2 mile
Hooksett	○ 3				1328 Hooksett Rd, 03106 / 603-644-8144 • *Lat:* 43.0548 *Lon:* -71.4421 I-93 Exit 9N follow US-3 N 2.5 miles
Hudson	■		℞	🚐	7 Wal Mart Blvd, 03051 / 603-882-4600 • *Lat:* 42.7259 *Lon:* -71.4278 I-495 Exit 35 take US-3 N 10.2 miles to Exit 2 toward Rt-3A for 1.6 miles, S on Rt-3A .2 mile & W on WalMart Blvd .2 mile
	○ 1		℞		254 Lowell Rd, 03051 / 603-598-4226 • *Lat:* 42.7261 *Lon:* -71.4239 From Everett Tpk Exit 2 go E 1 mile to SH-3A then S .2 mile on Lowell Rd (SH-3A)
Keene	○				350 Winchester St, 03431 / 603-357-7200 • *Lat:* 42.9236 *Lon:* -72.2900 Jct US-12 & SH-101 (S of town) follow SH-12/101 W .8 mile & N on Winchester St
Littleton	○ 1		℞		615 Meadow St, 03561 / 603-444-6300 • *Lat:* 44.3048 *Lon:* -71.8035 I-93 Exit 42 merge onto US-302 W .2 mile
Manchester	□ 1			🚐	200 John E Devine Dr, 03103 / 603-641-9220 • *Lat:* 42.9591 *Lon:* -71.4412 I-293 Exit 1 take SH-28 N .2 mile then W on Devine Dr .2 mile
	○ 1		℞		300 Keller St, 03103 / 603-621-9666 • *Lat:* 42.9515 *Lon:* -71.4398 I-293 Exit 1 take SH-28 S .2 mile & W on Auto Center Rd .1 mile
Newington	○ 2		℞		2200 Woodbury Ave, 03801 / 603-430-9985 • *Lat:* 43.1002 *Lon:* -70.8044 I-95 Exit 7 take Market St W .7 mile, continue W on Woodbury Ave 1.3 miles
North Conway	○		℞		46 North-South Rd, 03860 / 603-356-0130 • *Lat:* 44.0742 *Lon:* -71.1403 Jct US-302 & SH-16 (S of town) take US-302 N 2.8 miles, Seavey St E .2 mile & North-South Rd N
Plaistow	○ 3		℞		58 Plaistow Rd, 03865 / 603-382-2839 • *Lat:* 42.8278 *Lon:* -71.1074 I-495 Exit 51B (in MA) go N on SH-125 for 2.1 miles
Plymouth	◇ 3	🕐	℞	🚐	683 Tenney Mountain Hwy, 03264 / 603-536-5352 • *Lat:* 43.7709 *Lon:* -71.7443 I-93 Exit 26 merge onto SH-3A W 3 miles
Portsmouth	◇ 4		℞	🚐	2460 Lafayette Rd, 03801 / 603-433-6008 • *Lat:* 43.0332 *Lon:* -70.7840 I-95 Exit 5 take SH-16 S .6 mile then follow US-1 BYP S for 3.1 miles
Rindge	○		℞		750 US Rt 202, 03461 / 603-899-6882 • *Lat:* 42.7531 *Lon:* -72.0104 Jct SH-119 & US-202 (in West Rindge) go S on US-202 for .6 mile

○ Wal-Mart ◇ Supercenter □ Sam's Club ■ Gas ■ Gas & Diesel

City/Town	⬡	🕐	℞	🚐	Information
Rochester	◇			℞	🚐	116 Farmington Rd, 03867 / 603-332-4300 • *Lat:* 43.3354 *Lon:* -71.0100 From US-202 (toll) Exit 15 (N of town) go N on SH-11 for 1.4 miles
Salem	◇ 2	🕐	℞	🚐	300 N Broadway, 03079 / 603-894-5642 • *Lat:* 42.8002 *Lon:* -71.2406 I-93 Exit 3 follow SH-111 E for 1.4 miles then S on Broadway .4 mile
Seabrook	☐ 1		℞	🚐	11 Batchelder Rd, 03874 / 603-474-7474 • *Lat:* 42.8924 *Lon:* -70.8866 I-95 Exit 1 go W on SH-107 for .4 mile, S on Batchelder .1 mile & E at Sams Dr .2 mile
	◯ 2		℞		270 Lafayette Rd, 03874 / 603-474-2037 • *Lat:* 42.8803 *Lon:* -70.8672 I-95 Exit 1 merge onto SH-107 E .5 mile then US-1 S .9 mile
Somersworth	◆	🕐	℞		430 High St, 03878 / 603-692-6346 • *Lat:* 43.2353 *Lon:* -70.8812 Spaulding Tpk (toll) Exit 9 go E on Indian Brook Dr .6 mile then continue on SH-9 for .7 mile
Tilton	◯ 1		℞	🚐	39 E Main St, 03276 / 603-286-7673 • *Lat:* 43.4456 *Lon:* -71.5758 I-93 Exit 20 follow US-3 SW .4 mile
West Lebanon	◯ 1		℞		285 Plainfield Rd, 03784 / 603-298-5014 • *Lat:* 43.6243 *Lon:* -72.3255 I-89 Exit 20 take SH-12A S .5 mile
Woodsville	◇ 5	🕐	℞	🚐	4901 Dartmouth College Hwy, 03785 / 603-747-8250 • *Lat:* 44.1416 *Lon:* -72.0244 I-91 Exit 17 (in Vermont) follow US-302 E 4.3 miles then SH-10 S .1 mile

◯ Wal-Mart ◇ Supercenter ☐ Sam's Club ▣ Gas ▰ Gas & Diesel

New Jersey

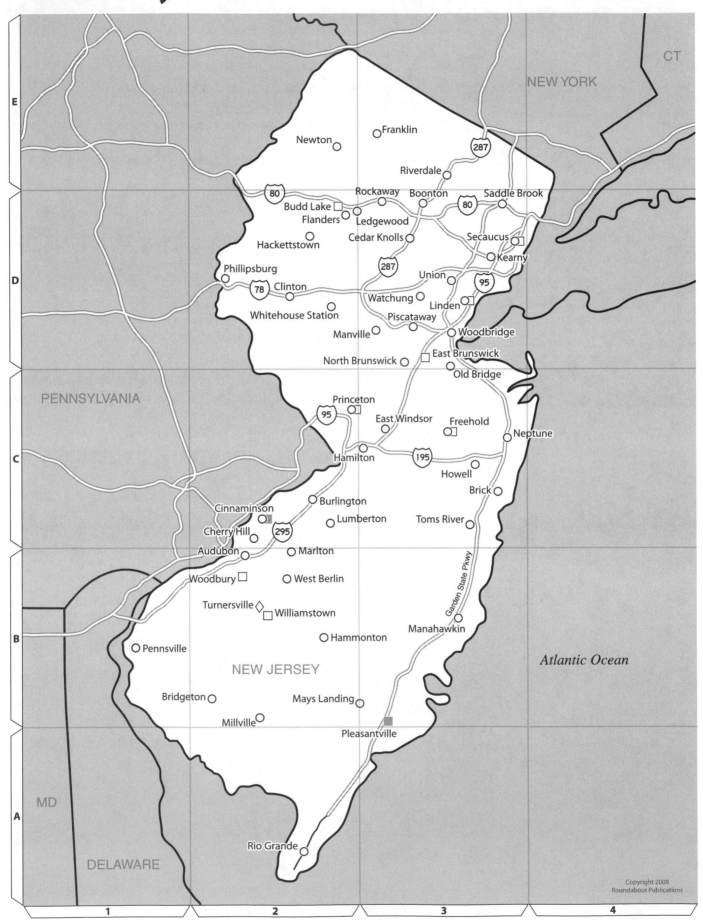

CT

NEW YORK

E

○ Franklin

Newton ○

287

Riverdale ○

80
Rockaway ○   Boonton ○   Saddle Brook ○
Budd Lake □   80
Flanders ○   Ledgewood ○
Cedar Knolls ○   Secaucus □
Hackettstown ○   Kearny ○
287

Phillipsburg ○
78   Clinton ○   Union ○   95
Watchung ○   Linden ○
Whitehouse Station ○   Piscataway ○
Manville ○   Woodbridge ○

D

North Brunswick ○   East Brunswick □
Old Bridge ○

PENNSYLVANIA

Princeton ○
95   East Windsor ○   Freehold ○
Neptune ○

Hamilton ○   195
Howell ○
Brick ○

C

Burlington ○
Cinnaminson ○▧   Lumberton ○   Toms River ○
Cherry Hill ○   295
Audubon ○   Marlton ○
Woodbury □   West Berlin ○

Turnersville ◇ □ Williamstown

Garden State Pkwy

Manahawkin ○

B

Hammonton ○

Pennsville ○

NEW JERSEY

Atlantic Ocean

Bridgeton ○   Mays Landing ○
Millville ○
Pleasantville ■

A

MD

DELAWARE

Rio Grande ○

1   2   3   4

City/Town	🛡	🕐	℞	🚗	Information
Audubon	○	2	℞		130 Black Horse Pike, 08106 / 856-310-1470 • *Lat:* 39.8906 *Lon:* -75.0899 I-295 Exit 28 go N 1.3 miles on Black Horse Pike (or 2 miles north of NJ Tpk Exit 3)
Boonton	○	1	℞		300 Wootton St, 07005 / 973-299-3943 • *Lat:* 40.9098 *Lon:* -74.4037 I-287 Exit 45 merge onto Park Ave W .1 mile then Wootton St W .4 mile
Brick	○		℞		1872 Rt 88, 08724 / 732-840-7772 • *Lat:* 40.0708 *Lon:* -74.1235 Garden State Pkwy Exit 88 take SH-70 E 2.5 miles & SH-88 NE .4 mile
Bridgeton	○		℞	🚗	1130 Hwy 77, 08302 / 856-453-0418 • *Lat:* 39.4699 *Lon:* -75.2068 From SH-55 Exit 32B follow SH-56 W 7.8 miles then SH-77 S 1 mile
Budd Lake	□	2	℞	🚗	81 International Dr S, 07828 / 973-448-8811 • *Lat:* 40.8891 *Lon:* -74.7176 I-80 Exit 27 take US-206 S for .3 mile & W on International Dr 1.5 miles
Burlington	○	1	℞	🚗	2106 Mount Holly Rd, 08016 / 609-386-8400 • *Lat:* 40.0501 *Lon:* -74.8400 I-295 Exit 47B merge onto Burlington/Mt Holly Rd .5 mile
Cedar Knolls	○	2			235 Ridgedale Ave, 07927 / 973-889-8646 • *Lat:* 40.8118 *Lon:* -74.4567 I-287 Exit 36B merge onto Lafayette Rd W .4 mile & Ridgedale Ave N 1.3 miles
Cherry Hill	○		℞	🚗	500 Rt 38, 08002 / 856-665-5430 • *Lat:* 39.9360 *Lon:* -75.0522 New Jersey Tpk (toll) Exit 4 merge onto SH-73 N 1.9 miles then SH-38 W 4.2 miles
Cinnaminson	▨	7	℞	🚗	2521 Route 130 S, 08077 / 856-303-2192 • *Lat:* 39.9879 *Lon:* -75.0101 I-295 Exit 43 take Creek Rd W 3.5 miles, NW on Bridgeboro .1 mile & S on US-13 for 2.8 miles
	○	6	℞	🚗	2501 Rt 130 S, 08077 / 856-303-2119 • *Lat:* 39.9879 *Lon:* -75.0101 I-295 Exit 43 take Creek Rd W 3.6 miles, Bridgeboro St N .4 mile & US-130 S 1.4 miles
Clinton	○	1	℞		1 Wal-Mart Plaza, 08809 / 908-730-8665 • *Lat:* 40.6281 *Lon:* -74.9192 I-78 Exit 15 take CR-513 S .1 mile then E on Frontage Dr and immediate right
East Brunswick	□	3	℞	🚗	290 State Route 18, 08816 / 732-613-6500 • *Lat:* 40.4584 *Lon:* -74.4017 I-95/NJ Tpk Exit 9 take SH-18 SE for 2.5 miles
East Windsor	○		℞	🚗	839 Rt 130, 08520 / 609-443-6159 • *Lat:* 40.2548 *Lon:* -74.5542 New Jersey Tpk (toll) Exit 8 take SH-33 W .9 mile, Main St S .1 mile, Stockton St W .8 mile & US-130 S .9 mile
Flanders	○	1	℞	🚗	40 International Dr S, 07836 / 973-347-7400 • *Lat:* 40.8836 *Lon:* -74.7057 I-80 Exit 27 take US-206 S .3 mile then Int'l Dr W .5 mile
Franklin	○		℞		230 State Rt 23, 07416 / 973-209-4242 • *Lat:* 41.1164 *Lon:* -74.5808 Jct CR-631/Franklin Ave & SH-23 (E of town) go N on SH-23 for .7 mile
Freehold	□	8	℞	🚗	320 W Main St, 07728 / 732-780-3943 • *Lat:* 40.2430 *Lon:* -74.3002 I-195 Exit 28 take US-9 N 5.6 miles, W on SH-33 for 1.3 miles & SW on Main St .4 mile
	○	9	℞	🚗	326 W Main St, 07728 / 732-780-3048 • *Lat:* 40.2429 *Lon:* -74.3003 I-195 Exit 16B take CR-537 E 8.7 miles
Hackettstown	○	8	℞		1885 NJ Hwy 57, 07840 / 908-979-9342 • *Lat:* 40.8154 *Lon:* -74.8414 I-80 Exit 19 follow CR-517 S 6 miles then SH-57 S 1.8 miles
Hamilton	○	2	℞	🚗	700 Marketplace Blvd, 08691 / 609-585-1463 • *Lat:* 40.1965 *Lon:* -74.6388 I-195 Exit 5A take US-130 S 1.2 miles, Crosswicks Rd E .2 mile & Marketplace Blvd N .6 mile
Hammonton	○		℞		55 S White Horse Pike, 08037 / 609-567-2700 • *Lat:* 39.6464 *Lon:* -74.7867 Atlantic City Expy Exit 28 take SH-54 N 3.2 miles & US-30 E .1 mile
Howell	○	3	℞		4900 US Hwy 9, 07731 / 732-886-9100 • *Lat:* 40.1491 *Lon:* -74.2104 I-195 Exit 28A merge onto US-9 S 2.4 miles
Kearny	○	1	℞	🚗	150 Harrison Ave, 07032 / 201-955-0280 • *Lat:* 40.7484 *Lon:* -74.1434 I-280 Exit 17B follow CR-508 W .6 mile
Ledgewood	○	2	℞		461 State Rt 10 Ledgewood Mall #29, 07852 / 973-252-7666 • *Lat:* 40.8837 *Lon:* -74.6613 I-80 Exit 28 take CR-631 S .2 mile then US-46 E .9 mile & SH-10 E .2 mile

○ Wal-Mart ◇ Supercenter □ Sam's Club ▨ Gas ■ Gas & Diesel

City/Town	◌	🕐	℞	🚗	Information
Linden	☐	2	℞	🚗	1900 E Linden Ave, 07036 / 908-587-9820 • *Lat:* 40.6470 *Lon:* -74.2312 I-95 Exit 14 go W .6 mile on Bayway Ave, S .5 mile on US-1, W .2 mile on Park Ave
	◯		℞		1601 W Edgar Rd, 07036 / 908-474-9055 • *Lat:* 40.6116 *Lon:* -74.2570 Garden State Pkwy Exit 135 follow CR-613 E 2.7 miles, Grand Ave E .1 mile & US-1 N .6 mile
Lumberton	◯		℞	🚗	1740 Rt 38, 08048 / 609-702-9200 • *Lat:* 39.9784 *Lon:* -74.7651 New Jersey Tpk (toll) Exit 5 follow CR-541 S 3.8 miles then SH-38 E 2.1 miles
Manahawkin	◯		℞		525 Rt 72 W, 08050 / 609-978-8300 • *Lat:* 39.7038 *Lon:* -74.2734 Garden State Pkwy Exit 63 follow SH-72 E 1.9 miles
Manville	◯	3	℞		100 N Main St, 08835 / 908-575-8997 • *Lat:* 40.5450 *Lon:* -74.5867 I-287 Exit 13B take SH-28 W 1 mile, Finderne Ave S 1.1 miles, & CR-533 S .7 mile
Marlton	◯		℞		150 E Rt 70, 08053 / 856-983-2100 • *Lat:* 39.8942 *Lon:* -74.9137 New Jersey Tpk (toll) Exit 4 take SH-70 E 1 mile
Mays Landing	◯		℞	🚗	4620 Black Horse Pike, 08330 / 609-625-8200 • *Lat:* 39.4546 *Lon:* -74.6540 Atlantic City Expy Exit 17 take SH-50 S 2.8 miles then US-322 E 3.4 miles
Millville	◯		℞		2291 N 2nd St, 08332 / 856-825-4200 • *Lat:* 39.4229 *Lon:* -75.0394 From SH-55 Exit 27 take SH-47 S .4 mile
Neptune	◯		℞	🚗	3575 Rt 66, 07753 / 732-922-8084 • *Lat:* 40.2236 *Lon:* -74.0836 Garden State Pkwy (toll) Exit 100A take SH-66 E .6 mile
Newton	◯		℞		26 Hampton House Rd, 07860 / 973-300-1859 • *Lat:* 41.0766 *Lon:* -74.7376 I-80 Exit 34B take SH-15 N 15.2 miles then SW on SH-94 for 3.6 miles
North Brunswick	◯		℞		979 Rt 1, 08902 / 732-545-4499 • *Lat:* 40.4509 *Lon:* -74.4815 New Jersey Tpk (toll) Exit 9 take US-1 S 2.8 miles
Old Bridge	◯		℞	🚗	1126 US Hwy 9, 08857 / 732-525-8030 • *Lat:* 40.4371 *Lon:* -74.3011 Garden State Pkwy (toll) Exit 123 take US-9 S 4.8 miles
Pennsville	◯	5	℞		709 S Broadway, 08070 / 856-935-8200 • *Lat:* 39.6133 *Lon:* -75.5023 I-295 Exit 1C go S on N Hood Rd 4.4 miles then S on Broadway .1 mile
Phillipsburg	◯	5	℞	🚗	1236 US Hwy 22, 08865 / 908-454-3622 • *Lat:* 40.6903 *Lon:* -75.1661 I-78 Exit 3 merge onto US-22 W 3.1 miles then US-22 E 1.6 miles
Piscataway	◯	1	℞	🚗	1303 Centennial Ave, 08854 / 732-562-1771 • *Lat:* 40.5527 *Lon:* -74.4413 I-287 Exit 5 go S on Stelton Rd .2 mile & W on Centennial Ave .5 mile
Pleasantville	▨			🚗	1025 Black Horse Pike, 08232 / 609-485-2277 • *Lat:* 39.3950 *Lon:* -74.5421 Jct Atlantic City Expy & US-9 (north of town) take US-9 S for .9 mile then W on Black Horse Pike .7 mile
Princeton	☐	3		🚗	301 Nassau Park Blvd, 08540 / 609-452-5959 • *Lat:* 40.3039 *Lon:* -74.6770 I-295 Exit 67 take US-1 NE for 2.1 miles, W on Quakerbridge Rd .4 mile & N on Nassau Park Blvd .4 mile
	◯	3	℞		101 Nassau Park Blvd, 08540 / 609-987-0202 • *Lat:* 40.3031 *Lon:* -74.6759 I-95 Exit 67 take US-1 N 2.1 miles, Quakerbridge Rd W .4 mile & Nassau Park Blvd N .5 mile
Rio Grande	◯		℞	🚗	3159 Rt 9 S, 08242 / 609-465-2204 • *Lat:* 39.0201 *Lon:* -74.8709 From Garden State Pkwy Exit 4 go W on Delsea Dr .6 mile then N on US-9 .5 mile
Riverdale	◯	1	℞		48 State Rt 23, 07457 / 973-835-5812 • *Lat:* 40.9916 *Lon:* -74.3101 I-287 Exit 52A take SH-23 S .5 mile
Rockaway	◯	2	℞		220 Enterprise Dr, 07866 / 973-361-6089 • *Lat:* 40.9076 *Lon:* -74.5630 I-80 Exit 35 take Mt Hope Ave S .5 mile, Mt Pleasant Ave W .9 mile & Enterprise Ave N .4 mile

◯ Wal-Mart ◇ Supercenter ☐ Sam's Club ▨ Gas ▮ Gas & Diesel

City/Town	⬠	🕐	℞	🚐	Information
Saddle Brook	◯ 2		℞		189 State Rt 46, 07663 / 201-226-0575 • *Lat:* 40.9036 *Lon:* -74.0956 I-80 Exit 62B take Railroad Ave E .2 mile, Rochelle Ave & Main St S .7 mile, Outwater Ln W .5 mile & US-46 W .4 mile
Secaucus	☐ 1		℞	🚐	300 Park Pl, 07094 / 201-974-0702 • *Lat:* 40.7904 *Lon:* -74.0436 I-95/NJ Tpk Exit 17, N .6 mile on Harmon Meadow Blvd
	◯ 2		℞	🚐	400 Park Pl, 07094 / 201-325-9280 • *Lat:* 40.7962 *Lon:* -74.0512 I-95 Exit 16E take Harmon Meadow Blvd N 1.1 miles & Park Pl W .1 mile
Toms River	◯		℞		950 Rt 37 W, 08755 / 732-349-6000 • *Lat:* 39.9739 *Lon:* -74.2403 Garden State Pkwy (toll) Exit 82A follow SH-97 W 4.6 miles
Turnersville	◇ 9	🕐	℞		3501 Rt 42, 08012 / 856-629-3888 • *Lat:* 39.7298 *Lon:* -75.0334 Jct I-295 & I-76 take I-76 S 1.3 miles, continue S on SH-42 for 7 miles
Union	◯		℞		900 Springfield Rd, 07083 / 908-624-0644 • *Lat:* 40.6876 *Lon:* -74.2989 Garden State Pkwy (toll) Exit 140A follow US-22 W 2.6 miles
Watchung	◯ 3		℞		1501 US Hwy 22, 07069 / 908-756-1925 • *Lat:* 40.6403 *Lon:* -74.4177 I-78 Exit 41 take Plainfield Ave E .9 mile, Bonnie Burn Rd E 1 mile then US-22 S .8 mile
West Berlin	◯		℞		265 N Rt 73, 08091 / 856-753-8787 • *Lat:* 39.8131 *Lon:* -74.9302 New Jersey Tpk (toll) Exit 4 take SH-73 S for 9.8 miles
Whitehouse Station	◯ 3		℞		3576 Rt 22 W, 08889 / 908-534-7377 • *Lat:* 40.6085 *Lon:* -74.7642 I-78 Exit 24 take CR-523 S 2.1 miles & US-22 E .2 mile
Williamstown	☐		℞	🚐	2080 N Black Horse Pike, 08094 / 856-875-7836 • *Lat:* 39.7189 *Lon:* -75.0220 Atlantic City Expy Exit 41 go SW on CR-689 for 1.2 miles then S on Black Horse Pike .1 mile
Woodbridge	◯		℞		306 US Hwy 9 N, 07095 / 732-826-4652 • *Lat:* 40.5357 *Lon:* -74.2964 Jct SH-440 & US-9 (S of town) take US-9 N 1.5 miles
Woodbury	☐			🚐	1500 Almonesson Rd Ste 18, 08096 / 856-228-9469 • *Lat:* 39.8239 *Lon:* -75.0998 From town center go E 3.2 miles on Cooper St then N .3 mile on Almonesson Rd

◯ Wal-Mart ◇ Supercenter ☐ Sam's Club ▨ Gas ■ Gas & Diesel

New Mexico

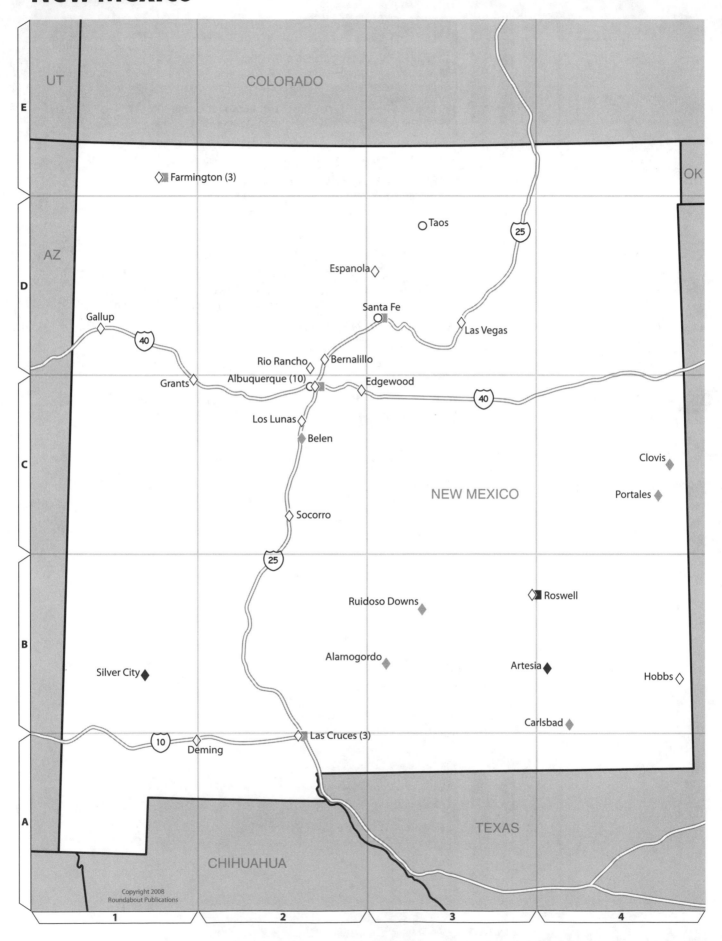

○ Wal-Mart ◇ Supercenter ☐ Sam's Club ▨ Gas ■ Gas & Diesel

UT

COLORADO

OK

AZ

Farmington (3)

Taos

25

Espanola

Santa Fe

Gallup

40

Las Vegas

Rio Rancho

Bernalillo

Grants

Albuquerque (10)

Edgewood

40

Los Lunas

Belen

NEW MEXICO

Clovis

Portales

Socorro

25

Ruidoso Downs

Roswell

B

Alamogordo

Artesia

Hobbs

Silver City

Carlsbad

Las Cruces (3)

10

Deming

A

TEXAS

CHIHUAHUA

1   2   3   4

City/Town	⬟	🕐	℞	🚗	Information
Alamogordo	◆		🕐	℞ 🚗	233 S New York Ave, 88310 / 505-434-5870 • *Lat:* 32.8895 *Lon:* -105.9593 Jct US-54 & US-70 (S of town) go N on US-54/70/82 for 1.4 miles then E on New York Ave .2 mile
Albuquerque	▣ 1			℞ 🚗	1421 N Renaissance Blvd NE, 87107 / 505-344-0051 • *Lat:* 35.1377 *Lon:* -106.6149 I-25 Exit 228 W on Montano Rd .5 mile then NE on Renaissance Blvd .5 mile
	▣ 1			℞ 🚗	300 Eubank Blvd NE, 87123 / 505-298-5308 • *Lat:* 35.0765 *Lon:* -106.5320 I-40 Exit 165 S on Eubank for .4 mile
	▣ 7			℞ 🚗	10600 Coors Bypass NW, 87114 / 505-922-0046 • *Lat:* 35.2079 *Lon:* -106.6583 I-25 Exit 232 go W on Paseo Del Norte 4.5 miles, N on Coors Blvd/Bypass 2 miles
	○ 3			℞	8000 Academy Rd NE, 87111 / 505-856-5274 • *Lat:* 35.1460 *Lon:* -106.5534 I-25 Exit 230 go S on San Mateo Blvd .3 mile then E on Academy Rd 1.9 miles
	◇ 1		🕐	℞ 🚗	2701 Carlisle Blvd NE, 87110 / 505-884-6650 • *Lat:* 35.1112 *Lon:* -106.6044 I-40 Exit 160 go N on Carlisle Blvd .6 mile
	◇ 1		🕐	℞ 🚗	2550 Coors Bldv NW, 87120 / 505-352-1870 • *Lat:* 35.1401 *Lon:* -106.7086 I-40 Exit 155 merge onto Coors Blvd NW .2 mile
	◇ 1		🕐	℞	400 Eubank Blvd NE, 87123 / 505-293-8878 • *Lat:* 35.0782 *Lon:* -106.5320 I-40 Exit 165 go S on Eubank Blvd .5 mile
	◇ 2		🕐	℞	301 San Mateo Blvd SE, 87108 / 505-268-6611 • *Lat:* 35.0756 *Lon:* -106.5865 I-40 Exit 161A go S on San Mateo Blvd 1.8 miles
	◇ 5		🕐	℞ 🚗	3500 Coors Blvd SW, 87121 / 505-877-2254 • *Lat:* 35.0274 *Lon:* -106.7095 I-25 Exit 220 go W on Rio Bravo 4 miles
	◇ 8		🕐	℞ 🚗	10224 Coors Byp NW, 87114 / 505-897-1228 • *Lat:* 35.2021 *Lon:* -106.6598 I-40 Exit 155 follow Coors Blvd NW 7.9 miles
Artesia	◆		🕐	℞ 🚗	604 N 26th St, 88210 / 505-746-2184 • *Lat:* 32.8474 *Lon:* -104.4297 Jct US-285 & US-82 (in town) take US-82 W 1.9 miles & 26th St N .3 mile
Belen	◆ 2		🕐	℞ 🚗	01 I-25 Interchange, 87002 / 505-864-9114 • *Lat:* 34.6958 *Lon:* -106.7699 I-25 Exit 195 take I-25 BR E 1.4 miles
Bernalillo	◇ 3		🕐	℞ 🚗	460 NM Hwy 528, 87004 / 505-771-4867 • *Lat:* 35.3214 *Lon:* -106.5746 I-25 Exit 242 follow US-550 W 2.4 miles then SH-528 S .6 mile
Carlsbad	◆		🕐	℞ 🚗	2401 S Canal St, 88220 / 505-885-0727 • *Lat:* 32.3967 *Lon:* -104.2218 Jct US-285 & US-180 (S of town) go N on US-285/Pecos Hwy 3.5 miles
Clovis	◆		🕐	℞ 🚗	3728 N Prince St, 88101 / 505-769-2261 • *Lat:* 34.4360 *Lon:* -103.1967 Jct US-60/70/84 & SH-209/Prince St (in town) go N on Prince St 2.6 miles
Deming	◇ 1		🕐	℞ 🚗	1021 E Pine St, 88030 / 505-546-6045 • *Lat:* 32.2688 *Lon:* -107.7468 I-10 Exit 82A go S .1 mile on Pearl St then E .4 mile on Pine St
Edgewood	◇ 1		🕐	℞ 🚗	66 State Rd 344, 87015 / 505-286-3043 • *Lat:* 35.0703 *Lon:* -106.1913 I-40 Exit 187 take SH-344 N .5 mile
Espanola	◇		🕐	℞ 🚗	1610 N Riverside Dr, 87532 / 505-747-0414 • *Lat:* 36.0161 *Lon:* -106.0647 Jct US-285/84 & SH-68 (in town) take SH-68/N Riverside Dr for 1.8 miles
Farmington	▣			℞ 🚗	4500 E Main St, 87402 / 505-326-3500 • *Lat:* 36.7643 *Lon:* -108.1539 Jct US-550 & US-64 take US-64 W for 10 miles & N on SH-516 for 4 miles
	◇		🕐	℞	1400 W Main St, 87401 / 505-327-1243 • *Lat:* 36.7313 *Lon:* -108.2273 Jct SH-170 & US-64 (W of town) follow US-64 E 2 miles
	◇		🕐	℞ 🚗	4600 E Main St, 87402 / 505-326-1100 • *Lat:* 36.7653 *Lon:* -108.1523 Jct US-64 & SH-516 (E of town) follow SH-516 N 3 miles
Gallup	◇ 1		🕐	℞ 🚗	1650 W Maloney Ave, 87301 / 505-722-2296 • *Lat:* 35.5303 *Lon:* -108.7594 I-40 Exit 20 take US-491 N .1 mile then E on Maloney Ave

○ Wal-Mart ◇ Supercenter ☐ Sam's Club ▣ Gas ■ Gas & Diesel

City/Town	⬡	🕐	℞	🚐	Information
Grants	◇ 2	🕐	℞		1000 Robert Rd, 87020 / 505-285-3350 • *Lat:* 35.1351 *Lon:* -107.8362 I-40 Exit 85 take I-40 BR W .8 mile & W on Robertas Rd .6 mile
Hobbs	◇	🕐	℞	🚐	3800 N Lovington Hwy, 88240 / 505-492-0120 • *Lat:* 32.7417 *Lon:* -103.1620 Jct US-180/62 & W County Rd (W of town) follow County Rd N 3.5 miles then SH-18 NW 3.2 miles
Las Cruces	■ 1		℞	🚐	2711 N Telshor Blvd, 88011 / 505-521-7858 • *Lat:* 32.3459 *Lon:* -106.7657 I-25 Exit 6 take US-82 E .2 mile & SW on Telshore Blvd .3 mile
	◇ 1	🕐	℞	🚐	571 Walton Blvd, 88001 / 505-525-1222 • *Lat:* 32.3162 *Lon:* -106.7521 I-25 Exit 3 go W on Lohman Ave .2 mile & N on Walton Blvd
	◇ 1	🕐	℞	🚐	1550 S Valley Dr, 88005 / 505-523-4924 • *Lat:* 32.2917 *Lon:* -106.7848 I-10 Exit 140 take SH-28 N .4 mile then I-10 BR E .1 mile
Las Vegas	◇ 4	🕐	℞		2609 7th St, 87701 / 505-425-5242 • *Lat:* 35.6213 *Lon:* -105.2257 I-25 Exit 347 merge onto I-25 BR S 1.3 miles, SH-329/Mills Ave W .7 mile & SH-519/7th St N 1.1 miles
Los Lunas	◇ 1	🕐	℞	🚐	2250 Main St NW, 87031 / 505-565-4611 • *Lat:* 34.8154 *Lon:* -106.7639 I-25 Exit 203 take SH-6 W .1 mile
Portales	◆	🕐	℞		1604 E Spruce St, 88130 / 505-359-3420 • *Lat:* 34.2006 *Lon:* -103.3190 Jct SH-467 & US-70 (NE of town) continue S on Kilgore Ave .1 mile & W on Spruce St
Rio Rancho	◇ 10	🕐	℞	🚐	901 Unser Blvd SE, 87124 / 505-962-9227 • *Lat:* 35.2445 *Lon:* -106.6971 I-25 Exit 233 follow SH-528 W 5 miles, Coors Blvd N 2.2 miles, Southern Blvd W 2.3 miles, and Unser Blvd N .2 mile
Roswell	■		℞	🚐	4400 N Main St, 88201 / 505-627-9852 • *Lat:* 33.4504 *Lon:* -104.5235 Jct US-380 & US-70 (west of town) take US-70 NE for 5 miles, SH-246 E 1.7 miles & S on Main St .1 mile
	◇	🕐	℞	🚐	4500A N Main St, 88201 / 505-623-2062 • *Lat:* 33.4529 *Lon:* -104.5236 Jct US-70 & US-285 (N of town) take Main St S 1.9 miles
Ruidoso Downs	◆	🕐	℞	🚐	1800 W Hwy 70, 88346 / 505-378-8050 • *Lat:* 33.3259 *Lon:* -105.6128 Jct SH-48 & US-70 (W of town) go E on US-70 for .9 mile
Santa Fe	■ 4		℞	🚐	4201 Rodeo Rd, 87507 / 505-471-8825 • *Lat:* 35.6390 *Lon:* -106.0085 I 25 Exit 278 take SH-14 NE 3 miles then E on Rodeo Rd .6 mile
	○ 4		℞		3251 Cerrillos Rd, 87507 / 505-474-4727 • *Lat:* 35.6506 *Lon:* -105.9998 I-25 Exit 278B merge onto Cerrillos Rd 4 miles
Silver City	◆	🕐	℞	🚐	2501 Hwy 180 E, 88061 / 505-538-2222 • *Lat:* 32.7873 *Lon:* -108.2482 2.4 miles northeast of town center via SH-90 and US-180
Socorro	◇ 3	🕐	℞		700 6th St N, 87801 / 505-838-1415 • *Lat:* 34.0638 *Lon:* -106.8912 I-25 Exit 147 take I-25 BR N 2 miles then E at Neal Ave
Taos	○		℞		926 Paseo Del Pueblo Sur, 87571 / 505-758-1136 • *Lat:* 36.3874 *Lon:* -105.5846 2 miles south of town along SH-68

○ Wal-Mart   ◇ Supercenter   ☐ Sam's Club   ■ Gas   ■ Gas & Diesel

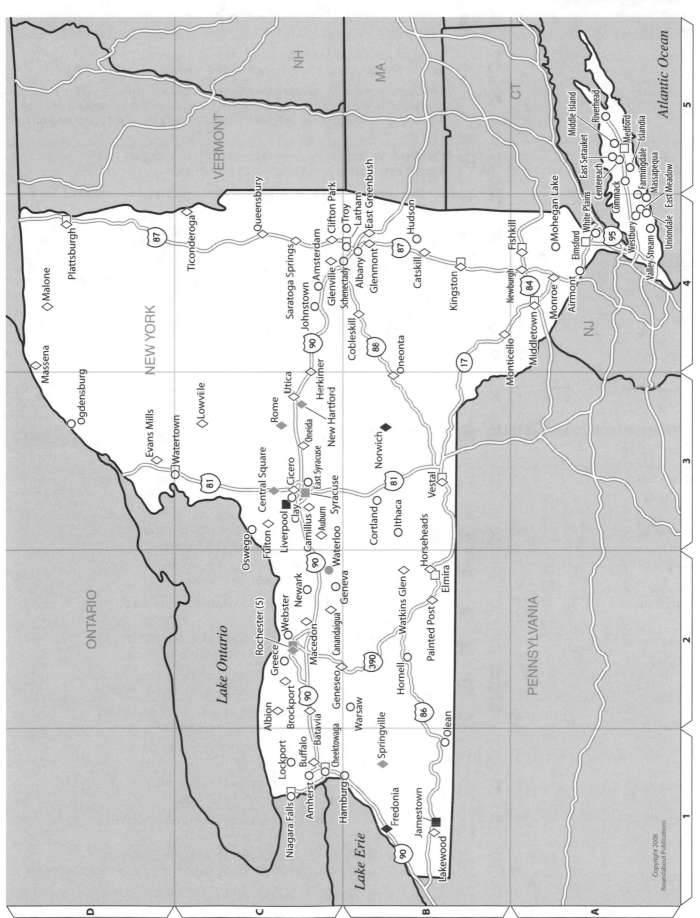

New York

Legend: ○ Wal-Mart ◇ Supercenter ☐ Sam's Club ▨ Gas ■ Gas & Diesel

Atlantic Ocean

NH
VERMONT
MA
CT
NEW YORK
NJ
ONTARIO
Lake Ontario
PENNSYLVANIA
Lake Erie

Middle Island
Riverhead
East Setauket
Medford
Islandia
Centereach
Farmingdale
Commack
Massapequa
Westbury
East Meadow
Uniondale
Valley Stream
White Plains
Elmsford
Mohegan Lake
Airmont
Monroe
Fishkill
Newburgh
Middletown
Monticello
Kingston
Catskill
Hudson
East Greenbush
Glenmont
Albany
Latham
Troy
Schenectady
Glenville
Clifton Park
Amsterdam
Queensbury
Ticonderoga
Plattsburgh
Malone
Massena
Ogdensburg
Evans Mills
Watertown
Lowville
Saratoga Springs
Johnstown
Rome
Utica
Herkimer
New Hartford
Oneida
Coxsackie
Cobleskill
Oneonta
Norwich
Vestal
Central Square
Cicero
East Syracuse
Syracuse
Liverpool
Clay
Camillus
Auburn
Waterloo
Cortland
Ithaca
Horseheads
Oswego
Fulton
Newark
Geneva
Webster
Rochester (5)
Greece
Macedon
Canandaigua
Geneseo
Warsaw
Watkins Glen
Elmira
Painted Post
Hornell
Olean
Springville
Jamestown
Lakewood
Fredonia
Albion
Brockport
Batavia
Cheektowaga
Lockport
Buffalo
Amherst
Hamburg
Niagara Falls

87
87
90
90
88
81
81
17
84
95
390
86
90

D   C   B   A

1   2   3   4   5

City/Town	⬡	🕐	℞	🚗	Information
Airmont	○ 1		℞		250 Rt 59, 10901 / 845-368-4705 • *Lat:* 41.1119 *Lon:* -74.1074 I-87 Exit 14B take Airmont Rd S .3 mile & SH-59 E .3 mile
Albany	○ 2		℞		141 Washington Ave Ext, 12205 / 518-869-4694 • *Lat:* 42.6960 *Lon:* -73.8488 Eastbound travelers turn right at I-90 Exit 2 and follow Washington Ave 1.6 miles; Westbound travelers turn left on Fuller Rd from I-90 Exit 2 then right at Washington Ave 1.3 miles
Albion	◇	🕐	℞	🚗	13858 Rt 31 W, 14411 / 585-589-0608 • *Lat:* 43.2421 *Lon:* -78.2047 I-90 Exit 48 take SH-98 N 15.6 miles & SH-31 W 1.7 miles
Amherst	○ 1		℞	🚗	2055 Niagara Falls Blvd, 14228 / 716-691-0195 • *Lat:* 43.0097 *Lon:* -78.8220 I-290 Exit 3B take US-62 N .8 mile
Amsterdam	○		℞	🚗	101 Sanford Farms Shpg Ctr, 12010 / 518-843-6890 • *Lat:* 42.9657 *Lon:* -74.1845 NY State Thruway (toll) Exit 27 take SH-30 N 2.9 miles & E at Miami Ave .1 mile
Auburn	◇	🕐	℞	🚗	297 Grant Ave, 13021 / 315-255-0532 • *Lat:* 42.9547 *Lon:* -76.5444 I-81 Exit 15 take US-20 W 21.3 miles, SH-86 N 1.8 miles, Gates Rd W .9 mile & SH-5 S .4 mile
Batavia	◇ 1	🕐	℞	🚗	4133 Veterans Memorial Dr, 14020 / 585-345-1050 • *Lat:* 43.0172 *Lon:* -78.2034 I-90 (toll) Exit 48 take Park Rd W .3 mile, continue on Veterans Memorial Dr .3 mile
Brockport	◇	🕐	℞	🚗	6265 Brockport Spencerport Rd, 14420 / 585-637-6331 • *Lat:* 43.1982 *Lon:* -77.9309 1.8 miles southeast of town along SH-31
Buffalo	◇ 3	🕐	℞	🚗	5033 Transit Rd, 14221 / 716-565-0250 • *Lat:* 42.9841 *Lon:* -78.6968 I-90 (toll) Exit 49 take SH-78/Transit Rd N 2.6 miles
Camillus	◇ 5	🕐	℞	🚗	5399 W Genesee St, 13031 / 315-487-0121 • *Lat:* 43.0410 *Lon:* -76.2743 I-690 Exit 6 take SH-695 S 1.9 miles, SH-5 W 1.5 miles, Hinsdale Rd S 1 mile & CR-98 W .5 mile
Canandaigua	◇ 7		℞	🚗	4238 Recreation Dr, 14424 / 585-394-5300 • *Lat:* 42.8780 *Lon:* -77.2423 I-90 (toll) Exit 43 take SH-21 S 5.2 miles, CR-22 S .5 mile, CR-4 E .1 mile, CR-10 S 1.7 miles & Recreation Dr E .6 mile
Catskill	◇ 3	🕐	℞	🚗	265 W Bridge St, 12414 / 518-943-9423 • *Lat:* 42.2144 *Lon:* -73.8822 I-87 (toll) Exit 21 take CR-23B S 1.7 miles then US-9 W 1 mile
Centereach	○ 4		℞	🚗	161 Centereach Mall, 11720 / 631-467-4825 • *Lat:* 40.8706 *Lon:* -73.0806 I-495 Exit 62 take CR-97 N 2.9 miles & SH-25 E .4 mile
Central Square	◆ 1	🕐	℞	🚗	3018 East Ave, 13036 / 315-668-0400 • *Lat:* 43.2868 *Lon:* -76.1352 I-81 Exit 32 take SH-49 W .2 mile
Cheektowaga	☐ 2		℞	🚗	3735 Union Rd, 14225 / 716-681-5195 • *Lat:* 42.9159 *Lon:* -78.7541 I-90 Exit 52E go E on Walden Ave .6 mile & N on Union Rd .6 mile
	○ 1		℞	🚗	100 Thruway Plaza Dr, 14225 / 716-896-3669 • *Lat:* 42.9062 *Lon:* -78.7805 I-90 (toll) Exit 52 take Walden Ave W .7 mile then S at Thruway Plaza Dr
Cicero	◇ 1	🕐	℞	🚗	8064 Brewerton Rd, 13039 / 315-698-0130 • *Lat:* 43.1602 *Lon:* -76.1206 I-481 Exit 10 take Circle Dr W .1 mile then US-11 N .8 mile
Clay	○		℞		3949 Rt 31, 13041 / 315-622-5401 • *Lat:* 43.1759 *Lon:* -76.1774 From SH-481 Exit 12 go W on SH-31 .8 mile
Clifton Park	◇ 3	🕐	℞	🚗	1549 Rt 9, 12065 / 518-373-8457 • *Lat:* 42.8452 *Lon:* -73.7494 I-87 Exit 9E take SH-146 E .6 mile then US-9 S 1.5 miles
Cobleskill	◇ 3	🕐	℞	🚗	139 Merchant Pl, 12043 / 518-234-1090 • *Lat:* 42.6810 *Lon:* -74.4575 I-88 Exit 22 take SH-145 W 2 miles & N on Merchant Pl
Commack	○ 1		℞	🚗	85 Crooked Hill Rd, 11725 / 631-851-0468 • *Lat:* 40.8107 *Lon:* -73.2925 I-495 Exit 52 take Commack Rd/CR-4 N .3 mile, Henry St E .2 mile & Crooked Hill Rd N .2 mile

○ Wal-Mart ◇ Supercenter ☐ Sam's Club ▨ Gas ▧ Gas & Diesel

City/Town	⬡	🕐	℞	🚗	Information
Cortland	◯ 5		℞		872 NY Hwy 13, 13045 / 607-756-1776 • *Lat:* 42.5733 *Lon:* -76.2175 I-81 Exit 12 take US-11 W .4 mile. SH-281 S 3.8 miles, continue on SH-13 for .5 mile
East Greenbush	◇ 1	🕐	℞	🚗	279 Troy Rd, 12061 / 518-283-3055 • *Lat:* 42.6149 *Lon:* -73.7028 I-90 Exit 9 take US-4 S .5 mile
East Meadow	◯		℞		2465 Hempstead Tpke, 11554 / 516-579-3307 • *Lat:* 40.7248 *Lon:* -73.5446 From Southern Pkwy Exit 27N merge onto Wantaugh Pkwy N 2.3 miles then SH-24 W .4 mile
East Setauket	◯ 6		℞	🚗	3990 Nesconset Hwy, 11733 / 631-474-3287 • *Lat:* 40.8995 *Lon:* -73.0808 I-495 Exit 62 take CR-97 N 4.3 miles, E at Hawkins Rd to Wireless Rd N 1.2 miles then E at Nesconsett Hwy
East Syracuse	◯ 1		℞	🚗	6438 Basile Rowe, 13057 / 315-434-9873 • *Lat:* 43.0625 *Lon:* -76.0611 I-690 Exit 17 take Bridge St N .2 mile, Chevy Dr S .1 mile & Basile Rowe E .3 mile
Elmira	☐ 1			🚗	830 County Road 64 , 14903 / 607-739-2883 • *Lat:* 42.1541 *Lon:* -76.8823 I-86 Exit 51 go S on Chambers Rd .1 mile then W on CR-64 .3 mile
Elmsford	☐ 1		℞	🚗	333 Saw Mill River Rd, 10523 / 914-592-0023 • *Lat:* 41.0825 *Lon:* -73.8188 I-287 Exit 2 N on SH-9A for .5 mile
Evans Mills	◇ 5	🕐	℞	🚗	25737 US Rt 11, 13637 / 315-629-2124 • *Lat:* 44.0881 *Lon:* -75.8253 I-81 Exit 48 take SH-342 E 3.9 miles then US-11 N .4 mile
Farmingdale	◯		℞	🚗	965 Broadhollow Rd, 11735 / 631-752-8768 • *Lat:* 40.7282 *Lon:* -73.4237 From Southern Pkwy Exit 32N go N on Broad Hollow Rd (SH 110) for 1.5 miles
Fishkill	☐ 1		℞	🚗	56 W Merritt Blvd, 12524 / 845-896-4980 • *Lat:* 41.5291 *Lon:* -73.8968 I-84 Exit 13 take US-9N .6 mile then W on Merritt Blvd .2 mile
	◇ 1	🕐	℞		26 W Merritt Blvd, 12524 / 845-896-8192 • *Lat:* 41.5286 *Lon:* -73.8988 I-84 Exit 13 take US-9 N .6 mile then W on Merritt Blvd .3 mile
Fredonia	◆ 1	🕐	℞	🚗	10401 Bennett Rd, 14063 / 716-679-3150 • *Lat:* 42.4548 *Lon:* -79.3104 I-90 (toll) Exit 59 go S on Bennett Rd .4 mile
Fulton	◇	🕐	℞	🚗	1818 State Rt 3, 13069 / 315-598-1773 • *Lat:* 43.3247 *Lon:* -76.4443 2 miles west of town along SH-3 at Hannibal St
Geneseo	◇ 4	🕐	℞	🚗	4235 Veteran Dr, 14454 / 585-243-4090 • *Lat:* 42.7989 *Lon:* -77.7853 I-390 Exit 8 take US-20A S 3.2 miles, Volunteer Rd W .1 mile & Veteran Dr S .1 mile
Geneva	◯ 7		℞		990 Rt 5 & 20, 14456 / 315-781-3253 • *Lat:* 42.8580 *Lon:* -77.0225 I-90 (toll) Exit 42 take SH-14 S 5.6 miles & E on Lake St/Lake Front St .9 mile
Glenmont	◇ 2	🕐	℞	🚗	311 Rt 9 W, 12077 / 518-432-6120 • *Lat:* 42.6084 *Lon:* -73.7899 I-87 (toll) Exit 23 take US-9W S 1.9 miles
Glenville	◇ 3	🕐	℞	🚗	200 Dutch Meadows Ln, 12302 / 518-344-7035 • *Lat:* 42.8408 *Lon:* -73.9425 I-890 Exit 4C follow SH-5 NW 1 mile, SH-50 N 1 mile & Dutch Meadow Ln E .6 mile
Greece	◯ 5		℞		100 Elmridge Center Dr, 14626 / 585-227-0720 • *Lat:* 43.2148 *Lon:* -77.7272 I-490 Exit 8 merge onto SH-531 W .7 mile, SH-386 N 3.9 miles & E at Elm Ridge Center Dr
Hamburg	◯ 3		℞	🚗	4255 McKinley Pkwy, 14075 / 716-646-0682 • *Lat:* 42.7692 *Lon:* -78.8112 I-90 (toll) Exit 56 take SH-179 E .5 mile & McKinley Pkwy S 1.6 miles
Herkimer	◇ 1	🕐	℞	🚗	103 N Caroline St, 13350 / 315-717-0023 • *Lat:* 43.0232 *Lon:* -74.9935 I-90 Exit 30 follow SH-28 N .7 mile
Hornell	◯ 2		℞	🚗	1000 NY Hwy 36, 14843 / 607-324-7019 • *Lat:* 42.3482 *Lon:* -77.6676 I-86 Exit 34 merge onto SH-36 S 1.9 miles
Horseheads	◇	🕐	℞	🚗	1400 County Route 64, 14845 / 607-739-1714 • *Lat:* 42.1595 *Lon:* -76.8605 I-86 Exit 51A go S .2 mile on Chambers Rd then E 1 mile on CR-64/Big Flats Rd
Hudson	◯		℞	🚗	351 Fairview Ave, 12534 / 518-822-0160 • *Lat:* 42.2719 *Lon:* -73.7605 Jct SH-66/Union Tpk & US-9 (E of town) go N on US-9 for 1.9 miles

◯ Wal-Mart   ◇ Supercenter   ☐ Sam's Club   ▨ Gas   ▧ Gas & Diesel

City/Town	⬭	🕐	℞	🚗	Information
Islandia	◯ 1		℞	🚗	1850 Veterans Memorial Hwy, 11749 / 631-851-0468 • *Lat:* 40.7933 *Lon:* -73.1676 I-495 Exit 57 take SH-454 E .6 mile
Ithaca	◯		℞	🚗	135 Fairgrounds Memorial Pkwy, 14850 / 607-277-4510 • *Lat:* 42.4275 *Lon:* -76.5120 Jct SH-13A/Five Mile Dr & SH-13/34 (S of town) go N on SH-13/34 for 1.3 miles then W at Fairgrounds Memorial Pkwy
Jamestown	⬛ 4			🚗	720 Fairmount Ave, 14701 / 716-483-1508 • *Lat:* 42.0974 *Lon:* -79.2805 I-86 Exit 12 take SH-60 S 1.7 miles then W on SH-394 for 2 miles
Johnstown	◯ 5		℞		233 W 5th Ave, 12095 / 518-773-8544 • *Lat:* 42.9956 *Lon:* -74.3758 I-90 (toll) Exit 28 follow SH-30A 4.1 miles then N on Melcher St .2 mile
Kingston	▢			🚗	801 Frank Sottile Blvd, 12401 / 845-382-1320 • *Lat:* 41.9702 *Lon:* -73.9849 4 miles north of town via US-9W
	◇	🕐	℞	🚗	601 Frank Sottile Blvd, 12401 / 845-336-4159 • *Lat:* 41.9620 *Lon:* -73.9837 Jct US-209 & US-9W (N of town) take US-9W S .1 mile then E on Frank Sottile Blvd .9 mile
Lakewood	◇ 5	🕐	℞	🚗	350 E Fairmount Ave, 14750 / 716-763-0945 • *Lat:* 42.0991 *Lon:* -79.3025 I-86 Exit 12 take SH-60 S 1.7 miles then SH-394 W 3.2 miles
Latham	▢ 1			🚗	579 Troy Schenectady Rd, 12110 / 518-783-1481 • *Lat:* 42.7492 *Lon:* -73.7691 I-87 Exit 6 go SE on SH-7 for .3 mile
	◯ 1		℞		579 Troy Schenectady Rd, 12110 / 518-783-4086 • *Lat:* 42.7520 *Lon:* -73.7665 I-87 Exit 7 merge onto SH-7 E .4 mile, take US-9 Exit & merge onto Sparrowbush Rd .2 mile
Liverpool	⬛ 7			🚗	3895 State Route 31, 13090 / 315-652-8676 • *Lat:* 43.1870 *Lon:* -76.2424 I-81 Exit 30 take SH-31 W for 6.6 miles, N on Dell Center .1 mile
Lockport	◯		℞	🚗	5783 S Transit Rd, 14094 / 716-438-2404 • *Lat:* 43.1440 *Lon:* -78.6967 I-90 (toll) Exit 49 take SH-78/Transit Rd N 13.6 miles
Lowville	◇	🕐	℞	🚗	7155 State Rt 12, 13367 / 315-376-7030 • *Lat:* 43.7820 *Lon:* -75.4778 Jct SH-26 & SH-12 (S of town) go S on SH-12 for 3.9 miles
Macedon	◇ 7	🕐	℞	🚗	425 NY Hwy 31, 14502 / 315-986-1584 • *Lat:* 43.0645 *Lon:* -77.3566 I-490 Exit 26 go E 6.7 miles on SH-31 (Pittsford-Palmyra Rd)
Malone	◇	🕐	℞	🚗	3222 NY Hwy 11, 12953 / 518-483-5968 • *Lat:* 44.8471 *Lon:* -74.3285 Jct CR-28/Town Line Rd & US-11 (N of town) take US-11 N 1.5 miles
Massapequa	◯		℞		200 Sunrise Mall, 11758 / 516-799-2697 • *Lat:* 40.6818 *Lon:* -73.4326 From Southern Pkwy Exit 32S take SH-110 S 1.3 miles, SH-27 E .7 mile & Hemlock St E .1 mile
Massena	◇	🕐	℞	🚗	43 Stephenville St, 13662 / 315-769-1072 • *Lat:* 44.9254 *Lon:* -74.8769 1.3 miles southeast of town center along SH-37/Seaway Trail
Medford	▢ 1		℞	🚗	2950 Horseblock Rd, 11763 / 631-447-0227 • *Lat:* 40.8271 *Lon:* -72.9933 I-495 Exit 64 go N on SH-112 for .3 mile then E at CR-16
Middle Island	◯ 7		℞	🚗	750 Middle Country Rd, 11953 / 631-924-0081 • *Lat:* 40.8823 *Lon:* -72.9448 I-495 Exit 64 take SH-112 N 3.3 miles & SH-25 E 3 miles
Middletown	▢ 2		℞	🚗	300 N Galleria Dr, 10941 / 845-692-5100 • *Lat:* 41.4620 *Lon:* -74.3714 I-84 Exit 4 take SH-17 W for 1 mile then N at SH-211 for .3 mile & E on Galleria Dr
	◇ 2	🕐	℞	🚗	470 Rt 211 E, 10940 / 845-342-0222 • *Lat:* 41.4556 *Lon:* -74.3817 I-84 Exit 4W take SH-17 NW 1 mile then SH-211 W .5 mile
Mohegan Lake	◯		℞		3133 E Main St, 10547 / 914-526-1100 • *Lat:* 41.3117 *Lon:* -73.8706 Jct SH-35/Bear Mountain State Pkwy & US-6 (S of town) take US-6 N 1.2 miles
Monroe	◇ 2	🕐	℞	🚗	288 Larkin Dr, 10950 / 845-783-3505 • *Lat:* 41.3194 *Lon:* -74.1468 I-87 (toll) Exit 16 go W .2 mile on SH-17 then S .3 mile on SH-32 then W .6 mile on Larkin Dr

City/Town	🛡	⏰	Rx	🚐	Information
Monticello	◇		⏰	Rx	🚐	41 Anawana Rd, 12701 / 845-796-7202 • *Lat:* 41.6676 *Lon:* -74.6779 From SH-17 Exit 105B (N of town) take SH-42 N .1 mile & CR-103 W .2 mile
New Hartford	◆ 5	⏰	Rx	🚐	4765 Commercial Dr, 13413 / 315-736-4932 • *Lat:* 43.0951 *Lon:* -75.3055 From I-790 at SH-5A (Oriskany St) in Utica, go W 2.2 miles on Oriskany St then S 2.1 miles on Commercial Dr
Newark	○		Rx		6788 NY Hwy 31 E, 14513 / 315-331-5081 • *Lat:* 43.0541 *Lon:* -77.0579 I-90 (toll) Exit 42 take SH-14 N 7.6 miles then SH-31 W 3.9 miles
Newburgh	◇ 3	⏰	Rx		1201 Union Ave Rt 300, 12550 / 845-567-6007 • *Lat:* 41.5381 *Lon:* -74.0719 I-87 (toll) Exit 17 take SH-300 N 1.8 miles, Gardnertown Rd NW .3 mile & Union Ave N .2 mile
Niagara Falls	☐ 1			🚐	5535 Porter Rd, 14304 / 716-298-1580 • *Lat:* 43.1071 *Lon:* -78.9998 I-190 Exit 23 go W on Porter Rd .5 mile
	○ 1		Rx		5555 Porter Rd, 14304 / 716-298-4484 • *Lat:* 43.1071 *Lon:* -78.9996 I-190 Exit 23 take Porter Rd W .3 mile
Norwich	◆	⏰	Rx	🚐	5396 NY Hwy 12, 13815 / 607-334-5553 • *Lat:* 42.4982 *Lon:* -75.5285 Jct SH-32A/Hale St & SH-12 (S of town) take SH-12 S 1.8 miles
Ogdensburg	○		Rx	🚐	3000 Ford St Ext, 13669 / 315-394-8990 • *Lat:* 44.7059 *Lon:* -75.4574 Jct SH-68 & SH-37 (E of town) go N on SH-37 for 1.4 miles then W on Ford St
Olean	○ 3		Rx	🚐	1869 Plaza Dr, 14760 / 716-373-2781 • *Lat:* 42.0789 *Lon:* -78.4690 I-86 Exit 25 go S on Buffalo St .6 mile, continue on 12th St .3 mile, SH-417 W 1.2 miles & Plaza Dr N .2 mile
Oneida	◇ 6	⏰	Rx	🚐	2024 Genesee St, 13421 / 315-361-1037 • *Lat:* 43.0762 *Lon:* -75.6919 I-90 (toll) Exit 34 take SH-13 S 1.3 miles & SH-5 E 4.4 miles
Oneonta	◇ 1	⏰	Rx	🚐	5054 NY Hwy 23, 13820 / 607-431-9557 • *Lat:* 42.4489 *Lon:* -75.0425 I-88 Exit 15 merge onto SH-28/23 E .4 mile
Oswego	○		Rx		341 State Rt 104 E, 13126 / 315-342-6210 • *Lat:* 43.4475 *Lon:* -76.4867 I-81 Exit 34 follow SH-104 W 18.7 miles
Painted Post	◇ 1	⏰	Rx	🚐	3217 Silverback Ln, 14870 / 607-937-9627 • *Lat:* 42.1800 *Lon:* -77.1373 I-86 Exit 44 take Silverback Ln S .5 mile
Plattsburgh	☐ 1			🚐	7 Consumer Sq, 12901 / 518-566-7769 • *Lat:* 44.6962 *Lon:* -73.4877 I-87 Exit 37 go E on Blake Rd .4 mile then S at Consumer Square
	◇ 1	⏰	Rx		25 Consumer Sq, 12901 / 518-561-0195 • *Lat:* 44.6961 *Lon:* -73.4877 I-87 Exit 37 take SH-3 E .4 mile then S on Consumer Sq
Queensbury	◇ 1	⏰	Rx	🚐	891 NY Hwy 9, 12804 / 518-793-0309 • *Lat:* 43.3341 *Lon:* -73.6753 I-87 Exit 19 take SH-254 E .6 mile & US-9 N .4 mile
Riverhead	○ 3		Rx		765 Old Country Rd, 11901 / 631-369-1041 • *Lat:* 40.9344 *Lon:* -72.6678 I-495 Exit 73 follow CR-58 E 2.6 miles
Rochester	■ 1		Rx	🚐	1600 Marketplace Dr, 14623 / 585-427-8880 • *Lat:* 43.0866 *Lon:* -77.6295 I-390 Exit 13 go NW on Hylan Dr .1 mile & N on Marketplace Dr .1 mile
	☐ 3		Rx	🚐	700 Elm Ridge Center Dr, 14626 / 585-225-3180 • *Lat:* 43.2154 *Lon:* -77.7301 I-390 Exit 24 go W on Ridge Rd 2.8 miles then N on Elm Ridge Center Dr
	◆ 7	⏰	Rx	🚐	1490 Hudson Ave, 14621 / 585-266-2000 • *Lat:* 43.1935 *Lon:* -77.5998 I-490 Exit 21 take SH-590 N 3.9 miles, follow SH-104 W 2.8 miles & N on Hudson Ave
	◇ 1	⏰	Rx		1200 Marketplace Dr, 14623 / 585-292-6000 • *Lat:* 43.0806 *Lon:* -77.6244 I-390 Exit 13 go W on Highland Dr .1 mile & N on Marketplace Dr .3 mile
	◇ 2	⏰	Rx	🚐	2150 Chili Ave, 14624 / 585-429-9640 • *Lat:* 43.1308 *Lon:* -77.6906 I-390 Exit 18B follow SH-204 W 1.8 miles

○ Wal-Mart   ◇ Supercenter   ☐ Sam's Club   ■ Gas   ■ Gas & Diesel

City/Town		🛡	🕘	Rx	🚚	Information
Rome	◆		🕘	Rx	🚚	5815 Rome Taberg Rd, 13440 / 315-338-7900 • *Lat:* 43.2355 *Lon:* -75.5030 Jct SH-49 & SH-69 (NW of town) follow SH-69 NW for .5 mile
Saratoga Springs	◇	1	🕘	Rx	🚚	16 Old Gick Rd, 12866 / 518-581-8035 • *Lat:* 43.1026 *Lon:* -73.7497 I-87 Exit 15 take SH-50 E .3 mile then N on Old Gick Rd .2 mile
Schenectady	○	3		Rx	🚚	1320 Altamont Ave, 12303 / 518-355-2596 • *Lat:* 42.7861 *Lon:* -73.9428 I-890 Exit 6 take Brandywine N 1 mile, SH-146 E .4 mile & Altamont Ave S .9 mile
Springville	◆		🕘	Rx	🚚	317 S Cascade Dr, 14141 / 716-592-1460 • *Lat:* 42.4999 *Lon:* -78.6902 Jct SH-39 & US-219 (W of town) go S on US-219 for .7 mile
Syracuse	■	1			🚚	2649 Erie Blvd E, 13224 / 315-449-9233 • *Lat:* 43.0545 *Lon:* -76.0992 I-690 Exit 16 go S on Thompson Rd .2 mile then W on Erie Blvd .8 mile
Ticonderoga	◇		🕘	Rx		1134 Wicker St, 12883 / 518-585-3060 • *Lat:* 43.8566 *Lon:* -73.4380 I-87 Exit 28 take SH-74 E 17.3 miles then Wicker St S .1 mile
Troy	○	4		Rx	🚚	760 Hoosick Rd, 12180 / 518-279-0685 • *Lat:* 42.7464 *Lon:* -73.6402 I-787 Exit 9E merge onto SH-7 E 3.3 miles
Uniondale	○			Rx		1123 Jerusalem Ave, 11553 / 516-505-1508 • *Lat:* 40.6942 *Lon:* -73.5781 From Southern Pkwy Exit 24N take Merrick Ave N .1 mile then Jerusalem Ave E .8 mile
Utica	◇	1	🕘	Rx		710 Horatio St, 13502 / 315-738-1155 • *Lat:* 43.1312 *Lon:* -75.2225 From I-90 at SH-8/SH-12 go N .7 mile on SH-8/SH-12 to Horatio St
Valley Stream	○			Rx		77 Green Acres Rd, 11581 / 516-887-0127 • *Lat:* 40.6617 *Lon:* -73.7233 From Belt Pkwy Exit 23B take SH-27 E 1.9 miles & S on Green Acres Rd .1 mile
Vestal	□			Rx	🚚	2441 Vestal Pkwy E, 13850 / 607-770-6200 • *Lat:* 42.0945 *Lon:* -76.0122 SH-17 Exit 67S to SH-434 (Vestal Pkwy) and go E 1.8 miles
	◇		🕘	Rx		2405 Vestal Pkwy E, 13850 / 607-798-1011 • *Lat:* 42.0944 *Lon:* -76.0140 From SH-17 Exit 70S merge onto SH-201S 2 miles then SH-434 W 2.3 miles
Warsaw	○			Rx		2348 State Rt 19 N, 14569 / 585-786-0700 • *Lat:* 42.7390 *Lon:* -78.1564 Jct US-20A & SH-19 (in town) go N on SH-19 1.8 miles
Waterloo	●	5		Rx		1855 US Rt 20, 13165 / 315-539-2560 • *Lat:* 42.9100 *Lon:* -76.8757 I-90 (toll) Exit 41 take SH-414 S 4.3 miles then US-20 W .2 mile
Watertown	□	1			🚚	21341 Sams Dr, 13601 / 315-786-8602 • *Lat:* 43.9752 *Lon:* -75.9602 I-81 Exit 45 go W .6 mile on SH-3
	○	1		Rx	🚚	20823 NY Hwy 3, 13601 / 315-786-0145 • *Lat:* 43.9744 *Lon:* -75.9578 I-81 Exit 45 take SH-3 W .5 mile
Watkins Glen	◇		🕘	Rx	🚚	515 E 4th St, 14891 / 607-535-3108 • *Lat:* 42.3822 *Lon:* -76.8672 I-86 Exit 46 follow SH-414 N 20.5 miles
Webster	○	6		Rx		1902 Empire Blvd, 14580 / 585-787-1370 • *Lat:* 43.1911 *Lon:* -77.5031 I-490 Exit 21 merge onto SH-590 N 2.4 miles then Empire Blvd/SH-404 NE 2.9 miles
Westbury	○			Rx		1220 Old Country Rd, 11590 / 516-794-7280 • *Lat:* 40.7458 *Lon:* -73.5987 From Northern Pkwy Exit 31A take Meadowbrook Pkwy S 1.4 miles, then Exit M1 for Old Country Rd E .7 mile
White Plains	○	2		Rx		275 Main St, 10601 / 914-285-1070 • *Lat:* 41.0339 *Lon:* -73.7637 I-287 Exit 8, Westchester Ave W 1.2 miles, SH-22 S .1 mile, Martine Ave E .2 mile, SH-125 N & Main St E .2 mile

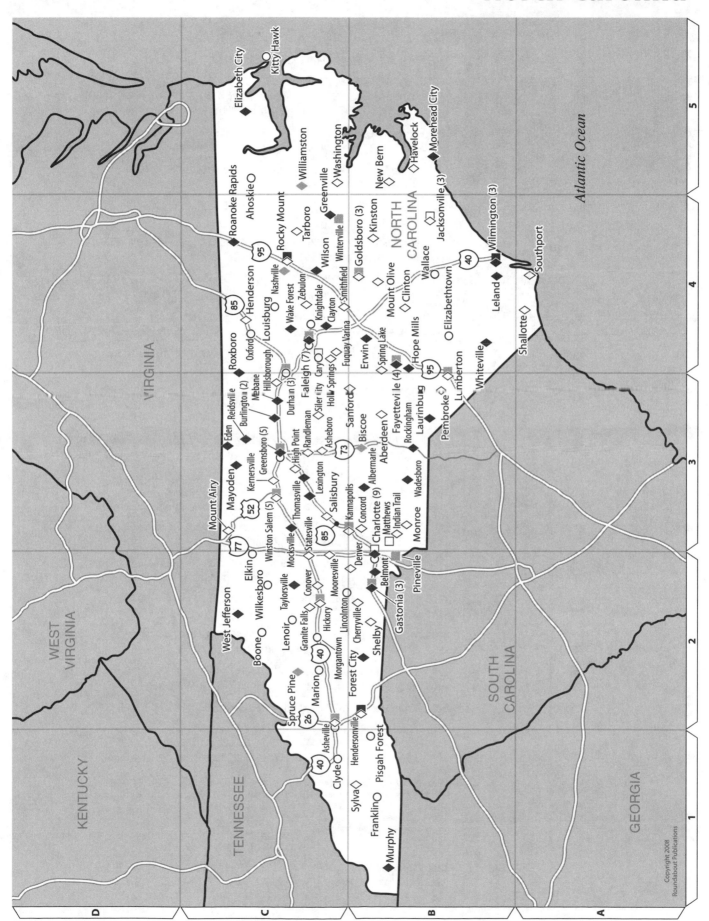

North Carolina

Wal-Mart ◇ Supercenter ☐ Sam's Club ▨ Gas ■ Gas & Diesel

City/Town	⬡	🕐	℞	🚐	Information
Aberdeen	◇		🕐	℞	🚐	250 Turner St, 28315 / 910-695-1255 • *Lat:* 35.1617 *Lon:* -79.4213 Jct US-1 & US-15/501 (in Midtown) take US-15/501 NE .7 mile then W on Commerce Ave
Ahoskie	○			℞		1532 Memorial Dr E, 27910 / 252-332-7773 • *Lat:* 36.2722 *Lon:* -76.9710 Jct US-13 & SH-561 (SE of town) go NW on US-13 for .6 mile
Albemarle	◆		🕐	℞	🚐	781 Leonard Ave, 28001 / 704-983-6830 • *Lat:* 35.3435 *Lon:* -80.1780 Jct US-52 & SH-27 (S of town) go E on SH-27/Spaulding St .9 mile then N on Leonard Ave
Asheboro	◇	3	🕐	℞	🚐	1226 E Dixie Dr, 27203 / 336-626-0004 • *Lat:* 35.6954 *Lon:* -79.7918 Jct I-73/74 & US-64 take US-64 E 2.5 miles
Asheville	■	2		℞	🚐	645 Patton Ave, 28806 / 828-251-9791 • *Lat:* 35.5890 *Lon:* -82.5816 I-40 Exit 44 go NE on US-19/23 for 1.9 miles
	○	4		℞		1636 Hendersonville Rd, 28803 / 828-274-9283 • *Lat:* 35.5124 *Lon:* -82.5267 I-40 Exit 50A merge onto US-25 S 3.4 miles
	◇	2	🕐	℞	🚐	125 Bleachery Blvd, 28805 / 828-298-8092 • *Lat:* 35.6113 *Lon:* -82.5172 I-240 Exit 8 take US-74A W .4 mile then Bleachery Blvd N .8 mile
Belmont	◆	1	🕐	℞	🚐	701 Hawley Ave, 28012 / 704-825-8885 • *Lat:* 35.2508 *Lon:* -81.0333 I-85 Exit 26 take Main St S .3 mile, Wilkerson Blvd E .5 mile & Hawley Ave S .2 mile
Biscoe	◆	1	🕐	℞		201 Montgomery Xing, 27209 / 910-428-1851 • *Lat:* 35.3656 *Lon:* -79.7764 I-73/74 Exit 33 take SH-27/24 W .9 mile
Boone	○			℞		200 Watauga Village Dr, 28607 / 828-262-0254 • *Lat:* 36.1969 *Lon:* -81.6576 Jct SH-105 & US-221/321 (S of town) take US-221/321 S .8 mile & SW on Watauga Village Dr .1 mile
Burlington	◆	3	🕐	℞	🚐	530 S Graham Hopedale Rd, 27217 / 336-226-1819 • *Lat:* 36.1350 *Lon:* -79.4083 I-40/I-85 Exit 148 take SH-54 NW 1.1 miles, Main St N .8 mile, W on Providence/N on Washington .2 mile, Graham Hopedale Rd N .7 mile
	◇	1	🕐	℞		3141 Garden Rd, 27215 / 336-584-6400 • *Lat:* 36.0692 *Lon:* -79.4994 I-40/I-85 Exit 141 take Huffman Mill Rd N .2 mile & Garden Rd W .2 mile
Cary	□	1			🚐	1801 N Harrison Ave, 27513 / 919-677-0225 • *Lat:* 35.8293 *Lon:* -78.7691 I-40 Exit 287 go S on Harrison Ave .2 mile
	○	6		℞	🚐	2010 Kildaire Farm Rd, 27518 / 919-852-0651 • *Lat:* 35.7376 *Lon:* -78.7802 I-40 Exit 293 follow US-1 S 4.2 miles then Tryon Rd/US-64 E 1 mile & Kildaire Rd S .1 mile
Charlotte	□	1		℞	🚐	8909 JW Clay Blvd, 28262 / 704-593-0227 • *Lat:* 35.3129 *Lon:* -80.7530 I-85 Exit 45 take SH-24 SE .2 mile then N on J W Clay Blvd .3 mile
	○	1		℞	🚐	8709 JW Clay Blvd, 28262 / 704-547-0525 • *Lat:* 35.3100 *Lon:* -80.7535 I-85 Exit 45A merge onto SH-24 E .2 mile then Clay Blvd N .4 mile
	○	3		℞		3209 Pineville Matthews Rd, 28226 / 704-541-7292 • *Lat:* 35.0990 *Lon:* -80.7818 I-485 Exit 57 take SH-16 N 2.8 miles then Pineville Rd W .2 mile
	○	3		℞		9101 Albemarle Rd, 28227 / 704-531-6588 • *Lat:* 35.2118 *Lon:* -80.6893 I-485 Exit 41 take SH-24/27 W 2.7 miles
	○	4		℞		3304 Eastway Dr, 28205 / 704-535-3708 • *Lat:* 35.2101 *Lon:* -80.7826 I-277 Exit 2B take US-74 E 3 miles then Exit 234B/Eastway Dr N .7 mile
	◆	3	🕐	℞	🚐	1830 Galleria Blvd, 28270 / 704-844-1066 • *Lat:* 35.1375 *Lon:* -80.7350 I-485 Exit 52 take John St N 1.9 miles, continue on Monroe Rd .8 mile & E on Galleria .3 mile
	◇	1	🕐	℞	🚐	8180 S Tryon St, 28273 / 704-588-2656 • *Lat:* 35.1435 *Lon:* -80.9297 I-485 Exit 1 take Tryon St/SH-49 N .2 mile
	◇	2	🕐	℞	🚐	3240 Wilkinson Blvd, 28208 / 704-392-2311 • *Lat:* 35.2246 *Lon:* -80.8936 I-277 Exit 1 take Wilkinson Blvd/US-74 W 1.6 miles

○ Wal-Mart   ◇ Supercenter   □ Sam's Club   ■ Gas   ■ Gas & Diesel

City/Town	⛊	⏱	℞	🚐	Information
	◇	9	⏱ ℞	🚐	9820 Callabridge Ct, 28216 / 704-392-3338 • *Lat:* 35.3284 *Lon:* -80.9464 I-77 Exit 11B take SH-16 N 8.1 miles, Mt Holly Rd E .2 mile & Callabridge Ct N .2 mile
Cherryville	◇		⏱ ℞		2505 Lincolnton Hwy, 28021 / 704-435-4449 • *Lat:* 35.3987 *Lon:* -81.3397 2.6 miles east of town center along SH-150
Clayton	◆	6	⏱ ℞	🚐	805 Town Centre Blvd, 27520 / 919-550-5600 • *Lat:* 35.6717 *Lon:* -78.5108 I-40 Exit 306 merge onto US-70 E 5.6 miles
Clinton	◇		⏱ ℞	🚐	1415 Sunset Ave, 28328 / 910-592-1818 • *Lat:* 34.9915 *Lon:* -78.3498 I-40 Exit 364 follow SH-24/US-701 BR W 13.2 miles
Clyde	◯	3	℞		157 Paragon Pkwy, 28721 / 828-456-4828 • *Lat:* 35.5259 *Lon:* -82.9540 I-40 Exit 27 follow US-74 W 2.4 miles
Concord	◇	6	⏱ ℞	🚐	150 Concord Commons Pl SW, 28027 / 704-788-3135 • *Lat:* 35.3918 *Lon:* -80.6243 I-85 Exit 58 follow US-29 S 5.4 miles
Conover	◇	1	⏱ ℞	🚐	201 Zelkova Ct NW, 28613 / 828-464-4441 • *Lat:* 35.7079 *Lon:* -81.1838 I-40 Exit 132 take Thornberg Dr NW .3 mile & SH-16 S .2 mile
Denver	◇	9	⏱ ℞	🚐	7131 Hwy 73, 28037 / 704-827-8911 • *Lat:* 35.4507 *Lon:* -81.0056 I-77 Exit 25 take SH-73 W 8.7 miles
Durham	▪	3	℞	🚐	4005 Durham Chapel Hill Blvd, 27707 / 919-489-8160 • *Lat:* 35.9698 *Lon:* -78.9561 I-40 Exit 270 take US-15 NE 1.9 miles & US-15BR for .6 mile
	◯	1	℞	🚐	5450 New Hope Commons Dr, 27707 / 919-489-4412 • *Lat:* 35.9538 *Lon:* -78.9962 I-40 Exit 270 take US-501 NE .3 mile, Mt Moriah Rd W .1 mile & New Hope Dr S .1 mile
	◯	3	℞		3500 N Roxboro St, 27704 / 919-220-7660 • *Lat:* 36.0360 *Lon:* -78.8936 I-85 Exit 176B take US-501 N 1.4 miles, Carver St E .4 mile & Roxboro St S .5 mile
Eden	◆		⏱ ℞	🚐	304 E Arbor Ln, 27288 / 336-623-8981 • *Lat:* 36.4897 *Lon:* -79.7350 Jct SH-700/770 & SH-14 (in town) take SH-14 S 1.2 miles then Arbor Ln E
Elizabeth City	◆		⏱ ℞	🚐	101 Tanglewood Pkwy, 27909 / 252-338-3367 • *Lat:* 36.2859 *Lon:* -76.3016 From US-17 BYP Exit 258 go E on Halstead Blvd 2.3 miles, Forest Park Rd NE 1 mile, Main St NW .6 mile & Tanglewd Dr E
Elizabethtown	◯		℞		1347 W Broad St, 28337 / 910-862-8424 • *Lat:* 34.6323 *Lon:* -78.6199 Jct US-701 & SH-41 (N of town) go W on SH-41 for .8 mile
Elkin	◯	3	℞		2099 N Bridge St, 28621 / 336-526-2636 • *Lat:* 36.2869 *Lon:* -80.8529 I-77 Exit 83 take US-21 BYP N 2.4 miles, Poplar Springs Rd W .1 mile & Bridge St S .1 mile
Erwin	◆	4	⏱ ℞	🚐	590 E Jackson Blvd, 28339 / 910-892-0445 • *Lat:* 35.3248 *Lon:* -78.6492 I-95 Exit 73 follow US-421 N 3.2 miles
Fayetteville	▪		℞	🚐	1450 Skibo Rd, 28303 / 910-864-7080 • *Lat:* 35.0831 *Lon:* -78.9537 I-95 Exit 58 go W on I-295 7.2 miles, S on US-401 for 3.5 miles & W on Country Club Dr 4.9 miles
	◆	3	⏱ ℞	🚐	4601 Ramsey St, 28311 / 910-488-1800 • *Lat:* 35.1235 *Lon:* -78.8797 Jct I-295 & US-401 (N of town) take US-401 S 2.2 miles
	◆		⏱ ℞	🚐	7701 S Raeford Rd, 28304 / 910-864-6575 • *Lat:* 35.0266 *Lon:* -79.0501 I-95 Exit 46 take SH-87 5.5 miles to Exit 104 then US-401 BR W 9.5 miles
	◇	9	⏱ ℞	🚐	1550 Skibo Rd, 28303 / 910-868-6434 • *Lat:* 35.0808 *Lon:* -78.9554 Jct I-295 & US-401 (N of town) take US-401 S 3.5 miles & US-401 BYP S 5.1 miles
Forest City	◆	3	⏱ ℞	🚐	197 Plaza Dr, 28043 / 828-287-7458 • *Lat:* 35.3338 *Lon:* -81.8949 From I-74 Exit 181 (S of town) take US-74 ALT N 2.4 miles & Plaza Dr W .1 mile
Franklin	◯		℞		305 Holly Springs Plz, 28734 / 828-524-9111 • *Lat:* 35.2070 *Lon:* -83.3259 Jct US-64 & US-441 (E of town) take US-441 N 1 mile, Cat Creek Rd NE 2 miles & Holly Springs Rd N .8 mile

◯ Wal-Mart ◇ Supercenter ▢ Sam's Club ▪ Gas ▪ Gas & Diesel

City/Town	⬭	🕐	℞	🚐	Information
Fuquay Varina	◇		🕐	℞	🚐	1051 E Broad St, 27526 / 919-567-2350 • *Lat:* 35.5926 *Lon:* -78.7827 I-40 Exit 312 follow SH-42 W 12.9 miles, Judd Pkwy N .1 mile & Broad St W .2 mile
Gastonia	◼ 1			℞	🚐	3540 E Franklin Blvd, 28056 / 704-866-4752 • *Lat:* 35.2579 *Lon:* -81.1166 I-85 Exit 22 go S on Main St .3 mile, W on Wilkerson Blvd .4 mile, continue on Franklin Blvd .2 mile
	◆ 2	🕐	℞	🚐	223 N Myrtle School Rd, 28052 / 704-864-6776 • *Lat:* 35.2610 *Lon:* -81.2234 I-85 Exit 14 take SH-274 S .7 mile, Crescent Ln W & Myrtle School Rd S .5 mile
	◇ 1	🕐	℞		3000 E Franklin Blvd, 28056 / 704-867-2440 • *Lat:* 35.2594 *Lon:* -81.1255 I-85 Exit 20 take SH-279 S .5 mile & Franklin Blvd E .4 mile
Goldsboro	◼				🚐	2811 N Park Dr, 27534 / 919-778-9775 • *Lat:* 35.3857 *Lon:* -77.9406 5 miles east of town center via US-13/US-70
	◇	🕐	℞		2908 US Hwy 70 W, 27530 / 919-736-7332 • *Lat:* 35.4291 *Lon:* -78.0649 5 miles west of town on US-70 at SH-581
	◇	🕐	℞		1002 N Spence Ave, 27534 / 919-778-3324 • *Lat:* 35.3860 *Lon:* -77.9474 Jct SH-111 & US-70/13 (SE of town) take US-70/13 N 3.1 miles then Spence Ave E .2 mile
Granite Falls	◇ 6	🕐	℞	🚐	4780 Hickory Blvd, 28630 / 828-396-3170 • *Lat:* 35.7776 *Lon:* -81.3951 I-40 Exit 123B take US-321 N 5.9 miles
Greensboro	◼ 1			℞	🚐	4418 W Wendover Ave, 27407 / 336-852-6212 • *Lat:* 36.0558 *Lon:* -79.8991 I-40 Exit 214 go SW on Wendover Ave .5 mile
	○ 7			℞		3738 Battleground Ave, 27410 / 336-282-6754 • *Lat:* 36.1347 *Lon:* -79.8589 I-40 Exit 213 take College Rd N 2.2 miles, then follow New Garden Rd NE 3.8 miles and US-220 NW .4 mile
	◆ 6	🕐	℞	🚐	2107 Pyramid Village Blvd, 27405 / 336-375-5445 • *Lat:* 36.1127 *Lon:* -79.7535 I-840 Exit 21 take US-70 W 3.8 miles, US-29 N 1.5 miles, then E .2 mile on Cone Blvd
	◇ 1	🕐	℞	🚐	121 W Elmsley St, 27406 / 336-370-0775 • *Lat:* 36.0035 *Lon:* -79.7962 I-85 Exit 124 take Eugene St N .2 mile & Elmsley Dr W .2 mile
	◇ 1	🕐	℞		4424 W Wendover Ave, 27407 / 336-292-5070 • *Lat:* 36.0559 *Lon:* -79.9000 I-40 Exit 214 go S on Wendover Ave .6 mile
Greenville	◆	🕐	℞	🚐	210 Greenville Blvd SW, 27834 / 252-355-2441 • *Lat:* 35.5746 *Lon:* -77.3874 Jct SH-11 & US-264 ALT (S of town) go NE on US-264 ALT .7 mile
Havelock	◇	🕐	℞		566 US Hwy 70 W, 28532 / 252-444-2055 • *Lat:* 34.9102 *Lon:* -76.9364 3 miles north of town along US-70 at Catawba Rd
Henderson	◇ 1	🕐	℞	🚐	200 N Cooper Dr, 27536 / 252-438-9004 • *Lat:* 36.3353 *Lon:* -78.4413 I-85 Exit 213 take US-158 BYP .7 mile to Dabney Dr E & Cooper Dr S .1 mile
Hendersonville	◼ 2			℞	🚐	300 Highlands Square Dr, 28792 / 828-698-6889 • *Lat:* 35.3488 *Lon:* -82.4410 I-26 Exit 49 take US-64 E .7 mile then N at Highlands Square Dr .5 mile
	◇ 1	🕐	℞	🚐	250 Highlands Square Dr, 28792 / 828-696-8285 • *Lat:* 35.3478 *Lon:* -82.4365 I-26 Exit 49A take US-64 N .5 mile then W at Highlands Sq Dr .2 mile
Hickory	◼ 1			℞	🚐	2435 US Hwy 70 SE, 28602 / 828-326-8699 • *Lat:* 35.7016 *Lon:* -81.2907 I-40 Exit 126 go S .4 mile on McDonald Pkwy then E .3 mile on US-70
	◇ 1	🕐	℞		2525 US Hwy 70 SE, 28602 / 828-326-7060 • *Lat:* 35.7011 *Lon:* -81.3598 I-40 Exit 126 take McDonald Pkwy SE .3 mile & US-70 E .4 mile
High Point	◇ 3	🕐	℞		2628 S Main St, 27263 / 336-869-9633 • *Lat:* 35.9270 *Lon:* -79.9877 I-85 Exit 111 take US-311 NW 2.5 miles
Hillsborough	◇ 1	🕐	℞	🚐	501 Hampton Pointe, 27278 / 919-732-9172 • *Lat:* 36.0567 *Lon:* -79.0831 I-85 Exit 165 take SH-86 S .2 mile then W at Hampton Point Dr .1 mile
Holly Springs	◇	🕐	℞		7016 GB Alford Hwy, 27540 / 919-557-9181 • *Lat:* 35.6368 *Lon:* -78.8306 From US-1 Exit 95 (N of town) take SH-55 S 6 miles

○ Wal-Mart ◇ Supercenter □ Sam's Club ◼ Gas ◼ Gas & Diesel

City/Town	⬢	⏰	℞	🚗	Information
Hope Mills	◆	4	⏰	℞	🚗	3030 N Main St, 28348 / 910-429-7401 • Lat: 34.9832 Lon: -78.9643 I-95 Exit 41 go NW on SH-59 for 4 miles
Indian Trail	◇	4	⏰	℞	🚗	2101 Younts Rd, 28079 / 704-882-5566 • Lat: 35.0785 Lon: -80.6480 I-485 Exit 51 follow US-74 SE 3.4 miles, Indian Trail Rd E .2 mile & Younts Rd N .1 mile
Jacksonville	☐				🚗	1170 Western Blvd, 28546 / 910-346-2148 • Lat: 34.7824 Lon: -77.3972 Jct US-17 & SH-58 (northeast of town) take US-17 S for 12.7 miles then NW .4 mile on Western Blvd
	◇		⏰	℞		561 Yopp Road, 28540 / 910-346-1889 • Lat: 34.7518 Lon: -77.4620 Jct US-258 & SH-24 (W of town) take US-258 E .5 mile then Yopp Rd S .4 mile
	◇		⏰	℞		2025 N Marine Blvd, 28546 / 910-455-2358 • Lat: 34.7782 Lon: -77.3919 Jct SH-24 & US-17 (S of town) take Marine Blvd/US-17 N 4.7 miles
Kannapolis	▦	1		℞	🚗	2421 Supercenter Dr NE, 28083 / 704-792-9000 • Lat: 35.4636 Lon: -80.5924 I-85 Exit 60 go W on Dale Earnhardt Blvd .2 mile & S on Roxie St .3 mile
	◇	1	⏰	℞	🚗	2420 Supercenter Dr NE, 28083 / 704-792-9800 • Lat: 35.4641 Lon: -80.5934 I-85 Exit 60 go W on Dale Earnhardt Blvd .2 mile & S on Roxie St .3 mile
Kernersville	◇	6	⏰	℞	🚗	1130 S Main St, 27284 / 336-992-2343 • Lat: 36.1081 Lon: -80.0976 I-40 Exit 206 merge onto I-40 BR W 4.5 miles to Exit 14 - Main St S .6 mile
Kinston	◇		⏰	℞		4101 W Vernon Ave, 28504 / 252-527-3100 • Lat: 35.2621 Lon: -77.6467 Jct US-70 & US-258 (W of town) take US-70 E .3 mile
Kitty Hawk	◯			℞		5400 N Croatan Hwy, 27949 / 252-261-6011 • Lat: 36.0988 Lon: -75.7204 Jct US-64 & US-158 (S of Nags Head) take US-158 N for 15.3 miles
Knightdale	◯	2		℞		7106 Knightdale Blvd, 27545 / 919-217-0490 • Lat: 35.7982 Lon: -78.4916 I-540 Exit 24B take US-64 BR E 1.6 miles
Laurinburg	◆		⏰	℞	🚗	901 US Hwy 401 Byp S, 28352 / 910-277-7770 • Lat: 34.7631 Lon: -79.4820 Jct US-74 & US-401 (S of town) take US-401 S .5 mile
Leland	◆		⏰	℞	🚗	1112 New Pointe Blvd, 28451 / 910-383-1769 • Lat: 34.2115 Lon: -78.0240 Jct US-74/76 & US-17 (S of town) follow US-17 S 1.2 miles
Lenoir	◯			℞	🚗	845 Blowing Rock Blvd, 28645 / 828-754-0763 • Lat: 35.9273 Lon: -81.5268 I-40 Exit 123 take US-321 N 19.4 miles
Lexington	◆	1	⏰	℞	🚗	160 Lowes Blvd, 27292 / 336-243-3051 • Lat: 35.7912 Lon: -80.2612 I-85 Exit 91 take SH-8 N .5 mile & E on Lowes Blvd
Lincolnton	◯			℞	🚗	401 N Generals Blvd, 28092 / 704-732-3090 • Lat: 35.4861 Lon: -81.2437 I-40 Exit 123 take US-321 S 15.8 miles to Exit 28 then SH-155 S 3.3 miles
Louisburg	◯			℞		279 Franklin Plz, 27549 / 919-496-2221 • Lat: 36.0908 Lon: -78.2991 1 mile south of town center along US-401/SH-39
Lumberton	▦	1		℞	🚗	5085 Dawn Dr, 28360 / 910-738-7366 • Lat: 34.6662 Lon: -79.0077 I-95 Exit 22, west of exit to Dawn Dr
	◇	1	⏰	℞	🚗	5070 Fayetteville Rd, 28358 / 910-738-2595 • Lat: 34.6675 Lon: -79.0032 I-95 Exit 22 take Fayettville Rd E .2 mile
Marion	◯	7		℞		364 US 70 W, 28752 / 828-659-3200 • Lat: 35.7040 Lon: -82.0373 I-40 Exit 86 take SH-226 N 6.1 miles then US-70 W
Matthews	☐	3		℞	🚗	1801 Windsor Square Dr, 28105 / 704-847-6742 • Lat: 35.1344 Lon: -80.7104 I-485 Exit 51 go NW on US-74 for 2.3 miles then N on Windsor Sq Dr .1 mile
Mayodan	◆		⏰	℞	🚗	6711 NC Hwy 135, 27027 / 336-548-6540 • Lat: 36.4173 Lon: -79.9370 Jct US-220 & SH-135 (E of town) take SH-135 W 1.3 miles
Mebane	◆	1	⏰	℞	🚗	1318 Mebane Oaks Rd, 27302 / 919-304-0171 • Lat: 36.0684 Lon: -79.2698 I-40/I-85 Exit 154 go S on Mebane Oaks Rd .3 mile

◯ Wal-Mart ◇ Supercenter ☐ Sam's Club ▦ Gas ◼ Gas & Diesel

City/Town			⏰	℞	🚐	Information
Mocksville	◆	1	⏰	℞	🚐	261 Cooper Creek Dr, 27028 / 336-751-1266 • *Lat:* 35.9259 *Lon:* -80.5877 I-40 Exit 170 take US-601 N .3 mile then Cooper Creek Dr E .4 mile
Monroe	◇		⏰	℞	🚐	2406 W Roosevelt Blvd, 28110 / 704-289-5478 • *Lat:* 35.0105 *Lon:* -80.5641 I-485 Exit 51 follow US-74 E 10.5 miles
Mooresville	◇	1	⏰	℞	🚐	169 Norman Station Blvd, 28117 / 704-664-5238 • *Lat:* 35.5918 *Lon:* -80.8559 I-77 Exit 36 take SH-150 E .3 mile then Norman Station Blvd S .1 mile
Morehead City	◆		⏰	℞	🚐	300 NC Hwy 24, 28557 / 252-247-0511 • *Lat:* 34.7341 *Lon:* -76.8103 Jct US-70 & SH-24 (W of town) take SH-24 W .6 mile
Morganton	○	1		℞		1227 Burkemont Ave, 28655 / 828-433-7696 • *Lat:* 35.7253 *Lon:* -81.6925 I-40 Exit 103 take US-64 S .2 mile
Mount Airy	◇	2	⏰	℞	🚐	2241 Rockford St, 27030 / 336-719-2300 • *Lat:* 36.4736 *Lon:* -80.6207 I-74 Exit 11 take US-601 N 1.6 miles
Mount Olive	◇	10	⏰	℞	🚐	308 NC Hwy 55 W, 28365 / 919-658-1701 • *Lat:* 35.2125 *Lon:* -78.0719 I-40 Exit 355 take I-40 Connector N 5 miles, US-117 N 4.4 miles, SH-55 W .5 mile
Murphy	◆		⏰	℞	🚐	2330 US 19, 28906 / 828-837-9184 • *Lat:* 35.0669 *Lon:* -84.0607 Jct US-64/74 & US-129/19 (S of town) take US-19 S 1.9 miles
Nashville	◆	4	⏰	℞		1205 Eastern Ave, 27856 / 252-459-0020 • *Lat:* 35.9708 *Lon:* -77.9372 I-95 Exit 138 follow US-64 W 3.2 miles, S .3 mile on US-64 BR, then E .1 mile on Eastern Ave/Sunset Ave
New Bern	◇		⏰	℞		3105 Martin Luther King Jr Blvd, 28562 / 252-637-6699 • *Lat:* 35.1025 *Lon:* -77.0877 Jct US-70 & US-17 (W of town) take MLK Jr Blvd/US-17 S .3 mile
Oxford	○	1		℞		714 Granville Corners, 27565 / 919-693-2900 • *Lat:* 36.2977 *Lon:* -78.5873 I-85 Exit 204 go N on SH-96 for .5 mile then S at Easy St
Pembroke	◇	8	⏰	℞	🚐	930 Hwy 711 E, 28372 / 910-522-1321 • *Lat:* 34.6929 *Lon:* -79.1847 I-95 Exit 17 follow SH-711 W 7.9 miles
Pineville	■	1		℞	🚐	11425 Carolina Place Pkwy, 28134 / 704-541-1234 • *Lat:* 35.0787 *Lon:* -80.8750 I-485 Exit 64B go SW on SH-51 for .4 mile then S on Carolina Pkwy .6 mile
Pisgah Forest	○			℞		400 Forest Gate Ctr, 28768 / 828-885-7900 • *Lat:* 35.2749 *Lon:* -82.7028 3.4 miles northeast of Brevard near US-276/US-64 jct
Raleigh	■	1		℞	🚐	2537 S Saunders St, 27603 / 919-839-1700 • *Lat:* 35.7503 *Lon:* -78.6487 I-40 Exit 298 go S on US-401 for .2 mile
	□	4		℞	🚐	3001 Calvary Dr, 27604 / 919-874-0112 • *Lat:* 35.8458 *Lon:* -78.5869 I-440 Exit 11 take US-1 N for 3.1 miles then W on Calvary Dr .4 mile
	○	3		℞		1527 Garner Station Blvd, 27603 / 919-772-8751 • *Lat:* 35.7246 *Lon:* -78.6530 I-40/I-440 Exit 298 take US-401 S 2 miles then Garner Station Blvd W .4 mile
	○	3		℞		6600 Glenwood Ave, 27612 / 919-783-5552 • *Lat:* 35.8602 *Lon:* -78.7080 I-440 Exit 7 take US-70 W 2.9 miles
	◆	2	⏰	℞	🚐	4431 New Bern Ave, 27610 / 919-212-6442 • *Lat:* 35.7987 *Lon:* -78.5621 I-440 Exit 13B merge onto New Bern Ave E 1.6 miles
	◇	1	⏰	℞	🚐	1725 New Hope Church Rd, 27609 / 919-790-6910 • *Lat:* 35.8362 *Lon:* -78.6110 I-440 Exit 10 take Wake Forest Rd N .9 mile & New Hope Rd E .1 mile
	◇	1	⏰	℞	🚐	10050 Glenwood Ave, 27617 / 919-596-5790 • *Lat:* 35.9102 *Lon:* -78.7780 I-540 Exit 4B take US-70 W .7 mile
Randleman	◇	1	⏰	℞	🚐	1021 High Point St, 27317 / 336-495-6278 • *Lat:* 35.8224 *Lon:* -79.8226 I-73/I-74 Exit 66 take Academy St E .4 mile & S at High Pt St
Reidsville	◆		⏰	℞	🚐	1624 NC Hwy 14, 27320 / 336-349-6569 • *Lat:* 36.3432 *Lon:* -79.6708 Jct US-29 & US-158 (NE of town) take US-158 W/SH-14 N 5.8 miles

○ Wal-Mart ◇ Supercenter □ Sam's Club ■ Gas ■ Gas & Diesel

City/Town	🛡	⏱	Rx	🚐	Information
Roanoke Rapids	♦ 1	⏱	Rx	🚐	251 Premier Blvd, 27870 / 252-535-3151 • *Lat:* 36.4265 *Lon:* -77.6323 I-95 Exit 173 take US-158 W .1 mile & Premier Blvd S .4 mile
Rockingham	♦	⏱	Rx	🚐	720 E US Hwy 74, 28379 / 910-582-3996 • *Lat:* 34.9389 *Lon:* -79.7656 Jct US-220 & US-74 BR (in town) take US-74 BR N 1 mile
Rocky Mount	■ 4		Rx	🚐	300 Tarrytown Ctr, 27804 / 252-443-4044 • *Lat:* 35.9601 *Lon:* -77.8222 I-95 Exit 138 go E 3.1 miles on US-64 then S .4 mile on US-301
	◇ 6	⏱	Rx	🚐	1511 Benvenue Rd, 27804 / 252-985-2254 • *Lat:* 35.9807 *Lon:* -77.8091 I-95 Exit 138 merge onto US-64 E 4.3 miles then SH-43/48 N 1.4 miles
Roxboro	♦	⏱	Rx	🚐	1049 Durham Rd, 27573 / 336-597-2909 • *Lat:* 36.3776 *Lon:* -78.9832 Jct US-158 & US-501 (S of town) take US-501 S .1 mile
Salisbury	◇ 1	⏱	Rx	🚐	323 S Arlington St, 28144 / 704-639-9718 • *Lat:* 35.6592 *Lon:* -80.4625 I-85 Exit 76 take Innes St W .1 mile & Arlington St S .3 mile
Sanford	◇	⏱	Rx		3310 NC 87 S, 27330 / 919-776-9388 • *Lat:* 35.4442 *Lon:* -79.1282 2.4 miles southeast of town along SH-87
Shallotte	◇	⏱	Rx	🚐	4540 Main St, 28470 / 910-754-2880 • *Lat:* 33.9815 *Lon:* -78.3736 Jct SH-130 & US-17 (in town) take US-17 BR NE 1.3 miles
Shelby	◇	⏱	Rx	🚐	705 E Dixon Blvd, 28152 / 704-484-0021 • *Lat:* 35.2748 *Lon:* -81.5296 I-85 Exit 10B merge onto US-74 W 11.7 miles, continue on US-74 BYP 3 miles
Siler City	◇	⏱	Rx	🚐	14215 US Hwy 64 W, 27344 / 919-663-6000 • *Lat:* 35.7346 *Lon:* -79.4272 From US-421 Exit 171 (E of town) go E on US-64 for .3 mile
Smithfield	◇ 2	⏱	Rx	🚐	1299 N Brightleaf Blvd, 27577 / 919-989-6455 • *Lat:* 35.5200 *Lon:* -78.3113 I-95 Exit 97 go W on US-70 for .6 mile then US-301 S .7 mile
Southport	◇	⏱	Rx	🚐	1675 N Howe St, 28461 / 910-454-9909 • *Lat:* 33.9440 *Lon:* -78.0300 Jct SH-133/Dosher Cutoff & SH-211 (N of town) take SH-211/Howe St S .4 mile
Spring Lake	◇	⏱	Rx	🚐	670 Lillington Hwy, 28390 / 910-436-1199 • *Lat:* 35.1745 *Lon:* -78.9694 .5 mile northeast of town on SH-210
Spruce Pine	◆	⏱	Rx	🚐	2514 Halltown Rd, 28777 / 828-766-9991 • *Lat:* 35.8692 *Lon:* -82.0435 I-40 Exit 86 follow SH-226 N for 19.4 miles then E at Halltown Rd .2 mile
Statesville	◇ 1	⏱	Rx	🚐	1116 Crossroads Dr, 28625 / 704-871-9833 • *Lat:* 35.8110 *Lon:* -80.8743 I-40 Exit 151 take US-21 N .3 mile
Sylva	◇	⏱	Rx		210 Wal-Mart Plz, 28779 / 828-586-0211 • *Lat:* 35.3616 *Lon:* -83.2032 From US-23/74 Exit 85 (N of town) take US-23 BR 1.8 miles, SH-107 S 1.1 miles & Connor Rd W
Tarboro	◇	⏱	Rx	🚐	110 River Oaks Dr, 27886 / 252-824-8170 • *Lat:* 35.8836 *Lon:* -77.5481 From US-64 Exit 485 (S of town) go S on US-258 for .3 mile
Taylorsville	♦	⏱	Rx		901 NC Hwy 16 S, 28681 / 828-632-4176 • *Lat:* 35.9053 *Lon:* -81.1777 Jct SH-90 & SH-16 (NW of town) go N on SH-16 for 1.3 miles
Thomasville	♦ 1	⏱	Rx	🚐	1585 Liberty Dr, 27360 / 336-474-2239 • *Lat:* 35.8565 *Lon:* -80.0681 I-85 Exit 103 take SH-109 E .3 mile then N at Liberty Dr .2 mile
Wadesboro	♦		Rx	🚐	2004 US Hwy 74 W, 28170 / 704-694-6530 • *Lat:* 34.9792 *Lon:* -80.1007 1.7 miles west of town on US-74
Wake Forest	♦ 7	⏱	Rx	🚐	2114 S Main St, 27587 / 919-562-2921 • *Lat:* 35.9487 *Lon:* -78.5338 I-540 Exit 16 take US-1 N 6 miles & NE on Main St .4 mile
Wallace	○ 5		Rx		715 N Norwood St, 28466 / 910-285-2078 • *Lat:* 34.7433 *Lon:* -77.9958 I-40 Exit 390 take US-117 N 5 miles
Washington	◇	⏱	Rx	🚐	570 Pamlico Plz, 27889 / 252-975-2083 • *Lat:* 35.5589 *Lon:* -77.0526 Jct US-17 & SH-32/3rd St (in town) go S on SH-32 for 2.9 miles then E at Pamlico Dr .2 mile

○ Wal-Mart ◇ Supercenter □ Sam's Club ▨ Gas ■ Gas & Diesel

City/Town	⬡	🕐	℞	🚌	Information
West Jefferson	◆		🕐 ℞	🚌	1489 Mount Jefferson Rd, 28694 / 336-246-3920 • *Lat:* 36.3911 *Lon:* -81.4819 From US-221/SH-163 jct (south of town) go N .6 mile on US-221 and turn right at SH-1250, continue N .2 mile Mount Jefferson Rd
Whiteville	◆		🕐 ℞	🚌	200 Columbus Corners Dr, 28472 / 910-640-1393 • *Lat:* 34.2954 *Lon:* -78.7042 Jct US-701 BR & SH-130 (in S Whiteville) continue S on US-701 BR .2 mile
Wilkesboro	◯		℞	🚌	1834 Winkler St, 28697 / 336-667-7691 • *Lat:* 36.1508 *Lon:* -81.1915 Jct SH-16 & US-421 (W of town) go E on US-421/SH-16 for 2.4 miles & N on Winkler Rd
Williamston	◆		🕐 ℞		1529 Washington St, 27892 / 252-792-9033 • *Lat:* 35.8343 *Lon:* -77.0667 1.5 miles south of town center via US-17 BR
Wilmington	■ 3		℞	🚌	412 S College Rd, 28403 / 910-392-2995 • *Lat:* 34.2323 *Lon:* -77.8760 I-40 Exit 420 take US-117 S for 2.8 miles
	◆ 3		🕐 ℞	🚌	5226 Sigmon Rd, 28403 / 910-392-4034 • *Lat:* 34.2438 *Lon:* -77.8759 I-40 Exit 420 continue on US-117 S 2.2 miles, Imperial Dr W .1 mile, Van Campen Blvd N .3 mile & Sigmon Rd W
	◆ 10		🕐 ℞	🚌	5135 Carolina Beach Rd, 28412 / 910-452-0944 • *Lat:* 34.1465 *Lon:* -77.8995 I-40 Exit 420 continue S on US-117 for 9.3 miles then US-421 N .6 mile
Wilson	◆ 4		🕐 ℞		2500 Forest Hills Rd W, 27893 / 252-243-9300 • *Lat:* 35.7342 *Lon:* -77.9519 I-95 Exit 121 take US-264 ALT E 3.7 miles then S on SH-1183 for .3 mile
Winston Salem	■ 1		℞	🚌	930 Hanes Mall Blvd, 27103 / 336-765-3590 • *Lat:* 36.0645 *Lon:* -80.3119 I-40 Exit 189 take US-158 S .1 mile then W at Hanes Mall Blvd
	■ 8		℞	🚌	284 Summit Square Blvd, 27105 / 336-377-2820 • *Lat:* 36.1876 *Lon:* -80.2738 I-40 Exit 6 take US-52 NW 7 miles, at Exit 155 go NE on University Pkwy .2 mile & N on Summit Sq .2 mile
	◇ 2		🕐 ℞	🚌	4550 Kester Mill Rd, 27103 / 336-760-9868 • *Lat:* 36.0692 *Lon:* -80.3407 I-40 Exit 188 take US-421 N 1 mile to Exit 239-Jonestown Rd S .3 mile
	◇ 2		🕐 ℞	🚌	1330 W Clemmonsville Rd, 27127 / 336-771-1011 • *Lat:* 36.0401 *Lon:* -80.2624 I-40 Exit 193A take US-52 S .3 mile then W on Clemmonsville Rd 1.5 miles
	◇ 10		🕐 ℞	🚌	320 E Hanes Mill Rd, 27105 / 336-377-9194 • *Lat:* 36.1896 *Lon:* -80.2744 I-40 Exit 193B take US-52 N 9.2 miles then Exit 115A-University Pkwy .5 mile N to Hanes Mill Rd E
Winterville	■		℞	🚌	4240 State Hwy 11 S, 28590 / 252-439-0400 • *Lat:* 35.5467 *Lon:* -77.4053 3.7 miles south of town via SH-11
Zebulon	◇		🕐 ℞		841 East Gannon Ave, 27597 / 919-269-2221 • *Lat:* 35.8290 *Lon:* -78.2963 1 mile east of town center via SH-97/Gannon Ave near jct with US-64

◯ Wal-Mart   ◇ Supercenter   ☐ Sam's Club   ▩ Gas   ■ Gas & Diesel

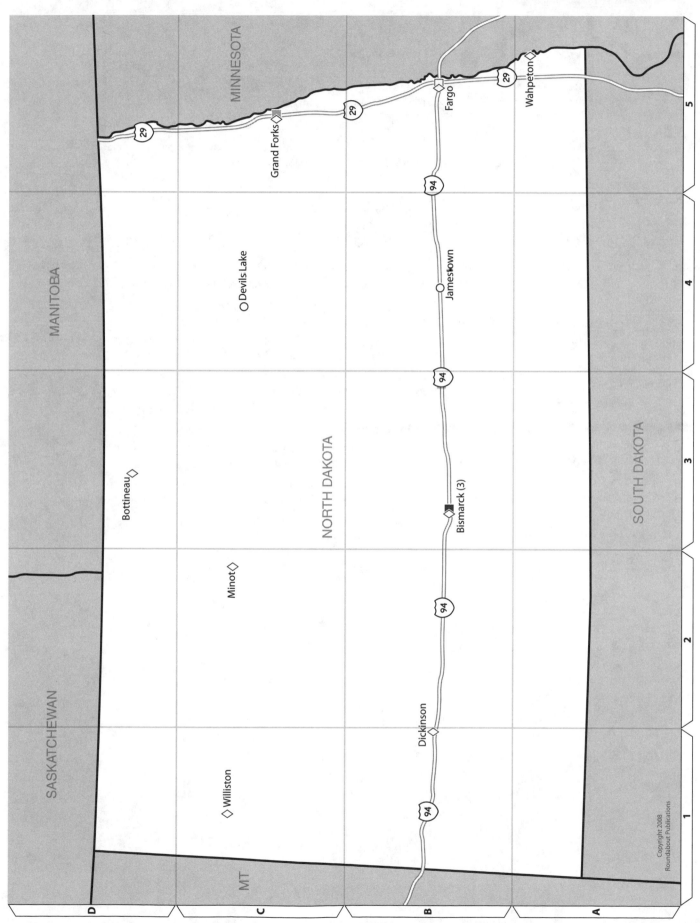

North Dakota

○ Wal-Mart ◇ Supercenter ☐ Sam's Club ▨ Gas ■ Gas & Diesel

MINNESOTA

MANITOBA

SASKATCHEWAN

NORTH DAKOTA

SOUTH DAKOTA

MT

Grand Forks ◇

Fargo ◇

29

29

Wahpeton ◇

94

Devils Lake ○

Jamestown ○

Bottineau ◇

Bismarck (3) ■

Minot ◇

94

Dickinson ◇

Williston ◇

94

94

D   C   B   A

5   4   3   2   1

City/Town	♡	🕐	℞	🚐	Information
Bismarck	■ 3			🚐	2821 Rock Island Pl, 58504 / 701-222-1101 • *Lat:* 46.7945 *Lon:* -100.7417 I-94 Exit 161 go S on Bismarck Expy 2.7 miles then S on Rock Island Pl .1 mile
	◇ 2	🕐		🚐	1400 Skyline Blvd, 58503 / 701-323-0530 • *Lat:* 46.8561 *Lon:* -100.7723 I-94 Exit 159 go N 1.7 miles on US-83
	◇ 3	🕐		🚐	2717 Rock Island Pl, 58503 / 701-223-3066 • *Lat:* 46.7950 *Lon:* -100.7479 I-94 Exit 161 go S 2.9 miles on Bismarck Expy
Bottineau	◇	🕐	℞		912 11th St E, 58318 / 701-228-5276 • *Lat:* 48.8208 *Lon:* -100.4346 .5 mile east of town along SH-5
Devils Lake	○				210 Hwy 2 W, 58301 / 701-662-5203 • *Lat:* 48.1271 *Lon:* -98.8667 Jct SH-20 & US-2 (SE of town) go W on US-2 for .2 mile
Dickinson	◇ 1	🕐		🚐	2456 3rd Ave W, 58601 / 701-225-8504 • *Lat:* 46.9081 *Lon:* -102.7895 I-94 Exit 61 take SH-22 N .8 mile
Fargo	□ 2			🚐	4831 13th Ave S, 58103 / 701-282-7997 • *Lat:* 46.8621 *Lon:* -96.8677 1.3 miles north of I-94 Exit 348 or 1.3 miles west of I-29 Exit 64
	◇ 2	🕐		🚐	4731 13th Ave S, 58103 / 701-281-3971 • *Lat:* 46.8621 *Lon:* -96.8653 I-94 Exit 348 go N on 45th St 1.1 miles then W on 13th Ave .2 mile
Grand Forks	■ 2			🚐	2501 32nd Ave S, 58201 / 701-795-9449 • *Lat:* 47.8894 *Lon:* -97.0630 I-29 Exit 138 go E on 32nd Ave 1.1 miles
	◇ 1	🕐			2551 32nd Ave S, 58201 / 701-746-7225 • *Lat:* 47.8894 *Lon:* -97.0639 I-29 Exit 138 take 32nd Ave E 1 mile
Jamestown	○ 1				921 25th St SW, 58401 / 701-252-6778 • *Lat:* 46.8819 *Lon:* -98.7213 I-94 Exit 258 take US-281 S .2 mile then 25th St W .2 mile
Minot	◇	🕐		🚐	3900 S Broadway, 58701 / 701-838-2176 • *Lat:* 48.1946 *Lon:* -101.2963 Jct US-2 & US-83 (S of town) take US-83 S 1 mile
Wahpeton	◇	🕐			1625 Commerce Dr, 58075 / 701-642-9086 • *Lat:* 46.2824 *Lon:* -96.6307 I-29 Exit 23A follow SH-13 E 10 miles, SH-210 N 1.3 miles, W at 16th Ave .2 mile
Williston	◇	🕐		🚐	4001 2nd Ave W, 58801 / 701-572-8550 • *Lat:* 48.1800 *Lon:* -103.6255 Jct 2nd Ave/US-2 & 28th St (N of town) go N on 2nd Ave for .8 mile

○ Wal-Mart ◇ Supercenter □ Sam's Club ▨ Gas ■ Gas & Diesel

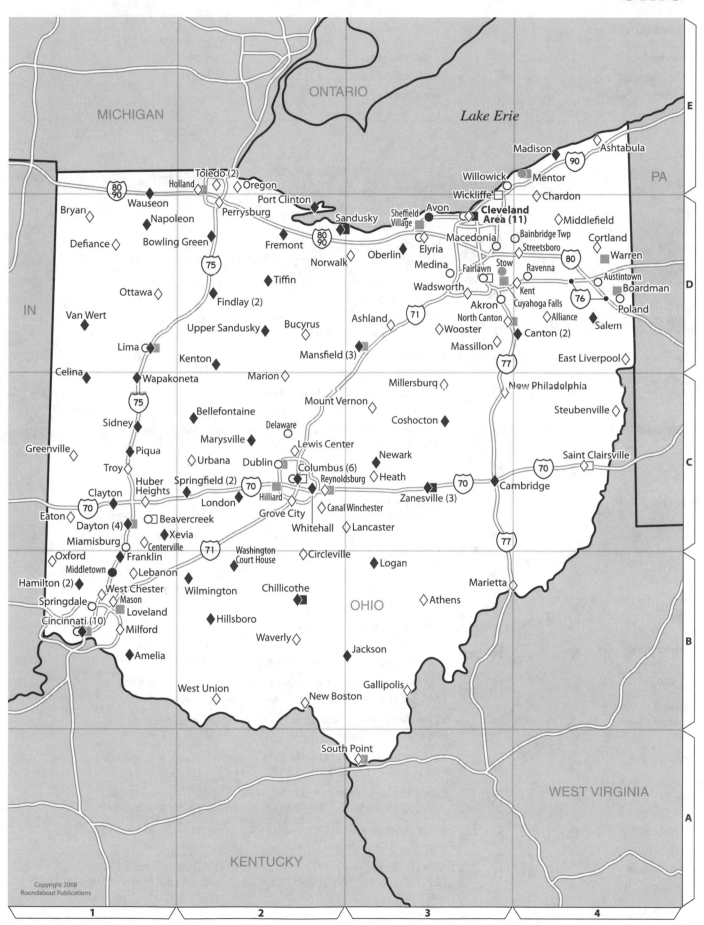

Ohio

Legend: ○ Wal-Mart ◇ Supercenter □ Sam's Club ▨ Gas ■ Gas & Diesel

MICHIGAN

ONTARIO

Lake Erie

PA

IN

OHIO

WEST VIRGINIA

KENTUCKY

Bryan
Wauseon
Holland
Toledo (2)
Oregon
Perrysburg
Port Clinton
Sandusky
Napoleon
Defiance
Bowling Green
Fremont
Norwalk
Oberlin
Elyria
Sheffield Village
Avon
Macedonia
Cleveland Area (11)
Madison
Ashtabula
Willowick
Mentor
Wickliffe
Chardon
Middlefield
Cortland
Warren
Ottawa
Tiffin
Findlay (2)
Medina
Fairlawn
Stow
Bainbridge Twp
Streetsboro
Ravenna
Austintown
Boardman
Van Wert
Upper Sandusky
Bucyrus
Ashland
Wadsworth
Akron
Kent
Cuyahoga Falls
Poland
Lima
Kenton
Mansfield (3)
North Canton
Wooster
Alliance
Salem
Celina
Wapakoneta
Marion
Massillon
Canton (2)
East Liverpool
Sidney
Bellefontaine
Mount Vernon
Millersburg
Coshocton
New Philadelphia
Steubenville
Greenville
Marysville
Delaware
Lewis Center
Newark
Saint Clairsville
Piqua
Troy
Urbana
Dublin
Columbus (6)
Reynoldsburg
Heath
Cambridge
Huber Heights
Springfield (2)
Hilliard
Zanesville (3)
Clayton
London
Grove City
Canal Winchester
Eaton
Dayton (4)
Beavercreek
Whitehall
Lancaster
Miamisburg
Xevia
Centerville
Washington Court House
Circleville
Logan
Marietta
Oxford
Franklin
Lebanon
Wilmington
Chillicothe
Athens
Middletown
Hamilton (2)
West Chester
Mason
Loveland
Hillsboro
Springdale
Milford
Waverly
Cincinnati (10)
Amelia
Jackson
West Union
Gallipolis
New Boston
South Point

1   2   3   4

Cleveland Area

Bedford	◇	Garfield Heights	○	Oakwood Village ■
Cleveland (3)	○ ◇ ■	Mayfield Heights	○	Parma ○
Cleveland Heights	○	North Olmsted	○	Strongsville ○

City/Town	🛡	🕐	℞	🚐	Information
Akron	○	1			🚐	2887 S Arlington Rd, 44312 / 330-645-9556 • *Lat:* 40.9916 *Lon:* -81.4922 I-77 Exit 120 go N on Arlington Rd .3 mile
Alliance	◇		🕐	℞	🚐	2700 W State St, 44601 / 330-821-0026 • *Lat:* 40.9019 *Lon:* -81.1597 Jct US-62F & US-62 (W of town) go E on US-62/State St for .5 mile
Amelia	◆	7	🕐	℞	🚐	1815 E Ohio Pike, 45102 / 513-797-5700 • *Lat:* 39.0183 *Lon:* -84.1976 I-275 Exit 65 go SE on SH-125 for 6.8 miles
Ashland	◇	3	🕐	℞	🚐	1996 E Main St, 44805 / 419-281-9537 • *Lat:* 40.8684 *Lon:* -82.3093 I-71 Exit 186 take US-250 W 2.5 miles
Ashtabula	◇	5	🕐	℞	🚐	3551 N Ridge Rd E, 44004 / 440-998-4000 • *Lat:* 41.8807 *Lon:* -80.7497 I-90 Exit 228 merge onto SH-46 N 3.9 miles then US-20 E .7 mile
Athens	◇		🕐	℞	🚐	929 E State St, 45701 / 740-594-3398 • *Lat:* 39.3366 *Lon:* -82.0669 From US-50 Exit 16A (E of town) go N on US-33 for .2 mile then E on State St .7 mile
Austintown	○	3		℞	🚐	6001 Mahoning Ave, 44515 / 330-270-0001 • *Lat:* 41.0995 *Lon:* -80.7731 I-80 Exit 224 merge onto SH-11 S 1.8 miles then Mahoning Ave W 1 mile
Avon	●	1		℞	🚐	35901 Chester Rd, 44011 / 440-937-4750 • *Lat:* 41.4672 *Lon:* -82.0176 I-90 Exit 153 take US-83 N .2 mile then Chester Rd E .2 mile
Bainbridge Township	○			℞	🚐	7235 Market Place Dr, 44023 / 330-562-0000 • *Lat:* 41.3542 *Lon:* -81.3868 Jct US-422 & SH-91/Som Center Rd, follow SH-91 S .6 mile, Aurora Rd SE 3.4 miles
Beavercreek	□	1		℞	🚐	3446 New Germany Trebein Rd, 45431 / 937-426-1511 • *Lat:* 39.7713 *Lon:* -84.0579 I-675 Exit 17 go S on Fairfield Rd .4 mile & W on New Germany Rd .3 mile
	○	1		℞	🚐	3360 New Germany Trebein Rd, 45431 / 937-426-8227 • *Lat:* 39.7710 *Lon:* -84.0561 I-675 Exit 17 take Fairfield Rd S .4 mile then New Germany Trebein Rd E .5 mile
Bedford	◇	2	🕐	℞	🚐	22209 Rockside Rd, 44146 / 216-587-0110 • *Lat:* 41.4093 *Lon:* -81.5327 I-271 Exit 26A (southbound use Exit 26) go W on Rockside Rd 1.4 miles
Bellefontaine	◆		🕐	℞	🚐	2281 S Main St, 43311 / 937-592-4700 • *Lat:* 40.3286 *Lon:* -83.7612 2.3 miles south of town center on US-68
Boardman	■	1		℞	🚐	6361 South Ave, 44512 / 330-965-1643 • *Lat:* 41.0335 *Lon:* -80.6344 I-680 Exit 11 take US 224 W for .3 mile then N on South Ave .6 mile
Bowling Green	◆	2	🕐	℞	🚐	131 W Gypsy Lane Rd, 43402 / 419-352-3776 • *Lat:* 41.3566 *Lon:* -83.6507 I-75 Exit 179 merge onto US-6 W 1.4 miles then US-25 N .5 mile
Bryan	◇		🕐	℞	🚐	1215 S Main St, 43506 / 419-636-1535 • *Lat:* 41.4610 *Lon:* -84.5507 I-80/90 (toll) Exit 13 take SH-15 S 10.4 miles
Bucyrus	◇		🕐	℞		1875 E Mansfield St, 44820 / 419-562-8101 • *Lat:* 40.8124 *Lon:* -82.9463 Jct US-30 & CR-330/US-30 BR (E of town) go W on US-30 BR .7 mile
Cambridge	◆	1	🕐	℞	🚐	61215 Southgate Rd, 43725 / 740-439-5743 • *Lat:* 39.9888 *Lon:* -81.5738 I-70 Exit 178 take SH-209 S .5 mile
Canal Winchester	◇	6	🕐	℞	🚐	6674 Winchester Blvd, 43110 / 614-833-3930 • *Lat:* 39.8547 *Lon:* -82.8261 I-270 Exit 46B merge onto US-33 E 5 miles then SH-674 S .2 mile & Winchester Blvd E .1 mile

○ Wal-Mart ◇ Supercenter □ Sam's Club ▨ Gas ■ Gas & Diesel

City/Town	⬟	🕐	℞	🚌	Information
Canton	◆ 2	🕐	℞	🚌	4004 Tuscarawas St W, 44708 / 330-479-9620 • *Lat:* 40.7967 *Lon:* -81.4222 I-77 Exit 105 take SH-172 W 1.3 miles
	◆ 5	🕐	℞	🚌	3200 Atlantic Blvd NE, 44705 / 330-489-9035 • *Lat:* 40.8365 *Lon:* -81.3284 I-77 Exit 107B merge onto US-62 E 4.1 miles
Celina	◆	🕐	℞	🚌	1950 Havemann Rd, 45822 / 419-586-3777 • *Lat:* 40.5564 *Lon:* -84.5366 I-75 Exit 11 take US-33 & SH-29 W for 19.6 miles
Centerville	◇ 1	🕐	℞	🚌	6244 Wilmington Pike, 45459 / 937-848-3188 • *Lat:* 39.6484 *Lon:* -84.1103 I-675 Exit 7 take Wilmington Pike S .4 mile
Chardon	◇ 7	🕐	℞	🚌	223 Meadowlands Dr, 44024 / 440-286-2250 • *Lat:* 41.5834 *Lon:* -81.2238 I-90 Exit 200 take SH-44 S 6 miles then W on Meadowlands Dr .3 mile
Chillicothe	■		℞	🚌	1270 N Bridge St, 45601 / 740-779-6700 • *Lat:* 39.3615 *Lon:* -82.9764 Jct US-35 & US-23BR (east of town) go N on Bridge St .9 mile
	◆	🕐	℞	🚌	85 River Trace, 45601 / 740-774-4800 • *Lat:* 39.3303 *Lon:* -82.9761 Jct US-35 & SH-159/Bridge St (N of town) go S on Bridge St .2 mile & E on River Trace .1 mile
Cincinnati	■ 1		℞	🚌	4825 Marburg Ave, 45209 / 513-631-4732 • *Lat:* 39.1628 *Lon:* -84.4299 Northbound travelers use I-71 Exit 8A to Marburg Ave; Southbound travelers use I-71 Exit 8, turn left at Highland Ave .2 mile, left at Ridge Ave .6 mile, right at Alamo Ave .2 mile to Marburg Ave.
	▦ 1		℞	🚌	5375 N Bend Rd, 45247 / 513-661-0800 • *Lat:* 39.1872 *Lon:* -84.6026 I-74 Exit 14, north of exit
	■ 2		℞	🚌	815 Clepper Ln, 45245 / 513-753-4865 • *Lat:* 39.0922 *Lon:* -84.2625 I-275 Exit 63 go SE on SH-32 for 1.6 miles then S at Glen Este Rd .2 mile
	□ 1		℞	🚌	800 Kemper Commons Cir, 45246 / 513-671-2016 • *Lat:* 39.2876 *Lon:* -84.4558 I-275 Exit 42 take SH-747S .4 mile then E on Kemper Rd .5 mile
	○ 1		℞		3430 Highland Ave, 45213 / 513-351-9818 • *Lat:* 39.1706 *Lon:* -84.4216 I-71 Exit 8 go W .2 mile then N on Highland Ave
	○ 4		℞	🚌	2322 Ferguson Rd, 45238 / 513-922-8881 • *Lat:* 39.1284 *Lon:* -84.6007 I-74 Exit 17 take Montana Ave SW 2.3 miles, Boudinot Ave S 1.4 miles & Glenhills Way E .3 mile
	◆ 2	🕐	℞	🚌	1143 Smiley Ave, 45240 / 513-825-4423 • *Lat:* 39.2970 *Lon:* -84.5227 I-275 Exit 39 follow Winton Rd S 1.2 miles then NE at Smiley Ave .2 mile
	◇ 1	🕐	℞	🚌	2801 Cunningham Dr, 45241 / 513-769-1124 • *Lat:* 39.2544 *Lon:* -84.4275 I-75 Exit 14 go E .8 mile on Glendale Milford Rd
	◇ 2	🕐	℞	🚌	4370 Eastgate Square Dr, 45245 / 513-753-3200 • *Lat:* 39.0944 *Lon:* -84.2690 I-275 Exit 63B merge onto SH-32 E 1.3 miles then S at Eastgate Sq Dr .1 mile
	◇ 3	🕐	℞	🚌	8451 Colerain Ave, 45239 / 513-245-9458 • *Lat:* 39.2236 *Lon:* -84.5873 I-275 Exit 33 go SE on US-27 (Colerain Ave) 2.4 miles
Circleville	◇	🕐	℞	🚌	1470 S Court St, 43113 / 740-477-3678 • *Lat:* 39.5852 *Lon:* -82.9527 Jct US-22/Main St & CR-188/Court St (in town) take Court St S 1.2 miles
Clayton	◆ 1	🕐	℞	🚌	7725 Hoke Rd, 45315 / 937-836-9405 • *Lat:* 39.8577 *Lon:* -84.3308 I-70 Exit 26 go N on Hoke Rd .1 mile
Cleveland	■ 1		℞	🚌	10250 Brookpark Rd, 44130 / 216-265-0012 • *Lat:* 41.3773 *Lon:* -81.7832 I-480 Exit 13 go S on Tiedeman Rd .5 mile & E on Brookpark Rd
	○ 1		℞	🚌	10000 Brookpark Rd, 44130 / 216-741-7340 • *Lat:* 41.4185 *Lon:* -81.7544 I-480 Exit 13 go S .5 mile on Tiedeman Rd then E .2 mile on Brookpark Rd
	◇ 1	🕐	℞	🚌	3400 Steelyard Dr, 44109 / 216-661-2406 • *Lat:* 41.4624 *Lon:* -81.6902 I-71 Exit 247A (northbound exit only) follow Steelyard Dr E .2 mile and then S .4 mile

○ Wal-Mart ◇ Supercenter □ Sam's Club ■ Gas ■ Gas & Diesel

City/Town	⛊	🕐	℞	🚗	Information
Cleveland Heights	○ 6		℞		3606 Mayfield Rd, 44118 / 216-382-1657 • *Lat:* 41.5204 *Lon:* -81.5497 I-271 Exit 34 take US-322 W 5.3 miles
Columbus	□ 1		℞	🚗	3950 Morse Rd, 43219 / 614-476-4224 • *Lat:* 40.0579 *Lon:* -82.9120 I-270 Exit 32 go W on Morse Rd for .6 mile
	○ 2		℞		3579 S High St, 43207 / 614-409-0683 • *Lat:* 39.8893 *Lon:* -82.9979 I-270 Exit 52A merge onto US-23 N 1.2 miles
	◆ 1	🕐	℞	🚗	5200 Westpointe Plaza Dr, 43228 / 614-876-7850 • *Lat:* 39.9820 *Lon:* -83.1456 I-70 Exit 91B take Hilliard-Rome Rd N .1 mile & Renner Rd E .4 mile
	◇ 1	🕐	℞	🚗	3900 Morse Rd, 43219 / 614-476-2070 • *Lat:* 40.0580 *Lon:* -82.9142 I-270 Exit 32 go W on Morse Rd .7 mile
	◇ 1	🕐	℞	🚗	1221 Georgesville Rd, 43228 / 614-275-9811 • *Lat:* 39.9279 *Lon:* -83.1170 I-270 Exit 5 take Georgesville Rd N .6 mile
	◇ 4	🕐	℞		2700 Bethel Rd, 43220 / 614-326-0083 • *Lat:* 40.0651 *Lon:* -83.0908 I-270 Exit 20 take Sawmill Rd S 2.8 miles, Resler Rd E .3 mile, Picforde Dr S .2 mile & Bethel Rd W .2 mile
Cortland	◇	🕐	℞	🚗	2016 Millenium Blvd, 44410 / 330-372-1772 • *Lat:* 41.2758 *Lon:* -80.7740 3.7 miles northeast of Warren via Elm Rd and SH-5
Coshocton	◆	🕐	℞	🚗	23605 Airport Rd, 43812 / 740-622-1278 • *Lat:* 40.3324 *Lon:* -81.9101 I-77 Exit 65 take US-36 W 16.6 miles
Cuyahoga Falls	■ 6		℞	🚗	1189 Buchholzer Blvd, 44221 / 330-929-3789 • *Lat:* 41.1181 *Lon:* -81.4711 I-76 Exit 23 take SH-8 N 4.1 miles, then E on Howe Ave .9 mile & S on Buchholzer .3 mile
Dayton	■ 1		℞	🚗	6955 Miller Ln, 45414 / 937-454-6200 • *Lat:* 39.8479 *Lon:* -84.1922 I-75 Exit 59 go W at Benchwood Rd .1 mile then N on Miller .4 mile
	■ 3			🚗	1111 Miamisburg Centerville Rd, 45459 / 937-436-0299 • *Lat:* 39.6301 *Lon:* -84.1911 I-75 Exit 44 go E 2 miles on SH 725 then N on Lyons Rd
	◆ 2	🕐	℞	🚗	1701 W Dorothy Ln, 45439 / 937-643-2124 • *Lat:* 39.7092 *Lon:* -84.2040 I-75 Exit 50A go S .6 mile on Dryden Rd, E .4 mile on Northlawn Ave, N .3 mile on Springboro Rd, E .7 mile on Dorothy Ln
	◇ 1	🕐	℞	🚗	3465 York Commons Blvd, 45414 / 937-454-6240 • *Lat:* 39.8448 *Lon:* -84.1954 I-75 Exit 59 take Benchwood Rd W .2 mile, Commerce Center N .2 mile & York Commons W .1 mile
Defiance	◇	🕐	℞	🚗	1804 N Clinton St, 43512 / 419-784-2390 • *Lat:* 41.3021 *Lon:* -84.3608 1 mile north of town along SH-66 (Clinton St)
Delaware	○ 10		℞	🚗	1760 Columbus Pike, 43015 / 740-363-9931 • *Lat:* 40.2661 *Lon:* -83.0700 I-71 Exit 131 take US-36 W 7.5 miles then US-23 S 2.4 miles
Dublin	■ 2		℞	🚗	5870 Sawmill Rd, 43017 / 614-760-7771 • *Lat:* 40.0875 *Lon:* -83.0918 I-270 Exit 20 go S on Sawmill Rd 1.5 miles
	○ 1		℞	🚗	5900 Britton Pkwy, 43016 / 614-717-9660 • *Lat:* 40.0733 *Lon:* -83.1392 I-270 Exit 15 take Tuttle Blvd W .3 mile & Britton Pkwy S .2 mile
East Liverpool	◇	🕐	℞	🚗	16280 Dresden Ave, 43920 / 330-386-4002 • *Lat:* 40.6635 *Lon:* -80.5894 Jct US-30 & SH-170 (N of town) go E on SH-170 & S on Dresden Ave .1 mile
Eaton	◇ 6	🕐	℞	🚗	100A E Washington Jackson Rd, 45320 / 937-456-1777 • *Lat:* 39.7663 *Lon:* -84.6374 I-70 Exit 10 take US-127 S 4.9 miles & Washington Jackson Rd W .6 mile
Elyria	○ 2		℞	🚗	149 Midway Blvd, 44035 / 440-324-4104 • *Lat:* 41.3989 *Lon:* -82.1028 I-80 Exit 145 take SH-57 N .5 mile & Midway Blvd E .8 mile
	◇ 7	🕐	℞	🚗	1000 Chestnut Commons Dr, 44035 / 440-365-0135 • *Lat:* 41.3487 *Lon:* -82.0669 I-80 Exit 145 follow SH-57 S 5.8 mile, E .1 mile on Chestnut Ridge Rd, N .3 mile on Chestnut Commons Dr

○ Wal-Mart ◇ Supercenter □ Sam's Club ■ Gas ■ Gas & Diesel

City/Town	⬭	🕐	Rx	🚐	Information
Fairlawn	☐ 1		Rx	🚐	3750 W Market St Unit J, 44333 / 330-665-5336 • *Lat:* 41.1253 *Lon:* -81.5706 I-77 Exit 137 go E on SH-18 for 1 mile
	◯ 1		Rx		3750 W Market St, 44333 / 330-668-1129 • *Lat:* 41.1357 *Lon:* -81.6342 I-77 Exit 137A follow SH-18 E .7 mile
Findlay	◆ 1	🕐	Rx	🚐	1161 Trenton Ave, 45840 / 419-425-2186 • *Lat:* 41.0584 *Lon:* -83.6729 I-75 Exit 159 take US-224 W .3 mile
	◇ 5	🕐	Rx		2500 Tiffin Ave, 45840 / 419-425-1300 • *Lat:* 41.0557 *Lon:* -83.5950 I-75 Exit 157 follow SH-12 West & North 1.2 miles, Center St E .3 mile, continue on Tiffin Ave 2.7 miles
Franklin	◆ 1	🕐	Rx	🚐	1275 E 2nd St, 45005 / 937-704-0568 • *Lat:* 39.5635 *Lon:* -84.2774 I-75 Exit 38 take 2nd St W .4 mile
Fremont	◆ 2	🕐	Rx	🚐	2052 N State Rt 53, 43420 / 419-334-3190 • *Lat:* 41.3785 *Lon:* -83.1173 I-80/90 (toll) Exit 91 merge onto SH-53 S 1.7 miles
Gallipolis	◇	🕐	Rx	🚐	2145 Eastern Ave, 45631 / 740-441-0406 • *Lat:* 38.8231 *Lon:* -82.1729 Jct US-35 & SH-7 (N of town) take SH-7/Eastern Ave S 2.2 miles
Garfield Heights	◯ 1		Rx	🚐	5638 Transportation Blvd, 44125 / 216-663-2884 • *Lat:* 41.4139 *Lon:* -81.6161 I-480 Exit 21 take Transportation Blvd E .3 mile
Greenville	◇	🕐	Rx	🚐	1501 Wagner Ave, 45331 / 937-547-9644 • *Lat:* 40.1239 *Lon:* -84.6207 Jct US-36 & US-127 (E of town) take US-127 N 1.5 miles, SH-153 W .9 mile & CR-98 N .2 mile
Grove City	◇ 1	🕐	Rx	🚐	1693 Stringtown Rd, 43123 / 614-539-8560 • *Lat:* 39.8786 *Lon:* -83.0436 I-71 Exit 100 take Stringtown Rd E .2 mile
Hamilton	◆ 9	🕐	Rx	🚐	3201 Princeton Rd, 45011 / 513-869-8400 • *Lat:* 39.3909 *Lon:* -84.5092 I-75 Exit 24 take SH-129 W 7.8 miles & SH-4 BYP N .3 mile
	◇	🕐	Rx	🚐	1505 Main St, 45013 / 513-737-0564 • *Lat:* 39.4262 *Lon:* -84.5968 I-75 Exit 24 take SH-129 W 12.2 miles, continue W on Main St 1.8 miles
Heath	◇ 7	🕐	Rx	🚐	911 Hebron Rd, 43056 / 740-522-5841 • *Lat:* 40.0282 *Lon:* -82.4438 I-70 Exit 129B take SH-79 N 6.6 miles
Hilliard	▧ 1		Rx	🚐	1755 Hilliard Rome Rd, 43026 / 614-921-0057 • *Lat:* 39.9663 *Lon:* -83.1470 I-70 Exit 91 go N on Hilliard-Rome Rd for .5 mile
Hillsboro	◆	🕐	Rx	🚐	540 Harry Sauner Rd, 45133 / 937-840-0208 • *Lat:* 39.2267 *Lon:* -83.6192 Jct US-50 & US-62 (in town) take US-62 N 1.9 miles & Sauner Rd W .5 mile
Holland	▧ 1		Rx	🚐	1300 E Mall Dr, 43528 / 419-866-8366 • *Lat:* 41.6231 *Lon:* -83.7265 I-475 Exit 8 take SH-2 W for .2 mile, N at Spring Meadows then NW at Centers Dr & Mall Dr for .5 mile
	◇ 1	🕐	Rx	🚐	1355 S McCord Rd, 43528 / 419-867-0155 • *Lat:* 41.6179 *Lon:* -83.7032 I-475 Exit 8B follow SH-2 W .5 mile & McCord Rd N .4 mile
Huber Heights	◇ 1	🕐	Rx	🚐	7680 Brandt Pike, 45424 / 937-237-1988 • *Lat:* 39.8637 *Lon:* -84.1027 I-70 Exit 38 take SH-201 S .2 mile
Jackson	◆	🕐	Rx	🚐	100 Wal-Mart Dr, 45640 / 740-288-2700 • *Lat:* 39.0328 *Lon:* -82.6235 1.9 miles southeast of town center via SH-93
Kent	◇ 1	🕐	Rx	🚐	250 Tallmadge Rd, 44240 / 330-673-3142 • *Lat:* 41.1002 *Lon:* -81.3841 I-76 Exit 31 take Tallmadge Rd W .4 mile
Kenton	◆	🕐	Rx	🚐	1241 E Columbus St, 43326 / 419-675-1156 • *Lat:* 40.6482 *Lon:* -83.6066 Jct US-68 & SH-67 (in town) take SH-67 E .7 mile
Lancaster	◇	🕐	Rx	🚐	2687 N Memorial Dr, 43130 / 740-687-0323 • *Lat:* 39.7394 *Lon:* -82.6349 2.6 miles northwest of town center via US-33 BR/Memorial Dr

◯ Wal-Mart ◇ Supercenter ☐ Sam's Club ▧ Gas ▨ Gas & Diesel

City/Town	🛡	🕐	℞	🚐	Information
Lebanon	◇ 5	🕐	℞	🚐	1530 Wal-Mart Dr, 45036 / 513-932-4236 • Lat: 39.4556 Lon: -84.1758 I-71 Exit 32 follow SH-123 W 2.4 miles then US-42 BYP N 1.9 miles & US-42 N .2 mile
Lewis Center	◇ 5	🕐	℞	🚐	8659 Columbus Pike, 43035 / 740-657-1341 • Lat: 40.1649 Lon: -83.0197 I-270 Exit 23 take US-23 N 4.4 miles
Lima	■ 1			🚐	1150 Greely Chapel Rd, 45804 / 419-222-4050 • Lat: 40.7268 Lon: -84.0700 I-75 Exit 125B take SH-117 E .3 mile, S on Bellefontaine .3 mile & SE on Greely Chapel .3 mile
	○ 7		℞		975 N Cable Rd, 45805 / 419-224-3168 • Lat: 40.7532 Lon: -84.1473 I-75 Exit 120 take Breese Rd W 1.4 miles, Shawnee Rd N 3 miles & Cable Rd N 1.7 miles
	◆ 1	🕐	℞	🚐	2400 Harding Hwy, 45804 / 419-222-4466 • Lat: 40.7307 Lon: -84.0615 I-75 Exit 175 follow SH-309 E .6 mile
Logan	◆	🕐	℞	🚐	12910 OH Hwy 664 S, 43138 / 740-380-1472 • Lat: 39.5403 Lon: -82.4399 Jct US-33 & SH-664 (W of town) take SH-664 N .3 mile
London	◆ 5	🕐	℞	🚐	375 Lafayette St, 43140 / 740-852-1507 • Lat: 39.9083 Lon: -83.4262 I-70 Exit 79 take US-42 S 4.5 miles
Loveland	■ 2		℞	🚐	9570 Fields Ertel Rd, 45140 / 513-677-5020 • Lat: 39.2903 Lon: -84.2936 I-71 Exit 19 go E on Fields Ertel Rd 1.2 miles
Macedonia	○ 1		℞	🚐	8160 Macedonia Commons Blvd, 44056 / 330-468-0200 • Lat: 41.3133 Lon: -81.5146 I-271 Exit 19 take Macedonia Commons Blvd SW .1 mile
Madison	◆ 5	🕐	℞	🚐	6067 N Ridge Rd, 44057 / 440-417-0010 • Lat: 41.8018 Lon: -81.0717 I-90 Exit 212 follow SH-528 N 3 miles & US-20 W 1.2 miles
Mansfield	■ 10			🚐	1070 N Lexington Springmill Rd, 44906 / 419-747-9939 • Lat: 40.7817 Lon: -82.5901 I-71 Exit 176 go W 9.4 miles on US-30 to Lexington Springmill Rd, south of highway
	◆ 1	🕐	℞	🚐	2485 Possum Run Rd, 44903 / 419-756-2850 • Lat: 40.6850 Lon: -82.5111 I-71 Exit 169 take SH-13 E .2 mile & Possum Run Rd S .3 mile
	◇	🕐	℞	🚐	359 N Lexington Springmill Rd, 44906 / 419-529-2950 • Lat: 40.7614 Lon: -82.5905 Jct US-30 & Lexington Springmill Rd (NW of town) go S on Lexington Springmill Rd .8 mile
Marietta	◇ 1	🕐	℞	🚐	804 Pike St, 45750 / 740-376-9030 • Lat: 39.4068 Lon: -81.4186 I-77 Exit 1 take SH-7 E .5 mile
Marion	◇	🕐	℞	🚐	1546 Marion Mount Gilead Rd, 43302 / 740-389-3404 • Lat: 40.5813 Lon: -83.0872 Jct US-23 & SH-95 (E of town) take SH-95 W .6 mile
Marysville	◆	🕐	℞	🚐	555 Colemans Crossing, 43040 / 937-644-2800 • Lat: 40.2287 Lon: -83.3396 I-270 Exit 17B take US-33 NW 15.6 miles, Delaware Ave W .3 mile & Colemans Crossing S .6 mile
Mason	◇ 2	🕐	℞	🚐	5303 Bowen Dr, 45040 / 513-583-9330 • Lat: 39.3114 Lon: -84.3160 I-71 Exit 19 go N on Mason-Montgomery Rd 1.2 miles then W at Bowen Dr .2 mile
Massillon	◇ 8	🕐	℞	🚐	1 Massillon Marketplace Dr SW, 44646 / 330-834-0500 • Lat: 40.7677 Lon: -81.5233 I-77 Exit 104 take US-30 W 7.2 miles, SH-21 N .6 mile & Erie St S .2 mile
Mayfield Heights	○ 1		℞		6594 Mayfield Rd, 44124 / 440-446-0668 • Lat: 41.5200 Lon: -81.4414 I-271 Exit 34 merge onto US-322 E .2 mile
Medina	○ 5		℞	🚐	4141 Pearl Rd, 44256 / 330-723-1122 • Lat: 41.1621 Lon: -81.8621 I-71 Exit 222 take SH-3 W 2 miles, Fenn Rd W 2.4 miles & Pearl Rd S .6 mile
Mentor	■ 8		℞	🚐	5600 Emerald Ct, 44060 / 440-352-7430 • Lat: 41.7162 Lon: -81.2972 I-90 Exit 193 take SH-306 N 1.7 miles then SH-2 NE 5.5 miles, S on Heisley & E on Diamond Centre .2 mile, N on Emerald Ct
	● 4		℞		9303 Mentor Ave, 44060 / 440-974-3300 • Lat: 41.6785 Lon: -81.3065 I-90 Exit 195 take SH-615 N 1.5 miles then US-20 E 1.9 miles

○ Wal-Mart   ◇ Supercenter   □ Sam's Club   ■ Gas   ■ Gas & Diesel

City/Town	🛡	🕐	℞	🚗	Information
Miamisburg	○ 2		℞	🚗	8480 Springboro Pike, 45342 / 937-435-2222 • *Lat:* 39.6271 *Lon:* -84.2260 I-75 Exit 44 take SH-725 E .5 mile & Springboro Pike S .7 mile
Middlefield	◇	🕐	℞	🚗	15050 S Springdale Ave, 44062 / 440-632-0383 • *Lat:* 41.4596 *Lon:* -81.0835 Jct CR-608/State Ave & SH-87/High St (in town) take High St W .6 mile then Springdale Ave S .3 mile
Middletown	● 1		℞	🚗	2900 Towne Blvd, 45044 / 513-423-6785 • *Lat:* 39.4854 *Lon:* -84.3291 I-75 Exit 32 take SH-122 W .1 mile then Towne Blvd S .7 mile
Milford	◇ 1	🕐	℞	🚗	201 Chamber Dr, 45150 / 513-248-0067 • *Lat:* 39.1607 *Lon:* -84.2782 I-275 Exit 59 take Milford Pkwy W .7 mile then left at Chamber Dr
Millersburg	◇	🕐	℞	🚗	1640 S Washington St, 44654 / 330-674-2888 • *Lat:* 40.5354 *Lon:* -81.9169 Jct US-62 & SH-83 (S of town) take SH-83 N 1.6 miles
Mount Vernon	◇	🕐	℞	🚗	1575 Coshocton Ave, 43050 / 740-392-3800 • *Lat:* 40.4026 *Lon:* -82.4414 Jct CR-308 & US-36 (E of town) take US-36 W 1.8 miles
Napoleon	◆	🕐	℞	🚗	1815 Scott St, 43545 / 419-599-1973 • *Lat:* 41.4028 *Lon:* -84.1322 I-80/90 (toll) Exit 34 follow SH-108 S 13.8 miles
New Boston	◇	🕐	℞	🚗	4490 Gallia St, 45662 / 740-456-8257 • *Lat:* 38.7550 *Lon:* -82.9275 .5 mile east of town on US-52
New Philadelphia	◇ 1	🕐	℞	🚗	231 Bluebell Dr NW, 44663 / 330-339-3991 • *Lat:* 40.4935 *Lon:* -81.4726 I-77 Exit 81 take SH-250 BR E .2 mile & Bluebell Dr N .2 mile
Newark	◆	🕐	℞	🚗	1315 N 21st St, 43055 / 740-364-9090 • *Lat:* 40.0840 *Lon:* -82.4279 I-70 Exit 132 follow SH-13 N 8.2 miles, Granville St NW 1.2 miles & 21st St N 1.3 miles
North Canton	▩ 1		℞	🚗	4790 Portage St NW, 44720 / 330-497-5295 • *Lat:* 40.8796 *Lon:* -81.4361 I-77 Exit 111 go W on Portage St .3 mile
	○ 1		℞	🚗	4572 Mega St NW, 44720 / 330-305-9527 • *Lat:* 40.8724 *Lon:* -81.4344 I-77 Exit 111 take Portage St W .2 mile, Strip Ave S .6 mile & Mega St W .1 mile
North Olmsted	○ 1		℞		24801 Brookpark Rd, 44070 / 440-979-9234 • *Lat:* 41.4187 *Lon:* -81.8972 I-480 Exit 6B take SH-252 N .3 mile then Brookpark Rd E .2 mile
Norwalk	◇ 6	🕐	℞	🚗	340 Westwind Dr, 44857 / 419-663-2212 • *Lat:* 41.2613 *Lon:* -82.6119 I-80/90 (toll) take US-250 S 5.9 miles
Oakwood Village	■ 1			🚗	23300 Broadway Ave, 44146 / 440-232-2582 • *Lat:* 41.3684 *Lon:* -81.5122 I-480 Exit 23 go S on SH-14 for .2 mile
Oberlin	◆ 10	🕐	℞	🚗	46440 US Hwy 20, 44074 / 440-774-6720 • *Lat:* 41.2868 *Lon:* -82.2173 I-80/90 (toll) take Baumhart Rd S 7.3 miles then US-20 E 2.6 miles
Oregon	◇ 2	🕐	℞	🚗	3721 Navarre Ave, 43616 / 419-698-2034 • *Lat:* 41.6374 *Lon:* -83.4589 I-280 Exit 7 take SH-2 E 1.7 miles
Ottawa	◇	🕐	℞		1720 N Perry St, 45875 / 419-523-6995 • *Lat:* 41.0352 *Lon:* -84.0365 Jct SH-15 & SH-65 (N of town) go N on SH-65 for .9 mile
Oxford	◇	🕐	℞	🚗	5720 College Corner Pike, 45056 / 513-524-4122 • *Lat:* 39.5312 *Lon:* -84.7743 Jct CR-732/N Main St & W Church St (in town) take Church St W .4 mile then US-27 NW for 1.8 miles
Parma	○ 7		℞	🚗	8303 W Ridgewood Dr, 44129 / 440-884-5641 • *Lat:* 41.3845 *Lon:* -81.7423 I-77 Exit 153 take Pleasant Valley Rd W 4.4 miles, Ridge Rd N 1.4 miles & Ridgewood Dr W .4 mile
Perrysburg	◇ 1	🕐	℞		10392 Fremont Pike, 43551 / 419-874-0291 • *Lat:* 41.5462 *Lon:* -83.5934 I-75 Exit 193 take US-20 E .5 mile
Piqua	◆ 1	🕐	℞	🚗	1300 E Ash St, 45356 / 937-615-9924 • *Lat:* 40.1505 *Lon:* -84.2087 I-75 Exit 82 take US-36 E .7 mile

○ Wal-Mart ◇ Supercenter □ Sam's Club ▩ Gas ■ Gas & Diesel

City/Town	♡	🕐	℞	🚌	Information
Poland	○ 1		℞	🚌	1300 Doral Dr, 44514 / 330-758-0011 • Lat: 41.0282 Lon: -80.6316 I-680 Exit 11 take US-224 W .3 mile, Tiffany Blvd N .3 mile & Doral Dr W
Port Clinton	♦	🕐	℞	🚌	2826 E Harbor Rd, 43452 / 419-732-3369 • Lat: 41.5199 Lon: -82.8784 Jct US-2 & SH-163 (E of town) take SH-163 E 1.4 miles
Ravenna	○ 6		℞	🚌	2600 OH Hwy 59, 44266 / 330-677-0338 • Lat: 41.1577 Lon: -81.2996 I-76 Exit 38 take Prospect St N 2.6 miles then SH-59 W 3.1 miles
Reynoldsburg	■ 1		℞	🚌	2675 Taylor Road Ext, 43068 / 614-866-5369 • Lat: 39.9369 Lon: -82.7829 I-70 Exit 112 take SH-256 N .3 mile then E on Taylor Rd .4 mile
	◇ 1	🕐	℞	🚌	2793 Taylor Rd Ext, 43068 / 614-367-1015 • Lat: 39.9372 Lon: -82.7873 I-70 Exit 112 take SH-256 N .2 mile & Taylor Rd E .1 mile
Saint Clairsville	□ 1			🚌	50555 Valley Plaza Dr, 43950 / 740-695-0198 • Lat: 40.0764 Lon: -80.8729 I-70 Exit 218 go NW on Mall Rd .5 mile, US-40 W for .2 mile, S at Valley Plaza
	◇ 1	🕐		🚌	50739 Valley Plaza Dr, 43950 / 740-695-8410 • Lat: 40.0751 Lon: -80.8732 I-70 Exit 218 take Mall Rd N .4 mile & Valley Centre Blvd W .3 mile
Salem	♦	🕐	℞	🚌	2875 E State St, 44460 / 330-337-8313 • Lat: 40.9002 Lon: -80.8196 2 miles east of town center along SH-14
Sandusky	■		℞	🚌	614 Crossings Rd, 44870 / 419-626-6563 • Lat: 41.4020 Lon: -82.6655 4 miles southeast of town at US-250/SH-2 jct
	♦ 7	🕐	℞	🚌	5500 Milan Rd, 44870 / 419-627-8778 • Lat: 41.4018 Lon: -82.6572 I-80/90 (toll) take US-250 N 6.8 miles
Sheffield Village	■ 1		℞	🚌	5225 Cobblestone Rd, 44035 / 440-934-7567 • Lat: 41.4186 Lon: -82.0848 I-90 Exit 148 take SH-254 E .2 mile, Abbe Rd N .3 mile & W at Cobblestone .4 mile
Sidney	♦ 1	🕐	℞	🚌	2400 Michigan St, 45365 / 937-498-2371 • Lat: 40.2879 Lon: -84.1921 I-75 Exit 92 take SH-47 W .5 mile
South Point	■ 4		℞	🚌	432 Private Drive 288, 45680 / 740-894-3296 • Lat: 38.4129 Lon: -82.5229 I-64 Exit 6 (in WV) follow US-52 NW 3.5 miles
	◇	🕐	℞		223 County Rd 410, 45680 / 740-894-3235 • Lat: 38.4096 Lon: -82.5233 Jct US-52 & CR-18 (N of town) take US-52 E 3.3 miles & S on CR-410
Springdale	○ 2		℞	🚌	600 Kemper Commons Cir, 45246 / 513-671-3023 • Lat: 39.2900 Lon: -84.4606 I-275 Exit 42 take SH-747 S .4 mile, Kemper Rd E .5 mile & Kemper Commons N .4 mile
Springfield	♦ 4	🕐	℞	🚌	200 Tuttle Rd, 45503 / 937-325-2111 • Lat: 39.9244 Lon: -83.7501 I-70 Exit 62 merge onto US-40 W 3.4 miles then Tuttle Rd N .2 mile
	◇ 4	🕐	℞	🚌	2100 N Bechtle Ave, 45504 / 937-399-0370 • Lat: 39.9269 Lon: -83.8334 I-70 Exit 52 take US-68 N 2.1 miles, US-40 E 1 mile & Bechtle Ave N .4 mile
Steubenville	◇	🕐	℞	🚌	100 Mall Dr, 43952 / 740-266-7136 • Lat: 40.3710 Lon: -80.6701 Jct SH-43 & US-22 (W of town) take US-22 E 2.4 miles, Lovers Ln S 1.5 miles & Mall Dr E .5 mile
Stow	● 8		℞	🚌	3520 Hudson Dr, 44224 / 330-923-8232 • Lat: 41.1651 Lon: -81.4771 I-76 Exit 23B take SH-8 N 7.4 miles, Graham Rd W .4 mile & Hudson Dr N .1 mile
Streetsboro	◇ 1	🕐	℞	🚌	905 Singletary Dr, 44241 / 330-626-9990 • Lat: 41.2503 Lon: -81.3640 I-80 (toll) Exit 187, south of exit
Strongsville	○ 1		℞		8585 Pearl Rd, 44136 / 440-826-0004 • Lat: 41.3462 Lon: -81.8238 I-71 Exit 234 take US-42 SW .8 mile
Tiffin	♦	🕐	℞	🚌	2801 W OH Hwy 18, 44883 / 419-448-4402 • Lat: 41.1109 Lon: -83.2235 Jct US-224 & SH-18 (W of town) take SH-18 N .2 mile
Toledo	◇ 1	🕐	℞	🚌	5821 W Central Ave, 43615 / 419-536-9105 • Lat: 41.6763 Lon: -83.6811 I-475 Exit 13 take US-20 E .8 mile

○ Wal-Mart　◇ Supercenter　□ Sam's Club　■ Gas　■ Gas & Diesel

City/Town	⬥	🕐	℞	🚐	Information
	◇ 5	🕐	℞	🚐	2925 Glendale Ave, 43614 / 419-380-0994 • *Lat:* 41.6121 *Lon:* -83.6130 I-75 Exit 201A take SH-25 S 3.5 miles then Glendale Ave W .9 mile
Troy	◇ 1	🕐	℞		1801 W Main St, 45373 / 937-339-7211 • *Lat:* 40.0544 *Lon:* -84.2370 I-75 Exit 74 take SH-41 W .4 mile
Upper Sandusky	◆	🕐	℞	🚐	1855 E Wyandot Ave, 43351 / 419-294-3404 • *Lat:* 40.8355 *Lon:* -83.2371 Jct US-23/30 & CR-182 (W of town) take US-23/30 N .2 mile then Wyandot Ave E .1 mile
Urbana	◇	🕐	℞	🚐	1840 E US Hwy 36, 43078 / 937-653-5313 • *Lat:* 40.1074 *Lon:* -83.7658 Jct SH-29 & US-36 (E of town) go E on US-36 for .6 mile
Van Wert	◆	🕐	℞	🚐	301 Town Center Blvd, 45891 / 419-238-5662 • *Lat:* 40.8518 *Lon:* -84.5632 Jct US-127 & SH-116 (S of town) go W on Fox Rd .9 mile
Wadsworth	◇ 1	🕐	℞	🚐	222 Smokerise Dr, 44281 / 330-336-5170 • *Lat:* 41.0524 *Lon:* -81.7335 I-76 Exit 9 take SH-94 N .4 mile & Smokerise Dr W .2 mile
Wapakoneta	◆ 1	🕐	℞	🚐	1257 Bellefontaine St, 45895 / 419-738-0474 • *Lat:* 40.5646 *Lon:* -84.1781 I-75 Exit 111 go W on Bellefontaine Rd .4 mile
Warren	▧ 8		℞	🚐	1040 Niles Cortland Rd SE, 44484 / 330-856-7411 • *Lat:* 41.2270 *Lon:* -80.7407 I-80 Exit 228 take SH-11 N 5.5 miles, SH-82 W 1.7 miles, S on Niles-Corltland .2 mile
Washington Crt Hse	◆	🕐	℞	🚐	1397 Leesburg Ave, 43160 / 740-333-3171 • *Lat:* 39.5267 *Lon:* -83.4547 I-71 Exit 65 take US-35 E 10.1 miles & US-62 N .5 mile
Wauseon	◆ 2	🕐	℞	🚐	485 Airport Hwy, 43567 / 419-337-8900 • *Lat:* 41.5879 *Lon:* -84.1077 I-80 (toll) Exit 34 take SH-108 S 1.3 miles then US-20 ALT E .4 mile
Waverly	◇	🕐	℞		990 W Emmitt Ave, 45690 / 740-947-1700 • *Lat:* 39.1175 *Lon:* -82.9956 Jct SH-220 & US-23 (in town) go S on US-23 .7 mile
West Chester	◇ 1	🕐	℞	🚐	8288 Cincinnati Dayton Rd, 45069 / 513-777-2397 • *Lat:* 39.3456 *Lon:* -84.3955 I-75 Exit 21 go N on Cincinnati Dayton Rd .2 mile
West Union	◇	🕐	℞	🚐	11217 OH Hwy 41, 45693 / 937-544-7198 • *Lat:* 38.7773 *Lon:* -83.5699 Jct SH-125 & SH-41 (W of town) take SH-41 S 1.6 miles
Whitehall	◆ 4	🕐	℞	🚐	3657 E Main St, 43213 / 614-239-7509 • *Lat:* 39.9560 *Lon:* -82.8995 I-270 Exit 41 follow US-40 W 3.4 miles
Wickliffe	☐ 1			🚐	27853 Chardon Rd, 44092 / 440-944-5747 • *Lat:* 41.5829 *Lon:* -81.4858 I-90 Exit 187 take SH-84 S .5 mile & W on Chardon .2 mile
Willowick	○ 5		℞	🚐	34440 Vine St, 44095 / 440-269-8827 • *Lat:* 41.6424 *Lon:* -81.4432 I-90 Exit 185 take SH-2 E 3.5 miles, SH-91 N .5 mile & Vine St W .3 mile
Wilmington	◆ 8	🕐	℞	🚐	2825 S OH Hwy 73, 45177 / 937-382-4919 • *Lat:* 39.4511 *Lon:* -83.7817 I-71 Exit 50 follow US-68 SE 5.2 miles, US-22 E 2.6 miles & SH-73 S .2 mile
Wooster	◇	🕐	℞		3883 Burbank Rd, 44691 / 330-345-8955 • *Lat:* 40.8469 *Lon:* -81.9445 I-71 Exit 204 follow SH-83 E 10.9 miles
Xenia	◆ 9		℞	🚐	70 Hospitality Dr, 45385 / 937-376-9878 • *Lat:* 39.6882 *Lon:* -83.9645 I-675 Exit 13A take US-35 E 6.9 miles, US-35 BR E 1.1 miles & S on Progress Dr/ W on Harner
Zanesville	▪ 4		℞	🚐	3724 Northpointe Dr, 43701 / 740-452-7183 • *Lat:* 39.9927 *Lon:* -82.0296 I-70 Exit 153A N on Blue Ave .3 mile, NW on SH-146 for 2.8 miles then NW on Northpointe Dr .9 mile
	◆ 5	🕐	℞	🚐	2850 Maysville Pike, 43701 / 740-452-3282 • *Lat:* 39.8928 *Lon:* -82.0440 I-70 Exit 155 take SH-146/60 S .6 mile, follow US-22 S 4.2 miles
	◇ 3	🕐	℞	🚐	2850 Maple Ave, 43701 / 740-455-9001 • *Lat:* 39.9752 *Lon:* -82.0130 I-70 Exit 153B merge onto Maple Ave N 2.1 miles

○ Wal-Mart ◇ Supercenter ☐ Sam's Club ▨ Gas ▪ Gas & Diesel

Oklahoma

○ Wal-Mart ◇ Supercenter □ Sam's Club ▦ Gas ■ Gas & Diesel

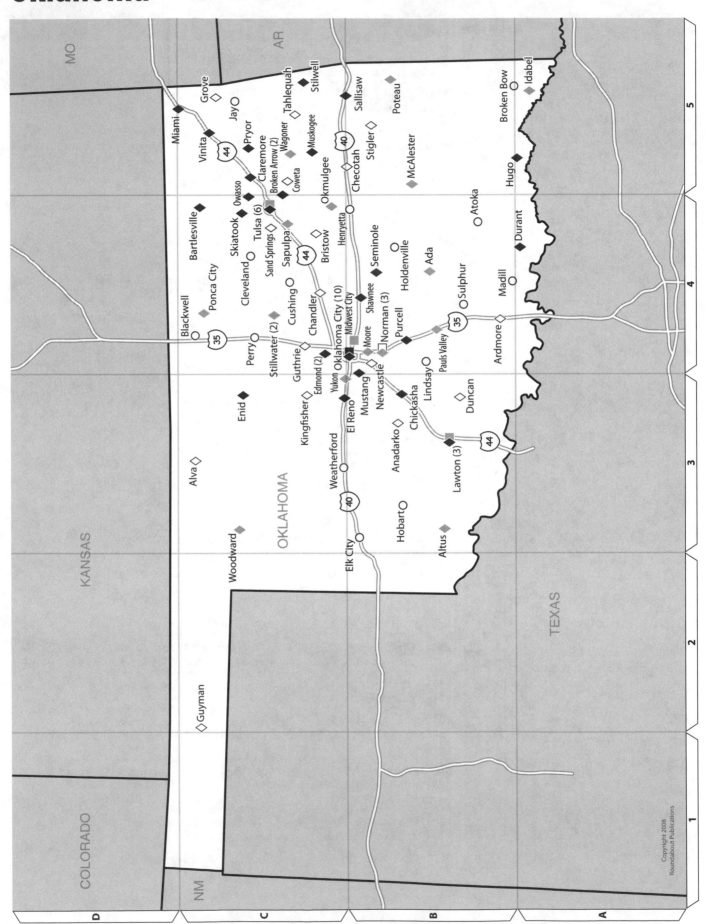

City/Town	⬡	🕐	℞	🚗	Information
Ada	◆		🕐	℞ 🚗	1419 N Country Club Rd, 74820 / 580-332-2232 • *Lat:* 34.7892 *Lon:* -96.6526 Jct SH-1 & US-377 (N of town) go E on US-377 for .5 mile, continue E on Abbott Blvd 1 mile & Country Club Rd S .1 mile
Altus	◆		🕐	℞ 🚗	2500 N Main St, 73521 / 580-482-8189 • *Lat:* 34.6631 *Lon:* -99.3336 Jct SH-62 & US-283 (in town) take US-283 N 1.7 miles
Alva	◇		🕐	℞	914 E Oklahoma Blvd, 73717 / 580-327-4021 • *Lat:* 36.7977 *Lon:* -98.6490 At Jct US-64 & US-281 (E of town)
Anadarko	◇		🕐	℞	1201 W Petree Rd, 73005 / 405-247-2535 • *Lat:* 35.0580 *Lon:* -98.2445 Jct US-62 & SH-8 (E of town) take SH-8/7th St S 1 mile then Petree Rd W .6 mile
Ardmore	◇ 2		🕐	℞ 🚗	1715 N Commerce St, 73401 / 580-226-1257 • *Lat:* 34.1931 *Lon:* -97.1433 I-35 Exit 33 take SH-142 E 1.3 miles & US-77 S .7 mile
Atoka	○			℞	1901 S Mississippi Ave, 74525 / 580-889-6676 • *Lat:* 34.3686 *Lon:* -96.1392 Jct SH-7 & US-75/69 (S of town) go S on US-75/69 for .5 mile
Bartlesville	◆		🕐	℞ 🚗	4000 SE Green Country Rd, 74006 / 918-335-6600 • *Lat:* 36.7393 *Lon:* -95.9324 Jct US-60 & US-75 (E of town) take US-75 S .2 mile & Green Country Rd E .2 mile
Blackwell	○ 3			℞	1219 W Doolin Ave, 74631 / 580-363-4111 • *Lat:* 36.8113 *Lon:* -97.2984 I-35 Exit 222 take SH-11 E 2.2 miles
Bristow	◇ 7		🕐	℞ 🚗	105 W Hwy 16, 74010 / 918-367-3335 • *Lat:* 35.7407 *Lon:* -96.2281 I-44 (toll) Exit 196 take SH-48 S 1.3 miles & follow SH-16 S 5.3 miles
Broken Arrow	◆		🕐	℞ 🚗	6310 S Elm Pl, 74011 / 918-455-4354 • *Lat:* 35.9913 *Lon:* -95.7976 From I-44 at Exit 34 follow Creek Tpk for 15 miles to Elm Pl then go S .2 mile
	◆		🕐	℞ 🚗	2301 W Kenosha St, 74012 / 918-259-9126 • *Lat:* 36.0608 *Lon:* -95.8192 Jct US-169 & SH-51 (NE of town) take SH-51 E 2.5 miles & Aspen Ave S 1.2 miles
Broken Bow	○			℞	501 S Park Dr, 74728 / 580-584-3324 • *Lat:* 34.0227 *Lon:* -94.7393 Jct SH-3 & US-259/70 (S of town) go S on US-259/70 for .2 mile
Chandler	◇ 2		🕐	℞	3100 E 1st St, 74834 / 405-258-0541 • *Lat:* 35.7097 *Lon:* -96.8583 I-44 (toll) Exit 166 follow SH-18 S .7 mile then E on 1st St 1 mile
Checotah	◇		🕐	℞ 🚗	131 Paul Carr Dr, 74426 / 918-473-2201 • *Lat:* 35.4711 *Lon:* -95.5373 I-40 Exit 264B take US-69 N 1.2 miles & US-266 E to Paul Carr Dr (frontage road)
Chickasha	◆ 1		🕐	℞ 🚗	2001 S 1st St, 73018 / 405-224-1867 • *Lat:* 35.0306 *Lon:* -97.9324 I-44 (toll) Exit 80 merge onto US-277 N .5 mile then Grand Ave E .1 mile
Claremore	◆ 3		🕐	℞ 🚗	1500 S Lynn Riggs Blvd, 74017 / 918-341-2765 • *Lat:* 36.2949 *Lon:* -95.6292 I-44 (toll) Exit 255 go W 1.4 miles on Will Rogers Blvd, S 1.2 miles on Lynn Riggs Blvd and left onto frontage road
Cleveland	○			℞	1004 N Broadway St, 74020 / 918-358-3553 • *Lat:* 36.3178 *Lon:* -96.4644 Jct US-64 & SH-99 (S of town) go N on SH-99 for .8 mile
Coweta	◇		🕐	℞ 🚗	11207 S Hwy 51, 74429 / 918-486-6511 • *Lat:* 36.0026 *Lon:* -95.6790 From Muskogee Tpk Exit 13 go W on SH-51 for 7 miles
Cushing	○			℞	2004 E Main St, 74023 / 918-225-0578 • *Lat:* 35.9854 *Lon:* -96.7440 Jct SH-18 & SH-33 (N of town) go E on SH-33 for 1.7 miles
Duncan	◇		🕐	℞ 🚗	1845 N Hwy 81, 73533 / 580-255-5455 • *Lat:* 34.5265 *Lon:* -97.9672 Jct SH-7 & US-81 (N of town) take US-81 S 4.7 miles
Durant	◆		🕐	℞ 🚗	3712 W Main St, 74701 / 580-920-0234 • *Lat:* 33.9985 *Lon:* -96.4152 Jct US-69 & US-70 (W of town) take US-70 W .6 mile
Edmond	◆ 7		🕐	℞ 🚗	2200 W Danforth Rd, 73003 / 405-216-0520 • *Lat:* 35.6674 *Lon:* -97.5127 I-35 Exit 143 take Covell Rd W 4.4 miles, Kelly Ave S 1 mile & Danforth Rd W .9 mile
	◇ 1		🕐	℞	1225 W I-35 Frontage Rd, 73034 / 405-348-8005 • *Lat:* 35.6445 *Lon:* -97.4253 I-35 Exit 140 go N on I-35 W Frontage Rd .4 mile

○ Wal-Mart ◇ Supercenter ☐ Sam's Club ▧ Gas ▨ Gas & Diesel

City/Town	⬟	🕐	℞	🚐	Information
El Reno	◆ 1	🕐	℞	🚐	2400 S Country Club Rd, 73036 / 405-262-7354 • *Lat:* 35.5126 *Lon:* -97.9729 I-40 Exit 123 go N on Country Club Rd .2 mile
Elk City	○ 6		℞	🚐	3105 W 3rd St, 73644 / 580-225-3003 • *Lat:* 35.4118 *Lon:* -99.4425 I-40 Exit 41 merge onto I-40 BR W 5.1 miles
Enid	◆	🕐	℞	🚐	5505 W Owen K Garriott Rd, 73703 / 580-237-7963 • *Lat:* 36.3906 *Lon:* -97.9457 Jct US-81 & US-60 (S of town) take US-60 W 3.3 miles
Grove	◇	🕐	℞	🚐	2115 S Main St, 74344 / 918-786-8561 • *Lat:* 36.5784 *Lon:* -94.7689 I-44 (toll) Exit 302 follow US-59 S 16.1 miles
Guthrie	◇ 3	🕐	℞	🚐	1608 S Division St, 73044 / 405-282-7900 • *Lat:* 35.8625 *Lon:* -97.4253 I-35 Exit 153 follow US-77 N 3 miles
Guymon	◇	🕐	℞	🚐	2600 N Hwy 64, 73942 / 580-338-1611 • *Lat:* 36.7051 *Lon:* -101.4852 1.7 miles north of town center along US-64/US-412
Henryetta	○ 1		℞		605 E Main St, 74437 / 918-652-9676 • *Lat:* 35.4397 *Lon:* -95.9748 I-40 Exit 240B follow I-40 BR W .3 mile
Hobart	○		℞		923 W 11th St, 73651 / 580-726-5693 • *Lat:* 35.0158 *Lon:* -99.1015 Jct US-183 & SH-9 (SE of town) go W on SH-9 for 2.3 miles
Holdenville	○		℞		500 E Hwy 270, 74848 / 405-379-6688 • *Lat:* 35.0869 *Lon:* -96.3823 Jct US-270 & US-270 BR (W of town) continue W on US-270 BR .8 mile
Hugo	◆	🕐	℞		1911 E Jackson St, 74743 / 580-326-6494 • *Lat:* 34.0107 *Lon:* -95.4966 Jct SH-93 & US-70 (E of town) take US-70 W .4 mile & US-70 BR NW 1 mile
Idabel	◆	🕐	℞		1907 SE Washington St, 74745 / 580-286-6696 • *Lat:* 33.8956 *Lon:* -94.8004 Jct SH-3 & US-259 (E of town) take SH-3 W 1.1 miles
Jay	○		℞		1107 S Main St, 74346 / 918-253-4861 • *Lat:* 36.4183 *Lon:* -94.8058 Jct SH-127 & US-59 (SW of town) go N on US-59 for .3 mile
Kingfisher	◇	🕐	℞		200 Starlite Dr, 73750 / 405-375-5743 • *Lat:* 35.8276 *Lon:* -97.9340 2.3 miles south of town center along US-81
Lawton	■ 3			🚐	802 NW Sheridan Rd, 73505 / 580-248-3400 • *Lat:* 34.6178 *Lon:* -98.4226 I-44 Exit 39 go W on Cache Rd for 2 miles then S on Sheridan Rd .4 mile
	◆ 5	🕐	℞	🚐	6301 NW Quannah Parker Trl, 73505 / 580-510-9130 • *Lat:* 34.6306 *Lon:* -98.4678 I-44 (toll) Exit 39A follow Old US-62 W 4.7 miles
	◇ 3	🕐	℞	🚐	1002 NW Sheridan Rd, 73505 / 580-355-9070 • *Lat:* 34.6190 *Lon:* -98.4226 I-44 (toll) Exit 39A merge onto NW Cache Rd W 2 miles & Sheridan Rd S .3 mile
Lindsay	○		℞		401 Linwood Plz, 73052 / 405-756-9535 • *Lat:* 34.8207 *Lon:* -97.5864 Jct CR-1490 & SH-76 (N of town) take CR-1490 E .6 mile, 4th St S .3 mile & Oakwd Dr E
Madill	○		℞		903 S 1st St, 73446 / 580-795-7383 • *Lat:* 34.0812 *Lon:* -96.7655 Jct US-377 & US-70 (S of town) take US-70 S .2 mile
McAlester	◆	🕐	℞	🚐	432 S George Nigh Expy, 74501 / 918-423-8585 • *Lat:* 34.9136 *Lon:* -95.7452 From Indian Nation Tpk Exit 63 take US-69 N 5.6 miles
Miami	◆ 4	🕐	℞	🚐	2415 N Main St, 74354 / 918-542-6654 • *Lat:* 36.9034 *Lon:* -94.8778 I-44 (toll) Exit 313 take SH-10 W 1.4 miles & US-69 N 2.3 miles
Midwest City	■ 1		℞	🚐	6521 SE 29th St, 73110 / 405-741-0012 • *Lat:* 35.4354 *Lon:* -97.4127 I-40 Exit 157B go N on Air Depot Blvd .1 mile then W on 29th St .4 mile
Moore	◆ 1	🕐	℞	🚐	501 SW 19th St, 73160 / 405-790-0021 • *Lat:* 35.3202 *Lon:* -97.4929 I-35 Exit 116 take 19th St W .1 mile
Muskogee	◆	🕐	℞	🚐	1000 W Shawnee St, 74401 / 918-687-0058 • *Lat:* 35.7699 *Lon:* -95.3744 Jct SH-165 & US-62 (NW of town) take US-62 W 4 miles
Mustang	◆ 9	🕐	℞	🚐	951 E OK Hwy 152, 73064 / 405-376-4549 • *Lat:* 35.3918 *Lon:* -97.7055 I-44 Exit 116B take SH-152 W 8.8 miles

○ Wal-Mart ◇ Supercenter □ Sam's Club ■ Gas ■ Gas & Diesel

City/Town	🛡	⏰	℞	🚙	Information
Newcastle	◇ 1	⏰	℞	🚙	3300 Tri City Dr, 73065 / 405-387-3400 • Lat: 35.2922 Lon: -97.6048 I-44 Exit 108 take SH-37 W .1 mile then N on Tri City Dr .1 mile
Norman	□ 1		℞	🚙	3400 W Main St, 73072 / 405-307-8374 • Lat: 35.2182 Lon: -97.4923 I-35 Exit 109 go W on Main St .7 mile
	◆ 2	⏰	℞	🚙	333 N Interstate Dr, 73069 / 405-329-4000 • Lat: 35.2210 Lon: -97.4847 I-35 Exit 109 merge E onto Main St .9 mile & N on Interstate Dr .3 mile
	◆ 5	⏰	℞	🚙	601 12th Ave NE, 73071 / 405-579-5203 • Lat: 35.2258 Lon: -97.4233 I-35 Exit 109 take Main St W 4.2 miles
Oklahoma City	■		℞	🚙	9000 NW Passage, 73132 / 405-773-3602 • Lat: 35.5607 Lon: -97.6509 John Kilpatrick Tpk at SH-3 go SE 2.5 miles
	▦ 1		℞	🚙	5510 SW 5th St, 73128 / 405-943-9810 • Lat: 35.4587 Lon: -97.6135 I-40 Exit 144 go S on MacArthur .1 mile then E on 5th St .3 mile
	▦		℞	🚙	1900 W Memorial Rd, 73134 / 405-748-7109 • Lat: 35.6084 Lon: -97.5462 Jct US-77 & Kilpatrick Tpk go W on Kilpatrick 2.8 miles, exit at Penn Ave S to Memorial Rd .3 mile
	◆ 1	⏰	℞	🚙	100 E I-240 Service Rd, 73149 / 405-631-0746 • Lat: 35.3915 Lon: -97.5114 I-240 Exit 5 go NW to Service Rd .2 mile
	◆ 5	⏰	℞	🚙	9011 NE 23rd St, 73141 / 405-769-2164 • Lat: 35.4931 Lon: -97.3705 I-35 Exit 130 take US-62 E 4.8 miles
	◇ 1	⏰	℞	🚙	5401 Tinker Diagonal St, 73115 / 405-670-1007 • Lat: 35.4468 Lon: -97.4254 I-40 Exit 156A merge onto Tinker Diagonal W .3 mile
	◇ 1	⏰	℞	🚙	1801 Belle Isle Blvd, 73118 / 405-841-6502 • Lat: 35.5248 Lon: -97.5384 I-44 Exit 125C take Belle Isle Blvd E .3 mile
	◇ 1	⏰	℞	🚙	6100 W Reno Ave, 73127 / 405-491-0320 • Lat: 35.4641 Lon: -97.6218 I-40 Exit 144 take MacArthur Blvd N .3 mile & Reno Ave W .3 mile
	◇ 7	⏰	℞	🚙	7800 NW Expressway St, 73132 / 405-773-2625 • Lat: 35.5636 Lon: -97.6516 I-44 Exit 125C follow SH-3 NW for 6.9 miles
	◇ 9	⏰	℞	🚙	2000 W Memorial Rd, 73134 / 405-752-1900 • Lat: 35.6084 Lon: -97.5483 I-44 Exit 123B take SH-74 N 6.8 miles, Kilpatrick Tpk (toll) W 1.3 miles & Penn Ave/Memorial Rd W .2 mile
Okmulgee	◆	⏰	℞	🚙	1800 S Wood Dr, 74447 / 918-756-6790 • Lat: 35.6055 Lon: -95.9620 I-40 Exit 240B follow US-75 N 12.6 miles
Owasso	◆ 10	⏰	℞	🚙	12101 E 96th St N, 74055 / 918-272-6609 • Lat: 36.2931 Lon: -95.8380 I-244 Exit 13C take US-169 N 9.4 miles & 96th St W .4 mile
Pauls Valley	◆ 2	⏰	℞	🚙	2008 W Grant Ave, 73075 / 405-238-7353 • Lat: 34.7389 Lon: -97.2450 I-35 Exit 72 take SH-19 E 1.1 miles
Perry	○ 2		℞		1506 Fir St, 73077 / 580-336-4491 • Lat: 36.2896 Lon: -97.3001 I-35 Exit 186 take Fir St/US-64 E 1.5 miles
Ponca City	◆	⏰	℞	🚙	1101 E Prospect Ave, 74601 / 580-762-0395 • Lat: 36.7387 Lon: -97.0726 Jct US-60 & US-60 BR (W of town) take US-60 BR E 3.1 miles, Union St N 2.4 miles & Prospect St E .7 mile
Poteau	◆	⏰	℞	🚙	3108 N Broadway St, 74953 / 918-647-5040 • Lat: 35.0730 Lon: -94.6286 Jct SH-112 & US-59 (N of town) take US-59 S .1 mile
Pryor	◆	⏰	℞	🚙	4901 S Mill St, 74361 / 918-825-6000 • Lat: 36.3048 Lon: -95.3197 I-44 (toll) Exit 255 take US-20 E 15.4 miles & US-69 S 3.2 miles
Purcell	◆ 1	⏰	℞	🚙	2015 S Green Ave, 73080 / 405-527-5621 • Lat: 34.9930 Lon: -97.3677 I-35 Exit 91 take SH-74 N .7 mile

○ Wal-Mart ◇ Supercenter □ Sam's Club ▦ Gas ■ Gas & Diesel

City/Town	🛡		🕐	℞	🚍	Information
Sallisaw	◆	1	🕐	℞	🚍	1101 W Ruth Ave, 74955 / 918-775-4492 • *Lat:* 35.4497 *Lon:* -94.8038 I-40 Exit 308 take US-59 N .2 mile
Sand Springs	◇	10	🕐	℞	🚍	220 S Hwy 97, 74063 / 918-245-0213 • *Lat:* 36.1358 *Lon:* -96.1697 I-44 (toll) Exit 215 follow SH-97 N 9.1 miles
Sapulpa	◆	3	🕐	℞	🚍	1002 W Taft St, 74066 / 918-224-8080 • *Lat:* 35.9882 *Lon:* -96.1261 I-44 (toll) Exit 215 take SH-97 S 1.8 miles then SH-117 E .7 mile
Seminole	◆		🕐	℞	🚍	1500 E Wrangler Blvd, 74868 / 405-382-5290 • *Lat:* 35.2466 *Lon:* -96.6533 I-40 Exit 200 take US-377 S 9.4 miles then SH-9 E .9 mile
Shawnee	◆	1	🕐	℞	🚍	196 Shawnee Mall Dr, 74804 / 405-275-1030 • *Lat:* 35.3845 *Lon:* -96.9182 I-40 Exit 186 go W to Shawnee Mall Dr .6 mile
Skiatook	◆		🕐	℞	🚍	700 W Rogers Blvd, 74070 / 918-396-1244 • *Lat:* 36.3687 *Lon:* -96.0097 Jct US-75 & SH-20 (E of town) follow SH-20 W 5.1 miles
Stigler	◇		🕐	℞		1312 E Main, 74462 / 918-967-4637 • *Lat:* 35.2541 *Lon:* -95.1101 1 mile east of town along SH-9 (Main St)
Stillwater	◆		🕐	℞	🚍	111 N Perkins Rd, 74075 / 405-372-2897 • *Lat:* 36.1236 *Lon:* -97.0512 Jct SH-51 & US-177 (E of town) take US-177 N .5 mile
	◇		🕐	℞	🚍	4545 W 6th Ave, 74074 / 405-707-0744 • *Lat:* 36.1157 *Lon:* -97.1192 Jct SH-51 & US-177 (E of town) take SH-51 W 3.8 miles
Stilwell	◆		🕐	℞		RR 6 Box 1895, 74960 / 918-696-3141 • *Lat:* 35.8133 *Lon:* -94.6328 Jct US-59 & SH-100 (SE of town) take SH-100 E 2 miles then N4730 Rd N 1.1 miles
Sulphur	○			℞	🚍	2108 W Broadway Ave, 73086 / 580-622-6146 • *Lat:* 34.5064 *Lon:* -96.9947 I-35 Exit 55 take SH-7 E 10.5 miles
Tahlequah	◇		🕐	℞	🚍	2020 S Muskogee Ave, 74464 / 918-456-8804 • *Lat:* 35.8883 *Lon:* -94.9772 Jct SH-51 & US-62 (S of town) go S on US-62 for .1 mile
Tulsa	▪	1		℞	🚍	4420 S Sheridan Rd, 74145 / 918-627-1443 • *Lat:* 36.0993 *Lon:* -95.9047 I-44 Exit 230 go E on 41st for .2 mile then S on Sheridan for .3 mile
	▪	6		℞	🚍	6922 S Mingo Rd, 74133 / 918-252-9503 • *Lat:* 36.0635 *Lon:* -95.8687 I-44 Exit 231 take US-64 SE 2.5 miles, US-169 S 2.6 miles, W on 71st St .4 mile & N on Mingo Rd .2 mile
	◆	1	🕐	℞	🚍	207 S Memorial Dr, 74112 / 918-834-8700 • *Lat:* 36.1585 *Lon:* -95.8865 I-244 Exit 12A take Memorial Dr S .4 mile
	◆	8	🕐	℞	🚍	10938 S Memorial Dr, 74133 / 918-394-4000 • *Lat:* 36.0059 *Lon:* -95.8869 I-44 Exit 231 follow US-64 SE 7.8 miles
	◆	6	🕐	℞	🚍	2019 E 81st St, 74137 / 918-488-8791 • *Lat:* 36.0465 *Lon:* -95.9609 I-44 Exit 229 take Yale Ave S 2.3 miles, 71st St W 2 miles, Lewis Ave S 1 mile & 81st St W .2 mile
	◇	4	🕐	℞	🚍	6625 S Memorial Dr, 74133 / 918-294-3800 • *Lat:* 36.0674 *Lon:* -95.8861 I-44 Exit 231 take SH-51 S .9 mile then Memorial Dr S 2.9 miles
Vinita	◆	1	🕐	℞		268 S 7th St, 74301 / 918-256-7505 • *Lat:* 36.6376 *Lon:* -95.1432 I-44 (toll) Exit 289 take US-60/69 W .3 mile then S4410 Rd/7th St S .2 mile
Wagoner	◆		🕐	℞	🚍	410 S Dewey Ave, 74467 / 918-485-9515 • *Lat:* 35.9574 *Lon:* -95.3954 Jct SH-51 & US-69 (W of town) take US-69 S .1 mile
Weatherford	○	1		℞		800 E Main St, 73096 / 580-772-1408 • *Lat:* 35.5259 *Lon:* -98.6984 I-40 Exit 82 merge onto I-40 BR W .6 mile
Woodward	◆		🕐	℞	🚍	3215 Williams Ave, 73801 / 580-254-3331 • *Lat:* 36.4148 *Lon:* -99.3821 Jct US-412 & US-270 (in town) go S on US-270 for 1.4 miles
Yukon	◆	1	🕐	℞	🚍	1200 Garth Brooks Blvd, 73099 / 405-350-1900 • *Lat:* 35.4913 *Lon:* -97.7604 I-40 Exit 136 take SH-92 N .4 mile

○ Wal-Mart   ◇ Supercenter   □ Sam's Club   ▪ Gas   ■ Gas & Diesel

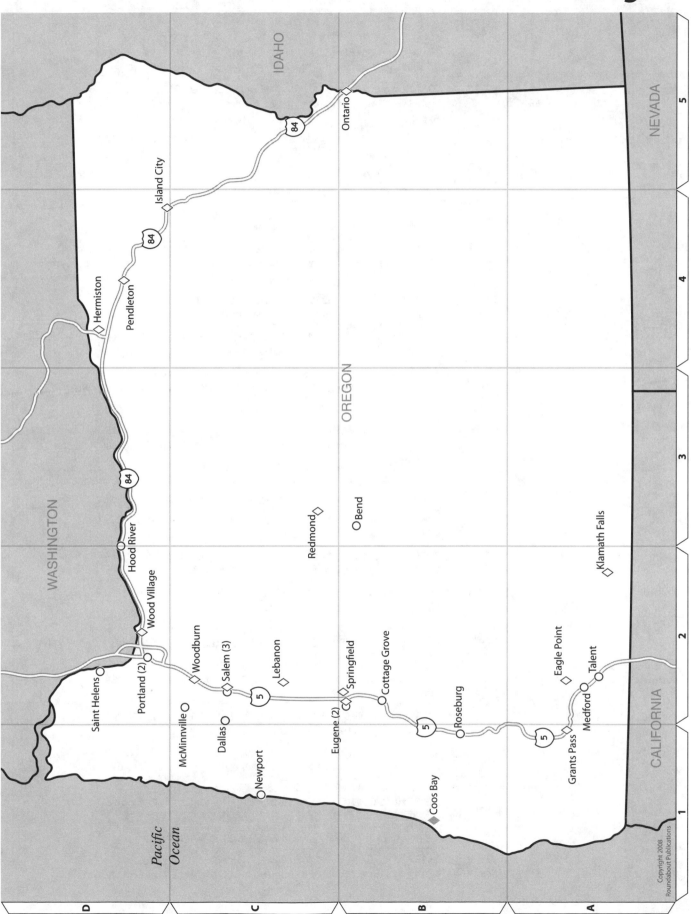

Oregon

Legend: ○ Wal-Mart ◇ Supercenter □ Sam's Club ▨ Gas ▦ Gas & Diesel

IDAHO

NEVADA

OREGON

WASHINGTON

CALIFORNIA

Pacific Ocean

Ontario

Island City

84

Hermiston

Pendleton

84

84

Hood River

Wood Village

Redmond

Bend

Klamath Falls

Saint Helens

Portland (2)

Woodburn

Salem (3)

Lebanon

Springfield

Cottage Grove

Eagle Point

Talent

McMinnville

Dallas

Eugene (2)

Roseburg

Medford

Newport

Grants Pass

Coos Bay

5

5

5

5

City/Town	⬭	🕐	℞	🚐	Information
Bend	○		℞	🚐	20120 Pinebrook Blvd, 97702 / 541-389-8184 • *Lat:* 44.0215 *Lon:* -121.3181 2.5 miles south of town center off Bend Pkwy at Pinebrook Blvd
Coos Bay	◆	🕐	℞	🚐	2051 Newmark Ave, 97420 / 541-888-5488 • *Lat:* 43.3915 *Lon:* -124.2505 From US-101 at Newmark St, go W 1.6 miles on Newmark St (which becomes Newmark Ave)
Cottage Grove	○ 1		℞	🚐	901 Row River Rd, 97424 / 541-942-4600 • *Lat:* 43.8006 *Lon:* -123.0399 I-5 Exit 174, east of exit
Dallas	○		℞	🚐	321 NE Kings Valley Hwy, 97338 / 503-623-0490 • *Lat:* 44.9320 *Lon:* -123.3076 1 mile northeast of town center on Kings Valley Hwy
Eagle Point	◇ 10	🕐	℞	🚐	11500 Hannon Rd, 97524 / 541-826-2210 • *Lat:* 42.4720 *Lon:* -122.8132 I-5 Exit 30 go N 9.6 miles on Crater Lake Hwy (SH-62)
Eugene	○ 3		℞		1040 Green Acres Rd, 97408 / 541-343-6977 • *Lat:* 44.0931 *Lon:* -123.0924 I-5 Exit 195B go W 2.4 miles on Beltline Hwy, N .1 mile on Delta Hwy, and E .3 mile on Green Acres Rd
	◇	🕐	℞	🚐	4550 W 11th Ave, 97402 / 541-344-2030 • *Lat:* 44.0480 *Lon:* -123.1709 4 miles west of town along SH-126, east of the Beltline Hwy
Grants Pass	◇ 1	🕐	℞	🚐	135 NE Terry Ln, 97526 / 541-471-2822 • *Lat:* 42.4347 *Lon:* -123.3033 I-5 Exit 55 go W .5 mile on Grants Pass Pkwy
Hermiston	◇ 8	🕐	℞	🚐	1350 N 1st St, 97838 / 541-567-4854 • *Lat:* 45.8504 *Lon:* -119.2900 I-84 Exit 188 take US-395 N for 7.6 miles (located on US-395 north of town)
Hood River	○ 1		℞		2700 Wasco St, 97031 / 541-387-2300 • *Lat:* 45.7112 *Lon:* -121.5378 I-84 Exit 62, go S .5 mile to Wasco St and turn left
Island City	◇ 1		℞		11619 Island Ave, 97850 / 541-963-6783 • *Lat:* 45.3376 *Lon:* -118.0588 I-84 Exit 261, go NE .7 mile on Island Ave
Klamath Falls	◇	🕐	℞	🚐	3600 Washburn Way, 97603 / 541-885-6890 • *Lat:* 42.1937 *Lon:* -121.7573 From Jct US-97/SH-140, E on SH-140 2.5 miles, N on Washburn Way 1.4 miles
Lebanon	◇ 10	🕐	℞	🚐	3290 S Santiam Hwy, 97355 / 541-258-7400 • *Lat:* 44.5174 *Lon:* -122.8991 I-5 Exit 228 go E 7.7 miles on SH-34 then S 2.3 miles on US-20
McMinnville	○		℞		2375 NE Hwy 99W, 97128 / 503-434-9233 • *Lat:* 45.2282 *Lon:* -123.1749 2 miles northeast of town center along SH-99W
Medford	○ 2		℞	🚐	3615 Crater Lake Hwy, 97504 / 541-770-2010 • *Lat:* 42.3670 *Lon:* -122.8561 I-5 Exit 30, follow SH-62 (Crater Lake Hwy) NE about 2 miles
Newport	○		℞		160 NW 25th St, 97365 / 541-265-6560 • *Lat:* 44.6548 *Lon:* -124.0546 From Jct US-20 & US-101 in Newport, follow US-101 N for 1.3 miles, turn left at NW 25th St
Ontario	◇ 1	🕐	℞		1775 E Idaho Ave, 97914 / 541-889-7400 • *Lat:* 44.0248 *Lon:* -116.9398 I-84 Exit 376B go N .4 mile
Pendleton	◇ 1	🕐	℞	🚐	2203 SW Court Pl, 97801 / 541-966-9970 • *Lat:* 45.6667 *Lon:* -118.8075 I-84 Exit 209 go N to SW 20th St and turn left .3 mile
Portland	○ 1		℞	🚐	4200 SE 82nd Ave, 97266 / 503-788-0200 • *Lat:* 45.4920 *Lon:* -122.5788 I-205 Exit 19 go W .6 mile on Powell Blvd then S .4 mile on 82nd Ave
	○ 1		℞		10000 SE 82nd Ave, 97286 / 503-788-4748 • *Lat:* 45.4502 *Lon:* -122.5788 I-205 Exit 16 go W .3 mile on Johnson Creek Blvd then S .4 mile on 82nd Ave
Redmond	◇	🕐	℞	🚐	300 NW Oaktree Ln, 97756 / 541-923-5972 • *Lat:* 44.2910 *Lon:* -121.1706 1.5 miles north of town center, east of US-97 at Maple Ave
Roseburg	○ 1		℞	🚐	2125 NW Stewart Pkwy, 97470 / 541-957-8550 • *Lat:* 43.2346 *Lon:* -123.3722 I-5 Exit 125 go W .7 mile on Garden Valley Blvd then N .2 mile on Stewart Pkwy

○ Wal-Mart ◇ Supercenter ☐ Sam's Club ▬ Gas ▬ Gas & Diesel

City/Town	⬭	🕐	℞	�	Information
Saint Helens	○		℞	�	2295 Gable Rd, 97051 / 503-366-5866 • *Lat:* 45.8482 *Lon:* -122.8311 2 miles southwest of town center at US-30/Gable Rd jct
Salem	○ 2		℞		5250 Commercial St SE, 97306 / 503-378-1336 • *Lat:* 44.8795 *Lon:* -123.0284 I-5 Exit 252 go W 1.6 miles on Kuebler Blvd then S .2 mile on Commercial St
	◇ 1	🕐	℞	�	1940 Turner Rd SE, 97302 / 503-391-0394 • *Lat:* 44.9134 *Lon:* -122.9974 I-5 Exit 253 go W .8 mile on SH-22 then S .6 mile on Turner Rd
	◇ 2	🕐	℞		3025 Lancaster Dr NE, 97305 / 503-378-7424 • *Lat:* 44.9647 *Lon:* -122.9837 I-5 Exit 256 go E .3 mile on Market St then N 1 mile on Lancaster Dr
Springfield	◇ 4	🕐	℞	�	2659 Olympic St, 97477 / 541-744-3004 • *Lat:* 44.0595 *Lon:* -122.9873 I-5 Exit 194A go E 2.4 miles on OR-126 (McKenzie Hwy), S .2 mile on Mohawk Blvd, E .6 mile on Olympic St
Talent	○ 1		℞	�	300 Valley View Rd, 97540 / 541-535-9170 • *Lat:* 42.2455 *Lon:* -122.7789 I-5 Exit 21, west of exit
Wood Village	◇ 1	🕐	℞	�	23500 NE Sandy Blvd, 97060 / 503-665-9200 • *Lat:* 45.5428 *Lon:* -122.4212 I-84 Exit 16 go N .2 mile on 238th Dr then W .2 mile on Sandy Blvd
Woodburn	◇ 1	🕐	℞		3002 Stacey Allison Way, 97071 / 503-981-9622 • *Lat:* 45.1488 *Lon:* -122.8827 I-5 Exit 271 go E .1 mile on Newberg Hwy, S .1 mile on Lawson Ave, W .2 mile on Stacey Allison Way

○ Wal-Mart   ◇ Supercenter   ☐ Sam's Club   ▨ Gas   ▮ Gas & Diesel

Pennsylvania

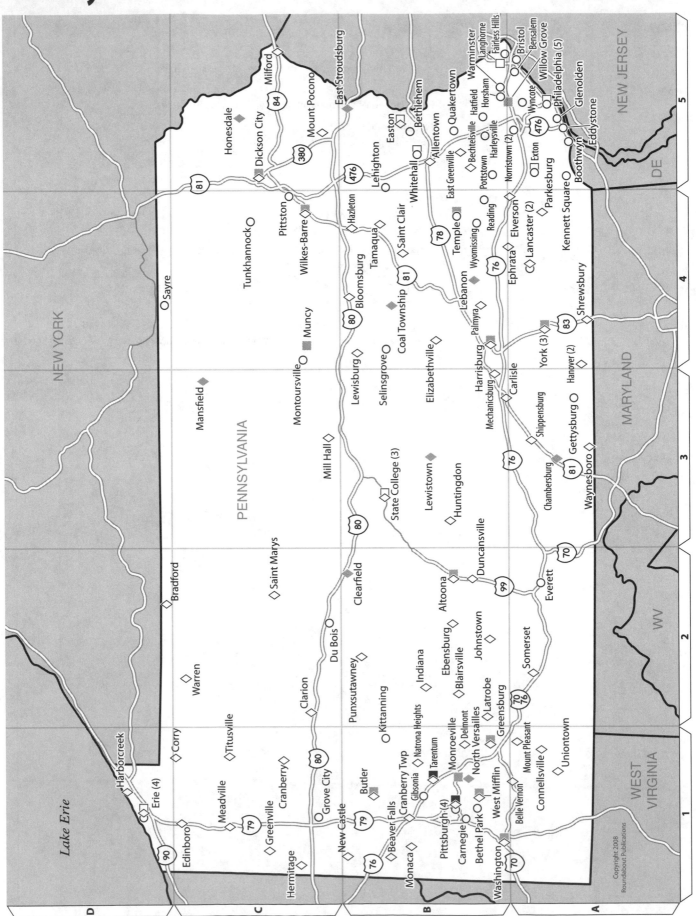

Wal-Mart ◇ Supercenter □ Sam's Club ▨ Gas ■ Gas & Diesel

NEW JERSEY

NEW YORK

PENNSYLVANIA

Lake Erie

MARYLAND

WEST VIRGINIA

WV

DE

Milford
Honesdale
Dickson City
Mount Pocono
East Stroudsburg
Bethlehem
Warminster
Langhorne
Fairless Hills
Bristol
Bensalem
Willow Grove
Wyncote
Philadelphia (5)
Glenolden
Eddystone
Boothwyn
Kennett Square
Quakertown
Hatfield
Horsham
Bechtelsville
Harleysville
Norristown (2)
Exton
Parkesburg
Easton
Allentown
Whitehall
East greenville
Pottstown
Elverson
Lancaster (2)
Shrewsbury
Lehighton
Saint Clair
Tamaqua
Reading
Temple
Wyomissing
Ephrata
Hazleton
Pittston
Wilkes-Barre
Bloomsburg
Coal Township
Lebanon
Palmyra
Harrisburg
Carlisle
York (3)
Hanover (2)
Shippensburg
Gettysburg
Chambersburg
Waynesboro
Tunkhannock
Sayre
Muncy
Montoursville
Lewisburg
Selinsgrove
Elizabethville
Mechanicsburg
Mansfield
Mill Hall
State College (3)
Lewistown
Huntingdon
Duncansville
Altoona
Everett
Bradford
Saint Marys
Clearfield
Du Bois
Warren
Punxsutawney
Kittanning
Indiana
Ebensburg
Blairsville
Johnstown
Latrobe
Greensburg
Somerset
Mount Pleasant
Connellsville
Uniontown
Corry
Titusville
Clarion
Natrona Heights
Delmont
North Versailles
Belle Vernon
Harborcreek
Erie (4)
Edinboro
Meadville
Greenville
Cranberry
Grove City
Butler
Cranberry Twp
Gibsonia
Tarentum
Monroeville
Hermitage
New Castle
Beaver Falls
Monaca
Pittsburgh (4)
Carnegie
Bethel Park
West Mifflin
Washington

84
380
81
476
476
78
76
80
80
80
81
83
99
70
76
81
76
70
79
79
76
90

City/Town	⬟	🕐	℞	🚐	Information
Allentown	◇ 4	🕐	℞	🚐	1091 Millcreek Rd, 18106 / 610-530-1400 • *Lat:* 40.5646 *Lon:* -75.5708 I-78 Exit 49A take SH-100 S 1.9 miles, continue S on Trexlertown Rd .2 mile then E on Cetronia Rd 1.1 miles
Altoona	■ 1		℞	🚐	2500 Plank Rd Commons, 16601 / 814-949-8950 • *Lat:* 40.4590 *Lon:* -78.4086 I-99 Exit 31, S on Plank Rd .5 mile
	◇ 1	🕐	℞	🚐	2600 Plank Rd Commons, 16601 / 814-949-8980 • *Lat:* 40.4566 *Lon:* -78.4095 I-99 Exit 31 take Plank Rd S .6 mile
Beaver Falls	◇ 7	🕐	℞	🚐	100 Chippewa Town Ctr, 15010 / 724-843-1100 • *Lat:* 40.7783 *Lon:* -80.3845 I-76 Exit 10 take SH-60 (toll) S 5.6 miles to Exit 29-SH-51 N 1.4 miles
Bechtelsville	◇	🕐	℞	🚐	567 Rt 100 N, 19505 / 610-367-1005 • *Lat:* 40.3524 *Lon:* -75.6284 Jct US-422 & SH-100 (S of town) follow SH-100 N 10.6 miles
Belle Vernon	◇ 1	🕐	℞	🚐	100 Sara Way / Rostraver Square, 15012 / 724-929-2424 • *Lat:* 40.1447 *Lon:* -79.8345 I-70 Exit 43A take SH-201 S .2 mile & W at Sara Way .2 mile
Bensalem	◯ 3		℞	🚐	3461 Horizon Blvd, 19020 / 215-942-4005 • *Lat:* 40.1073 *Lon:* -74.9388 I-276 (toll) Exit 351 take US-1 S .8 mile, SH-132 N .2 mile, Old Lincoln Hwy E .8 mile & Rockhill Dr S .3 mile
Bethel Park	◯ 8		℞		5055 Library Rd, 15102 / 412-831-0459 • *Lat:* 40.3385 *Lon:* -80.0259 I-79 Exit 54 go E .2 mile on SH-50, N .4 mile on Washington Pike, E 1.6 miles on Bower Hill Rd, turn right and continue E 2.4 miles on Painters Run Rd/Gilkeson Rd, continue E 2.2 miles on Connor Rd/Yellow Belt, then S .5 mile on Library Rd/PA-88
Bethlehem	◯ 8		℞		3926 Linden St, 18020 / 610-867-1300 • *Lat:* 40.6758 *Lon:* -75.3440 I-78 Exit 71 take SH-33 N 3.9 miles, US-22 W 3.1 miles & SH-191 S .3 mile
Blairsville	◇	🕐	℞		300 Resort Plaza Dr, 15717 / 724-459-3349 • *Lat:* 40.4422 *Lon:* -79.2287 Jct US-119 & US-22 (E of town) go W on US-22 for .6 mile then S at Resort Plaza Dr
Bloomsburg	◇ 1	🕐	℞	🚐	100 Lunger Dr, 17815 / 570-389-5750 • *Lat:* 41.0110 *Lon:* -76.4890 I-80 Exit 232 go E on Lunger Dr .3 mile
Boothwyn	◯ 3		℞		605 Conchester Hwy, 19061 / 610-494-2535 • *Lat:* 39.8501 *Lon:* -75.4487 I-95 Exit 3A take US-322 W 2.3 miles
Bradford	◇	🕐	℞	🚐	50 Foster Brook Blvd, 16701 / 814-368-4600 • *Lat:* 41.9809 *Lon:* -78.6170 Jct SH-219 & SH-346 (N of town) take Jackson Ave SW 1.5 miles, School St W .4 mile & Interstate Pkwy NW .2 mile
Bristol	◯ 3		℞		100 Commerce Cir, 19007 / 215-788-5600 • *Lat:* 40.1026 *Lon:* -74.8714 I-95 Exit 40 follow SH-413 S 2.4 miles then E at Commerce Cir .2 mile
Butler	■		℞	🚐	200 Moraine Pointe Plz, 16001 / 724-282-3525 • *Lat:* 40.8771 *Lon:* -79.9516 I-79 Exit 99 take US-422 SE for 11.7 miles then S on SH-356 for .4 mile
	◇	🕐	℞	🚐	400 Butler Commons, 16001 / 724-282-4060 • *Lat:* 40.8764 *Lon:* -79.9428 2.8 miles northwest of town center along SH-356
Carlisle	◇ 1	🕐	℞	🚐	60 Noble Blvd, 17013 / 717-258-1250 • *Lat:* 40.1909 *Lon:* -77.1921 I-81 Exit 47B take SH-34 N .2 mile then W on Noble Blvd
Carnegie	◯ 1		℞		2200 Washington Pike, 15106 / 412-429-1285 • *Lat:* 40.3846 *Lon:* -80.0933 I-79 Exit 55 follow US-50 N 1 mile
Chambersburg	◆ 2	🕐	℞		1730 Lincoln Way E, 17201 / 717-264-2300 • *Lat:* 39.9231 *Lon:* -77.6054 I-81 Exit 16 take US-30 E 1.6 miles
Clarion	◇ 1	🕐	℞	🚐	63 Perkins Rd, 16214 / 814-226-0809 • *Lat:* 41.2023 *Lon:* -79.3663 I-80 Exit 62 go N on SH-68 for .5 mile
Clearfield	◆ 1	🕐	℞	🚐	100 Supercenter Dr, 16830 / 814-765-8089 • *Lat:* 41.0308 *Lon:* -78.4028 I-80 Exit 120 go S on SH-879
Coal Township	◆	🕐	℞	🚐	3300 State Rt 61, 17866 / 570-648-6700 • *Lat:* 40.7876 *Lon:* -76.5569 Jct SH-901 & SH-61 (SE of town) go E on SH-61 for .8 mile

◯ Wal-Mart   ◇ Supercenter   ☐ Sam's Club   ▩ Gas   ■ Gas & Diesel

City/Town	🛡	🕐	℞	🚐	Information
Connellsville	◇		🕐	℞	🚐	1450 Morrell Ave, 15425 / 724-626-4470 • *Lat:* 40.0021 *Lon:* -79.6045 Jct SH-201/Vanderbilt Rd & US-119/Morrell Rd (S of town) follow US-119 S 1 mile
Corry	◇		🕐	℞		961 Rt 6, 16407 / 814-663-8070 • *Lat:* 41.9179 *Lon:* -79.7158 Jct SH-957 & US-6 (E of town) take US-6 W 1.2 miles
Cranberry	◇		🕐	℞	🚐	10 Kimberly Ln, 16319 / 814-678-0037 • *Lat:* 41.3505 *Lon:* -79.7188 Jct SH-257 & US-322 (N of town) take US-322 W .4 mile then Ross Dr S
Cranberry Twp	◇ 2		🕐	℞		20245 Rt 19, 16066 / 724-772-4550 • *Lat:* 40.6878 *Lon:* -80.1023 I-79 Exit 78 take SH-228 W .4 mile, Dutilh Rd N .6 mile & US-19 S .3 mile
Delmont	◇		🕐	℞	🚐	6700 Hollywood Blvd, 15626 / 724-468-6274 • *Lat:* 40.3993 *Lon:* -79.5921 I-76 (toll) Exit 57 follow US-22 E 10.1 miles then Hollywood Blvd S .6 mile
Dickson City	■ 1			℞	🚐	921 Viewmont Dr, 18519 / 570-347-4847 • *Lat:* 41.4617 *Lon:* -75.6268 I-81 Exit 190 go NW on Main Ave .2 mile, W on Viewmont .3 mile
	◇ 2		🕐	℞	🚐	900 Commerce Blvd, 18519 / 570-383-2354 • *Lat:* 41.4641 *Lon:* -75.6404 I-81 Exit 191A take US-6 BR E .8 mile, Viewmont Dr S .2 mile & Commerce Blvd E .4 mile
Du Bois	○ 3			℞		20 Industrial Dr, 15801 / 814-375-5000 • *Lat:* 41.1279 *Lon:* -78.7360 I-80 Exit 101 merge onto SH-255 S 1.8 miles & Industrial Dr N .8 mile
Duncansville	◇		🕐	℞		200 Commerce Dr, 16635 / 814-693-0531 • *Lat:* 40.3715 *Lon:* -78.4303 I-99 at Exit 23, east of exit
East Greenville	◇ 6		🕐	℞	🚐	620 Gravel Pike, 18041 / 215-679-2782 • *Lat:* 40.4129 *Lon:* -75.5081 I-476 Exit 44 take SH-663 W 4.5 miles, Quakertown Ave W .4 mile, Main St N .1 mile & Gravel Pike N .1 mile
East Stroudsburg	◆ 1		🕐	℞		355 Lincoln Ave, 18301 / 570-424-8415 • *Lat:* 40.9913 *Lon:* -75.1825 I-80 Exit 308 merge onto Prospect St W .1 mile & N on Forge Rd/Lincoln Ave .9 mile
Easton	□ 7				🚐	3796 Easton Nazareth Hwy, 18045 / 610-923-7350 • *Lat:* 40.7137 *Lon:* -75.2838 I-78 Exit 71 take SH-33 N for 6.3 miles, then SE on SH-248 for .2 mile
	◇ 10		🕐	℞	🚐	3722 Easton Nazareth Hwy, 18045 / 610-250-8603 • *Lat:* 40.7116 *Lon:* -75.2815 I-78 Exit 3 follow US-22 W 7.9 miles & SH-248 NW 2.2 miles
Ebensburg	◇		🕐	℞	🚐	300 Wal-Mart Dr, 15931 / 814-471-0200 • *Lat:* 40.4730 *Lon:* -78.7485 I-99 Exit 28 go N on US-32 .8 mile then US-22 W 19.3 miles
Eddystone	○ 2			℞	🚐	1570 Chester Pike, 19022 / 610-447-1860 • *Lat:* 39.8670 *Lon:* -75.3403 I-95 Exit 8 take Stewart Ave W .2 mile & US-13 S .9 mile
Edinboro	◇ 1		🕐	℞	🚐	108 Washington Towne Blvd N, 16412 / 814-734-0900 • *Lat:* 41.8794 *Lon:* -80.1729 I-79 Exit 166 take US-6 N .5 mile
Elizabethville	◇		🕐	℞	🚐	200 Kocher Ln, 17023 / 717-362-3696 • *Lat:* 40.5576 *Lon:* -76.7901 1.4 miles northeast of town center via US-209
Elverson	◇ 2		🕐	℞	🚐	100 Crossings Blvd, 19520 / 610-913-2000 • *Lat:* 40.1581 *Lon:* -75.8227 I-76 (toll) Exit 298 follow SH-10 E .3 mile, Quarry Rd S .4 mile, Morgan Way W .2 mile & Main St E .7 mile
Ephrata	◇		🕐	℞		890 E Main St, 17522 / 717-721-6680 • *Lat:* 40.1655 *Lon:* -76.1602 Jct US-222 & US-322 (SE of town) go NW on US-322 for .6 mile
Erie	□ 1				🚐	7200 Peach St, 16509 / 814-866-1074 • *Lat:* 42.0549 *Lon:* -80.0878 I-90 Exit 24 take US-19 N .6 mile
	○ 2			℞	🚐	1900 Keystone Dr, 16509 / 814-864-7330 • *Lat:* 42.0567 *Lon:* -80.0867 I-79 Exit 180 take Interchange Rd E .7 mile, US-19 S .8 mile & Keystone Dr E .1 mile
	○ 5			℞	🚐	4950 W 23rd St, 16506 / 814-835-0556 • *Lat:* 42.0693 *Lon:* -80.1896 I-79 Exit 182 take US-20 W 4.2 miles then 23rd St N
	◇ 5		🕐	℞	🚐	2711 Elm St, 16504 / 814-459-3625 • *Lat:* 42.1219 *Lon:* -80.0429 I-79 Exit 182 take US-20/26th St E 4.7 miles then S on Elm St

○ Wal-Mart ◇ Supercenter □ Sam's Club ▩ Gas ■ Gas & Diesel

City/Town	⬡	🕐	℞	🚚	Information
Everett	◯ 5		℞		72 Bedford Sq, 15537 / 814-623-3332 • *Lat:* 40.0186 *Lon:* -78.4628 Jct I-99/US-220 & US-30 (W of town) take US-30 E 4.5 miles & S at Bedford Sq
Exton	▢ 5		℞	🚚	280 Indian Run St, 19341 / 484-875-0469 • *Lat:* 40.0221 *Lon:* -75.6308 I-76 Exit 312 take SH-100 SE 3.7 miles, Commerce Dr W .3 mile & Indian Run S .2 mile
	◯		℞	🚚	270 Indian Run St, 19341 / 484-875-9053 • *Lat:* 40.0227 *Lon:* -75.6310 Jct US-202 & US-30 (E of town) take US-30 W .4 mile, Lincoln Hwy W 2 miles, Commerce Dr S .3 mile & Indian Run W .1 mile
Fairless Hills	◯ 10		℞	🚚	495 S Oxford Valley Rd, 19030 / 215-949-6600 • *Lat:* 40.1709 *Lon:* -74.8515 I-276 Exit 351 merge onto US-1 N 7.7 miles then follow Oxford Valley Rd SE 2.2 miles
Gettysburg	◯		℞		1270 York Rd, 17325 / 717-334-2000 • *Lat:* 39.8441 *Lon:* -77.2015 Jct US-15 & US-30 (E of town) go W on US-30 .5 mile
Gibsonia	◯ 1		℞	🚚	300 Wal-Mart Dr, 15044 / 724-449-2700 • *Lat:* 40.6212 *Lon:* -79.9447 I-76 (toll) Exit 39 take SH-8 N .6 mile then W at Theater Dr
Glenolden	◯ 6		℞		50 N Macdade Blvd, 19036 / 610-583-2682 • *Lat:* 39.9057 *Lon:* -75.2911 I-476 (toll) Exit 3 follow E Baltimore Pike E 1.9 miles, Woodland/Kedron Ave SE 1.8 miles & Macdade Blvd E 1.4 miles
Greensburg	◼ 5		℞	🚚	6211 State Rt 30, 15601 / 724-850-7490 • *Lat:* 40.2271 *Lon:* -79.5267 I-76 Exit 67 take US-30 E for 5 miles
	◇ 6	🕐	℞	🚚	2200 Greengate Centre Cir, 15601 / 724-830-2440 • *Lat:* 40.3086 *Lon:* -79.5804 I-76 Exit 67 take US-30 E 5.5 miles then Greengate Centre Dr N .2 mile
Greenville	◇	🕐	℞	🚚	45 Williamson Rd, 16125 / 724-589-0211 • *Lat:* 41.4143 *Lon:* -80.3597 I-79 Exit 130 follow SH-358 W 11.8 miles then Williamson Rd N .1 mile
Grove City	◯ 4		℞		1566 W Main St Ext, 16127 / 724-458-5877 • *Lat:* 41.1688 *Lon:* -80.1118 I-79 Exit 113 take SH-208 NE 2 miles, Irishtown Rd N 1.3 miles & Main St S .6 mile
Hanover	◇	🕐	℞		495 Eisenhower Dr, 17331 / 717-632-8444 • *Lat:* 39.8250 *Lon:* -76.9792 Jct US-15 & US-30 (NW of town) take US-30 E 9 miles, SH-94 S 3.7 miles & Eisenhower Dr E 1 mile
	◇	🕐	℞	🚚	1881 Baltimore Pike, 17331 / 717-630-8211 • *Lat:* 39.7615 *Lon:* -76.9591 Jct Grandview Rd & SH-94 (S of town) go S on SH-94 for .9 mile
Harborcreek	◇ 5	🕐	℞	🚚	5741 Buffalo Rd, 16421 / 814-899-6255 • *Lat:* 42.1602 *Lon:* -79.9707 I-90 Exit 32 take SH-430 N .3 mile, Hannon Rd N 2.9 miles & US-20 W .9 mile
Harleysville	◯ 4		℞		651 Main St, 19438 / 215-513-0205 • *Lat:* 40.2857 *Lon:* -75.3959 I-476 (toll) Exit 31 take SH-63 NW 3.9 miles
Harrisburg	◼ 3		℞	🚚	6781 Grayson Rd, 17111 / 717-558-4200 • *Lat:* 40.2626 *Lon:* -76.7685 I-83 Exit 47 take US-322 E for 2.3 miles, Mushroom Hill Rd N .2 mile & Grayson Rd E .4 mile
	◇ 3	🕐	℞		6535 Grayson Rd, 17111 / 717-561-8402 • *Lat:* 40.2622 *Lon:* -76.7730 I-83 Exit 47 take US-322 E 2.7 miles, Mushroom Hill Rd N .2 mile & Grayson Rd E .1 mile
Hatfield	◯		℞		1515 Bethlehem Pike, 19440 / 215-997-2929 • *Lat:* 40.2869 *Lon:* -75.2641 I-276 (toll) Exit 339 take SH-309 N 12.4 miles then E on Hilltown Pike .2 mile
Hazleton	◇ 2	🕐	℞	🚚	87 Airport Rd, 18202 / 570-454-8322 • *Lat:* 40.9881 *Lon:* -76.0142 I-81 Exit 145 go E .5 mile on SH-93 then N .7 mile on Airport Rd
Hermitage	◇ 6	🕐	℞	🚚	1275 N Hermitage Rd, 16148 / 724-346-5940 • *Lat:* 41.2492 *Lon:* -80.4501 I-80 Exit 4B take SH-60 N .8 mile & SH-18 N 4.6 miles
Honesdale	◆	🕐	℞	🚚	777 Old Willow Ave, 18431 / 570-251-9543 • *Lat:* 41.5552 *Lon:* -75.2248 I-84 Exit 30 take SH-402 N 4.5 miles, follow US-6 N 11.6 miles & E at Brook Rd .3 mile
Horsham	◯ 2		℞		200 Blair Mill Rd, 19044 / 215-672-1300 • *Lat:* 40.1797 *Lon:* -75.1197 I-276 (toll) Exit 343 take SH-611 N .4 mile & Blair Mill Rd E .7 mile

◯ Wal-Mart   ◇ Supercenter   ▢ Sam's Club   ◼ Gas   ◼ Gas & Diesel

City/Town	⬦	🕐	℞	🚌	Information
Huntingdon	◇		🕐	℞	🚌	6716 Towne Center Blvd, 16652 / 814-644-6910 • *Lat:* 40.4918 *Lon:* -78.0418 1.8 miles west of town center via SH-26
Indiana	◇		🕐	℞	🚌	3100 Oakland Ave, 15701 / 724-349-3565 • *Lat:* 40.5999 *Lon:* -79.1951 Jct US-422 & SH-286 (S of town) take SH-286/Oakland Ave N .2 mile
Johnstown	◇		🕐	℞	🚌	150 Town Centre Dr, 15904 / 814-266-6996 • *Lat:* 40.2801 *Lon:* -78.8417 Jct US-219 & SH-756 (SE of town) go E on SH-756 for .2 mile & S at Town Center Dr
Kennett Square	○			℞		516 School House Rd, 19348 / 610-444-2268 • *Lat:* 39.8590 *Lon:* -75.6896 Jct US-1/Kennett Oxford Bypass & SH-82 go S on SH-82 for 1 mile & E at Mulberry St
Kittanning	○			℞		1 Hilltop Plz, 16201 / 724-543-2023 • *Lat:* 40.8148 *Lon:* -79.5454 From SH-28 Exit 19 (S of town) take US-422 W .8 mile, US-422 BR E .6 mile & N at Hilltop Plaza .3 mile
Lancaster	○			℞		2030 Fruitville Pike, 17601 / 717-581-0200 • *Lat:* 40.0762 *Lon:* -76.3252 From US-30 (NW of town) take Fruitviille Pike N .6 mile
	◇		🕐	℞	🚌	2034 Lincoln Hwy E, 17602 / 717-390-1738 • *Lat:* 40.0323 *Lon:* -76.2422 Jct US-222 & US-30 (NE of town) take US-30 E for 4.1 miles & Lincoln Hwy E .2 mile
Langhorne	▢ 1				🚌	1717 E Lincoln Hwy, 19047 / 215-949-6501 • *Lat:* 40.1732 *Lon:* -74.8892 I-95 Exit 44 go NE on SH-413 for .6 mile
Latrobe	◇		🕐	℞	🚌	100 Colony Ln, 15650 / 724-537-0928 • *Lat:* 40.2856 *Lon:* -79.3845 Jct SH-982 & US-30 (S of town) take US-30 W .9 mile & S at Colony Lane
Lebanon	◆ 10		🕐	℞	🚌	1355 E Lehman St, 17046 / 717-228-1221 • *Lat:* 40.3477 *Lon:* -76.3886 I-76 (toll) Exit 266 follow SH-72 N 7.4 miles, US-422 E 1.8 miles, Cumberland St .3 mile, 11th Ave N .2 mile & Lehman St E .3 mile
Lehighton	○ 5			℞	🚌	1204 Blakeslee Dr E, 18235 / 570-386-3356 • *Lat:* 40.8154 *Lon:* -75.7343 I-476 (toll) Exit 74 merge onto US-209 S 2.8 miles then SH-443 W 1.8 miles
Lewisburg	◇ 6		🕐	℞	🚌	120 AJK Blvd, 17837 / 570-522-8200 • *Lat:* 40.9801 *Lon:* -76.8857 I-80 Exit 210A follow US-15 S 5.2 miles
Lewistown	◆		🕐	℞		10180 US Hwy 522 S, 17044 / 717-242-6201 • *Lat:* 40.5831 *Lon:* -77.6125 Jct US-22 & US-522 (in town) go SW on US-522/US-22 BR 2.8 miles
Mansfield	◆		🕐	℞		1169 S Main St, 16933 / 570-662-1115 • *Lat:* 41.7830 *Lon:* -77.0695 Jct SH-660 & US-15 (S of town) take SH-660/US-15 BR N 1.1 miles
Meadville	◇ 3		🕐	℞		16086 Conneaut Lake Rd, 16335 / 814-724-6267 • *Lat:* 41.6201 *Lon:* -80.2159 I-79 Exit 147B take US-6 W 2.3 miles
Mechanicsburg	◇ 2		🕐	℞		6520 Carlisle Pike, 17050 / 717-691-3150 • *Lat:* 40.2465 *Lon:* -77.0241 I-81 Exit 57 follow SH-114 E 1.7 miles & US-11 E .2 mile
Milford	◇ 1		🕐	℞	🚌	220 Rt 6 & 209, 18337 / 570-491-4940 • *Lat:* 41.3409 *Lon:* -74.7656 I-84 Exit 46 merge onto US-6 E .5 mile
Mill Hall	◇ 6		🕐	℞	🚌	167 Hogan Blvd, 17751 / 570-893-4627 • *Lat:* 41.1173 *Lon:* -77.4754 I-80 Exit 178 take US-220 N 4.8 miles then Mill Hall Rd/SH-150 N .7 mile
Monaca	◇		🕐	℞		3942 Brodhead Rd, 15061 / 724-773-2929 • *Lat:* 40.6807 *Lon:* -80.3030 I-76 (toll) Exit 10 take SH-60 S 13.8 miles then SH-18 E 1.7 miles
Monroeville	▮ 3			℞	🚌	3621 William Penn Hwy, 15146 / 412-856-7162 • *Lat:* 40.4329 *Lon:* -79.7999 I-376 Exit 10B go SE on US-22BR/William Penn Hwy 3 miles
Montoursville	○ 1			℞		1015 N Loyalsock Ave, 17754 / 570-368-5450 • *Lat:* 41.2612 *Lon:* -76.9158 I-180 Exit 21 take Loyalsock Ave S .3 mile
Mount Pleasant	◇ 9		🕐	℞	🚌	2100 Summit Ridge Plz, 15666 / 724-542-7300 • *Lat:* 40.1273 *Lon:* -79.5480 I-70/76 (toll) Exit 75 follow US-119 S 7.5 miles & SH-819 NE .6 mile
Mount Pocono	◇ 2		🕐	℞		500 Rt 940, 18344 / 570-895-4700 • *Lat:* 41.1273 *Lon:* -75.3440 I-380 Exit 3 take SH-940 E 1.9 miles

○ Wal-Mart ◇ Supercenter ▢ Sam's Club ▮ Gas ▮ Gas & Diesel

City/Town	🛡	⏰	℞	🚌	Information
Muncy	▣ 1			🚌	611 Lycoming Mall Cir, 17756 / 570-546-6699 • *Lat:* 41.2404 *Lon:* -76.8302 I-80 Exit 17, S on Lycoming Mall Rd .2 mile & E onto Lycoming Mall Cir
Natrona Heights	◇	⏰	℞	🚌	4015 Freeport Rd, 15065 / 724-226-6949 • *Lat:* 40.6461 *Lon:* -79.7096 From SH-28 Exit 15 go E .8 mile on Burtner Rd then N 1.2 miles on Freeport Rd
New Castle	◇	⏰	℞	🚌	2501 W State St, 16101 / 724-657-9390 • *Lat:* 41.0107 *Lon:* -80.3910 I-80 Exit 4A take SH-60 S 13.5 miles & US-224 E .3 mile
Norristown	◯ 4		℞		53 W Germantown Pike, 19401 / 610-275-0222 • *Lat:* 40.1444 *Lon:* -75.3163 I-276 (toll) Exit 333 take Plymouth Rd E .2 mile & Germantown Pike NW 2.9 miles
	◯ 5		℞	🚌	650 S Trooper Rd, 19403 / 610-631-6750 • *Lat:* 40.1282 *Lon:* -75.4040 I-76 Exit 328A take US-422 W 3 miles then follow SH-363 N 1.5 miles
North Versailles	◆ 10	⏰	℞	🚌	100 Wal-Mart Dr, 15137 / 412-816-0301 • *Lat:* 40.3865 *Lon:* -79.8218 I-76 (toll) Exit 67 take US-30 W 9 miles & Greensburg Ave N .6 mile
Palmyra	◇ 9	⏰	℞	🚌	100 N Londonderry Sq, 17078 / 717-838-0800 • *Lat:* 40.3199 *Lon:* -76.5622 I-81 Exit 85 follow SH-934 S 5 miles, Clearspring Rd S 2 miles, and US-422 W 1.2 miles
Parkesburg	◇	⏰	℞	🚌	100 Commons Dr, 19365 / 610-857-0500 • *Lat:* 39.9818 *Lon:* -75.9324 Jct US-30 & SH-10 (N of town) go S on SH-10/Octorara Trl .1 mile
Philadelphia	☐ 2			🚌	1000 Franklin Mills Cir, 19154 / 215-632-2299 • *Lat:* 40.0856 *Lon:* -74.9592 I-95 Exit 35 take SH-63 W 1.1 miles then E to Franklin Mills .6 mile
	◯ 1		℞		1601 S Columbus Blvd, 19148 / 215-468-4220 • *Lat:* 39.9273 *Lon:* -75.1446 I-95 Exit 20 take Columbus Blvd S 1 mile
	◯ 2		℞		1 Franklin Mills Blvd, 19154 / 215-281-3159 • *Lat:* 40.0827 *Lon:* -74.9658 I-95 Exit 35 merge onto SH-63 W 1.1 miles then Milbrook Rd N .3 mile
	◯ 4		℞	🚌	9745 Roosevelt Blvd, 19114 / 215-698-0350 • *Lat:* 40.0875 *Lon:* -75.0216 I-95 Exit 32 take Academy Rd N 2.2 miles, Grant Ave W 1.4 miles & Roosevelt Blvd N .4 mile
	◯ 6		℞		4600 Roosevelt Blvd, 19124 / 215-288-0700 • *Lat:* 40.0287 *Lon:* -75.1008 I-76 Exit 340B merge onto US-1 N 6 miles
Pittsburgh	■ 1		℞	🚌	289 Mount Nebo Rd, 15237 / 412-364-1572 • *Lat:* 40.5338 *Lon:* -80.0711 I-279 Exit 15 go NE .4 mile on Camp Horne Rd/Green Belt then left at Mt Nebo Rd .2 mile
	▣ 5		℞	🚌	249 Summit Park Dr, 15275 / 412-494-4140 • *Lat:* 40.4483 *Lon:* -80.1777 I-79 Exit 60B take SH-60 W 3.8 miles to Exit 1, W on Summit Pk Dr .4 mile
	◯ 8		℞		877 Freeport Rd, 15238 / 412-782-4444 • *Lat:* 40.4868 *Lon:* -79.8912 From I-579 take SH-28 N 7.3 miles to Exit 8, then Freeport Rd E .5 mile
	◇ 5	⏰	℞	🚌	250 Summit Park Dr, 15275 / 412-788-9055 • *Lat:* 40.4482 *Lon:* -80.1774 I-79 Exit 59B take US-22 W 4 miles, US-60 N .3 mile to Exit 1, follow Summit Park Dr W .6 mile
Pittston	◯ 1		℞		1201 Oak St, 18640 / 570-883-9400 • *Lat:* 41.3075 *Lon:* -75.7688 I-81 Exit 175 take SH-315 N .3 mile & W on Oak St .3 mile
Pottstown	◯		℞		233 Shoemaker Rd, 19464 / 610-327-3204 • *Lat:* 40.2550 *Lon:* -75.6628 Jct US-422 & SH-100 (S of town) take SH-100 N .9 mile then W at Shoemaker Rd .2 mile
Punxsutawney	◇	⏰	℞		21920 Rt 119, 15767 / 814-938-3500 • *Lat:* 40.9544 *Lon:* -78.9777 Jct SH-36 & US-119 (in town) take US-119 S 1.2 miles
Quakertown	◯ 4		℞	🚌	195 N West End Blvd, 18951 / 215-529-7689 • *Lat:* 40.4441 *Lon:* -75.3524 I-476 (toll) Exit 44 follow SH-663 E 3.5 miles then N on West End Blvd .2 mile
Reading	◯ 4		℞		5900 Perkiomen Ave, 19606 / 610-582-0505 • *Lat:* 40.2962 *Lon:* -75.8398 I-176/Morgantown Expy Exit 11A merge onto US-422 E 3.5 miles
Saint Clair	◇ 5	⏰	℞	🚌	500 Terry Rich Blvd, 17970 / 570-429-1959 • *Lat:* 40.7239 *Lon:* -76.1926 I-81 Exit 124A follow SH-61 S 4.4 miles

◯ Wal-Mart   ◇ Supercenter   ☐ Sam's Club   ▣ Gas   ■ Gas & Diesel

City/Town	🛡	🕐	℞	🚐	Information
Saint Marys	◇		🕐	℞ 🚐	1102 Million Dollar Hwy, 15857 / 814-781-1344 • *Lat:* 41.3902 *Lon:* -78.5586 Jct SH-120 & SH-255 (in town) go S on SH-255 for 2.6 miles
Sayre	○			℞ 🚐	1887 N Elmira St, 18840 / 570-888-9791 • *Lat:* 41.9758 *Lon:* -76.5415 Jct US-220 & SH-17 (NW of town) take US-220 S .4 mile, E .1 mile on Wilawana Rd, then S 1 mile on Elmira St.
Selinsgrove	○			℞ 🚐	980 N Susquehanna Trl, 17870 / 570-374-1230 • *Lat:* 40.8181 *Lon:* -76.8531 I-80 Exit 210 merge onto US-15 S 17.9 miles
Shippensburg	◇ 1		🕐	℞ 🚐	100 S Conestoga Dr, 17257 / 717-532-4240 • *Lat:* 40.0596 *Lon:* -77.4968 I-81 Exit 29 take SH-174 W .9 mile then N at Conestoga Dr .1 mile
Shrewsbury	◇ 1		🕐	℞ 🚐	698 Shrewsbury Commons Ave, 17361 / 717-235-6363 • *Lat:* 39.7689 *Lon:* -76.6690 I-83 Exit 4 merge onto SH-851 W .2 mile & S on Mt Airy Rd .3 mile
Somerset	◇ 3		🕐	℞ 🚐	2028 N Center Ave, 15501 / 814-443-6962 • *Lat:* 40.0517 *Lon:* -79.0748 I-70/76 (toll) Exit 110 go N on Center Ave 2.5 miles
State College	☐			🚐	381 Benner Pike, 16801 / 814-235-9404 • *Lat:* 40.8308 *Lon:* -77.8048 I-80 Exit 161 take US-220 S 6.9 miles then SH-150 S 3.8 miles
	◇		🕐	℞ 🚐	373 Benner Pike, 16801 / 814-235-9306 • *Lat:* 40.8307 *Lon:* -77.8048 I-80 Exit 161 follow US-220 S 7.2 miles to Exit 78A, SH-150 S for 3.3 miles
	◇		🕐	℞	1665 N Atherton St, 16803 / 814-237-8401 • *Lat:* 40.8083 *Lon:* -77.8967 I-80 Exit 161 follow US-220 S 14.9 miles, Waddle Rd S .8 mile & Vaero Rd W .2 mile
Tamaqua	◇		🕐	℞ 🚐	35 Plaza Dr, 18252 / 570-668-2054 • *Lat:* 40.8339 *Lon:* -75.9877 2.9 miles north of town via SH-309
Tarentum	■			℞ 🚐	2000 Village Center Dr, 15084 / 724-274-1734 • *Lat:* 40.5660 *Lon:* -79.8023 5 miles southwest of town via SH-28 at Pittsburgh Mills Blvd
	◇		🕐	℞ 🚐	2010 Village Center Dr, 15084 / 724-274-0260 • *Lat:* 40.5631 *Lon:* -79.8031 From SH-28/Allegheny Valley Expy Exit 12A go W .5 mile on Pittsburgh Mills Blvd then S at Village Center Dr .3 mile
Temple	▨			℞ 🚐	5314 Allentown Pike, 19560 / 610-929-4321 • *Lat:* 40.4128 *Lon:* -75.9238 I-78 Exit 29 take SH-61 S 12.3 miles, NE on Tuckerton Rd .5 mile & N on 5th St .4 mile
	◇		🕐	℞ 🚐	5370 Allentown Pike, 19560 / 610-939-0601 • *Lat:* 40.4174 *Lon:* -75.9189 I-78 Exit 29A take SH-61 S 12.3 miles, Tuckerton Rd E .5 mile & 5th St N .6 mile
Titusville	◇		🕐	℞	11415 Hydetown Rd, 16354 / 814-827-0850 • *Lat:* 41.6341 *Lon:* -79.6973 Jct SH-27 & SH-8 (in town) go NW on SH-8 for 1.4 miles
Tunkhannock	○			℞	809 State Rd 29 S, 18657 / 570-836-8064 • *Lat:* 41.5206 *Lon:* -75.9396 Jct US-6 & US-29 (in town) go S on SH-29/Bridge St for 1.1 miles
Uniontown	◇		🕐	℞ 🚐	355 Wal-Mart Dr, 15401 / 724-438-3344 • *Lat:* 39.9158 *Lon:* -79.7515 2 miles northwest of town center along US-40, west side of highway
Warminster	○ 8			℞	100 E Street Rd, 18974 / 215-442-5670 • *Lat:* 40.1953 *Lon:* -75.0800 I-276 (toll) Exit 351 take US-1 S .6 mile & SH-132 N 7.3 miles
Warren	◇		🕐	℞ 🚐	2901 Market St, 16365 / 814-723-2640 • *Lat:* 41.8793 *Lon:* -79.1502 2.7 miles north of town via US-62
Washington	▨ 1			℞ 🚐	80 Trinity Point Dr, 15301 / 724-229-3500 • *Lat:* 40.1833 *Lon:* -80.2215 I-70 Exit 19 take US-19 NE .4 mile then S on Trinity Point Dr .3 mile
	◇ 1		🕐	℞ 🚐	30 Trinity Point Dr, 15301 / 724-229-4020 • *Lat:* 40.1833 *Lon:* -80.2232 I-70 Exit 19B take US-19 N .4 mile then Trinity Pt Dr E .3 mile
Waynesboro	◇		🕐	℞ 🚐	12751 Washington Township Blvd, 17268 / 717-762-2282 • *Lat:* 39.7404 *Lon:* -77.5266 3.3 miles east of town center via SH-16

○ Wal-Mart   ◇ Supercenter   ☐ Sam's Club   ▨ Gas   ■ Gas & Diesel

City/Town	🛡	🕐	℞	🚐	Information
West Mifflin	■ 9		℞	🚐	2251 Century Dr, 15122 / 412-653-8622 • *Lat:* 40.3443 *Lon:* -79.9480 I-279 Exit 5B take SH-51 S for 7.6 miles, SH-885 E 1 mile, Mt View Dr S .1 mile & Century Dr S .3 mile
	◇	🕐	℞	🚐	2351 Century Dr, 15122 / 412-655-3404 • *Lat:* 40.3438 *Lon:* -79.9435 Jct SH-51 & SH-885/Yellow Belt (W of town) take SH-885 E .2 mile & S on Mt View/Century Dr .5 mile
Whitehall	□ 8			🚐	2595 MacArthur Rd, 18052 / 610-266-5201 • *Lat:* 40.6443 *Lon:* -75.4919 I-476 Exit 56 take US-22 E 5.8 miles then SH-145 N 1.5 miles
	○		℞	🚐	2601 Macarthur Rd, 18052 / 610-266-9645 • *Lat:* 40.6446 *Lon:* -75.4922 I-78 Exit 71 take SH-33 N 4.2 miles, US-22 W 11.4 miles & Macarthur Rd N 1.4 miles
Wilkes Barre	■ 2		℞	🚐	441 Wilkes Barre Twnsp Blvd, 18702 / 570-821-5500 • *Lat:* 41.2342 *Lon:* -75.8654 I-81 Exit 165 take SH-309BR N 2 miles
	◇ 2	🕐	℞	🚐	2150 Wilkes Barre Township Market Pl, 18702 / 570-821-6180 • *Lat:* 41.2204 *Lon:* -75.8839 I-81 Exit 165 merge onto SH-309 N 1.3 miles
Willow Grove	■ 2		℞	🚐	3925 Welsh Rd, 19090 / 215-657-1837 • *Lat:* 40.1562 *Lon:* -75.1415 I-276 Exit 343 toward Jenkintown, W on Maryland .6 mile, SW on Compiter .5 mile & NW on Welsh .2 mile
Wyncote	○ 5		℞		1000 Easton Rd, 19095 / 215-887-6737 • *Lat:* 40.0808 *Lon:* -75.1699 I-276 (toll) Exit 339 follow SH-309 S 4.5 miles, exit at Easton Rd and go SW .3 mile
Wyomissing	○		℞		1135 Berkshire Blvd, 19610 / 610-376-5848 • *Lat:* 40.3137 *Lon:* 75.9756 Jct US-422 & US-222, take US-222 S .7 mile, Papermill Rd W .3 mile, Woodland Rd S .2 mile, Ridgewood Rd W .2 mile
York	■ 1		℞	🚐	2801 E Market St, 17402 / 717-840-0111 • *Lat:* 39.9755 *Lon:* -76.6730 I-81 Exit 19 take SH-462 E 1 mile
	◇ 2	🕐	℞		2801 E Market St, 17402 / 717-755-1600 • *Lat:* 39.9755 *Lon:* -76.6730 I-83 Exit 18 take SH-124 E .2 mile, Haines Rd N 1 mile, Mills St N .1 mile & SH-462 W .3 mile
	◇ 3	🕐	℞	🚐	1800 Loucks Rd, 17408 / 717-764-1485 • *Lat:* 39.9749 *Lon:* -76.7695 I-83 Exit 21B take US-30 W 2.3 miles, Kenneth Rd N .2 mile & Loucks Rd W .1 mile

○ Wal-Mart   ◇ Supercenter   □ Sam's Club   ■ Gas   ■ Gas & Diesel

Rhode Island

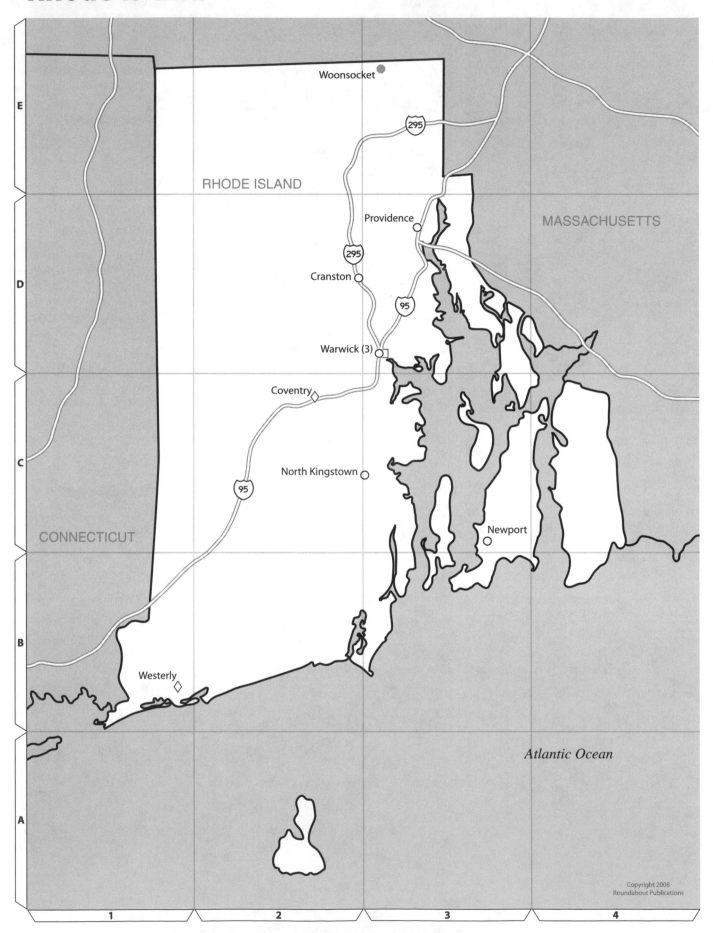

RHODE ISLAND

MASSACHUSETTS

Woonsocket

295

Providence

295

Cranston

95

Warwick (3)

Coventry

95

North Kingstown

CONNECTICUT

Newport

B

Westerly

Atlantic Ocean

E

D

C

B

A

1   2   3   4

City/Town	🛡	🕐	Rx	🚗	Information
Coventry	◇ 1		Rx	🚗	650 Centre Of New England Blvd, 02816 / 401-823-7780 • *Lat:* 41.6642 *Lon:* -71.5665 I-95 Exit 6A go N on Hopkins Hill Rd .8 mile & E on Centre Of New England Blvd .2 mile
Cranston	○ 1		Rx		1776 Plainfield Pike, 02921 / 401-946-2030 • *Lat:* 41.7901 *Lon:* -71.4997 I-295 Exit 4 take SH-14 E .1 mile
Newport	○		Rx		199 Connell Hwy, 02840 / 401-848-5167 • *Lat:* 41.5106 *Lon:* -71.3176 2 miles north of town center; from the Claiborne Pell Bridge, follow SH-138 1 mile to Admiral Kalbfus Rd then go W .2 mile and N .2 mile on Connell Hwy
North Kingstown	○		Rx		1031 Ten Rod Rd, 02852 / 401-294-0025 • *Lat:* 41.5811 *Lon:* -71.4930 From SH-4 Exit 5A (W of town) take SH-102 S .7 mile
Providence	○ 1		Rx		51 Silver Spring St, 02904 / 401-272-5047 • *Lat:* 41.8455 *Lon:* -71.4176 I-95 Exit 24 take Branch Ave W .4 mile & Silver Sprg St S .2 mile
Warwick	☐ 2			🚗	25 Pace Blvd, 02886 / 401-823-7070 • *Lat:* 41.7025 *Lon:* -71.4968 I-95 Exit 10 take SH-117 W 1.1 miles, NE on Inskip Blvd .1 mile & N on Pace .3 mile
	○ 1		Rx		650 Bald Hill Rd, 02886 / 401-821-1766 • *Lat:* 41.7206 *Lon:* -71.4830 I-295 Exit 2 merge onto Bald Hill Rd S .6 mile
	○ 3		Rx		840 Post Rd, 02888 / 401-781-2233 • *Lat:* 41.7524 *Lon:* -71.4158 I-95 Exit 14 take SH-37 E .9 mile & US-1 N 1.2 miles
Westerly	◇	🕐	Rx		258 Post Rd, 02891 / 401-322-0790 • *Lat:* 41.3519 *Lon:* -71.7614 Jct SH-78/Westerly BYP & US-1, follow US-1 NE 2.9 miles
Woonsocket	⬤ 6		Rx		1919 Diamond Hill Rd, 02895 / 401-762-0640 • *Lat:* 42.0149 *Lon:* -71.4708 I-295 Exit 9B take SH-99 N 2.8 miles, follow Mendon Rd N 2.3 miles & Diamond Hill Rd E .6 mile

South Carolina

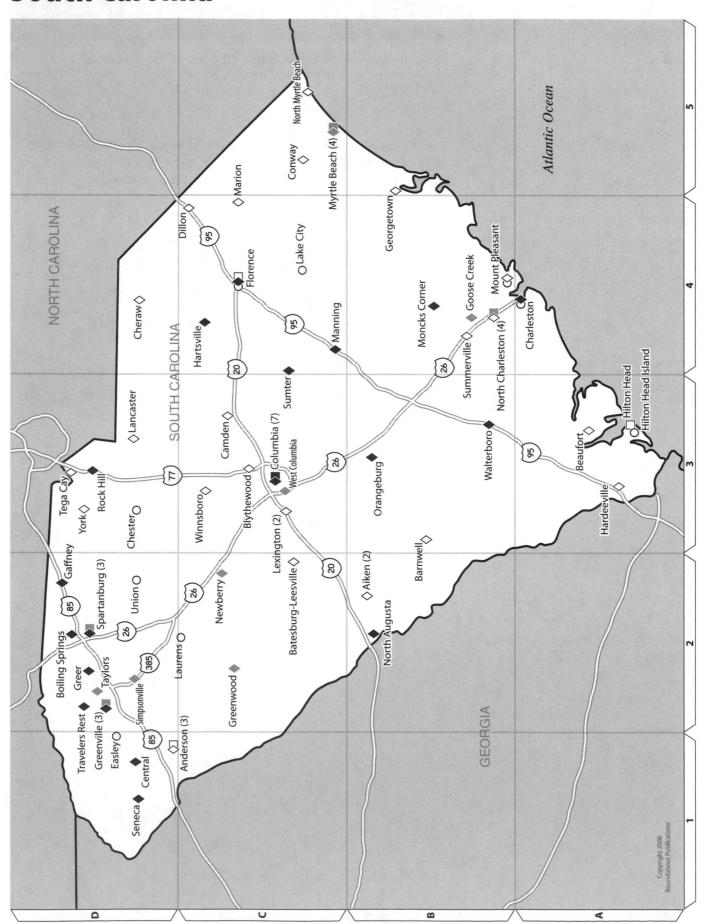

NORTH CAROLINA

SOUTH CAROLINA

GEORGIA

Atlantic Ocean

North Myrtle Beach

Conway

Marion

Myrtle Beach (4)

Georgetown

Dillon

95

Florence

Lake City

Goose Creek

Mount Pleasant

Cheraw

Hartsville

95

Manning

Moncks Corner

Summerville

North Charleston (4)

Charleston

20

26

Lancaster

Camden

Sumter

Columbia (7)

West Columbia

Orangeburg

Walterboro

Hilton Head

Hilton Head Island

77

Blythewood

26

95

Beaufort

Chester

Winnsboro

Lexington (2)

Batesburg-Leesville

Barnwell

Hardeeville

Gaffney

York

Rock Hill

Tega Cay

Union

Newberry

Aiken (2)

26

26

Spartanburg (3)

385

Laurens

20

North Augusta

85

Boiling Springs

Greer

Taylors

Simpsonville

Greenwood

Travelers Rest

Greenville (3)

Easley

Anderson (3)

85

Central

Seneca

City/Town	⬡	🕐	℞	🚗	Information
Aiken	◇ 10	🕐	℞	🚗	3581 Richland Ave W, 29801 / 803-648-5551 • *Lat:* 33.5633 *Lon:* -81.7687 I-20 Exit 18 take SH-19 S 4.4 miles, SH-118 SW 4.6 miles & US-1 E .6 mile
	◇	🕐	℞	🚗	2035 Whiskey Rd, 29803 / 803-648-9197 • *Lat:* 33.5193 *Lon:* -81.7175 I-20 Exit 22 take US-1 S 8.1 miles then SH-19 S 3 miles
Anderson	☐ 3			🚗	3812 Liberty Hwy Ste 6, 29621 / 864-261-7609 • *Lat:* 34.5535 *Lon:* -82.6795 I-85 Exit 21 go SE on US-178 for 2.2 miles
	◇ 3	🕐	℞	🚗	3812 Liberty Hwy, 29621 / 864-225-1800 • *Lat:* 34.5535 *Lon:* -82.6795 I-85 Exit 21 take US-178 E 2.2 miles
	◇ 8	🕐	℞	🚗	651 Hwy 28 Byp, 29624 / 864-261-7420 • *Lat:* 34.4852 *Lon:* -82.6693 I-85 Exit 19A go E on SH-28 for 1.9 miles & continue on SH-28 BYP 5.7 miles
Barnwell	◇	🕐	℞		11391 Dunbarton Blvd, 29812 / 803-259-2000 • *Lat:* 33.2402 *Lon:* -81.3915 Jct US-278 & SH-64 (W of town) go W on SH-64/Dunbarton Blvd 1.3 miles
Batesburg-Leesville	◇ 9	🕐	℞	🚗	115 E Church St, 29070 / 803-532-5332 • *Lat:* 33.9146 *Lon:* -81.5276 I-20 Exit 39 take US-178 N 5.1 miles, SH-245 N 3.1 miles & Church St W .8 mile
Beaufort	◇	🕐	℞	🚗	350 Robert Smalls Pkwy, 29906 / 843-522-8221 • *Lat:* 32.4241 *Lon:* -80.7319 Jct US-21 & US-17 (N of town) take US-21 S 11.8 miles, SH-280 S 1.2 miles & SH-170 SW .2 mile
Blythewood	◇ 1	🕐	℞	🚗	321 Killian Rd, 29016 / 803-754-8884 • *Lat:* 34.1365 *Lon:* -80.9606 I-77 Exit 22, east of exit
Boiling Springs	◆ 3	🕐	℞	🚗	4000 Hwy 9, 29316 / 864-814-2889 • *Lat:* 35.0342 *Lon:* -81.9775 I-85 Exit 75 follow SH-9 N 2.9 miles
Camden	◇ 5	🕐	℞	🚗	2240 W Dekalb St, 29020 / 803-425-5746 • *Lat:* 34.2491 *Lon:* -80.6486 I-20 Exit 98 merge onto US-521 N 2.6 miles then US-601 W 2.4 miles
Central	◆	🕐	℞	🚗	1286 Eighteen Mile Rd, 29630 / 864-639-2525 • *Lat:* 34.7073 *Lon:* -82.7593 I-85 Exit 19B follow US-76 W 6.4 miles, SH-28 BR W 1.3 miles, SH-88 NW 3.9 miles & SH-18 N 1.3 miles
Charleston	○ 7		℞		1231 Folly Rd, 29412 / 843-762-9034 • *Lat:* 32.7199 *Lon:* -79.9666 I-26 Exit 221A take US-17 S 1.8 miles & Folly Rd S 4.4 miles
	◆	🕐	℞	🚗	3951 W Ashley Cir, 29414 / 843-763-5554 • *Lat:* 32.6550 *Lon:* -79.9419 I-26 Exit 221A follow US-17 S 1.8 miles, Folly Rd/Center St S 9.3 miles & Ashley Ave W .9 mile
Cheraw	◇	🕐	℞	🚗	1040 Chesterfield Hwy #10, 29520 / 843-537-6381 • *Lat:* 34.6992 *Lon:* -79.9320 3 miles west of town along SH-9
Chester	○ 10		℞		1841 J A Cochran Byp, 29706 / 803-581-6278 • *Lat:* 34.7210 *Lon:* -81.2167 I-77 Exit 65 go W on SH-9 N 9.8 miles & N on US-321 BYP .2 mile
Columbia	■ 1		℞	🚗	350 Harbison Blvd, 29212 / 803-749-9838 • *Lat:* 34.0758 *Lon:* -81.1541 I-26 Exit 103 go S on Harbison .3 mile
	▨ 1		℞	🚗	5426 Forest Dr, 29206 / 803-790-1581 • *Lat:* 34.0234 *Lon:* -80.9529 I-77 Exit 12 go W on Forest Dr .4 mile
	◆ 1	🕐	℞	🚗	7520 Garners Ferry Rd, 29209 / 803-783-1277 • *Lat:* 33.9625 *Lon:* -80.9412 I-77 Exit 9B take US-378/US-76 E .2 mile
	◆ 4	🕐	℞	🚗	10060 Two Notch Rd, 29223 / 803-736-8123 • *Lat:* 34.1138 *Lon:* -80.8905 I-77 Exit 17 take US-1 NE 3.8 miles
	◇ 1	🕐	℞	🚗	5420 Forest Dr, 29206 / 803-782-0323 • *Lat:* 34.0234 *Lon:* -80.9531 I-77 Exit 12 take Forest Dr W .4 mile
	◇ 1	🕐	℞	🚗	1326 Bush River Rd, 29210 / 803-750-3097 • *Lat:* 34.0311 *Lon:* -81.1067 I-26 Exit 108A, west of exit

○ Wal-Mart ◇ Supercenter ☐ Sam's Club ▨ Gas ■ Gas & Diesel

City/Town	🛡	🕐	℞	🚌	Information
	◇ 1	🕐	℞	🚌	360 Harbison Blvd, 29212 / 803-781-0762 • *Lat:* 34.0764 *Lon:* -81.1537 I-26 Exit 103 take Harbison Blvd S .2 mile
Conway	◇	🕐	℞		2709 Church St, 29526 / 843-365-0303 • *Lat:* 33.8597 *Lon:* -79.0892 Jct US-378 & US-501 (in town) go N on US-501 for 2.7 miles
Dillon	◇ 1	🕐	℞	🚌	805 Enterprise Rd, 29536 / 843-841-9800 • *Lat:* 34.4353 *Lon:* -79.3750 I-95 Exit 193 go S .4 mile on SH-9/SH-57 then W .3 mile on Enterprise Rd
Easley	○		℞		1023 S Pendleton St, 29642 / 864-859-8595 • *Lat:* 34.8165 *Lon:* -82.6012 I-85 Exit 40 follow SH-153 W 5.4 miles, US-123 S 4.5 miles & SH-135 E .2 mile
Florence	☐ 2			🚌	200 N Beltline Dr, 29501 / 843-662-2769 • *Lat:* 34.1932 *Lon:* -79.8236 I-95 Exit 160A take I-20 Spur E for 1.4 miles then N on Beltline Dr for .4 mile
	○ 2		℞		2530 David H McLeod Blvd, 29501 / 843-664-2020 • *Lat:* 34.1885 *Lon:* -79.8294 I-95 Exit 160A merge onto I-20 Spur E 1.2 miles
	◆ 6	🕐	℞	🚌	2014 S Irby St, 29505 / 843-292-0862 • *Lat:* 34.1558 *Lon:* -79.7679 I-95 Exit 164 follow US-52 E 6 miles
Gaffney	◆ 1	🕐	℞	🚌	165 Walton Dr, 29341 / 864-487-3769 • *Lat:* 35.0886 *Lon:* -81.6639 I-85 Exit 92 follow SH-11 S .6 mile
Georgetown	◇	🕐	℞		1310 N Fraser St, 29440 / 843-527-9970 • *Lat:* 33.3908 *Lon:* -79.2889 Jct SH-51 & US-701 (N of town) go S on US-701 for 1.8 miles
Goose Creek	◆ 7	🕐	℞	🚌	605 Saint James Ave, 29445 / 843-553-5421 • *Lat:* 33.0300 *Lon:* -80.0588 I-26 Exit 199B take US-17Alt N 3.9 miles & US-176 E 3.1 miles
Greenville	◼ 1		℞	🚌	1211 Woodruff Rd, 29607 / 864-987-7220 • *Lat:* 34.8231 *Lon:* -82.2894 I-385 Exit 35 go E on Woodruff Rd .2 mile
	◆ 5	🕐	℞	🚌	6134 White Horse Rd, 29611 / 864-295-3181 • *Lat:* 34.8542 *Lon:* -82.4544 I-185 Exit 15 take US-25 W 4.2 miles
	◇ 1	🕐	℞	🚌	1451 Woodruff Rd, 29607 / 864-297-3031 • *Lat:* 34.8213 *Lon:* -82.2830 I-385 Exit 35 take SH-146 E .5 mile
Greenwood	◆	🕐	℞		508 Bypass 72 NW, 29649 / 864-229-2232 • *Lat:* 34.2092 *Lon:* -82.1837 Jct US-25 & SH-72 BYP (N of town) go S on SH-72 BYP .8 mile
Greer	◆ 8	🕐	℞	🚌	14055 E Wade Hampton Blvd, 29651 / 864-877-1928 • *Lat:* 34.9472 *Lon:* -82.2068 I-85 Exit 66 merge onto SH-29 S 7.3 miles
Hardeeville	◇ 1	🕐	℞	🚌	4400 US Hwy 278, 29927 / 843-208-3000 • *Lat:* 32.2666 *Lon:* -81.0642 I-95 Exit 8 take US-278 E .2 mile
Hartsville	◆	🕐	℞	🚌	1150 S 4th St, 29550 / 843-383-4891 • *Lat:* 34.3579 *Lon:* -80.0602 I-20 Exit 131 take SH-403 N 7.8 miles, US-15 N 4.3 miles & SH-151 BR NW .2 mile
Hilton Head	☐				95 Mathews Dr #1, 29926 / 843-681-7100 • *Lat:* 32.2128 *Lon:* -80.7025 I-95 Exit 8 go E 21 miles on US-278, E 2.5 miles on US-278 BR (William Hilton Pkwy), then S at Mathews Dr
Hilton Head Island	○		℞	🚌	25 Pembroke Dr, 29926 / 843-681-3011 • *Lat:* 32.2119 *Lon:* -80.7296 Jct US-278 & US-278 BR (W of town) take US-278 BR E .5 mile & Pembroke Dr S .2 mile
Lake City	○		℞		230 Kelley St, 29560 / 843-394-7405 • *Lat:* 33.8774 *Lon:* -79.7565 Jct US-378 & US-52 (N of town) take US-52 S 1.1 miles & E at Kelley St .2 mile
Lancaster	◇	🕐	℞	🚌	805 Lancaster Byp W, 29720 / 803-286-5445 • *Lat:* 34.7358 *Lon:* -80.7856 1.7 miles northwest of town center via US-521 and SH-9 Bypass
Laurens	○ 6		℞		917 E Main St, 29360 / 864-682-8100 • *Lat:* 34.4933 *Lon:* -81.9827 I-385 Exit 9 take SH-221 S 3.6 miles then US-76 BYP E 1.8 miles & US-76 for .1 mile
Lexington	◇ 4	🕐	℞	🚌	1780 S Lake Dr, 29073 / 803-957-2557 • *Lat:* 33.9139 *Lon:* -81.2266 I-20 Exit 55 go S on SH-6 for 3.4 miles

○ Wal-Mart ◇ Supercenter ☐ Sam's Club ◼ Gas ◼ Gas & Diesel

City/Town	⬡	🕐	℞	🚗	Information
	◇ 5	🕐	℞	🚗	5556 Sunset Blvd, 29072 / 803-808-3740 • *Lat:* 33.9960 *Lon:* -81.2237 I-20 Exit 61 merge onto US-378 W 4.9 miles
Manning	◆ 2		℞	🚗	2010 Paxville Hwy, 29102 / 803-435-4323 • *Lat:* 33.6981 *Lon:* -80.2277 I-95 Exit 119 take SH-261 E 1.2 miles
Marion	◇	🕐	℞	🚗	305 Commerce Dr, 29571 / 843-423-9444 • *Lat:* 34.1872 *Lon:* -79.3415 3.7 miles east of town center via US-76
Moncks Corner	◆	🕐	℞	🚗	511 N Hwy 52, 29461 / 843-899-5701 • *Lat:* 33.2084 *Lon:* -79.9829 Jct SH-402 & US-52 (N of town) go S on US-52 1.1 miles
Mount Pleasant	○ 1		℞		1481 N Hwy 17, 29464 / 843-881-6100 • *Lat:* 32.8173 *Lon:* -79.8558 I-526 Exit 29 take US-17 S .1 mile & SE on Engals Blvd .3 mile
	◇ 5	🕐	℞	🚗	3000 Proprietors Pl, 29466 / 843-884-2844 • *Lat:* 32.8648 *Lon:* -79.7868 I-526 Exit 30 follow US-17 N 5 miles
Myrtle Beach	▨		℞	🚗	1946 10th Ave N, 29577 / 843-448-3887 • *Lat:* 33.7127 *Lon:* -78.8993 Jct US-501 & US-17 Bypass go N 1 mile on US-17 Bypass then E on 10th Ave
	◆	🕐	℞	🚗	10820 Kings Rd, 29572 / 843-449-0502 • *Lat:* 33.7846 *Lon:* -78.7701 Jct SH-22 & US-17 go E on Kings Rd .2 mile
	◇	🕐	℞		2751 Beaver Run Blvd, 29575 / 843-650-4800 • *Lat:* 33.6483 *Lon:* -78.9784 Jct US-501 & US-17 take US-17 S 5.3 miles then E at SH-544 .3 mile
	◇	🕐	℞	🚗	541 Seaboard St, 29577 / 843-445-7781 • *Lat:* 33.7049 *Lon:* 78.9120 Jct US-501 & US-17 go E on US-501 for .8 mile then S on Grissom Pkwy .5 mile & E on Pine Island Rd .3 mile
Newberry	◆ 3	🕐	℞	🚗	2812 Main St, 29108 / 803-276-4411 • *Lat:* 34.2825 *Lon:* -81.5946 I-26 Exit 76 take SH-219 S 3 miles
North Augusta	◆ 5	🕐	℞	🚗	1201 Knox Ave, 29841 / 803-279-0545 • *Lat:* 33.5007 *Lon:* -81.9595 I-20 Exit 5 follow US-25 S 4.6 miles
North Charleston	▨ 2		℞	🚗	4900 Centre Pointe Dr, 29418 / 843-529-9893 • *Lat:* 32.8759 *Lon:* -80.0175 I-26 Exit 213 (eastbound travelers use I-26 Exit 213A) go S .4 mile, W .4 mile on International Blvd, N .7 mile on Coliseum Dr
	◇ 1	🕐	℞		7400 Rivers Ave, 29406 / 843-572-9660 • *Lat:* 32.9374 *Lon:* -80.0378 I-26 Exit 209B go E .6 mile on Ashley Rd
	◇ 2	🕐	℞	🚗	4920 Centre Pointe Dr, 29418 / 843-740-1112 • *Lat:* 32.8760 *Lon:* -80.0175 I-26 Exit 213 (eastbound travelers use I-26 Exit 213A) go S .4 mile on Montague Ave, W .4 mile on International Blvd, N .7 mile on Coliseum Dr
	◇ 8	🕐	℞	🚗	9880 Dorchester Rd, 29418 / 843-871-3303 • *Lat:* 32.9490 *Lon:* -80.1561 I-26 Exit 209B go W 3.8 miles on Ashley Phosphate Rd then N 3.7 miles on Dorchester Rd
North Myrtle Beach	◇	🕐	℞	🚗	550 Hwy 17 N, 29582 / 843-281-8352 • *Lat:* 33.8327 *Lon:* -78.6742 Jct SH-22 & US-17 (S of town) take US-17 N 6.4 miles
Orangeburg	◆ 8	🕐	℞	🚗	2795 North Rd, 29118 / 803-533-0645 • *Lat:* 33.5295 *Lon:* -80.8938 I-26 Exit 149 take SH-33 S 3.5 miles & US-178 W 3.9 miles
Rock Hill	◆ 1	🕐	℞	🚗	2377 Dave Lyle Blvd, 29730 / 803-366-9431 • *Lat:* 34.9417 *Lon:* -80.9619 I-77 Exit 79 take SH-122 E .5 mile
Seneca	◆	🕐	℞	🚗	1636 Sandifer Blvd, 29678 / 864-885-0408 • *Lat:* 34.6889 *Lon:* -82.9956 Jct SH-59 & Wells Hwy (S of town) go NW on Wells Hwy 3 miles then S on Sandifer Blvd .2 mile
Simpsonville	◆ 1	🕐	℞	🚗	3950 Grandview Dr, 29680 / 864-963-0049 • *Lat:* 34.7089 *Lon:* -82.2447 I-385 Exit 26 merge onto Harrison Bridge Rd W .5 mile & N at Grandview Dr .3 mile

○ Wal-Mart   ◇ Supercenter   □ Sam's Club   ▨ Gas   ▧ Gas & Diesel

City/Town	🛡	🕐	℞	🚐	Information
Spartanburg	■ 1		℞	🚐	200 Peachwood Centre Dr, 29301 / 864-574-3480 • *Lat:* 34.9348 *Lon:* -81.9991 I-26 Exit 21 take US-29 W .6 mile, S on Franklin Ave .1 mile & E on Peachwood Centre .1 mile
	◆ 4	🕐	℞	🚐	2151 E Main St, 29307 / 864-529-0156 • *Lat:* 34.9727 *Lon:* -81.8835 I-585 Exit 25B continue on Pine St 1.2 miles then Main St NE 2.4 miles
	◇ 1	🕐	℞	🚐	141 Dorman Centre Dr, 29301 / 864-574-6452 • *Lat:* 34.9344 *Lon:* -81.9866 I-26 Exit 21B take US-29 N .6 mile & Dorman Centre Dr E .2 mile
Summerville	◇ 1	🕐	℞	🚐	1317 N Main St, 29483 / 843-821-1991 • *Lat:* 33.0369 *Lon:* -80.1540 I-26 Exit 199A take US-17 ALT S .1 mile
Sumter	◆	🕐	℞	🚐	1283 Broad St, 29150 / 803-905-5500 • *Lat:* 33.9569 *Lon:* -80.3882 I-95 Exit 135 merge onto US-378 W 18.5 miles
Taylors	◆ 5	🕐	℞	🚐	3027 Wade Hampton Blvd, 29687 / 864-292-8155 • *Lat:* 34.9072 *Lon:* -82.3296 I-385 Exit 40A take SH-291 N 1.6 miles then Wade Hampton Blvd NW 2.5 miles
Tega Cay	◇ 2	🕐	℞	🚐	1151 Stone Crest Blvd, 29708 / 803-578-4140 • *Lat:* 35.0486 *Lon:* -80.9912 I-77 Exit 85 go W 2 miles on SH-160
Travelers Rest	◆	🕐	℞	🚐	9 Benton Rd, 29690 / 864-834-7179 • *Lat:* 34.9624 *Lon:* -82.4258 I-185 Exit 15 take US-25 N 17 miles
Union	○		℞		441 N Duncan Bypass, 29379 / 864-429-0598 • *Lat:* 34.7222 *Lon:* -81.6396 Jct SH-49 & US-176 (W of town) go N on US-176 for 1 mile
Walterboro	◆ 1	🕐	℞	🚐	2110 Bells Hwy, 29488 / 843-539-1550 • *Lat:* 32.9329 *Lon:* -80.6982 I-95 Exit 57 take SH-64 W .4 mile
West Columbia	◆ 1	🕐	℞	🚐	2401 Augusta Rd, 29169 / 803-796-9144 • *Lat:* 33.9828 *Lon:* -81.0983 I-26 Exit 111B merge onto US-1 N .4 mile
Winnsboro	◇ 8		℞		721 US Hwy 321 Byp S, 29180 / 803-712-9601 • *Lat:* 34.3585 *Lon:* -81.0971 I-77 Exit 34 take SH-34 W 6.3 miles then US-321 N 1.3 miles
York	◇	🕐	℞	🚐	970 E Liberty St, 29745 / 803-684-5486 • *Lat:* 34.9855 *Lon:* -81.2151 I-77 Exit 82 follow SH-161 W 12.8 miles & continue on SH-161 BR .8 mile

○ Wal-Mart   ◇ Supercenter   □ Sam's Club   ■ Gas   ■ Gas & Diesel

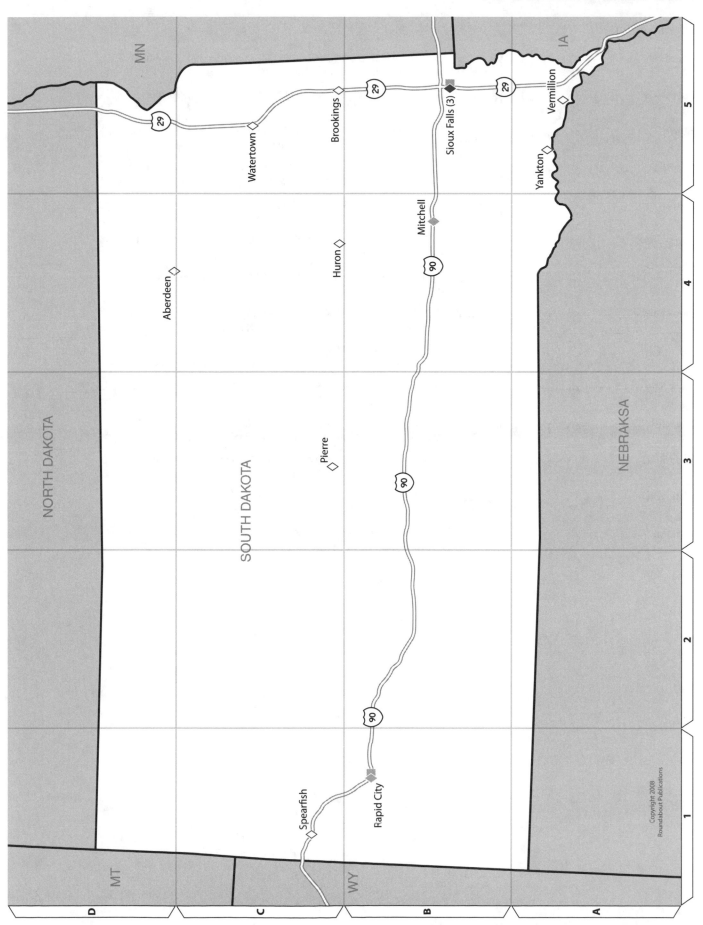

South Dakota

○ Wal-Mart ◇ Supercenter ☐ Sam's Club ▨ Gas ■ Gas & Diesel

MN

IA

SOUTH DAKOTA

NORTH DAKOTA

NEBRAKSA

MT

WY

29 Watertown

29 Brookings

29 Vermillion

Sioux Falls (3)

Yankton

Huron

Mitchell

90

Aberdeen

Pierre

90

90

Spearfish

Rapid City

Copyright 2008
Roundabout Publications

5

4

3

2

1

D

C

B

A

City/Town	♡	🕐	℞	🚗	Information
Aberdeen	◇		🕐	℞ 🚗	3820 7th Ave SE, 57401 / 605-229-2345 • *Lat:* 45.4590 *Lon:* -98.4357 2.5 miles east of town center along US-12
Brookings	◇ 1		🕐	℞ 🚗	2233 6th St, 57006 / 605-692-6332 • *Lat:* 44.3116 *Lon:* -96.7668 I-29 Exit 132 take US-14 W .3 mile
Huron	◇		🕐	℞ 🚗	2791 Dakota Ave S, 57350 / 605-353-0891 • *Lat:* 44.3346 *Lon:* -98.2145 Jct US-14 & SH-37 (N of town) take SH-37 S for 2.5 miles
Mitchell	◆ 1		🕐	℞ 🚗	1101 E Spruce St, 57301 / 605-995-6840 • *Lat:* 43.6875 *Lon:* -98.0214 I-90 Exit 332 take SH-37 S .4 mile & W on Spruce St .6 mile
Pierre	◇		🕐	℞ 🚗	1730 N Garfield Rd, 57501 / 605-224-8830 • *Lat:* 44.3927 *Lon:* -100.3137 Jct SH-34/Wells Ave & US-18 (SE of town) go N on US-18 BYP 2.4 miles
Rapid City	■ 1			🚗	1020 N Lacrosse St, 57701 / 605-355-9066 • *Lat:* 44.0837 *Lon:* -103.2136 I-90 Exit 59 go S on La Crosse St .8 mile
	◆ 1		🕐	℞ 🚗	1200 N Lacrosse St, 57701 / 605-342-9444 • *Lat:* 44.0960 *Lon:* -103.2016 I-90 Exit 59 take La Crosse St S .5 mile
Sioux Falls	■ 1			℞ 🚗	3201 S Louise Ave, 57106 / 605-362-0119 • *Lat:* 43.5154 *Lon:* -96.7713 I-29 Exit 77 go E on 41st St .4 mile then N at Louise Ave
	◇ 2		🕐	℞ 🚗	3209 S Louise Ave, 57106 / 605-362-1002 • *Lat:* 43.5154 *Lon:* -96.7713 I-29 Exit 78 go W on 26th St .4 mile & continue on Louise Ave .7 mile
	◆ 2		🕐	℞ 🚗	5521 E Arrowhead Pkwy, 57110 / 605-367-3140 • *Lat:* 43.5438 *Lon:* -96.6588 I-229 Exit 6 follow SH-42 E 1.7 miles
Spearfish	◇ 1		🕐	℞ 🚗	2825 1st Ave, 57783 / 605-642-2460 • *Lat:* 44.4803 *Lon:* -103.8122 I-90 Exit 14 go N .2 mile on 27th St then 1st Ave E .2 mile
Vermillion	◇ 9		🕐	℞ 🚗	1207 Princeton Ave, 57069 / 605-624-0215 • *Lat:* 42.7907 *Lon:* -96.9390 I-29 Exit 42 take SH-50 W 7.7 miles & Princeton Ave N 1.2 miles
Watertown	◇ 1		🕐	℞ 🚗	1201 29th St SE, 57201 / 605-882-0801 • *Lat:* 44.8878 *Lon:* -97.0679 I-29 Exit 177 take US-212 W .6 mile then 29th St S .2 mile
Yankton	◇		🕐	℞ 🚗	3001 Broadway Ave, 57078 / 605-665-1425 • *Lat:* 42.9052 *Lon:* -97.3979 Jct SH-50 & US-81 (N of town) take US-81 S for .3 mile

Tennessee

○ Wal-Mart ◇ Supercenter ☐ Sam's Club ▦ Gas ■ Gas & Diesel

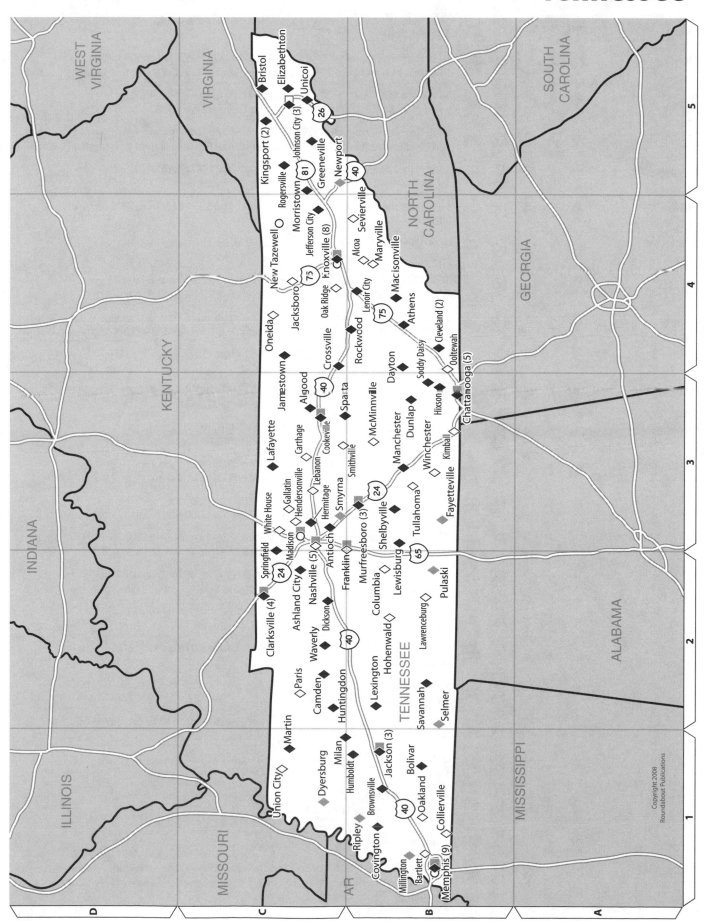

City/Town	♡	⏱	℞	🚐	Information
Alcoa	◇ 5	⏱	℞	🚐	1030 Hunters Crossing, 37701 / 865-984-1099 • *Lat:* 35.7712 *Lon:* -83.9896 I-140 Exit 11A take US-129 S 4.8 miles then Louisville Rd W & Hunters Crossing S .1 mile
Algood	◆ 4	⏱	℞	🚐	589 W Main St, 38501 / 931-537-3880 • *Lat:* 36.1843 *Lon:* -85.4579 I-40 Exit 288 take SH-111 N 3.3 miles, then E on Main St .3 mile
Antioch	◆ 3	⏱	℞	🚐	3035 Hamilton Church Rd, 37013 / 615-360-2228 • *Lat:* 36.0616 *Lon:* -86.6315 I-24 Exit 59 take SH-254 NE 1.2 miles, Zelida Ave E .3 mile & Hamilton Church N .6 mile
Ashland City	◆	⏱	℞	🚐	1626 Hwy 12 S, 37015 / 615-792-7782 • *Lat:* 36.2944 *Lon:* -87.0703 Jct SH-249/49 & SH-12 (in town) take SH-12 SE 2.6 miles
Athens	◆ 2	⏱	℞	🚐	1815 Decatur Pike, 37303 / 423-745-0395 • *Lat:* 35.4545 *Lon:* -84.6284 I-75 Exit 49 take SH-30 E 1.3 miles
Bartlett	◇ 1	⏱	℞	🚐	8400 US Hwy 64, 38133 / 901-382-6101 • *Lat:* 35.2114 *Lon:* -89.7984 I-40 Exit 18 merge onto US-64 W .8 mile
Bolivar	◆	⏱	℞		1604 W Market St, 38008 / 731-658-7794 • *Lat:* 35.2676 *Lon:* -89.0127 Jct SH-100 & US-64 (NW of town) go SE on US-64 for 8.3 miles
Bristol	◆ 2	⏱	℞	🚐	220 Century Blvd, 37620 / 423-968-2777 • *Lat:* 36.5427 *Lon:* -82.2343 I-81 Exit 69 take SH-394 SE 3.9 miles, Exide Dr E 1.5 miles & US-11E N 1.9 miles
Brownsville	◆	⏱	℞	🚐	1100 S Dupree Ave, 38012 / 731-772-9551 • *Lat:* 35.5858 *Lon:* -89.2419 US-40 Exit 60 follow SH-19 NW 3.6 miles
Camden	◆	⏱	℞	🚐	2200 Hwy 641 N, 38320 / 731-584-4445 • *Lat:* 36.0872 *Lon:* -88.1101 3.2 miles north of town center along US-641 at McKelvy Rd
Carthage	◇ 5	⏱	℞		1 Myers St, 37030 / 615-735-2049 • *Lat:* 36.2420 *Lon:* -85.9433 I-40 Exit 258 go N 4.7 miles on SH-53/Gordonsville Hwy
Chattanooga	■ 2		℞	🚐	6101 Lee Hwy, 37421 / 423-954-1746 • *Lat:* 35.0274 *Lon:* -85.1906 I-75 Exit 4 take SH-153 N .8 mile then SW on Lee Hwy .6 mile
	◇ 1	⏱	℞	🚐	2020 Gunbarrel Rd, 37421 / 423-899-7021 • *Lat:* 35.0323 *Lon:* -85.1544 I-75 Exit 5 go E .4 mile on Shallowford Rd then S .6 mile on Gunbarrel Rd
	◇ 5	⏱	℞	🚐	601 Signal Mountain Rd, 37405 / 423-756-7202 • *Lat:* 35.0946 *Lon:* -85.3289 I-24 Exit 178 follow US-27 N 4 miles then Signal Mountain Rd W .9 mile
	◆ 2	⏱	℞	🚐	490 Greenway View Dr, 37411 / 423-892-8911 • *Lat:* 35.0089 *Lon:* -85.2093 I-24 Exit 184 take Moore Rd N .4 mile, Brainerd Rd E 1.1 miles & Greenway View S .3 mile
	◇ 1	⏱	℞	🚐	3550 Cummings Hwy, 37419 / 423-821-1556 • *Lat:* 35.0187 *Lon:* -85.3754 I-24 Exit 174 go E on Cummings Hwy/US-41 .5 mile
Clarksville	■ 2		℞	🚐	3315 Guthrie Hwy, 37040 / 931-552-0733 • *Lat:* 36.6074 *Lon:* -87.2725 I-24 Exit 4 go NE on US-79 for 1.1 miles
	◆ 1	⏱	℞	🚐	3050 Wilma Rudolph Blvd, 37040 / 931-553-8127 • *Lat:* 36.5934 *Lon:* -87.2894 I-24 Exit 4 take US-79 S .7 mile
	◆ 9	⏱	℞	🚐	1680 Fort Campbell Blvd, 37042 / 931-645-8439 • *Lat:* 36.5812 *Lon:* -87.4106 I-24 Exit 86 (in KY) follow Fort Campbell Blvd S 8.7 miles
	◆ 4	⏱	℞	🚐	2315 Madison St, 37043 / 931-552-1010 • *Lat:* 36.5084 *Lon:* -87.2714 I-24 Exit 11 merge onto SH-76 W/76 CONN W 3.5 miles
Cleveland	◆ 2	⏱	℞	🚐	4495 Keith St NW, 37312 / 423-472-1436 • *Lat:* 35.2011 *Lon:* -84.8459 I-75 Exit 27 take Huff Pkwy SE 1.4 miles
	◆ 5	⏱	℞	🚐	2300 Treasury Dr SE, 37323 / 423-472-9660 • *Lat:* 35.1282 *Lon:* -84.8664 I-75 Exit 20 follow SH-311 E 5 miles
Collierville	◇	⏱	℞	🚐	560 W Poplar Ave, 38017 / 901-854-5100 • *Lat:* 35.0460 *Lon:* -89.6806 I-240 Exit 16 merge onto Morris Pkwy E 12.5 miles then Byhalia Rd N .9 mile & Poplar Ave E .5 mile

○ Wal-Mart ◇ Supercenter □ Sam's Club ▨ Gas ■ Gas & Diesel

City/Town	♡	🕐	℞	🚌	Information
Columbia	◇	🕐	℞	🚌	2200 Brookmeade Dr, 38401 / 931-381-6892 • *Lat:* 35.5960 *Lon:* -87.0535 I-65 Exit 37 take SH-50 NW 11.6 miles & W at Brookmeade .1 mile
Cookeville	■ 1			🚌	1177 Sams St, 38506 / 931-528-2070 • *Lat:* 36.1339 *Lon:* -85.5034 I-40 Exit 287, south of exit
	◆ 1	🕐	℞	🚌	768 S Jefferson Ave, 38501 / 931-520-0232 • *Lat:* 36.1439 *Lon:* -85.5009 I-40 Exit 287 take SH-136 N .6 mile
Covington	◆	🕐	℞	🚌	201 Lanny Bridges Ave, 38019 / 901-476-4492 • *Lat:* 35.6117 *Lon:* -89.6227 I-40 Exit 35 follow SH-59 NW 17.2 miles, Main St/Sherrod Ave N 1.7 miles & E at College St .4 mile
Crossville	◆ 2	🕐	℞	🚌	2542 N Main St, 38555 / 931-484-9745 • *Lat:* 35.9823 *Lon:* -85.0384 I-40 Exit 317 take US-127 S 1.4 miles
Dayton	◆	🕐	℞	🚌	3034 Rhea County Hwy, 37321 / 423-775-4448 • *Lat:* 35.4593 *Lon:* -85.0470 Jct SH-60 & US-27 (S of town) take US-27 S 2.2 miles
Dickson	◆ 5	🕐	℞	🚌	175 Beasley Dr, 37055 / 615-446-4588 • *Lat:* 36.0641 *Lon:* -87.3846 I-40 Exit 172 take SH-46 N 3.7 miles & Beasley Dr W .5 mile
Dunlap	◆	🕐	℞		16773 Rankin Ave, 37327 / 423-949-7778 • *Lat:* 35.4039 *Lon:* -85.3696 Jct SH-111 & US-127 (in town) take US-127 S 2.1 miles
Dyersburg	◆ 1	🕐	℞	🚌	2650 Lake Rd, 38024 / 731-285-3700 • *Lat:* 36.0650 *Lon:* -89.3957 I-155 Exit 13 take SH-78 S .4 mile
Elizabethton	◆ 7	🕐	℞	🚌	1001 Over Mountain Dr, 37643 / 423-543-8133 • *Lat:* 36.3470 *Lon:* -82.2466 I-26 Exit 24 follow US-321 N 6.4 miles then W .2 mile on Over Mountain Dr
Fayetteville	◆	🕐	℞	🚌	1224 Huntsville Hwy, 37334 / 931-433-3010 • *Lat:* 35.1377 *Lon:* -86.5671 Jct SH-15 BYP & US-431 (SW of town) take US-431 S .4 mile
Franklin	■ 1		℞	🚌	3070 Mallory Ln, 37067 / 615-778-1401 • *Lat:* 35.9433 *Lon:* -86.8203 I-65 Exit 68 go W on Cool Springs Blvd & S on Mallory Ln .3 mile
	◇ 1	🕐	℞	🚌	3600 Mallory Ln, 37067 / 615-771-0929 • *Lat:* 35.9416 *Lon:* -86.8209 I-65 Exit 67 go W on McEwen Dr .3 mile & N on Mallory Ln .3 mile
Gallatin	◇	🕐	℞	🚌	1112 Nashville Pike, 37066 / 615-452-8452 • *Lat:* 36.3745 *Lon:* -86.4764 Jct SH-109 & US-31E (W of town) go SW on US-31E .5 mile
Greeneville	◆	🕐	℞	🚌	3755 E Andrew Johnson Hwy, 37745 / 423-639-8181 • *Lat:* 36.1857 *Lon:* -82.7610 I-81 Exit 30 take SH-70 S 10.1 miles then US-11 E 5.6 miles
Hendersonville	◇ 7	🕐	℞	🚌	204 N Anderson Ln, 37075 / 615-264-0770 • *Lat:* 36.3189 *Lon:* -86.6003 I-65 Exit 95-97 take SH-386 E 5.8 miles & Callender Ln/Indian Lake Blvd S 1 mile
Hermitage	◆ 4	🕐	℞	🚌	4424 Lebanon Pike, 37076 / 615-883-0201 • *Lat:* 36.2152 *Lon:* -86.6030 I-40 Exit 221 take SH-45 N 2.2 miles then Lebanon Pike E 1.5 miles
Hixson	◆	🕐	℞	🚌	5764 Hwy 153, 37343 / 423-870-1680 • *Lat:* 35.1547 *Lon:* -85.2486 I-75 Exit 4 take SH-153 N 10.5 miles
Hohenwald	◇	🕐	℞		612 E Main St, 38462 / 931-796-3282 • *Lat:* 35.5589 *Lon:* -87.5307 Jct SH-20 & US-412 (in town) take US-412 E 1.5 miles
Humboldt	◆	🕐	℞	🚌	2716 N Central Ave, 38343 / 731-784-0025 • *Lat:* 35.8403 *Lon:* -88.9148 I-40 Exit 80B take US-45 BYP N 4.6 miles then go N 9.6 miles on US-45/US-45-W
Huntingdon	◆	🕐	℞		180 Veterans Dr N, 38344 / 731-986-4439 • *Lat:* 36.0033 *Lon:* -88.4463 1.4 miles west of town center off US-70 at Veterans Dr
Jacksboro	◇ 4	🕐	℞	🚌	2824 Appalachian Hwy, 37757 / 423-566-5318 • *Lat:* 36.3334 *Lon:* -84.1800 I-75 Exit 134 go N 3.6 miles on US-25-W
Jackson	■ 2			🚌	2120 Emporium Dr, 38305 / 731-668-6958 • *Lat:* 35.6661 *Lon:* -88.8500 I-40 Exit 82 go W on Vann Dr 1.1 miles then SW on Emporium .1 mile

○ Wal-Mart   ◇ Supercenter   □ Sam's Club   ■ Gas   ■ Gas & Diesel

City/Town	🛡		🕐	℞	�	Information
	◆	1	🕐	℞	🚌	2171 S Highland Ave, 38301 / 731-422-1614 • *Lat:* 35.5504 *Lon:* -88.8073 I-40 Exit 82A merge onto US-45 S .8 mile
	◇	2	🕐	℞	🚌	2196 Emporium Dr, 38305 / 731-664-1157 • *Lat:* 35.6698 *Lon:* -88.8538 I-40 Exit 82B go N .1 mile on US-45 then W 1.6 miles on Vann Dr
Jamestown	◆		🕐	℞		539 E Central Ave, 38556 / 931-879-4767 • *Lat:* 36.4272 *Lon:* -84.9242 .4 mile east of town center on Central Ave near US-127 jct
Jefferson City	◆	8	🕐	℞	🚌	630 E Broadway Blvd, 37760 / 865-475-0730 • *Lat:* 36.1274 *Lon:* -83.4676 I-40 Exit 417 take SH-92 N 6.3 miles & US-11 E 1.5 miles
	☐	1			🚌	3060 Franklin Terrace Dr, 37604 / 423-282-2303 • *Lat:* 36.3524 *Lon:* -82.4019 I-26 Exit 36, south of exit
	◆	1	🕐	℞	🚌	3111 Browns Mill Rd, 37604 / 423-282-5376 • *Lat:* 36.3591 *Lon:* -82.3963 I-26 Exit 19 go NE on SH-381 for .2 mile then W on Browns Mill Rd .2 mile
	◆	4	🕐	℞	🚌	2915 W Market St, 37604 / 423-434-2250 • *Lat:* 36.3098 *Lon:* -82.4030 I-26 Exit 23 take SH-91 & US-11 W 3.3 miles
Kimball	◇	1	🕐	℞	🚌	525 Kimball Crossing Dr, 37347 / 423-837-6732 • *Lat:* 35.0395 *Lon:* -85.6837 I-24 Exit 152 take US-72 E .5 mile then S on Kimball Crossing .2 mile
Kingsport	◆	2	🕐	℞	🚌	2500 W Stone Dr, 37660 / 423-246-4676 • *Lat:* 36.5555 *Lon:* -82.6055 I-26 Exit 1 take Stone Dr W 1.4 miles
	◇	4	🕐	℞	🚌	3200 Fort Henry Dr, 37664 / 423-392-0600 • *Lat:* 36.5095 *Lon:* -82.5162 I-81 Exit 59 take SH-36 N 3.1 miles
Knoxville	☐	1		℞	🚌	2920 Knoxville Center Dr, 37924 / 865-637-2582 • *Lat:* 36.0321 *Lon:* -83.8737 I-640 Exit 8, north of exit, at Knoxville Center
	▨	1		℞	🚌	8435 Walbrook Dr, 37923 / 865-694-2168 • *Lat:* 35.9255 *Lon:* -84.0609 I-40/I-75 Exit 379 go NW on Wallbrook Dr
	○	5		℞	🚌	7340 Norris Fwy, 37918 / 865-922-6031 • *Lat:* 36.0829 *Lon:* -83.9332 I-75 Exit 112 take SH-131 NE 4.6 miles then N on Norris Fwy
	◇	3	🕐	℞	🚌	6777 Clinton Hwy, 37912 / 865-938-6760 • *Lat:* 36.0070 *Lon:* -84.0263 I-75 Exit 110 take Callahan Dr SW 1.8 miles & Clinton Hwy W .8 mile
	◆	7	🕐	℞	🚌	7420 Chapman Hwy, 37920 / 865-577-2596 • *Lat:* 35.9084 *Lon:* -83.8434 I-40 Exit 388 take US-441 S 7 miles
	◇	1	🕐	℞	🚌	8445 Walbrook Dr, 37923 / 865-690-8986 • *Lat:* 35.9246 *Lon:* -84.0638 I-40 Exit 379 merge onto Walbrook Dr N .1 mile
	◇	1	🕐	℞	🚌	3051 Kinzel Way, 37924 / 865-544-7710 • *Lat:* 36.0298 *Lon:* -83.8671 I-640 Exit 8 take Millertown Pike NE .1 mile & Kenzel Way S .2 mile
	◇	1	🕐	℞	🚌	10900 Parkside Dr, 37934 / 865-777-5171 • *Lat:* 35.9028 *Lon:* -84.1477 I-40/I-75 Exit 374 take SH-131 S .5 mile & Parkside Dr W .5 mile
Lafayette	◆		🕐	℞	🚌	419 Hwy 52 Byp W, 37083 / 615-666-2135 • *Lat:* 36.5207 *Lon:* -86.0369 Jct SH-10 & SH-52 (W of town) go W on SH-52 BYP for .2 mile
Lawrenceburg	◇		🕐	℞	🚌	2130 N Locust Ave, 38464 / 931-762-1094 • *Lat:* 35.2705 *Lon:* -87.3201 Jct US-64 & US-43 (in town) take US-43 N 2.4 miles
Lebanon	◇	1	🕐	℞	🚌	615 S Cumberland St, 37087 / 615-444-0471 • *Lat:* 36.1935 *Lon:* -86.2937 I-40 Exit 238 take US-231 N .9 mile
Lenoir City	◆	2	🕐	℞	🚌	911 Hwy 321 N, 37771 / 865-986-9002 • *Lat:* 35.8219 *Lon:* -84.2686 I-75 Exit 81 take US-321 S 1.1 miles
Lewisburg	◆	7	🕐	℞	🚌	1334 N Ellington Pkwy, 37091 / 931-359-9568 • *Lat:* 35.4698 *Lon:* -86.7935 I-65 Exit 32 take SH-373 E 3.7 miles, SH-417 NE 1.9 miles & US-431 SE .5 mile

○ Wal-Mart ◇ Supercenter ☐ Sam's Club ▨ Gas ■ Gas & Diesel

City/Town	⬟	🕐	℞	🚐	Information
Lexington	◆		🕐	℞ 🚐	547 W Church St, 38351 / 731-968-5212 •*Lat:* 35.6569 *Lon:* -88.4101 I-40 Exit 108 take SH-22 S 9.8 miles then US-412 W 1 mile
Madison	■ 2			℞ 🚐	2240 Gallatin Pike N, 37115 / 615-859-2023 •*Lat:* 36.3065 *Lon:* -86.6865 I-65 Exit 96 go E .8 mile on Rivergate Pkwy then N 1 mile on Gallatin Pike Rd
	○ 2			℞	2232 Gallatin Pike N, 37115 / 615-859-7212 •*Lat:* 36.3065 *Lon:* -86.6865 I-65 Exit 96 go E .8 mile on Rivergate Pkwy then N 1 mile on Gallatin Pike Rd
Madisonville	◆		🕐	℞ 🚐	4525 Hwy 411, 37354 / 423-442-5237 •*Lat:* 35.5161 *Lon:* -84.3598 Jct SH-68 & US-411 (in town) go N on US-411 for 1 mile
Manchester	◆ 1		🕐	℞ 🚐	2518 Hillsboro Blvd, 37355 / 931-728-6000 •*Lat:* 35.4553 *Lon:* -86.0462 I-24 Exit 114 take US-41 E .2 mile
Martin	◆		🕐	℞ 🚐	134 Courtright Rd, 38237 / 731-587-3843 •*Lat:* 36.3539 *Lon:* -88.8824 2 miles west of town center via University St (SH-431) at Courtright Rd
Maryvllle	◇		🕐	℞ 🚐	2410 US Hwy 411 S, 37801 / 865-982-3660 •*Lat:* 35.7168 *Lon:* -84.0144 3.3 miles southwest of town center via US-129/US-411
McMinnville	◇		🕐	℞ 🚐	915 N Chancery St, 37110 / 931-473-0826 •*Lat:* 35.6994 *Lon:* -85.7868 1.6 miles northwest of town center via Chancery St
Memphis	■ 1			℞ 🚐	1805 Getwell Rd, 38111 / 901-743-6401 •*Lat:* 35.0829 *Lon:* -89.9315 I-240 Exit 20 go N on Getwell Rd .1 mile
	□ 1			℞ 🚐	2150 Covington Pike, 38128 / 901-386-1004 •*Lat:* 35.1041 *Lon:* -89.8961 I-40 Exit 10 take SH-204 N for 1 mile
	■ 5			℞ 🚐	7475 Winchester Rd, 38125 / 901-754-0324 •*Lat:* 35.0505 *Lon:* -89.8145 I-240 Exit 16 go SE on SH-385 for 4.3 miles then W on Winchester Rd .2 mile
	■ 1			℞ 🚐	8480 US Hwy 64, 38133 / 901-384-9997 •*Lat:* 35.2114 *Lon:* -89.7984 I-40 Exit 18 take US-64 W for .6 mile
	○ 1			℞ 🚐	5000 American Way, 38115 / 901-366-6036 •*Lat:* 35.0756 *Lon:* -89.8946 I-240 Exit 17 take Mt Moriah Rd S .4 mile then American Way W .5 mile
	○ 4			℞ 🚐	3950 Austin Peay Hwy, 38128 / 901-377-1211 •*Lat:* 35.2329 *Lon:* -89.8973 I-40 Exit 8 follow SH-14 N 3.8 miles
	◆ 4		🕐	℞ 🚐	577 Germantown Pkwy, 38018 / 901-758-1591 •*Lat:* 35.1395 *Lon:* -89.7958 I-40 Exit 16A take SH-177 S 3.8 miles
	◇ 3		🕐	℞ 🚐	5255 Elvis Presley Blvd, 38116 / 901-346-4994 •*Lat:* 35.0049 *Lon:* -90.0255 I-55 Exit 2B take SH-175 W 1.1 miles then S on Presley Blvd 1.1 miles
	◇ 6		🕐	℞ 🚐	7525 Winchester Rd, 38125 / 901-757-1442 •*Lat:* 35.0503 *Lon:* -89.8125 I-240 Exit 16 take SH-385 E 5 miles then Winchester Rd W .1 mile
Milan	◆		🕐	℞ 🚐	15427 S First St, 38358 / 731-686-9557 •*Lat:* 35.8746 *Lon:* -88.7447 Jct SH-187 & US-45E (S of town) go S on US-45E .4 mile
Millington	◆		🕐	℞ 🚐	8445 US Hwy 51 N, 38053 / 901-872-6100 •*Lat:* 35.3419 *Lon:* -89.9042 I-40 Exit 2A take SH-300 W .7 mile & US-51 N 13.4 miles
Morristown	◆ 6		🕐	℞ 🚐	475 S Davy Crockett Pkwy, 37813 / 423-587-0495 •*Lat:* 36.2121 *Lon:* -83.2612 I-81 Exit 8 take US-25E N 5.7 miles
Murfreesboro	■ 1			🚐	125 John R Rice Blvd, 37129 / 615-895-4246 •*Lat:* 35.8476 *Lon:* -86.4403 I-24 Exit 78 take SH-96 W .4 mile then N on Rice Blvd
	◆ 1		🕐	℞ 🚐	2000 Old Fort Pkwy, 37129 / 615-893-0175 •*Lat:* 35.8470 *Lon:* -86.4269 I-24 Exit 78B take SH-96 E .8 mile
	◆ 5		🕐	℞ 🚐	2900 S Rutherford Blvd, 37130 / 615-896-4650 •*Lat:* 35.8317 *Lon:* -86.3501 I-24 Exit 81B take US-231 N .8 mile then NE on Rutherford Blvd 3.6 miles

○ Wal-Mart   ◇ Supercenter   □ Sam's Club   ■ Gas   ■ Gas & Diesel

City/Town			Rx		Information
Nashville	■	1	Rx	🚌	1300 Antioch Pike, 37211 / 615-834-9092 • *Lat:* 36.0867 *Lon:* -86.6914 I-24 Exit 56 take SH-255 E .5 mile then S on Antioch Pike
	■	1		🚌	615 Old Hickory Blvd, 37209 / 615-356-5545 • *Lat:* 36.1082 *Lon:* -86.9226 I-40 Exit 199 go S on Old Hickory .5 mile
	◇	1	🕐 Rx	🚌	7044 Charlotte Pike, 37209 / 615-352-1240 • *Lat:* 36.1294 *Lon:* -86.9049 I-40 Exit 201 take US-70 SW .3 mile
	◇	4	🕐 Rx	🚌	5824 Nolensville Pike, 37211 / 615-331-4666 • *Lat:* 36.0424 *Lon:* -86.7128 I-24 Exit 59 take SH-254 W 2.6 miles, continue W on Old Hickory Blvd .6 mile, then S on Nolensville Rd .2 mile
	◇	2	🕐 Rx		4040 Nolensville Pike, 37211 / 615-831-0133 • *Lat:* 36.0821 *Lon:* -86.7269 I-24 Exit 56 take SH-255 W 1.6 miles & N on Nolensville Rd .2 mile
New Tazewell	○		Rx		432 S Broad St, 37825 / 423-626-6550 • *Lat:* 36.4391 *Lon:* -83.6063 Jct US-25E & SH-33 (N of town) go S on SH-33 for 2.7 miles
Newport	◆	1	🕐 Rx	🚌	1075 Cosby Hwy, 37821 / 423-623-0429 • *Lat:* 35.9425 *Lon:* -83.2093 I-40 Exit 435 take US-321 S .5 mile
Oak Ridge	◇		🕐 Rx		373 S Illinois Ave, 37830 / 865-481-2503 • *Lat:* 36.0060 *Lon:* -84.2523 I-40 Exit 376 take SH-162 N 6.3 miles then SH-62 W 5.3 miles
Oakland	◇		🕐 Rx	🚌	105 Chickasaw Ridge Dr, 38060 / 901-465-0225 • *Lat:* 35.2290 *Lon:* -89.5235 I-40 Exit 25 take SH-205 S 4 miles then US-64 E 7.3 miles
Oneida	◇		🕐 Rx	🚌	19740 Alberta St, 37841 / 423-569-6228 • *Lat:* 36.5150 *Lon:* -84.5071 I-75 Exit 141 follow SH-63 W for 16.2 miles then US-27 N 8 miles
Ooltewah	◇	1	🕐 Rx	🚌	5588 Little Debbie Pkwy, 37363 / 423-238-1036 • *Lat:* 35.0829 *Lon:* -85.0646 I-75 Exit 11 take US-11 N .1 mile & E on Little Debbie .1 mile
Paris	◇		🕐 Rx	🚌	1210 Mineral Wells Ave, 38242 / 731-644-0290 • *Lat:* 36.2841 *Lon:* -88.3080 Jct US-79 & US-641 (in town) go S on US-641 for .7 mile
Pulaski	◆		🕐 Rx	🚌	1655 W College St, 38478 / 931-363-7618 • *Lat:* 35.2053 *Lon:* -87.0640 I-65 Exit 14 follow US-64 W 13.5 miles
Ripley	◆		🕐 Rx		628 Hwy 51 N, 38063 / 731-635-8904 • *Lat:* 35.7624 *Lon:* -89.5452 Jct SH-19 BYP & US-51 (SW of town) take US-51 N .8 mile
Rockwood	◆	6	🕐 Rx	🚌	1102 N Gateway Ave, 37854 / 865-354-0863 • *Lat:* 35.8794 *Lon:* -84.6668 I-40 Exit 347 follow US-27 S 5.2 miles
Rogersville	◆		🕐 Rx	🚌	4331 Hwy 66 S, 37857 / 423-272-7707 • *Lat:* 36.3974 *Lon:* -83.0164 I-81 Exit 23 take US-11E NW 3.8 miles then SH-66 NE 11.5 miles
Savannah	◆		🕐 Rx	🚌	175 Jl Bell Ln, 38372 / 731-925-3020 • *Lat:* 35.2409 *Lon:* -88.1731 Jct SH-128 & US-64 (E of town) take US-64 W 3.5 miles & Bell Ln S .2 mile
Selmer	◆		🕐 Rx	🚌	1017 Mulberry Ave, 38375 / 731-645-7938 • *Lat:* 35.1397 *Lon:* -88.5718 Jct US-64 & US-45 (S of town) go S on US-45 1.4 miles
Sevierville	◇		🕐 Rx	🚌	1414 Parkway, 37862 / 865-429-0029 • *Lat:* 35.8405 *Lon:* -83.5712 I-40 Exit 407 follow SH-66 S 8.5 miles then US-441 S 2.1 miles
Shelbyville	◆		🕐 Rx	🚌	1880 N Main St, 37160 / 931-685-0499 • *Lat:* 35.5137 *Lon:* -86.4554 I-24 Exit 81A take US-231 S 21.3 miles
Smithville	◇		🕐 Rx	🚌	515 W Broad St, 37166 / 615-215-7550 • *Lat:* 35.9582 *Lon:* -85.8278 I-40 Exit 273 take SH-56 S 13 miles then US-70 W .9 mile
Smyrna	◆	4	🕐 Rx	🚌	570 Enon Springs Rd E, 37167 / 615-355-1029 • *Lat:* 35.9777 *Lon:* -86.5248 I-24 Exit 70 take SH-102 NE 3.9 miles & Enon Springs Rd W .1 mile
Soddy Daisy	◆		🕐 Rx	🚌	9334 Dayton Pike, 37379 / 423-332-2412 • *Lat:* 35.2351 *Lon:* -85.2019 I-24 Exit 178 take US-27 N 17 miles, Harrison Ln W .3 mile & Dayton Pike S .2 mile

○ Wal-Mart ◇ Supercenter □ Sam's Club ■ Gas ■ Gas & Diesel

City/Town	⬭	🕐	Rx	🚗	Information
Sparta	◆		🕐	Rx 🚗	202 Sam Walton Dr, 38583 / 931-738-3225 • *Lat:* 35.9280 *Lon:* -85.5765 I-49 Exit 287 follow SH-136 S 15.7 miles
Springfield	◆		🕐	Rx 🚗	3360 Tom Austin Hwy, 37172 / 615-384-9561 • *Lat:* 36.4828 *Lon:* -86.8868 I-24 Exit 35 take US-431 N 11.7 miles
Tullahoma	◇		🕐	Rx 🚗	2111 N Jackson St, 37388 / 931-455-1382 • *Lat:* 35.3917 *Lon:* -86.2398 I-24 Exit 111 take SH-55 W 13.1 miles then US-41 ALT N 2.1 miles
Unicoi	◆	1	🕐	Rx	110 Rocky Bottom Dr, 37692 / 423-743-8780 • *Lat:* 36.1862 *Lon:* -82.3756 I-26 Exit 34, south of exit
Union City	◇	1	🕐	Rx 🚗	1601 W Reelfoot Ave, 38261 / 731-884-0114 • *Lat:* 36.4127 *Lon:* -89.0779 Jct SH-431 & US-51 (S of town) take US-51 S .7 mile
Waverly	◆		🕐	Rx	275 Walton Dr, 37185 / 931-296-9235 • *Lat:* 36.0827 *Lon:* -87.8321 2.2 miles west of town via US-70 at Browntown Rd
White House	◇	1	🕐	Rx 🚗	222 Wilkinson Ln, 37188 / 615-672-6773 • *Lat:* 36.4722 *Lon:* -86.6753 I-65 Exit 108 go E .4 mile on SH-76 then N on Wilkinson Ln .3 mile
Winchester	◇		🕐	Rx 🚗	2675 Decherd Blvd, 37398 / 931-967-0207 • *Lat:* 35.1962 *Lon:* -86.0989 I-24 Exit 127 follow SH-50 W 14 miles then US-41 ALT 1 mile

○ Wal-Mart   ◇ Supercenter   ☐ Sam's Club   ▨ Gas   ▬ Gas & Diesel

Texas

○ Wal-Mart ◇ Supercenter ▢ Sam's Club ▨ Gas ■ Gas & Diesel

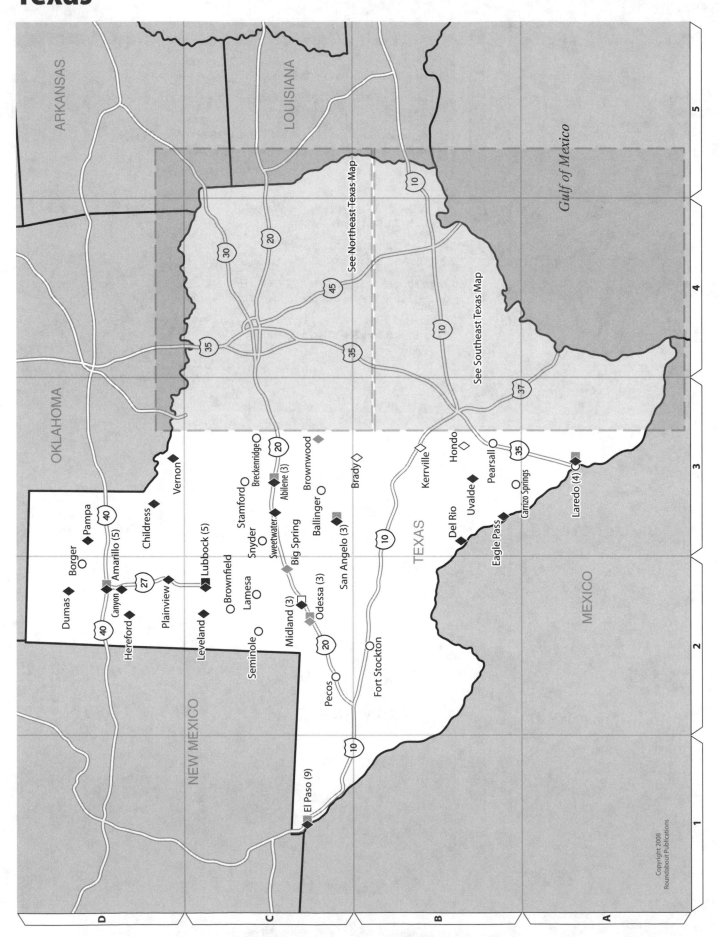

ARKANSAS

LOUISIANA

OKLAHOMA

NEW MEXICO

TEXAS

MEXICO

Gulf of Mexico

See Northeast Texas Map

See Southeast Texas Map

Dumas
Borger
Pampa
Canyon
Amarillo (5)
Hereford
Plainview
Leveland
Childress
Vernon
Brownfield
Lubbock (5)
Seminole
Lamesa
Snyder
Midland (3)
Odessa (3)
Pecos
Fort Stockton
El Paso (9)
Stamford
Breckenridge
Abilene (3)
Sweetwater
Big Spring
Ballinger
Brownwood
San Angelo (3)
Brady
Kerrville
Hondo
Pearsall
Uvalde
Del Rio
Eagle Pass
Carrizo Springs
Laredo (4)

40 27 35 30 20 45 35 10 37 10 20 10

Copyright 2008
Roundabout Publications

A B C D

1 2 3 4 5

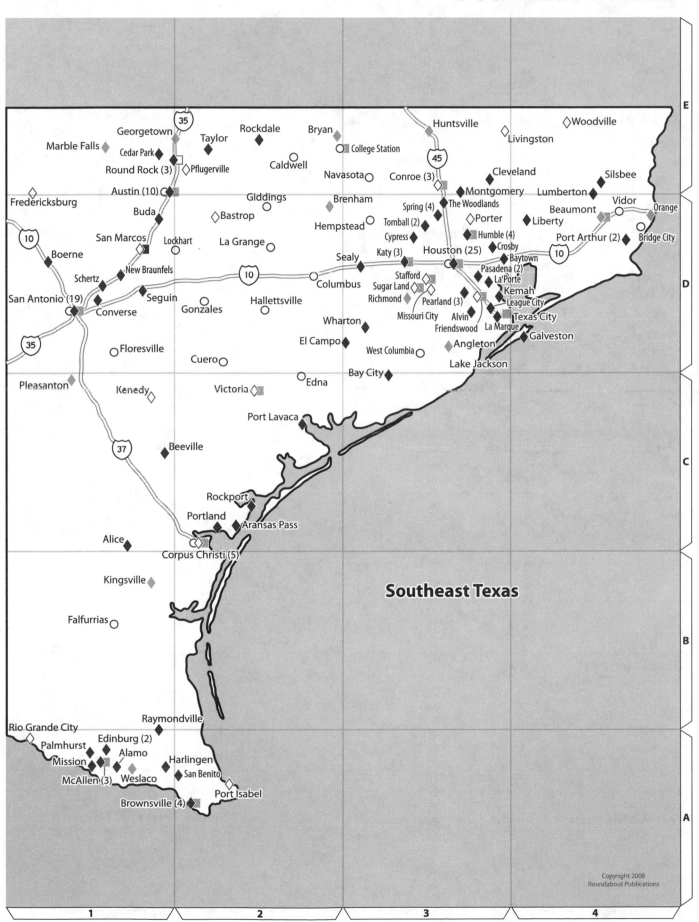

Southeast Texas

○ Wal-Mart ◇ Supercenter □ Sam's Club ▨ Gas ■ Gas & Diesel

Marble Falls
Georgetown
Cedar Park
Round Rock (3)
Pflugerville
Taylor
Rockdale
Bryan
College Station
Caldwell
Huntsville
Livingston
Woodville
Austin (10)
Fredericksburg
Buda
Giddings
Navasota
Conroe (3)
Cleveland
Silsbee
Lumberton
Brenham
Spring (4)
The Woodlands
Porter
Beaumont
Vidor
Orange
San Marcos
Lockhart
La Grange
Hempstead
Tomball (2)
Humble (4)
Liberty
Port Arthur (2)
Bridge City
Boerne
Cypress
Houston (25)
Crosby
Baytown
Schertz
New Braunfels
Sealy
Katy (3)
Pasadena (2)
San Antonio (19)
Seguin
Columbus
Sugar Land
Stafford
La'Porte
Kemah
Converse
Gonzales
Hallettsville
Richmond
Pearland (3)
League City
Texas City
Floresville
Missouri City
Alvin
La Marque
Wharton
Friendswood
Galveston
Cuero
El Campo
West Columbia
Angleton
Lake Jackson
Pleasanton
Kenedy
Victoria
Edna
Bay City
Port Lavaca
Beeville
Rockport
Portland
Aransas Pass
Alice
Corpus Christi (5)
Kingsville
Falfurrias

Southeast Texas

Rio Grande City
Raymondville
Palmhurst
Edinburg (2)
Alamo
Mission
Harlingen
McAllen (3)
Weslaco
San Benito
Port Isabel
Brownsville (4)

Northeast Texas

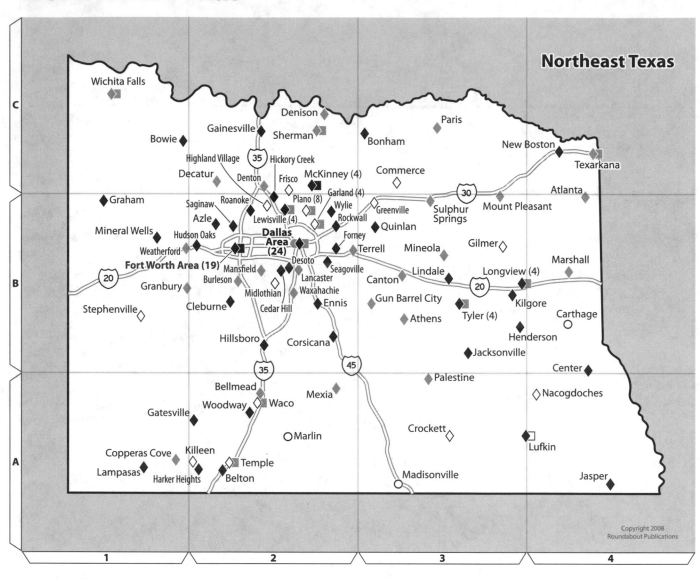

Northeast Texas

Wichita Falls
Denison
Paris
Gainesville
Sherman
Bonham
New Boston
Bowie
Texarkana
Highland Village
Hickory Creek
McKinney (4)
Commerce
Atlanta
Decatur
Denton
Frisco
Graham
Garland (4)
Mount Pleasant
Saginaw
Roanoke
Plano (8)
Wylie
Greenville
Sulphur
Springs
Gilmer
Azle
Lewisville (4)
Rockwall
Marshall
Mineral Wells
Dallas
Area
(24)
Forney
Quinlan
Longview (4)
Hudson Oaks
Terrell
Mineola
Weatherford
Fort Worth Area (19)
Desoto
Kilgore
Granbury
Mansfield
Seagoville
Lindale
Carthage
Burleson
Lancaster
Canton
Longview (4)
Stephenville
Midlothian
Waxahachie
Gun Barrel City
Henderson
Cleburne
Cedar Hill
Ennis
Athens
Tyler (4)
Hillsboro
Corsicana
Jacksonville
Center
Bellmead
Mexia
Palestine
Nacogdoches
Woodway
Waco
Gatesville
Crockett
Lufkin
Marlin
Copperas Cove
Killeen
Jasper
Lampasas
Temple
Madisonville
Harker Heights
Belton

Copyright 2008
Roundabout Publications

1   2   3   4

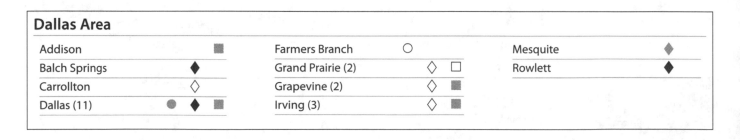

Dallas Area

Addison	▨		Farmers Branch	○		Mesquite	◆	
Balch Springs	◆		Grand Prairie (2)	◇ □		Rowlett	◆	
Carrollton	◇		Grapevine (2)	◇ ▨				
Dallas (11)	● ◆ ▨		Irving (3)	◇ ▨				

Fort Worth Area

Arlington (2)	◇		Hurst	◆		Richland Hills	▨
Bedford	◇ ▨		Lake Worth	◇		Westworth Village (2)	◇ ■
Fort Worth (9)	◆ ▨		North Richland Hills (2)	◆			

City/Town	⛉	🕐	℞	🚗	Information
Abilene	■ 4		℞	🚗	5301 S 1st St, 79605 / 325-691-5480 • *Lat:* 32.4525 *Lon:* -99.7928 I-20 Exit 283 take US-277 S 2.7 miles, W on 7th St .5 mile, N on Ruidosa Dr .6 mile & E on 1st St .2 mille
	♦ 1	🕐	℞	🚗	1650 TX Hwy 351, 79601 / 325-677-5584 • *Lat:* 32.4784 *Lon:* -99.6979 I-20 Exit 288 on SH-351 N of I-20
	◇ 6	🕐	℞	🚗	4350 Southwest Dr, 79606 / 325-695-3092 • *Lat:* 32.4108 *Lon:* -99.7774 I-20 Exit 283A follow US-83 S 4.3 miles then Southwest Dr W 1 mile
Addison	■ 2		℞	🚗	4150 Belt Line Rd, 75001 / 972-934-9274 • *Lat:* 32.9542 *Lon:* -96.8409 I-635 Exit 23 follow Midway Rd N 1.8 miles, then W .1 mile on Belt Line Rd
Alamo	♦	🕐	℞	🚗	1421 Frontage Rd, 78516 / 956-782-0034 • *Lat:* 26.1917 *Lon:* -98.1286 Jct US-281 & US-83 (W of town) go E on US-83 for 3.5 miles, exit toward Alamo Rd to S Frontage Rd .1 mile
Alice	♦	🕐	℞	🚗	2701 E Main St, 78332 / 361-668-0441 • *Lat:* 27.7667 *Lon:* -98.0427 Jct SH-459 & SH-44 (E of town) merge onto SH-359 W/SH-44 W 1.8 miles
Alvin	♦ 10	🕐	℞	🚗	400 Hwy 35 Byp N, 77511 / 281-585-2825 • *Lat:* 29.4191 *Lon:* -95.2478 I-45 Exit 19 take FM-517 W 9 miles, CR-142 S .6 mile & SH-6 N .4 mile
Amarillo	■ 1			🚗	2201 Ross-Osage St, 79103 / 806-374-6653 • *Lat:* 35.1896 *Lon:* -101.8164 I-40 Exit 71 go S on Ross-Osage St for .2 mile
	♦ 1	🕐	℞	🚗	3700 E I-40, 79103 / 806-342-3030 • *Lat:* 35.1925 *Lon:* -101.7943 I-40 Exit 72B take Interstate Dr E .2 mile
	♦ 2	🕐	℞	🚗	5730 W Amarillo Blvd, 79106 / 806-354-9454 • *Lat:* 35.2122 *Lon:* -101.9026 I-40 Exit 66 go N on Bell St 1.5 miles
	♦ 1	🕐	℞	🚗	4215 Canyon Dr, 79110 / 806-352-6360 • *Lat:* 35.1727 *Lon:* -101.8605 I-27 Exit 121A merge onto Canyon Dr N .3 mile
	♦ 1	🕐	℞	🚗	4610 S Coulter St, 79119 / 806-354-9300 • *Lat:* 35.1598 *Lon:* -101.9203 I-27 Exit 115 take Sundown Ln W .2 mile & Coulter Rd S .6 mile
Angleton	♦	🕐	℞	🚗	1801 N Velasco St, 77515 / 979-849-4604 • *Lat:* 29.1827 *Lon:* -95.4332 Jct FM-523 & SH-288 BR (N of town) go S on SH-288 BR 1.4 miles
Aransas Pass	♦	🕐	℞	🚗	2501 W Wheeler Ave, 78336 / 361-758-2920 • *Lat:* 27.9231 *Lon:* -97.1744 Jct FM-136 & SH-35 (W of town) take SH-35 E 5 miles then SH-35 BR SE .9 mile
Arlington	◇ 2	🕐	℞	🚗	915 E Randol Mill Rd, 76011 / 817-274-1040 • *Lat:* 32.7500 *Lon:* -97.0969 I-30 Exit 29 take Ballpark Way S .9 mile & Randol Mill Rd W .9 mile
	◇ 2	🕐	℞	🚗	4801 S Cooper St, 76017 / 817-465-1000 • *Lat:* 32.6689 *Lon:* -97.1341 I-20 Exit 449 follow FM-157 S 1.2 miles
Athens	♦	🕐	℞	🚗	1405 E Tyler St, 75751 / 903-677-5400 • *Lat:* 32.2115 *Lon:* -95.8295 Jct FM-317 Loop & SH-31 (NE of town) go SW on SH-31/Tyler St 1.5 miles
Atlanta	♦	🕐	℞	🚗	201 US Hwy 59 Loop, 75551 / 903-796-7916 • *Lat:* 33.1143 *Lon:* -94.1826 Jct FM-2328 & US-59 (SW of town) follow US-59 N 3.5 miles
Austin	□		℞	🚗	4970 W Hwy 290, 78735 / 512-358-8695 • *Lat:* 30.2338 *Lon:* -97.8191 I-35 Exit 230 take US-290 W 15.1 miles
	■ 1			🚗	5107 S I-35, 78744 / 512-444-0363 • *Lat:* 30.2042 *Lon:* -97.7586 I-35 at Exit 230 (southbound travelers use I-35 Exit 230A), store is on east side of highway at Teri Rd
	■		℞	🚗	9700 N Capital Of Texas Hwy, 78759 / 512-343-8262 • *Lat:* 30.3901 *Lon:* -97.7442 Jct SH-1 Loop & Capital of Texas Hwy, go W on Capital of Texas Hwy for .6 mile
	○		℞		5017 W Hwy 290, 78735 / 512-892-6086 • *Lat:* 30.2550 *Lon:* -97.8539 I-35 Exit 230 follow US-290 W 10.1 miles

○ Wal-Mart   ◇ Supercenter   □ Sam's Club   ■ Gas   ■ Gas & Diesel

City/Town	🛡	⏱	℞	🚐	Information
	◇		⏱ ℞ 🚐		8201 N FM 620, 78726 / 512-249-6666 • *Lat:* 30.4179 *Lon:* -97.8466 I-35 Exit 250B merge onto SH-45 (toll) W 8.4 miles & continue W on FM-620 for 4.6 miles
	◇ 8		⏱ ℞ 🚐		13201 FM 620 N, 78717 / 512-331-9924 • *Lat:* 30.4691 *Lon:* -97.7895 I-35 Exit 250 follow SH-45 (toll) and FM-620 W for 7.1 miles then go S .1 mile on Lake Creek Pkwy
	◆ 1		⏱ ℞ 🚐		1030 Norwood Park Blvd, 78753 / 512-339-6060 • *Lat:* 30.3384 *Lon:* -97.6923 I-35 Exit 241 go E on Norwood Park Blvd .4 mile
	◆ 1		⏱ ℞ 🚐		12900 N I-35, 78753 / 512-837-9886 • *Lat:* 30.4142 *Lon:* -97.6738 I-35 Exit 245 (southbound travelers) follow I-35 service road S .4 mile. Northbound travelers use I-35 Exit 246, W on Howard Ln then S .7 mile on I-35 service road
	◆ 2		⏱ ℞ 🚐		710 E Ben White Blvd, 78704 / 512-443-6601 • *Lat:* 30.2190 *Lon:* -97.7552 I-35 Exit 231 (southbound travelers) follow I-35 service road S 1.1 miles then go W .3 mile on Ben White Blvd. Northbound travelers use I-35 Exit 230, go N on service road 1.1 miles then W .3 mile on Ben White Blvd.
	◆ 1		⏱ ℞ 🚐		9300 S I-35, 78748 / 512-292-6973 • *Lat:* 30.1641 *Lon:* -97.7884 On West side of I-35 at Slaughter Ln (northbound travelers use Exit 227, southbound use Exit 226B)
Azle	◆		⏱ ℞ 🚐		721 Boyd Rd, 76020 / 817-270-5716 • *Lat:* 32.9039 *Lon:* -97.5437 I-820 Exit 10A follow SH-199 W 11.1 miles then FM-730 N .3 mile
Balch Springs	◆ 1		⏱ ℞ 🚐		12300 Lake June Rd, 75180 / 972-286-8600 • *Lat:* 32.7339 *Lon:* -96.6158 I-635 Exit 2 go W on Lake June Rd .3 mile
Ballinger	○		℞		2005 Hutchins Ave, 76821 / 325-365-5731 • *Lat:* 31.7256 *Lon:* -99.9591 Jct US-83 & US-67 (in town) go S on US-67 for 1.1 miles
Bastrop	◇		⏱ ℞ 🚐		488 Hwy 71 W, 78602 / 512-321-2288 • *Lat:* 30.1110 *Lon:* -97.3576 Jct FM-969 & SH-71 (W of town) go E on SH-71 for 1.7 miles
Bay City	◆		⏱ ℞ 🚐		4600 7th St, 77414 / 979-245-0196 • *Lat:* 28.9865 *Lon:* -95.9338 Jct FM-457 & SH-35 (E of town) go N on SH-35 for .4 mile
Baytown	◆ 2		⏱ ℞ 🚐		4900 Garth Rd, 77521 / 281-421-4859 • *Lat:* 29.7767 *Lon:* -94.9775 I-10 Exit 792 take Garth Rd S 2 miles
Beaumont	■ 1		℞ 🚐		1615 I-10 S, 77701 / 409-842-5071 • *Lat:* 30.0613 *Lon:* -94.1341 I-10 at Exit 851
	◆ 3		⏱ ℞ 🚐		4145 Dowlen Rd, 77706 / 409-899-9203 • *Lat:* 30.1216 *Lon:* -94.1654 I-10 Exit 853A take US-287 N 2.2 miles then Dowlen Rd W .8 mile
Bedford	◇ 8		⏱ ℞ 🚐		4101 Hwy 121, 76021 / 817-571-7928 • *Lat:* 32.8659 *Lon:* -97.1025 I-820 Exit 22B follow SH-121 NE 7.8 miles & W at Cheek-Sparger Rd
Beeville	◆		⏱ ℞ 🚐		502 E FM 351, 78102 / 361-358-4764 • *Lat:* 28.4289 *Lon:* -97.7443 I-37 Exit 56 follow US-59 N 16.7 miles then FM-351 NW 2.6 miles
Bellmead	◆ 1		⏱ ℞ 🚐		1521 I-35 N, 76705 / 254-867-8084 • *Lat:* 31.5972 *Lon:* -97.1084 I-35 Exit 338B go N .5 mile
Belton	◆ 3		⏱ ℞ 🚐		2604 N Main St, 76513 / 254-939-0962 • *Lat:* 31.0814 *Lon:* -97.4579 I-35 Exit 294A take Central Ave W .6 mile & SH-317 N 1.8 miles
Big Spring	◆ 4		⏱ ℞ 🚐		201 W Marcy Dr, 79720 / 432-267-3363 • *Lat:* 32.2287 *Lon:* -101.4706 I-20 Exit 179 take I-20 BR W 1.6 miles & US-87 S 1.6 miles
Boerne	◆ 1		⏱ ℞ 🚐		1381 S Main St, 78006 / 830-249-6195 • *Lat:* 29.7788 *Lon:* -98.7281 I-10 Exit 540 take SH-46 E .6 mile then US-87 BR S .1 mile
Bonham	◆		⏱ ℞		2021 N TX Hwy 121, 75418 / 903-583-9591 • *Lat:* 33.6254 *Lon:* -96.1891 Jct US-82 & SH-121 (NW of town) take SH-121 N .9 mile

○ Wal-Mart   ◇ Supercenter   □ Sam's Club   ■ Gas   ■ Gas & Diesel

City/Town	🛡	🕐	℞	🚗	Information
Borger	○		℞		1404 W Wilson St, 79007 / 806-274-7257 • *Lat:* 35.6598 *Lon:* -101.4086 1.6 miles southwest of town on SH-136
Bowie	◆	🕐	℞		8420 US Hwy 287 N Access Rd, 76230 / 940-872-1166 • *Lat:* 33.5401 *Lon:* -97.8358 1.8 miles southeast of town at US-81/US-287 jct
Brady	◇	🕐	℞		2207 S Bridge St, 76825 / 325-597-3406 • *Lat:* 31.1097 *Lon:* -99.3337 1.8 miles south of town center via US-87
Breckenridge	○		℞	🚗	3732 W Walker St, 76424 / 254-559-6579 • *Lat:* 32.7592 *Lon:* -98.9443 Jct US-183 & US-180 (in town) take US-180 W 2.5 miles
Brenham	◆	🕐	℞	🚗	203 Hwy 290 W, 77833 / 979-836-1118 • *Lat:* 30.1929 *Lon:* -96.4070 Jct SH-36 & US-290 (S of town) go E on US-290 for .2 mile
Bridge City	○ 8		℞		795 Texas Ave, 77611 / 409-735-2417 • *Lat:* 30.0235 *Lon:* -93.8438 I-10 Exit 873 follow SH-73 S 7.1 miles
Brownfield	○				1405 Tahoka Rd, 79316 / 806-637-8778 • *Lat:* 33.1812 *Lon:* -102.2567 Jct US-385 & US-380 (in town) take US-380 E 1 mile
Brownsville	▪		℞	🚗	3570 W Alton Gloor Blvd, 78520 / 956-350-6917 • *Lat:* 25.9651 *Lon:* -97.5390 From US-77/83 (northwest of town) go SW on FM-3248 for 1.9 miles
	◇	🕐	℞	🚗	3500 W Alton Gloor Blvd, 78520 / 956-350-2022 • *Lat:* 25.9642 *Lon:* -97.5392 Jct US-83/77 & FM-3248/Alton Gloor Blvd (N of town) go W on Gloor Blvd .2 mile
	◆	🕐	℞	🚗	2721 Boca Chica Blvd, 78521 / 956-544-0394 • *Lat:* 25.9218 *Lon:* -97.4801 Jct US-83/77 & SH-48/Boca Chica Blvd (in town) go E on Boca Chica .7 mile
	◆	🕐	℞	🚗	7480 Padre Island Hwy, 78521 / 956-832-0376 • *Lat:* 25.9160 *Lon:* -97.4505 Jct FM-511/Indiana Ave & Padre Island Hwy (NE of town) go S on Padre Island Hwy .5 mile
Brownwood	◆	🕐	℞	🚗	401 W Commerce St, 76801 / 325-643-9727 • *Lat:* 31.7290 *Lon:* -98.9839 Jct US-183 & US-84 (NE of town) follow US-84 SW 1.2 miles
Bryan	◆	🕐	℞	🚗	2200 Briarcrest Dr, 77802 / 979-776-6441 • *Lat:* 30.6587 *Lon:* -96.3327 Jct SH-6/Rudder Fwy & FM-1179/Briarcrest Dr (E of town) go W on FM-1179 for .5 mile
Buda	◆ 1	🕐	℞	🚗	690 Old San Antonio Rd, 78610 / 512-295-1670 • *Lat:* 30.0864 *Lon:* -97.8222 I-35 Exit 220 go W .5 mile on Cabelas Dr then turn right .5 mile at Old San Antonio Rd
Burleson	◆ 3	🕐	℞	🚗	951 SW Wilshire Blvd, 76028 / 817-572-9574 • *Lat:* 32.5293 *Lon:* -97.3397 I-35W Exit 36 take SH-50 Spur W .8 mile & SH-174 S 1.3 miles
Caldwell	○		℞		475 TX Hwy 36 N, 77836 / 979-567-9807 • *Lat:* 30.5437 *Lon:* -96.7050 Jct SH-21 & SH-36 (N of town) go NW on SH-36 for .1 mile
Canton	◆ 3	🕐	℞	🚗	603 E Hwy 243, 75103 / 903-567-5744 • *Lat:* 32.5457 *Lon:* -95.8552 I-20 Exit 528 take FM-17 S 1.6 miles, SH-64 SE .4 mile & SH-243 W .5 mile
Canyon	◆ 4	🕐	℞	🚗	1701 N 23rd St, 79015 / 806-655-1175 • *Lat:* 34.9846 *Lon:* -101.9193 I-27 Exit 110 follow US-87 S 4 miles
Carrizo Springs	○		℞		2214 N 1st St, 78834 / 830-876-2462 • *Lat:* 28.5348 *Lon:* -99.8514 Jct US-277 & US-83 (in town) take US-83 N 1 mile
Carrollton	◇ 3	🕐	℞	🚗	1213 E Trinity Mills Rd, 75006 / 972-466-2228 • *Lat:* 32.9843 *Lon:* -96.9043 I-35E Exit 445 take Bush Tpk (toll) E 1.4 miles then Josey Ln N .4 mile & Trinity Mills W .8 mile
Carthage	○		℞		423 W Loop 436, 75633 / 903-693-8881 • *Lat:* 32.1520 *Lon:* -94.3701 2.6 miles west of town center via US-79-BR and LaSalle Pkwy/SH-149
Cedar Hill	◆ 7	🕐	℞	🚗	621 Uptown Blvd, 75104 / 469-272-7344 • *Lat:* 32.5962 *Lon:* -96.9454 I-20 Exit 464 follow US-67 S 5.9 miles. FM-1382 W .4 mile & Uptown Blvd S .3 mile
Cedar Park	◆ 9	🕐	℞	🚗	201 Walton Way, 78613 / 512-528-8746 • *Lat:* 30.5221 *Lon:* -97.8322 I-35 Exit 257 take FM-1431 W 8.7 miles & Walton Way N .2 mile

○ Wal-Mart ◇ Supercenter ☐ Sam's Club ▪ Gas ▪ Gas & Diesel

City/Town	⬡	🕐	℞	🚗	Information
Center	◆		🕐	℞	🚗	810 Hurst St, 75935 / 936-598-6131 • *Lat:* 31.8074 *Lon:* -94.1918 Jct SH-87 & US-96 (NW of town) go S on US-96/Hurst St .2 mile
Childress	◆		🕐	℞	🚗	2801 Avenue F NW, 79201 / 940-937-6166 • *Lat:* 34.4376 *Lon:* -100.2358 Jct US-62 & US-287/Ave F (NW of town) go NW on Ave F .8 mile
Cleburne	◆		🕐	℞	🚗	1616 W Henderson St, 76033 / 817-645-1575 • *Lat:* 32.3381 *Lon:* -97.4144 I-35W Exit 26 follow US-67 W 6.3 miles & US-67-BR W 6.2 miles
Cleveland	◆		🕐	℞	🚗	831 Hwy 59 S, 77327 / 281-592-2654 • *Lat:* 30.3767 *Lon:* -95.0697 Jct SH-105 & US-59 (SW of town) take US-59 S 1.6 miles
College Station	■				🚗	1405 Earl Rudder Fwy S, 77845 / 979-693-2828 • *Lat:* 30.6323 *Lon:* -96.3026 2 miles northeast of town center at jct of SH-6 and SH-30
	○			℞	🚗	1815 Brothers Blvd, 77845 / 979-693-3095 • *Lat:* 30.5962 *Lon:* -96.3000 Jct SH-6 & FM-2818 (E of town) take FM-2818 W .7 mile, Texas Ave S .3 mile & Brothers Blvd W .2 mile
Columbus	○	1		℞		2103 Milam St, 78934 / 979-732-8341 • *Lat:* 29.6948 *Lon:* -96.5401 I-10 Exit 696 take SH-71 BR N .1 mile to Milam St N
Commerce	◇	9	🕐	℞		2701 TX Hwy 50, 75428 / 903-886-3108 • *Lat:* 33.2346 *Lon:* -95.9129 2 miles southwest of town center on SH-50 at SH-178 -or- I-30 Exit 101 go N 9 miles on SH-50
Conroe	■	1		℞	🚗	19091 I-45 S, 77385 / 936-271-1732 • *Lat:* 30.1821 *Lon:* -95.4516 I-45 Exit 76 N of Tamina Rd, E side of highway
	■	1		℞	🚗	2000 Westview Blvd, 77304 / 936-756-5778 • *Lat:* 30.3286 *Lon:* -95.4820 I-45 Exit 88 take SH-336 Loop W .2 mile then S on Westview .3 mile
	◇	1	🕐	℞	🚗	1407 N Loop 336 W, 77304 / 936-788-5400 • *Lat:* 30.3328 *Lon:* -95.4801 I-45 Exit 88 take SH-336 Loop W .2 mile
Converse	◆	4	🕐	℞	🚗	8315 FM 78, 78109 / 210-666-6066 • *Lat:* 29.5119 *Lon:* -98.3082 I-35 Exit 172 take SH-1604 S 2.8 miles then FM-78 SW 1.2 miles
Copperas Cove	◆		🕐	℞	🚗	2720 E Hwy 190, 76522 / 254-542-7600 • *Lat:* 31.1206 *Lon:* -97.8720 Jct FM-116 & US-190 (in town) go E on US-190 for 1 mile
Corpus Christi	■	5		℞	🚗	4949 Greenwood Dr, 78416 / 361-857-0151 • *Lat:* 27.7450 *Lon:* -97.4402 I-37 Exit 4A go SE on SH-358 for 4.7 miles then N on Greenwood Dr .3 mile
	○	9		℞	🚗	4833 S Padre Island Dr, 78411 / 361-994-9010 • *Lat:* 27.7139 *Lon:* -97.3839 I-37 Exit 4 merge onto South Padre Island Dr SE 9 miles
	○			℞	🚗	10241 S Padre Island Dr, 78418 / 361-937-2643 • *Lat:* 27.6689 *Lon:* -97.2840 I-37 Exit 4 take South Padre Island Dr SE 15.8 miles
	◇	2	🕐	℞	🚗	3829 US Hwy 77, 78410 / 361-387-0599 • *Lat:* 27.8530 *Lon:* -97.6304 I-37 Exit 14 follow US-77 S 1.4 miles
	◇	6	🕐	℞	🚗	1821 S Padre Island Dr, 78416 / 361-854-0943 • *Lat:* 27.7404 *Lon:* -97.4383 I-37 Exit 4 merge onto South Padre Island Dr SE 5.2 miles
Corsicana	◆	5	🕐	℞	🚗	3801 W TX Hwy 31, 75110 / 903-872-6691 • *Lat:* 32.0688 *Lon:* -96.5068 I-45 Exit 231 merge onto Frontage Rd S .3 mile then SH-31 W 4.4 miles
Crockett	◇		🕐	℞		1225 E Loop 304, 75835 / 936-544-5121 • *Lat:* 31.3164 *Lon:* -95.4365 Jct US-287 & SH-304 Loop (SE of town) go N on SH-304 for .8 mile
Crosby	◆	8	🕐	℞	🚗	14215 FM 2100 Rd, 77532 / 281-328-4836 • *Lat:* 29.8920 *Lon:* -95.0635 I-10 Exit 787 take I-10 Frontage W .4 mile then FM-2100 N 7 miles
Cuero	○			℞	🚗	1202 E Broadway St, 77954 / 361-275-5796 • *Lat:* 29.0880 *Lon:* -97.2733 Jct US-183 & US-87 (in town) take US-87 E 1.1 miles
Cypress	◆		🕐	℞	🚗	26270 Northwest Fwy, 77429 / 281-256-8038 • *Lat:* 29.9721 *Lon:* -95.7015 I-10 Exit 747A take Fry Rd N 14.1 miles & US-290 E .2 mile

○ Wal-Mart ◇ Supercenter ☐ Sam's Club ■ Gas ■ Gas & Diesel

City/Town	🛡	⏰	℞	🚗	Information
Dallas	■ 2		℞	🚗	12000 McCree Rd, 75238 / 214-342-9810 • *Lat:* 32.8687 *Lon:* -96.6751 I-635 Exit 13 S on LBJ Fwy .9 mile, W at Executive Dr, S on McCree Rd .2 mile
	■ 1		℞	🚗	1959 W Northwest Hwy, 75220 / 972-556-0831 • *Lat:* 32.8684 *Lon:* -96.9109 I-35E Exit 436 go W on Northwest Hwy for .7 mile
	■ 1		℞	🚗	2900 W Wheatland Rd, 75237 / 972-283-1704 • *Lat:* 32.6474 *Lon:* -96.8673 I-20 Exit 465 go E on Wheatland Rd .3 mile
	■ 1		℞	🚗	5555 S Buckner Blvd, 75228 / 214-320-2839 • *Lat:* 32.7936 *Lon:* -96.6852 I-30 Exit 52 go S on Buckner Blvd .1 mile
	□ 4		℞	🚗	8282 Park Ln, 75231 / 214-373-3058 • *Lat:* 32.8713 *Lon:* -96.7631 I-635 Exit 19A take US-75 S 3.1 miles then E on Park Ln .5 mile
	● 2		℞		13739 N Central Expy, 75243 / 972-437-9146 • *Lat:* 32.9359 *Lon:* -96.7520 I-635 Exit 19A take US-75 N 1.8 miles
	◆ 1	⏰	℞	🚗	1521 N Cockrell Hill Rd, 75211 / 214-330-7249 • *Lat:* 32.7628 *Lon:* -96.8954 I-30 Exit 39 go S on Cockrell Hill Rd .3 mile
	◇ 1	⏰	℞	🚗	7401 Samuell Blvd, 75228 / 214-319-2616 • *Lat:* 32.7926 *Lon:* -96.6887 I-30 Exit 52B take Thornton Fwy E .1 mile, St Francis Ave S .1 mile & Samuell Blvd E .2 mile
	◆ 1	⏰	℞	🚗	3155 W Wheatland Rd, 75237 / 972-709-1400 • *Lat:* 32.6477 *Lon:* -96.8715 I-20 Exit 465 take Wheatland Rd W .4 mile
	◇ 2	⏰	℞	🚗	15220 Montford Rd, 75248 / 972-233-0430 • *Lat:* 32.9560 *Lon:* -96.8183 I-635 Exit 22C take Dallas North Tollway (toll) N 1.4 miles, Belt Line Rd E .2 mile & Montford Dr N .1 mile
	◆ 4	⏰	℞	🚗	18121 Marsh Ln, 75287 / 972-307-6978 • *Lat:* 32.9974 *Lon:* -96.8559 I-35E Exit 445B take Bush Tpk (toll) E 3.5 miles, Frankford Rd E .2 mile & Marsh Ln S .1 mile
Decatur	◆	⏰	℞	🚗	800 S Hwy 287, 76234 / 940-627-5546 • *Lat:* 33.2518 *Lon:* -97.5507 Jct US-380 & US-81 (W of town) go S on US-81 for .6 mile
Del Rio	◆	⏰	℞	🚗	2410 Dodson Ave, 78840 / 830-774-6034 • *Lat:* 29.3970 *Lon:* -100.8999 Jct US-90 & US-277 (E of town) go N on Bedell Ave 1.1 miles then N on Dodson 1.1 miles
Denison	◆	⏰	℞	🚗	401 N US Hwy 75, 75020 / 903-465-9744 • *Lat:* 33.7545 *Lon:* -96.5861 Jct SH-503 & US-75 (S of town) take US-75 N 2.2 miles
Denton	◆ 1	⏰	℞	🚗	1515 S Loop 288, 76205 / 940-484-1717 • *Lat:* 33.1943 *Lon:* -97.0937 I-35E Exit 462 take SH-288 Loop E 1 mile
Desoto	◆ 4	⏰	℞	🚗	951 W Belt Line Rd, 75115 / 972-223-1711 • *Lat:* 32.5900 *Lon:* -96.8785 I-35 Exit 414 take FM-1382 W 3.2 miles
Dumas	◆	⏰	℞	🚗	2003 S Dumas Ave, 79029 / 806-935-9075 • *Lat:* 35.8425 *Lon:* -101.9733 Jct FM-722 & US-287/87 (S of town) go S on US-287/87 for .6 mile
Eagle Pass	◆	⏰	℞	🚗	496 S Bibb Ave, 78852 / 830-773-9403 • *Lat:* 28.7011 *Lon:* -100.4835 Jct US-277 & FM-375 (in town) take FM-375/Bibb Ave S .4 mile
Eastland	◆ 1	⏰	℞		1410 E Main St, 76448 / 254-629-3371 • *Lat:* 32.4018 *Lon:* -98.7942 I-20 Exit 343 take FM-570 W .3 mile
Edinburg	◆	⏰	℞	🚗	1724 W University Dr, 78539 / 956-381-6674 • *Lat:* 26.3038 *Lon:* -98.1798 Jct US-281 & SH-107/University Dr (in town) go W on University Dr 2 miles
	◆	⏰	℞	🚗	4101 S McColl Rd, 78539 / 956-618-2018 • *Lat:* 26.2726 *Lon:* -98.2005 Jct US-83 & SH-2061/McColl Rd (in McAllen) take McColl Rd N 7 miles
Edna	○		℞		1002 N Wells St, 77957 / 361-782-5223 • *Lat:* 28.9874 *Lon:* -96.6507 At Jct US-59 & SH-111 (N of town)
El Campo	◆	⏰	℞	🚗	3413 W Loop St, 77437 / 979-543-7286 • *Lat:* 29.2183 *Lon:* -96.2879 Jct US-59 & SH-525 Loop (SW of town) take SH-525 E 1.5 miles then N at FM-2765 for 2.5 miles

○ Wal-Mart ◇ Supercenter □ Sam's Club ■ Gas ■ Gas & Diesel

City/Town	⬡	🕐	℞	🚌	Information
El Paso	■ 2		℞	🚌	11360 Pellicano Dr, 79936 / 915-591-6688 • *Lat:* 31.7470 *Lon:* -106.3152 I-10 Exit 30 N on Lee Travino Dr 1.6 miles then E on Pellicano .2 mile
	■ 1		℞	🚌	7001 Gateway Blvd W, 79925 / 915-771-0004 • *Lat:* 31.7767 *Lon:* -106.3878 I-10 Exit 26 W on Gateway Blvd .7 mile
	■ 1		℞	🚌	7970 N Mesa St, 79932 / 915-585-2433 • *Lat:* 31.8406 *Lon:* -106.5753 I-10 Exit 11 W on Mesa St .4 mile
	◆ 9	🕐	℞	🚌	4530 Woodrow Bean Dr, 79924 / 915-757-0151 • *Lat:* 31.8985 *Lon:* -106.4375 I-10 Exit 22B go N on US-54/Patriot Fwy for 8 miles to Exit 9 then go E on SH-375 Loop .2 mile
	◆ 3	🕐	℞	🚌	9441 Alameda Ave, 79907 / 915-860-7171 • *Lat:* 31.6831 *Lon:* -106.3151 I-10 Exit 34 take SH-375 Loop S 2.2 miles then Alameda Ave W .2 mile
	◇ 1	🕐	℞		7555 N Mesa St, 79912 / 915-833-1335 • *Lat:* 31.8382 *Lon:* -106.5650 I-10 Exit 11 take Mesa St E .2 mile
	◇ 1	🕐	℞	🚌	7101 Gateway Blvd W, 79925 / 915-779-6664 • *Lat:* 31.7766 *Lon:* -106.3874 I-10 Exit 26 merge onto Gateway Blvd W .8 mile
	◆ 1	🕐	℞	🚌	10727 Gateway Blvd W, 79935 / 915-594-0243 • *Lat:* 31.7507 *Lon:* -106.3416 I-10 Exit 28B merge onto Gateway Blvd W .1 mile
	◆ 4	🕐	℞	🚌	1850 N Zaragoza Rd, 79936 / 915-855-6405 • *Lat:* 31.7579 *Lon:* -106.2719 I-10 Exit 34 merge onto Gateway Blvd W 2.1 miles then Zaragosa Rd S 1.3 miles
Ennis	◆ 1	🕐	℞	🚌	700 E Ennis Ave, 75119 / 972-875-9671 • *Lat:* 32.3311 *Lon:* -96.6207 I-45 Exit 251B go W on Ennis Ave .4 mile
Falfurrias	○		℞		2399 S US Hwy 281, 78355 / 361-325-3601 • *Lat:* 27.2105 *Lon:* -98.1431 1 mile south of town along US-281
Farmers Branch	○ 1		℞		13307 Midway Rd, 75244 / 972-980-2195 • *Lat:* 32.9262 *Lon:* -96.8393 I-635 Exit 23 take Midway Rd N .4 mile
Floresville	○		℞		534 10th St, 78114 / 830-393-4417 • *Lat:* 29.1532 *Lon:* -98.1657 Jct SH-97 & US-181 (NE of town) take US-181 N .8 mile
Forney	◆ 5	🕐	℞	🚌	802 E US Hwy 80, 75126 / 972-564-1867 • *Lat:* 32.7516 *Lon:* -96.4610 I-20 Exit 490 take FM-741 N 2.8 miles, FM-548 N 1.2 miles & US-80 W .9 mile
Fort Stockton	○ 2		℞		1700 W Dickinson Blvd, 79735 / 432-336-3389 • *Lat:* 30.8940 *Lon:* -102.8965 I-10 Exit 259B take SH-18 S 1 mile & I-10 BR W .7 mile
Fort Worth	■ 1		℞	🚌	2440 SE Loop 820, 76140 / 817-293-9225 • *Lat:* 32.6638 *Lon:* -97.2956 I-20 Exit 439 go S on Campus Dr .2 mile
	■ 1		℞	🚌	4400 Bryant Irvin Rd, 76132 / 817-989-1992 • *Lat:* 32.6873 *Lon:* -97.4136 I-20 Exit 431 go N on Bryant Irvin Rd .5 mile
	■ 1		℞	🚌	8351 Anderson Blvd, 76120 / 817-459-4581 • *Lat:* 32.7626 *Lon:* -97.1720 I-30 Exit 24 N on Eastchase .1 mile & W on Anderson Blvd .3 mile
	◆ 1	🕐	℞	🚌	9500 Clifford St, 76108 / 817-367-0042 • *Lat:* 32.7640 *Lon:* -97.4817 I-820 Exit 5A go W on Clifford St .4 mile
	◆ 2	🕐	℞	🚌	3851 Airport Fwy, 76111 / 817-759-2047 • *Lat:* 32.7740 *Lon:* -97.2911 I-30 Exit 16C go N on Beach St 1.8 miles then W at Airport Fwy .2 mile
	◇ 1	🕐	℞	🚌	8401 Anderson Blvd, 76120 / 817-276-9021 • *Lat:* 32.7626 *Lon:* -97.1713 I-30 Exit 24, north of exit
	◆ 3	🕐	℞	🚌	7451 McCart Ave, 76133 / 817-361-6032 • *Lat:* 32.6361 *Lon:* -97.3695 I-35W Exit 43 go W on Sycamore School Rd 2.8 miles then N at McCart Ave
	◆ 3	🕐	℞		8520 N Beach St, 76137 / 817-514-9793 • *Lat:* 32.8960 *Lon:* -97.2894 I-35W Exit 61 (northbound travelers) go E 1.6 miles on Tarrant Pkwy then N .2 mile on

○ Wal-Mart ◇ Supercenter □ Sam's Club ■ Gas ■ Gas & Diesel

City/Town	🛡	🕐	℞	🚗	Information
					Beach St. Southbound travelers use I-35W Exit 63 go W 1.6 miles on Heritage Trace Pkwy then S 1.3 miles on Beach St
	◇ 2	🕐	℞	🚗	6300 Oakmont Blvd, 76132 / 817-263-4065 • *Lat:* 32.6631 *Lon:* -97.4046 I-20 Exit 433 take Hulen St S 1.4 miles then W at Oakmont Blvd
Fredericksburg	◇	🕐	℞	🚗	1435 E Main St, 78624 / 830-997-2633 • *Lat:* 30.2576 *Lon:* -98.8524 Jct US-87 & US-290 (in town) go S on US-290 for 1.3 miles
Friendswood	■ 1		℞	🚗	155 W El Dorado Blvd, 77546 / 281-286-4471 • *Lat:* 29.5556 *Lon:* -95.1510 I-45 Exit 27 go W on El Dorado .2 mile
	◇ 1	🕐	℞	🚗	150 W El Dorado Blvd, 77546 / 281-480-6134 • *Lat:* 29.5552 *Lon:* -95.1509 I-45 Exit 27 take El Dorado Blvd W .2 mile
Frisco	◇	🕐	℞	🚗	12220 FM 423, 75034 / 469-362-8542 • *Lat:* 33.1795 *Lon:* -96.8872 From Dallas North Tollway at Eldorado Pkwy go W 2.8 miles on Eldorado Pkwy then N .1 mile on FM-423
Gainesville	◆ 2	🕐	℞	🚗	1800 Lawrence St, 76240 / 940-668-6898 • *Lat:* 33.6423 *Lon:* -97.1370 I-35 Exit 498A take US-82 E 1.1 miles
Galveston	◆ 2	🕐	℞	🚗	6702 Seawall Blvd, 77551 / 409-744-8677 • *Lat:* 29.2636 *Lon:* -94.8319 I-45 Exit 1A take 61st St S 1.6 miles then Seawall Blvd S .4 mile
Garland	■ 8		℞	🚗	5150 N Garland Ave, 75040 / 972-496-3956 • *Lat:* 32.9622 *Lon:* -96.6459 I-635 Exit 12 go NE on Garland Ave 7.3 miles
	◇	🕐	℞	🚗	5302 N Garland Ave, 75040 / 972-496-2711 • *Lat:* 32.9631 *Lon:* -96.6448 I-635 Exit 19A take US-75 N 7 miles, Bush Tpk (toll) E 4.3 miles & Garland Ave S .4 mile
	◇ 1	🕐	℞		3159 S Garland Ave, 75041 / 972-278-8077 • *Lat:* 32.8778 *Lon:* -96.6610 I-635 Exit 13 take SH-78 N .9 mile
	◇ 1	🕐	℞	🚗	555 W I-30, 75043 / 972-303-5865 • *Lat:* 32.8390 *Lon:* -96.5995 I-30W at Exit 59
Gatesville	◆	🕐	℞	🚗	2805 S TX Hwy 36, 76528 / 254-865-8991 • *Lat:* 31.4267 *Lon:* -97.7176 Jct US-84 & SH-36 (S of town) take SH-36 S 1.8 miles
Georgetown	◆ 1	🕐	℞	🚗	620 S I-35, 78626 / 512-863-4855 • *Lat:* 30.6454 *Lon:* -97.6896 I-35 Exit 261, west side of highway
Giddings	○		℞	🚗	2374 E Austin St, 78942 / 979-542-1375 • *Lat:* 30.1696 *Lon:* -96.9329 Jct US-77 & US-290 (in town) take US-290 E 1.4 miles
Gilmer	◇	🕐	℞		1923 N Wood St, 75644 / 903-797-6501 • *Lat:* 32.7571 *Lon:* -94.9402 Jct SH-155 & US-271 (in town) take US-271 N 1.7 miles
Gonzales	○ 10		℞	🚗	1620 E Sarah Dewitt Dr, 78629 / 830-672-7573 • *Lat:* 29.5207 *Lon:* -97.4349 I-10 Exit 642 take SH-304 S 7.6 miles, SH-97 S 2.1 miles & US-90-ALT E .1 mile
Graham	◆	🕐	℞	🚗	2121 Hwy 16 S, 76450 / 940-549-7714 • *Lat:* 33.0827 *Lon:* -98.5832 Jct SH-380 & SH-16 (N of town) go S on SH-16 for 2.2 miles
Granbury	◆	🕐	℞	🚗	735 E Hwy 377, 76048 / 817-573-3791 • *Lat:* 32.4342 *Lon:* -97.7807 Jct US-377 & SH-144 (in town) go E on US-377 for .8 mile
Grand Prairie	□ 1		℞	🚗	2325 W I-20, 75052 / 972-660-3405 • *Lat:* 32.6764 *Lon:* -97.0376 I-20 Exit 456 go S on Carrier Pkwy & E on Westchester Dr .7 mile
	◇ 1	🕐	℞	🚗	2225 W I-20, 75052 / 972-660-4200 • *Lat:* 32.6754 *Lon:* -97.0371 I-20 Exit 454, south of exit on I-20 service road
Grapevine	■ 7		℞	🚗	1701 W State Hwy 114, 76051 / 817-416-5434 • *Lat:* 32.9295 *Lon:* -97.0950 I-635 Exit 36 take SH-114 W 6.1 miles
	◇ 6	🕐	℞	🚗	1601 W TX Hwy 114, 76051 / 817-421-4770 • *Lat:* 32.9295 *Lon:* -97.0950 I-635 Exit 36A take SH-121 S 1.4 miles, SH-114 W 4 miles, exit at Southlake Blvd W .1 mile & E at SH-114 for .2 mile

○ Wal-Mart ◇ Supercenter □ Sam's Club ■ Gas ■ Gas & Diesel

City/Town	🛡	⏰	℞	🚐	Information
Greenville	◇ 1	⏰	℞	🚐	7401 I-30, 75402 / 903-455-1792 • *Lat:* 33.0932 *Lon:* -96.1083 I-35 Exit 93A, south of exit
Gun Barrel City	◆	⏰	℞	🚐	1200 W Main St, 75156 / 903-887-4180 • *Lat:* 32.3310 *Lon:* -96.1339 Jct US-175 & FM-85 (E of town) take FM-85 W 5.4 miles
Hallettsville	○		℞		1506 N Texana St, 77964 / 361-798-4377 • *Lat:* 29.4588 *Lon:* -96.9397 Jct US-90A & US-77 (in town) take US-77 N 1 mile
Harker Heights	◆	⏰	℞	🚐	2020 Heights Dr, 76548 / 254-699-1021 • *Lat:* 31.0697 *Lon:* -97.6738 From Central Texas Expy/US-190 at FM-2410 go S .2 mile, turn right at Triangle Rd 318 feet then Commercial Dr W .2 mile
Harlingen	◆	⏰	℞	🚐	1801 W Lincoln St, 78552 / 956-428-0734 • *Lat:* 26.1816 *Lon:* -97.7171 Jct US-83 & US-77 (W of town) go S on US-77/83 for .4 mile & Lincoln St W .1 mile
Hempstead	○		℞		625 Hwy 290 E, 77445 / 979-826-3344 • *Lat:* 30.0962 *Lon:* -96.0654 Jct US-290 & SH-6 (N of town) take US-290 S .5 mile
Henderson	◆	⏰	℞	🚐	2121 US Hwy 79 S, 75654 / 903-657-5707 • *Lat:* 32.1325 *Lon:* -94.8035 Jct US-259 & US-79 (S of town) take US-79 SW 1 mile
Hereford	◆	⏰	℞	🚐	300 W 15th St, 79045 / 806-364-5712 • *Lat:* 34.8368 *Lon:* -102.4083 Jct US-60 & US-385 (in town) take US-385 N 1.8 miles then W on 15th St .2 mile
Hickory Creek	◆ 1	⏰	℞	🚐	1035 Hickory Creek Blvd, 75065 / 940-321-5363 • *Lat:* 33.1152 *Lon:* -97.0305 I-35E Exit 457B take Swisher Rd W .3 mile & Hickory Creek Blvd S .1 mile
Highland Village	◇ 4	⏰	℞		3060 Justin Rd, 75077 / 972-317-4951 • *Lat:* 33.0738 *Lon:* -97.0754 I-35E Exit 454A take Justin Rd/FM-407 W 3.2 miles
Hillsboro	◆ 1	⏰	℞	🚐	401 Coke Ave, 76645 / 254-582-2523 • *Lat:* 32.0071 *Lon:* -97.0985 I-35 Exit 368A take SH-171/22 W .3 mile & S at Coke Ave
Hondo	◇	⏰	℞	🚐	109 22nd St, 78861 / 830-426-4356 • *Lat:* 29.3440 *Lon:* -99.1312 Jct US-90 & SH-173 (E of town) take US-90 W .9 mile then S on Ave D .3 mile
Houston	■ 1		℞	🚐	1025 Hwy 6 N, 77079 / 281-578-9884 • *Lat:* 29.7857 *Lon:* -95.6451 I-10 Exit 751 at SH-6
	■ 1		℞	🚐	10488 Old Katy Rd, 77043 / 713-468-5146 • *Lat:* 29.7851 *Lon:* -95.5589 I-10 Exit 756 go N on Sam Houston Tollway .1 mile & E on Old Katy Rd .3 mile
	■ 1		℞	🚐	11101 Fuqua St, 77089 / 713-941-8484 • *Lat:* 29.6130 *Lon:* -95.2214 I-45 Exit 33 take Fuqua St W .5 mile
	■		℞	🚐	12205 West Rd, 77065 / 281-955-2071 • *Lat:* 29.9030 *Lon:* -95.5960 I-10 Exit 763 N on I-610 for 1.6 miles then US-290 NW 11.5 miles & E at West Rd .2 mile
	■ 1		℞	🚐	13600 East Fwy, 77015 / 713-450-2592 • *Lat:* 29.7783 *Lon:* -95.1819 I-10 Exit 780 at Market St
	■ 1		℞	🚐	1615 South Loop W, 77054 / 713-796-8599 • *Lat:* 29.6785 *Lon:* -95.4024 I-610 Exit 1B at Fannin St
	■ 4		℞	🚐	2827 Dunvale Rd, 77063 / 713-780-3494 • *Lat:* 29.7356 *Lon:* -95.5140 I-610 Exit 88 take FM-1093 W 3.4 miles then S at Dunvale Rd .1 mile
	☐ 1		℞	🚐	325 E Richey Rd, 77073 / 281-821-8777 • *Lat:* 29.9984 *Lon:* -95.4197 I-45 Exit 64 go E on Richey Rd .5 mile
	■ 1		℞	🚐	5310 S Rice Ave, 77081 / 832-778-9736 • *Lat:* 29.7242 *Lon:* -95.4683 I-610 Exit 8 go W on Westpark Dr .5 mile & S at Rice Ave
	☐ 9		℞	🚐	7950 FM 1960 Rd W, 77070 / 832-237-8269 • *Lat:* 29.9618 *Lon:* -95.5461 I-45 Exit 66 take FM-1960 SW 8.1 miles
	○ 1		℞	🚐	13750 I-10 E, 77015 / 713-453-5018 • *Lat:* 29.7702 *Lon:* -95.1778 I-10 Exit 780 (westbound travelers), south of exit; eastbound travelers use I-10 Exit 780 and follow the frontage road E for 1 mile

○ Wal-Mart ◇ Supercenter ☐ Sam's Club ■ Gas ■ Gas & Diesel

City/Town	⬡	🕐	℞	🚗	Information
	○ 1		℞		9555 S Post Oak Rd, 77096 / 713-551-9148 • *Lat:* 29.6766 *Lon:* -95.4587 I-610 Exit 4A take Post Oak Rd S .4 mile
	○ 1		℞	🚗	10750 Westview Dr, 77043 / 713-984-2773 • *Lat:* 29.7910 *Lon:* -95.5649 I-10 Exit 756A take Houston Pkwy N .4 mile then Westview Dr W .1 mile
	◇ 1	🕐	℞	🚗	10411 North Fwy #45, 77037 / 281-999-9920 • *Lat:* 29.9182 *Lon:* -95.4137 I-45 Exit 59 (southbound travelers) follow frontage road S .6 mile; northbound travelers use Exit 60A
	◆ 8	🕐	℞	🚗	9460 W Sam Houston Pkwy S, 77099 / 281-568-3710 • *Lat:* 29.6767 *Lon:* -95.5607 I-10 Exit 756B take Houston Pkwy (toll) S 7.3 miles & Beltway S .6 mile
	◆ 3	🕐	℞	🚗	5655 E Sam Houston Pkwy N, 77015 / 713-450-2222 • *Lat:* 29.8049 *Lon:* -95.1632 I-10 Exit 781B take Houston Pkwy N 2.4 miles then Beltway N .3 mile
	◇ 5	🕐	℞	🚗	13484 Northwest Fwy, 77040 / 713-690-0666 • *Lat:* 29.8525 *Lon:* -95.5108 I-610 Exit 13B take US-290 NW 4.5 miles, exit at Tidwell & continue on NW Fwy .5 mile
	◇ 5	🕐	℞	🚗	2727 Dunvale Rd, 77063 / 713-977-2099 • *Lat:* 29.7370 *Lon:* -95.5140 I-10 Exit 760 take Bingle Rd/Voss Rd S 3.4 miles then Westheimer Rd W .8 mile
	◆	🕐	℞	🚗	12353 FM 1960 Rd W, 77065 / 832-912-7320 • *Lat:* 29.9229 *Lon:* -95.6023 I-10 Exit 756B take Houston Tollway N 6.4 miles, US-29 NW 4.9 miles & FM-1960 E .9 mile
	◆ 4	🕐	℞	🚗	3450 FM 1960 Rd W, 77068 / 281-440-4482 • *Lat:* 29.9974 *Lon:* -95.4816 I-45 Exit 66 take FM-1960 W 3.8 miles then Walters Rd N .2 mile
	◆ 8	🕐		🚗	7075 FM 1960 Rd W, 77069 / 281-893-1707 • *Lat:* 29.9676 *Lon:* -95.5349 I-45 Exit 66 take FM-1960 W 7.5 miles
	◆ 1	🕐	℞	🚗	9598 Rowlett Rd, 77075 / 832-386-0103 • *Lat:* 29.6314 *Lon:* -95.2344 I-45 Exit 34 take Gulf Fwy S .4 mile then Rowlett Rd S .1 mile
	◇ 3	🕐	℞	🚗	2700 S Kirkwood Rd, 77077 / 281-558-5670 • *Lat:* 29.7360 *Lon:* -95.5889 I-10 Exit 754 take Kirkwood Rd S 2.7 miles
	◆ 5	🕐	℞	🚗	3506 Hwy 6 S, 77082 / 281-561-0866 • *Lat:* 29.7197 *Lon:* -95.6444 I-10 Exit 753A take SH-6 S 4.3 miles
	◆ 7	🕐	℞	🚗	15955 FM 529 Rd, 77095 / 281-855-1604 • *Lat:* 29.8790 *Lon:* -95.6503 I-10 Exit 753A take SH-6 N 6.5 miles then FM-529 W .3 mile
Hudson Oaks	◆ 2	🕐	℞	🚗	2801 E I-20, 76087 / 817-599-7490 • *Lat:* 32.7558 *Lon:* -97.7099 I-20 Exit 413 (eastbound travelers) go N .1 mile on Lakeshore Dr then W .8 mile on I-20 Service Rd; westbound travelers use Exit 414 and continue W .8 mile on US-180/Fort Worth Hwy, S .1 mile on Lakeshore Dr then W .8 mile on I-20 Service Rd
Humble	■ 10		℞	🚗	9665 FM 1960 Bypass Rd W, 77338 / 281-548-1211 • *Lat:* 30.0051 *Lon:* -95.2771 I-45 Exit 66 take FM-1960 E 9.4 miles
	◆ 10	🕐	℞	🚗	9235 N Sam Houston Pkwy E, 77396 / 281-441-2209 • *Lat:* 29.9351 *Lon:* -95.2507 I-45 Exit 60B (northbound use Exit 60D) go E 10 miles on Sam Houston Pkwy
	◇ 10	🕐	℞	🚗	9451 FM 1960 Bypass Rd W, 77338 / 281-540-8838 • *Lat:* 30.0051 *Lon:* -95.2811 I-45 Exit 66 take FM-1960 E 7.3 miles, continue on FM-1960A BR E 1.9 miles
	◆	🕐	℞	🚗	6626 FM 1960 Rd E, 77346 / 281-852-4648 • *Lat:* 29.9984 *Lon:* -95.1760 I-45 Exit 66 take FM-1960 E 10.7 miles
Huntsville	◆ 2	🕐	℞	🚗	141 I-45 S, 77340 / 936-293-1066 • *Lat:* 30.7159 *Lon:* -95.5690 I-45 Exit 118 go S on I-45 Service Rd/US-190 for 1.7 miles
Hurst	◆ 3	🕐	℞	🚗	1732 Precinct Line Rd, 76054 / 817-503-7152 • *Lat:* 32.8454 *Lon:* -97.1860 I-820 Exit 22B take SH-121/183 E 1.8 miles then Precinct Line Rd N .5 mile
Irving	■ 1		℞	🚗	1213 Market Pl, 75063 / 972-401-0143 • *Lat:* 32.9182 *Lon:* -96.9614 I-635 Exit 31 N on Stanton Dr .1 mile & E on Market Pl

○ Wal-Mart   ◇ Supercenter   □ Sam's Club   ■ Gas   ■ Gas & Diesel

City/Town	🛡	🕐	℞	🚌	Information
	◇ 1	🕐	℞	🚌	1635 Market Pl, 75063 / 214-574-4517 • *Lat:* 32.9193 *Lon:* -96.9678 I-635 Exit 31 take Olympus Blvd N .5 mile & Market Pl E .4 mile
	◇ 7	🕐	℞	🚌	4100 W Airport Fwy, 75062 / 972-313-0707 • *Lat:* 32.8364 *Lon:* -97.0076 I-635 Exit 29A follow Bush Tpk & SH-161 S 6 miles then Airport Fwy E .8 mile
Jacksonville	◆	🕐	℞	🚌	1311 S Jackson St, 75766 / 903-589-3434 • *Lat:* 31.9522 *Lon:* -95.2641 Jct US-79 & US-69 (in town) take US-69 S .9 mile
Jasper	◆	🕐	℞	🚌	800 W Gibson St, 75951 / 409-384-1707 • *Lat:* 30.9064 *Lon:* -94.0140 Jct US-96 & US-190 (in town) go W on US-190 for 1.2 miles
Katy	■ 1		℞	🚌	20424 Katy Fwy, 77449 / 281-578-7846 • *Lat:* 29.7858 *Lon:* -95.7268 I-10 at Exit 747 N of the freeway
	◇ 1	🕐	℞	🚌	1313 N Fry Rd, 77449 / 281-579-3373 • *Lat:* 29.7875 *Lon:* -95.7192 I-10 Exit 747A take Fry Rd N .2 mile
	◆ 1	🕐	℞	🚌	25108 Market Place Dr, 77494 / 281-644-6404 • *Lat:* 29.7823 *Lon:* -95.8021 I-10 Exit 741 take US-90 W .1 mile, cross over to I-10 Service Rd E .3 mile then Katy Fort Bend Rd S .2 mile
Kemah	◆ 7	🕐	℞	🚌	255 FM 518 Rd, 77565 / 281-538-9778 • *Lat:* 29.5371 *Lon:* -95.0194 I-45 Exit 22 take Calder Dr N 1.1 miles then follow FM-518 E 5.8 miles
Kenedy	◇	🕐	℞		200 Business Park Blvd, 78119 / 830-583-9825 • *Lat:* 28.8304 *Lon:* -97.8634 1 mile northwest of town along US-181
Kerrville	◇ 3	🕐	℞	🚌	1216 Junction Hwy, 78028 / 830-895-7900 • *Lat:* 30.0611 *Lon:* -99.1682 I-10 Exit 505 take FM-783 S 2.8 miles then W on SH-27 .2 mile
Kilgore	◆ 4	🕐	℞	🚌	1201 Stone St, 75662 / 903-983-1494 • *Lat:* 32.3921 *Lon:* -94.8665 I-20 Exit 587 take SH-42 S 2.9 miles & E on Stone St .2 mile
Killeen	◇	🕐	℞	🚌	1400 Lowes Blvd, 76542 / 254-526-4102 • *Lat:* 31.0903 *Lon:* -97.7239 I-35 Exit 293A take US-190 W 17 miles, exit S at Trimmel Rd to US-190 E .3 mile & S at Wal-Mart Blvd .1 mile
Kingsville	◆	🕐	℞	🚌	1133 E General Cavazos Blvd, 78363 / 361-595-4146 • *Lat:* 27.4960 *Lon:* -97.8422 Jct SH-425 & US-77 (S of town) take US-77 S .6 mile then W on Cavazos Blvd .5 mile
La Grange	○		℞		2125 W Travis St, 78945 / 979-968-8426 • *Lat:* 29.9038 *Lon:* -96.9087 2 miles west of town center via Travis St (SH-71-BR)
La Marque	◆ 1	🕐	℞	🚌	6410 I-45, 77568 / 409-986-6000 • *Lat:* 29.4025 *Lon:* -95.0352 I-45 Exit 15, west of exit
La Porte	◆	🕐	℞	🚌	9025 Spencer Hwy, 77571 / 281-479-9636 • *Lat:* 29.6643 *Lon:* -95.0977 I-10 Exit 781B follow Houston Pkwy S 7.2 miles then E on Spencer Hwy 3.5 miles
Lake Jackson	◆	🕐	℞	🚌	121 Hwy 332 W, 77566 / 979-297-9757 • *Lat:* 29.0480 *Lon:* -95.4600 Jct FM-2004 & SH-288 (NW of town) take FM-2004 S .8 mile, Lake Rd S .3 mile & SH-332 E .2 mile
Lake Worth	◇ 2	🕐	℞	🚌	6360 Lake Worth Blvd, 76135 / 817-237-0400 • *Lat:* 32.8106 *Lon:* -97.4257 I-820 Exit 10A take SH-199 W 1.6 miles
Lamesa	○				2406 Lubbock Hwy, 79331 / 806-872-9576 • *Lat:* 32.7549 *Lon:* -101.9490 Jct US-180 & US-87 (in town) take US-87 N 1 mile
Lampasas	◆	🕐	℞		1710 Central Texas Expy, 76550 / 512-556-8217 • *Lat:* 31.0638 *Lon:* -98.1615 Jct US-183 & US-190 (S of town) go E on US-190 for 1.2 miles
Lancaster	◆ 1	🕐	℞	🚌	150 N Beckley St, 75146 / 972-223-9791 • *Lat:* 32.5914 *Lon:* -96.8218 I-35E Exit 414 merge onto Beckley Ave N .7 mile
Laredo	■ 1			🚌	4810 San Bernardo Ave, 78041 / 956-725-5300 • *Lat:* 27.5437 *Lon:* -99.5045 I-35 Exit 3A W on Calton Rd & S on San Bernardo

City/Town	⬮	⬭	🕙	℞	🚌	Information
	○	1		℞	🚌	5610 San Bernardo Ave, 78041 / 956-718-2441 • *Lat:* 27.5490 *Lon:* -99.5045 I-35 Exit 3B merge onto San Bernardo Ave S .4 mile
	◆	4	🕙	℞	🚌	2320 Bob Bullock Loop, 78043 / 956-791-3303 • *Lat:* 27.5207 *Lon:* -99.4476 I-35 Exit 2 take US-59 E 3.5 miles & Bullock Loop S .5 mile
	◇		🕙	℞	🚌	4401 S Zapata Hwy, 78046 / 956-727-0492 • *Lat:* 27.4535 *Lon:* -99.4773 5.7 miles southeast of town center via US-83
League City	◆	1	🕙	℞	🚌	1701 W FM 646 Rd, 77573 / 281-337-9700 • *Lat:* 29.4685 *Lon:* -95.0870 I-45 Exit 20 take FM-646 SW 1 mile
Levelland	◆		🕙	℞	🚌	407 E State Rd 114, 79336 / 806-894-2993 • *Lat:* 33.5941 *Lon:* -102.3625 Jct US-385 & SH-114 (N of town) take SH-114 E .3 mile
Lewisville	▪	1		℞	🚌	751 W Main St, 75067 / 972-436-6684 • *Lat:* 33.0462 *Lon:* -97.0114 I-35E Exit 452 W on Main St .2 mile
	◇	2	🕙	℞	🚌	4691 TX Hwy 121, 75056 / 972-625-6000 • *Lat:* 33.0651 *Lon:* -96.8893 I-35E Exit 448A take SH-121 W 1.1 miles
	◇	1	🕙	℞	🚌	801 W Main St, 75067 / 972-436-3099 • *Lat:* 33.0457 *Lon:* -97.0125 I-35E Exit 452 take FM-1171 W .2 mile
	◆	2	🕙	℞	🚌	190 E Round Grove Rd, 75067 / 972-315-3398 • *Lat:* 33.0034 *Lon:* -96.9897 I-35E Exit 448B take FM-3040 W 1.4 miles
Liberty	◆		🕙	℞	🚌	2121 Hwy 146 Byp, 77575 / 936-336-5601 • *Lat:* 30.0776 *Lon:* -94.7735 From town center go E 1.5 miles on US-90/SH-146 then N 1.3 miles on SH-146
Lindale	◆	1	🕙	℞	🚌	105 Centennial Blvd, 75771 / 903-882-0740 • *Lat:* 32.5182 *Lon:* -95.4379 I-20 Exit 556 take US-69 N .5 mile
Livingston	◇		🕙	℞	🚌	1620 W Church St, 77351 / 936-327-6370 • *Lat:* 30.7112 *Lon:* -94.9509 Jct US-59 & US-190 (W of town) take US-190 W .2 mile
Lockhart	○			℞	🚌	1703 S Colorado St, 78644 / 512-398-2333 • *Lat:* 29.8648 *Lon:* -97.6687 1.5 miles south of town center on US-183
Longview	▪	8			🚌	3310 N 4th St, 75605 / 903-663-5588 • *Lat:* 32.5414 *Lon:* -94.7306 I-20 Exit 599 take SH-281 N 7.4 miles then N on 4th St
	◆	10	🕙	℞	🚌	2440 Gilmer Rd, 75604 / 903-297-1121 • *Lat:* 32.5328 *Lon:* -94.7888 I-20 Exit 589B take SH-31 NE 4.5 miles, SH-281 Loop N 4.7 miles then SH-300 N .7 mile
	◇	8	🕙	℞	🚌	515 E Loop 281, 75605 / 903-663-4446 • *Lat:* 32.5408 *Lon:* -94.7304 I-20 Exit 599 take SH-281 Loop NW 7.4 miles
	◆	1	🕙	℞	🚌	4006 Estes Pkwy, 75603 / 903-236-0947 • *Lat:* 32.4333 *Lon:* -94.7166 I-20 Exit 595A take SH-322 S .8 mile
Lubbock	▪	7		℞	🚌	4303 W Loop 289, 79407 / 806-793-7182 • *Lat:* 33.5572 *Lon:* -101.9405 I-27 Exit 1A take SH-289 W 5.9 miles, Franford Ave Exit .1 mile then S on 289 Loop
	◆	1	🕙	℞	🚌	1911 4th St, 79415 / 806-747-3454 • *Lat:* 33.5901 *Lon:* -101.8565 I-27 Exit 4 go W 1 mile on 4th St (US-82)
	◇	6	🕙	℞	🚌	702 W Loop 289, 79416 / 806-793-9686 • *Lat:* 33.5896 *Lon:* -101.9352 I-27 Exit 6B take SH-289 Loop W 4.5 miles, merge onto Service Rd W 1.1 miles
	◆	3	🕙	℞	🚌	4215 S Loop 289, 79423 / 806-793-2091 • *Lat:* 33.5295 *Lon:* -101.9039 I-27 Exit 1A take SH-289 Loop W 2.6 miles
	◆	3	🕙	℞	🚌	6315 82nd St, 79424 / 806-698-6394 • *Lat:* 33.5197 *Lon:* -101.9530 I-27 Exit 1 continue on US-87 S .8 mile then 82nd St W 1.7 miles
Lufkin	☐					407 Brentwood Dr, 75901 / 936-639-1700 • *Lat:* 31.2919 *Lon:* -94.7314 From US-59 (north of town) take Loop 287 S for 6.1 miles, FM-58 S 2.4 miles & Brentwood Dr W .1 mile

○ Wal-Mart ◇ Supercenter ☐ Sam's Club ▪ Gas ■ Gas & Diesel

City/Town	⬟	🕐	℞	🚗	Information
	◆		🕐	℞ 🚗	2500 Daniel McCall Dr, 75904 / 936-639-9600 • *Lat:* 31.2978 *Lon:* -94.7287 Jct SH-287 Loop & US-59 (S of town) continue S on US-59 for .4 mile then McCall Dr W .2 mile
Lumberton	◆		🕐	℞ 🚗	100 N LHS Dr, 77657 / 409-755-1963 • *Lat:* 30.2559 *Lon:* -94.2170 I-10 Exit 853A follow US-69 N 12.1 miles
Madisonville	○	1		℞	1620 E Main St, 77864 / 936-348-3715 • *Lat:* 30.9574 *Lon:* -95.8955 I-45 Exit 142 take US-190 W .9 mile
Mansfield	◆	8	🕐	℞ 🚗	930 N Walnut Creek Dr, 76063 / 817-473-1189 • *Lat:* 32.5786 *Lon:* -97.1324 I-20 Exit 444 take US-287 S 7.9 miles & S at Walnut Creek Dr .1 mile
Marble Falls	◆		🕐	℞ 🚗	2700 N Hwy 281, 78654 / 830-693-4461 • *Lat:* 30.5986 *Lon:* -98.2699 Jct SH-71 & US-281 (S of town) take US-281 N 6.7 miles
Marlin	○			℞ 🚗	600 N State Hwy 6, 76661 / 254-883-5556 • *Lat:* 31.3050 *Lon:* -96.8754 1.5 miles east of town center at SH-6/SH-7 jct
Marshall	◆	5	🕐	℞ 🚗	1701 E End Blvd N, 75670 / 903-938-0072 • *Lat:* 32.5570 *Lon:* -94.3502 I-20 Exit 617 follow US-59 N 4.8 miles
McAllen	■			℞ 🚗	1400 E Jackson Ave, 78503 / 956-618-3363 • *Lat:* 26.1907 *Lon:* -98.2067 Jct US-281 & US-83 (east of town) go SW on US-83 for 1.8 miles, E on Jackson .3 mile
	◆		🕐	℞ 🚗	2800 Nolana Ave, 78504 / 956-687-8285 • *Lat:* 26.2393 *Lon:* -98.2233 Jct US-83 & US-281 (in town) take US-281 N 2 miles & SH-3461/Nolana Blvd W 3.5 miles
	◇		🕐	℞ 🚗	1200 E Jackson Ave, 78503 / 956-686-4311 • *Lat:* 26.1910 *Lon:* -98.2087 Jct US-281 & US-83 (in town) take US-83 W 2 miles then E at Jackson Ave .1 mile
McKinney	■			℞ 🚗	1670 W University Dr, 75069 / 469-952-2417 • *Lat:* 33.2167 *Lon:* -96.6307 From George Bush Tpk & US-75 take US-75 N 15.8 miles then US-380 E .3 mile
	◇		🕐	℞ 🚗	2041 N Redbud Blvd, 75069 / 972-542-9585 • *Lat:* 33.2212 *Lon:* -96.6281 From US-75 Exit 41 (N of town) go E at Bray Dr .4 mile & S at Rosebud Blvd .1 mile
	◆		🕐	℞ 🚗	5001 McKinney Ranch Pkwy, 75070 / 972-529-5046 • *Lat:* 33.1589 *Lon:* -96.6809 From US-75 Exit 38A (in town) take SH-121 SW 2.4 miles, Lake Forest Dr N 1 mile & McKinney Pkwy W .2 mile
	◆		🕐	℞ 🚗	1721 N Custer Rd, 75071 / 972-548-7270 • *Lat:* 33.2170 *Lon:* -96.7335 From US-75 Exit 41 take US-380 W 5.6 miles
Mesquite	◆	2	🕐	℞ 🚗	200 US Hwy 80 E, 75149 / 972-329-0191 • *Lat:* 32.7879 *Lon:* -96.5835 I-635 Exit 6B merge onto US-80 E 2 miles
Mexia	◆		🕐	℞ 🚗	1406 E Milam St, 76667 / 254-562-3831 • *Lat:* 31.6856 *Lon:* -96.4574 I-45 Exit 219A take SH-14 S 16.1 miles, CR-243 SE 1.8 miles then US-84 E 1 mile
Midland	□	4		🚗	1500 Tradewinds Blvd, 79706 / 432-699-5933 • *Lat:* 31.9942 *Lon:* -102.1570 I-20 Exit 131 take SH-158 N 2.4 miles then Thomason Dr W .3 mile & Tradewinds Blvd N .7 mile
	◆	1	🕐	℞ 🚗	200 W I-20, 79701 / 432-684-3910 • *Lat:* 31.9755 *Lon:* -102.0727 I-20 Exit 136, north of exit
	◆	7	🕐	℞ 🚗	4517 N Midland Dr, 79707 / 432-697-0871 • *Lat:* 32.0303 *Lon:* -102.1462 I-20 Exit 131 take SH-250 Loop NE 6.1 miles, Northcrest Dr N .3 mile, Briarwood E .2 mile & Midland Dr S .1 mile
Midlothian	◇		🕐	℞ 🚗	400 N Hwy 67, 76065 / 972-775-6755 • *Lat:* 32.4856 *Lon:* -97.0087 I-20 Exit 464B take US-67 S 14.6 miles
Mineola	◆		🕐	℞ 🚗	135 NE Loop 564, 75773 / 903-569-0180 • *Lat:* 32.6879 *Lon:* -95.4815 Jct US-80 & FM-564 Loop NE 2.5 miles
Mineral Wells	◆		🕐	℞ 🚗	601 FM 1821, 76067 / 940-325-7808 • *Lat:* 32.8131 *Lon:* -98.0831 I-20 Exit 386 take US-281 N 14.3 miles, US-180 E 1.8 miles & FM-1821 N .2 mile

○ Wal-Mart ◇ Supercenter □ Sam's Club ▨ Gas ■ Gas & Diesel

City/Town	⬤	🕐	℞	🚐	Information
Mission	◆		🕐	℞	🚐	2410 E Expressway 83, 78572 / 956-580-3393 • *Lat:* 26.1951 *Lon:* -98.2829 Jct SH-107 & US-83 (in town) take US-83 E 2.6 miles
Missouri City	◇		🕐	℞	🚐	5501 Hwy 6, 77459 / 281-403-5000 • *Lat:* 29.5742 *Lon:* -95.5733 Jct US-59 & SH-6 (W of town) go E on SH-6 for 3.4 miles
Montgomery	◆		🕐	℞	🚐	18700 Hwy 105 W, 77356 / 936-582-1551 • *Lat:* 30.2823 *Lon:* -95.3227 I-45 Exit 88 take SH-336 Loop W 1.3 miles & SH-105 W 10.2 miles
Mount Pleasant	◆ 4		🕐	℞	🚐	2311 S Jefferson Ave, 75455 / 903-572-0018 • *Lat:* 33.1342 *Lon:* -94.9679 I-30 Exit 160 follow US-271 S 3.4 miles
Nacogdoches	◇		🕐	℞	🚐	4810 North St, 75965 / 936-560-6969 • *Lat:* 31.6501 *Lon:* -94.6553 Jct US-59 & US-259 (N of town) take US-59 BR S 2.5 miles
Navasota	◯			℞		1712 E Washington Ave, 77868 / 936-825-7541 • *Lat:* 30.3966 *Lon:* -96.0717 Jct FM-3455 & SH-90 (E of town) go W on SH-90 for 1.5 miles
New Boston	◆ 1		🕐	℞	🚐	800 James Bowie Dr, 75570 / 903-628-5557 • *Lat:* 33.4728 *Lon:* -94.4062 I-30 Exit 201 take SH-8 S .1 mile & Bowie Dr E .2 mile
New Braunfels	◆ 1		🕐	℞	🚐	1209 S I-35, 78130 / 830-629-0129 • *Lat:* 29.6850 *Lon:* -98.1275 I-35 at Exit 186 on E Service Rd
North Richland Hills	◆ 7		🕐	℞	🚐	9101 N Tarrant Pkwy, 76180 / 817-605-1717 • *Lat:* 32.9041 *Lon:* -97.1887 I-820 Exit 22B take SH-121 N 1.8 miles, Precinct Line Rd N 4.5 miles & Tarrant Pkwy W .1 mile
	◇ 1		🕐	℞	🚐	6401 NE Loop 820, 76180 / 817-577-2100 • *Lat:* 32.8407 *Lon:* -97.2485 I-820 Exit 20B merge onto NE Loop 820 Service Rd .5 mile
Odessa	◼ 4				🚐	4230 John Ben Shepperd Pkwy, 79762 / 432-550-9191 • *Lat:* 31.8947 *Lon:* -102.3342 I-20 Exit 121 take SH-338 N 2.3 miles then SH-191 W .9 mile & N on Shepperd Pkwy
	◇ 4		🕐	℞	🚐	4210 John Ben Shepperd Pkwy, 79762 / 432-363-9663 • *Lat:* 31.8945 *Lon:* -102.3341 I-20 Exit 121 take Loop 338 N 2.3 miles then SH-191 W .9 mile
	◆ 3		🕐	℞	🚐	2450 NW Loop 338, 79763 / 432-332-6016 • *Lat:* 31.8556 *Lon:* -102.4120 I-20 Exit 113 take SH-338 Loop N 3 miles
Orange	◆ 4		🕐	℞	🚐	3115 Edgar Brown Dr, 77630 / 409-883-5244 • *Lat:* 30.0935 *Lon:* -93.7659 I-10 Exit 877 follow SH-87 S 3.2 miles
Palestine	◆		🕐	℞	🚐	2223 S Loop 256, 75801 / 903-729-4441 • *Lat:* 31.7343 *Lon:* -95.6149 Jct US-84 & SH-256 Loop (W of town) go E on SH-256 Loop 2.6 miles
Palmhurst	◆		🕐	℞	🚐	215 E Mile 3 Rd, 78573 / 956-519-8453 • *Lat:* 26.2584 *Lon:* -98.3181 Jct US-281 & US-83 go W on US-83 for 5.3 miles, Ware Rd N 3.8 miles & 3 Mile Rd W 1.3 miles
Pampa	◆		🕐	℞	🚐	2801 Charles St, 79065 / 806-665-0727 • *Lat:* 35.5605 *Lon:* -100.9664 Jct SH-171 Loop & SH-70 (N of town) go S on SH-70 for 1.2 miles
Paris	◆		🕐	℞	🚐	3855 Lamar Ave, 75462 / 903-785-7168 • *Lat:* 33.6620 *Lon:* -95.5066 Jct US-82 & SH-286 Loop (E of town) continue E on US-82/Lamar Ave .2 mile
Pasadena	◆ 9		🕐	℞	🚐	5200 Fairmont Pkwy, 77505 / 281-998-1077 • *Lat:* 29.6495 *Lon:* -95.1627 I-10 Exit 781A take SH-8/Houston Pkwy S 8.4 miles, then Fairmont Pkwy W .3 mile
	◇ 9		🕐	℞		1107 Shaver St, 77506 / 713-534-6660 • *Lat:* 29.6942 *Lon:* -95.2112 I-10 Exit 781A take SH-8 S 4 miles, SH-225 W 3.4 miles & Shaver St S 1.2 miles
Pearland	◆ 7		🕐	℞	🚐	1919 N Main St, 77581 / 281-485-0877 • *Lat:* 29.5736 *Lon:* -95.2861 I-45 Exit 32 take Houston Tollway W 4.4 miles then SH-35 S 1.9 miles
	◆ 5		🕐	℞	🚐	1710 Broadway St, 77581 / 281-482-5016 • *Lat:* 29.5479 *Lon:* -95.2347 I-45 Exit 31 take Dixie Farm Rd W 3.9 miles & Broadway St W .2 mile
	◇		🕐	℞	🚐	10505 Broadway St, 77584 / 713-436-2899 • *Lat:* 29.5560 *Lon:* -95.3888 I-45 Exit 32 take Houston Tollway W 9 miles, FM-865 S 2.8 miles & FM-518 W 2.1 miles

◯ Wal-Mart   ◇ Supercenter   ☐ Sam's Club   ◼ Gas   ◼ Gas & Diesel

City/Town	⬭	🕐	℞	🚌	Information
Pearsall	◯ 4		℞		819 N Oak St, 78061 / 830-334-9451 • *Lat:* 28.9001 *Lon:* -99.0929 I-35 Exit 104 take I-35 BR S 3.1 miles
Pecos	◯ 1		℞		1903 S Cedar St, 79772 / 432-445-4231 • *Lat:* 31.4089 *Lon:* -103.4866 I-20 Exit 42 take US-285 W .7 mile
Pflugerville	◇ 6	🕐	℞	🚌	1548 FM 685, 78660 / 512-252-0112 • *Lat:* 30.4529 *Lon:* -97.6038 I-35 Exit 247 follow FM-1825 E 3.7 miles then FM-685 N 1.3 miles
Plainview	◆ 1	🕐	℞	🚌	1501 N I-27, 79072 / 806-293-4278 • *Lat:* 34.1961 *Lon:* -101.7504 I-27 Exit 49 take the W Service Rd N 1 mile
Plano	▪		℞	🚌	1200 E Spring Creek Pkwy, 75074 / 972-516-8520 • *Lat:* 33.0568 *Lon:* -96.6887 I-635 Exit 19A take US-75 N 11.2 miles then E at Exit 31 for Spring Pkwy .3 mile
	▪ 9		℞	🚌	301 Coit Rd, 75075 / 972-612-8041 • *Lat:* 33.0014 *Lon:* -96.7681 I-635 Exit 19A take US-75 N for 6.3 miles, Exit 28B to Bush Tpk W 2.3 miles, N on Coit Rd .2 mile
	▪		℞	🚌	8621 Ohio Dr, 75024 / 469-633-0026 • *Lat:* 33.0947 *Lon:* -96.7971 I-35E Exit 448 take SH-121 NE 12.4 miles then Ohio Dr S .4 mile
	◇	🕐	℞	🚌	6001 N Central Expy, 75023 / 972-422-3000 • *Lat:* 33.0567 *Lon:* -96.6950 I-635 Exit 19A take US-75 N 10.4 miles
	◇	🕐	℞		6000 Coit Rd, 75023 / 972-612-9637 • *Lat:* 33.0556 *Lon:* -96.7702 From US-75 Exit 28B take Bush Tpk (toll) W 2.3 miles then Coit Rd N 3.9 miles
	◇	🕐	℞	🚌	8801 Ohio Dr, 75024 / 972-731-9576 • *Lat:* 33.0972 *Lon:* -96.7971 I-35E Exit 448A take SH-121 NE 12.4 miles then Ohio Dr S .2 mile
	◇	🕐	℞	🚌	425 Coit Rd, 75075 / 972-599-1650 • *Lat:* 33.0035 *Lon:* -96.7681 From US-75 Exit 28B take Bush Tpk (toll) W 2.3 miles then Coit Rd N .7 mile
	◇ 8	🕐	℞	🚌	1700 Dallas Pkwy, 75093 / 972-931-9846 • *Lat:* 33.0267 *Lon:* -96.8290 I-635 Exit 22C take Dallas Tollway N 7.4 miles
Pleasanton	◆ 8	🕐	℞	🚌	2151 W Oaklawn Rd, 78064 / 830-569-3879 • *Lat:* 28.9399 *Lon:* -98.5130 I-37 Exit 103 take US-281 N 5.1 miles then SH-97 W 2.2 miles
Port Arthur	◆	🕐	℞	🚌	8585 Memorial Blvd, 77640 / 409-727-4667 • *Lat:* 29.9436 *Lon:* -93.9914 I-10 Exit 849 follow US-287 S 12.7 miles
	◆	🕐	℞	🚌	4999 N Twin City Hwy, 77642 / 409-962-7858 • *Lat:* 29.9404 *Lon:* -93.9395 I-10 Exit 849 take US-287 S 5.5 miles then SH-347 E 9.1 miles
Port Isabel	◇	🕐	℞	🚌	1401 Hwy 100, 78578 / 956-943-1387 • *Lat:* 26.0715 *Lon:* -97.2220 1 mile west of town center via SH-100
Port Lavaca	◆	🕐	℞	🚌	400 Tiney Browning Blvd, 77979 / 361-552-4116 • *Lat:* 28.6333 *Lon:* -96.6268 From town center go N .9 mile on FM-1090/Virginia St then E .8 mile on SH-35
Porter	◇	🕐	℞	🚌	23561 Hwy 59, 77365 / 281-354-3400 • *Lat:* 30.0741 *Lon:* -95.2458 Jct FM-1960 & US-59 (S of town) take US-59 N 6.2 miles
Portland	◆	🕐	℞	🚌	2000 Hwy 181, 78374 / 361-643-5342 • *Lat:* 27.8895 *Lon:* -97.3129 Jct FM-2986 & US-181 (in town) go N on US-181 .4 mile
Quinlan	◆	🕐	℞	🚌	8801 Hwy 34 S, 75474 / 903-356-1000 • *Lat:* 32.9070 *Lon:* -96.1057 I-30 Exit 85 take FM-36 S 8.7 miles then SH-276 W 2.6 miles
Raymondville	◆	🕐	℞	🚌	14091 FM 490, 78580 / 956-689-6571 • *Lat:* 26.4522 *Lon:* -97.7793 Jct SH-186 & US-77 (in town) take US-77 S 2.2 miles
Richland Hills	▪ 1		℞	🚌	6375 NE Loop 820, 76180 / 817-428-3700 • *Lat:* 32.8407 *Lon:* -97.2494 I-820 Exit 20 on N side of Loop
Richmond	◆	🕐	℞	🚌	5330 FM 1640 Rd, 77469 / 281-232-8396 • *Lat:* 29.5582 *Lon:* -95.7652 Jct US-59 & FM-762 (E of town) take FM-762 NW 1.3 miles & FM-1640 W .3 mile

◯ Wal-Mart   ◇ Supercenter   ☐ Sam's Club   ▪ Gas   ■ Gas & Diesel

City/Town	🛡	🕐	℞	🚗	Information
Rio Grande City	◇		🕐	℞	🚗	4534 E Hwy 83, 78582 / 956-487-0090 • *Lat:* 26.3672 *Lon:* -98.7941 On US-83/2nd St E of town
Roanoke	◆ 3		🕐	℞	🚗	1228 N Hwy 377, 76262 / 682-831-9338 • *Lat:* 33.0128 *Lon:* -97.2205 I-35W Exit 74 take FM-1171 E 2.6 miles then US-377 S .2 mile
Rockdale	◆		🕐	℞		709 W US Hwy 79, 76567 / 512-446-5851 • *Lat:* 30.6567 *Lon:* -97.0000 Jct US-77 & US-79 (E of town) take US-79 E .5 mile
Rockport	◆		🕐	℞	🚗	2401 Hwy 35 N, 78382 / 361-729-9277 • *Lat:* 28.0472 *Lon:* -97.0427 Jct FM-3036 & SH-35 BR (NE of town) take SH-35 BR S 1 mile
Rockwall	◆ 1		🕐	℞	🚗	782 E I-30, 75087 / 972-771-8309 • *Lat:* 32.9001 *Lon:* -96.4615 I-30 Exit 68 take the Service Rd/US-67 S 1 mile
Round Rock	☐ 1			℞	🚗	130 Sundance Pkwy Ste 300, 78681 / 512-828-0534 • *Lat:* 30.4825 *Lon:* -97.6910 I-35 Exit 251 go W at Hester's Crossing .9 mile & S on Sundance
	◆ 5		🕐	℞	🚗	4700 E Palm Valley Blvd, 78664 / 512-218-1018 • *Lat:* 30.5321 *Lon:* -97.6142 I-35 Exit 253 take Palm Valley Blvd W 4.6 miles, continue on US-79 E .3 mile
	◇ 1		🕐	℞	🚗	2701 S I-35, 78664 / 512-310-9024 • *Lat:* 30.4825 *Lon:* -97.6721 I-35 Exit 250 (northbound travelers) follow I-35 Service Rd N 1 mile; southbound travelers use Exit 250B or Exit 251
Rowlett	◆ 6		🕐	℞	🚗	2501 Lakeview Pkwy, 75088 / 214-607-9839 • *Lat:* 32.9080 *Lon:* -96.5785 I-30 Exit 60A take Rosehill Rd N .7 mile, Rowlett Rd NE 3.9 miles & SH-66 W .5 mile
Saginaw	◆ 5		🕐	℞	🚗	1401 N Saginaw Blvd, 76179 / 817-306-1468 • *Lat:* 32.8875 *Lon:* -97.3879 I-820 Exit 13 take US-287 BR N 4.5 miles
San Angelo	▪			℞	🚗	5749 Sherwood Way, 76901 / 325-223-9373 • *Lat:* 31.4280 *Lon:* -100.5120 5 miles southwest of town via US-67
	◆		🕐	℞	🚗	610 W 29th St, 76903 / 325-655-4949 • *Lat:* 31.4858 *Lon:* -100.4607 1.6 miles north of town center off US-87 at 29th St
	◆		🕐	℞	🚗	5501 Sherwood Way, 76904 / 325-949-9201 • *Lat:* 31.4282 *Lon:* -100.5116 Jct SH-306 Loop & US-67 (SW of town) take US-67 S .5 mile
San Antonio	▪ 1			℞	🚗	12349 N I-35, 78233 / 210-646-8188 • *Lat:* 29.5524 *Lon:* -98.3564 I-35 Exit 170 (northbound travelers use I-35 Exit 170A), west of highway
	☐ 4			℞	🚗	12919 San Pedro Ave, 78216 / 210-496-9924 • *Lat:* 29.5602 *Lon:* -98.4844 I-410 Exit 21 take US-281 N 2.5 miles, W on Bitters Rd .1 mile then S on San Pedro .9 mile
	▪ 2			℞	🚗	3150 SW Military Dr, 78224 / 210-927-3593 • *Lat:* 29.3572 *Lon:* -98.5489 I-35 Exit 150 go W on SH-13/Military Dr 1.4 miles
	▪ 1			℞	🚗	5055 NW Loop 410, 78229 / 210-680-9425 • *Lat:* 29.4876 *Lon:* -98.5873 I-410 near Exit 14 on the N side of the Loop
	▪ 1			℞	🚗	5565 De Zavala Rd, 78249 / 210-641-4810 • *Lat:* 29.5632 *Lon:* -98.5940 I-10 Exit 558 go W on De Zavala .2 mile
	○ 1			℞	🚗	5025 NW Loop 410, 78229 / 210-523-1091 • *Lat:* 29.4878 *Lon:* -98.5865 I-410 Exit 14A take Service Rd W .6 mile
	◇ 5		🕐	℞	🚗	11210 Potranco Rd, 78253 / 210-679-7184 • *Lat:* 29.4352 *Lon:* -98.7135 I-410 Exit 9 take SH-151 W 1.4 miles then Potranco Rd W 3.1 miles
	◇ 10		🕐	℞	🚗	1515 N Loop 1604 E, 78258 / 210-491-0291 • *Lat:* 29.6105 *Lon:* -98.4718 I-35 Exit 72 follow SH-1604-LOOP W for 9.7 miles
	◆ 2		🕐	℞	🚗	1430 Austin Hwy, 78209 / 210-637-1700 • *Lat:* 29.4919 *Lon:* -98.4373 I-410 Exit 24 take Wurzbach Rd S 1.6 miles & Austin Hwy W .2 mile
	◆ 3		🕐	℞	🚗	1603 Vance Jackson Rd, 78213 / 210-738-8218 • *Lat:* 29.4884 *Lon:* -98.5352 I-10 Exit 565B follow Vance Jackson Rd N 2 miles

○ Wal-Mart   ◇ Supercenter   ☐ Sam's Club   ▪ Gas   ■ Gas & Diesel

City/Town	🛡	🕐	℞	🚐	Information
	◆ 4	🕐	℞		1200 SE Military Dr, 78214 / 210-921-0800 • *Lat:* 29.3548 *Lon:* -98.4795 I-35 Exit 135 take SH-13 W 3.7 miles
	◆ 2	🕐	℞		8500 Jones Maltsberger Rd, 78216 / 210-377-1899 • *Lat:* 29.5156 *Lon:* -98.4831 I-410 Exit 20 take 410 Service Rd E 1.1 miles then Jones Maltsberger Rd S .3 mile
	◆ 1	🕐	℞	🚐	2100 SE Loop 410, 78220 / 210-648-7194 • *Lat:* 29.4009 *Lon:* -98.3886 I-410 Exit 35 take Service Rd N .3 mile
	◇ 1	🕐	℞	🚐	3302 SE Military Dr, 78223 / 210-337-1946 • *Lat:* 29.3516 *Lon:* -98.4330 I-37 Exit 135 take SH-13 W .3 mile
	◆ 1	🕐	℞	🚐	8923 W Military Dr, 78245 / 210-675-5092 • *Lat:* 29.4481 *Lon:* -98.6463 I-410 Exit 9A go W on Military Dr .7 mile
	◆ 3	🕐	℞	🚐	16503 Nacogdoches Rd, 78247 / 210-646-6077 • *Lat:* 29.5903 *Lon:* -98.3553 I-35 Exit 172 take SH-1604 Loop W 2.5 miles then FM-2252 W .3 mile
	◇ 1	🕐	℞	🚐	5555 De Zavala Rd, 78249 / 210-558-2007 • *Lat:* 29.5632 *Lon:* -98.5939 I-10 Exit 558 merge N onto McDermott Fwy .5 mile then E on DeZavala Rd .3 mile
	◆ 4	🕐	℞	🚐	8030 Bandera Rd, 78250 / 210-520-6517 • *Lat:* 29.5161 *Lon:* -98.6330 I-410 Exit 13A take Bandera Rd/SH-16 N 3.1 miles
	◆ 9	🕐	℞	🚐	6703 Leslie Rd, 78254 / 210-688-3626 • *Lat:* 29.5004 *Lon:* -98.7023 I-10 Exit 556A follow SH-1604 (Charles Anderson Loop) W 9 miles
San Benito	◆	🕐	℞	🚐	1126 W Hwy 77, 78586 / 956-399-1373 • *Lat:* 26.1316 *Lon:* -97.6182 From US-77 take SH-486 E 1 mile then US-77 BR S .8 mile
San Marcos	■ 1		℞	🚐	1350 Leah Ave, 78666 / 512-392-1963 • *Lat:* 29.8544 *Lon:* -97.9501 I-35 Exit 202 on E side of I-35 at FM 3407 (Wonder World Dr)
	◇ 1	🕐	℞	🚐	1015 Hwy 80, 78666 / 512-353-0617 • *Lat:* 29.8821 *Lon:* -97.9166 I-35 Exit 205 take SH-80 E .3 mile
Schertz	◆ 1	🕐	℞	🚐	6102 FM 3009, 78154 / 210-651-8217 • *Lat:* 29.6045 *Lon:* -98.2794 I-35 Exit 175 take FM-3009 W .3 mile
Seagoville	◆ 7	🕐	℞	🚐	220 N Hwy 175, 75159 / 972-287-3917 • *Lat:* 32.6478 *Lon:* -96.5349 I-20 Exit 479B take US-175 S 6.7 miles
Sealy	◆ 1	🕐	℞	🚐	310 Overcreek Way, 77474 / 979-627-7758 • *Lat:* 29.7590 *Lon:* -96.1502 I-10 Exit 720, go S .4 mile on SH-36
Seguin	◆ 3	🕐	℞	🚐	550 S Hwy 123 Byp, 78155 / 830-372-5993 • *Lat:* 29.5644 *Lon:* -97.9418 I-10 Exit 610 take SH-123 S 2.6 miles
Seminole	○		℞		2000 Hobbs Hwy, 79360 / 432-758-9225 • *Lat:* 32.7234 *Lon:* -102.6658 1.3 miles west of town center along US-62/US-180
Sherman	■		℞	🚐	3333 N US Hwy 75, 75090 / 903-813-0444 • *Lat:* 33.6733 *Lon:* -96.6065 North of town at US-75/US-82 jct
	◆	🕐	℞	🚐	401 E US Hwy 82, 75090 / 903-813-4825 • *Lat:* 33.6407 *Lon:* -96.6055 From US-75 Exit 63 (N of town) take US-82 W .3 mile
Silsbee	◆	🕐	℞	🚐	1100 Hwy 96 S, 77656 / 409-385-0782 • *Lat:* 30.3340 *Lon:* -94.1545 Jct US-96 & US-96 BR (S of town) take US-96 BR N 1.7 miles
Snyder	○		℞		4515 College Ave, 79549 / 325-573-1967 • *Lat:* 32.6967 *Lon:* -100.9194 Jct SH-1605/37th St & SH-350 (S of town) take SH-350/College Ave S .6 mile
Spring	◇ 1	🕐	℞	🚐	155 Louetta Crossing, 77373 / 281-651-9963 • *Lat:* 30.0645 *Lon:* -95.3955 I-45 Exit 68 take Louetta Rd E .4 mile, Whitewood Dr S .3 mile & Louetta Crossing W .1 mile
	◆ 5	🕐	℞	🚐	21150 Kuykendahl Rd, 77379 / 281-288-6437 • *Lat:* 30.0772 *Lon:* -95.5165 I-45 Exit 70 take FM-2920 W 4.7 miles & Kuykendahl Rd N .3 mile

○ Wal-Mart ◇ Supercenter □ Sam's Club ■ Gas ■ Gas & Diesel

City/Town	🛡	🕐	℞	🚗	Information
	♦ 10	🕐	℞	🚗	10001 Woodlands Pkwy, 77382 / 281-419-0162 • *Lat:* 30.1815 *Lon:* -95.5390 I-45 Exit 76B take Woodlands Pkwy W 9.9 miles
	◇ 1	🕐	℞	🚗	1025 Sawdust Rd, 77380 / 281-298-4306 • *Lat:* 30.1265 *Lon:* -95.4575 I-45 Exit 73 take Sawdust Rd W 1 mile
Stafford	■ 10		℞	🚗	12300 Southwest Fwy, 77477 / 281-295-2500 • *Lat:* 29.6432 *Lon:* -95.5780 I-610 Exit 8A take US-59 SW 9.1 miles, exit toward Kirkwood Rd .3 mile then Southwest Fwy .3 mile
	◇ 10	🕐	℞	🚗	11210 W Airport Blvd, 77477 / 281-933-7800 • *Lat:* 29.6420 *Lon:* -95.5725 I-610 Exit 8A take US-59 S 8.7 miles then Wilcrest Dr/FM-1092 S .8 mile & Airport Blvd W .5 mile
Stamford	○		℞		1608 N Swenson St, 79553 / 325-773-2775 • *Lat:* 32.9617 *Lon:* -99.8027 Jct SH-283 & US-277 BR (N of town) take US-277 BR S .2 mile
Stephenville	◇	🕐	℞	🚗	2765 W Washington St, 76401 / 254-965-7766 • *Lat:* 32.2049 *Lon:* -98.2367 Jct SH-108 & S Loop US-87 (S of town) go W on US-87 for 2.6 miles
Sugar Land	■		℞	🚗	351 Hwy 6, 77478 / 281-295-2525 • *Lat:* 29.6122 *Lon:* -95.6449 I-610 Exit 8A take US-59 SW for 13.1 miles then SH-6 W for 1.6 miles
	◇	🕐	℞	🚗	345 Hwy 6, 77478 / 281-340-0900 • *Lat:* 29.6101 *Lon:* -95.6442 I-610 Exit 8A take US-59/SW Fwy S 13.6 miles then SH-6 S 1.5 miles
Sulphur Springs	♦ 1	🕐	℞	🚗	1750 S Broadway St, 75482 / 903-439-3144 • *Lat:* 33.1059 *Lon:* -95.5969 I-30 Exit 124 take SH-154 S .8 mile
Sweetwater	♦ 1	🕐	℞		407 NE Georgia Ave, 79556 / 325-236-9562 • *Lat:* 32.4537 *Lon:* -100.3911 I-20 Exit 246 merge onto Service Rd W 1 mile
Taylor	♦	🕐	℞	🚗	3701 N Main St, 76574 / 512-352-5505 • *Lat:* 30.6000 *Lon:* -97.4164 Jct SH-29 & SH-95 (N of town) take SH-95 S 3.5 miles
Temple	■ 3			🚗	1414 Marlandwood Rd, 76502 / 254-774-8402 • *Lat:* 31.0650 *Lon:* -97.3716 I-35 Exit 299 take US-190 E 2.1 miles, S on Lowes Dr .7 mile & E at Marlandwood Rd
	◇ 2	🕐	℞	🚗	3401 S 31st St, 76502 / 254-778-9235 • *Lat:* 31.0678 *Lon:* -97.3699 I-35 Exit 299 take US-190 E 1.6 miles then FM-1741 S .3 mile
Terrell	♦ 2	🕐	℞	🚗	1900 W Moore Ave, 75160 / 972-563-7638 • *Lat:* 32.7373 *Lon:* -96.3065 I-20 Exit 499A take FM-148 N 1.5 miles then Moore Ave W .2 mile
Texarkana	■ 1			🚗	3610 Saint Michael Dr, 75503 / 903-838-4338 • *Lat:* 33.4579 *Lon:* -94.0860 I-30 Exit 220 NW on FM-559 .1 mile then E on St. Michael Dr .1 mile
	♦ 1	🕐	℞	🚗	4000 New Boston Rd, 75501 / 903-838-4007 • *Lat:* 33.4436 *Lon:* -94.1004 I-30 Exit 220A take US-59 S .7 mile, Bishop Rd S & New Boston Rd W .1 mile
Texas City	■ 1		℞	🚗	9300 Emmett F Lowry Expy, 77591 / 409-986-9100 • *Lat:* 29.4005 *Lon:* -95.0144 I-45 Exit 16 take FM-1764 E 1 mile
The Woodlands	♦ 1	🕐	℞	🚗	3040 College Park Dr, 77384 / 936-321-9922 • *Lat:* 30.2075 *Lon:* -95.4587 I-45 Exit 79 take College Pk Dr W .2 mile
Tomball	♦	🕐	℞	🚗	27650 Tomball Pkwy, 77375 / 281-351-2616 • *Lat:* 30.0754 *Lon:* -95.6276 From town center go W 1.1 miles on Main St then S 1 mile on SH-249 (Tomball Pkwy)
	♦	🕐	℞	🚗	22605 Tomball Pkwy, 77375 / 281-374-9449 • *Lat:* 30.0146 *Lon:* -95.5922 From town center go W 1.1 miles on Main St then S 5.7 miles on SH-249 (Tomball Pkwy)
Tyler	■		℞	🚗	2025 S Southwest Loop 323, 75701 / 903-597-2296 • *Lat:* 32.3277 *Lon:* -95.3414 I-20 Exit 556 take US-69 SE 6.9 miles then Loop 323 S 4.1 miles
	◇	🕐	℞	🚗	6801 S Broadway Ave, 75703 / 903-581-4296 • *Lat:* 32.2754 *Lon:* -95.3068 Jct SH-49 & US-69 (S of town) take US-69 N 2.6 miles
	♦	🕐	℞	🚗	3820 TX Hwy 64 W, 75704 / 903-597-2888 • *Lat:* 32.3533 *Lon:* -95.3440 Jct FM-2661 & SH-64 (W of town) go E on SH-64 for 1.1 miles

○ Wal-Mart ◇ Supercenter □ Sam's Club ■ Gas ■ Gas & Diesel

City/Town	⬟	🕐	Rx	🚌	Information
	◆	🕐	Rx	🚌	5050 Troup Hwy, 75707 / 903-534-1333 • *Lat:* 32.2965 *Lon:* -95.2625 Jct SH-64 & SW Loop 323 (W of town) go E on Loop 323 for 7.3 miles & S on SH-110 for 1.3 miles
Uvalde	◆	🕐	Rx	🚌	3100 E Main St, 78801 / 830-278-9117 • *Lat:* 29.2259 *Lon:* -99.7602 Jct US-83 & US-90 (in town) take US-90 E 2.2 miles
Vernon	◆	🕐	Rx	🚌	3800 US Hwy 287 W, 76384 / 940-552-8029 • *Lat:* 34.1376 *Lon:* -99.3163 Jct US-283/183 & US-287/70 (N of town) go W on N Frontage Rd 1.2 miles
Victoria	◼			🚌	9202 N Navarro St, 77904 / 361-572-0043 • *Lat:* 28.8803 *Lon:* -96.9962 5 miles north of town via US-77
	◇	🕐	Rx	🚌	9002 N Navarro St, 77904 / 361-573-0041 • *Lat:* 28.8778 *Lon:* -96.9969 Jct SH-463 & US-77 (N of town) go N on US-77 1 mile
Vidor	◯ 1		Rx	🚌	1350 N Main St, 77662 / 409-769-6233 • *Lat:* 30.1435 *Lon:* -94.0160 I-10 Exit 861A take FM-105 N .8 mile
Waco	◼ 1			🚌	2301 E Waco Dr, 76705 / 254-799-2408 • *Lat:* 31.5850 *Lon:* -97.1075 I-35 Exit 338 take US-84 E .1 mile
	◇ 3	🕐	Rx	🚌	4320 Franklin Ave, 76710 / 254-751-0464 • *Lat:* 31.5227 *Lon:* -97.1685 I-35 Exit 331 take New Rd W 2.1 miles then Franklin Ave N .1 mile
Waxahachie	◆ 5	🕐	Rx	🚌	1200 N Hwy 77, 75165 / 972-937-3460 • *Lat:* 32.4167 *Lon:* -96.8408 I-35 Exit 397 merge onto US-77 N for 4.6 miles
Weatherford	◆ 1	🕐	Rx	🚌	1836 S Main St, 76086 / 817-594-9193 • *Lat:* 32.7363 *Lon:* -97.7962 I-20 Exit 408 take SH-171 N .5 mile
Weslaco	◆	🕐	Rx	🚌	1310 N Texas Blvd, 78596 / 956-968-6357 • *Lat:* 26.1713 *Lon:* -97.9907 Jct US-83 & SH-88 go S on SH-88/Texas Blvd .1 mile
West Columbia	◯		Rx		301 N Columbia Dr, 77486 / 979-345-3147 • *Lat:* 29.1495 *Lon:* -95.6592 Jct FM-1301 & SH-36 (W of town) go N on SH-36 for .2 mile
Westworth Village	◼ 3		Rx	🚌	6760 Westworth Blvd, 76114 / 817-763-9621 • *Lat:* 32.7594 *Lon:* -97.4236 I-30 Exit 7B go NE on SH-183 for 2.9 miles
	◇ 3	🕐	Rx	🚌	6770 Westworth Blvd, 76114 / 817-570-9538 • *Lat:* 32.7594 *Lon:* -97.4236 I-30 Exit 7B follow SH-183 N 2.2 miles
Wharton	◆	🕐	Rx	🚌	10388 US 59 Road, 77488 / 979-532-3986 • *Lat:* 29.3274 *Lon:* -96.1228 1.5 miles west of town at US-59/SH-102 jct
Wichita Falls	◼			🚌	3801 Kell Blvd, 76308 / 940-691-0632 • *Lat:* 33.8793 *Lon:* -98.5436 4 miles southwest of town center via US-82
	◆ 1	🕐	Rx	🚌	2700 Central Fwy, 76306 / 940-851-0629 • *Lat:* 33.9510 *Lon:* -98.5265 I-44 Exit 3C merge onto Central Fwy S .2 mile
	◇ 6	🕐	Rx	🚌	3130 Lawrence Rd, 76308 / 940-692-0771 • *Lat:* 33.8773 *Lon:* -98.5401 I-44 Exit 3C take US-287 S 1.8 miles & follow US-82 W 2.8 miles then Lawrence Rd N .7 mile
	◆	🕐	Rx	🚌	5131 Greenbriar Rd, 76302 / 940-397-9650 • *Lat:* 33.8541 *Lon:* -98.4998 South of town center about .5 mile west of US-281 via SH-369
Woodville	◇	🕐	Rx	🚌	115 Cobb Mill Rd, 75979 / 409-283-8248 • *Lat:* 30.7664 *Lon:* -94.4271 Jct US-190 & S Beech St (in town) take S Beech St .6 mile then Cobb Rd E .2 mile
Woodway	◆ 4	🕐	Rx	🚌	600 Hewitt Dr, 76712 / 254-666-9021 • *Lat:* 31.4925 *Lon:* -97.2151 I-35 Exit 328 take Sun Valley Dr W 1.7 miles & Hewitt Dr NW 2.1 miles
Wylie	◆	🕐	Rx	🚌	2050 N Hwy 78, 75098 / 972-429-3526 • *Lat:* 33.0229 *Lon:* -96.5148 Jct CR-434 & SH-78 (N of town) go W on SH-78 for 1.5 miles

◯ Wal-Mart ◇ Supercenter ◻ Sam's Club ◼ Gas ◼ Gas & Diesel

Utah

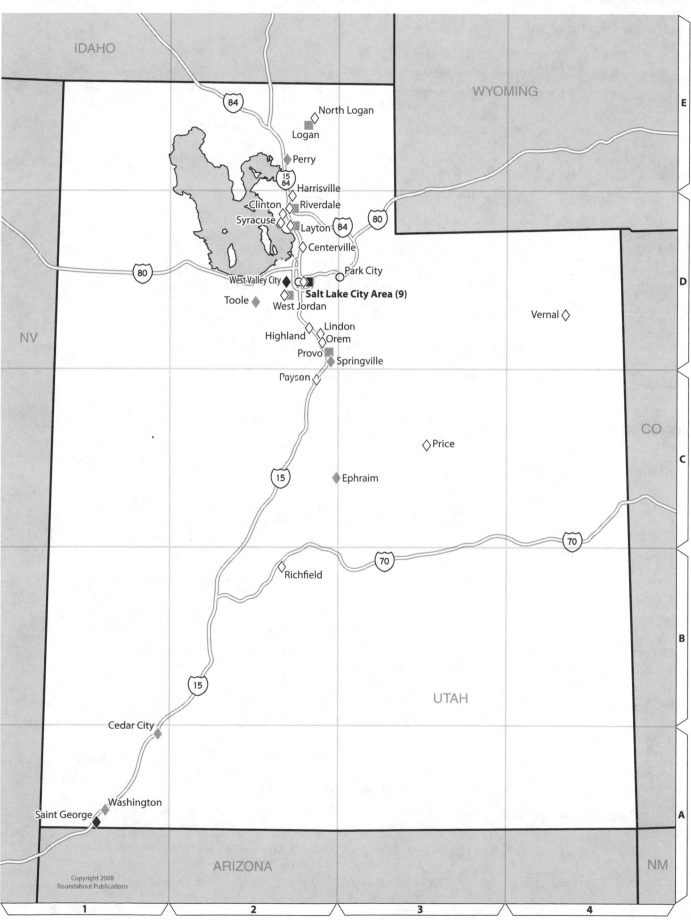

○ Wal-Mart ◇ Supercenter ☐ Sam's Club ▨ Gas ■ Gas & Diesel

IDAHO

WYOMING

North Logan

Logan

Perry

15
84

Harrisville

Clinton
Riverdale

Syracuse

Layton
84

80

Centerville

Park City

West Valley City

Salt Lake City Area (9)

Toole

West Jordan

Vernal

Lindon

Highland
Orem

Provo
Springville

Payson

Price

NV

80

84

15

Ephraim

CO

15

70

70

Richfield

UTAH

15

Cedar City

Washington

Saint George

ARIZONA

NM

Copyright 2008
Roundabout Publications

E

D

C

B

A

1   2   3   4

Salt Lake City Area

Midvale	○	Salt Lake City (4)	◇ ■	South Jordan	◇
Murray	■	Sandy	◇	Taylorsville	◇

City/Town	🛡		🕐	℞	🚗	Information
Cedar City	◆	1	🕐	℞	🚗	1330 S Providence Center Dr, 84720 / 435-586-0172 • *Lat:* 37.6543 *Lon:* -113.0854 I-15 Exit 57 go W on Sage Way .1 mile & S at Providence Center Dr
Centerville	◇	1	🕐	℞	🚗	221 W Parrish Ln, 84014 / 801-294-0587 • *Lat:* 40.9214 *Lon:* -111.8835 I-15 Exit 319 go E on Parrish Ln .4 mile
Clinton	◇	3	🕐	℞	🚗	1632 N 2000 W, 84015 / 801-779-3165 • *Lat:* 41.1375 *Lon:* -112.0643 I-15 Exit 335 take SH-126 N .2 mile, W800N W 2 miles & Two Mile Rd N .8 mile
Ephraim	◆		🕐	℞		777 N Main St, 84627 / 435-283-8189 • *Lat:* 39.3726 *Lon:* -111.5872 Jct SH-132 & US-89 (N of town) take US-89 S for 3.8 miles
Harrisville	◇	4	🕐	℞	🚗	534 N Harrisville Rd, 84404 / 801-737-0092 • *Lat:* 41.2684 *Lon:* -111.9753 I-15 Exit 344 take W1200S E 1.9 miles, Wall Ave N 1.6 miles, North Rd E .2 mile & Harrisville Rd N .1 mile
Highland	◇	1	🕐	℞	🚗	949 W Grassland Dr, 84003 / 801-492-1102 • *Lat:* 40.3866 *Lon:* -111.8236 I-15 Exit 279 take SH-73 E .4 mile, US-89 S .2 mile
Layton	■	1		℞	🚗	1055 W Hill Field Rd, 84041 / 801-546-5206 • *Lat:* 41.0718 *Lon:* -111.9845 I-15 Exit 331 go W on SH-232 for .5 mile
	◇	1	🕐	℞	🚗	745 W Hill Field Rd, 84041 / 801-546-1992 • *Lat:* 41.0730 *Lon:* -111.9780 I-15 Exit 331 take SH-232 W .1 mile
Lindon	◇	3	🕐	℞	🚗	585 N State St, 84042 / 801-785-7683 • *Lat:* 40.3484 *Lon:* -111.7279 I-15 Exit 273 take W1600N E 1.1 miles & US-89 N 1.8 miles
Logan	■			℞	🚗	145 W Cache Valley Blvd, 84341 / 435-787-0063 • *Lat:* 41.7544 *Lon:* -111.8306 1.3 miles north of town center along US-91
Midvale	○	1		℞	🚗	7250 Union Park Ave, 84047 / 801-255-0224 • *Lat:* 40.6196 *Lon:* -111.8569 I-215 Exit 9 merge onto Union Park Ave S 1 mile
Murray	■	1		℞	🚗	6525 S State St, 84107 / 801-262-6444 • *Lat:* 40.6304 *Lon:* -111.8895 I-215 Exit 11 go S on US-89 for .1 mile
North Logan	◇		🕐	℞	🚗	1550 N Main St, 84341 / 435-753-0880 • *Lat:* 41.7604 *Lon:* -111.8341 Jct SH-30 & US-91 (S of town) go N on US-91 for 4.4 miles, E on SH-237 for .7 mile & N on Main St .3 mile
Orem	◇	1	🕐	℞	🚗	1355 Sandhill Rd, 84058 / 801-221-0600 • *Lat:* 40.2723 *Lon:* -111.7117 I-15 Exit 269 take SH-265 E .3 mile & Sandhilol Rd S .2 mile
Park City	○	1		℞		6545 Landmark Dr, 84098 / 435-647-9909 • *Lat:* 40.7268 *Lon:* -111.5474 I-80 Exit 145 take SH-224 S .2 mile & Landmark Dr NW .2 mile
Payson	◇	1	🕐	℞	🚗	1052 Turf Farm Rd, 84651 / 801-465-8246 • *Lat:* 40.0272 *Lon:* -111.7547 I-15 Exit 248 take W800S E .2 mile & Turf Farm Rd S .3 mile
Perry	◆	2	🕐	℞	🚗	1200 S Commerce Way, 84302 / 435-734-9660 • *Lat:* 41.4853 *Lon:* -112.0285 I-15 Exit 362 merge onto US-91 E 1.3 miles & S at Commerce Way
Price	◇		🕐	℞	🚗	255 S Hwy 55, 84501 / 435-637-6712 • *Lat:* 39.5953 *Lon:* -110.7906 Jct SH-10 & US-6/191 (S of town) take US-6/191 E 1.1 miles & US-6 BR N .8 mile
Provo	■	1		℞	🚗	1313 S University Ave, 84601 / 801-374-9700 • *Lat:* 40.2162 *Lon:* -111.6588 I-15 Exit 263 take US-189 N .5 mile

○ Wal-Mart ◇ Supercenter □ Sam's Club ■ Gas ■ Gas & Diesel

City/Town	🛡	🕐	℞	🚗	Information
Richfield	◇	4	🕐	℞ 🚗	10 E 1300 S, 84701 / 435-893-8164 • Lat: 38.7864 Lon: -112.0468 I-70 Exit 40 take I-70 BR S 1.2 miles, SH-119 E .8 mile & SH-118 NE 1.4 miles
Riverdale	■	1		℞ 🚗	4949 S 900 W, 84405 / 801-612-3465 • Lat: 41.1738 Lon: -112.0003 I-84 Exit 81 take SH-26 NE .4 mile then S on 900W .3 mile
	◇	1	🕐	℞ 🚗	4848 S 900 W, 84405 / 801-627-0066 • Lat: 41.1758 Lon: -112.0007 I-84 Exit 81 go E .5 mile on SH-26 (Riverdale Rd) then S .1 mile on S900W Rd
Saint George	◆	1	🕐	℞ 🚗	2610 Pioneer Rd, 84790 / 435-674-0459 • Lat: 37.0537 Lon: -113.5888 I-15 Exit 4 go W .3 mile then S on Pioneer Rd .5 mile
Salt Lake City	■	2		℞ 🚗	1905 S 300 W, 84115 / 801-478-2400 • Lat: 40.7289 Lon: -111.8995 I-15/I-80 Exit 305 go E on 1300S .3 mile then S on 300W .9 mile
	◇	1	🕐	℞	350 Hope Ave, 84115 / 801-484-7311 • Lat: 40.7390 Lon: -111.9012 I-15 Exit 305C go E on W1300S .1 mile & S on S400W .2 mile
	◇	3	🕐	℞	4627 S 900 E, 84117 / 801-261-3695 • Lat: 40.6701 Lon: -111.8652 I-15 Exit 301 take SH-266 E 1.9 miles & S900E S .3 mile
	◇	6	🕐	℞ 🚗	5675 W 6200 S, 84118 / 801-965-0125 • Lat: 40.6385 Lon: -112.0263 I-215 Exit 13 take SH-68 S .6 mile then W6200S W 4.6 miles
Sandy	◇	2	🕐	℞ 🚗	9151 S Quarry Blvd, 84094 / 801-352-4200 • Lat: 40.5863 Lon: -111.8620 I-15 Exit 295 take SH-209 E 2 miles
South Jordan	◇	2	🕐	℞ 🚗	11328 S Jordan Gateway, 84095 / 801-553-2200 • Lat: 40.5457 Lon: 111.8985 I-15 Exit 293 take SH-151 W .2 mile then Jordan Gateway S 1.1 miles
Springville	◆	1	🕐	℞ 🚗	660 S 1750 W, 84663 / 801-489-6293 • Lat: 40.1569 Lon: -111.6422 I-15 Exit 260 take SH-77 E .4 mile & S1750W S .3 mile
Syracuse	◇	5	🕐	℞ 🚗	2228 W 1700 S, 84075 / 801-775-9688 • Lat: 41.0893 Lon: -112.0692 I-15 Exit 332 follow SH-108 W 3.9 miles & continue on W1700S .2 mile
Taylorsville	◇	2	🕐	℞ 🚗	5469 S Redwood Rd, 84123 / 801-264-9666 • Lat: 40.6518 Lon: -111.9386 I-15 Exit 297 take W7200/W7000 W 1.8 miles
Tooele	◆		🕐	℞ 🚗	99 W 1280 N, 84074 / 435-833-9017 • Lat: 40.5565 Lon: -112.2956 I-80 Exit 99 merge onto SH-36 S 10.5 miles then E at W1280N
Vernal	◇		🕐	℞ 🚗	1851 W Hwy 40, 84078 / 435-789-9784 • Lat: 40.4401 Lon: -109.5637 Jct US-191 & US-40 (in town) go W on US-191/US-40 for 2.3 miles
Washington	◆	1	🕐	℞ 🚗	625 W Telegraph St, 84780 / 435-628-2802 • Lat: 37.1285 Lon: -113.5197 I-15 Exit 10 go E .1 mile on Green Spring Dr then N .2 mile on SH-212 (Telegraph St)
West Jordan	■	6		℞ 🚗	7571 S 3800 W, 84084 / 801-282-5600 • Lat: 40.6115 Lon: -111.9802 I-15 Exit 295 go W on 9000S 4 miles, N on SH-154 for 1.5 miles, W on 7800W .3 mile & S on 3800W .1 mile
	◇	6	🕐	℞ 🚗	7671 S 3800 W, 84084 / 801-282-4066 • Lat: 40.6092 Lon: -111.9814 I-15 Exit 295 take SH-209 W 4 miles, SH-154 N 1.5 miles, W7800S W .3 mile & S3800W S .1 mile
West Valley City	◆	5	🕐	℞ 🚗	3180 S 5600 W, 84120 / 801-966-2986 • Lat: 40.7021 Lon: -112.0251 I-215 Exit 18B take SH-171 W 3.8 miles & S5600W N .4 mile

○ Wal-Mart ◇ Supercenter □ Sam's Club ■ Gas ■ Gas & Diesel

Vermont

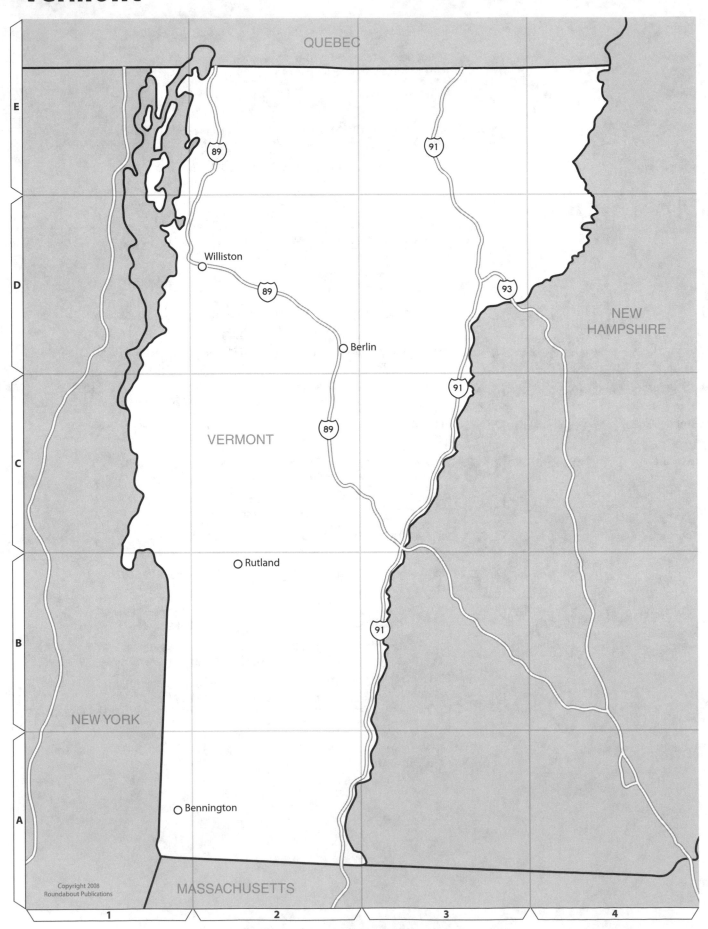

QUEBEC

89

91

E

D

Williston

89

NEW
HAMPSHIRE

93

Berlin

91

VERMONT

89

C

91

Rutland

B

91

NEW YORK

A

91

Bennington

MASSACHUSETTS

1   2   3   4

City/Town	⬡	🕐	℞	🚌	Information
Bennington	○		℞		210 Northside Dr, 5201 / 802-447-1614 • *Lat:* 42.9005 *Lon:* -73.2114 From US-7 Exit 2 (N of town) go S on SH-7A for 1.6 miles
Berlin	○	2	℞		282 Berlin Mall Rd, 5602 / 802-229-7792 • *Lat:* 44.2151 *Lon:* -72.5659 I-89 Exit 7 take SH-62 E .9 mile then N on Berlin Mall Rd .2 mile
Rutland	○		℞		1 Rutland Shopping Plz, 5701 / 802-773-0200 • *Lat:* 43.6053 *Lon:* -72.9786 From town center go S .3 mile on Main St (US-4/US-7) then W .3 mile on Washington St
Williston	○	1	℞		863 Harvest Ln, 5495 / 802-878-5233 • *Lat:* 44.4433 *Lon:* -73.1213 I-89 Exit 12 take SH-2A N .3 mile, Marshall Ave W .3 mile & Harvest Ln S .3 mile

○ Wal-Mart   ◇ Supercenter   □ Sam's Club   ▨ Gas   ▪ Gas & Diesel

Virginia

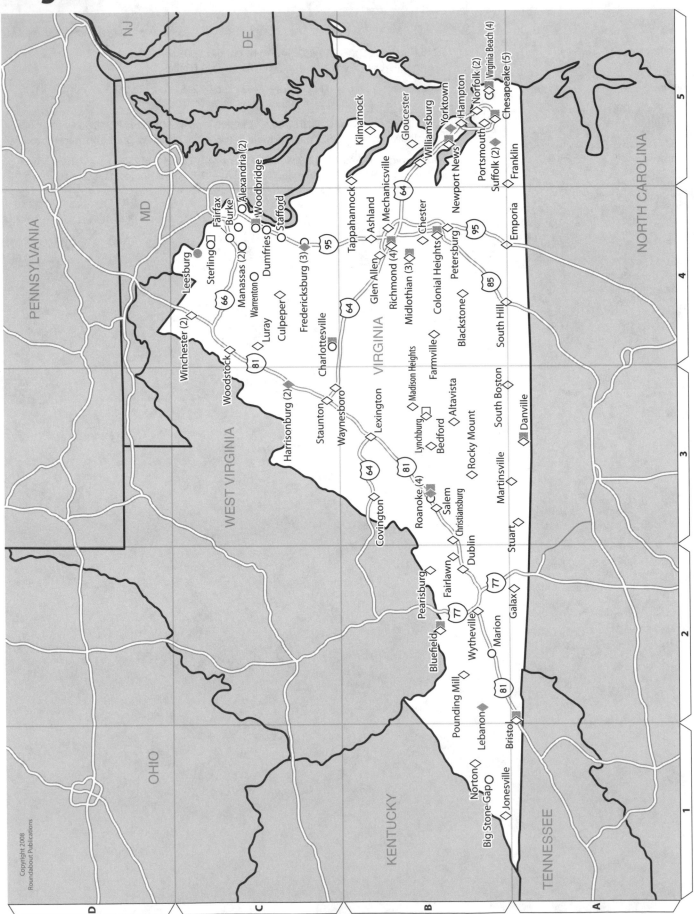

○ Wal-Mart ◇ Supercenter □ Sam's Club ▬ Gas ▬ Gas & Diesel

City/Town	⬭	🕐	℞	🚐	Information
Alexandria	◯ 5		℞		7910 Richmond Hwy, 22306 / 703-799-8815 • *Lat:* 38.7433 *Lon:* -77.0851 I-95 Exit 177 take US-1 S 4.5 miles
	◯ 2		℞	🚐	5800 Kingstowne Ctr, 22315 / 703-924-8800 • *Lat:* 38.7723 *Lon:* -77.1354 I-95 Exit 173 follow Van Dorn St S 1.3 miles then SW on Keystone Pkwy .3 mile
Altavista	◇	🕐	℞	🚐	125 Clarion Rd, 24517 / 434-309-2245 • *Lat:* 37.1383 *Lon:* -79.2686 Jct SH-43 & US-29 (W of town) take US-29 N 2 miles & S on Clarion Rd .3 mile
Ashland	◇ 3	🕐	℞		145 Hill Carter Pkwy, 23005 / 804-798-2511 • *Lat:* 37.7508 *Lon:* -77.4619 I-95 Exit 89 take Lewistown Rd E .4 mile, Ashcake Rd NW 2 miles & Hill Carter Pkwy N .6 mile
Bedford	◇	🕐	℞	🚐	1126 E Lynchburg Salem Tpke, 24523 / 540-586-6176 • *Lat:* 37.3240 *Lon:* -79.4974 Jct US-221 & US-460 (SE of town) take US-460 E .4 mile
Big Stone Gap	◯				1941 Neeley Rd, 24219 / 276-523-5026 • *Lat:* 36.8593 *Lon:* -82.7565 From town center, follow US-23-BR/US-23-ALT E 1.2 miles then go S .2 mile on Neely Rd
Blackstone	◇	🕐	℞		1451 S Main St, 23824 / 434-292-5898 • *Lat:* 37.0615 *Lon:* -78.0067 Jct SH-46 & SH-40 (S of town) go W on SH-40 for .2 mile
Bluefield	▨ 9			🚐	601 Commerce Dr, 24605 / 276-326-1583 • *Lat:* 37.2409 *Lon:* -81.2497 2 miles south of town near jct of US-450 and SH-102
	◇ 10	🕐	℞	🚐	4001 College Ave, 24605 / 276-322-3144 • *Lat:* 37.2441 *Lon:* -81.2452 I-77 Exit 66 take SH-598 W 6.3 miles, US-460 W 2.2 miles & SH-102 NW 1.4 miles
Bristol	▨ 1		℞	🚐	13249 Lee Hwy, 24202 / 276-466-7390 • *Lat:* 36.6317 *Lon:* -82.1406 I-81 Exit 5 go NE .8 mile on US-11 (Lee Hwy)
	◇ 1	🕐	℞	🚐	13245 Lee Hwy, 24202 / 276-466-0290 • *Lat:* 36.6380 *Lon:* -82.1128 I-81 Exit 7 go W on Old Airport Rd .1 mile & NW on Lee Hwy .7 mile
Burke	◯ 8		℞		6000 Burke Commons Rd, 22015 / 703-250-9280 • *Lat:* 38.7916 *Lon:* -77.2992 I-95 Exit 169 take SH-644 W 5.5 miles, SH-643 W 1.7 miles & N on Burke Commons Rd .3 mile
Charlottesville	▨ 8		℞	🚐	970 Hilton Heights Rd, 22901 / 434-978-2122 • *Lat:* 38.0976 *Lon:* -78.4651 I-64 Exit 118B take US-29 N for 7.7 miles then W at Hilton Heights Rd
	◯ 8		℞		975 Hilton Heights Rd, 22901 / 434-973-1412 • *Lat:* 38.0974 *Lon:* -78.4652 I-64 Exit 118 follow US-29 N 7.7 miles
Chesapeake	▨ 1		℞	🚐	1501 Sam's Cir, 23320 / 757-436-7119 • *Lat:* 36.7696 *Lon:* -76.2508 I-64 Exit 290 take SH-168 S .3 mile then E on WalMart Way
	▨ 2		℞	🚐	2444 Chesapeake Square Ring Rd, 23321 / 757-465-0082 • *Lat:* 36.8293 *Lon:* -76.4152 I-664 Exit 11B take SH-337 E 1.1 miles, N at Capri Cir .2 mile & NE on Chesapeake Sq .4 mile
	◇ 1	🕐	℞		1521 Sams Cir, 23320 / 757-436-6055 • *Lat:* 36.7712 *Lon:* -76.2512 I-64 Exit 290B take SH-168 BR S .1 mile & E at Wal-Mart Way
	◇ 2	🕐	℞	🚐	2448 Chesapeake Square Ring Rd, 23321 / 757-488-6098 • *Lat:* 36.8290 *Lon:* -76.4157 I-664 Exit 11B take SH-337 E 1.1 miles, Capri Cir N .2 mile & Ring Rd N .4 mile
	◇ 4	🕐	℞	🚐	632 Grassfield Pkwy, 23322 / 757-312-8309 • *Lat:* 36.7173 *Lon:* -76.3226 I-464 Exit 15B take US-17 S 3.4 miles & Grassfield Pkwy E .2 mile
Chester	◇ 5	🕐	℞		12000 Iron Bridge Rd, 23831 / 804-768-0060 • *Lat:* 37.3520 *Lon:* -77.4830 I-95 Exit 61B follow SH-10 W 4.7 miles
Christiansburg	◇ 6	🕐	℞	🚐	2400 N Franklin St, 24073 / 540-381-3705 • *Lat:* 37.1618 *Lon:* -80.4232 I-81 Exit 118 take US-460 W 4.2 miles then US-460 BR W 1.2 miles
Colonial Heights	▨ 1			🚐	735 Southpark Blvd, 23834 / 804-520-0508 • *Lat:* 37.2486 *Lon:* -77.3884 I-95 Exit 53 NE on Southpark Blvd .5 mile

◯ Wal-Mart ◇ Supercenter ▢ Sam's Club ▨ Gas ■ Gas & Diesel

City/Town	⬡	🕐	℞	🚌	Information
	◇ 1	🕐	℞	🚌	671 Southpark Blvd, 23834 / 804-526-0844 • *Lat:* 37.2465 *Lon:* -77.3893 I-95 Exit 53 take Southpark Blvd NE .3 mile
Covington	◇ 1	🕐	℞		313 Thacker Ave, 24426 / 540-962-6670 • *Lat:* 37.7705 *Lon:* -79.9921 I-64 Exit 14 take SH-154 S .1 mile, continue S on Durant Rd .1 mile
Culpeper	◇	🕐	℞	🚌	801 James Madison Hwy, 22701 / 540-825-2723 • *Lat:* 38.4816 *Lon:* -77.9758 Jct US-15/29 & US-15/29 BR (E of town) take US-15/29 BR W 2.1 miles
Danville	▪		℞	🚌	215 Piedmont Pl, 24541 / 434-797-3029 • *Lat:* 36.5854 *Lon:* -79.4328 From the Danville Expy (US-29/US-58) at Main St, go N 3 miles on Main St then W .6 mile on Piedmont Dr
	◇	🕐	℞	🚌	515 Mount Cross Rd, 24540 / 434-799-6902 • *Lat:* 36.5953 *Lon:* -79.4282 Jct US-58 & US-29 (S of town) take US-29 BR N 3.3 miles, Piedmont Dr NW 1.3 miles & Mt Cross Rd W .1 mile
Dublin	◇ 1	🕐	℞	🚌	5225 Alexander Rd, 24084 / 540-674-5385 • *Lat:* 37.0849 *Lon:* -80.6935 I-81 Exit 98 take SH-100 N .4 mile then W at Alexander Rd .2 mile
Dumfries	◯ 2		℞		17041 Jefferson Davis Hwy, 22026 / 703-221-4116 • *Lat:* 38.5815 *Lon:* -77.3105 I-95 Exit 152A take SH-234 SE .8 mile & US-1 N .6 mile
Emporia	◇ 1	🕐	℞		303 Market Dr, 23847 / 434-336-9269 • *Lat:* 36.7030 *Lon:* -77.5438 I-95 Exit 11A take US-58 E .5 mile & Market Dr N .2 mile
Fairfax	◯ 2		℞		13059 Fair Lakes Pkwy, 22033 / 703-631-9450 • *Lat:* 38.8556 *Lon:* -77.3981 I-66 Exit 55B follow SH-7100 N .7 mile then W on Fair Lakes Pkwy .9 mile
Fairlawn	◇ 6	🕐	℞	🚌	7373 Peppers Ferry Blvd, 24141 / 540-731-3378 • *Lat:* 37.1497 *Lon:* -80.5836 I-81 Exit 105 take SH-232 N 3.9 miles, US-11 NW 1.1 miles & SH-114 N .3 mile
Farmville	◇	🕐	℞	🚌	1800 Peery Dr, 23901 / 434-392-5334 • *Lat:* 37.2782 *Lon:* -78.3989 1.8 miles south of town center via US-15-BR
Franklin	◇	🕐	℞	🚌	1500 Armory Dr, 23851 / 757-562-6776 • *Lat:* 36.6682 *Lon:* -76.9525 Jct US-58 & SH-671 (W of town) go NE on SH-671/Armory Dr .5 mile
Fredericksburg	◯ 5		℞	🚌	125 Washington Square Plz, 22405 / 540-899-8890 • *Lat:* 38.2854 *Lon:* -77.4379 I-95 Exit 13A take SH-3 E 4.4 miles & S at Washington Sq .1 mile
	◆ 3	🕐	℞	🚌	1800 Carl D Silver Pkwy, 22401 / 540-786-2090 • *Lat:* 38.3066 *Lon:* -77.5110 I-95 Exit 130B take SH-3 W .9 mile, Bragg Ave/Fan Hill Ave N 1.1 miles & Silver Pkwy SE .2 mile
	◇ 1	🕐	℞	🚌	10001 Southpoint Pkwy, 22407 / 540-834-4142 • *Lat:* 38.2328 *Lon:* -77.5037 I-95 Exit 126 take US-17 S .3 mile & Southpoint Pkwy W .6 mile
Galax	◇ 8	🕐	℞	🚌	1140 E Stuart Dr, 24333 / 276-236-7113 • *Lat:* 36.6896 *Lon:* -80.8833 I-77 Exit 14 follow US-58 W 7.4 miles
Glen Allen	◇ 1	🕐	℞		11400 W Broad St, 23060 / 804-360-9777 • *Lat:* 37.6533 *Lon:* -77.6111 I-64 Exit 178A take US-250 W 1 mile
Gloucester	◇	🕐	℞	🚌	6819 Walton Ln, 23061 / 804-694-0110 • *Lat:* 37.4145 *Lon:* -76.5294 Jct US-17 & SH-216 take US-17 S 1.8 miles then W at Walton St
Hampton	◇ 2	🕐	℞		1900 Cunningham Dr, 23666 / 757-826-6377 • *Lat:* 37.0423 *Lon:* -76.3807 I-64 Exit 263 merge onto SH-134 SE 1.2 miles & S on Cunningham Dr
Harrisonburg	◆ 1	🕐	℞	🚌	171 Burgess Rd, 22801 / 540-433-0808 • *Lat:* 38.4329 *Lon:* -78.8537 I-81 Exit 247A merge onto US-33 E .4 mile & S at Burgess Rd .2 mile
	◇ 3	🕐	℞	🚌	2160 John Wayland Hwy, 22801 / 540-438-0349 • *Lat:* 38.4303 *Lon:* -78.9102 I-81 Exit 245 take Pt Republic Rd/Maryland Ave W .9 mile & SH-42 SW 1.6 miles
Jonesville	◇	🕐	℞	🚌	RR 2 Box 3160, 24263 / 276-346-2860 • *Lat:* 36.7244 *Lon:* -83.1000 From town center, follow Main St E .6 mile then go NE 3.1 miles on US-58-ALT

◯ Wal-Mart ◇ Supercenter ☐ Sam's Club ▪ Gas ▪ Gas & Diesel

City/Town	⬢	🕐	℞	🚌	Information
Kilmarnock	◇	🕐	℞		200 Old Fairgrounds Way, 22482 / 804-435-6148 • *Lat:* 37.7262 *Lon:* -76.3893 1.2 miles north of town along SH-3
Lebanon	◆	🕐	℞	🚌	1050 Regional Park Rd, 24266 / 276-889-1654 • *Lat:* 36.9034 *Lon:* -82.0460 Jct SH-656 & US-19 (N of town) take US-19 S 1.7 miles, US-19 BR S .6 mile & S at Cedar Heights .2 mile
Leesburg	●		℞		950 Edwards Ferry Rd NE, 20176 / 703-779-0102 • *Lat:* 39.1158 *Lon:* -77.5398 1.4 miles east of town center via Edwards Ferry Rd at US-15
Lexington	◇ 1	🕐	℞		1233 N Lee Hwy, 24450 / 540-464-3535 • *Lat:* 37.8041 *Lon:* -79.4084 I-64 Exit 55 take US-11 N .5 mile
Luray	◇ 9	🕐	℞		1036 US Hwy 211 W, 22835 / 540-743-4111 • *Lat:* 38.6616 *Lon:* -78.4846 I-81 Exit 264 follow US-211 E 8.4 miles
Lynchburg	☐			🚌	3912 Wards Rd, 24502 / 434-237-5234 • *Lat:* 37.3510 *Lon:* -79.1850 6 miles southwest of town at US-460/US-29 jct, across from Liberty University
	◇	🕐	℞		3900 Wards Rd, 24502 / 434-832-0304 • *Lat:* 37.3513 *Lon:* -79.1848 Jct US-29 & US-460 (SE of town) go N on US-29 BR for 1.1 miles
Madison Heights	◇	🕐	℞	🚌	197 Madison Heights Sq, 24572 / 434-846-9650 • *Lat:* 37.4612 *Lon:* -79.1182 Jct US-29 & Amelon Hwy (NE of town) go W on Amelon Hwy 2 miles then S on US-29 BR .5 mile
Manassas	◯ 1		℞		7412 Stream Walk Ln, 20109 / 703-330-5253 • *Lat:* 38.7975 *Lon:* -77.5237 I-66 Exit 47 merge onto SH-234 BR S .2 mile then Balls Ford Rd W .3 mile
	◯ 8		℞		9401 Liberia Ave, 20110 / 703-257-0403 • *Lat:* 38.7513 *Lon:* -77.4484 I-66 Exit 53A follow SH-28 S 6.6 miles then Liberia Ave E 1 mile
Marion	◯ 2		℞		1193 N Main St, 24354 / 276-783-4244 • *Lat:* 36.8446 *Lon:* -81.5010 I-81 Exit 47 follow US-11 S 1.1 miles
Martinsville	◇	🕐	℞	🚌	976 Commonwealth Blvd, 24112 / 276-634-5110 • *Lat:* 36.6973 *Lon:* -79.8536 Jct US-58 & US-58 BR (E of town) go W on US-58 BR 4.6 miles then N on Chatham Rd .3 mile
Mechanicsville	◇ 1	🕐	℞	🚌	7430 Bell Creek Rd, 23111 / 804-730-8877 • *Lat:* 37.6116 *Lon:* -77.3547 I-295 Exit 37A go E .3 mile on US-360, N .1 mile on Sandy Ln, E .1 mile on Bell Creek Rd
Midlothian	■		℞	🚌	901 Wal Mart Way, 23113 / 804-378-7654 • *Lat:* 37.5037 *Lon:* -77.6280 Jct SH-288 & US-60 go N on US-60 for 3.7 miles, N on Walmart Way
	◇	🕐	℞	🚌	12200 Chattanooga Plz, 23112 / 804-744-8437 • *Lat:* 37.4320 *Lon:* -77.6198 I-95 Exit 62 take SH-288 NW 12.6 miles then Warbro Rd N .1 mile
	◇	🕐	℞		900 Wal-Mart Way, 23113 / 804-378-9001 • *Lat:* 37.5036 *Lon:* -77.6283 I-64 Exit 175 take SH-288 S 11.4 miles then US-60 E 3.7 miles & N at Wal-Mart Way
Newport News	■ 1		℞	🚌	12407 Jefferson Ave, 23602 / 757-875-0243 • *Lat:* 37.1217 *Lon:* -76.5070 I-64 Exit 255 N on Jefferson Ave 1 mile
	◇ 1	🕐	℞		12401 Jefferson Ave, 23602 / 757-874-4434 • *Lat:* 37.1214 *Lon:* -76.5068 I-64 Exit 255 take SH-143 W .9 mile
Norfolk	◇ 2	🕐	℞	🚌	1170 N Military Hwy, 23502 / 757-461-6330 • *Lat:* 36.8623 *Lon:* -76.2090 I-64 Exit 281 follow Military Hwy S 1.3 miles (or from I-264 Exit 13B go N 1.3 miles on Military Hwy)
	◇ 1	🕐	℞	🚌	7530 Tidewater Dr, 23505 / 757-480-0587 • *Lat:* 36.9125 *Lon:* -76.2550 I-64 Exit 277B merge onto Tidewater Dr NE .7 mile
Norton	◇	🕐	℞	🚌	780 Commonwealth Dr, 24273 / 276-679-7327 • *Lat:* 36.9573 *Lon:* -82.6050 2 miles northeast of town via US-23 at SH-657
Pearisburg	◇	🕐	℞		160 Kinter Way, 24134 / 540-921-1204 • *Lat:* 37.3280 *Lon:* -80.7081 Jct US-460 & US-460 BR (E of town) go W on US-460 BR 1 mile & N on Kinter Way

◯ Wal-Mart   ◇ Supercenter   ☐ Sam's Club   ■ Gas   ■ Gas & Diesel

City/Town	🛡		🕐	℞	🚗	Information
Petersburg	◇	2	🕐	℞	🚗	3500 S Crater Rd, 23805 / 804-957-6444 • *Lat:* 37.1794 *Lon:* -77.3644 I-95 Exit 48B take Wagner Rd W .4 mile & Crater Rd/US-301 S .7 mile
Portsmouth	◇	1	🕐	℞	🚗	1098 Fredrick Blvd, 23707 / 757-399-1795 • *Lat:* 36.8298 *Lon:* -76.3402 I-264 Exit 5 take US-17 N 1 mile
Pounding Mill	◇		🕐	℞	🚗	13320 Governor G C Peery Hwy, 24637 / 276-596-9706 • *Lat:* 37.0637 *Lon:* -81.7232 Jct SH-16 ALT & US-460/US-19 (NE of town) take US-460/US-19 SW 7.7 miles
Richmond	■	3		℞	🚗	9440 W Broad St, 23294 / 804-346-3031 • *Lat:* 37.6393 *Lon:* -77.5563 I-64 Exit 181 take SH-73 E 1.2 miles & NW on Broad St 1.3 miles
	◇		🕐	℞	🚗	2501 Sheila Ln, 23225 / 804-320-6991 • *Lat:* 37.5341 *Lon:* -77.5324 I-95 Exit 67 take SH-150 NW 10.8 miles then Forest Hill Ave W .2 mile & Sheila Ln S .2 mile
	◇	1	🕐	℞	🚗	7901 Brook Rd, 23227 / 804-553-8432 • *Lat:* 37.6317 *Lon:* -77.4585 I-95 Exit 83B go W .4 mile on SH-73/Parham Rd then S .2 mile on US-1/Brook Rd
	◇	2	🕐	℞		1504 N Parham Rd, 23229 / 804-270-6034 • *Lat:* 37.6021 *Lon:* -77.5642 I-64 Exit 181 take Parham Rd S 1.6 miles
Roanoke	■	1		℞	🚗	1455 Towne Square Blvd NW, 24012 / 540-563-2620 • *Lat:* 37.3185 *Lon:* -79.9651 I-581 Exit 3 take SH-101 E .5 mile, N on Aviation Rd .1 mile & E on Town Sq Blvd
	○			℞		4210 Franklin Rd SW, 24014 / 540-772-3892 • *Lat:* 37.2238 *Lon:* -79.9683 I-81 Exit 143 take I-581 S 6.9 miles, continue on US-220 S 4.1 miles
	◆	1	🕐	℞	🚗	4807 Valley View Blvd NW, 24012 / 540-265-5600 • *Lat:* 37.3039 *Lon:* -79.9598 I-581 Exit 3E take SH-101 E .4 mile then Valley View Blvd S .6 mile
	◇	6	🕐	℞	🚗	4524 Challenger Ave, 24012 / 540-977-3745 • *Lat:* 37.3282 *Lon:* -79.8666 I-81 Exit 150A take US-220 S 5.1 miles & US-221 S .7 mile
Rocky Mount	◇		🕐	℞	🚗	550 Old Franklin Tpke, 24151 / 540-484-1002 • *Lat:* 37.0082 *Lon:* -79.7800 Jct SH-122 & SH-40 (NE of town) go E on SH-40 for 4.8 miles
Salem	◇	1	🕐	℞		1851 W Main St, 24153 / 540-375-2919 • *Lat:* 37.2887 *Lon:* -80.0884 I-81 Exit 137 take SH-112 S .4 mile & US-11/US-460 E .4 mile
South Boston	◇		🕐	℞		3471 Old Halifax Rd, 24592 / 434-575-0680 • *Lat:* 36.7336 *Lon:* -78.9102 Jct US-501 & SH-129 (NW of town) take SH-129 E .4 mile
South Hill	◇	1	🕐	℞	🚗	315 Furr St, 23970 / 434-447-3610 • *Lat:* 36.7112 *Lon:* -78.1076 I-85 Exit 12A take US-58 E .1 mile
Stafford	○	1		℞	🚗	217 Garrisonville Rd, 22554 / 540-720-0059 • *Lat:* 38.4727 *Lon:* -77.4158 I-95 Exit 143B take SH-610 W 1 mile
Staunton	◇	1	🕐	℞	🚗	1028 Richmond Ave, 24401 / 540-886-8566 • *Lat:* 38.1382 *Lon:* -79.0477 I-81 Exit 222 take US-250 W 1 mile
Sterling	□			℞	🚗	45425 Dulles Crossing Plz, 20166 / 571-434-8711 • *Lat:* 39.0242 *Lon:* -77.4287 I-66 Exit 53 take SH-28 N 13.1 miles, Nokes Blvd E .3 mile, Atlantic Blvd .2 mile & Dulles Crossing W .2 mile
	○			℞	🚗	45415 Dulles Crossing Plz, 20166 / 571-434-9434 • *Lat:* 39.0242 *Lon:* -77.4291 I-66 Exit 53 go N 13 miles on SH-28, E .3 mile on Nokes Blvd, S .2 mile on Atlantic Blvd
Stuart	◇		🕐	℞		19265 Jeb Stuart Hwy, 24171 / 276-694-2520 • *Lat:* 36.6416 *Lon:* -80.2463 2 miles east of town along US-58
Suffolk	◆		🕐	℞		1200 N Main St, 23434 / 757-925-0224 • *Lat:* 36.7471 *Lon:* -76.5830 I-664 Exit 13A take US-460 W 5.8 miles then follow US-460 BR 4 miles & N on Main St .7 mile
	◇	1	🕐	℞	🚗	6259 College Dr, 23435 / 757-483-8860 • *Lat:* 36.8807 *Lon:* -76.4252 I-664 Exit 8B take SH-135 S .2 mile
Tappahannock	◇		🕐	℞		1660 Tappahannock Blvd, 22560 / 804-443-1188 • *Lat:* 37.9022 *Lon:* -76.8674 Jct US-360 & US-17 (S of town) take US-360/US-17 N .8 mile

○ Wal-Mart ◇ Supercenter □ Sam's Club ■ Gas ■ Gas & Diesel

City/Town	⬡	🕐	℞	🚐	Information
Virginia Beach	▨ 1		℞	🚐	3345 Virginia Beach Blvd, 23452 / 757-631-9791 • *Lat:* 36.8415 *Lon:* -76.0887 I-264 Exit 18 go E on Virginia Beach Blvd .5 mile
	◯ 1		℞		657 Phoenix Dr, 23452 / 757-498-9633 • *Lat:* 36.8239 *Lon:* -76.0688 I-264 Exit 19A merge onto SH-414 S .6 mile, Guardian Ln W/Phoenix Dr S .2 mile
	◇ 6	🕐	℞		2021 Lynnhaven Pkwy, 23456 / 757-416-3480 • *Lat:* 36.7922 *Lon:* -76.1205 I-264 Exit 19A follow SH-414 S 5.1 miles
	◇ 8	🕐	℞	🚐	1149 Nimmo Pkwy, 23456 / 757-430-1836 • *Lat:* 36.7614 *Lon:* -76.0070 I-264 Exit 20 follow 1st Colonial Rd/SH-615 S 4.2 miles, continue on SH-615 S 2.4 miles & E at Nimmo Pkwy .5 mile
Warrenton	◯		℞	🚐	8278 James Madison Hwy, 20186 / 540-341-3568 • *Lat:* 38.6918 *Lon:* -77.7894 I-66 Exit 28 follow US-17 S 13 miles
Waynesboro	◇ 1	🕐	℞	🚐	116 Lucy Ln, 22980 / 540-932-2500 • *Lat:* 38.0656 *Lon:* -78.9347 I-64 Exit 94 take US-340 N .4 mile
Williamsburg	◇ 2	🕐	℞	🚐	731 E Rochambeau Dr, 23188 / 757-220-2772 • *Lat:* 37.3507 *Lon:* -76.7349 I-64 Exit 234 take SH-199 E .8 mile & Rochambeau Dr E .3 mile
Winchester	◇ 1	🕐	℞	🚐	2300 S Pleasant Valley Rd, 22601 / 540-667-9111 • *Lat:* 39.1588 *Lon:* -78.1717 I-81 Exit 313B take US-50 W .3 mile then Pleasant Valley Rd S .6 mile
	◇ 5	🕐	℞	🚐	501 Wal-Mart Dr, 22603 / 540-545-8730 • *Lat:* 39.2061 *Lon:* -78.1909 I-81 Exit 317 take SH-37 S 4 miles, US-50 W .3 mile & Echo Ln N
Woodbridge	▨ 2		℞	🚐	14050 Worth Ave, 22192 / 703-491-2662 • *Lat:* 38.6466 *Lon:* -77.2947 I-95 Exit 158B go W on Prince William Pkwy 1.3 miles then S on Worth Ave
	◯ 2		℞		14000 Worth Ave, 22192 / 703-497-2590 • *Lat:* 38.6476 *Lon:* -77.2948 I-95 Exit 158B follow Prince William Pkwy W 1 mile then go S at Worth Ave .3 mile
Woodstock	◇ 1	🕐	℞		461 W Reservoir Rd, 22664 / 540-459-9229 • *Lat:* 38.8704 *Lon:* -78.5245 I-81 Exit 283 take SH-42 E .3 mile
Wytheville	◇ 1	🕐	℞	🚐	345 Commonwealth Dr, 24382 / 276-228-2190 • *Lat:* 36.9579 *Lon:* -81.0976 I-81 Exit 70 take US-21 S .1 mile then W on Commonwealth Dr
Yorktown	◆ 3	🕐	℞	🚐	2601 George Washington Mem Hwy, 23693 / 757-867-8004 • *Lat:* 37.1151 *Lon:* -76.4399 I-64 Exit 258B merge onto US-17 N 2.5 miles

◯ Wal-Mart   ◇ Supercenter   □ Sam's Club   ▨ Gas   ▰ Gas & Diesel

Washington

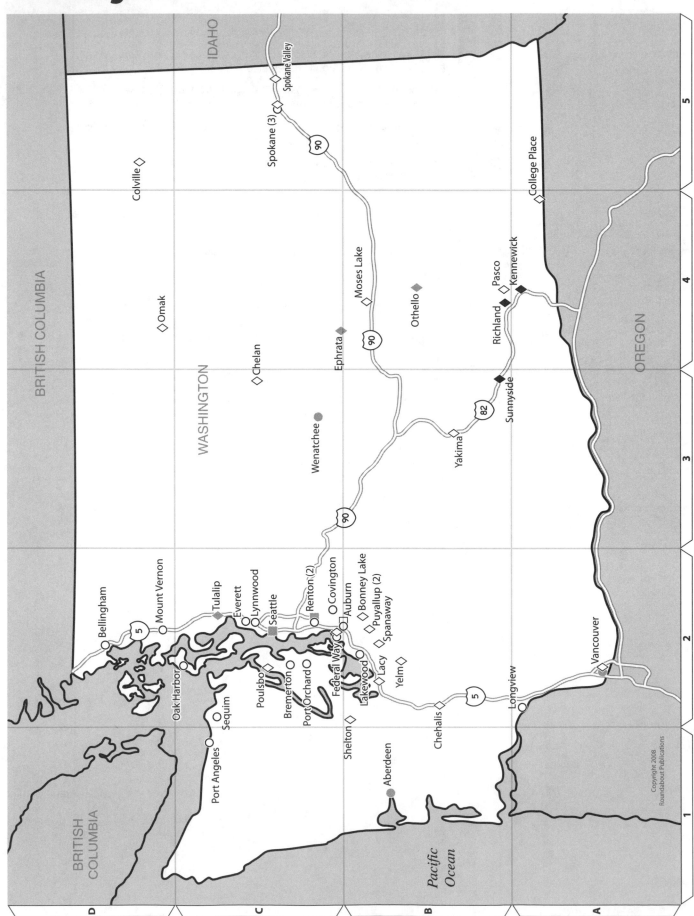

IDAHO

Spokane Valley

Spokane (3)

90

Colville

College Place

Kennewick

Pasco

Moses Lake

Richland

Othello

BRITISH COLUMBIA

Omak

90

82

Sunnyside

Chelan

Ephrata

Yakima

WASHINGTON

Wenatchee

OREGON

90

90

Bellingham

Mount Vernon

Tulalip

Everett

Lynnwood

Seattle

Renton (2)

Covington

Auburn

Bonney Lake

Puyallup (2)

Spanaway

5

Oak Harbor

Poulsbo

Bremerton

Port Orchard

Federal Way

Lakewood

Lacy

Yelm

Vancouver

Sequim

Shelton

Chehalis

Longview

5

Port Angeles

Aberdeen

Pacific Ocean

BRITISH COLUMBIA

A B C D

1 2 3 4 5

City/Town	⬡	🕐	Rx	🚐	Information
Aberdeen	●		Rx		909 E Wishkah St, 98520 / 360-532-7595 • *Lat:* 46.9772 *Lon:* -123.8071 From Jct US-101 & US-12 in town, go E on US-12 for .3 mile
Auburn	□ 5		Rx	🚐	1101 Supermall Way Ste 1275, 98001 / 253-333-1026 • *Lat:* 47.2965 *Lon:* -122.2453 I-5 Exit 142 take SH-18 E 3.8 miles, S on C St .5 mile, W on 15th .6 mile & N at Market St
	○ 4		Rx		1425 Supermall Way, 98001 / 253-735-1855 • *Lat:* 47.2969 *Lon:* -122.2501 I-5 Exit 142A go E 2.6 miles on SH-18, S .5 mile on Valley Hwy, E .5 mile on 15th St, N at Supermall Dr
Bellingham	○ 2		Rx	🚐	4420 Meridian St, 98226 / 360-647-1400 • *Lat:* 48.8008 *Lon:* -122.4858 I-5 Exit 256, go N on SH-539 for 1.2 miles, then E on Stuart Rd .2 mile
Bonney Lake	◇	🕐	Rx	🚐	19205 WA Hwy 410 E, 98391 / 253-826-9144 • *Lat:* 47.1696 *Lon:* -122.1728 I-5 Exit 127, go E 12 miles on SH-512, N .4 mile on SH-167, E 5.4 miles on SH-410
Bremerton	○		Rx	🚐	6797 WA Hwy 303 NE, 98311 / 360-698-2889 • *Lat:* 47.6259 *Lon:* -122.6305 4.2 miles north of town center via SH-303
Chehalis	◇ 1	🕐	Rx	🚐	1601 NW Louisiana Ave, 98532 / 360-748-1240 • *Lat:* 46.6750 *Lon:* -122.9782 I-5 Exit 79, go W at Chamber Way .3 mile, then S on NW Louisiana Ave
Chelan	◇	🕐	Rx	🚐	108 Apple Blossom Dr, 98816 / 509-682-4291 • *Lat:* 47.8411 *Lon:* -119.9907 1.3 miles east of town center via US-97-ALT
College Place	◇	🕐	Rx	🚐	1700 SE Meadowbrook Blvd, 99324 / 509-525-3468 • *Lat:* 46.0348 *Lon:* -118.3818 From Walla Walla, S on SH-125 (9th St) for 3.3 miles, then W on SE Meadowbrook
Colville	◇	🕐	Rx	🚐	810 N Hwy, 99114 / 509-684-3209 • *Lat:* 48.5517 *Lon:* -117.9153 From Jct SH-20 & US-395 go S on US-395 for 9.6 miles
Covington	○		Rx		17432 SE 270th Pl, 98042 / 253-630-7791 • *Lat:* 47.3598 *Lon:* -122.1096 I-5 Exit 142A follow SH-18 NE for 11.4 miles, 272nd St/SH-516 E .4 mile, N at 172nd Ave and E on 270th Pl
Ephrata	◆	🕐	Rx	🚐	1399 Southeast Blvd, 98823 / 509-754-8837 • *Lat:* 47.3033 *Lon:* -119.5394 I-90 Exit 151 take SH-283 NE for 14.8 miles, N on SH-28 for 4.5 miles, E on SH-282 for 1 mile
Everett	○ 3		Rx	🚐	11400 Evergreen Way, 98204 / 425-923-1740 • *Lat:* 47.9020 *Lon:* -122.2541 I-5 Exit 189 go SE on Everett Mall Way for 2.1 miles then E on Evergree Way
Federal Way	○ 1		Rx	🚐	1900 S 314th St, 98003 / 253-941-9974 • *Lat:* 47.3201 *Lon:* -122.3091 I-5 Exit 143 go W on 320th St for .5 mile, N on 20th Ave for .4 mile, W at 314th St
	◇ 1	🕐	Rx	🚐	34520 16th Ave S, 98003 / 253-835-4965 • *Lat:* 47.2922 *Lon:* -122.3133 I-5 Exit 142B take SH-18 W for .3 mile then N at 16th Ave S
Kennewick	◆ 3	🕐	Rx	🚐	2720 S Quillan St, 99337 / 509-586-1554 • *Lat:* 46.1832 *Lon:* -119.1741 I-82 Exit 113 go N on US-395 for 2 miles, E on W 27th Ave for .1 mile, S at South Quillan St
Lacey	◇ 1	🕐	Rx		1401 Galaxy Dr NE, 98516 / 360-456-6550 • *Lat:* 47.0601 *Lon:* -122.7691 I-5 Exit 111 follow signs for Marvin Rd/SH-510 E for .5 mile then S at Galaxy Dr
Lakewood	○ 3		Rx	🚐	7001 Bridgeport Way W, 98499 / 253-513-0949 • *Lat:* 47.1933 *Lon:* -122.5194 I-5 Exit 129 go W on 74th St for 2.4 miles, W on 75th St .3 mile then N on Bridgeport Way .3 mile
Longview	○ 7		Rx	🚐	3715 Ocean Beach Hwy, 98632 / 360-414-9656 • *Lat:* 46.1545 *Lon:* -122.9817 I-5 Exit 36 take SH-432 W for 5.6 miles then S at Ocean Beach Hwy for 1.4 miles
Lynnwood	○ 1		Rx		1400 164th St SW, 98087 / 425-741-9445 • *Lat:* 47.8496 *Lon:* -122.2527 I-5 Exit 183 go E on 164th St SW for .5 mile
Moses Lake	◇ 4	🕐	Rx	🚐	1005 N Stratford Rd, 98837 / 509-765-8979 • *Lat:* 47.1416 *Lon:* -119.2782 I-90 Exit 179 go NW on SH-17 for 3.6 miles then S on Stratford Rd for .2 mile
Mount Vernon	○ 1		Rx	🚐	2021 Market St, 98273 / 360-428-7000 • *Lat:* 48.4364 *Lon:* -122.3381 I-5 Exit 227 go E on College Way for .2 mile then N on Riverside Dr for .2 mile, W at Riverside Ln .1 mile & S on Market St

○ Wal-Mart ◇ Supercenter □ Sam's Club ▨ Gas ▬ Gas & Diesel

City/Town	⬡	🕐	℞	🚐	Information
Oak Harbor	○		℞	🚐	1250 SW Erie St, 98277 / 360-279-0665 • *Lat:* 48.2878 *Lon:* -122.6629 From town center go W .7 mile on Pioneer Way and SH-20 then go N .1 mile on Erie St
Omak	◇	🕐	℞	🚐	902 Engh Rd, 98841 / 509-826-6002 • *Lat:* 48.4243 *Lon:* -119.4839 From town travel NE on US-97 for 2 miles, E on Sandflat Rd for .3 mile, S on Vista Vu Dr for .5 mile, E on Engh Rd
Othello	◆	🕐	℞		1860 E Main St, 99344 / 509-488-9295 • *Lat:* 46.8262 *Lon:* -119.1488 1.2 miles east of town center on Main St/SH-24
Pasco	◇ 1	🕐	℞	🚐	4820 N Rd 68, 99301 / 509-543-7934 • *Lat:* 46.2718 *Lon:* -119.1857 I-182 Exit 9 go N on Road 68 for .5 mile
Port Angeles	○		℞	🚐	3500 E Hwy 101, 98362 / 360-452-1244 • *Lat:* 48.1093 *Lon:* -123.3600 From the Olympic National Park Visitor Center (south of town) go N on Race St for 1 mile then E on US-101 for 2.8 miles
Port Orchard	○		℞	🚐	3497 Bethel Rd SE, 98366 / 360-874-9060 • *Lat:* 47.5163 *Lon:* -122.6310 From town center go E .5 mile on Bay St then S 1.8 miles on Bethel Ave
Poulsbo	◇	🕐	℞	🚐	21200 Olhava Way NW, 98370 / 360-697-3670 • *Lat:* 47.7573 *Lon:* -122.6595 From town center go N 1 mile on Front St, W .9 mile on Lindvig Way/Flinn Hill Rd, then N .3 mile on Olhava Way; near SH-3/SH-305 jct
Puyallup	◇ 10	🕐	℞		310 31st Ave SE, 98374 / 253-770-4399 • *Lat:* 47.1620 *Lon:* -122.2894 I-5 Exit 127 go E on SH-512 for 8.7 miles, S on SH-161 for .3 mile, N on Meridian and E on 31st Ave
	◇	🕐	℞	🚐	16502 Meridian E, 98375 / 253-446-1741 • *Lat:* 47.1073 *Lon:* -122.2936 I-5 Exit 127 take SH-512 E for 8.7 miles then SH-161 (Meridian) S for 3.1 miles
Renton	■ 1		℞	🚐	901 S Grady Way, 98057 / 425-793-7443 • *Lat:* 47.4741 *Lon:* -122.2064 I-405 Exit 2 go NE on Grady Way .6 mile
	○ 1		℞	🚐	743 Rainier Ave S, 98057 / 425-227-0407 • *Lat:* 47.4726 *Lon:* -122.2177 I-405 Exit 2 go N on Rainier Ave for .5 mile
Richland	◆ 1	🕐	℞	🚐	2801 Duportail St, 99352 / 509-628-8420 • *Lat:* 46.2611 *Lon:* -119.3071 I-182 Exit 3B go N on Queensgate Dr for .2 mile then E on Duportail
Seattle	■ 2		℞	🚐	13550 Aurora Ave N, 98133 / 206-362-6700 • *Lat:* 47.7278 *Lon:* -122.3449 I-5 Exit 174 go W on 130th St 1 mile then N on Aurora Ave .3 mile
Sequim	○		℞	🚐	1284 W Washington St, 98382 / 360-683-9346 • *Lat:* 48.0779 *Lon:* -123.1338 1.4 miles west of town center via Washington St
Shelton	◇	🕐	℞	🚐	100 E Wallace Kneeland Blvd, 98584 / 360-427-6226 • *Lat:* 47.2313 *Lon:* -123.1268 2 miles northwest of town off US-101 at Wallace Kneeland Blvd
Spanaway	◇ 9	🕐	℞	🚐	20307 Mountain Hwy E, 98387 / 253-846-6008 • *Lat:* 47.0730 *Lon:* -122.4205 I-5 Exit 127 take SH-512 E for 2.1 miles then SH-7 S for 6.1 miles
Spokane	○ 6		℞		2301 W Wellesley Ave, 99205 / 509-327-0404 • *Lat:* 47.7006 *Lon:* -117.4447 I-90 Exit 281 go N on US-2 for 3.2 miles then W on W Wellesley for 2.5 miles
	◇ 7	🕐	℞	🚐	9212 N Colton St, 99218 / 509-464-2173 • *Lat:* 47.7415 *Lon:* -117.4059 I-90 Exit 281 go N on US-2/US-395 for 5.8 miles, E at Magnesium Rd and N at Colton St for .4 mile
	◇ 4	🕐	℞		1221 S Hayford Rd, 99224 / 509-459-0602 • *Lat:* 47.6448 *Lon:* -117.5605 I-90 Exit 277B go W 3.7 miles on US-2 then N .1 mile on Hayford Rd
Spokane Valley	◇ 1	🕐	℞	🚐	15727 E Broadway Ave, 99037 / 509-922-8868 • *Lat:* 47.6652 *Lon:* -117.1919 I-90 Exit 291B go S .4 mile on Sullivan Rd then E .2 mile on Broadway Ave
Sunnyside	◆ 1	🕐	℞	🚐	2675 E Lincoln Ave, 98944 / 509-839-7339 • *Lat:* 46.3167 *Lon:* -119.9869 I-82 Exit 69 take SH-241 N for .4 mile then E at Yakima Valley Hospital for .4 mile, N on Lincoln

○ Wal-Mart   ◇ Supercenter   □ Sam's Club   ▨ Gas   ■ Gas & Diesel

City/Town	🛡	🕐	℞	🚐	Information
Tulalip	◆	1	🕐	℞ 🚐	8924 Quilceda Blvd, 98271 / 360-657-1192 • *Lat:* 48.0773 *Lon:* -122.1868 I-5 Exit 200, west of exit
Vancouver	●	1		℞ 🚐	9000 NE Hwy 99, 98665 / 360-571-0300 • *Lat:* 45.6876 *Lon:* -122.6598 I-5 Exit 4 go NE on 78th St & N at SH-99 for .7 mile
	◇	1	🕐	℞ 🚐	221 NE 104th Ave, 98664 / 360-885-0734 • *Lat:* 45.6223 *Lon:* -122.5652 I-205 Exit 28 go W on Mill Plain Blvd for .8 mile then N on 104th Ave
	◇	4	🕐	℞ 🚐	430 SE 192nd Ave, 98683 / 360-256-0109 • *Lat:* 45.6191 *Lon:* -122.4762 I-205 Exit 28 go E on Mill Plain Blvd for 3 miles, E on Southeast 1st St for .9 mile then S on Southeast 192nd Ave
Wenatchee	●			℞	2000 N Wenatchee Ave, 98801 / 509-664-2448 • *Lat:* 47.4542 *Lon:* -120.3367 3.2 miles northwest of town center via SH-285
Yakima	◇	1	🕐	℞ 🚐	1600 E Chestnut Ave, 98901 / 509-248-3448 • *Lat:* 46.6030 *Lon:* -120.4814 I-82 Exit 33 go E .3 mile on Yakima Ave/Terrace Heights Dr then S .1 mile on 17th St
Yelm	◇		🕐	℞ 🚐	17100 State Route 507 SE, 98597 / 360-400-8050 • *Lat:* 46.9332 *Lon:* -122.5784 1.6 miles southeast of town center via SH-507

○ Wal-Mart ◇ Supercenter □ Sam's Club ▬ Gas ▬ Gas & Diesel

West Virginia

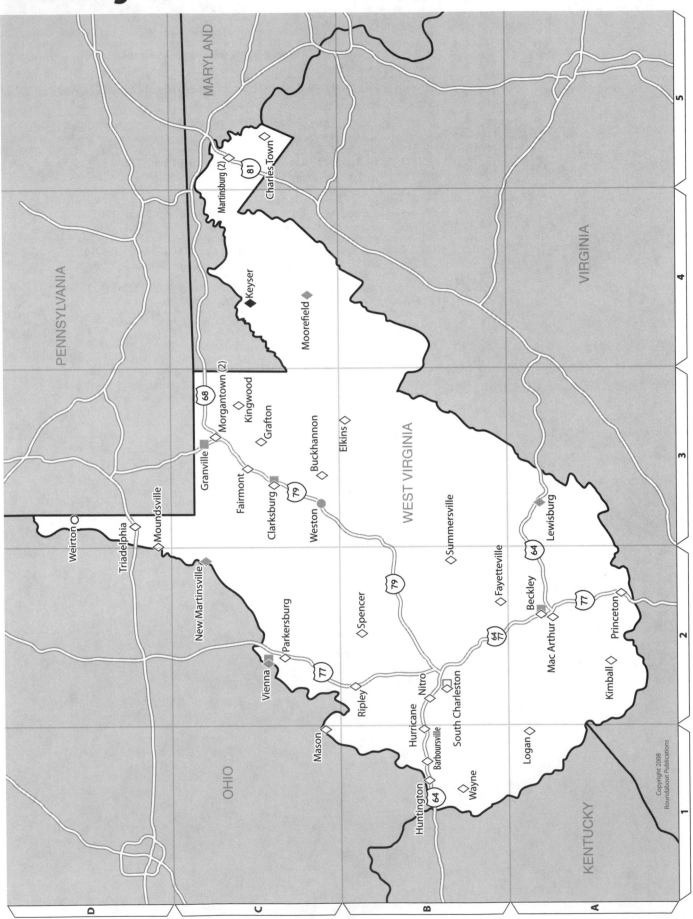

MARYLAND

PENNSYLVANIA

VIRGINIA

OHIO

KENTUCKY

WEST VIRGINIA

Charles Town

Martinsburg (2) 81

Keyser

Moorefield

Morgantown (2) 68

Kingwood

Grafton

Granville

Fairmont

Buckhannon

Elkins

Clarksburg 79

Weston

Moundsville

Weirton ○

Triadelphia

New Martinsville

Summersville

Lewisburg 64

Fayetteville

Beckley

77

Princeton

Parkersburg

Spencer 79

64 77

Mac Arthur

Kimball

Vienna

77

Ripley

Nitro

South Charleston

Logan

Mason

Hurricane

Barboursville

Wayne

Huntington 64

City/Town	🛡	⏱	R_X	🚐	Information
Barboursville	◇	1	⏱	R_X 🚐	25 Nichols Dr, 25504 / 304-733-0789 • *Lat:* 38.4257 *Lon:* -82.2589 I-64 Exit 20 go N on E Mall Rd for .4 mile, then E on Melody Farms Rd
Beckley	▨	4		R_X 🚐	1220 N Eisenhower Dr, 25801 / 304-252-6508 • *Lat:* 37.8013 *Lon:* -81.1804 I-64 Exit 124 take US-19 N 3.2 miles
	◇	4	⏱	R_X 🚐	1330 N Eisenhower Dr, 25801 / 304-255-7800 • *Lat:* 37.8045 *Lon:* -81.1834 I-64 Exit 124 take US-19 N for 3.6 miles
Buckhannon	◇		⏱	R_X	100 Buckhannon Cross Roads, 26201 / 304-472-2589 • *Lat:* 39.0108 *Lon:* -80.2363 I-79 Exit 99 take US-33 E for 12 miles
Charles Town	◇		⏱	R_X	96 Patrick Henry Way, 25414 / 304-728-2720 • *Lat:* 39.2987 *Lon:* -77.8296 I-81 Exit 5 go E on SH-51 for 12.4 miles, then N on US-340 BR for 1 mile
Clarksburg	▨	1		🚐	200 Emily Dr, 26301 / 304-623-6410 • *Lat:* 39.2807 *Lon:* -80.2780 I-79 Exit 119 take US-50 E .5 mile then S at Emily Dr
	◇	1	⏱	R_X 🚐	550 Emily Dr, 26301 / 304-622-1954 • *Lat:* 39.2805 *Lon:* -80.2780 I-79 Exit 119 go E on US-50 for .5 mile, S on Emily
Elkins	◇		⏱	R_X	721 Beverly Pike, 26241 / 304-636-2138 • *Lat:* 38.8938 *Lon:* -79.8463 2.2 miles south of town center via US-219/US-250
Fairmont	◇	1	⏱	R_X	32 Tygart Mall Loop, 26554 / 304-366-0444 • *Lat:* 39.4255 *Lon:* -80.1949 I-79 Exit 132 go E on US-250 (Fairmont Ave) for .5 mile then left at the mall
Fayetteville	◇		⏱	R_X 🚐	100 Fayette Town Ctr, 25840 / 304-574-1086 • *Lat:* 38.0320 *Lon:* -81.1228 I-64/I-77 Exit 48 take US-19 N for 16 miles
Grafton	◇		⏱	R_X	1 Wal-Mart Ln, 26354 / 304-265-6294 • *Lat:* 39.3597 *Lon:* -79.9945 2.7 miles northeast of town center via US-119
Granville	■	1		R_X 🚐	6001 University Town Centre Dr, 26501 / 304-598-3042 • *Lat:* 39.6488 *Lon:* -80.0022 I-79 Exit 155, E .3 mile, S on University Town Centre Dr
Huntington	◇	1	⏱	R_X 🚐	3333 US Hwy 60, 25705 / 304-525-8889 • *Lat:* 38.4113 *Lon:* -82.3855 I-64 Exit 15 go .5 mile W on US-60/Midland Trail
Hurricane	◇	1	⏱	R_X 🚐	167 Progress Way, 25526 / 304-562-0475 • *Lat:* 38.4402 *Lon:* -82.0211 I-64 Exit 34, north of exit
Keyser	◆		⏱	R_X 🚐	RR 4 Box 82, 26726 / 304-788-8160 • *Lat:* 39.3994 *Lon:* -79.0089 3.4 miles southwest of town center via US-220
Kimball	◇		⏱	R_X	61 Plaza Dr, 24853 / 304-585-7800 • *Lat:* 37.4140 *Lon:* -81.5221 2 miles southwest of town center via US-52
Kingwood	◇		⏱	R_X 🚐	100 Wal-Mart Dr, 26537 / 304-329-4020 • *Lat:* 39.4856 *Lon:* -79.7339 3 miles west of town center via SH-7
Lewisburg	◆	1	⏱	R_X 🚐	520 N Jefferson St, 24901 / 304-645-5280 • *Lat:* 37.8125 *Lon:* -80.4318 I-64 Exit 169, south of exit
Logan	◇		⏱	R_X 🚐	77 Norman Morgan Blvd, 25601 / 304-752-7391 • *Lat:* 37.8607 *Lon:* -82.0477 4 miles west of town center along US-119
Mac Arthur	◇	1	⏱	R_X 🚐	1881 Robert C Byrd Dr, 25873 / 304-256-6480 • *Lat:* 37.7516 *Lon:* -81.2200 I-64/I-77 Exit 42, south of exit about .7 mile
Martinsburg	◇	1	⏱	R_X	800 Foxcroft Ave, 25401 / 304-263-6061 • *Lat:* 39.4578 *Lon:* -77.9878 I-81 Exit 13 go .3 mile on CR-15 then S on Foxcroft
	◇	1	⏱	R_X	5680 Hammonds Mill Rd, 25404 / 304-274-5176 • *Lat:* 39.5438 *Lon:* -77.9090 I-81 Exit 20, east of exit
Mason	◇		⏱	R_X	320 Mallard Lane, 25260 / 304-773-9125 • *Lat:* 39.0111 *Lon:* -82.0356 .7 mile south of town center via SH-62

○ Wal-Mart ◇ Supercenter ☐ Sam's Club ▨ Gas ■ Gas & Diesel

City/Town	🍎		🕐	℞	🚐	Information
Moorefield	◆		🕐	℞		11 Harness Rd, 26836 / 304-538-3490 • *Lat:* 39.0869 *Lon:* -78.9613 1.8 miles north of town center via US-220
Morgantown	◇	1	🕐	℞	🚐	6051 University Town Centre Dr, 26501 / 304-598-3239 • *Lat:* 39.6458 *Lon:* -80.0016 I-79 Exit 155 go E .4 mile on Chaplin Hill Rd/Osage Rd then S 1 mile on University Town Centre Blvd
	◇	2	🕐	℞	🚐	215 Four H Camp Rd, 26508 / 304-292-4786 • *Lat:* 39.5731 *Lon:* -79.9726 I-68 Exit 1 go S on US-119 for .3 mile the W on CR-7 for 1.2 miles
Moundsville	◇	10	🕐	℞	🚐	240 Lafayette Ave, 26041 / 304-843-1580 • *Lat:* 39.9255 *Lon:* -80.7504 I-470 Exit 1 take SH-2 S for 9.5 miles
New Martinsville	◆		🕐	℞		1142 S Bridge St, 26155 / 304-455-6522 • *Lat:* 39.6563 *Lon:* -80.8583 1 mile north of town off SH-2 (3rd St) at Russell Ave
Nitro	◇	1	🕐	℞	🚐	100 Nitro Marketplace, 25143 / 304-769-0100 • *Lat:* 38.4126 *Lon:* -81.8089 I-64 Exit 47A go S .2 mile on Golf Mountain Rd, W .4 mile on Lakeview Dr, S .2 mile on Nitro Blvd
Parkersburg	◇	4	🕐	℞	🚐	2900 Pike St, 26101 / 304-489-1905 • *Lat:* 39.2308 *Lon:* -81.5413 I-77 Exit 170 go NW on SH-14 for 3.4 miles
Princeton	◇	1	🕐	℞	🚐	201 Greasy Ridge Rd, 24740 / 304-431-2100 • *Lat:* 37.3622 *Lon:* -81.0462 I-77 Exit 9 take US-460 E for .3 mile, then S on Greasy Rideg Rd
Ripley	◇	1	🕐	℞	🚐	200 Academy Dr, 25271 / 304-372-4482 • *Lat:* 38.8276 *Lon:* -81.7240 I-77 Exit 138 go E .2 mile on US-33 then N .5 mile on Accademy Dr
South Charleston	☐	4		℞	🚐	2500 Mountaineer Blvd, 25309 / 304-746-1700 • *Lat:* 38.3227 *Lon:* -81.7141 I-64 Exit 54 take SH-601 S 1.6 miles, US-119 S 1.8 miles, E at Southridge & N on Mountaineer .2 mile
	◇	4	🕐	℞	🚐	2700 Mountaineer Blvd, 25309 / 304-746-1720 • *Lat:* 38.3210 *Lon:* -81.7158 I-64 Exit 54 follow SH-601 S 1.6 miles to US-119 and continue 1.8 mile S to Southridge Blvd and turn left
Spencer	◇		🕐	℞		97 Williams Dr, 25276 / 304-927-6920 • *Lat:* 38.7995 *Lon:* -81.3485 .3 mile east of town center off Main St/US-33 at Williams Dr
Summersville	◇		🕐	℞		200 Wal St, 26651 / 304-872-6734 • *Lat:* 38.3019 *Lon:* -80.8341 3 miles northeast of town center along US-19
Triadelphia	◇	1	🕐	℞	🚐	450 Stewart Ln, 26059 / 304-547-1726 • *Lat:* 40.0587 *Lon:* -80.6021 I-70 Exit 10 go W .6 mile on Cabela Dr
Vienna	■	6			🚐	1100 Grand Central Ave, 26105 / 304-295-0280 • *Lat:* 39.3104 *Lon:* -81.5527 I-77 Exit 179 take SH-68 S 3.5 miles, W at West Virginia Ave .7 mile & N on SH-14 1.3 miles
	◆	4	🕐	℞	🚐	701 Grand Central Ave, 26105 / 304-422-3522 • *Lat:* 39.3057 *Lon:* -81.5511 I-79 Exit 179 go W on SH-68 for 3.5 miles, N on Virginia Ave & NW at Murdock Ave
Wayne	◇	8	🕐	℞		100 McGinnis Dr, 25570 / 304-272-3633 • *Lat:* 38.2237 *Lon:* -82.4450 I-64 Exit 8 go S on SH-152 for 7.2 miles, then W on Moore Rd
Weirton	○			℞	🚐	243 Three Springs Dr, 26062 / 304-723-3445 • *Lat:* 40.4003 *Lon:* -80.5498 3 miles southeast of town, north of US-22 Exit 4
Weston	●	1		℞		110 Berlin Rd, 26452 / 304-269-1549 • *Lat:* 39.0199 *Lon:* -80.4160 I-79 Exit 99 go E on US-33 for .9 mile then N on Berlin Rd

○ Wal-Mart　◇ Supercenter　☐ Sam's Club　■ Gas　■ Gas & Diesel

Wisconsin

○ Wal-Mart   ◇ Supercenter   □ Sam's Club   ▨ Gas   ◆ Gas & Diesel

Lake Superior

MINNESOTA

MICHIGAN

Superior ◇

◇ Ashland

②

⑤①

WISCONSIN

Hayward ◆

○ Minocqua

Rice Lake ◇

◇ Rhinelander

◇ Saint Croix Falls

◇ Ladysmith

⑤①

◇ New Richmond

Medford ◇

Merrill ◇

◆ Antigo

Marinette ◇

Menomonie ◇

⑨④

◇ Chippewa Falls

Wausau □

Shawano ◇

Sturgeon Bay ○

Hudson ○

Eau Claire □

Marshfield ◆

Plover ◇

Green Bay □

⑨④

Wisconsin Rapids ◇

New London ○

De Pere ◇

Black River Falls ◇

③⑨

Appleton (3) □

Manitowoc ◇

Tomah ◆

Neenah ◇

Onalaska □

Sparta ◇

⑨⓪

Oshkosh ◇

Chilton ◇

La Crosse ◇

⑨⓪
⑨④

Berlin ○

Sheboygan (2) ▨

Wisconsin Dells ◆

Fond du Lac ◇

Plymouth ◇

Lake Michigan

Viroqua ◇

Portage ◇

Beaver Dam ◇

West Bend ◇

④③

Baraboo ◇

Saukville ◇

Richland Center ◇

Hartford ◇

Germantown ○

Sun Prairie ◇

Watertown ◇

Pewaukee ◇

Waukesha (2) ◇

Prairie du Chien ◆

Madison (3) □

⑨④

Delafield ○

Milwaukee Area (8) ○

Dodgeville ◇

Monona □

Whitewater ◇

New Berlin ○

Greenfield ◇

Platteville ◇

Stoughton ○

③⑨
⑨⓪

Mukwonago ◇

⑨④

Monroe ○

Janesville ◇

Delavan ◇

④③

Burlington ◇

Racine □

Sturtevant ◇

IOWA

Beloit ◇

Lake Geneva ◇

Kenosha ○

ILLINOIS

Copyright 2008
Roundabout Publications

E   D   C   B   A

1   2   3   4

Milwaukee Area

Franklin (2) ○ □	Milwaukee (5) ○ □	West Allis □

City/Town	🍎	🕐	℞	🚌	Information
Antigo	◆		🕐	℞	🚌	200 State Hwy 64, 54409 / 715-627-1382 • *Lat:* 45.1621 *Lon:* -89.1442 From town center go N 1.6 miles on US-45 then E .2 mile on SH-64
Appleton	□			℞	🚌	1000 N Westhill Blvd, 54914 / 920-733-4655 • *Lat:* 44.2700 *Lon:* -88.4610 US-41 Exit 138 go E on Wisconsin Ave .5 mile then S at Westhill Blvd
	◇		🕐	℞		955 Mutual Way, 54913 / 920-954-6300 • *Lat:* 44.2683 *Lon:* -88.4777 US-41 Exit 137 take College Ave W for .5 mile then S at Casaloma Dr
	◇		🕐	℞	🚌	3701 E Calumet St, 54915 / 920-996-0573 • *Lat:* 44.2437 *Lon:* -88.3531 US-41 Exit 134 take SH-441 NE for 6.2 miles then E on Calumet
Ashland	◇		🕐	℞	🚌	2500 Lake Shore Dr E, 54806 / 715-682-9699 • *Lat:* 46.6059 *Lon:* -90.8527 2 miles northeast of town along US-2
Baraboo	◇	8	🕐	℞	🚌	920 US Hwy 12, 53913 / 608-356-1765 • *Lat:* 43.4562 *Lon:* -89.7447 I-90/94 Exit 92 take US-12 SE for 7.4 miles
Beaver Dam	◇		🕐	℞	🚌	120 Frances Ln, 53916 / 920-887-8900 • *Lat:* 43.4876 *Lon:* -88.8092 2.9 miles northeast of town center; from US-151 Exit 135 go E .3 mile on Gateway Dr then N .2 mile on Frances Ln
Beloit	◇	1	🕐	℞	🚌	2785 Milwaukee Rd, 53511 / 608-362-0057 • *Lat:* 42.5241 *Lon:* -88.9849 I-90 Exit 185A go W on Milwaukee Rd for .4 mile
Berlin	○			℞		822 Broadway St, 54923 / 920-361-1600 • *Lat:* 43.9681 *Lon:* -88.9763 US-41 Exit 116 take SH-91 W for 17.8 miles, continue on Huron St/Broadway for 2.5 miles
Black River Falls	◇	3	🕐	℞	🚌	611 WI Hwy 54, 54615 / 715-284-2434 • *Lat:* 44.2821 *Lon:* -90.8057 I-94 Exit 116 go SW on SH-54 for 2.6 miles
Burlington	◇		🕐	℞	🚌	1901 Milwaukee Ave, 53105 / 262-767-9520 • *Lat:* 42.7024 *Lon:* -88.2532 I-43 Exit 29 go E on SH-11 for 11.8 miles & N on Milwaukee Ave for 2 miles
Chilton	◇		🕐	℞	🚌	810 S Irish Rd, 53014 / 920-849-9551 • *Lat:* 44.0247 *Lon:* -88.1427 1.5 miles southeast of town center along US-151 at Irish Rd
Chippewa Falls	◇		🕐	℞	🚌	2786 Commercial Blvd, 54729 / 715-738-2254 • *Lat:* 44.8863 *Lon:* -91.4184 I-94 Exit 70 go N on SH-53 for 9.1 miles, N on SH-53 BR for 1 mile & E at Commercial Blvd
De Pere	◇		🕐	℞	🚌	1415 Lawrence Dr, 54115 / 920-336-3416 • *Lat:* 44.4345 *Lon:* -88.1048 US-41 Exit 161, go E on Scheiring Rd for .2 mile, then N on Lawrence Dr
Delafield	○	1		℞		2863 Heritage Dr, 53018 / 262-646-8858 • *Lat:* 43.0488 *Lon:* -88.3704 I-94 Exit 287 go S on US-83 for .5 mile, then E on Heritage
Delavan	◇	1	🕐	℞	🚌	1819 E Geneva St, 53115 / 262-740-1815 • *Lat:* 42.6281 *Lon:* -88.6072 I-43 Exit 21 go W on SH-50 for 1 mile
Dodgeville	◇			℞	🚌	601 Leffler, 53533 / 608-935-2723 • *Lat:* 42.9745 *Lon:* -90.1212 From Governor Dodge State Park (north of town) go S on SH-23 for 3 miles, then E on Leffler St
Eau Claire	□	2			🚌	4001 Gateway Dr, 54701 / 715-836-9585 • *Lat:* 44.7756 *Lon:* -91.4316 I-94 Exit 70 take US-53 N .9 mile, Golf Rd E .1 mile & Gateway Dr S .2 mile
	◇	2	🕐	℞		3915 Gateway Dr, 54701 / 715-834-0733 • *Lat:* 44.7758 *Lon:* -91.4318 I-94 Exit 70 take US-53 N for 1.5 miles to Golf Rd E to Gateway Dr

○ Wal-Mart ◇ Supercenter □ Sam's Club ▬ Gas ▬ Gas & Diesel

City/Town	🛡	🕐	℞	🚌	Information
Fond Du Lac	◇		🕐	℞	🚌	377 N Rolling Meadows Dr, 54937 / 920-921-6311 • *Lat:* 43.7867 *Lon:* -88.4860 US-41 Exit 99 go W on SH-23 for .2 mile then N on Rolling Meadows Dr
Franklin	□ 2			℞	🚌	6705 S 27th St, 53132 / 414-761-0088 • *Lat:* 42.9240 *Lon:* -87.9500 I-94 Exit 320 go W on Rawson Ave .6 mile & N on 27th .5 mile
	○ 3			℞		6701 S 27th St, 53132 / 414-761-9560 • *Lat:* 42.9241 *Lon:* -87.9500 I-43 Exit 9 go S on 27th St for 2.6 miles
Germantown	◇			℞	🚌	W190 N9855 Appleton Ave, 53022 / 262-255-1285 • *Lat:* 43.1978 *Lon:* -88.1453 US-41 Exit 54 go W on Lannon Rd for .8 mile, then S on Appleton for 1 mile
Green Bay	□ 1			℞	🚌	2470 W Mason St, 54303 / 920-497-2112 • *Lat:* 44.5242 *Lon:* -88.0928 I-41 Exit 168 take SH-54 W .9 mile
	○ 3			℞		2292 Main St, 54311 / 920-465-1333 • *Lat:* 44.4807 *Lon:* -87.9701 I-43 Exit 183 go W on CR-V for 1.7 miles, then S on Main St for .7 mile
	◇		🕐	℞	🚌	2440 W Mason St, 54303 / 920-499-9897 • *Lat:* 44.5242 *Lon:* -88.0914 US-41 Exit 168 take SH-54 W for .6 mile
Greenfield	○ 1			℞		4500 S 108th St, 53228 / 414-529-0455 • *Lat:* 42.9625 *Lon:* -88.0476 I-43 Exit 60 go .5 mile S on 108th St
Hartford	◇		🕐	℞	🚌	1220 Thiel St, 53027 / 262-670-5803 • *Lat:* 43.3229 *Lon:* -88.4026 US-41 Exit 64B take SH-60 W 8 miles
Hayward	◆		🕐	℞		15594 State Rd 77, 54043 / 715-634-8228 • *Lat:* 46.0171 *Lon:* -91.4735 .7 mile northeast of town center, east of US-63/SH-77 jct
Hudson	○ 1			℞		2222 Crest View Dr, 54016 / 715-386-1101 • *Lat:* 44.9609 *Lon:* -92.7252 I-94 Exit 2 go S on Carmichael for .1 mile, then W on Crest View
Janesville	□ 2			℞	🚌	3900 Deerfield Dr, 53546 / 608-741-2367 • *Lat:* 42.7204 *Lon:* -88.9846 I-39/I-90 Exit 171A, east of highway
	◇ 1		🕐	℞	🚌	3800 Deerfield Dr, 53546 / 608-754-7800 • *Lat:* 42.7204 *Lon:* -88.9846 I-39/I-90 Exit 171A, east of highway
Kenosha	○ 5			℞		4404 52nd St, 53144 / 262-652-1039 • *Lat:* 42.5886 *Lon:* -87.8621 I-94 Exit 342 go E on 52nd St for 4.7 miles
La Crosse	◇ 8		🕐	℞	🚌	4622 Mormon Coulee Rd, 54601 / 608-788-1870 • *Lat:* 43.7674 *Lon:* -91.2121 I-90 Exit 3 go S on SH-35 for 7.8 miles
Ladysmith	◇		🕐	℞		800 W 10th St S, 54848 / 715-532-2039 • *Lat:* 45.4556 *Lon:* -91.1123 From town center go W .5 mile on US-8, S .7 mile on SH-27, W .2 mile on College Ave
Lake Geneva	◇ 9		🕐	℞	🚌	201 S Edwards Blvd, 53147 / 262-248-2266 • *Lat:* 42.5929 *Lon:* -88.4139 I-43 Exit 27A take US-12 SE for 8.1 miles (to Exit 330A) then W on SH-50 for .4 mile
Madison	□				🚌	7050 Watts Rd, 53719 / 608-273-2146 • *Lat:* 43.0503 *Lon:* -89.5046 I-39/I-90 Exit 142 take US-12 W 11.8 miles, S on Gammon Rd .3 mile & W on Watts Ave
	○ 1			℞	🚌	4198 Nakoosa Trl, 53714 / 608-241-8808 • *Lat:* 43.1097 *Lon:* -89.3118 I-39/I-90 Exit 138B take Stoughton Rd N for .6 mile, then E on Commercial Ave
	○			℞		7202 Watts Rd, 53719 / 608-276-9393 • *Lat:* 43.0507 *Lon:* -89.5084 I-39/I-90 Exit 142A take US-12 W 11.6 miles to Exit 255, S on Gammon Rd .3 mile, W on Watts Rd .3 mile
Manitowoc	◇ 1		🕐	℞		4115 Calumet Ave, 54220 / 920-684-4214 • *Lat:* 44.0799 *Lon:* -87.6965 I-43 Exit 149 take US-151 NE for 1 mile
Marinette	○			℞		2700 Roosevelt Rd, 54143 / 715-735-5117 • *Lat:* 45.0869 *Lon:* -87.6605 2.3 miles southwest of town, north of US-41 at Roosevelt Rd
Marshfield	◆		🕐	℞	🚌	2001 N Central Ave, 54449 / 715-486-9440 • *Lat:* 44.6875 *Lon:* -90.1579 1.6 miles northeast of town center via SH-97

○ Wal-Mart ◇ Supercenter □ Sam's Club ▨ Gas ■ Gas & Diesel

City/Town	🛡	🕐	℞	🚗	Information
Medford	◇		🕐	℞		1010 N 8th St, 54451 / 715-748-9000 • *Lat:* 45.1508 *Lon:* -90.3343 From town center go E .6 mile on SH-64 (Broadway Ave) then go N .6 mile on SH-13 (8th St)
Menomonie	◇ 1		🕐	℞	🚗	180 Cedar Falls Rd, 54751 / 715-235-6565 • *Lat:* 44.9117 *Lon:* -91.9324 I-94 Exit 41, go N on Broadway .2 mile then E on Cedar Falls Rd
Merrill	○			℞		3500 E Main St, 54452 / 715-536-2414 • *Lat:* 45.1780 *Lon:* -89.6546 From US-51 Exit 208 take SH-64 W for .5 mile
Milwaukee	□ 7			℞	🚗	7701 W Calumet Rd, 53223 / 414-365-3700 • *Lat:* 43.1559 *Lon:* -88.0058 I-43 Exit 82 follow SH-100 W 3.5 miles, 60th St S 1 mile, Bradley Rd W 1 mile, 76th St S .5 mile
	○ 1			℞		401 E Capitol Dr, 53212 / 414-967-7804 • *Lat:* 43.0890 *Lon:* -87.9060 I-43 Exit 76A go E on Capitol Dr for .9 mile
	○ 2			℞	🚗	3355 S 27th St, 53215 / 414-383-1113 • *Lat:* 42.9840 *Lon:* -87.9486 I-43 Exit 9 go N on 27th St for 1.6 miles
	○ 4			℞	🚗	5825 W Hope Ave, 53216 / 414-445-3930 • *Lat:* 43.0934 *Lon:* -87.9851 I-43 Exit 76 go W on Capitol Dr for 3.2 miles & N on 60th St for .2 mile
	○ 5			℞		8700 N Servite Dr, 53223 / 414-355-0892 • *Lat:* 43.1754 *Lon:* -88.0103 I-43 Exit 82B take SH-100 W for 4.7 miles then S on Servite Dr
Minocqua	○			℞		8705 Blumenstein Rd, 54548 / 715-356-1609 • *Lat:* 45.8909 *Lon:* -89.7197 From Jct US-51 & SH-70 take SH-70 W for .8 mile then N on Blumenstein
Monona	◇ 4		🕐	℞	🚗	2151 Royal Ave, 53713 / 608-226-0913 • *Lat:* 43.0422 *Lon:* -89.3527 I-39/I-90 Exit 142A follow US-12/US-18 W 3.5 miles to Exit 264 then go S .1 mile on Towne Dr and left onto Royal Ave
Monroe	○			℞		424 W 8th St, 53566 / 608-325-7701 • *Lat:* 42.6034 *Lon:* -89.6632 From US-69 (south of town) go W on SH-11 BR/8th St for .6 mile
Mukwonago	◇ 1		🕐	℞	🚗	250 Wolf Run, 53149 / 262-363-7500 • *Lat:* 42.8466 *Lon:* -88.3230 I-43 Exit 43 go SE on SH-83 for .3 mile, then N on Wolf Run
Neenah	◇		🕐	℞	🚗	1155 W Winneconne Ave, 54956 / 920-722-0782 • *Lat:* 44.1820 *Lon:* -88.4652 US-41 Exit 131 go E on Winneconne Ave .6 mile
New Berlin	○ 2			℞		15333 W National Ave, 53151 / 262-796-1620 • *Lat:* 42.9784 *Lon:* -88.1052 I-43 Exit 57 go 1.6 miles N on South Moorland Rd then E on National Ave
New London	○			℞		1717 N Shawano St, 54961 / 920-982-7525 • *Lat:* 44.4116 *Lon:* -88.7416 1.5 miles north of town via US-45-BR
New Richmond	◇		🕐	℞	🚗	250 W Richmond Way, 54017 / 715-246-5509 • *Lat:* 45.1008 *Lon:* -92.5399 I-94 Exit 10 follow SH-65 N 10.8 miles then go W .1 mile on Richmond Way
Onalaska	□ 2				🚗	1211 Crossing Meadows Dr, 54650 / 608-781-1670 • *Lat:* 43.8700 *Lon:* -91.2161 I-90 Exit 4 take SH-157 S .6 mile, CR-SS W .4 mile, 12th Ave N .1 mile & E on Crossng Meadows
	◇ 1		🕐	℞	🚗	3107 Market Pl, 54650 / 608-781-8282 • *Lat:* 43.8786 *Lon:* -91.1857 I-90 Exit 5 take SH-16 NE for .5 mile
Oshkosh	◇		🕐	℞	🚗	351 S Washburn St, 54904 / 920-231-1575 • *Lat:* 44.0148 *Lon:* -88.5829 US-41 Exit 117 take W 9th Ave for .2 mile then N at Washburn
Pewaukee	○ 3			℞	🚗	411 Pewaukee Rd, 53072 / 262-695-1847 • *Lat:* 43.0751 *Lon:* -88.2253 I-94 Exit 294 go N on Pewaukee Rd 2.7 miles
Platteville	◇		🕐	℞	🚗	1800 Progressive Pkwy, 53818 / 608-348-4888 • *Lat:* 42.7330 *Lon:* -90.4390 2 miles east of town at US-151 Exit 21, west of exit
Plover	◇ 1		🕐	℞	🚗	250 Crossroads Dr, 54467 / 715-345-7855 • *Lat:* 44.4928 *Lon:* -89.5130 I-39 Exit 156 go E on CR-HH for .2 mile then S on Crossroads Dr

○Wal-Mart ◇Supercenter □Sam's Club ▨Gas ▥Gas & Diesel

City/Town	⬭	🕐	℞	🚗	Information
Plymouth	◇ 10	🕐	℞	🚗	428 Walton Dr, 53073 / 920-892-7523 • *Lat:* 43.7535 *Lon:* -87.9429 I-43 Exit 126 take SH-23 W for 8.9 miles, SH-57 S for .4 mile
Portage	◇ 1	🕐	℞	🚗	2950 New Pinery Rd, 53901 / 608-742-1432 • *Lat:* 43.5712 *Lon:* -89.4698 I-39 Exit 92 take US-51 S for 1 mile
Prairie Du Chien	◆	🕐	℞	🚗	38020 US Hwy 18, 53821 / 608-326-2408 • *Lat:* 43.0179 *Lon:* -91.1101 3 miles south of town center along US-18
Racine	□ 8			🚗	6200 Regency West Dr, 53406 / 262-554-2052 • *Lat:* 42.7024 *Lon:* -87.8557 I-94 Exit 333 take SH-20 E 5.6 miles, SH-31 S 1.3 miles & W at Regency West Dr .2 mile
Rhinelander	◇	🕐	℞	🚗	2121 Lincoln St, 54501 / 715-362-8550 • *Lat:* 45.6334 *Lon:* -89.3814 From Jct US-8 & SH-17 (W of town) take US-8 E for .7 mile & US-8 BR for 2.9 miles
Rice Lake	◇	🕐	℞	🚗	2501 West Ave, 54868 / 715-234-6990 • *Lat:* 45.5274 *Lon:* -91.7648 US-53 Exit 143 take SH-48 W for .2 mile then S on West Ave
Richland Center	◇	🕐	℞	🚗	2401 US Hwy 14 E, 53581 / 608-647-7141 • *Lat:* 43.3623 *Lon:* -90.4054 From Jct SH-60 & US-14 (in Gotham) take US-14 NE for 7.4 miles
Saint Croix Falls	◇	🕐	℞	🚗	2212 Glacier Dr, 54024 / 715-483-1399 • *Lat:* 45.3978 *Lon:* -92.5857 3 miles east of town via US-8
Saukville	○ 1		℞		825 E Green Bay Ave, 53080 / 262-284-9616 • *Lat:* 43.3848 *Lon:* -87.9235 I-43 Exit 96 take SH-33 SW for .2 mile
Shawano	◇	🕐	℞	🚗	1244 E Green Bay St, 54166 / 715-524-5980 • *Lat:* 44.7818 *Lon:* -88.5805 1.4 miles east of town center; from SH-29 Exit 225 go N 2 miles on SH-22 then E 1.4 miles on Green Bay St
Sheboygan	◇ 1	🕐	℞	🚗	3711 S Taylor Dr, 53081 / 920-459-9300 • *Lat:* 43.7154 *Lon:* -87.7579 I-43 Exit 123 go E .2 mile then S at Taylor Rd
	◇ 1	🕐	℞	🚗	4433 Vanguard Dr, 53083 / 920-459-9410 • *Lat:* 43.7943 *Lon:* -87.7683 I-43 Exit 128, west of exit
Sparta	◇ 2	🕐	℞	🚗	1600 W Wisconsin St, 54656 / 608-269-7501 • *Lat:* 43.9391 *Lon:* -90.8321 I-90 Exit 25 take SH-27 N for 1.4 miles then W at SH-16 for .6 mile
Stoughton	○ 8		℞		1800 US Hwy 51, 53589 / 608-873-5453 • *Lat:* 42.9181 *Lon:* -89.2426 I-39/I-90 Exit 156 take US-51 W for 7.9 miles
Sturgeon Bay	○		℞		1536 Egg Harbor Rd, 54235 / 920-746-0402 • *Lat:* 44.8497 *Lon:* -87.3588 1.3 miles northeast of town center on Egg Harbor Rd
Sturtevant	◇ 5	🕐	℞	🚗	3049 S Oakes Rd, 53177 / 262-598-8702 • *Lat:* 42.6965 *Lon:* -87.8664 I-94 Exit 335 go E 4.4 miles on Durand Ave/SH-11
Sun Prairie	○ 4		℞		1905 McCoy Rd, 53590 / 608-837-6339 • *Lat:* 43.1761 *Lon:* -89.2452 I-39/90 Exit 135 follow US-151 N 3.3 miles to Exit 101 then E .2 mile on Main St
Superior	◇ 6	🕐	℞	🚗	3705 Tower Ave, 54880 / 715-392-6060 • *Lat:* 46.6939 *Lon:* -92.1043 I-35 (in Minnesota) Exit 253A take US-2 E for 2.7 miles, N at Belknap St for .7 mile & E on Tower Ave for 1.8 miles
Tomah	◆ 1	🕐	℞	🚗	222 W McCoy Blvd, 54660 / 608-372-7900 • *Lat:* 44.0178 *Lon:* -90.5105 I-94 Exit 143 take SH-21 E for .2 mile
Viroqua	◇	🕐	℞		1133 N Main St, 54665 / 608-637-8511 • *Lat:* 43.5696 *Lon:* -90.8889 .8 mile north of town center on Main St (US-14/US-61)
Watertown	◇ 9	🕐	℞	🚗	1901 Market Way, 53094 / 920-261-7270 • *Lat:* 43.1936 *Lon:* -88.7245 I-94 Exit 267 take SH-26 N for 7.8 miles, E on SH-19 for .6 mile
Waukesha	□ 1		℞	🚗	600 N Springdale Rd, 53186 / 262-798-1490 • *Lat:* 43.0418 *Lon:* -88.1857 I-94 Exit 297 take US-18/Bluemont Rd W .5 mile & N at Springdale Rd .1 mile
	○ 2		℞		W226 S 1500 Hwy 164, 53186 / 262-521-1815 • *Lat:* 43.0172 *Lon:* -88.1996 I-94 Exit 297 take SH-164 S for 2 miles

○ Wal-Mart ◇ Supercenter □ Sam's Club ▨ Gas ■ Gas & Diesel

City/Town	🛡	🕐	Rx	🚗	Information
Wausau	□			🚗	4000 Rib Mountain Dr, 54401 / 715-359-0044 • *Lat:* 44.9206 *Lon:* -89.6522 US-51 Exit 188 go N on Rib Mountain Dr for .9 mile
	◇	1	🕐 Rx	🚗	4300 Rib Mountain Dr, 54401 / 715-359-2282 • *Lat:* 44.9180 *Lon:* -89.6500 I-39 Exit 188 go E on Rib Mountain Dr for .6 mile
West Allis	□	1	Rx	🚗	1540 S 108th St, 53214 / 414-453-5806 • *Lat:* 43.0143 *Lon:* -88.0464 I-894 Exit 1 go W on SH-59 .5 mile & S on 108th .3 mile
West Bend	◇		🕐 Rx	🚗	1515 W Paradise Dr, 53095 / 262-334-5760 • *Lat:* 43.3977 *Lon:* -88.1965 From Jct US-41 & US-45 go N on US-45 for 9.7 miles then W on Paradise Dr for .4 mile
Whitewater	○		Rx		1362 W Main St, 53190 / 262-473-7744 • *Lat:* 42.8347 *Lon:* -88.7573 1.4 miles west of town center via Main St
Wisconsin Dells	◆	1	🕐 Rx	🚗	130 Commerce St, 53965 / 608-253-3490 • *Lat:* 43.6301 *Lon:* -89.8376 I-90/94 Exit 89 take SH-23 W for .2 mile
Wisconsin Rapids	◇		🕐 Rx	🚗	4331 8th St S, 54494 / 715-423-1900 • *Lat:* 44.3532 *Lon:* -89.8155 3 miles south of town center along SH-3

○ Wal-Mart ◇ Supercenter □ Sam's Club ▬ Gas ■ Gas & Diesel

Wyoming

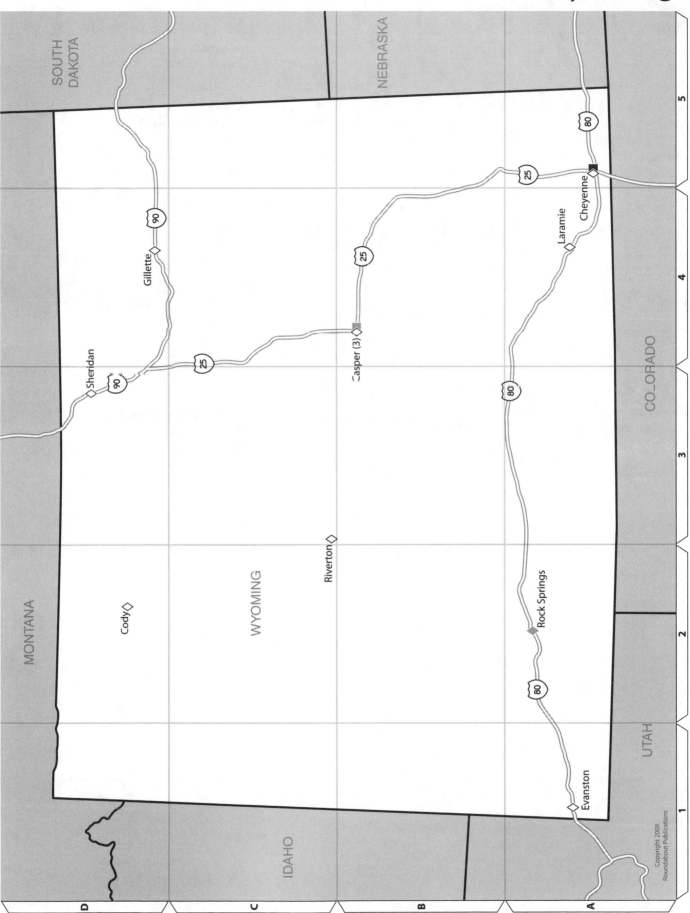

SOUTH DAKOTA

NEBRASKA

MONTANA

IDAHO

UTAH

COLORADO

WYOMING

Sheridan

Gillette

Cody

Riverton

Casper (3)

Rock Springs

Evanston

Laramie

Cheyenne

Copyright 2008
Roundabout Publications

City/Town	⬡ 🕐 ℞ 🚐		Information
Casper	▪ 1	🚐	4600 E 2nd St, 82609 / 307-237-8877 • *Lat:* 42.8491 *Lon:* -106.2666 I-25 Exit 185 go S on Wyoming Blvd .4 mile then E on 2nd St .2 mile
	◇ 4 🕐 ℞	🚐	4255 Cy Ave, 82604 / 307-232-9593 • *Lat:* 42.8188 *Lon:* -106.3750 I-25 Exit 188B take SH-220 SW for 1.6 miles, S on Cy Ave 2.4 miles
	◇ 1 🕐 ℞		4400 E 2nd St, 82609 / 307-237-0991 • *Lat:* 42.8491 *Lon:* -106.2694 I-25 Exit 185 go S on SH-258 for .4 mile, E on 2nd St
Cheyenne	■ 5	🚐	1948 Dell Range Blvd, 82009 / 307-637-3771 • *Lat:* 41.1603 *Lon:* -104.7933 I-80 Exit 364 go N on College Dr 2.5 miles & W on Dell Range Blvd 1.7 miles
	◇ 5 🕐 ℞	🚐	2032 Dell Range Blvd, 82009 / 307-632-4330 • *Lat:* 41.1603 *Lon:* -104.7912 I-80 Exit 364 go N on SH-212 for 2.5 miles, W at Dell Range Rd for 1.6 miles
Cody	◇	🕐 ℞ 🚐	321 Yellowstone Ave, 82414 / 307-527-4673 • *Lat:* 44.5166 *Lon:* -109.0904 2.2 miles west of town center via Yellowstone Ave (US-14/US-16/US-20)
Evanston	◇ 1	🕐 ℞ 🚐	125 N 2nd St, 82930 / 307-789-0010 • *Lat:* 41.2623 *Lon:* -110.9575 I-80 Exit 5 go NW on Front St .3 mile, S on 2nd St
Gillette	◇ 1	🕐 ℞ 🚐	2300 S Douglas Hwy, 82718 / 307-686-4060 • *Lat:* 44.2707 *Lon:* -105.4939 I-90 Exit 126 take SH-59 S for .3 mile
Laramie	◇ 1	🕐 ℞ 🚐	4308 E Grand Ave, 82070 / 307-745-6100 • *Lat:* 41.3048 *Lon:* -105.5411 I-80 Exit 316 go N on Grand Ave for 1 mile
Riverton	◇	🕐 ℞ 🚐	1733 N Federal Blvd, 82501 / 307-856-3261 • *Lat:* 43.0429 *Lon:* -108.3806 1.3 miles north of town center on Federal Blvd (US-26)
Rock Springs	◆ 1	🕐 ℞ 🚐	201 Gateway Blvd, 82901 / 307-362-1957 • *Lat:* 41.5784 *Lon:* -109.2499 I-80 Exit 102 go E on Dewar Dr for .5 mile, then N at Gateway Blvd
Sheridan	◇ 1	🕐 ℞	1695 Coffeen Ave, 82801 / 307-674-6492 • *Lat:* 44.7794 *Lon:* -106.9414 I-90 Exit 25 take US-14 W for .3 mile then N on Coffeen for .5 mile

○ Wal-Mart ◇ Supercenter ☐ Sam's Club ▪ Gas ■ Gas & Diesel

Notes

Notes

Notes

Notes